Witness to History
1929-1969

Witness to History

1929-1969

CHARLES E. BOHLEN

W · W · NORTON & COMPANY · INC ·

NEW YORK

Copyright © 1973 by W. W. Norton & Company, Inc.

FIRST EDITION

ALL RIGHTS RESERVED

Published simultaneously in Canada
by George J. McLeod Limited, Toronto

Library of Congress Cataloging in Publication Data

Bohlen, Charles Eustis, 1904-
  Witness to history, 1929–1969.

  1. United States—Foreign relations—Russia.
2. Russia—Foreign relations—United States.
I. Title.
E748.B64A38   327'.2'0924 [B]   72–13407
ISBN 0–393–07476–5

PRINTED IN THE UNITED STATES OF AMERICA
Book Design by Robert Freese

1 2 3 4 5 6 7 8 9 0

To Avis

Contents

PART IV—The Ambassador

PART V—The Final Years

Illustrations

Secretary of State Dulles, President Eisenhower, and the author after Senate confirmation of Mr. Bohlen as Ambassador to USSR, 1953

These photographs follow page 370.

Ambassador and Mrs. Bohlen with their three children, 1953
The new Ambassador presents his credentials at the Kremlin
The author with Bulganin at a picnic near Moscow, 1955
July 4 reception at Spaso House, Moscow, 1956
Porgy and Bess troupe, Leningrad, 1956
The Ambassador in his office in the Embassy, Moscow, 1956
The author calls on President Eisenhower, 1957
The author in a contemplative mood
The author with President Carlos P. Garcia of the Philippines, 1958
Secretary of State Rusk bids farewell to new Ambassador to France, 1962
President de Gaulle and Foreign Minister Couve de Murville receive the new Ambassador
Hubert Humphrey, accompanied by Ambassador Bohlen, calls on de Gaulle
Shooting pheasants in France, 1963
Off for Berlin with Vice President Johnson
President Kennedy and Ambassador Bohlen
The author confers with President Johnson, 1967
With President and Mrs. Nixon at White House, 1969
Ambassador and Mrs. Bohlen in France

Editor's Note

This book was written in an unusual way. Chip Bohlen does not type, and his handwriting, the product of St. Paul's and Harvard, is illegible. Thus he turned, as others have, to a tape recorder. He dictated some 600,000 to 700,000 words, following fairly closely the chronology of his career. Then began an eleven-month chore in which I asked questions—probing, needling, pleading—in an attempt to clarify thoughts, correct errors, fill in holes. The replies were taped, transcribed, and worked into the original manuscript, which was then re-edited and boiled down to perhaps 400,000 words. Over the next year and a half, we went through this process two more times, with me asking questions, Chip dictating answers into the recorder, and me re-editing the manuscript. The final product, this book of about 220,000 words, is truly Chip's—he did the research, he wrote the words, he checked the facts. As the catalytic agent and surgeon, I can express only admiration for his dogged performance and unfailing good humor under a waspish tongue and sharp knife.

ROBERT H. PHELPS

Foreword

This book is a collection of personal reminiscences and observations based on nearly forty years in the United States Foreign Service. It is a memoir of a diplomat lucky enough to have witnessed and participated in every major development in American-Soviet relations from 1929 to 1969.

This book is not, nor does it attempt to be, a history of American-Soviet relations, although every paragraph is wrapped in the history of those momentous years. While fate presented me with an unusual observation point, at the side of great leaders as they made decisions of incalculable consequences, every witness is limited. Other eyes see a different picture; other ears hear a different sound; other minds conceive a different situation. Thus I recognize that this book cannot truly be a balanced history.

This book is also not an analysis of the merits and demerits of American and Soviet policy, although I have not hesitated to point out mistakes that were made by myself, as well as others. My memoirs are not designed to be an apology for American policy or an attack on revisionist historians. I have tried only to relate, explain, and interpret events as I saw them.

The impressions I have sought to convey of the men I worked for in the American government—Presidents, Secretaries of State, and other high officials—are contemporary with their periods of service. I have sought whenever possible to avoid hindsight and ex post facto judgment of individuals. Therefore, my appraisals of the men who led the United States during this period should not be considered conclusive. They represent the opinion of one who had the privilege of working closely with them.

Because the material I had to work with was so vast, selection had to be somewhat brutal. Personal experiences were included only if they were germane to the general theme of American-Soviet relations. My ambassadorships to the Philippines and France were given relatively less space than the years there would seem to call for. It was not possible to mention all my associates. Therefore I would like to pay tribute here to the excellence and loyalty of my staff, both Foreign Service officers and clerical personnel, at the three Embassies I headed, in Moscow, Manila, and Paris, as well as my assistants during my tours of duty in the Department of State.

My appreciation and gratitude also go to three men who read an early draft of the manuscript and offered many useful comments and criticisms. They are George F. Kennan and the late Llewellyn E. Thompson, both former ambassadors to the Soviet Union, who served with distinction in the Foreign Service, and Larry Smith, a historian at Dartmouth College who is now administrative assistant to Senator Thomas J. McIntyre of New Hampshire.

My thanks also go to Evan Thomas, vice-president of W. W. Norton & Company, who encouraged me to write the book and helped me over many a hump.

Finally, I find it difficult to express my deep gratitude to Robert H. Phelps, news editor of the Washington Bureau of *The New York Times*, without whose invaluable assistance and constant help this book would never have been written.

CHARLES E. BOHLEN

PART ONE

The Apprenticeship

CHAPTER ONE

The Smell of Makhorka

As dusk was settling on the Russian plains, the train from Warsaw to Moscow pulled into the Soviet border village of Negoreloye, and we jumped down to the station platform. It was my first step on Soviet territory, marking the beginning of my Russian experience, which was to last on and off, mostly on, for more than thirty-four years. No one can read the future—not even a shaman with his Siberian magic—and on that bright, snowy day of March 7, 1934, I was too excited by our arrival to look much beyond the opening in a few days of the first American Embassy in the Soviet Union. Ahead, however, was a close-up view of some of the major historic events of the twentieth century—Stalin's great purges; the Nazi-Soviet pact; the World War II summit conferences at Teheran, Yalta, and Potsdam; the Marshall Plan; the cold war; the Berlin blockade; the downing of the U-2 spy plane; the Cuban missile crisis. The Soviet Union became the central factor of my life in the Foreign Service.

I had planned it that way, selecting the Soviet Union as my specialty and spending five years, from the time I entered the Foreign Service in 1929, preparing for a career dealing with Russian-American relations. I selected my specialty only after deciding to become a diplomat, and I cannot remember when or why I decided on such a career. Diplomacy certainly was not a popular career in the late 1920s, when isolationism prevailed in the United States. At that time of booming prosperity, most of my friends at Harvard, where I graduated in 1927 with a bachelor of arts degree, planned to go into the stock market, banking, or the law, with the overriding purpose of acquiring a fortune. Such a future did not appeal to me; I had no interest in business, no inclination toward any of the professions.

I did, however, possess a somewhat more cosmopolitan upbringing than most of my contemporaries, and this background may have predisposed me toward diplomacy. The second of three children, I was born in the family's summer home in Clayton, New York, on one of the Thousand Islands, on August 30, 1904. Both my father, Charles, a gentleman of leisure who had inherited a little money, and my mother, Celestine Eustis, who had been from her birth in New Orleans pro-French, enjoyed traveling in Europe, and usually took me and my brother and sister with them. My first trip there was made when I was eight years old; we spent the winter of 1912–13 in Vevey, Switzerland, where I was tutored by a Monsieur Robert, practiced my French, slid down snowy hills on my sled, and got fat on Swiss chocolate.

In succeeding years, I visited most of the Western European countries. My mother, who was by far more influential than my father with me, always made sure that France was on our itinerary. Her love for France stemmed from her French ancestry and from her four years in the American Embassy in Paris. Her father, a United States senator from Louisiana, had been named the first American ambassador to France by President Cleveland in 1893. Up to that time, all our representatives had held no rank higher than Minister. During his ambassadorship, my mother acted as hostess for the Embassy because my grandmother was dead. Her love for France sometimes bordered on the ludicrous, as her children well knew. Once, on a train from Cherbourg to Paris in the early 1920s, she pointed to a group of cows in a field and said, to our indignation, "You must admit that they are prettier than cows in America."

Thus I became oriented toward foreign countries at an early age. Even in college, this leaning did not result in any decision to become a diplomat, and on graduation, undecided about what I wanted to do, I jumped at the chance to work as an apprentice seaman on a tramp steamer which was making a six-month trip around the world. Nothing happened on the trip to end my uncertainty. On my return, I discussed on and off for the next few months various career possibilities with my family and friends. Someone suggested the Foreign Service and mentioned that my cousin, Mrs. William C. Eustis, who lived in Washington, knew people in the State Department. Mrs. Eustis arranged for me to see William R. Castle, the Assistant Secretary of State for European Affairs. It was this conversation at the end of the summer of 1928 that finally fixed me in my decision to become a diplomat.

An attractive, urbane gentleman, Castle spoke to me with frankness and understanding about the problems of the Foreign Service. He pointed out that with the passage of the Rogers Act of 1924, which established the career Foreign Service, the State Department could at last offer a respectable future to a young man with a genuine interest in foreign affairs. I was particularly concerned about pay. I was under the erroneous impression—popular even to this day—that without a private income no one could make a go of a career in diplomacy. Castle explained that the 1924 law provided for pay and allowances which, while not lavish, were sufficient for a decent living. There was every indication, he said, that conditions would continue to improve. He swept away my doubts, and I decided to try for the Foreign Service.

It was necessary then, as now, to pass an examination, written and oral. It was considered wise to attend a tutoring school in Georgetown run by an estimable gentleman from Virginia named Crawford with a fondness for bourbon whiskey and the Democratic party. He was a man of some erudition who usually had the will power to refrain from drinking during the two months of his course. In the presidential election of 1928, however, Herbert Hoover, a Republican, carried Virginia. The day after the election, Crawford came to class drunk, delivered an impassioned lecture on the "black shame of the Dominion of Virginia," then disappeared for a week.

With the help of Crawford's tutoring, I had no trouble with the written part of the test. In those days, the written examination was much easier than it is now. The questions I had to answer called for simple factual knowledge—such as matching a list of important military battles with dates. A revision of the exam, made soon thereafter by Professor Joseph Green of Princeton, was aimed at testing the ability of an applicant to reason and to write rather than to recall facts, and required essay-type answers.

The oral exam, which followed a few weeks after the written test, was not stiff, either. One question I answered incorrectly asked what percentage of the population of the United States lived on farms. The questions were put to me by a panel of representatives of the State Department, the Civil Service Commission, and the Department of Commerce. For me, the anticipation of this appearance was nerve-racking. I took a drink of bootleg gin in my apartment before going to the exam to give me courage. Apparently, someone on the board smelled the alcohol on my breath and argued, when my application was considered, that anyone who violated the nation's Prohibition laws should be barred from the Foreign Service. Luckily, Castle was on the board and was able to persuade the other members to pass me.

Having successfully completed the exams, I was accepted into the Foreign Service on March 26, 1929. The first step in my training was a four-month stint at the Foreign Service School, which, like the rest of the State Department, was housed next door to the White House in a building of unsurpassed ugliness but of exceptional comfort. Now known as the Executive Office Building, it is an annex of the White House. At the Foreign Service School, the courses were primarily pragmatic, dealing with procedures such as handling visa applications and making out invoices. There was little discussion of foreign policy in general. The prevailing isolationist philosophy of the country was reflected in classes on how a diplomat should report political events overseas. He should report objectively and succinctly but under no circumstances take sides.

After Foreign Service School, the next step in my apprenticeship was to acquire some of the basic skills of the diplomatic art. The department believed that the best way to learn was under the watchful eye of an experienced officer. I was assigned for a few months to the staff of J. Theodore Marriner, the chief of the Division of European Affairs. Marriner, tall and courtly and possessed of great patience, taught me the rudiments of answering correspondence from American citizens. His constant admonition was to keep controversial issues quiet. There was a run of letters at that time from hard-shelled Protestants who feared that the United States was going to send a diplomatic mission to the Pope. Under Marriner's guidance, I drafted innocuous replies assuring those who had written warnings about the Pope that the State Department would consider their views.

Marriner was typical of the old-line diplomats who filled key positions in the department. Steeped in isolationism, they were interested in doing a good job for their country. (Marriner was killed in 1937 by a disappointed visa-seeker in Beirut, where he was consul general.) But the old-timers thought that America's responsibilities were not very great. The world seemed secure to them and the United States safe from attack as long as it kept its nose out of other nations' business. The two dominant world powers—Britain and France—were considered friendly, even though America had traditionally opposed colonialism, because they shared the same basic Western Christian democratic view of society. The other big countries—Germany, Italy, the Soviet Union, Japan, and China—posed no apparent threat at that time. There was no need for the United States to assume a big power's responsibility.

As a result, the work load at State was light and there were few crises to worry about. Virtually the only contact with Congress was the annual review of the budget, which totaled only $14 million in 1929, with half of that returned to the Treasury in the form of passport and visa fees and charges for other services. Regular public hearings, closed-door briefings, and the constant interchange of views which are now a regular part of the relations between State and Congress were unknown in 1929.

As a bachelor in a city with many single girls, I enjoyed those charming days. As far as I remember, neither I nor any of the other young Foreign Service officers dissented from the prevailing head-in-the-sand policies of the United States government. I never dreamed that within a few years the United States would be involved in every area of the globe and that the tranquil life of the Foreign Service officer would be a relic of the 1920s.

My first doubts were not whether the department was relevant to the world but whether it was made up of eccentrics and misfits, as some Americans believed then and still do. That summer, a Foreign Service officer whom I had known, but not well, was arrested on a streetcar in Washington for indecent exposure. Then a consul general in Australia was thrown off a boat in Sydney harbor for molesting two boys. Finally, a consul general in Prague suffered a mental breakdown and shut himself in his hotel room, where he lived on beer and raw beef. When he got word that the consul was coming to take him into custody, he jumped in a taxicab and headed for Carlsbad, scattering hunks of beef on the way, presumably to divert his pursuers.

I soon learned that those were isolated incidents, by no means typical of the Foreign Service. The department was so small (there were only 614 people working for State in Washington in 1929 compared with 6,396 in 1972) that I soon got to know, like, and respect most of them, although I never even saw the first two Secretaries of State I worked under, Frank B. Kellogg and Henry L. Stimson. The small size of the Foreign Service produced an intimacy that helped a great deal in personnel matters. The boards of promotion or review, as well as personnel officers, came to know and were able to give much more time to the consideration of the personal qualities of each officer and his problems. I suppose it is nostalgia, but it seems to me that a smaller, more compact, more intimately integrated Foreign Service would be better than the vast sprawling mass of people who now administer the government's foreign policy.

The third step in my training was to decide whether to be a generalist, as most Foreign Service officers were, or to specialize. I decided to specialize.

One of the difficulties in the Foreign Service in those days was that an officer would spend two, three, or even four years in one country and then be transferred to another without really having much opportunity to acquire a serious knowledge of the first country's customs, institutions, and history. This skipping around like a water bug from one country to another had produced a certain superficiality in our career officers. To increase the knowledge of certain countries and areas, a program of regional specialization had been established. After some thought, I decided to concentrate on Russia. Although this was one of the most important decisions of my life, I am not sure why I chose Russia. At Harvard, my general field had been modern European history, and this naturally included courses on Russia. I imagine it was during this period that my interest in Russian affairs began. But I did no special work or reading on the Bolshevik Revolution. I do not recall any deep interest in what the Bolsheviks were trying to do, and I shared the common American ignorance of what was going on in the Soviet Union. Thus I did not join any pro-Soviet group, as some of my contemporaries did, much to their eventual regret.

I did see, however, the growing importance of the Soviet Union, and realized that the United States would need experts to deal with the Communist state. Another freshman Foreign Service officer, Edward Page, who later became Minister to Bulgaria, also decided to specialize in Russian affairs. We were the third group of two to select Russia under the specialization program.

Before beginning my specialization, I was sent to Prague for two years for some on-the-job training in general diplomatic work. Another purpose of this preliminary assignment, I suppose, was to test whether I was cut out to be a diplomat before investing in specialized training for me.

In Prague, I went through the usual routine of a new vice-consul. To get experience, I was rotated through jobs in various sections of the Consulate—visas, invoices, passports, commercial reporting, and, finally, political reporting. The work was generally routine.

At that time, the demand for United States immigration visas was very great. One of our constant efforts was to find and destroy fraudulent visas, which were sold in many capitals of Europe. In some cases, local officials would falsify birth certificates and facts to enable an applicant to get a legitimate visa. One day, a Czech man and his wife came into the Consulate with several children, apparently of minor ages. One of the "boys," although rather large, was dressed in short pants and bounced a ball along the corridor. Suspicious, we had him examined by a doctor, who said the "boy" was actually a man. He did not get a visa.

One of the most interesting experiences of my tour was a trip I took with a member of the Consulate to Ruthenia, or Podkarpaska Rus, as it was known then. In my report, my first for the Foreign Service, I found the Czech administration of the predominantly Hungarian and Ukrainian region to be relatively just.

Life in Prague in 1929, 1930, and 1931 was pleasant. In the winter I went skiing in Schpindelmühle in northern Czechoslovakia. In the summer I visited Slovakia, the Tatra Mountains, and the entire area of Bohemia. There was as yet no threat from Germany; in fact, except for the age-old enmity of the Hungarians and, to a lesser extent, hostility from the Rumanians, the Czech Republic had little trouble with her neighbors.

In September, 1931, I was transferred to the Ecole Nationale des Langues Orientales Vivantes in Paris. It was to Paris that most of our officers were sent for language study, since the majority knew French. Paris was a perfect choice for me, even though I was learning Russian, because, with my mother's teaching, I already spoke French fluently.

Life in Paris was sheer delight. Prices were down because of the worldwide depression, and we could get along nicely on our $2,500 a year State Department salaries. Page, who was starting his language study at the same time, and I rented a plush apartment on the Rue de Lille. We ate in good restaurants and enjoyed all that Paris offers young bachelors. This splendid existence ended abruptly when the dollar was devalued in the spring of 1933. This meant a 40 percent cut in the purchasing power of our salaries overnight. Page and I had to give up our luxurious flat (it was only after months of wrangling that we were able to terminate the lease without a lawsuit) and move into a cheaper apartment. We were forced to forgo the better restaurants and eat in those of the fourth or fifth category. It was then that I learned of the French system under which class A restaurants served food only on the day it came from the market. Food that was not used was sold to class B restaurants, who offered it two days from market, and then was passed down the line, day by day, progressively more distant from the market, to the lower-grade restaurants.

I spent two and a half years in Paris studying the Russian language, history, customs, geography, and economics, with particular reference to the Soviet period, which at that time was hardly fourteen years old. The work load was heavy but interesting and enjoyable. Most of the classroom instruction was in Russian. There were a few lectures on Marxism and Russian history by French professors, but most of our study of such subjects came from books, almost all anti-Communist, that we were supposed to read on our own time. Naturally, I began to follow news about the Bolshevik government. Many reports came from Riga, Latvia, which served as a listening post for the Soviet Union then just as Hong Kong did for Communist China decades later.

Our Russian-language teacher was Paul Boyer, the director of the school, who conducted his classes with brilliance and a sardonic wit. Possessed of an *esprit gaulois*, he gave a slightly indecent twist to many Russian expressions. For example, the Russian word for marriage, to marry "on" someone, expressed, he said, the *"idée physique du mariage."*

The Russian language is complex, but not too difficult to learn if you have time to devote to it, as I did. The grammar looks extremely complicated at first, with six cases and two forms of the verb; but under Professor Boyer apparent contradictions straightened themselves out, and on the whole it became quite a logical language. It is a beautiful language, too, excellent for music and poetry because of the many vowels. I never had any particular problem in learning Russian, and I still get pleasure out of reading and speaking it.

Of course, practice is important in acquiring a vocabulary and fluency in any language. In the summer, I was sent to Estonia, which was independent then, to live in a Russian pension, where I immersed myself in the sound and feel of Russian. The pension was in Narva Joesu, a former Russian resort with a magnificent beach, about four hours from Tallin. Under the name of Hungerburg, it had been the chief summer resort for St. Petersburg. Life in the Serebryakovy sisters' pension undoubtedly followed the centuries-old style of the leisure class of Czarist Russia. In the morning there were language lessons. Lunch was very late, around four o'clock. Then we took a nap, followed by a walk, often to gather mushrooms in the forest. After a late supper, the samovar would be set on a table outdoors. Then we would converse for two or three hours like characters in the stories of Chekhov, discussing philosophy and morals, reciting poetry, talking politics, and sipping tea.

The Serebryakovy sisters came from Leningrad, which they always referred to by its pre-war name of St. Petersburg. Both were strongly anti-Bolshevik and lived in the hope that someday the nightmare would pass away and they would return to old Russia, complete with Czar and aristocracy. One of the sisters was well educated and had been a teacher in the Smolny Institute, a school for the daughters of the Russian nobility which the Bolsheviks had seized and used as a headquarters before the October Revolution. It was she who inspired my interest in Russian literature—the classics of Tolstoy, Dostoevsky, Turgenev, Chekhov, and others.

One engaging feature of life in Narva Joesu was the beach. It was divided into two sections by lines in the sand. On the left the females bathed in the nude; on the right the males bathed in suits. I spent many an hour on the beach, but I could never get over the novelty of being greeted by a bevy of naked Estonian beauties. The Estonian people are a singularly handsome race of Scandinavian origin—tall, blond, and well built in comparison with Russians.

Once when a friend from America visited me for a week or so, we decided to go up to the Soviet frontier. We walked along a dusty road until we came to the Estonian frontier post. Standing there, we looked into Russia. It was my first glimpse of the soil of that country. We could see the Soviet sentries and a guards' tower, but we never got close enough to talk to any Russian.

When the summer was over, I went to Tallin and lived about a month with the family of a man who had been a big timber merchant in Russia before the war and who still carried on the business from Tallin. The family was immensely Russian, full of the curiosity which characterized the pre-Revolution Russian intelligentsia, and obsessed with deep and unworkable philosophical concepts.

I passed two summers in Estonia. They were delightful, but, more important, they enabled me to become relatively fluent in Russian, since, from the time I set foot in Estonia at the end of June until I left in the middle of September, I spoke hardly a word of English.

Life was so pleasant during those two and a half years in school that I only dimly realized the basic changes stirring in Europe and America. However, I did undergo two experiences that opened my eyes to the kind of world that I would soon have to deal with as a diplomat. On February 7, 1934, I saw the class conflict in action in Paris. Right-wingers staged a spectacular demonstration in the Place de la Concorde. A motor bus had been overturned and set on fire, covering the area with a pall of dark smoke which reflected the street lights and searchlights that intermittently lit up the action. The demonstrators were relatively well behaved until the Garde Mobile opened fire to prevent their crossing the bridge leading to the Chamber of Deputies; then they turned ugly. They began to throw rocks at the policemen and to hamstring the horses of the Garde Républicaine with razors tied to sticks. The rioting lasted until late that night. The next night it was the turn of the left, and the crowds rioted and robbed along the Rue de Rivoli. The unrest of February, 1934, led to cooperation between the Communists and the Socialists in France, a coalition known as the Popular Front. This tactic was officially adopted in 1935 by the Russian-dominated Third International.

The second experience involved a young German army officer whom I met on the steamer from Stettin to Tallin. His English was barely passable, and my German was rudimentary, but as we played chess we were able to carry on a discussion about Germany. He lived for one goal, to revenge the humiliations of the World War I settlement, which he contended had been forced on Germany by treachery. It was clear that he had been deeply influenced by Nazi propaganda—at that time Hitler was maneuvering to assume power—and my feeble attempts to set the historical record straight were greeted tolerantly, ironically, and pityingly. He said that he fully expected to die on the battlefield, that every young German of his age felt the same way. War was inevitable, he said, but this time Germany would be adequately prepared and would have the morale and the will to prevail. Blaming the Bolsheviks for the destruction of the fabric of German social life, he envisaged war with the Soviet Union.

In the United States, there was also strong interest in the Soviet Union, but of a different kind. Not long after becoming president, Franklin D. Roosevelt had decided to end the sixteen years of estrangement—an "anomaly," he termed it—between the two countris and extend diplomatic recognition to the Soviet Union. I was visiting Washington in 1933 when the President and William C. Bullitt, who was to be our first ambassador to the Soviet Union, were conferring with Maxim Litvinov, the Soviet Foreign Commissar, over the terms of recognition.

Obviously, I was delighted with the decision to recognize the Soviet Union. It seemed clear to me that the time had long passed when the two potentially most powerful nations of the earth should not be officially speaking to each other, especially in view of the rise of the Hitler and Mussolini dictatorships in Europe and the truculent nature of Japan's actions in the Far East.

THE SMELL OF MAKHORKA

I was chosen by Ambassador Bullitt to be a member of the new Embassy, and subsequently ordered to join his party of some fifteen persons leaving Paris on February 27, 1934, by train and stopping off in Warsaw for two or three days. Slowed by a mild blizzard, the train took well over twenty-four hours to travel from Warsaw to the Soviet border. There, at Negoreloye, where we changed trains, we were met by a Soviet Assistant Chief of Protocol. The dank smell of the station in Negoreloye—the odor of wet sheepskin coats, of sawdust spread on the floors to absorb moisture, of disinfectant, of pink soap, of human sweat, and of the cheap Russian tobacco known as Makhorka—still remains for me the smell of the Soviet Union.

CHAPTER TWO

The Shattering of Illusions

As our train drew into Moscow station on March 8, 1934, Ambassador Bullitt, noting a band on the platform, put on his hat and overcoat and prepared for a small welcoming ceremony. But when he stepped down from the train, he saw that the band, instead of being opposite his compartment, was facing the third-class cars. The musicians were there not to welcome him but to greet a delegation of Communist women arriving for the celebration of Red International Women's Day. The only Russians meeting the Ambassador and his staff were the Soviet Chief of Protocol and George Andreychin, an old friend of Bullitt's. This trivial incident turned out to be a symbol of Bullitt's mission—the great expectation and the dashed hopes.

Never showing his disappointment over the small welcome, Bullitt smilingly posed for news photographers while Russian porters with white aprons ran around picking up luggage. As we came out of the dark, cavernous station, I had my first view of Moscow. The city was appallingly drab, disorderly, and somber. There were piles of dirty snow on the sidewalks, and most of the people walked with their heads down. We got into automobiles and drove to Spaso House, the Ambassador's Residence, in the western part of the city. Our route took us through the center of the city, and I was impressed by the crowds—especially the large numbers of people clinging to dull brown streetcars, which were then the chief method of transportation in Moscow.

At Spaso House, Bullitt spoke a few words of inspiration to the staff. Then he took those of us who were going to live there on a tour of our new home. (Since I was a bachelor and spoke Russian, I was invited to live in a room in the residence until an apartment-office

14

building on Mokhavaya Street was completed.) A large and relatively elegant mansion built for a merchant, Spaso House stood in a garden on Spasopeskovskaya Ploshchad (Square of the Sacred Sands). It was made of stucco, with a columned, rounded balcony in front, and could have been a house in Italy. There was no question about the main feature of the mansion—an immense central hall, two stories high, with marble columns all around and a gigantic chandelier hanging from the ceiling. It was ideal for entertaining. Through the years, this room was the scene of impromptu performances by the cast of *Porgy and Bess*, art shows, balls, church services, children's pageants, and concerts by American artists.

To one side was a large wing, constructed as a music room, which we found useful for a badminton court, Christmas parties, dance studio, schoolroom, and various other purposes. The rooms on the second floor opened on a gallery running around the chandelier room, and it was on this floor that the Ambassador and his family had their living quarters. Perhaps the most intriguing part of Spaso was the basement, a warren of cubicles, including storerooms, so necessary in Moscow, where a three-or-four-month supply of food and liquor, purchased in Western Europe, had to be kept under lock and key. Also in the basement were the kitchen, servants' rooms, furnaces, and many mysterious passages.

Here, too, was the apartment of the caretaker, Sergei, and his wife. Sergei, a slight, short Russian, always wore a pleasant expression. His wife, who was one of the maids, was rather good-looking and high-spirited. It was generally assumed from the beginning that Spaso House was insecure and that Sergei was an agent of the Soviet security police. Thus we did not transact much official business there. We suspected that Sergei's apartment contained espionage devices, but his door was always locked and we had no key to it. Years later, when I was ambassador and Sergei was still caretaker, I insisted on having a key. After a delay of several weeks, one was produced, but the apartment had been cleaned out. Sergei and his wife soon went into retirement.

As we walked through Spaso House, Bullitt told us he wanted the Embassy to be a model for the American diplomatic service. The Ambassador was a man of great appeal. Slight, of medium height, with a round face and a bald head, he had an effervescent personality, which he could turn on and off at will. His brilliant smile and his eloquence, coupled with his wide knowledge, usually succeeded in charming even the dubious. He was convinced that it was possible to establish friendly relations with the Soviet Union, and had played a major role in the 1933 negotiations that led to American recognition. On the train from Paris to Moscow, he had fascinated us with accounts of his 1919 visit to the new Soviet state, which was then fighting a civil war against a strong White Russian army, and of his conversations with Lenin. Bullitt had been sent from the peace conference at Versailles to Moscow by Colonel Edward M. House, President Wilson's trusted aide, presumably with the consent of Wilson, on a purely fact-finding mission. It is almost certain that Bullitt stretched his instructions. He had several interviews with Lenin and brought back a plan which, had it been accepted and put into effect, could have changed the history of the world. It called for a cease-fire between all warring factions on Russian soil, a recognition of the authority of each army over the areas under its control, and a peace conference among all major contenders. When one considers that at that moment the White Army controlled most of the country, it is obvious that this was not a plan preferred by the Bolsheviks. Still, it was one which would have given them time to recover some strength. It was a good example of Bolshevik realism in taking account of the correlation of forces in Russia and in arriving at the conclusion that it was best over the long haul to make a temporary truce on the soil of Russia. It is also possible that the plan was proposed by the Bolsheviks with the idea that it would be rejected and thereby increase their popular appeal as the party of peace.

Bullitt returned to Versailles to find that the atmosphere of the conference had radically changed from interest to downright hostility. Given the anti-Bolshevik mood of the conference, the idea of any deal with Lenin was anathema, and Bullitt was repudiated by President Wilson and Lloyd George, the British Prime Minister. Bullitt resigned in anger, writing a letter to Wilson in which he castigated the Treaty of Versailles in prophetic terms.

Fifteen years later, because he was so eager to make a success of his mission, Bullitt handpicked all the officers of the first American Embassy staff, either from personal acquaintance or on recommendation of people he trusted. We had been chosen, I think, in the belief that we would view the Soviet scene impartially and objectively in the light only of the interest of the United States. The quality of the people he selected is shown by the fact that five officers of that first staff eventually became chiefs of mission.

The Counselor, as the number-two man in the Embassy was known then, was John C. Wiley, an experienced diplomat of many years' standing. He was a tall, impressive man with a deep voice and a good sense of humor. He was a pragmatic diplomat with an extensive knowledge of the policies and attitudes of the European countries, although he was new to the Russian scene and did not speak the language. Wiley's steadiness was a good offset to Bullitt's exuberance and tendency to go to extremes. Wiley eventually became ambassador to a number of countries, including Portugal, Iran, Colombia, and Panama.

The First Secretary of the Embassy was Loy W. Henderson. Although he spoke only a little Russian, he had been studying the Soviet Union for a number of years and had pronounced views on the need for taking great care in our dealing with the Bolsheviks. A man with a high sense of duty and honesty, he would go to any trouble to help a younger staff officer, of which I was one, to learn his trade. Henderson was the chief political officer of the Embassy. He was also, in effect, the administrator of the Embassy, since neither Bullitt nor Wiley was particularly gifted in that field. During Stalin's great purges, when Henderson was chargé d'affaires for at least two years, he wrote some brilliant dispatches from Moscow. Eventually, Henderson became ambassador to Iraq, Iran, and India.

Of the rest of the Foreign Service officers, three of us were Russian-language officers—George Kennan, Bertel T. Kuniholm, and I, all Third Secretaries. We three constituted half of the Russian-language officers in the State Department at that time. Kuniholm, a man of great ambition, reported on economic affairs. Kennan and I were assigned to the political section and worked under Henderson.

Kennan was probably the outstanding individual of the Embassy staff. Although young, he looked distinguished because he was tall, thin, and slightly balding, with a faintly ascetic expression. The fine qualities of his mind were already apparent to the rest of us. He was an excellent political reporter and analyst, but even in 1934 I felt that his interest in literature equaled his interest in Soviet political affairs. We frequently went together to lectures and concerts. While Kennan achieved a distinguished career in letters, I think it was unfortunate that he never wrote the biography of Chekhov he thought of doing in 1934. Kennan, who went on to become a brilliant policy planner in the State Department, ambassador in Moscow for a short time, and eventually, under President Kennedy, ambassador to Yugoslavia, was and remained one of my best friends. Through decades of turmoil, we kept in touch and generally thought similarly about Soviet policy.

One of my closest friends in the Embassy was Elbridge Durbrow, who was in charge of the Consulate. Durbrow was a man of irrepressible energy and good humor. When I moved from the Embassy, we shared an apartment and he became and has remained a close friend. He was ambassador to South Vietnam under President Eisenhower, before American involvement in the war there.

Another member of the staff was Charles Thayer, my future brother-in-law, who had been in Moscow as a tourist and had been hired as a clerk the preceding December during a visit by Bullitt.* Blue-eyed, round-faced, Thayer was unabashed by authority and kept us in good humor with his marvelous sense of the ridiculous. He wrote a number of books about Russia. Although he was a West Point graduate, Thayer left the Army in 1933 and joined the Foreign Service in 1937. During the war, he was head of the American team maintaining liaison with Marshal Tito, the Communist guerrilla leader, the future President of the Yugoslav Republic. In 1953, Thayer fell victim to Senator Joseph R. McCarthy's witch-hunting and left the Foreign Service.

Among the others in the Embassy in 1934, the most talented was Lieutenant Thomas D. White, an assistant military attaché, who became Chief of Staff of the Air Force after World War II.

Right from the beginning, the Moscow Embassy was different from other American missions overseas. Every Embassy is charged with a half-dozen general tasks, the most fundamental of which is to transact official business between the two governments. To carry out this mission, information on the political situation in the country must be collected and analyzed to determine the direction of foreign policy; military data must be gathered to estimate how much force a government can marshal to back up its policy. In addition, every Embassy must service American travelers and foreigners who want to visit or emigrate to the United States, and help in trade matters.

In Moscow, our emphasis was quite different from the established missions in other countries. One factor that made a difference was the fact that there were few American travelers in Russia and almost no attempt by individual Russians to overcome Bolshevik restrictions on emigration. As a result, the new Embassy was relieved of two of the chores that consume so much of the time of our missions in Western Europe.

This was indeed fortunate, because we had to spend a great deal of time in the early days just getting temporary headquarters set up in

---

*Bullitt presented his letters of credence in December, 1933, and then returned to Washington to collect his staff.

the run-down Savoy Hotel. Almost all of us were kept busy on house-keeping matters—locating shipments of furniture and supplies, trying to get goods cleared through customs, making sure living quarters had a decent amount of hot water. As a result, no regular office hours were kept at first. Official business was intermittent, to say the least.

An inordinate amount of time also went into finding the consumer goods our staff needed to put up with life in Moscow. The shortage of such goods was striking. Living conditions in general were difficult and complicated even for American diplomats, who were in a privi-leged position in the months following our arrival in Moscow.

Among the many things lacking in Spaso House were clothes hang-ers. Bullitt's two French servants, who had on their arrival become instantly disillusioned with Moscow, insisted that hangers for the Ambassador's clothes must be obtained at all cost. Thayer had hired a Russian named Grisha, who, in some obscure manner, had become the owner of a motorcycle with a sidecar. Charlie, Grisha, and I careened around the muddy streets of Moscow all one day in search of clothes hangers (I had to look up the Russian word—*veselka*—in the diction-ary). Eventually, we discovered a limited number of wooden hangers and took them back in triumph to Spaso.

Even obtaining rubles for the Embassy staff to make purchases was a major problem. Every foreign mission in Moscow was operating on the black market, for if an attempt had been made to adhere to the official rate of exchange, which was about two rubles to the dollar, no government could have afforded to maintain an embassy. In addition to the official and black-market rates—about sixty to the dollar—there were at least three other methods of calculating the value of the ruble. There was the Torgsin ruble, named for the stores that accepted only foreign currency and thus gave a rough estimate of the real value of goods; the foreign-trade ruble, and the special interest rate for Soviet enterprises. In a conversation he had had with the Commissar for Finance, G. F. Grinko, on his previous visit to Moscow in December, Bullitt had been assured that it would be possible to work out a legiti-mate means of obtaining rubles for the use of the Embassy. He was soon to be disillusioned. Not only the Commissar for Finance but also the Commissar for Foreign Affairs, Litvinov, curtly informed him that there could be no exception to the Soviet rate of exchange. Finally Litvinov, admitting that the American attempt to play fair was becoming embarrassing, told Bullitt, "If worst comes to worst, you know that we shall have no possible objection to your obtaining paper rubles in any way you think fit." The American Embassy then did as other foreign missions did and obtained rubles by purchasing them abroad and bringing them in by diplomatic pouch. Warsaw and Harbin were the chief sources of supply, I believe.

The new Embassy also differed from American missions in other countries in its preoccupation with security. While Bullitt was enamored of the Russian people, he realized that the Soviet police would do everything they could to learn our secrets. At his urging, Moscow became the first American Embassy with Marine guards. In the beginning, the six Marines performed little guard duty because of the chaotic nature of our operation, and they found feminine companionship, as they had in other countries. One day as I sat in the lobby of the Savoy Hotel, a highly painted Russian woman walked up to the desk and said she wished to go up to Sergeant O'Dean's room. The Russian room clerk looked at her suspiciously and asked, "Why do you want to visit Sergeant O'Dean?" She replied airily. "I am his Russian teacher." A few months later, after the Embassy offices were moved to the Mokhavaya Building, security was tightened.

Another difference was the emphasis that Bullitt put on the development of close ties with the Russian people. Convinced that the basis for a solid political relationship was understanding between people, he constantly urged us to mix with the Russians. As a bachelor, I eagerly carried out his instructions. Contact with the average Russian was relatively easy, and among others the young members of the ballet corps always seemed willing to accept a date from a foreigner, particularly an American. One evening, Bullitt invited the director of the Moscow Ballet to Spaso House for dinner to show her a film of Balinese dancing. The director, much impressed, commented that it might be useful to show the film to the corps de ballet. Whereupon, Bullitt, with a lordly manner, turned to Thayer and me and said, "Arrange a showing for the corps de ballet." Thinking that we were going to be plunged into a mass of pulchritudinous young ladies, we put more than our normal energy into arranging the evening. To our dismay a dreary, scrubby-looking group of young ladies appeared. They were abominably dressed, their faces plain, without makeup; their hair indifferently combed. Nevertheless, the evening was gay and we made a number of pleasant acquaintances.

After that, there were usually two or three ballerinas running around the Embassy. They would go there for lunch and supper and would sit around talking and drinking until dawn. One of them, a short, plain little girl named Charnotskaya, was a true believer of the Communist doctrine and would spend hours trying to indoctrinate us in the glories of the Soviet Union. She told me once that any automobile produced by any Communist was always superior to any automobile produced by any capitalist.

In those days, the ballerinas were given free run of the diplomatic corps, and many temporary liaisons were formed. One of the girls had an unrequited passion for Bullitt, and she spent hours talking of her undying love for the Ambassador, describing him as her sun, her moon, and her stars.

Once, a group of earnest young theater workers came to the Embassy and asked if we would help them out in the production of the American play *The Front Page*. Kennan and I went down to the theater once or twice a week to advise them on how to achieve an authentic American mood for the production. Some of the misconceptions about the United States which Communist propaganda had succeeded in creating in the minds of these young Russians were amusing. In their version of the play, the city editor wore a top hat and tailcoat to work. These young Russians assumed that this was the normal dress of anybody in a position of importance in a capitalist society. We thoroughly enjoyed this brief incursion into the Soviet theater, especially an opening-night party backstage. It was typical of most Russian parties—relaxed, with no one caring about the rank of any guest. There were brisk exchanges of ideas and a general feeling of ease and familiarity. This party was one of our first introductions to the Russian habit of interminable speechmaking. Everybody made a speech, including Kennan and me. Although we spoke haltingly, we did speak Russian. The variety of food was limited, but the amount of liquor was exceptional. There was vodka, Caucasian wine, and Caucasian cognac, all liberally imbibed.

One of the Russians I met and became relatively friendly with was Mikhail Bulgakov, at that time the outstanding playwright in Russia. He had a round, Ukrainian face, a reddish snub nose, and a gregarious personality enhanced by his bright, twinkly eyes. He did not hesitate to express his opinions about the Soviet system. He had had an extraordinarily successful yet controversial career in the Soviet theater. His plays had been consistently popular. He had also had an uninterrupted series of conflicts with the Soviet censorship. He once told me he would never put a Communist in any of his plays, since he considered them to be nothing but two-dimensional figures.

The coup de grâce was administered to Bulgakov after he had written a story titled "The Fateful Egg." It concerned a professor who inadvertently put a growth drug he had developed into the wrong eggs, which hatched reptiles. The reptiles kept growing and turned into monsters a hundred meters long. They quickly multiplied and began ravaging the countryside. The Red Army was called out but was decisively defeated. Just when disaster seemed inevitable, a sharp frost miraculously came and killed all the monsters. *Nedra*, a minor literary journal, printed the entire story before the editors realized it was a parody on Bolshevism, which turned men into monsters who were destroying Russia and who could be stopped only by the intervention of God.

When the real meaning of the story was understood, a campaign of denunciation was unleashed against Bulgakov. Cartoons appeared in the press with such captions as "Stamp out Bulgakovism on the cultural front." Bulgakov used these cartoons attacking him to cover the walls of his apartment. As a result of the campaign, all his plays were banned and he could no longer obtain any employment. He applied for an exit visa. He told me that one day he was in his apartment, feeling depressed, when his telephone rang and a voice said, "Comrade Stalin wishes to speak to you." Bulgakov thought it was a joke of some friend and, giving a suitable answer, hung up. A few minutes later, the telephone rang again and the same voice said, "I am quite serious. It is indeed Comrade Stalin." It was. Stalin asked Bulgakov why he wished to desert his motherland. Bulgakov explained that since he was a playwright by profession but could not work at it in the Soviet Union, he wished to do so abroad. Stalin told him, "Do not act hastily. We will fix up something." In a few days, Bulgakov was appointed assistant director of the First Moscow Art Theater, and one of his plays, *The Days of the Turbines*, an excellent revolutionary play, was restaged at the same theater. Bulgakov, however, could never leave well enough alone and was soon in difficulty again with the theater. He was working as an assistant librettist at the Bolshoi Theater in Moscow when he died. In a freer society, Bulgakov would undoubtedly have been recognized as a great playwright.

Another Soviet citizen whom we saw a good deal was Bullitt's friend, George Andreychin. His dark face and bushy gray hair fitted the stereotype of the radical. But Andreychin, although he believed theoretically in the Revolution, was not a man of violence; in fact, he had a gentle, almost sweet nature. He was articulate and had much to talk about. The son of a Macedonian peasant, he had been recommended by his local priest to the King of Bulgaria as a bright youth who would be worth educating at the expense of the Crown. The idea was that he would become a pillar of the royal establishment. But

Andreychin soon became a Marxist and a revolutionary. Eventually, he was brought to the King, who told him that his course would lead to his arrest. They parted on apparently friendly terms, with Andreychin heading toward a long period of arrests, imprisonment, and all the other experiences of a revolutionary at the beginning of the twentieth century. By curious coincidence, the two met again, shortly after the Russian Revolution, in a small station in Switzerland. Having been deposed, the King was going into exile, while Andreychin, the ex-peasant boy, was going to Russia to become an official of the Soviet government.

Before World War I, when Andreychin had been in the United States, he was active in the "Wobblies," the revolutionary Industrial Workers of the World. He was arrested, and Bullitt, I believe, was one of those who put up bail for him. Andreychin, however, fled the country. Shortly after his arrival in Moscow, Bullitt wrote President Roosevelt to inquire into the possibility of having the old indictment against Andreychin quashed. Replying in a jocular letter, Roosevelt stated that while he could understand Bullitt's feelings, nevertheless it was quite impossible for the President to lift the indictment for Bullitt's "little playmate."

In our early days in Moscow, Soviet authorities assigned Andreychin, who spoke English perfectly, to be the companion of Americans. He was working for Intourist, and often had to shepherd important visitors around. Despite Soviet propaganda about elevating the status of women, one of Andreychin's tasks was to keep some important visitors supplied with girls.

In his enthusiasm for contacts with the people, Bullitt prodded us to teach the Russians to play baseball. He sent to the United States for bats, balls, and gloves, and about once a week we would gather in a park to instruct the Russians, who were only mildly interested. Apparently, they had been ordered to play with the Americans. Their interest declined even further when a Russian who was learning to catch missed a fast ball. The ball hit him in the head and knocked him out. Finally the baseball school was abandoned.

Thayer had the same bad luck in trying to introduce polo. He did succeed, at a dinner where large quantities of vodka were consumed, in persuading Marshal Semyon M. Budenny, Inspector General of the Cavalry, to start polo in the Red Army. Charlie sent a telegram to a cousin in England ordering equipment for two teams. Budenny assigned a group of Cossacks to Charlie, who had played polo at West Point. The Cossacks were beautiful riders but did not have the foggiest notion of how to hit the ball and absolutely no sense of boundaries. They would hit the ball and charge off in a cloud of dust with Charlie behind them on a horse yelling, "Back, back" in Russian. When the teams had been trained, there was a formal opening of the polo matches. Bullitt was referee and Marshal Klimenti E. Voroshilov, Commissar for Defense, was guest of honor. The proceedings were slightly marred when half of his honor guards, while parading in front of Bullitt, misunderstood a command to turn right and turned left. Some of the Soviet officials saw polo as a trick to insinuate capitalist propaganda into the Soviet Union. The game was played no more than two or three times, and even before Bullitt's departure the venture was dropped.

One of the principal objects of that early people-to-people campaign of Bullitt's was meeting Soviet officials. It was relatively easy in those days before the purge to meet some political figures. One night in the summer of 1934, Bullitt invited Nikolai I. Bukharin, one of the genuine old Bolsheviks and an original member of Lenin's first Politburo, to dinner. Bukharin had become the leader of the "right opposition" to Stalin in 1930 and had been defeated and removed from his high Party positions while still retaining his Party membership. By 1934, Bukharin had been partially reinstated and was editor of *Izvestia*.

With Bukharin that evening was Karl B. Radek, a prominent but not leading Bolshevik in the early days of the Revolution. He was a man of surpassing ugliness, with a brilliant and cynical mind. Of Polish extraction, Radek had been a useful publicist for the Bolsheviks. Having been closely associated with Trotsky, he was sent to Siberia, where he recanted. In Moscow on what was, in effect, probation, he wrote editorials for various Soviet newspapers. Commenting on an observation by Ambassador Bullitt, Radek said to me in Russian, "You Westerners will never understand Bolshevism. You consider Bolshevism as a hot bath whose temperature can be raised and lowered to suit the taste of the bather. This is not true. You are either a hundred percent in the bath and a hundred percent for it, or you are a hundred percent outside and a hundred percent against it." Radek knew what he was talking about. Both he and Bukharin were victims of the purge a few years later.

Our early days were so taken up with the establishment of the Embassy that we had little opportunity to follow Bullitt's advice to carry his people-to-people campaign out of Moscow to other parts of Russia. By the end of October, our duties had eased sufficiently for

Thayer and me to go to the Caucasus. Andreychin, as an Intourist official, arranged an itinerary to take us north of Baku on the Caspian Sea for some hunting, then back across the peninsula to Batumi to catch a boat for Istanbul.

We found the Moscow-Baku express exceptionally comfortable, although the wooden cars were all of pre-World War I vintage. Because of the wide Russian tracks, the cars were roomier than American trains and the berths were placed across the compartments instead of lengthwise, minimizing the roll and making it easier to sleep. The dining car was reasonably clean, and although the menu was limited, there always seemed to be a supply of good, hot soup. The express was not noted for its speed, and took three days to go approximately a thousand miles.

On the train, we found Marshal Budenny, who was a hero of the Russian civil war and the leader of the Red cavalry forces. It was he who had cooperated in the polo venture. He seemed delighted that we were on the train, and we invited him to our compartment to drink American whiskey. After we had a drink or two, Budenny said that he really liked our American *vino* very much (in Russian *vino* applies to spirits as well as to wine). Budenny, who was on his way south to Gagry, where he was going boar hunting with Stalin, was, as always, in a talkative mood, and gave an earthy account of his early life. The inefficiency of the Czar's army, the indifference of the officers, and the total lack of discipline and organization as he described them were appalling.

Budenny also told us about the capture of a White Russian officer in the civil war. The officer, Budenny said, had ordered the execution of some of Budenny's young relatives in a captured village by picking the children up by their heels and slamming their heads against a stone wall. Stroking his abundant mustache, Budenny said, "I dealt appropriately with that swine."

As the evening wore on, Budenny became somewhat incoherent. Turning to international politics, he stated that the Soviet Union and the United States had a great destiny and that they should become friends with China, which he called a marvelous country. It was not quite clear in what context he placed China, but nevertheless he wrote on a piece of paper that within ten years China would be a great power and that relations between the Soviet Union and the United States would bear witness to that development. I am inclined to think his prediction was the result of his intoxicated imagination rather than prescience.

The next morning about dawn, after having sat up all night, he asked the conductor to let him know when the train arrived at his station. The attendant replied that we had already passed that station. Budenny exploded into a rich flow of oaths (of which no language contains a better supply than Russian) and almost hit the attendant. Typically, the attendant was wrong and we had not reached Budenny's station. When we arrived, he stood up, took a deep breath, buttoned up his tunic, and stepped off the train, apparently sober.

On arriving in Baku, Thayer and I were immediately put in touch with the director of Intourist, an estimable gentleman named Badaev, who proceeded to drop everything he was doing (he was at that time also head of the timber trust of the Baku area) and promptly organized an expedition for us.

Our party, consisting of Badaev, his body servant, a Soviet business official, and Charlie and me, started out from Baku in a car. We were followed by an autobus filled with Caucasians wearing black fuzzy hats and carrying shotguns. There was a large barrel of beer on the bus, and a number of times, along the Caspian Sea, we stopped, bought some *raki*, or crayfish, sold by venders, and had a tasty snack and drink.

Our destination was the big steppe area where the small gazelle, known to the Russians as *djiran*, live. When we reached the steppe, the two vehicles moved along side by side. Men on the roof of the bus watched, and when they saw the white tails of the *djiran* bobbing along, a great shout went up. The vehicles plunged forward, sometimes reaching fifty miles per hour, which was slightly faster than the gazelles could run. We shot from the speeding automobile. I was on one side, Charlie on the other, so we each had a relatively free shot at the bounding gazelles. I brought down two or three and so did Charlie. In the middle of the rear seat, the Russian would shoot between the heads of our host and his servant, who was driving the car, much to our concern.

Given such opportunities for direct contact with the people, I soon came to appreciate the qualities of the Russians. I know of no one who has been in Russia, whatever his attitude toward the regime, who has felt anything but affection for the Russian people as a whole. They are simple and unaffected—primitive in the best sense of the word—and dislike many of the niceties of more sophisticated societies. They are natural, their characters and attitudes not having been frozen into molds by centuries of convention. I have always felt that a Russian is an individualist who gives his personal reaction to situations and people, with nothing stylized or conventional. There is also the well-known tendency of the Russians to accept with passivity harsh dictatorial authority over their lives. This is only apparently inconsistent with their individuality. The whole Russian tradition indicates that the people have built a wall between themselves and the authorities. In Russia, authority is considered as remote as the weather, with no direct connection between an individual's personal life and the decisions of those in command. It is, however, possible for the Soviet citizen to surround his personal life with a large degree of protection against the psychological effects of authority.

Probably the most remarkable example of the Russians' tacit acceptance of authority was their passivity during Stalin's purge of millions from 1935 to 1939. Such a mindless and all-pervading bloodbath could take place only in a country where the actions of the authorities are outside the influence of the ordinary citizen. But even during the terror, the Soviet citizen was able to maintain a considerable degree of privacy in his personal life. It is true, of course, that Soviet authorities have sought to penetrate this private area, and millions of Soviet citizens suffered personal tragedy, but still, any foreigner who has lived in Russia and has had an opportunity to see Russians under the Soviet regime is struck by the extent to which their lives go on without being affected by the policies, if not the actions, of the regime.

Except in moments of great violence—and Russian history records times of extreme violence and ruthlessness—the average Russian is an easygoing person with a certain distaste for sustained labor. There is no doubt that climate plays a part in forming this character. It is not only the cold itself but also its duration. Winter in Moscow lasts seven months, the days are short, the sky is slate gray with lowering clouds, and the countryside around the city is shrouded in an endless expanse of snow, as though in a sleep of death. In tiny villages, a few wisps of smoke rising from the peasants' *isbas* are the only sign of life. There are such long periods when no work can be done, when even visiting a neighbor is a major undertaking, that Russians have come to believe that they are living an existence over which they have no control. The result is lethargy, broken by outbursts of energy, and occasionally by violence. Despite basic changes in the city and the industrial complexes created by the Soviets, life in the Russian countryside is relatively unchanged—as almost every writer has observed. The Russian peasant still has months of inactivity on his hands in winter.

There are many aspects of Russian personality that baffle the foreigner, particularly the Anglo-Saxon. One such trait is the attitude toward compromise. To the Russian, a compromise is frequently the equivalent of betrayal or surrender. To the Anglo-Saxon, compromise is a normal way of life. One reason for this is that Russia has never had much trade in goods with the outside world. There are authorities who believe that the Anglo-Saxon trait of compromise is due to the fact that England was a trading nation almost from its inception. The Russians have concentrated on the acquisition of land, seizing and holding territory, and dealing primarily with border states as tributaries. Such a relationship does not produce the spirit of compromise. Since the Revolution, the arbitrary and intolerant nature of Bolshevik thought has reinforced the Russian tendency to shy away from compromise as an operating principle in their official lives and particularly in their dealings with foreign states.

Russians are like Americans in the sense that both are products of entire continents. The fact that both have had large horizons to move around in and new lands to conquer has given each a boldness of thought and imagination and an unwillingness to accept some of the conventional limitations that seem to form and control the Western Europeans. Russians, as well as Americans, tend to neglect detail (we perhaps too much so in the conduct of diplomatic business). And our sense of humor often coincides.

On the other hand, the average Russian is unquestionably on a lower level of cultural development than the average American. The Russian intelligentsia before the Revolution constituted one of the most remarkable collections of men that the world has seen, and an educated Russian today is an interesting person. Unlike the average American, however, the average Russian has not shed the traits of his past; the Russian is still the victim of many superstitions, gullibility, and other characteristics of his peasant ancestors, who lived for centuries in darkness. In fact, the Russian expression for peasantry used to be *chorny narod*, "the dark people."

So many Americans are quicker, more nervous, more active, while Russians generally are slower, more thoughtful, more patient. The American lacks the endurance of the Russian, especially his extraordinary stoicism in bearing hardship. It is the Russian's friendliness and warmheartedness that are most appealing to Americans—just as American frankness and generosity appeal to the Russians. In those early days, whenever ideological barriers were missing, friendship and mutual acceptance flowered. The American is untrammeled by convention and tradition, friendly, and ready to believe people are good until proved otherwise. The Russian is also friendly, but wary and suspicious of all things alien, and, conscious of his country's backwardness, he is apt to have an inferiority complex in relation to foreigners. Soviet leaders, with humble backgrounds and only partially educated, are especially sensitive on this subject.

The Russian's past is always with him. The basic peasant quality of suspicion was demonstrated in the first days of our arrival in Moscow. We had hired a contingent of Russians to help us move equipment into the offices. As an incentive to work, we sometimes gave them their pay in foreign currency, which could be used to buy goods not available for Russian money. One day, a workman showed me a battered Polish zloty piece. He explained that he had been given it as part of his pay the day before but some of his fellow workmen had doubted it was genuine. To test the coin, they placed it on a rock and hit it with a sledgehammer. In proving it was real, they destroyed the coin, thus fulfilling the curious Russian logic of destroying that which they desire.

Mixing with the people and talking with the Bolshevik leaders gave me a little experience in reporting on political conditions in the new Soviet society. Henderson, Kennan, and I realized that we had arrived in Moscow at an opportune time, for 1934 may be seen as the most optimistic year in Soviet history. The isolation of the Soviet Union was ending. Not only had the United States recognized Moscow, but Moscow was moving to enter the League of Nations. The great famine, which has resulted from Stalin's decision to collectivize agriculture and which had cost millions of lives, was over. The average citizen we saw in Moscow felt that the Bolshevik Revolution had been won and the rule of the Bolsheviks was secure. Many Muscovites believed that they could logically look forward to a period of increasing freedom and personal security, that the Soviet Union was about to move toward democratic forms inherent in the Marxist philosophy. Russian youth, in the cities at least, still retained a measure of enthusiasm for the Soviet idea. Students would give up their Saturdays to work in the fields or the mines or to help build factories, and seemed to do so without any sign of real compulsion.

The character of Stalin was hidden not only from the Russian people but also from the prying eyes of foreign diplomats. The only time he appeared in public was to review a parade on May Day or some other holiday, and then he was only a dim figure atop the Lenin mausoleum on Red Square. An audience with Stalin was a rare privilege for a foreign diplomat. (Bullitt had seen him in December of 1933 when Stalin dropped in on a dinner at the Kremlin.) To the few who talked with him, Stalin—always on his best behavior on such occasions—appeared as a leader who surveyed the Russian scene with tolerance, if not with kindliness. He was the legendary figure standing above the strife, intervening only when a problem could not be resolved by underlings. Stalin was, on the whole, popular because of the controlled press, which at the time was waging a widespread campaign to present him as a thoughtful and compassionate genius concerned only for the welfare and happiness of the Soviet people. A typical photo showed Stalin holding a young Uzbek girl in his arms, with the slogan, "Life, comrades, is becoming happier and gayer." This campaign, ludicrously transparent to skeptical Russians and foreigners who understood Soviet propaganda, was clearly designed to dim the memory of the famine. In 1934, not even the skeptics realized Stalin's almost paranoid hostility and suspicion, which were shortly to become manifest in the purges.

We were much more aware of the *militzionair*, the ordinary cop on the beat, than we were of the OGPU (Organized State Political Direction), as the secret police were called early in 1934 and are still called in loose usage. The Soviet citizen seemed to have no fear of the *militzionair*. He was fearful of the OGPU, but certainly not as much as he would be of its successor, the NKVD (Peoples' Commissariat of Internal Affairs), during the purges, and not as much as he had been of its predecessor, the CHEKA (Extraordinary Commission), during the 1920s. Bullitt, however, was followed everywhere by four plainclothesmen. They sat outside the Residence when he was there, even when he was sleeping at night; they followed him to the office and everywhere else he went. One beautiful June evening, Bullitt and I decided to go for a row on the Moscow River, so we hired a rowboat and set off. Looking back, we saw the "boys," as we called the plainclothesmen, standing on the float where the boats were tied up, scratching their heads. It was obvious that they did not know how to row a boat. Russian officials insisted that these men were for Bullitt's protection, and there was some truth in what they said. Ever since the assassination of the German ambassador in 1918, the Soviet government had worried about attempts on the lives of envoys. The main reason for police surveillance, however, was to keep track of what ambassadors were doing and the Russians they met. Thus it was established practice for Soviet security police to follow all ambassadors. Only in 1953, when I was ambassador, was the practice abandoned.

It was illustrative of the atmosphere of 1934 that when the government, in July, changed the name of the secret police from OGPU to

NKVD, Litvinov, then Foreign Commissar, told Bullitt that this change marked a definite step in the liberalization of the Soviet regime. It indicated, he said, that the Revolution had conquered and Soviet power was established. He predicted that the NKVD would hold no more terror for the Soviet citizens than the New York police did for the citizens of New York—a staggering misstatement. I am sure Litvinov spoke with complete sincerity, because he, like many other Soviet leaders, was unaware of the dark recesses of Stalin's mind.

Housekeeping, people-to-people relations, and political-reporting duties took up most of my time, but the most important task of the Embassy was the establishment of friendly and meaningful diplomatic dealings with the Soviet government. Despite a surface friendliness, negotiations foundered almost from the beginning. One of the first tasks Bullitt assigned me was the negotiation of a lease for a property on the banks of the Moscow River. The site, which Bullitt had earlier been promised by Stalin, was a beautiful piece of land on a high bluff with a splendid view of the city. It was a wooded plot and sloped down to the river. Here the United States hoped to build an Embassy modeled, curiously enough, after Monticello—a compound to provide residential and office space for all American Embassy personnel. Shortly after our arrival in Moscow, Litvinov told Bullitt that the property would not be available. Bullitt became very cross, and Litvinov backtracked, informing us that the property could be leased. Once this decision was made, negotiations were transferred to the Moscow Soviet, which controlled all property in the city.

I immediately ran into difficulties. One of the obstacles was the blind refusal of the Moscow Soviet to permit the United States to cut down trees on the property without a specific authorization for each tree. Since well over a hundred trees would have to be cut down at one time or another, we were soon acquainted with the muscle-bound nature of Moscow bureaucracy. There were also complications involving the right of the United States to import workers and how they were to be housed, paid, and fed. The sensitivity of Soviet officials to any implications that conditions in the Soviet Union were less than perfect came out frequently during these discussions. The most formidable difficulty was Soviet insistence that we buy building materials, such as brick, cement, and wood, at the official rate of exchange. This would have meant that practically the entire allocation of $1,250,000 appropriated by Congress for the construction of the Embassy would have been used for these basic materials. I would call on officials at the Moscow Soviet to discuss the problems, and, while they were pleasant enough, they would not yield on the simplest matter. It soon became apparent that the Russians did not want us to build on the site Bullitt had selected, and eventually the project was dropped. The real reason for the Soviet obstructionism is obscure, but it did save us from the mistake of erecting a building like Monticello, which, with its flat roof, would not have been suitable for the heavy snows of Moscow.

Other diplomatic problems with the Russians were more basic than failure to find an acceptable site for a new Embassy. The troubles related to Soviet violation of the 1933 Roosevelt-Litvinov accord on diplomatic recognition. In that pact, the Soviet Union agreed to three special United States requests. Moscow acknowledged the indebtedness of the pre-Soviet regime, agreed to ban organizations seeking the overthrow of the American government, and pledged freedom of religious worship for Americans living in the Soviet Union. The freedom of worship provision caused no problem; it was the other agreements that led to the cooling of relations and to a change in Bullitt's heart. The trouble was that the memo of understanding on the debts was a carelessly drafted document—a fault which, repeated later, was to cost the United States heavily in its World War II dealings with the Soviet Union. The memo (it remained secret until 1945) referred to a "loan" to be credited to Moscow by Washington. In his discussions with Bullitt in the spring, summer, and fall of 1934, Litvinov insisted that the word "loan" meant that the United States had promised to extend to the Soviet Union funds to use wherever and however it chose. The United States always held the contrary view that any money made available to the Soviet Union would be in the form of a credit to be spent in the United States. The memorandum was also deficient in that it made no reference to the Export-Import Bank's control of credits to the Soviet Union. Bullitt always maintained that this control had been part of the basic assumption under which he and the President had been operating. The Export-Import Bank was created to finance Soviet-American trade.

With difficulties piling up, Bullitt tended more and more to believe that Litvinov was acting on his own and was not giving a full account of the discussions to Stalin. His face flushing and his eyes popping, Bullitt told me one day of his suspicions that Litvinov was double-crossing him. Of course, it would have been possible to mislead the dictator, but it would have been dangerous and unlikely, especially for anyone as powerless as Litvinov, who was not even a member of the Politburo. It was even more unlikely to believe, as Bullitt apparently did, that Litvinov was carrying out his own policy. Bullitt went to the length of enlisting the old Bolshevik Radek to check on what Litvinov was telling Stalin. When one considers that Radek had been exiled to Siberia in 1927 for his Trotskyist views, it is incredible that he apparently had access to Stalin's files seven years later. He told Bullitt that Litvinov's reporting was without any noteworthy distortions. Bullitt, however, continued to make a sharp differentiation between Litvinov and the other Soviet leaders and thought that a lot of the troubles were due entirely to the Commissar's intransigence.

It is probable that Litvinov's shifts of position and concentration on specific details such as "loan" versus "credit" reflected not the Foreign Commissar's personal views but a change in the Soviet government's attitude on foreign policy. In 1933, at the time of recognition, Stalin told Bullitt that Japan was planning to attack the Soviet Union in the near future. Stalin, with his lack of knowledge of American traditions, probably felt that the United States might sign some agreement in opposition to Japanese expansion. This was impossible for the United States, given our traditional refusal to join in any pacts aimed at any countries. While it is true that isolationism as a doctrine was born with our eye on Europe and did not have the same connotation for Asia or Latin America, nevertheless a pact with Russia, a European country and Communist to boot, which would cover Asia was politically out of the question. By the end of 1934, however, Soviet fears of Japan had diminished, and an accord with us on Asia had lost its urgency. Meanwhile, the Soviet Union was being urged by some European countries, notably France, to join the League of Nations (as it did in 1934) and to take part in some form of collective-security arrangement against Nazi Germany. Under these circumstances, the Soviet Union was not prepared, and said so, to make an arrangement with the United States for the payment of relatively minor debts, when much larger amounts were owed France and Britain.

Bullitt's final break with his illusions came in the summer of 1935, after I had left the Soviet Union. The Soviets held the seventh—and, as it turned out, the last—Communist International, or Comintern, Congress, which proclaimed the policy of Communist parties' joining their bitter foes, the Social Democrats, in Popular Fronts against Fascists, but still maintained their goal of undermining the capitalist democracies. Furious, Bullitt protested that the 1933 Litvinov-Roosevelt agreement obligated the Soviet Union not to permit meetings on its soil of any groups dedicated to the overthrow of the United States government by force. The cynical manner in which Litvinov brushed aside the protests—he denied that he or Stalin knew the Comintern was going to meet—convinced Bullitt that the Soviet Union lacked the qualities that made for decent relations between governments.

Eventually, Bullitt became so bitter an enemy of the Soviet Union that he favored a Franco-German rapprochement. It was not until the British-French sellout of Czechoslovakia to Hitler in Munich in 1938 that Bullitt concluded that constructive relations with Nazi Germany were impossible. While he was dead wrong in suggesting an agreement with Hitler, Bullitt's final advice as ambassador on relations with the Soviet Union still makes sense. In a message written on April 20, 1936, Bullitt counseled Secretary of State Cordell Hull:

> We should neither expect too much or despair of getting anything at all. We should take what we can get when the atmosphere is favorable and do our best to hold on to it when the wind blows the other way. We should remain unimpressed in the face of expansive professions of friendliness and unperturbed in the face of slights and underhand opposition. We should make the weight of our influence felt steadily over a long period of time in the directions which best suit our interests. We should never threaten. We should act and allow the Bolsheviks to draw their own conclusions as to the causes of our acts.
>
> Above all, we should guard the reputation of Americans for businesslike efficiency, sincerity and straightforwardness. We should never send a spy to the Soviet Union. There is no weapon at once so disarming and effective in relations with the Communists as sheer honesty. They know very little about it.

I don't believe that anything could have changed Bullitt's mind, given his temperament and the reality of the Soviet scene. He harbored too many illusions from his brief visit to Moscow in March, 1919, the idealistic period of the Revolution. The Russian Revolution had changed, and the change violated his idealism and his old-fashioned American morality. Bullitt's personal attitude had no lasting effect on Soviet-American relations. It was the character of the Bolshevik government, not the personalities of men, that prevented the development of better relations.

In 1933, Soviet leaders thought that they were going to develop friendly relations with the United States. They expected the United States to possess the sophistication of the Europeans in dealing with the reality of the Soviet system, not trying to push in directions where no result could be expected. Soviet officials all felt that they were dealing with a temporary phenomenon, a capitalist nation that had only a temporary life. This ideological belief was not translated into personal animosity. In fact, as far as Americans were concerned, we were, for a while, popular; we were the new boys in town and an object of interest. Working in our favor was the fact that America had pushed away from Europe; we did not fall into the category of the wicked old European nations. Eventually, the novelty wore off and we were viewed as just another capitalist nation.

Bullitt's change of heart cannot be understood unless it is accompanied by some knowledge of his background, particularly his experience with the Soviet government in 1919. At that time, he had a definite pro-Soviet slant to his thinking. As early as 1918, while the war was still on and before he had even visited the Soviet Union, Bullitt had written in a private note to himself that one thing that seemed to make the future worth while was the Russian Revolution, stating that "as a nation they had become brotherly, open-hearted, free from conventions and unafraid of life."

Like Bullitt, I, too, suffered disillusionment during that first year. But I had fewer illusions to lose, partly because I had never been exposed to the inspiring early days of the Bolshevik Revolution and partly because I had read a good deal about the Soviet dictatorship. All of us on that first Embassy staff guarded our objectivity as we had been trained to do; we avoided statements that could not be supported by fact and were always scrupulous in giving the Russians a fair deal in analyzing their motives. Thus we did not fall prey to the Soviet propaganda attempt to put critics of the Soviet Union on the moral defensive. The Bolsheviks were quick to make a charge of "anti-Soviet prejudice" against any foreigner whose comments, however accurate or realistic, departed from the current Party line.

During this period, a British correspondent with the same sense of objectivity was approached by a "pink peer" when visiting Moscow, who belligerently accused him of "running around slandering the Soviet Union, saying that they have two sets of statistics—one secret set for themselves and a false set for the public." The correspondent replied to the peer, "I deny this absolutely. What I did say is that the Soviet system has two sets of statistics, and both are false." That we could laugh at Soviet practices did not mean we were anti-Russian.

I do not think that my first tour of duty in Moscow led me to form any hard attitude toward the Soviet Union. As I have pointed out, 1934 was a relatively mild, relaxed year. It was still possible to imagine that the Soviets were emerging out of the difficult years of the civil war, the collectivization, and the beginnings of industrialization and were entering a plateau of relatively stable, pacific development. When I left there in the spring of 1935, the purge was just beginning, but gave no indication of the terror that was coming. It was not until the extent of the purges became known and the Hitler-Stalin pact was signed that my attitude toward the Soviet Union hardened.

I did learn much from Bullitt's bitter response to Soviet reneging on the agreements. Actually, he was accurate in his prognostications and analysis of Soviet misbehavior. What he could be faulted for was his reacting with violence, prejudice, and unreason. I never forgot this lesson, which was particularly valuable during the McCarthy period.

While I had not yet learned the true nature of Stalin's regime, I do remember my elation on crossing the frontier with Charlie Thayer, leaving the Soviet Union on the way home for a vacation in the spring of 1935. It was like coming out into the fresh spring air from a room where the oxygen content was sufficient to sustain life but insufficient to produce any mental or spiritual animation. I believe that almost every foreigner has felt the same way on leaving Russia. In fact, in the summer of 1934 Bullitt had written a personal dispatch to the State Department urging that special money be made available for Embassy personnel to travel outside the Soviet Union. He described the possibilities of relaxed recreation in Moscow as about equivalent to getting a seat on the New York subway during the rush hour. It has now become established practice for American diplomats in Moscow to get out of the Soviet Union at least twice a year. This practice, I believe, has also been followed by diplomats of some other countries and by American correspondents in Moscow. Sitting for months in Moscow, reading the Soviet press, hearing nothing but one solid line of propaganda on the major questions of the day eventually affects your judgment, especially if you are introspective, unless you can look forward to "getting out"—a term that in itself indicates the closed nature of Soviet society. To this day, even strong sympathizers of the Soviet Union experience, when they cross the border, an enormous relief, a lightening of the spirits, a return of gaiety impossible in drab, dreary Moscow.

CHAPTER THREE

To Be Shot, To Be Shot, To Be Shot

Fully intending to return to Moscow after the expiration of my leave in the spring of 1935, I was surprised to learn on a visit to the State Department that I was being transferred to Washington. I had been in Moscow less than fifteen months and expected to stay at least another year. Bullitt requested the transfer, but since he had written laudatory efficiency reports on me, I do not believe there was any complaint because of my work. The most likely explanation is that I was part of a cut in the Embassy staff ordered by Bullitt as a result of the breakdown in negotiations with the Russians. A number of military attachés were sent home, and there were changes in the Consul General's office.

My disappointment at not returning to Moscow was soon forgotten as I set about becoming engaged to Avis Thayer, a sister of Charlie Thayer. When I was still at school, I had met Avis while visiting her older brother, George, my classmate, at their home in Villa Nova, Pennsylvania. Avis was then a child and made no particular impression on me. However, when she visited Charlie in Moscow in 1934, she had grown into a very attractive young lady and I saw a great deal of her. Avis was accompanied by her older sister and a friend. The three girls were on their first trip to the Soviet Union and were excited by everything they saw. One day Avis, after lunch at the house of the Secretary of the French Embassy, was walking back to her hotel carrying her camera. She stopped and took a picture of the Kremlin and was immediately accosted by two plainclothesmen, who seized her camera, exposed the film, and took her off to a police station. The only two Russian phrases she knew were "My brother speaks Russian," which was singularly useless, and the Embassy Residence telephone number. After four hours, the Russians telephoned the Embassy Residence, where the telephone operator, a man named Ilyin, rushed into Charlie's office and said, "Good gracious me, Jesus Christ, Mr. Thayer, your sister is arrested." She was soon released.

Avis's interest in world affairs, especially Russia, added to our interest in each other, and I saw a great deal of her in the early summer of 1935. The courtship was carried on in taxis and bars in New York and during an occasional visit to Villa Nova, where Avis lived. We became engaged in June and were married in Villa Nova on August 29, 1935. We went to Bermuda on our honeymoon and returned to live in an apartment on Sixteenth Street in Washington.

At the State Department, apparently on the theory that specialists, even before they become specialists, should broaden their views, I was assigned to the office of the Under Secretary, William Phillips, whose tall, thin frame and old-fashioned manners gave him an aristocratic bearing. He was a fine and able man, a credit to the old diplomatic school. As his assistant, my duties were varied. In addition to special jobs, I would summarize the letters, telegrams, and dispatches which poured into Mr. Phillips's office and answer some of the correspondence. The work was not exacting, and I felt somewhat sidetracked from Soviet affairs. I was pleased, therefore, in the summer of 1936, when I was transferred to the Division of Eastern European Affairs, where I could again concentrate on the Soviet Union.

My first task was to write a memorandum on the Bolshevik use of terror. There was wide interest in the subject because of the purges sweeping Russia. My main conclusions were that while the Bolsheviks had been adamant against the use of terror against individuals by Communists when they were not in office, they regarded terror as a perfectly legitimate instrument of class warfare once they were in power.

I also helped with the backup work for the trade negotiations in Moscow conducted by Loy Henderson. The talks for this first trade agreement with the Soviet Union presented no major problems. The only interesting aspect was recognition by the United States and acceptance by the Soviet Union of the fact that reciprocal tariff reductions would not work. Because the Soviet government was both the purchaser and the authority that levied the duties, any Soviet purchasing agent need not be concerned about tariffs. Reductions of Soviet tariffs on a wide range of American goods would neither stimulate nor restrict imports. The final agreement gave the Soviet Union "most-favored-nations" treatment for its goods sent to the United States. This meant that the tariff on Soviet goods was as low as that on those of any other country. In return, Moscow agreed to purchase $40 million worth of goods from us. This agreement, coming at a time when relations between the two countries were chilly, was an indication that some business was still possible with Moscow. The agreement also recognized the fact that Soviet-American trade would not balance off, since there was little produced in the Soviet Union that the United States needed.

While working on these talks, I found myself on the periphery of a struggle between the State Department's old-line officers and powerful figures in the White House over American policy toward the Soviet Union. The question then, as it was destined to be right after World War II and is today, was whether the United States and the Soviet Union could develop normal cooperative relations.

The Eastern European Division was headed by Robert F. Kelly, who believed that the possibility of developing meaningful relations with the Soviet Union was limited because of Bolshevik ideology and the close ties between the Moscow government and the Communist International. In no way was the tall, taciturn Kelly an anti-Soviet crusader. He had done exhaustive research on the Soviet Union in the 1920s and, as a result, insisted that because of the emotional controversy that surrounded the Soviet Union, the Eastern European Division should train its people not only to be objective but also to take special pains to make sure to verify every fact with substantial evidence. From Moscow's point of view, this attitude was anti-Soviet, but from an American perspective it was valuable training.

Kelly's refusal to accept Moscow statements at face value, a realistic attitude that was shared by most others in the Russian section of the division, was cited in private to the President by some in the White House (we thought then that Mrs. Roosevelt and Harry Hopkins were among them, but now I am not certain) as an impediment to good relations between the two countries. The anti-Kelly group was worried that the United States might lose an opportunity to work with the Soviet Union to counter the growing menace of Hitler. The White House people were impressed by the fact that the Soviet Union had signed mutual-assistance treaties with France and Czechoslovakia in 1935, and that the Comintern had proclaimed the Popular Front. What the anti-Kelly group did not understand was that the 180-degree turn by the Communist parties of the world from violent opposition to cooperation with Social Democrats in Western countries could just as easily be reversed. The essential element of Stalin's policy was to protect, above all, the Bolshevik regime in Russia.

The main line of Soviet interest was also obscure to the pro-Soviet elements when Hitler sent German troops into the demilitarized Rhineland on March 7, 1936. Foreign Commissar Litvinov called on the League of Nations to take some action and warned, in an immortal phrase, that "peace is indivisible." The White House group was so impressed by Litvinov's rhetoric that they were deaf to hints by both Litvinov and Premier Vyacheslav M. Molotov of collaboration with Hitler, and were blind to the fact that the Soviet leaders did nothing to urge France to expel German occupation troops from the Rhineland—a step that might have toppled Hitler early and saved the world from a terrible war.

To neutralize Kelly, the White House group ordered a hoary bureaucratic solution—that the Eastern European Division be merged with the European Division, with a resulting diminution in the Russian experts' influence.

As one of the developing Russian experts in the department, I was pulled somewhat in both directions. The move made sense because Russia was becoming part of Europe. And I realized that for years in the 1920s the Eastern European Division under Kelly had produced evidence to support the view that the Soviet Union should not be recognized by the United States. I also realized, on the other hand, that it was Kelly who wrote the basic paper that guided the United States in talks with the Soviets on recognition. There was no doubt in my mind that Roosevelt was right in believing that the Soviet Union would be an important factor in the world and that a fresh view was needed in the State Department to deal with this fact. After all, I represented new blood. Yet I could not but be fearful of accepting the Bolsheviks at face value. Kelly's skepticism was healthy. My first tour of duty in Moscow had taught me that. My feelings were shared by most of the young Soviet specialists, including Kennan.

One of the younger officers in the Eastern European Division did side with those who were more favorably disposed toward the Soviet Union. He was Norris B. Chipman, who had studied Russian with me in Paris. He told me that our reporting from Moscow appeared to be slanted against the Russians. He attributed this bias to the poor living conditions that Americans had to put up with in the Soviet Union. I insisted that he was wrong, that we were reporting the situation as it really was behind the propaganda smoke screen. It was not long before he was transferred to Moscow, and within a month he was reporting exactly the way we had.

The Russians themselves, I believe, took part in the campaign against Kelly. I picked up from a number of sources reports that Soviet officials, in both Moscow and Washington, were cutting up Kelly in private conversations.

In a few months, White House pressure triumphed and, as noted, the Eastern European Division was put under the European Division, headed by Pierrepont Moffat, who had no special interest in Soviet affairs. So strong did emotions run, however, that some of the anti-Kelly elements were not satisfied with this victory; they wanted to dispose of its valuable files and ship off for almost certain destruction the collection of newspapers, periodicals, and other literature that had been painstakingly assembled over the years. The preservation of this invaluable collection of revolutionary documents was my first concern. The original intention had been to store them in the attic of the State Department Library. Under such a condition, the documents would have soon disintegrated. Librarians in the department told me that the Library of Congress was the only place with the facilities to preserve old documents. After a good deal of work and talking to various people, I was able to get the collection transferred to the Library of Congress, where it still is.

In the spring of 1937, my junior status in the Service was brought home abruptly to me. I was assigned as secretary to the American delegation to the International Sugar Conference in London, which meant that I was charged with all of the physical arrangements—travel accommodations, clerical assistance, codes and communications, and finances. I found this a very arduous and boring job.

In the autumn of 1937, I was transferred back to Moscow with, however, an interim assignment as secretary of the American delegation to another meeting, this time one of more interest—the Conference of the Nine Powers to examine the problem created by the Japanese attack in Manchuria. The conference, held in Brussels, came to nothing, largely because of the unwillingness of all countries, particularly the United States and the Soviet Union, to be drawn into anything that might lead to military action. The conference produced so little news that the restless American correspondents began playing jokes on the delegates. One day, they bribed a streetwalker to accost the British Foreign Minister, Anthony Eden, when he came out of the hotel where the conference was being held. I sat with the newsmen in a café across the street and watched as the prostitute stuck her arm through Eden's, and then said something to him. Eden turned quite pink, brushed her off, jumped into his limousine, and dashed off. The prostitute became known as *"la poule des neuf puissances."*

My wife and I arrived in Moscow on January 4, 1938. We noted a few changes in the city. There was the same pervasive odor that everyone smelled on crossing the border. My wife detected in the combination of sheepskin, sawdust, pink soap, disinfectant, and tobacco another ingredient—a ghastly Russian perfume that foreigners had nicknamed "Stalin's breath." The completion of the central portion of the subway had made a difference. The stations were beautifully decorated with white marble and statues. I was told that the service was rapid and efficient. The trolleys were no longer crowded with people hanging from them like bunches of grapes. The people still walked along with their heads down as though preoccupied with their thoughts.

The purge had begun in a low key before I left Moscow in 1935. I had heard rumors of arrests in Leningrad after the murder the preceding December of Sergei Mironovich Kirov, the member of the Politburo in charge of the Leningrad area, by L. V. Nikolaiev, an ex-Bolshevik. That evening, December 1, 1934, we heard that Stalin, Commissar for Defense Voroshilov, and Premier Molotov had boarded the night train for Leningrad. Since this was the first time since 1918 that any leading Bolshevik had been the target of an assassination attempt and the first time that one had been murdered, and knowing a little bit about the pathological fears of the Bolshevik leaders, I realized that something was going to happen in the regime. The first official announcement, made several days after the murder, reported the execution of 103 Polish White Guards who had been in jail for many years and who obviously had nothing whatsoever to do with the Kirov case. The announcement of the executions apparently was designed to warn others against any acts of violence. Lacking information, we in the foreign colony could only speculate about the reason for the murder. An Austrian correspondent expressed a popular opinion when he said that the shot that killed Kirov came from the left—meaning from radicals who resented the growing conservatism of the Bolshevik system and longed for a return to a more revolutionary Party. Subsequent events did not bear this theory out, although some of the first victims of the purge were former Trotskyites and others theoretically to the left of Stalin.

It would be stretching the truth to say that anyone in the foreign colony seriously suspected at that time that Stalin himself was behind

Kirov's murder, as is now widely believed. Kirov was second only to Stalin in Party support, but was known to be loyal to the dictator. I can say, however, that from the first I was suspicious of the official reports of the existence of a "counterrevolutionary terrorist group." I even pointed out that the Russian Truth Brotherhood in Latvia, said by the authorities to have the same aims as the Leningrad terrorists, had been organized by Stalin's secret police—certainly a hint of official participation in Kirov's murder.

We had another secret-police link to the slaying. This report came from Dr. Jurgis Baltrusaitis, the Lithuanian Minister to the Soviet Union, who had been a resident of Moscow for forty years. He was a leading Russian poet, and because he wrote in Russian many Russians did not know he was Lithuanian. Bullitt cultivated Dr. Baltrusaitis and found his information reliable.

Dr. Baltrusaitis told a story of sex and intrigue that was somewhat fanciful, but he was one of the first to report the real dimensions of the arrests. He told Bullitt that "everyone in the slightest degree distasteful" to the Soviet government in Leningrad had been arrested. He put the number of those exiled from that city at 21,000. We had reports in April of 7,000. This was less than five months after Kirov's murder. No one realized that the number of arrests, exiles, and executions would eventually reach 9 to 10 million—the figure now generally accepted. One of the most inexplicable features of the purge was the onslaught against military leaders. Leading marshals and generals were secretly executed. It has been estimated that Stalin executed or sent to concentration camps at least 10,000 officers of the rank of colonel or higher during the period when Hitler's growing power threatened the Soviet Union.

As I had been told before returning to Moscow, the purge was everywhere. It even reached into the privacy of our apartment. As a Second Secretary and Consul of the Embassy, I was entitled to a four-room apartment, complete with institutional-type walnut-stained metal furniture, in the Mokhavaya Building. While the rooms were small, they were large enough by Russian standards for us to hire, through the Foreign Office, two servants. We were sure that both were required to report regularly to the secret police on our activities. The cook, Claudia, was a Tartar from Kazan—tough, talkative, and one of the few Russians unafraid of the purge. On returning from a day at the market, she often told us stories she had heard about arrests and exiles. The maid, Sonya, was a Volga German, small, neat, and clean, but constantly in fear of arrest. She told us nothing. (Like

43

other Volga Germans, she was arrested when Germany attacked Russia; we never learned what happened to her.)

At least twice the secret police came into the Mokhavaya Building to arrest Soviet citizens. In neither case did we know about the action until after the police had left. In one case we learned about the arrest because water came pouring down into one of the Embassy apartments. The apartment above was occupied by a genial old Bolshevik journalist, Pavel L. Mikhailsky, who wrote about the United States for *Izvestia* under the pen name Lapinsky. He had an exceptional knowledge of the United States, its customs, its people, and its institutions and was fair, within the limitations of Soviet ideology and objectives. On climbing the stairs to his apartment, we discovered the NKVD seals on the door. Our administrative officer, Angus I. Ward, broke the seals and we entered the apartment. The water tap had frozen and burst, causing the flooding. After stopping the leak, we looked around the apartment. Mikhailsky's substantial collection of books was scattered over the floor, and many pages had been ripped out. His clothing and other belongings were also in disarray. It was obvious that the police had conducted a minute search for incriminating evidence, probably at the usual period between midnight and dawn. Mikhailsky had been carted off. We sent the NKVD seals to the Foreign Office, explaining why it had been necessary to get into the apartment. The reaction of the Foreign Office was close to panic; they could not believe that anyone would dare to break the seals of the Commissariat of Internal Affairs. But no action was taken against us. Mikhailsky was never heard of again, and it must be assumed that he was shot.

On another occasion, we noticed that movers were taking furniture from an apartment occupied by a former Chief of Soviet Protocol, Dmitri T. Florinsky. We heard that he had been placed in charge of a girls' camp, a report that seemed unbelievable since he had been arrested on a charge of homosexuality.

The grim atmosphere did not stop me from going to the Foreign Office after each of these arrests to begin negotiating for the apartments. I felt like a vulture, but we were badly in need of space.

The purge had a dampening effect on the operation of the Embassy, which found its operations rigidly restricted. The Ambassador, Joseph E. Davies, who had succeeded Bullitt, made matters even worse. He had gone to the Soviet Union sublimely ignorant of even the most elementary realities of the Soviet system and of its ideology. He was determined, possibly with Bullitt's failure in mind, to maintain a Pollyanna attitude. He took the Soviet line on everything except issues between the two governments. He never even faintly understood the purges, going far toward accepting the official Soviet version of the existence of a conspiracy against the state. Moreover, he and his wife treated the staff as hired help and rarely listened to its views.

Most members of the staff were better than Davies deserved. In the absence of a counselor, the staff was headed by the First Secretary, Henderson, who had negotiated the trade agreement. He was soon replaced by Alexander Kirk, a superb diplomat who taught me a great deal. Stuart Grummon, a small, quiet man whose specialty was China and who at first was somewhat naïve about the Soviet Union, was a Second Secretary, replacing Kennan as the chief political reporter. Norris Chipman, a Third Secretary, reported on economic developments. Angus Ward, a vigorous man with a goatee, whose interests lay in Asia, headed the consular section, handling visas and passports, and performed other administrative duties. The weak link in the staff was the chief military attaché, Colonel Phillip R. Faymonville, a slender, pink-faced man with a fringe of white hair who had a definite pro-Russian bias. Chipman, Faymonville, and I were the only officers fluent in Russian.

The purge had brought a halt to one of the Embassy's principal functions—bettering relations through contacts with the Russian people and officials. I was eager to look up some of my acquaintances from my previous tour, but was immediately discouraged by other members of the Embassy. They pointed out that any attempt by a foreigner to get in touch with a Soviet citizen was the equivalent of signing an order for his arrest, if not his execution. Nor did I dare inquire into the whereabouts of George Andreychin, the Intourist official who had been so helpful in 1934. Andreychin had been arrested in January, 1935, a day or so after he had lunched with me in my apartment.

Just before my arrival in Moscow, the list of executed included Lev M. Karakhan, an Assistant Commissar for Foreign Affairs. Known as the dandy of the Bolshevik movement, he was handsome and well dressed and a favorite with the ladies. I had met him in 1934. Another victim, whom I had known even better, was Boris S. Steiger. Boris was a respectable bridge player and used to go around the diplomatic corps playing cards and dining. We could never figure whom he knew in the Kremlin, but for a time he obviously had the ear of people in authority. He was a good conversationalist, with a cynical turn of mind that always delighted members of the diplomatic corps. Even though he must have known he was a candidate for the purge, he could not pass up the opportunity to joke. I was told that one evening after a dinner, as he stepped out the doorway into the street, he rubbed the back of his neck and said, "One can't be too careful about the back of his neck in this type of weather." The favorite Soviet method of execution was a pistol shot in the back of the neck. He was on the list of those executed in December, 1937.

One evening, Alexander A. Troyanovsky, the first Soviet ambassador to the United States, and his wife came to dinner at Spaso House. Kirk, who was chargé d'affaires after the departure of Davies in June, 1938, had extended the invitation as a normal courtesy because some American doctors were visiting Moscow. Why Troyanovsky came I do not know. He must have had government permission, but that was not enough assurance in those days. I have rarely been through as painful an experience. Both Troyanovsky, a gentle, quiet man, and his wife were suffering from nervous shock, almost panic, and should have been in a hospital, the American doctors said. When a question was directed to them, they would jump as if startled, mumble a reply, then lapse into silence. Both were desperately afraid. They knew, but we did not learn until later, that they were under investigation for Trotskyist connections. Despite their fears, neither of the Troyanovskys was arrested.

Even the Russian man on the street, who in 1934, had been open and friendly, avoided all contact with foreigners. Once, my wife noticed a crowd inside a shop. She had learned that in Moscow the Russians lined up to buy even though they did not know what was being sold, because goods were so scarce. If the article was something they did not want or like, they could always sell it (perhaps for a profit) or exchange it for something else. On this particular day, fine linen tablecloths were being sold, and she decided to buy. But two women, noting her American fur coat (the Soviets sold their best fur abroad) and hearing her accent, quickly left the line, apparently afraid to be seen standing next to a foreigner.

With Soviet leaders not often visible to foreigners, there was not much political reporting for me to do. Two weeks after my return to Moscow, I did have an opportunity to observe the sycophantic attempts of Soviet officials to demonstrate their loyalty to Stalin. The occasion was a session of the Supreme Soviet. From the diplomatic gallery, I studied the Soviet leaders. Stalin had visibly aged since I had seen him from a distance at a parade three years before. His face was more deeply lined, and his hair had turned gray. He gave the appearance of general weariness and, at times, during the eight-day session, of strain that no one had reported before.

Andrei A. Zhdanov, the Leningrad leader, sat beside the dictator almost all the time and seemed to be his favorite, at least for the moment. Voroshilov was almost comical in his efforts to ingratiate himself, constantly changing his seat to get closer to Stalin and trying to engage him in conversation. A short, pudgy man with a round face and a big grin by the name of Nikita S. Khrushchev also clung close to Stalin. I noted in a memorandum to the State Department that Khrushchev was "less obviously boot-licking than Voroshilov." This was the first time that I mentioned Khrushchev in a dispatch to Washington.

Some embassies, such as the Greek, with sizable numbers of citizens living in the Soviet Union, spent much of the time endeavoring to protect people from the purge. We had only one incident of that kind. One day, we received word from an American tourist that a couple called Robinson had disappeared from their hotel. Inquiries at the hotel produced three stories, one that Robinson had gone off on a trip, another that Mrs. Robinson was in the hospital, and a third that Robinson himself was in a hospital in an iron lung. Repeated inquiries at the Foreign Office brought no answer whatsoever. Finally, the Foreign Office told us that Robinson had been arrested on charges of crimes against the Soviet state and his wife was being held as an accessory to these crimes. We had, of course, notified the State Department, which, after a check, informed us that Robinson's real name was Rubens, that he was not an American citizen, and that he had been traveling under a falsely acquired passport. While this information changed the legalities of the case, it did not diminish our interest in winning the Rubenses' release. After long months of arguing, Soviet authorities admitted that Rubens had been executed, but said that his wife would be released, and eventually she was.

My most important duty regarding the purge was observing, in March, 1938, the third, last, and most dramatic of the great show trials.*

The chief defendant in the third trial was Nikolai I. Bukharin, one

---

* At the first of these trials, held in August, 1936, Zinoviev and Kamenev confessed and were executed, along with fourteen others. Following a pattern which was to be established in subsequent trials, Zinoviev and Kamenev were accused of conspiring to overthrow the Soviet government, to murder Stalin, and to sabotage the Soviet economy. In addition to these accusations, charges of espionage on behalf of Germany and Japan were made against the defendants in the next two trials. In the second trial, in January, 1937, Y. L. Piatakov, a Lenin associate who had been an executive of the first Five Year Plan in heavy industry (and who had called for Zinoviev's death); Karl Radek, the journalist and an important second-level Bolshevik; and G. Y. Sokolnikov, a member of Lenin's first Politburo, were convicted, along with fourteen others. Most were shot.

of the original Bolsheviks and a member of the Politburo in the early days. The other principal defendants were A. I. Rykov, who had been Premier of the Soviet Union and also one of the original members of the Politburo, and G. G. Yagoda, the former head of the NKVD at the first two show trials, who had been removed for lack of zeal.

From the second day of the trial on, I attended all the sessions as Ambassador Davies's interpreter. The trial took place in the chandeliered, dome-ceilinged Hall of Columns of the former Nobles' Club of Moscow, which had been transformed into a courtroom for the occasion. The building was generally used as a meeting place for trade unions. We had to show our passes to three lines of guards before being admitted to the courtroom.

The room held about 250 to 300 spectators, who sat on cushioned benches divided into sections. We sat in the section reserved for ambassadors and their interpreters. There was a general section for carefully selected delegations of factory workers, government officials, and other Russian citizens invited to observe the trial. These groups were changed every day. In front of these benches was a table where the three military judges sat. At their right was a small table for the prosecutor, Andrei Y. Vishinsky, and one for the lawyers for the three defendants who did not waive counsel. On the judges' left sat the twenty-one defendants in the prisoners' box, which looked like a jury box in the United States. It was guarded at each corner by a blue-capped NKVD soldier with rifle and fixed bayonet. It seemed to me that the guards were changed every few minutes. The constant movement of the soldiers created the impression that the trial was taking place behind a screen of glittering bayonets. The three judges served as the jury.

Except for purposes of interpreting for Ambassador Davies (I could whisper to him during the proceedings), I did not take regular notes, since we knew from the two previous trials that the full transcript would be published in the Soviet press. There were morning and afternoon sessions; some of the afternoon sessions lasted from about four o'clock in the afternoon to well into the following morning, on occasion as late as five or six o'clock.

The prosecutor, Vishinsky, was one of the most unsavory products of Bolshevism. Originally one of the opposition Mensheviks, he had written an article about Bolshevik atrocities in the early days of the Revolution. Much of his bloodthirsty career can be traced to his desire to compensate for his anti-Bolshevik past. He was slight, of medium height, and had thinning reddish hair, a mustache, and a pointed nose that held steel-rimmed spectacles. He had a gift of oratory, particularly of invective, and was highly intelligent. Anyone who saw him, as I did, mercilessly pursuing, mocking, and prodding defendants will never forget the ferretlike quality of Vishinsky. Years later, I happened to mention to Vishinsky that I had been at the trial. He asked me, as a producer might ask about a stage set, "How did it look to you?" I said that there were many aspects of the trial that were puzzling. He seemed pleased with the public-relations effect of his performance.

The trial had only the trappings of justice. It was open to the press and public. The defendants had the right to counsel. Only three took advantage of this right. However, the defense lawyers played little part in the proceedings. They made no attempt to challenge the evidence or refute the charges in any way. I cannot remember any consultations between the accused and their lawyers during the entire trial. At the conclusion of the defense, the lawyers admitted the guilt of the accused and merely asked the court to show proletarian mercy. The defendants did have the opportunity to cross-examine witnesses, and Bukharin especially exercised that right.

Having met Bukharin, the chief defendant, in the summer of 1934, I was particularly interested in him. He was thinner, slightly paler, but not materially different. As I sat there, my thoughts went back to the dinner four years before. He still seemed like the same gentle scholar who proudly believed in the cause. He must have been deeply distressed by the events that were tearing the Bolshevik movement apart; if so, he never showed his worry. He was in complete command of himself throughout the trial and gave no noticeable signs of inner agitation or disturbance. This composure was true in general of all twenty-one of the defendants. Some, particularly Rykov, reminded me of actors of the First Moscow Art Theater performing in a particularly difficult character role.

So many episodes of the trial were fantastic. There was the witness who testified that Yagoda, the former head of the secret police, had, on his last day in the NKVD building, stood on chairs and sofas and sprayed the walls with a poisonous solution in order to assassinate N. I. Yezhov, his successor. This testimony was followed by the even more startling report from a committee of three leading Soviet doctors concluding that the method could be effective in poisoning an individual and, had it not been detected in time, could have caused the death of Comrade Yezhov. As it was, they said, Yezhov's health had been damaged. The mention of Yezhov's ill health was a clear clue that he, too, would be a victim of the purge; his downfall came in a few months.*

There was Yagoda's unbelievable testimony on how the murder of Maxim Gorky had been concealed in 1936. The old man was made drunk and then exposed to a roaring bonfire, with the result that the front of his body was overheated and the back was freezing—so Yagoda said. The temperature contrast was sufficient, according to the doctors, to produce an acute attack of pneumonia, which killed the great writer.

We were sure that force, threats, and promises had been used to obtain confessions, but were not certain which means were employed on each defendant. Once, when Vishinsky was questioning Yagoda about the death of Gorky's son, Yagoda looked at Vishinsky with baleful eyes and in a quiet voice said, "I would not advise the citizen prosecutor to pursue that line any further." Vishinsky immediately moved to another subject. What sensitive nerve had been touched, what aspect of the agreement between Yagoda and Vishinsky had been breached, we will never know.

On the first day of the trial, which I missed, one of the defendants, Nikolai N. Krestinsky, who had been a Vice-Commissar for Foreign Affairs, electrified the courtroom by suddenly announcing that his confession was false, that it had been given under threats and black-mail. This, I believe, was the first time that any defendant had repudiated his confession. Why Krestinsky did this is a matter of guess-work. A theory that I believe to be as valid as any is that Krestinsky, after his months in prison, concluded that the top officials of the Party did not know what had been going on, and a repudiation in open court would be the best method of bringing the truth to their attention. Vishinsky kept pointing out to Krestinsky that he had signed the confession, and asked how one could believe his repudiation if one could not believe what he had originally signed. I was at the opening of the second session of the trial when Krestinsky asked permission of the judge to make a voluntary statement. He said that he was unable to explain his sudden mental aberration of the preceding day. Possibly,

* We confirmed his removal with a device that newsmen in Moscow have used for decades—checking on the posters and pictures displayed at the May Day and November 7 celebrations. During these holidays, everyone in the Embassy would keep on the lookout for posters and pictures while driving or walking, and report his findings. Because wives had more free time, they were more assiduous at this tactic for gathering information. On parade days we would have parties in the Embassy building, which overlooked Red Square, and count the placards from the comfort of our offices. While journalists put great store in poster-watching, the Embassy never considered this more than a supplement to more serious methods of diplomatic reporting.

he said, the reason for his false repudiation of the confession was the shock of finding himself on the bench of the accused, indicted for a series of horrible crimes against country and Party. He again confessed to the crimes. It was an extremely weak explanation and did away with any suspicion that Krestinsky's recanting on the first day might have been planned by the authorities.

At 4 A.M. on March 13, the death sentences were read under kleig lights by the Judge of the Court, General Vasily V. Ulrich, who looked like a sadistic pig. With obvious relish, he intoned the names of the defendants, followed, in eighteen cases, with the refrain, "To be shot, to be shot, to be shot." It took more than an hour to read all the sentences, and by the time of the last "to be shot," I felt that the top of my head was coming off. I could not go to sleep easily for almost a month after that. Those eighteen executed included Bukharin, Rykov, Krestinsky, and Yagoda. The three other defendants received prison terms of fifteen to twenty-five years.

In the fall of 1938, with the appointment of Lavrenti P. Beria as Commissar for Internal Affairs, arrests slackened off, and by 1939 the terror was over. Not that Beria, as his subsequent actions showed, was a man of moderate views, but simply that Stalin had decided that the purge had gone far enough. There were still arrests for treason or anti-Soviet behavior; these began in November, 1917, and have never ceased. But the organized drive to root out all possible opposition to Stalin had ended.

Every bit of testimony at the Bukharin-Rykov trial was the subject of endless discussion in the Embassy. There was speculation over the reason the purges were started, what they were trying to accomplish, whether Stalin was mad, whether he had some other sinister plan in mind, how much truth there was in the accusations.

Ambassador Davies was not noted for an acute understanding of the Soviet system, and he had an unfortunate tendency to take what was presented at the trial as the honest and gospel truth. I still blush when I think of some of the telegrams he sent to the State Department about the trial. There were, for example, his comments on Krestinsky. Davies accepted Krestinsky's second-day story, in which he again confessed, as the true one. He commented on the "dignity" of the proceedings and said the "natural reaction to the first session is that if the charges are true a terrible, sordid picture of human nature at its worst is being unfolded." From the beginning, he believed in the defendants' guilt.

During one of the intermissions, Davies pompously asked a British correspondent, Alfred Chollerton of the *Daily Telegraph*, his opinion of the trial. Chollerton answered that the Soviet Union seemed to move only through convulsions, and that this, being the latest convulsion, was the most violent. As I remember the conversation, Davies said, "No, no, I am quite serious. I would like to have your opinion of this trial." Chollerton, tugging at his beard, looked at Davies with critical eyes and said, "Mr. Ambassador, I believe everything but the facts." Davies never did get the point of Chollerton's joke.

At the close of the trial, Davies sent a message to President Roosevelt and Secretary of State Hull in which he said that while he doubted the guilt of the three physicians on trial, sufficient facts were established regarding the eighteen political figures "to prove that these defendants had plotted to overthrow the present Soviet government and were willing to use any means available to overthrow the Union, and were therefore guilty of treason under Soviet law." It is only fair to point out that Davies did express shock over the lack of protection of the defendants' rights.

I did not have the opportunity to discuss Davies's views on the trial with him. I was still a junior officer, and he did not ask my opinion. I can only guess at the motivation for his reporting. He ardently desired to make a success of a pro-Soviet line and was probably reflecting the views of some of Roosevelt's advisers to enhance his political standing at home. I just don't know. I do not mean that the rest of us in the Embassy had a clear insight of what was going on. Except for Faymonville, the military attaché, we were dubious about the trials, but lacked the facts to support our suspicion.

A number of points that Stalin was trying to achieve through the trials were clear. One goal was to absolve himself and those of his followers who remained in power from any blame for the failure of the Five Year Plan to produce a significant increase in consumer goods and better living conditions for the people. While there was a logical explanation for this failure—the goals were unrealistically high—it was attributed at the trials to sabotage and willful neglect. In the case of Bukharin, there was a series of confessions about sabotaging shipments of eggs and blowing up vegetables consigned to the Moscow market. In a country that has a tendency to be naïve in its beliefs, such testimony was perhaps not so ludicrous as it sounded to us Americans.

The second point Stalin wanted the trials to make was that the accused were enraged because Stalin had gone ahead with plans they opposed but that turned out to be successful. A third strand of policy, which became increasingly evident as the trials progressed, was the danger of espionage. This was designed to exploit the traditional Bolshevik myth of the Soviet people surrounded by terrible enemies who were working to destroy the country out of hatred of its successes. The trials clearly instructed the Russian people not to associate with foreigners.

Over all, the purpose of the trials was to blacken the opposition to Stalin and render it incapable of organizing any movement against him.

While these aims of Stalin were transparent, I could not separate fact from fiction at the trial, nor could I come to any firm conclusions regarding Stalin's deeper motivations for the terror. In fact, an analytical dispatch on the trial was the only paper that I was unable to complete during my nearly forty years in the Foreign Service. I knew the trial was a phony, but I could not prove it; I could only intimate that it had no relevance to reality. Try as I did, and I tried for over a month, I was unable to present a convincing case. While the proceedings of the trial were published verbatim, you could not be sure what was true and what was untrue. It was never possible to tell whether a statement or an event was a total invention or had some semblance of fact behind it. In general, it seemed to me that those who were arranging and presenting the trial would try in every case to start with something that was true and then enlarge it out of all recognition into an indictment against the prisoner. For example, a meeting of three of the defendants for an exchange of views, possibly including some criticism of Stalin, would be turned into a conspiracy to murder him.

Bukharin added to my confusion and suspicion that something was wrong. While he made a general confession of guilt, he denied specific acts of crime. There were passages in his final statement at the trial in which he seemed to be speaking indirectly, in his Aesopian style, to indict Stalin. He talked of a duality of mind—a hint, certainly, of a veiled meaning in his words. He spoke, too, of reflecting during his year in prison on what he must die for, and added, "An absolutely black vacuity suddenly rises before you with startling vividness. There was nothing to die for if one wanted to die unrepentant and, on the contrary, everything positive that glistens in the Soviet Union acquires new dimensions in a man's mind." Ostensibly, Bukharin was saying that there was no place for him to turn, because he had been disloyal to the Party and he had to repent his sins. To those who knew Bukharin's style, he was saying something quite different. The "black vacuity" was Stalin's distorted version of the Bolshevik ideals, the oppressive state, the purges. His repentance was the expression of hope in the "positive"—non-Stalin—parts of the Soviet Union. Such veiled attacks not only fitted Bukharin's style, they were also in the Russian intellectual tradition.

As for Stalin's deeper motives, I could not accept any of the speculation. Some said he was mad. I found no evidence for a conclusion that he was mentally unbalanced in the usual sense of the term, although obviously there must have been something wrong with a man who would send millions of people to senseless deaths. The removal of opponents who might have overthrown him seemed to offer the best clue, but I could not understand why Stalin chose, at a time when the Soviet Union was imperiled by both Germany and Japan, to wreck the structure of officialdom that he had erected and to destroy the leadership of the Red Army.

One theory that, as time has passed, I have come more and more to hold is that Stalin purged the true believers in Communism from the ranks of the Soviet élite in order to avoid the possibility of a revolt against policies that he probably even then saw would be necessary if the Soviet Union as a system was to be saved. I do not maintain that he actually foresaw the deal with Nazi Germany, but it certainly must have been in his general thinking that in order to safeguard itself the Soviet government might be forced to make arrangements that would be repugnant to any true Bolshevik. Stalin probably recalled the violent opposition of the left Bolsheviks in 1918 to the treaty of Brest-Litovsk, under which Russia gave up one-third of her people to buy peace with Germany, and it did not take much imagination to realize that his opponents would be greater in number if he had to make a deal with Nazi Germany.

With the advantage of hindsight and all the evidence that has accumulated, particularly Khrushchev's secret speech to the Twentieth Party Congress in 1956 on Stalin's crimes, it is now apparent that the purge trials were complete frame-ups, that Stalin not only ordered them, he also directed them, and that great pressure was put on the accused to sign false confessions (Bukharin apparently confessed to save his young wife and son). But we still are not sure of Stalin's underlying motives.

The heritage of the purge still looms large in Russia. After a period when some, but by no means all, of the horrors were exposed, there has been a tendency to ease up on the disclosures. But the purge is a living memory to many Russians, especially to the thousands and thousands who spent time in concentration camps, and to the children of the thousands who were shot. It is not surprising that some of the dissidents in the Soviet Union today have a family background of being targets of the purge.

Furthermore, the purge had indirect effects. There is something to the thesis that men who succeeded to power were by no means of the caliber of those who were purged. Almost all the original Bolshevik leaders, such as Lenin and Trotsky, were men of considerable intellectual attainment. They were products of Western European civilization, against which they were in revolt; nevertheless, they were its children. Stalin was the one man in the original Bolshevik leadership who was purely a Russian-grown product. He was a Georgian and had little connection with the humane values of Western Christian civilization, even though his education was within that framework. The Revolution drove much of the Western-oriented upper class and middle class out of Russia. Stalin's purge nearly eliminated from the Communist Party those who, in the tradition of Lenin, possessed a Western-based intellect. Now the Moscow regime is rooted in an almost 100-percent Russian tradition, which in many respects is different in its attitude toward man and society than that of Christian Western Europe. One of the first results has been a sharp drop in the caliber of leadership of the Soviet Union since Stalin. It is true that his immediate successor, Georgi Malenkov, was a superior brain, but he, too, was basically a product of the West and he did not last long. As for Khrushchev, whatever admiration some of his policies deserve, he could hardly be considered a cultivated or a civilized human being. Even less could be said for Leonid Brezhnev and Alexei Kosygin. There is no question that in time the Russians can develop superb leaders; it is unfortunate that the purge eliminated those best qualified to run the Soviet Union after Stalin. Russia has suffered as a result.

CHAPTER FOUR

A Frustrating Year

In the summer of 1938, my duties expanded. Ambassador Davies was transferred to Brussels, and Alexander Kirk, as chargé d'affaires, assumed direction of the Embassy. These moves made me the senior Russian-language officer in charge of political reporting, a heavy responsibility at a time when Soviet intentions in regard to Hitler were critical. Stalin had two choices. He could join Britain and France in collective security against Germany, or he could seek an accommodation with Hitler to protect the Soviet Union's western border. It was my principal job to try to discover the trend of Stalin's thinking.

My task was made easier by Davies's departure. Davies had relied much more on the opinion of the American press than the judgments of his staff and had spent a lot of time ingratiating himself with American newsmen in Moscow. He was incurably optimistic in his reports to Washington, thereby misleading our government. His dispatches, while containing a good deal of information and shrewd observation, were almost always superficial and heavily slanted.

With Kirk in charge, Embassy working arrangements changed, and we settled down to a more serious routine. As a relatively junior officer with no special training in political reporting, I needed guidance. Kirk, who had served in many posts, was a hard taskmaster but understanding of the faults of youth. He insisted that the work be done in painstaking fashion and was infinitely patient in explaining any defects in a draft of a report. He had a sharp and witty tongue and would frequently use it. I owe a great deal to his wise guidance during the year he ran the Embassy.

The difficulties of accurate reporting from Moscow in 1938 were enormous. The Soviet government has always been secretive in the conduct of its business. Soviet officials as a rule never talk about what their government may or may not do, and there is no briefing after an event, as there is in Western capitals, to give foreign observers some inkling of the reasons for a decision. In addition, all means of public expression—the press, magazines, journals, and broadcasting—are controlled by the Communist regime. In 1938, the last year of the purge, the situation was even worse. There were virtually no contacts with any Russian, officially or unofficially, and consequently no possibility of testing by conversation any idea on Soviet policy that might be gleaned from the press. The official press and radio were the only source of news except for a very rare session of the Supreme Soviet plus gossip or information inside the diplomatic colony.

It must be remembered that in those days the United States information-gathering facilities were unsophisticated. There was no Central Intelligence Agency culling esoteric reports, monitoring broadcasts, taking photographs from reconnaissance planes and artificial satellites, sending secret agents into foreign countries. Washington depended almost completely on the Moscow Embassy. Everyone in the Embassy from Kirk on down was, of course, alert to any information he might pick up. Aside from me, however, the only members of the staff whose principal responsibility was gathering intelligence were military attachés, headed by Colonel Faymonville, who was not very useful because he was inclined to favor the Soviet regime in almost all its actions. At staff meetings (in those days staff meetings were a relative rarity in American missions), he would stoutly defend the purges, insisting that they were uprooting traitors and enemies of the people from the Red Army, and therefore did not weaken but, on the contrary, strengthened the military. He had had great influence on Ambassador Davies; they more or less thought alike. In Siberia in 1918 and 1919, he had seen the Bolsheviks fighting with some support from the people and had developed a deep sympathy for Russia as a nation and for her new rulers. I do not believe that Faymonville was in any sense of the word a Communist, or had even toyed with the idea of joining the American Communist Party. He was simply pro-Russian, which, under the circumstances of the 1930s, forced him into a pro-Bolshevik position. It did not take me long to discount Faymonville's views.

Like Kelly, Kirk believed that diplomatic reporting should be tentative and heavily qualified unless based on established fact or direct information. Thus Kirk reinforced the lessons I had learned from Kelly. With little hard information available in Moscow, my reports tended to be cautious and to avoid flat statements. In accordance with Kirk's teachings, I did not want to make any suppositions or assumptions that would mislead officials in Washington. There was an ever present danger of misinterpretation through oversimplification as reports moved through the State Department and White House bureaucracy. Kirk's guidelines were especially sound because our main interest was less the factual one of Soviet capability than the judgment of Soviet intent—would Stalin opt for an accord with Britain and France or make a deal with Hitler?

A series of events, beginning with German demands on Czechoslovakia in the summer of 1938, kept me puzzled about Stalin's intention for more than a year. We picked up hints that summer that the Soviet Union, which had for years been publicly urging a policy of collective security against Fascism, might be getting into a position to strike a deal with Hitler. In mid-June, I learned that an American correspondent in Moscow had been told by a reporter in Prague that Germany would soon approach the Soviet government with a view to improvement of relations. I asked a friend at the German Embassy whom I knew to be anti-Hitler (I did not sense the depth of his feeling until the next year) what he thought. He said that any such move was inconceivable "in view of the deep-seated personal antipathy" of Hitler toward Communism and the Soviet government. Significantly, however, the Soviet Foreign Office permitted the American correspondent to file a story through censorship saying that any such initiative by the Nazis "which would contribute to the cause of world peace" would probably meet with success, although there should be no attempt to break the "democratic front."

On June 23, the day after we reported this to the State Department, Litvinov added to my suspicion with a speech in Leningrad. In a commentary for the State Department, I pointed out that while Litvinov's speech, which denounced imperialism, contained nothing really new, it did disclose that "the Soviet Union does not consider itself an integral part of the present world system and charges the world with notice of the fact that if the countries with which it was heretofore contented to cooperate do not pursue policies in accordance with the desires of the Soviet government, even this slight cooperation may be withdrawn." Viewed against subsequent events, this speech could be taken as a warning of the possibility that the Soviet Union might make a deal with Germany, although in my caution I did not make such an interpretation. There was no question that the Soviet Union felt isolated, with Britain and France spurning Litvinov's overtures for collective action to forestall Hitler.

By late summer, we heard rumors that the Kremlin had assured the Czechs, in response to a request from President Eduard Benes, that help would be forthcoming in the event of a German attack. In fact, Litvinov, in a speech to the Council of the League of Nations on September 1, expressed the willingness of the Soviet Union to act "together with France ... by the way open to us" to aid Czechoslovakia. As we studied this statement, Kirk and I agreed that the two qualifications were important. One qualification required that France join in the action, as stated in the Soviet-Czech treaty. The other qualification was the form of aid—"by the way open to us." Since the two countries did not at that time border on each other, we doubted whether the Soviet Union could provide effective aid. In the middle of the crisis, Kirk called in Faymonville and asked him, as military attaché, for a cold-blooded judgment as to what the Soviet Union could do, on the assumption that it wanted to help the Czechs. Faymonville came back with a paper in which he said that all that the Soviet Union could do for Czechoslovakia would be to send them two of its forty-five squadrons of bombers—a few dozen planes. Kirk looked at the paper in astonishment and said, "Colonel, you cannot mean this. This is much too little." Faymonville replied, "This is what my serious calculation brings me to."

The Soviets have often cited Litvinov's speech to the League of Nations as evidence of a willingness to fight Hitler to save Czechoslovakia, but there was no solid information in 1938, nor have I seen any subsequently, that they ever gave any flat, firm commitment to Benes.

While I lacked sufficient information to make a solid judgment about Stalin's intentions during the Czech crisis, I was sure that the Soviet Union was not prepared to fight a major war. Internally, morale in the country was not high. It cannot be said that Stalin's reputation with the great mass of people had been seriously damaged during the purge. I believe that many Russians geniunely believed that he had unmasked a great conspiracy against the state and Revolution and was a hero for exposing and destroying it. Living standards were low, however, and people yearned for a better life. Inside the Party and within the intelligentsia, there was a much clearer understanding of what Stalin was up to, but everyone was much too terrorized to give vent to his feelings.

Above all, the army leadership, which had been decimated by the purge, was suffering; it would take years before the consequences could be overcome. Stalin knew this, although it is doubtful whether he fully realized the extent of the damage inflicted by the purge. It took the early setbacks of the Finnish War in the winter of 1939–40 to show how much the Red Army had suffered. Later, at the Teheran Conference, I heard Stalin tell Churchill and Roosevelt, in response to a toast to the victories of the Red Army, that in truth, in the Finnish War, the Red Army wasn't worth anything—*"nikomu ne goditsa."*

It is wrong to ascribe calculated dishonesty to the Russians regarding the 1938 Czech crisis, because Soviet policy does not lend itself to such analysis. If the Bolsheviks had considered the preservation of Czechoslovakia, or the halting of Hitler, as steps toward their main objective of the maintenance of the Soviet system in Russia, then they would undoubtedly have helped Czechoslovakia. On the other hand, there was doubt in the minds of the Soviet rulers as to whether Russia would not get involved alone in a war with Hitler. British and French vacillation on Hitler and pressure on Czechoslovakia added fuel to those doubts, as did widely expressed hopes in London and Paris that the Soviet Union and Germany would bleed each other white in a war. Stalin had no intention of fighting Hitler alone.

Underlying Soviet fears was a belief that in important matters the capitalist nations would join, despite their rivalries, to preserve their economic system. Therefore, the Soviets thought before the war that England, France, and Germany might find common cause to launch an attack on the Soviet Union. This was obviously a bogus belief, but it persisted even after Russia had been attacked. A Russian told me in 1943 that he and many others expected the British fleet to enter the Baltic Sea in 1941, against the Soviets in conjunction with the Nazis.

The Munich agreement of September 29, dismembering Czechoslovakia, was a sobering experience for the Soviet government. Kept out of all diplomatic procedures leading up to the conference and from the conference itself, the Soviet government found itself ignored. In the Embassy, Kirk and I could only guess at the feelings of Stalin and his associates, but they must have been gloomy. They probably saw the culmination of their traditional paranoid fear of a capitalist conspiracy against the Soviet Union, this time clothed in the reality of Nazi Germany and its armed might. Our views were set forth in a telegram to Washington on October 31, which offered the safe opinion that "for the moment at least the Kremlin is inclined to await the course of further developments abroad to assist it in determining its policy in relation to other countries, either singly or collectively, and to refrain from any definite commitment in policy until those developments are more clearly defined."

We had heard rumors at that time that Litvinov, who had become a symbol of collective security, would be fired. While we had little to go on, Kirk and I showed a little more confidence. We predicted he would be retained because there was no one qualified to replace him as Commissar for Foreign Affairs and because he did not make policy; Stalin did.

We were wrong in our prediction. In the spring of 1939, Litvinov was ousted. What we had not realized was that while Britain and France had learned, as a result of Munich, that appeasement of Hitler would not work, Stalin either had, or soon would, draw a different conclusion—that the Soviet Union must make an accommodation with Germany, regardless of the cost, to keep war from the Soviet state.

Shortly after Munich, we in the Embassy noticed some slackening of direct propaganda assaults on Germany in the Soviet press and radio. There had been fairly quiet periods before, and I did not report the slackening to Washington. While I studied the papers carefully and listened to many broadcasts, the Embassy had no facilities for systematically monitoring the Soviet press and radio. It was not until much later that I learned that the letup had been widespread and had been based on an agreement between the German and Soviet governments and that anti-Soviet propaganda in Berlin had abated, too. Had we known of this secret agreement at that time, we would have been much more alert to the possibility of a German-Soviet rapprochement. To call off propaganda, a subject that the Soviet government has in general refused even to discuss with other countries, was a very un-Soviet act and could only have been undertaken under conditions of extreme necessity. I still kick myself for missing this clue to Soviet policy.

With the Soviet Union's isolation, the Bolshevik leaders felt a little friendlier toward the United States. I noticed this when I picked up *Izvestia* on November 16 and read an editorial stressing the value of solidarity between the two countries. In an analysis written by Kirk, Grummon, and me, we said that circumstances might lead to settlement of some outstanding differences, such as the pre-Bolshevik debts, but we warned that "if the repeated utterances of Soviet leaders are considered, it may be assumed that the Kremlin does not envisage cordial relations with the capitalist governments on any permanent basis but rather as a temporary expedient dictated by the more immediate objectives of Soviet policy."

When this dispatch was read in Washington, Moffat, chief of the European Affairs Division, commented that the writers "seem to feel that no foreign government mapping out its foreign policies should place a dependence upon sustained Soviet cooperation or should consider Soviet gestures of friendship as other than opportunistic moves taken in order to meet some international exigency."

While it is true that the Embassy had little evidence to go on, the Nazi-Soviet pact eventually confirmed our view.

Over the winter, we sought in vain for clear clues to Soviet intentions. In March, Stalin himself, in a speech to the Eighteenth Congress of the Soviet Communist Party, gave us some indications. While the world nervously wondered whether Hitler would order his panzers to strike at Poland—which was the chief target of Nazi threats—or take over the rest of Czechoslovakia, or turn on some other helpless victim, like Switzerland or the Netherlands, Stalin told those Party members lucky enough to escape the purge that the Soviet Union wanted peace with all nations and that their task was to prevent Russia from being drawn into the conflict by the "provocateurs of war who are accustomed to using others as cats'-paws." The Soviet Union, he said in perhaps his most quoted line, would not get in a war "to pull somebody else's chestnuts out of the fire." He also denounced Western press reports regarding German designs on the Ukraine as an attempt to poison the atmosphere and produce a conflict with Germany without visible reason, and expressed satisfaction that Germany, instead of expanding eastward, was turning to the West and overseas. As always, the diplomatic corps was not invited to the Congress; we had to read about it in *Pravda*. In the following months this speech was studied and restudied.

Kirk, with my assistance, sent the State Department a telegram summing up initial reaction. We noted that members of the German Embassy had expressed satisfaction at the tone of Stalin's reference to the international situation, particularly to his denunciation of attempts to provoke a war between the two countries. The Germans whom I had talked with even offered the opinion that there was a possibility that if Stalin's remarks were properly presented to Hitler, an amelioration in the political situation between the Soviet Union and Germany might follow.

Would Stalin make such a move toward Hitler? We were extremely wary, arguing that the speech expressed Soviet policy only "in the light of the foreign situation which existed the day of its delivery." Stalin did say that the Soviet Union would maintain friendly relations with any country that did not directly threaten the interests of the Soviet Union, and he pointed out that he had indirectly associated those interests with Soviet frontiers. In our circumspection, we reached the somewhat banal conclusion that "the Soviet government has no intention of being drawn into a war with Germany in defense of the interests of other countries."

Our bafflement over Soviet policy increased five days after Stalin's speech with the sudden take-over by Hitler's armies of the parts of Czechoslovakia left after the dismemberment of Munich. The Soviet press made a generally routine denunciation of the aggression, and Moscow sent Berlin a note of protest, but it did not seem to us in the Embassy that the Russians had their heart in it. A week later, a Foreign Office communiqué denied "rumors" that the Soviet government had offered Poland and Rumania assistance in the event of a Nazi attack. Britain had asked the Soviet Union what it would do if Rumania were attacked, the communiqué noted, and the Soviet government had proposed, as it had previously, a conference of the representatives of Rumania, France, Poland, Turkey, Britain, and the Soviet Union.

When the British, however, turned down the proposal for a conference and proceeded unilaterally to guarantee Poland and Rumania against Nazi attack, Fitzroy MacLean, a Secretary in the British Embassy, who was later elected to Parliament and had a brilliant record of service with Tito in Yugoslavia during the war, confided his despair. He felt, and it seemed obvious, that the British government had given away all its bargaining chips. Prodded by Winston Churchill, Neville Chamberlain had switched from appeasement to a policy of seeking a united front against Hitler. But once Britain unilaterally guaranteed Poland—the traditional "invasion corridor" to Russia— there was little more Chamberlain could offer Stalin. Without receiving anything in return, Britain was in effect extending a guarantee to Russia. By this act, the Chamberlain government gave away all of the inducements which might conceivably have been valuable in an attempt to persuade the Soviet Union that its interests lay with an anti-Hitler coalition and not in a deal with Hitler. Thus Stalin could count on the division of the capitalist nations and be assured that they would not gang up against the Soviet Union.

With the benefit of hindsight, it is clear that the Chamberlain guarantee, instead of protecting Poland, doomed that country and led to the Nazi-Soviet pact. In our careful way, we in the Moscow Embassy would not go that far in the spring of 1939 in interpreting Soviet policy. In a telegram to Washington, Kirk and I noted signs of a possible inclination to reduce friction in Soviet relations with Germany, and emphasized the obvious—that "it is this change in the manifestation of Soviet attitude towards Germany which challenges attention at the present time" and safely forecast that Stalin would exercise "extreme caution."

One of the reasons we hesitated to jump to a conclusion was that, as always, what little evidence we had was contradictory. While softening Soviet policy toward Hitler, Stalin also raised anew with the British and French the possibility of a treaty to protect the rest of Eastern Europe against Nazi Germany. This time, Prime Minister Chamberlain and Premier Edouard Daladier responded positively but with so many qualifications that it was clear that the talks would be long and involved. It is now easy to see with clarity that Stalin made the move in an attempt to induce Hitler to make an offer. Stalin hardly needed Britain and France; together they could not guarantee his western border. Only a deal with Hitler could do that. But few saw through Stalin's maneuvering in the spring of 1939.

Even on May 3, when Stalin removed Litvinov as Foreign Commissar and appointed his faithful lackey, Molotov (who retained the premiership), in his place, we in the Embassy did not fully realize what was going on. The change was a major move in the process, which had developed after Munich, that led eventually to the deal with Germany. We believed that the change had been the result of a sudden decision, because the British Ambassador, Sir William Seeds, told us that he had talked to Litvinov a few hours before the announcement and saw no sign that he was about to be removed. Nor did other members of the diplomatic corps who had been in contact with the Foreign Office have any intimation that such a change was in progress, although there were rumors that the Germans were going to make some approach to the Russians.

In a cautious telegram to Washington, Kirk and I said that Litvinov's removal "might constitute a step away from the principle of collective security and one towards the establishment of relations with Germany." On the other hand, the report went on in typically prudent fashion, "the possibility cannot be excluded that the removal of Litvinov may be designed to produce, particularly in England, the impression of an immediate Soviet-German rapprochement" with the view to accelerating the British decision on the Soviet proposal for an anti-Nazi coalition. Hedging still more, the report said that whatever may have been the real reasons for Litvinov's removal, the action "is generally regarded as of major significance in Soviet foreign relations, the real direction and portent of which will only be apparent in light of further development."

When Bullitt, who was ambassador to France, heard about Litvinov, he called me from Paris. Realizing that the call would be monitored, we talked in baseball slang. Bullitt wondered whether his friends might be subject to a "shutout." I talked about the difficulty of knowing what a "pinch hitter" would do.

Lacking concrete information, we did not pretend to understand the full significance of Litvinov's removal. It was, of course, a subject of much speculation in the Embassy, and the fact that he was a Jew was not lost sight of in view of Hitler's anti-Semitism. In fact, the Embassy had already noted that one of the consequences of the purge had been the virtual elimination of Jews from positions of importance in Soviet foreign affairs.

As time went on, it became apparent that the entire staff of the Soviet Foreign Office had been changed immediately after the removal of Litvinov. Most of the new officials seem to have been selected because of their non-experience or non-connection with foreign affairs. Among the new officials mentioned in an Embassy dispatch was Andrei Gromyko. This was the first time, I think, that anyone had heard the name Gromyko in the foreign service of the Soviet Union. During this period, he came to lunch at Spaso House, and I think it was the first time he had ever had a meal with foreigners. It was quite apparent that Gromyko, a professor of economics, had virtually no knowledge of foreign affairs. He was ill at ease and obviously fearful of making some social blunder during the luncheon.

While the Embassy searched for the true direction of Soviet policy, Henderson, who had been transferred to Washington, wrote an impressive memorandum on July 22, pointing out that much of the discussion about Soviet policy was based on ignorance. He said that he thought that as long as Germany and Poland were at daggers drawn, the Soviet Union was relieved of danger of an attack from the West, and "as a result of this change, the Soviet Union has no longer any deep interest in the problem of the policy of collective security. It is also correct to state that if the Soviet Union does come to terms with Great Britain, it will do so only on a basis which will give them what amounts to hegemony over Eastern Europe and which will render impossible for at least many years to come a United Western Europe."

Henderson's views were quite accurate, but he left out one possibility—that Poland would be crushed with hardly a gesture of assistance from the Western Allies because they were not in any position to give it. I think this possibility loomed large in Stalin's mind as he considered what he might do to avoid clashing with the awesome Hitler war machine. Stalin's eventual solution was not long in coming. Since he was afraid of Hitler, Stalin joined him in the infamous pact that divided Poland. I was fortunate, after the frustration of my first year as a diplomatic reporter, to break through the cloud of secrecy in Moscow in 1939 and learn in detail about the private conversations between the Soviets and the Germans.

CHAPTER FIVE

A Source in the Nazi Embassy

One of the wisest investments that Americans at the Moscow Embassy made was leasing a dacha about seventeen kilometers west of Moscow. Our dacha was on a road that we dubbed the Georgian Military Highway because it led to Stalin's country place. It was a two-story frame and log house, painted light yellow, with four bedrooms, a living room, and a porch, with a beautiful view of the rolling countryside. The plumbing system provided hot water occasionally. In the rear was a small kitchen, and in the cellar a place where an incredible Russian named Panteleimon lived with a wife of whom we were unaware for years. How long she had lived in that dark hole we will never know.

Panteleimon, who was probably in his late fifties, was a somewhat scrawny peasant with a nondescript mustache. He wore the traditional peasant blouse and trousers, which were tucked into big boots. He was always dirty, invariably cheerful, and nauseatingly obsequious, bowing and calling us "Barin," the usual Russian title for the gentry. According to rumor, Panteleimon had fought on the wrong side of several battles in the civil war. Apparently, it was his peasant cunning that enabled him to survive.

We could attest to his slyness. He had charge of two lean horses, which were owned jointly by the Americans who leased the dacha, a member of the German Embassy, and Fitzroy MacLean, my friend in the British Embassy—a combination that led to some strain when war broke out. There was a continual argument with Panteleimon over the large amount of oats these horses ate. Finally, MacLean, who was the son of a colonel in the British Army, decided to deal with Panteleimon. Obtaining a copy of the British army regulations for the feeding of horses on active duty, he turned over to Panteleimon every week only the amount of oats set forth in the British rules. Panteleimon accepted the instructions in silence. But soon we began to notice that the horses were getting thinner. The battle went on for two months, with Panteleimon insisting that Russian horses must need more oats than British horses and MacLean arguing that they did not. Finally, when the health of the horses was beginning to be seriously affected, MacLean capitulated, and unlimited quantities of oats were again given to Panteleimon. We never did find out where Panteleimon was selling the oats.

The dacha was our principal place of recreation in those dreary days. Amusements were hard to find in Moscow. Of course, the ballet was magnificent, but the repertoire was always the same. (In my years in Moscow, I must have seen *Swan Lake* fifty times; I think I could dance every step.) There was some first-rate theater, but all of the plays were in the Russian classic style, nothing new or innovative. The movies were loaded with propaganda about happy peasants and factory workers and ultimate paradise in the Revolution. The exceptions were the Eisenstein films, of which there were very few. I especially remember the films *Peter the Great* and *Alexander Nevsky*. In any case, the movie theaters were so crowded and badly ventilated that it was more an ordeal than a pleasure to attend.

Travel was difficult. Distances were immense, and at that time all travel was by train; hotels were poor and the food was worse; it was a long process to get permission from the authorities to go outside the prescribed limits; the period when travel in northern Russia was feasible was limited because of the cold and the poor condition of the roads. However, we managed trips to Kiev and Leningrad.

As a result of lack of things to do and of the impossibility of getting to know any Russians, we were thrown a great deal into the company of other diplomats. Because of the Soviet Union's importance, most countries made a point of having exceptional members of their diplomatic service stationed there, so we were fortunate in having bright and interesting colleagues of all ages, as well as newspaper correspondents, as companions. There were the usual dinner parties, but they were more informal and more fun than those in other capitals. We went on expeditions into the countryside together, played tennis, and skied and skated on the paths of Gorky Park. Our dacha in the country was a meeting place every weekend in the summer for tennis and long walks in the forests, and in the winter for skiing on a gentle hill or cross-country and skating on the flooded tennis court. We held many parties at the dacha, and occasionally the waiters wore ice skates and skimmed around the rink, passing trays of drinks.

Among the most popular of the younger members of the diplomatic corps were Hans Heinrich Herwarth von Bittenfeld, usually called Johnny Herwarth, a Second Secretary of the German Embassy, whose pleasant brown eyes and easygoing personality were quite unlike the caricature of the blue-eyed, arrogant Nazi, and his wife, a Bavarian girl of considerable charm. They spent many a weekend with us at the dacha. Johnny was part owner of one of the horses, and we often went riding together.

Although Johnny had always seemed to be frank with me in discussing international affairs, I was somewhat surprised on May 16, 1939, when he returned from a trip to Iran and gave me some secret information. He had accompanied the German Ambassador to Moscow, Werner von der Schulenberg, to the wedding of the Shah's daughter in Teheran. Johnny came back alone. The day after his return, we went riding at the dacha. While we were waiting in the garden for Panteleimon to bring our horses, Johnny told me that, in Teheran, Schulenberg had received a personal message from Joachim von Ribbentrop, the German Foreign Minister, summoning him to Berlin for consultation with Hitler. Johnny said he did not know what could have caused this radical change in plans, or what particular aspect of foreign policy Hitler had in mind, although obviously it was related to the Soviet Union. But he thought that "something was up." I naturally expressed interest, and we speculated what the summons to the Ambassador meant. Johnny felt it had something to do with a shift in German policy on the Soviet Union, but, like Schulenberg, was completely in the dark regarding Hitler's reasons. Johnny thought he would soon know what was up because Schulenberg was arriving in Moscow the following day with instructions from the German government. Appointments had been made at Berlin's request for the Ambassador to see Molotov and V. P. Potemkin, Molotov's deputy.

Johnny also told me that a military attaché had been called to Berlin the previous week and had been asked by the German War Ministry whether there was any reason to believe that the Soviet Union was stronger in a military sense or in a better position to undertake offensive action than in September, 1938, and that the attaché had given a negative reply. It seemed that Berlin wanted to assess the possibility of a Soviet counteraction in the event that Germany attacked Poland, but Johnny did not know whether the two pieces of information were connected or not.

I did not understand why Johnny was giving me, the diplomat in charge of political reporting for a country unfriendly with Germany, secret information. From our acquaintance, I did know that Johnny was opposed to Nazi policy, although he was careful not to say so publicly. He was noted for the frankness and freedom with which he discussed international problems and, unlike the Nazis, was always willing to see the opposite side of the argument. In the Western diplomatic contingent in Moscow, he had a high reputation as an intelligent and forthright man. He was, in short, a civilized European.

Because of his reputation, I tended to believe Johnny, and, after talking the matter over with Grummon, the new chargé d'affaires, who had just replaced Kirk, I drafted and we sent a telegram to the State Department, informing it of Schulenberg's moves and emphasizing that the report had been given in "the strictest confidence." Eager to know what Germany was up to, and, of course, the Kremlin response, I kept in close touch with Johnny, and he did not let me down. At another meeting at the dacha, he told me that Ribbentrop had asked Schulenberg to feel the Soviets out on the possibility of closer relations. On May 20, we wired the following message to Washington:

> On his return to Berlin from Teheran the German Ambassador was told by Ribbentrop, obviously reflecting Hitler's views, that in the opinion of the German government, Communism had ceased to exist in the Soviet Union; that the Communist International was no longer a factor of importance in Soviet foreign relations, and that consequently it was felt that no real ideological barrier remained between Germany and Russia. Under the circumstances, it was desired that the Ambassador return to Moscow to convey very discreetly to the Soviet government the impression that Germany entertained no animosity toward it and to endeavor to ascertain the present Soviet attitude toward Soviet-German relations. Ribbentrop impressed upon the Ambassador the necessity of exercising the greatest caution in the premises, as any appearance of a German approach to the Soviet Union would alarm Japan, which in view of the special relationship existing between Germany and that country would be very undesirable.

In reply to the Ambassador's query as to whether in view of the

Soviet-British negotiations some more specific and direct approach would not be desirable, Ribbentrop replied that the German government was not alarmed at the prospect of an agreement between Great Britain and the Soviet Union as it was not convinced that England and France would be disposed to lend extensive or wholehearted military assistance to any country in Eastern Europe. Ribbentrop then told the Ambassador that Germany desired mediation to settle the question of Danzig and the auto-road across the corridor [to East Prussia] and that even in the event of a conflict with Poland, Germany had no intention of attempting to occupy the whole of that country. Ribbentrop's instructions were oral and they left to the Ambassador's discretion the manner of bringing the foregoing to the attention of the Soviet government. The impression, however, was received that without committing the German government to any line of action vis-a-vis the Soviet Government, he was to convey an indication of the change in attitude on the part of the higher circles in Berlin toward this country [the Soviet Union] as well as the assurance that Germany was in favor of the maintenance of an independent Poland. Despite Ribbentrop's statement to the contrary, it was believed that the purpose of this approach was not unconnected with the Soviet-British negotiations.

In conveying the above information it was emphasized that the Ambassador's instructions were general in nature and could not be taken as a definite German proposal to the Union of Soviet Socialist Republics, although a possible first step in that direction, and that future developments along this line would depend upon the reaction encountered by the Ambassador in his conversations here. In this connection it was stated that officials of the Soviet Embassy in Berlin especially the Counsellor, Astakhov, have intimated recently to members of the German Foreign Office that Soviet foreign policy was now on a new basis, a statement which has been repeated here to a German correspondent by the new Chief of the Press Section of the Commissariat for Foreign Affairs.

Ribbentrop's instructions made it clear that the Germans were probing with the aim of seeking an arrangement with the Soviet Union to eliminate the traditional nightmare of a war on two fronts, as in World War I.

The telegram concluded with a request that every effort be made to protect the source of information and its place of origin. Of course, I was very careful, too. During my conversations with Johnny, I would not take notes. Later, when I had a chance, I would jot down a specific fact on the back of an envelope or a scrap of paper. As soon as I returned to my office, I would write out a telegram in longhand. One of the reasons for writing in longhand rather than dictating was that we were never sure whether our office was bugged. This method occasionally led to some problems, because my handwriting is virtually illegible, even to me. Often I would have to puzzle over some of my hieroglyphics with the stenographers. But in reviewing the telegrams I wrote during this period, I did not find any serious garbles or any serious errors in fact. They were, I am happy to say, an accurate account of what Johnny told me. In those days, at least, I had a good memory and could recall almost verbatim words that had been spoken to me a day or so before. Once typewritten, the telegrams were submitted to Grummon and sent in code over his signature by regular commercial lines to Washington. (The information was too hot to go by slow diplomatic pouch.) The wires were sent, in the highest security classification we had available then, to Secretary of State Cordell Hull. It was up to Hull to decide who in the department should see the cables. In the Embassy, there were probably only about three people—Ambassador Laurence Steinhardt, following his arrival in August, Grummon, and my wife—who knew my source. We were less worried about leaks in Moscow (although our diplomatic code was not sophisticated) than we were of someone talking in Washington, a notoriously gossipy town.

We also were forced, somewhat to our discomfort, to observe strict secrecy with the British and the French diplomats in Moscow. The risk to the source was too great. We left the decision up to Washington. As it turned out, Hull, after receipt of the final telegram of this series, called in the British and French ambassadors and gave them details of the forthcoming Nazi-Soviet pact.

There were no near misses about security, no indications that there was any threat closing in on Johnny, even though some of our conversations took place in the German Embassy. The Soviets certainly had no idea that any German was passing information of this character to an American. They would have undoubtedly promptly relayed word to the Nazi government, which certainly would have taken swift and merciless action against him.

Although the Italians were allied with the Germans, the Italian Ambassador, Johnny told me, did not know of the secret talks. The Ambassador, Augosto Rosso, had been envoy to Washington for several years and had married an American. They entertained a great deal in Moscow and invited us to many of their parties. Rosso was strongly anti-Fascist and pro-American, but unfortunately, after the war, through a great error, he was labeled a pro-Nazi and was never given a responsible government job again.

Once we knew of the German plans for sounding out Moscow on a rapprochement, the question was how Schulenberg would carry out his instructions and what the Soviet reaction would be. It was a few days after Schulenberg's meetings with Molotov and Potemkin before Johnny could fill me in. On May 22, I cabled the information:

> The Ambassador, after commenting on the more favorable atmosphere in regard to the Soviet Union which he had found in Berlin, inquired of Molotov as to the possibility of continuing the economic negotiations which had been in abeyance for some months. In reply, Molotov expressed doubt as to the feasibility of the development of economic relations between the two countries in the absence of a "political base," and requested the Ambassador's views on this subject. The Ambassador, it was stated, replied that since as an Ambassador he did not determine policy, he could not offer any authoritative opinion on this matter, but that perhaps Molotov as Prime Minster of the Soviet Union would be in a position to explain exactly what the Soviet government envisaged by a "political basis." Molotov, however, evaded the question by a vague reference to the necessity of giving the matter further consideration.
>
> In his conversation with Potemkin, which consisted largely of an exchange of courtesies, the Ambassador again referred to his belief in the possibility of an improvement in Soviet-German relations at the present time.
>
> In general the impression was received, and I understand reported to Berlin, that Molotov was purposely reserved in regard to the general question of an improvement in Soviet-German relations and that only a definite proposal from the German government would be seriously considered here. Consequently, it was believed that any further developments along this line would depend upon whether the German government was prepared at the present time to make a clear and definite approach to the Soviet government, and the personal opinion was offered that in light of Ribbentrop's concern over the possible effect on Japan, such a step was doubtful at least pending the outcome of German-Japanese conversations which it was stated are now being carried on.

The "personal opinion" was Johnny's, of course, and he was right. Despite a clear signal from Molotov that a specific proposal for a deal would be welcome, Berlin instructed Schulenberg to take no further steps in approaching the Soviet government. Although Johnny told me that Berlin gave no reasons for this instruction, he reiterated his opinion that it was probably Ribbentrop's desire to avoid alarming Japan.

While the reason for the hesitation of the Germans was unclear, the delay did tend to confirm the accuracy of Herwarth's information. If Johnny had been feeding me material in a clever indirect move to mislead the French and British, there would have been no point in his reporting that Berlin had called a halt to the approach to Moscow.

The question of where Soviet foreign policy would go continued to be the subject of endless discussions in the diplomatic colony in Moscow. There was one school that clung to the belief that hints about a deal with Germany were designed to put pressure on the British and the French for an unequivocal commitment to protect the Soviet western frontier. There were others who took more seriously the indications of some desire for rapprochement with Germany.

Indicative of the division of opinion was the reaction to a half-page review in *Pravda* on March 21 of a book by a Soviet author predicting the outbreak of war between the Soviet Union and Nazi Germany. This review, which *Pravda* termed "realistic," took note of the "betrayal" of the bourgeois governments of France and England via a "second Munich," and it was only following the replacement of these governments by Popular Front governments in both England and France that the war proceeded to the inevitable victory of Soviet arms over the Fascist Germans. Why the Soviet regime published this article was unclear. There were those who believed it was to bait the Germans by making an advance to the Allies, and there were those who believed it was designed to prod the Allies to make an offer. There was no evidence to support either view.

There was virtually no Soviet-German activity in Moscow during June. A quietus appeared to have been placed on the German Ambassador by his government. On the Soviet side, hints were openly made that talks with the British and French, which were about to start, might produce a military agreement. Andrei Zhdanov, who was close to Stalin, in an interview in *Pravda* saw the possibility of creating a "mighty barrier against aggression." Such statements are not accidental in the Soviet Union; Zhdanov's looked like pressure on the Germans to speak more clearly about a deal.

During this lull, I was very much of two minds in regard to the eventual success of the Nazi-Soviet talks. I knew from Johnny that Ribbentrop was primarily concerned with getting the Japanese into the Anti-Comintern Pact and was prepared to sacrifice the possibility of a deal with the Soviet Union. But also present in my thinking was the knowledge that Schulenberg had always been of the school that believed that Germany's future lay in developing deeper relations with Eastern, not Western, Europe and sought a long-term rapprochement with the Soviet Union. In his eagerness for a deal, he exceeded his instructions. While he did not undertake new initiatives, he did maintain contacts with Molotov and kept the idea of a Soviet-Nazi pact alive. The pact was not abandoned, but for the moment it was being put on ice.

Then on June 28, Schulenberg, after another trip to Berlin, went to see Molotov again. Johnny filled me in a few days later, and I reported the following on July 1:

> The Ambassador told Molotov that following his visit to Berlin, he could assure him that Germany entertained no aggressive designs against the Soviet Union, and in confirmation thereof pointed out that the German press had ceased entirely the publication of any anti-Soviet views or articles; that acquiescence in the Hungarian annexation of Ruthenia could be regarded as proof that Germany entertained no designs on the Ukraine; and that furthermore the conclusion of non-aggression pacts with the Balkan countries was additional proof of the absence of any German intention to attack the Soviet Union. In respect of the nonaggression pacts with the Balkan states, Molotov remarked that these treaties were with third countries and not with the Soviet Union. The Ambassador therefore inquired whether the Soviet government desired a similar treaty with Germany. Molotov evaded the question. The Ambassador then remarked that the nonaggression treaty of 1926 between Germany and the Soviet Union was still in existence. To this Molotov replied that he was interested to hear the Ambassador say so inasmuch as the Soviet government had had certain doubts as to the continued validity of that treaty in view of subsequent agreements entered into by the German government. The Ambassador said that if Molotov referred to the German-Italian Alliance, he could assure him that this was in no way affecting the treaty. Molotov then stated that the denunciation of the nonaggression treaty with Poland had raised doubts of the value of such treaties at the present time, to which the Ambassador replied that the situation with respect to Poland was somewhat different in that the German government felt that Poland by joining the "encirclement" policy of Great Britain had in fact contravened the nonaggression pact with Germany.

The subject of the new commercial negotiations was then discussed, and Molotov informed the Ambassador that as he was not familiar with the details of this matter it would be better for the German Commercial Counselor to continue his discussion with [Foreign Trade Commissar Anastas I.] Mikoyan. Upon departing, the Ambassador inquired whether he was correct in assuming that the Soviet Union desired normal relations with all countries which did not transgress Soviet interests and whether this was equally applicable to Germany. Molotov replied in the affirmative.

As Johnny told me about these conversations, he commented that Molotov had again displayed a reserve with respect to Soviet-German relations, but had manifested a certain interest in the possibility of a concrete offer of a political character from Germany. To this extent Johnny noted an element of progress. In fact, Molotov had apparently abandoned his views that a political basis was a prerequisite of any improvement in commercial relations.

Although Johnny continued to feed me details of the Soviet-German talks, my uneasiness never left me. I wondered, but did not ask for fear of shutting him up, why he was giving me the information. While Johnny and I were friends, our two countries were at odds, and I was certainly not giving him any information in return. Eventually, I became convinced that initially Johnny did not understand the full importance of the May telegram regarding Hitler's change in views on the Soviet Union, and when the Nazi wooing of the Soviet Union went on, he found it difficult to hold back because of our friendship.

Johnny certainly realized the chance he was taking, but he gave no sign of any apprehension or nervousness. He did not adopt any conspiratorial manner, there were no guarded telephone calls, no whispered comments. All the discussions were perfectly natural—while we were riding horses or playing tennis at the dacha, or sitting around having a drink.

On July 10, the British and French delegations to negotiate a mutual defense pact with the Soviet Union arrived in Leningrad. They had come by boat, a fact that was much commented on by the diplomatic colony in Moscow, and had taken over two weeks to arrive in Leningrad. These delegations were headed by an elderly British admiral and a French general. Members of the British Embassy were appalled by this low-level delegation. It should have been headed by the French and British Foreign Ministers to demonstrate Paris's and London's seriousness about making a deal. The halfhearted British-French approach had the mark of failure on it right from the beginning.

That same day, I informed Washington that there had been no further developments in Soviet-German relations in Moscow and that Berlin had again instructed Ambassador Schulenberg to take no further steps toward an approach to the Soviet government. The German Embassy was also awaiting further instructions on renewal of commercial negotiations. In less than a week, however, Johnny told me that the Soviet Union had placed a five-million-mark order for turbines. He interpreted the fourteen-month delivery time as indicating "a certain confidence" of Moscow in the future stability of relations with Germany. At the same time, the Soviets told us that big orders for gun borers and lathes and probably anti-aircraft guns would be placed with German firms. The political importance of these transactions was not lost on Washington. A confidential commentary by the State Department noted that it would be "strange" for Germany to allow such sales if it contemplated an attack on Russia. The analysis saw the sales as providing "a certain substance" to reports of a German-Soviet rapprochement.

While we maintained regular contact with the British and the French during this period, I was not the officer detailed to do so. We got very little from them, since they were all under the seal of secrecy, but from what we did get it was apparent that the conversations were going slowly. Nevertheless, they were continuing. The chief problem seemed to be the unwillingness of Poland, or for that matter Rumania, to permit the free and easy passage of Soviet troops to get at Germany in the event of hostilities. The British and French were unwilling to consign to Soviet care a sphere of influence covering the Baltic states or to force the Poles—indeed, they were unable to do so—to grant rights which the Poles felt with some justification would mean the end of the independence of their country.

With the talks dragging on, Johnny told me that members of the German Embassy were confident that the Soviet Union would not sign an agreement with Britain and France because of the risk of provoking Hitler, and I so informed Washington.

Still, there was no hard evidence that Germany and the Soviet Union were drawing closer to a political agreement, and having been well trained by Kelly and Kirk, I still had doubts. Within two weeks, almost all these remaining doubts were swept aside. On August 5, at the dacha, Johnny told me that Ambassador Schulenberg had been to see Molotov two days before. For the first time, Johnny said, the Germans were convinced that Molotov was serious about negotiations.

On instructions from Berlin, the German Ambassador had assured Molotov that Germany entertained no aggressive designs against the Soviet Union, had no intention of impairing the status quo in the Baltic, and would respect all Soviet interests. Molotov expressed great interest and inquired whether the reference to the Baltic included Lithuania, which the Soviet Union considered in its sphere. The ambassador replied in the affirmative. Molotov then set forth the specific bases of Soviet distrust of Germany, which he outlined as follows:

1. The Anti-Comintern Pact.

2. The direct or indirect encouragement given by Germany to Japan in the Far East.

3. The apparent intention of Germany, since the advent of Hitler, to outlaw the Soviet Union as evidenced by the refusal of Germany to attend any European conference at which the Soviet Union was represented.

Schulenberg asserted that the Anti-Comintern Pact was in reality directed not against the Soviet Union but against England. Schulenberg's response was clearly an example of diplomatic double-talk. There was some faintly logical basis to his remark in that apparently Hitler had decided for purely tactical reasons that the Stalin regime was no longer a revolutionary government but simply the government of a big country. The Führer concluded therefore that the Soviets were no longer particularly interested in the spread of the Communist system and also, by inference, that the Anti-Comintern Pact had lost its immediate anti-Soviet objective. Since the major enemy was now Britain, London was the main target of the anti-Comintern nations. This explanation did not fool the Russians, but they were willing to accept it at face value in order to pursue their major objective—to keep war away from Soviet borders.

Schulenberg said that Germany was interested in developing good relations with Moscow, but if the Soviet Union allied itself with England and France, it would naturally expect to incur a share of the German hostility directed against these countries. Molotov replied that the Soviet government was interested in normalizing and improving its relations with Germany. At the same time, Moscow would continue its policy of attempting to assure a "genuine defense against aggression." Johnny said that Molotov's apparent acceptance of the Ambassador's assurances indicated a real possibility of an improvement of Soviet-German relations, but because of past German policy it would take some time to remove Soviet distrust, and there might be long and hard negotiations. Molotov's reference to the continuance of the Soviet policy of attempting to assure a "genuine" defense against aggression would appear to indicate that the Soviet Union was still seriously considering the conclusion of a pact with the British and the French, but only on Soviet terms. After their tardy start, negotiations for a military alliance between the Soviet Union and the Allies were speeding up.

By this time, in view of the wealth of information we had from Johnny in regard to the development of the Nazi-Soviet negotiations, the top people in the Embassy—Steinhardt, the new Ambassador, was filled in on his arrival—had pretty well come to the conclusion that something big was in the offing and that in all probability there would be a Soviet-German deal. It is not difficult to imagine with what eagerness I sought out Johnny Herwarth during this period.

Johnny was wrong about the length of time it would take Stalin to resolve his doubts about German intentions. Within two weeks, details of the deal which set off World War II were worked out. Johnny told me about the agreement at a ball the German Embassy gave on August 15 for all the young people of the diplomatic colony. With my wife and two visitors, Carmel Offie, the confidential secretary of Bullitt, who was then ambassador to France, and Joseph P. Kennedy, Jr., the son of our ambassador to Britain and the older brother of the future president, I arrived at the ball about ten o'clock. As we walked into the room, I saw Johnny standing in a corner, and he told me then that Schulenberg was not at the party; he was at the Soviet Foreign Office seeing Molotov after having received some very important instructions from Hitler himself. Johnny said he himself had not seen the instructions but he had heard that they went very far toward meeting Soviet desires. He said he would let me know as soon as Schulenberg returned from the Foreign Office. I was greatly excited. I remember thinking that a momentous event was taking place at the Kremlin while I was eating pâté de foie gras and drinking champagne at the German Embassy. I whiled away the time by dancing, conversing, and drinking. I watched my drinks because I wanted a clear head in order to obtain, to remember, and to transmit the information to Washington.

About an hour and a half later, Schulenberg appeared. He was the urbane, smiling host and gave no indication that he had just pulled off one of the greatest coups in modern diplomatic history. A little later, Johnny came up to me, and we went over to a corner of the room and sat down, drinking champagne. Against the background of dance music, he then briefly told me that the Nazis had agreed with the Russians that there should be a political basis for settling differences between the two countries, and outlined the general nature of the agreement.

He asked me to drop around to the German Embassy the next day, when he would have all the details. The following afternoon, I went to Johnny's office and he told me in a low voice the results of Schulenberg's meeting with Molotov. He said that he was leaving the next morning for Berlin by plane carrying a full record of the conversation with him. I went back to the Embassy and, after consulting with Steinhardt and Grummon, drafted the following telegram, which we sent to Washington:

> The German Ambassador saw Molotov last night for an hour and a half and under instructions from his government made to Molotov the following statement in respect to Germany policy towards the Soviet Union which it is understood emanated from Hitler himself:
>
> After reiterating that the German government had entertained no aggressive intentions whatsoever against the Soviet Union and that there was no conflict of interest between the countries from "the Baltic to the Black Sea," the statement continued that the German government was prepared to discuss in advance with the Soviet government "any territorial question in Eastern Europe"; that the German government felt that serious conversations between the two governments should begin soon, since events might otherwise develop which might adversely and unnecessarily affect Soviet-German relations. The statement concluded that the German government was prepared to send a high ranking official to discuss the question to Moscow. The Ambassador, I understand, left no written memorandum of this statement but his remarks were taken down verbatim by a stenographer. The Ambassador added that Hitler had requested that the contents of his statement be brought to the attention of Stalin himself.
>
> Molotov in reply, after promising to bring the contents of the statement immediately to Stalin's attention, added that for the first time the Soviet government was convinced of the seriousness of Germany's desire to improve its relations with the Soviet Union and he informed the Ambassador that the Soviet government would "welcome" the continuation of the political conversations but only if there was reasonable assurance that they would lead to definite and concrete results. As pos-

sible results, Molotov mentioned: (1) the conclusion of a non-aggression pact between the Soviet Union and Germany; (2) the cessation of any direct or indirect encouragement on the part of Germany to Japanese aggression in the Far East; and (3) regulations of mutual interests in the Baltic. Molotov felt that these three subjects should be discussed in preliminary conversations before the question of sending a German emissary to Moscow should be definitely decided. The results of the Ambassador's interview with Molotov were telegraphed to Berlin last night and a complete account is going forward by special courier from the German Embassy on Thursday.

In telling me about the agreement to conclude a treaty, Johnny said he thought that Ribbentrop would probably be the Nazi negotiator but that he was not certain, and therefore it would be best to leave the name out of my telegram (he obviously knew I was reporting the information) to avoid misleading the State Department. I am sorry I followed his advice, because Ribbentrop was chosen for the mission. Johnny said that while he had felt all along that there was a possibility of a Nazi-Soviet pact, now it was certain. He was depressed by the news, because he knew that this meant a quick attack on Poland. The Germans were anxious, he said, to have the treaty signed quickly so their mobile forces could profit from the good autumn weather. But the Soviets, as always, were a little more cautious, and said it was a mistake to send an emissary so quickly.

Despite the importance of the news, I did not hesitate to accept Herwarth's information as accurate. I was completely convinced of his reliability. I could not forget my training, however, and did hedge slightly in interpreting the Schulenberg-Molotov decision. The final section of the telegram said:

> Although it is possibly too soon to speak of a definite German-Soviet rapprochement at the present time . . . a steady progress can be noted in the conversations which the German Ambassador here has had with Molotov during the past two and a half months. Furthermore I have every reason to believe that the Soviet government has not in connection with the present negotiations informed the French and British governments of these developments in its relationship with Germany.

While I was sure in my mind that we had the basis of a Soviet-German deal of immense importance and that Poland would be the victim, I could not jump to conclusions in a telegram to Washington, because the agreement had not been signed. There were too many possibilities of last-minute hitches. Regardless of such possibilities, the important fact was that the Soviet Union had opted for an agreement with Germany rather than one with France and Britain.

My telegram was greeted with some skepticism in Washington. A memorandum was prepared in the Department of State expressing serious doubt that the Soviet Union, in view of its deep attachment to Marxism, would ever agree to make a deal of a political or military nature with the hated enemy, Nazi Germany. This doubt was a sign, I think, of too great a belief in the fidelity of the Soviet leaders to their anti-Fascist views and not enough realization that they put the preservation of the Soviet system high above every other consideration.

Regardless of the reception in some parts of the department, Secretary of State Hull called in the British and French ambassadors and gave them a summary of my telegram. Years later, at the Potsdam Conference, I had dinner with Anthony Eden, who had been the British Foreign Minister at that time, and he said that because of a Communist in the code room of the British Foreign Office, he did not receive the message from Washington forewarning the British of the impending Moscow visit of Ribbentrop until after the announcement had been made from Berlin. I have no knowledge of how the information was received in Paris, but the French government took no action.

With Johnny on his courier mission to Berlin, there was a break in the flow of information. Consequently, the Embassy received nothing in the week between Johnny's departure and Ribbentrop's arrival in Moscow, on August 23.

The Soviet government's about-face after six years of opposition to Hitler caused considerable confusion in the welcoming ceremonies for Ribbentrop. The Russians had no Nazi flags available to greet the German Foreign Minister and had to get them at a studio that had been making anti-Nazi films. These were the only flags with the hakenkreuz on them that could be found in Moscow. A Russian band hastily had to learn the "Horst Wessel Lied," which it played at the Moscow airport with the "Internationale." Surely no more contrasting situation could have been devised. After a brief welcome at the airport, Ribbentrop was whisked off to the Kremlin for the negotiations that resulted about 2 A.M. the next day in the Nazi-Soviet Nonaggression Pact.

In the morning, Johnny called and asked if I would go to the German Chancery to see him. While Ribbentrop was upstairs sleeping off his long night of successful negotiations and festivities at the

Kremlin, my friend gave me the details of the ten-year pact. He told me that "a full understanding" had also been embodied in a secret protocol whereby eastern Poland, Estonia, Latvia, and Bessarabia were recognized as spheres of Soviet vital interest, while western Poland would fall under German hegemony. Finland was not mentioned. The secret protocol also provided that the Soviet Union would be given territorial compensation if it so desired for any territorial changes that Germany might make in the countries lying between them. A provision of the basic agreement prohibiting each of the contracting parties from joining any group of powers directed against the other precluded Soviet adherence to the Anglo-French association as well as a German alliance with Japan.

I was amazed when I thought of the chances that Johnny Herwarth took in telling me this inside the German Chancery in Moscow. He must have felt quite secure; otherwise he could not possibly have run the risk to his life in talking so frankly about secret matters. In any event, nothing ever happened to him, and it was apparent that none of his transactions with me leaked.

Johnny said that the negotiations had been conducted personally by Stalin, who did not disguise from Ribbentrop that he had long been in favor of a Soviet-German rapprochement. When the treaty was concluded, Stalin drank a toast to Hitler, saying, "The Germans love their Führer," and called Hitler "*molodetz,*" a Russian slang expression meaning a "fine fellow."

Johnny was depressed by the pact. As he sat in his dark, paneled office, he clearly foresaw that this would mean war against Poland. He told me that he was going back to Germany to rejoin his regiment. He made this decision, I believe, on the advice of Ambassador Schulenberg, who felt that this was the safest and most prudent action for a German of Johnny's feelings.

Despite the wide publicity of Ribbentrop's visit, the British clung to their hope for an alliance with the Soviet Union until the terms of the pact were announced. It was rather pathetic to note in a telegram from Ambassador Steinhardt to Hull, just hours before the pact was announced, the naïveté of British Ambassador Seeds, who still believed Molotov's assurance that Ribbentrop was visiting Moscow only to "negotiate" with the Soviet government, that an agreement was not near, and that any agreement that might be signed would not be incompatible with a Soviet-Anglo-French alliance against aggression. This was downright dishonest on the part of the Soviets. Seeds seemed to view with some sardonic satisfaction the possibility that Ribbentrop would be given the same runaround by the Soviets as the British and French had received. It must have been embarrassing and caused Steinhardt considerable anguish to realize how uninformed the British Ambassador was, but I imagine he felt as I would have—that we could not possibly risk compromising our source by tipping the British off to what was going to happen.

In the light of subsequent information, it is quite apparent that Stalin and Molotov alone handled the negotiations with the Nazis, keeping the move from other members of the Politburo. This tight secrecy explains why Marshal Klimenti Voroshilov, who was negotiating with the British and French, was so upset by the news. The British told us that the usually effusive Voroshilov was drawn and ill at ease when he told them that the Soviet Union could not sign a pact because the one with Germany forbade it. This tactic was an example of Stalin's shrewdness. Obviously, Voroshilov would create an impression of sincerity if he believed that he was pursuing the real line of Soviet foreign policy. Had he been told that he was engaged in a cover plan, he would undoubtedly have been less effective as a negotiator.

I still doubt if Stalin would ever have agreed to an alliance with Britain and France. It cannot be repeated too often that to Bolshevik leaders the fate of the Soviet system was more important than the fate of Russia itself, and I cannot believe that Stalin would have banked on the will and the ability of England and France to exercise sufficient military pressure on Nazi Germany to forestall a German attack on the Soviet Union. In other words, it was very doubtful if the British-French mission then in Moscow ever had any real chance of success.

Actually, it was Nazi power and the consequences of non-agreement with Germany that impelled Stalin to go ahead and sign the pact. He did not want Hitler to take all of Poland and have the panzer divisions that much closer to Moscow. Besides, Ribbentrop had given him almost everything he asked, and if all went well, the Soviet Union was assured of an indefinite period of peace. On paper, the Soviets seemed to have got a sphere of influence over the eastern part of Poland and over the Baltic states and Bessarabia, and the Germans got virtually nothing in the territorial sense except what they would fight for. What the Germans did get that was vital to them, however, was the avoidance of a war on two fronts.

While Stalin was wrong on the time he had won (it turned out to be less than two years), he was able in that period to do much to improve the Red Army, which was still licking its wounds from the onslaughts of the purges. If the Nazi attack had come in 1939 instead of 1941, Russia might have been knocked out of the war and the Soviet system destroyed. All the subsequent evidence that has come to light indicates that Stalin believed that the Nazi-Soviet pact would be of long duration. He was very much surprised and shocked by the perfidy of the German attack in June, 1941. The British had long predicted the attack, but in Stalin's eyes the pact was a good deal, and he thought it was madness, as indeed it was, for Hitler to destroy a good thing for the sake of an imaginary and nonexistent threat.

The pact, except for the secret protocol, was published in the Soviet press the next day and stunned the world. The Russian people were bewildered after so many years of anti-Nazi propaganda, because there had been only a few tenuous indications in the Soviet press that something was up, and these were clues that would not have registered with the mass of readers. But the Russians are docile, and there was undoubted relief that the danger of war had abated. There was also a feeling among some Soviet officials that Stalin had pulled a slick trick. A member of the British Embassy who accompanied the Franco-British delegation to the railroad station said that, as the train pulled out, two Russians who had the assignment of saying good-bye looked at each other and burst into laughter.

As for me, I realized that the pact meant a Nazi attack on Poland, but I had no idea what the British and the French reaction would be. I doubt if many persons foresaw then the consequences of a general European war. At that time—and I imagine this view was shared by Stalin—the combined British and French forces were regarded as pretty much a match for Nazi Germany. The outcome of the German onslaught on France which was to come less than a year later was, of course, not considered or discussed.

The State Department was subsequently complimentary of the Embassy's ability to provide advance warning of the pact. We were the only government, aside from the Soviet Union and Germany, that had a full account of the negotiations, and therefore President Roosevelt and the State Department were prepared for the shock. Washington, as has been noted, tried to warn the British and French, but with no effect. In any event, Washington did not issue any statements or take any action that would have embarrassed the United States once the pact was announced.

It was not until after the war that I learned why Johnny Herwarth, a thoroughly patriotic German, took the risk of passing on highly secret information to me, the representative of a country on the opposite side of the fence if not yet in full alliance with Hitler's enemies. Johnny, who was one-quarter Jewish, explained that already in the spring of 1939, he was an active member of the resistance movement among upper-class Germans. He had hoped that if the West learned of the negotiations, something might be done to prevent a deal between Hitler and Stalin, because he was convinced that any such agreement would lead to World War II. He rather hoped that this information might have been used to galvanize the French and the British to be more liberal in their approach toward the Soviet Union. Johnny himself, however, felt, as I did, that there was very little chance of success for the British and French negotiations. He put it bluntly to me once after the war. He said, "We were able to make a deal with the Soviets because we were able without any problems with German opinion to deliver the Baltic states and eastern Poland to Russia. This the British and the French with their public opinions were unable to do."

The resistance movement to which Johnny belonged was not well organized and had not formed any plot. It was much more a question of sentiment. Schulenberg had definite sympathies in this direction, but he was not a member and apparently he did not know of the underground's existence then. I was very much an admirer of Schulenberg. He was a German of the old school—tall, handsome, with a white mustache, and a baldish head, courteous, affable, and, I think, very sensible. He knew a great deal about the Soviet Union, having been Consul General in Tiflis after World War I, and he was strongly opposed to the attack in 1941. In 1944, he joined the plot against Hitler, and when it failed he was seized, tortured, and executed.

Johnny Herwarth fought in the German army throughout the hostilities. He rejoined his regiment just before the Polish attack. It was a cavalry outfit that was later transformed into an armored infantry regiment. As a cavalryman, he participated throughout the entire three weeks of the Polish campaign and was then shifted to the Western front. His outfit was among those that kicked off the attack on the West on May 10, 1940, and ended up in Biarritz, having fought through the entire French campaign. As a front-line soldier, he participated in the initial German attack on the Soviet Union on June 22, 1941, and was at the front for two years. He thus fought through three major campaigns without suffering even a single scratch or being captured. The only time he came near to being hit was when some shrapnel went through the lining of his overcoat.

Eventually, Johnny was attached to the staff of General von Kostring, who was in charge of relations with German prisoners and with some of the minor Allies. He was in the Balkans at the time of the planned coup led by Count von Stauffenberg. Delayed by Allied air attacks in returning to Berlin, he heard about the coup days after the attempt. He found on his desk, in his office at Potsdam, where he was attached to the General Staff, five memos from his secretary telling him that Stauffenberg had called him urgently on the day of the attack. Johnny told me that this was the only time he lost his nerve. His legs gave way and he slumped to the floor. He realized that if the Gestapo had entered his office during this period, immediately after the attempt to assassinate Hitler, he certainly would have been executed out of hand.

After the war, Johnny returned to the diplomatic service and was West Germany's first ambassador to London. It was a tough job, but Johnny Herwarth was a brilliant success.

CHAPTER SIX

An Eye on the Collaborators

Once the Nazi-Soviet pact was signed, my role as chief political observer in the Embassy changed. The task that I now faced was to seek out the clues to the degree of cooperation between the two dictators. Would they be genuine allies, aiding each other economically and militarily and pledging to come to each other's defense? Would they divide Poland and then go their separate ways? Would they, as the British confidently predicted, soon fall into a quarrel, as thieves do? How long would they keep the pledge of nonaggression against each other?

In one way, my job was easy, because it was evident to me that the Soviet Union would not break the treaty as long as Germany remained strong. Stalin wanted at all cost to avoid a war, and he had made a handsome bargain to stay out. The crucial question in my mind was whether Hitler would stick with the agreement. That answer could come only from the Germans, and, with Johnny Herwarth gone, I had lost my invaluable source in the German Embassy. I soon acquired a new source there, Gebhardt von Walther, another Secretary, who after the war served as West Germany's ambassador to the North Atlantic Treaty Organization, Turkey, and the Soviet Union. He was a Nazi party member, but not a fanatic. He liked to get along with people. Much more reticent than Johnny, he never gave me secret material, but he did fill me in on events as diplomats normally do.

Another factor complicating my job was that the new American Ambassador, Steinhardt, knew little about the Soviet Union. He was a smooth New York lawyer, who had been a friend of Roosevelt's and ambassador to Sweden. Tall and thin, he was extremely energetic and had a lively and inquisitive mind. He was vain and highly egocentric, seemingly driven by a compulsion to make a reputation for himself, a characteristic that, as noted later, led him to the edge of fabrication reagarding the peace talks that ended the Soviet-Finnish War in the winter of 1939-40.

For seventeen months, until January, 1941, I kept as close an eye on Soviet-German relations as I could within the limitations imposed by the relative lack of information and by the need to leave Moscow three times owing to my wife's pregnancy. It was a kaleidoscopic period that in many ways remains a blur of disorder and grimness.

While I did not know it at the time, within days of the signing of the Nazi-Soviet pact, the Soviet government sent a number of telegrams to Berlin expressing worry lest Hitler should find some reason for postponing or calling off the attack on Poland. There was no need to worry, for Hitler launched his invasion on September 1, 1939, and smashed the Polish Army almost before Britain and France honored their commitments to Warsaw and declared war.

The people of Moscow, who had been shocked by the announcement of the pact, doubted the value of dealing with Hitler and were upset by the speed of the German advance. The people generally had no method for making known their anxiety and concern, but occasionally we picked up tidbits of information about public opinion at the Park of Culture and Rest, across the Moscow River. There representatives of the Party manned "agitation points" and answered questions. One evening about ten days after the German attack, I heard an elderly Russian, who said that he had fought against the Germans in World War I and had a deep distrust of their intentions, ask the Party spokesman what assurances the Soviet government had that the Germans would stop before reaching the Russian border. The old man was undoubtedly concerned because the Kremlin had announced a partial mobilization the previous day. The spokesman said he was sure the government had some reassurance in this regard, but was vague in his answer. He promised to return the following night with a clear answer to the question. The next night, he stated categorically that the Soviet government knew through their talks with the Germans that there would be no advance to the Soviet frontier. This answer only partially satisfied the old man.

In commenting on this incident, I told the State Department that the Soviet government would probably act to keep military operations from the vicinity of its frontiers. In a rare instance of prediction, I added, "It may be therefore anticipated that in furtherance of its ends Soviet policy will be directed towards hastening a German victory and the consequence of certain circumstances might even involve limited Soviet military action in Poland under the pretext of 'restoring order' in areas of that country inhabited by Russians."

At dawn on September 17, the Red Army moved into Poland to occupy the areas allocated to it by the Nazi-Soviet pact. According to rumors we picked up, when workers in the factories heard the news, they immediately assumed the Red Army was going to fight the Germans and, jumping on machines, cheered. A few minutes later, Communist Party representatives arrived and explained that the Red Army was not going to fight the Nazis but was taking over that part of the nonexistent Poland which the Soviet Union felt belonged to Russia because it was inhabited mostly by White Russians and Ukrainians.

Although the Soviet stab in Poland's back had no doubt been contemplated in the secret protocol to the nonaggression pact with the Nazis, there is evidence that the decision to move was taken precipitately. The Soviet style of operating called for a long period of propaganda, reports of "insurrections" in Poland, and appeals by "persecuted" White Russians and Ukrainians. The precipitate move was probably caused by the rapid advance of German troops close to areas allocated to the Soviets. The Embassy heard a rumor that the Germans had advised the Soviets to act quickly because the Poles were retreating into areas allocated to the Soviet Union. If the Soviets did not mop up the Poles, the Germans would have to. I could not confirm the rumor.

I did, however, pick up some information from von Walther on the second visit of Ribbentrop to Moscow. On September 27, the day Ribbentrop arrived, von Walther and I went riding at the dacha. He told me that the line of demarcation between the German and Soviet armies that had been agreed on was only temporary. The original line had run through the center of Warsaw. The Soviets had proposed a rectification, moving the boundary to the east to follow the course of the Vistula River. Stalin did not want the problem of controlling millions of Poles; he did, however, want Lithuania. Questions relating to the Far East were discussed, but I was not given any of the details. The conversations, von Walther said, had a strong anti-British tone. The communiqué bore out his information. It said that if the war continued, Britain and France would be responsible. Ominously hinting at an alliance, the communiqué said the Soviet and German governments "will then consult on necessary military measures to be taken in such an eventuality." There was also an agreement in principle to expand trade, with the Soviet Union supplying raw materials in return for Nazi promises of machinery and manufactured goods. As for Poland, the agreement set the line of demarcation along the Vistula River, as Stalin desired. Poland was wiped from the map, with the western half incorporated into the German Reich and the eastern half into the Soviet Union.

Despite the German-Soviet collaboration in Poland, the British still doubted that the arrangement would last long. As I was concerned primarily with the Kremlin point of view, I thought the pact would endure for a long time—a misjudgment springing from my inability to read Hitler's mind. I was not alone in this view. On October 4, Ambassador Steinhardt cabled Washington that "all evidence appears to foreshadow an extended period of Soviet-German cooperation."

After the collapse of Poland, I watched in sadness as Stalin consolidated his territorial barrier to Germany. The Baltic Ministers were summoned to Moscow to receive their instructions. First was the Estonian Foreign Minister, who went believing that he was to discuss improvement in trade relations and other matters of a technical nature. He was at the Bolshoi Ballet one Sunday night when he was suddenly ordered to go to the Kremlin, where Molotov demanded that Soviet troops be stationed in Estonia. At a second meeting, the number of troops was put at 35,000. The Estonian Foreign Minister protested that this would mean that the Soviet army would outnumber the Estonian army in that little country. A member of the Estonian legation told me that while they were arguing with Molotov, Stalin walked into the room and, in his benign role, asked what the difficulty was. Informed that it was the number of troops, Stalin gently chided Molotov, "Come, come, Molotov, you are rather harsh on our friends," and reduced the number of troops from 35,000 to 25,000. This was the figure in the final agreement. To the Estonians, this understanding attitude proved that Stalin was a moderating influence. To us in the American Embassy, this was a characteristic ploy of Stalin, who always wished to be known as genial, compromising, and easygoing in contrast with his tough, arbitrary, and disagreeable Commissars. The terse comment of the Embassy to Washington was that the ten-year treaty of mutual assistance amounted to "a Soviet military protectorate over Estonia."

The Estonian Minister was shortly followed by the Lithuanian and the Latvian Foreign Ministers, who received the same treatment. The entire operation was completed by the end of October, when the three Baltic states were firmly in Soviet hands. In a piece of ironical cynicism, the Soviets encouraged the Lithuanian government to take over from Poland the territory of Vilna, long an object of dispute. It was another year, after the collapse of France in 1940, before the final coup was administered to these three unfortunate little countries, which had had a brief but relatively happy and prosperous life in the period between the world wars. All were incorporated into the Soviet Union.

Early in October, when the Finns were also summoned to Moscow for consultations, I realized, from my talks at the Finnish Embassy, that the Soviets were in for some rough sessions. The Finns were tougher than the Baltic peoples, partly because of their geographic position, partly because of their innate ruggedness, which was to show itself time and time again throughout the three-month war with the Soviets in the winter of 1939-40. Moscow asked for leasing of naval bases, the moving back by about twenty-four miles of the frontier, which ran within twenty miles of Leningrad, and the Soviet occupation of Hanko, which guarded the entrance to the Finnish Gulf. In return, the Soviet Union would cede Finland some territory in Karelia. From the Soviet point of view, these demands were not unreasonable, for if a potential foe, such as Germany, made an alliance with Finland, it would have an ideal jumping-off place for an attack on Russia. From the Finnish point of view, the terms, particularly the ceding of Hanko, were unacceptable because Finland would not be able to defend herself. As the Soviet pact with the Baltic states demonstrated, the Finns' suspicion of Moscow's intention was justified.

During the entire period of negotiations, we were afforded accurate and timely information from the Finnish Legation in Moscow. The Counselor of the Finnish Embassy, Hjalmar J. Procope, was my friend and our principal source. It was apparent that the Finnish government had decided that it was in its national interest to keep the United States Embassy fully informed. The United States did have a special interest in Finland, stemming from its faithful repayment of its World War I debt. Just before the start of the negotiations, President Roosevelt sent a message to the Soviet President, M. I. Kalinin, and politely expressed the hope that Finland's independence and integrity would be maintained. Kalinin's reply was courteous, but later, in a speech to the Supreme Soviet, Molotov said that the United States had no business interfering in the negotiations.

At one point, my German informant, von Walther, told me of a conversation he had with Mikoyan. During an interval in the negotiations, Mikoyan, an Armenian, talking of the Russians in the third person, said he had warned the Finns, "You should be careful and not press the Russians too far. They have deep traditional feelings in regard to this part of the world and the threat to Leningrad, and I can only tell you that we Caucasians in the Politburo are having a great deal of difficulty in restraining the Russians." This sounded ominous to me, but the Finns took it as an empty threat.

Von Walther also told me that Molotov kept the Nazi Ambassador informed of what was going on during the negotiations. Throughout the talks, the Germans clung to the opinion that the Russians would be cautious and at one time thought that Stalin would eventually yield on the question of Hanko. When he did not yield, the Germans asked the Swedes to use their influence to persuade the Finns to cede the base. Walther told me that the Germans were urging moderation on the Russians, too.

Under such circumstances, I thought I could leave the Soviet Union for a few days at the end of November, even though negotiations were at an impasse. Steinhardt, who had been ambassador in Stockholm, planned to visit friends in Sweden. My wife and I accepted an invitation to accompany him so that she could take the opportunity to consult a competent Western doctor about her pregnancy. On November 30, while we were returning to Moscow on the night train from Riga, the radio loudspeaker broadcast the news that the Soviet Union had broken off relations with Finland. The next day the Soviet army attacked.

What I learned during the Finnish War was valuable to my diplomatic training in revealing basic aspects of Soviet thinking that were to recur after World War II. The troops that crossed the Soviet frontier were nothing but raw recruits from the garrisons of the northern part of Russia—untrained, untried, and unseasoned in battle. They carried placards and banners in Finnish saying that they had marched in to liberate the Finns from capitalist oppression. The night of the attack, the Soviets set up a new Finnish government at Terijoki, a frontier town that had been overrun by them. The setting up of a government which contained a leading Soviet-Finnish citizen, Otto W. Kuusinen, as a rival to the legitimate one at Helsinki was clear evidence that the Soviet Union intended to establish a protectorate, to put it mildly, over the entire territory of Finland. Far from welcoming the invaders, the efficient Finns, who realized they were fighting for the existence of their country, destroyed the first Soviet divisions. As weeks went by, repeated Soviet assaults against the Mannerheim Line did not succeed in making any great impression.

The effect in Russia was deep and must have been noted with considerable anxiety by the Soviet rulers. As the rumors of Soviet defeats percolated slowly through the population, a feeling of helplessness encompassed the people. Reports of Leningrad hospitals packed with soldiers suffering from wounds or frozen limbs permeated the population. Claudia, our cook, reflecting the gossip of the marketplaces and the shops, told us how dispirited people were. Although the Soviets never admitted any defeats, the tone of the official communiqués made it clear to anyone experienced in such matters that the war was going badly. Russians who listened to the BBC from London (in those days, no one had thought of jamming radio broadcasts) heard horrifying stories of whole Soviet divisions being shot to pieces in the cold. The reports were believed, because over the years the BBC had built a reputation for broadcasting facts, not propaganda.

Despite Soviet secrecy, foreign observers could easily see that the war, small as it was in terms of Russia's total resources and military power, had imposed a strain on the civilian distribution of food. There were shortages; lines formed outside food stores; there was some panic buying. Under all the unhappiness I thought I could detect a feeling that the war was unjust, that a tiny country had been attacked by a bully, and that Russia deserved the mauling it was getting.

Like other Americans, I was outraged by the Soviet attack on Finland. It was an unprovoked act of brutality. It was not until years later that I realized that the Finnish War, while morally unjustified, very probably saved the Soviet Union from defeat by Germany. It revealed to the Soviet high command and to Stalin himself the extent of the deficiencies of the Red Army. Some of the weaknesses had been known; the purges had ravaged the leadership. But the government apparently believed its own propaganda that the Red Army was invincible. Because of the Finnish War, serious measures were taken to remedy its deficiencies, and put it in much better condition to meet the German onslaught in 1941. Without the harsh lessons of Finland, it is improbable that the reforms would have been made. Considering how close the Soviet Union came to defeat in 1941, it is not too much to say that without those reforms the Soviet Union would have been crushed by Hitler.

In February, 1940, when the Soviet high command, using new divisions of well-trained troops and masses of artillery, launched a great assault, it became clear that the Finns were not going to be able to hold. In March, the Finnish peace treaty was signed. Finland lost the frontier zone near Leningrad, as well as Hanko, the Mannerheim Line was demolished, and the Finnish armed forces were reduced.

I was somewhat surprised by the terms of the treaty; they were less harsh than they might have been, given the military situation. But other considerations were weighing on Stalin's mind. The British and French were openly planning to send an expeditionary force to Finland. The war was a drain on Russia. All major objectives had been achieved, and the fighting could be brought to a swift conclusion.

There was no question that the brave Finnish resistance reduced the Soviet's immediate goals. The setting up of the "bungalow" government of Terijoki proved that the war was not just a question of the rectification of frontiers. It was an attempt, abandoned with the peace, to Sovietize Finland. This is an element in Soviet-Finnish relations that was conveniently forgotten when the USSR became an ally of the West.

The Finnish War chilled American relations with the Soviet Union, already shocked by the Nazi-Soviet rape of Poland. The two developments dealt a fatal blow to the ambitions of Ambassador Steinhardt, who was constantly looking for possibilities of enhancing his personal reputation in his dealing with the Soviet Union. After the Finnish War had been going on for a few weeks, Steinhardt thought he might become the great peacemaker and sought to insinuate himself via the Swedes into the role of a go-between. The idea never got very far, because the Finns were never enthusiastic. In any event, when the armistice was announced, Steinhardt drafted a telegram to Washington inventing a number of incidents that would look as if he had played a major role in the peace negotiations. At the last minute, he decided not to send the wire.

More than disenchanted with Moscow, I was pleased to read in February, 1940, that Roosevelt had told a Communist-front organization, the American Youth Congress, at the White House, "The Soviet Union, as everyone who has had the courage to face the fact knows, is run by a dictatorship as absolute as any other dictatorship in the world. It has allied itself with another dictatorship and it has invaded a neighbor so infinitesimally small that it could do no possible harm to the Soviet Union." The President was learning some of the hard facts about the Bolsheviks.

Roosevelt's reference to an alliance overstated the relationship between Moscow and Berlin. There was no agreement to go to each other's aid in a war. There was strong evidence, however, as seen from the telegrams that the Embassy was sending to Washington, that Soviet-German collaboration was increasing while Soviet relations with the West were falling to a low point. Our messages on the *City of Flint* incident illustrated both sides of the equation.

The *City of Flint* was an American merchant ship captured by the German pocket battleship *Deutschland* in the Atlantic in late October, 1939, as a prize of war because a portion of the cargo was deemed to be contraband. Instead of taking the ship to Germany, the Nazis sailed her to the Soviet port of Murmansk.

As the Soviet Foreign Office well knew, under international law a prize of war can be brought into a neutral port only on account of bad weather or damage to the ship or a lack of fuel or provisions. If the ship does not leave as soon as these conditions are corrected, the neutral power must release the vessel with its captured officers and crew and intern the prize crew. The Soviets did intern the German prize crew, and Steinhardt instructed me to go to Murmansk to interview the American master. But the Soviet authorities, obviously changing their mind under German pressure, began to talk ambiguously about broken boilers and the absence of suitable charts and provisions as the real reason for the ship's putting in at Murmansk, and threw up obstacles to my trip. The Soviets informed us that (1) there were no regular flights to Murmansk (a palpable lie, since regular service was listed), (2) all seats were booked on every flight, (3) bad weather had forced the cancellation of all flights.

On October 28, Steinhardt, on orders from the State Department, telephoned the dispatcher of the port of Murmansk. With me translating, the dispatcher completely contradicted what Steinhardt had been told by the Soviet Foreign Office and what I had been told by the German Embassy about the boiler breakdowns and the lack of charts and stores. It became increasingly apparent that the real reason the Nazis had sailed the *City of Flint* to Murmansk was to evade capture by British warships. The incident was terminated when the Soviets stretched the law, and in conformity with the desires of the Nazi government, released the German prize crew and permitted the vessel to leave Murmansk in the same condition under which it arrived. The *City of Flint* proceeded to a Norwegian port, where the German prize crew was interned and the ship released.

My watch on the growing Soviet-German cooperation was interrupted in early January, 1940, when I decided to take my pregnant wife to a West European city where she could catch a plane or ship to the United States. The trip would also give me an opportunity to confer with George Kennan in Berlin, where he was attached to the Embassy, and with Bullitt in Paris, where he was ambassador. It might also satisfy my curiosity about the "phony war," as hostilities were called because neither Germany nor the Allies had launched a major attack.

Avis and I left Moscow by sleeping car on the night of January 9, with the temperature 40 degrees below zero. It was still bitterly cold when we reached the German border. We were transferred to a German car, which stood on a siding in a snowfield. The car was virtually without heat, so I went into the buffet and bought a large bottle of raw Lithuanian vodka, returned to the compartment, piled fur coats upon my wife, and got into bed. We arrived in Berlin some forty hours late.

As we were walking in the lobby of the Adlon Hotel, we ran into a German officer, a friend of my Moscow days, who asked us to have a drink with him. We went to a bar, where, sitting in deep leather chairs, we chatted about old times. After a bit, he asked when and by what route I planned to return to Moscow. I said I was going back by the same route, through Belgium and Germany, between January 13 and 15. He raised his eyebrows and said he would not advise me to do that because his regiment, which was stationed along the Dutch border, was about to receive orders to be ready for offensive operations around January 13. He said there had been scares before and it was not possible to tell whether this would be another false alarm, but he thought that I should know that on January 13 there might be a full-fledged German attack on the West.

Avis and I left Berlin the next day. Again because of snow and extreme cold, the trains were delayed, and we arrived at Aachen after the frontier had shut. Confronted with the alternatives of spending the night in Aachen or trying to get to Belgium, we decided to make every effort to cross the frontier. Although my German was extremely limited, and my wife's was only a little better, we approached the young German lieutenant who was head of the patrol. I made much of the fact that "*meine Frau ist mit Kind,*" and finally the lieutenant suggested a way in which we could cross the frontier, despite the fact that it was technically illegal to do so. He advised us to take a German taxi to a café a few hundred yards across the border, where we could get transportation to Liège. The plan worked without difficulty, and we arrived in Brussels that night. There we checked into the hotel where the conference on the Far East had been held two years before. For some reason, the hotel employees remembered me and, although the dining room was closed, prepared a fine dinner of oysters and partridge—the best meal, Avis still says, we ever ate.

The next day, I telephoned the Embassy and passed on the report of the German military plans for the January 13 period with all the qualifications the circumstances dictated. In Paris, I gave the same information to Ambassador Bullitt, who immediately relayed the warning to Premiere Daladier. Possibly as a result, two divisions of French mechanized forces were moved up to the frontier. The tip was considered especially important because the French had found earlier that day, on the body of a German aviator who had been shot down, plans for an attack on the Western front on January 13. There was no attack on that date, but information at the end of the war from captured German documents revealed that January 13 had indeed been one of Hitler's target dates for the launching of Operation Yellow, the code name for the assault on the Low Countries and France.

During our visit with Bullitt, he told me, as we played bridge, that he thought the Soviet Union, although technically neutral, was genuinely allied with Germany. I expressed doubt that the Soviet Union was in fact allied with Germany, although agreeing that Moscow was doing everything to retain German favor. I conceded that if certain events developed, the Soviets might end up in a de facto alliance with the Nazis. If, for example, the British and French actually intervened in the Finnish War, they would find themselves at war with the Soviet Union. The effect would be to push Moscow closer to the Germans.

In Berlin, I had had a long conversation with Kennan. He was gloomy about the future, feeling that the Germans were preparing for an attack on the West with typical thoroughness and assiduity. Perhaps influenced by his views, I saw a certain gray-coated grimness in Germany, which indicated serious and efficient preparation for war. In contrast, France appeared only partly affected. Although there was a partial blackout in Paris, life appeared relatively unchanged. There was a startling contrast between the seriousness of the Germans and the carefree, almost frivolous, attitude of the French.

It had originally been planned that Avis was to fly back with Ambassador Bullitt on the new Pan American Clipper lines, but weather in the Azores and Portugal was so bad that the flights were canceled. I then decided to take her to Genoa and put her on the *America*, a ship of the United States Lines which was making her last sailing from Europe in January, 1940. In Genoa, I saw Avis aboard the *America* and headed back to Russia by way of Italy, Switzerland, and Germany. As we pulled into Munich late at night, I heard the burst of anti-aircraft fire and the roar of airplanes. The planes dropped no bombs; I assumed they dropped leaflets. In those days of the phony war, the British had the fantastic idea that a rain of propaganda might seriously shake the Hitler regime.

On my return to Moscow at the beginning of February, 1940, there was continued evidence of intimate Soviet-Nazi collaboration, particularly in the economic field. Franz Krapf, a German negotiator, told me that all of the Germans had been very much struck by the degree of Stalin's involvement in the most minute and relatively petty aspects of the negotiations. At one point, the issue was something like five thousand tons of copper, but before any decision could be reached, it had to be taken directly to Stalin. This refusal to delegate authority was due to Stalin's suspicious nature and lack of confidence in his subordinates. He felt the only way to get something done right was to do it himself. The result was an enormous work load for the dictator and incredibly slow decision-making.

In April, 1940, I again interrupted my search for clues to Soviet diplomatic plans, this time to return to the United States to visit my wife and daughter. There was a breathing spell in the European crisis. The Finnish War was over and the phony war was still on. It seemed like a safe time to go back.

Because of the Soviet agreement with Italy that set an artificial value on rubles, I was able to purchase my ticket from Moscow to New York for fifteen dollars. The reason was that the Embassy was still getting rubles on the black market at the rate of sixty or seventy to the dollar, while the ticket was written in lire at the official rate of 1.15 rubles per dollar. The ticket provided not only first-class rail accommodations from Moscow to Genoa but also first-class passage on the luxury liner *Conti di Savoia* to New York.

On the ship, a former Premier of Belgium, Paul van Zeeland, who unfortunately reflected the prevailing wishful thinking in Western Europe, asserted, while we were having a drink in the smoking room, that he knew for a fact that the steel in the German tanks could not resist bullets and the mechanism simply didn't work. As for the extraordinary success of the Nazis' Polish campaign, he said the reason lay not so much in the quality of the German army as in the ineffectiveness and inability of the Poles. Within weeks, his optimism was to be proved tragically misplaced by the collapse of France.

After a visit with my wife and daughter, Avis in Villa Nova, I went to Aiken, South Carolina, to see my mother and sister and was there when the Nazis attacked Holland, Belgium, and France. I remember hearing a broadcast by H. V. Kaltenborn, the radio commentator, in which he predicted that the German blitzkrieg would fail.

In the month after my return to Washington, I conferred with officers of the Eastern European Section on the effect on the Soviet Union of the fall of France and the withdrawal of the British from the Continent. Our general impression was that the Kremlin, which had been counting on a standoff between the Allies and the Axis, would now be even more careful not to offend the Nazis. Hitler might soon be free to turn on Russia.

Although I had dealt for some time with extremely sensitive political reporting, my junior status in the Foreign Service was made clear as I left the State Department on my way back to Moscow. I was ordered to pick up an undisclosed object in New York to take back with me. What I was directed to carry, alone, across war-torn Europe to Moscow, was a brown leather case, weighing more than fifty pounds, containing a copy of our most secret diplomatic code. I protested, pointing out that there was trouble all along my route. Portugal was infested with intelligence agents, France was swarming with Germans, the Nazis looked on the United States as an enemy, and we were at odds with the Soviet Union. It would be very difficult for me to guarantee the security of the code. Nevertheless, I was told to do it.

I took a Portuguese ship from New York to Lisbon, where I spent a few days, finding there by chance an old friend from Moscow, Elbridge Durbrow, who was then consul in charge of the visa section of the Consulate General. From Lisbon, I had a hair-raising train ride to Madrid, flew to Barcelona, and motored to Perpignan on the French border. The trip on a bus through France was sad. Everywhere there were demobilized soldiers standing like lost sheep. Switzerland, clean, prosperous, and peaceful, was a pleasant interlude. As we pulled into the railroad station at Munich, a little after midnight, the air-raid sirens sounded, and I could hear the engines of airplanes overhead and the anti-aircraft fire. This time the raid was not a fake; I heard bomb explosions. Only a few bombs were dropped.

The next day, I went to Berlin, where I saw a number of friends in the American Embassy, particularly Kennan. We agreed that there seemed to be little prospect of any change of Soviet policy in view of Stalin's anxiety to avoid war, and the question of what the Germans would do next was uncertain, although almost everyone believed the British Isles would be invaded. The Battle of Britain had not yet begun, and prognostications were gloomy. About the only good news was that Winston Churchill had become Prime Minister. To show me the Germans' high morale, Kennan took me to a German music hall, where the entertainers sang "Wir fahren nach England," to cheers and banging of beer mugs on the table. In my two or three days in Berlin, I heard no comments from Germans about the Soviet Union.

When I arrived at Davgopils, on the Latvian border, I felt as if I had run into the entire Red Army. The town was filled with soldiers, and there were no accommodations. I stayed in the station. For twenty-four hours I scarcely let go of the suitcase containing the secret code. Most of the time, I sat on a wooden bench with Russian soldiers. For several hours, I lay on a sofa in the stationmaster's anteroom. The soldiers were part of the increase in occupation forces in the Baltic states that the Soviets had ordered after Germany's victory over France. Filthy and tired, I finally boarded the Moscow train. Despite my apprehension, there was at no time any danger of losing the code; no one made any attempt to steal it.

I found Moscow comparatively unchanged and Soviet-German relations, on the surface, in good shape. In all probability, however, the fall of France shocked Soviet military analysts and produced concern over the danger of a German attack. Moving to shore up Russia's western border, Stalin incorporated the Baltic states, Bessarabia, and northern Bukovina into the Soviet Union. As a result of this action, I was detailed to go to the American Legation at Kaunas, Lithuania, to help close it. The experience was depressing. Russian soldiers were everywhere, and while on the whole they behaved well, they were inclined to get drunk, and when drunk a little obstreperous. The Lithuanian people, thoroughly cowed, foresaw nothing but disaster. In the week that I stayed there, I heard of a number of Lithuanians' committing suicide.

Our Minister to Lithuania was the Reverend Owen J. Norem,

who, I had been told, had been appointed because he had performed services for the Democratic party. Norem would give dinners at the hotel in Kaunas, and, when he felt sleepy, would leave and tell the waiters that further refreshments were to be charged to the guests and not to the American Legation. He was a man of monumental conceit. In early 1940, he had visited Moscow. Looking around Spaso House, he remarked, "Of course, I can have this post whenever I want it." Before the Soviet take-over, Norem, on a trip to Estonia, took up with the Foreign Minister the problem of war debts. Someone told me that one day, at a picnic with members of his staff, he was handed a letter from Secretary of State Hull. In a pleased voice, he said, "Oh, how nice, a letter from Cordell," and without stopping to see what the letter said, read it out loud. "My dear Mr. Ambassador," the letter is said to have begun, "you are hereby forbidden to make any reference in any public utterance or private conversation to the problem of war debts. This is one of the chief problems that the United States government has, and it cannot have individual Ambassadors expressing individual views on this subject which is exclusively a matter for handling in Washington."

One of the first signs that we in the Embassy detected of a rift between the Soviet Union and Germany was the sudden Nazi move in late August, 1940, in adjusting the border between Rumania and Hungary. Important pieces of Rumania were transferred to Hungary, apparently without consulting or informing the Soviet Union. Soviet displeasure was expressed by a note to the Germans, which commented in rather chilly terms on events in the Balkans. Within a month, the Kremlin was worried about another German move—the signing of a treaty with Italy and Japan in which each nation pledged to help either of the other two if it were attacked by a country not then involved in the war. The Soviets saw themselves as the target; the Germans said the United States was the foe in mind.

I had kept in close touch with von Walther, the Nazi Embassy Secretary, and in early November he told me that Molotov, still both Premier and Foreign Commissar, would visit Berlin and confer with Hitler. I hurriedly cabled the news to Washington, for I realized that the Molotov visit was of vital importance. It was an unprecedented Soviet act of friendship. Not one top Bolshevik had left the Soviet Union since the Stalin take-over in the late 1920s. The fact that Molotov, who had been a member of the Politburo since about 1918, was going to a foreign country demonstrated Stalin's deep desire to maintain amicable relations with Hitler. Either something was wrong that had to be patched up, or the Soviets and Germans were moving toward even closer collaboration. Von Walther said that pressure had come from Berlin, which was anxious to have Molotov return the two visits of Ribbentrop to Moscow. With Hitler the undisputed master of Europe, the Germans were interested in demonstrating to the world the "solidarity" of Soviet-German relations. Nevertheless, I had the feeling that there was some Soviet hesitancy about the visit. One bit of evidence was a report I had picked up that Communist Party propaganda orators had modified their pro-German lines and were emphasizing that the only country that could win the war was the Soviet Union. Another piece of evidence was a report from the Turkish Ambassador that an "unimpeachable source" had told him that Molotov tried at the last minute to call off the Berlin trip but that Schulenberg had insisted he go through with it.

Sir Stafford Cripps, the British Ambassador, was having dinner at Spaso House on November 9 when the Moscow radio announced that Molotov was going to Berlin. Cripps had not had the slightest intimation of the Molotov trip and exploded in a denunciation of the Soviet government and officials, who in his eyes were the personification of evil. He had been under an emotional strain because of the shabby treatment he had received. There had been high hopes in Britain when Churchill appointed Cripps, a Labour member of Parliament with leftist tendencies, as ambassador to Moscow. Instead of finding favor among the Bolsheviks, Cripps was practically ignored—the Kremlin knew that the Conservatives represented the London government. Molotov would not see Cripps; he had to do all of his business with Vishinsky, who had become Vice-Commissar for Foreign Affairs.

Another reason for Cripps's shock was his failure to face up to the possibility of continued Soviet-German collaboration. When we asked him at dinner whether the British government was prepared for such an eventuality, he conceded that he had persistently hoped, despite the rebuffs in Moscow, for some success in weaning the Russians away from Berlin and pulling them closer to London. He paused, then ominously added that if increased collaboration with the Nazis followed the Molotov visit, the possibility could not be excluded that "influential circles" in Great Britain might begin to press for a separate peace with Germany on an anti-Soviet basis. He did not name anyone, but apparently was referring to some officials in the Foreign Office. Cripps feared his position was becoming untenable.

The Molotov visit was undoubtedly one of the turning points in

Soviet-German relations. The Germans expected a great deal from the meeting. Before Molotov left, von Walther told me that while no new political accord would be signed, the visit indicated a decision "in principle" by the Soviet government to lay the foundations for closer collaboration, economic as well as political. The entire range of Soviet-German relations would be discussed.

Extraordinary security precautions were taken by the German authorities and the NKVD to protect Molotov. A German who went with him told me (he was probably exaggerating) that the railroad line from the Soviet border, which was then at the Latvian frontier, to Berlin was lined with troops, each man in sight of the next.

We received bits and pieces of general information from the German Embassy concerning the conversations of November 12–13. Von Walther reported inaccurately that Molotov had made an excellent impression in Berlin and Hitler had met the Russian's frankness with equal frankness. In a cable to the State Department on November 19, Steinhardt passed along the misleading report I had received from von Walther, then concluded, "I do not believe that there will be any immediate developments or early positive moves on the part of the Soviet Union as the discussions were apparently only of a preliminary nature. I am of the opinion, however, that a greater rather than a lesser degree of Soviet-German collaboration must be anticipated in the immediate future."

Obviously, we did not know at first that the talks had not gone well, that the Führer had been displeased, and that Molotov had been extremely stubborn and unyielding. The Russian was quite unresponsive to Hitler's blandishments, including the Führer's suggestion that the Soviet Union could share in the spoils from the British Empire if it turned toward the Indian Ocean, and asked questions about the stationing of German troops in Finland and Rumania.

It is conceivable that Hitler did not realize that under Bolshevik procedure even Molotov, who at that time was number two in the Soviet hierarchy, could not depart from Stalin's rigid instructions. Stalin did not trust anyone, even—or perhaps especially—his closest associates, and Molotov must have been strictly limited in what he could agree to with Hitler.

I have often wondered what would have happened if Hitler and Stalin had met during this period. Would it have been another Tilsit, with Stalin, as Alexander I did with Napoleon in 1807, agreeing to an alliance against England if England refused to come to terms? Or would it have ended in a row? I am rather inclined to think that given the nature of the two men, a far-reaching deal might easily have been struck that could have avoided the German attack in 1941. Stalin would have conceded much to avoid a war.

As later events proved, Molotov's granitelike resistance was a major factor in Hitler's decision to attack the Soviet Union. German documents made public after the war show that Hitler ordered increased preparations for Barbarossa, the code name for the attack on the Soviet Union, the day after Molotov left Berlin.

In Moscow we were unaware of all of this. Despite the strains, there was no conclusive evidence of any real rift in the Soviet-Nazi association. Within a few fateful months, after I left Moscow, the two nations would be locked in mortal combat, and not much later, when I was in Tokyo, Japan would attack the United States to expand the conflict into a war of world dimensions.

CHAPTER SEVEN

Internment in Tokyo

As 1940 came to a close, I was transferred to Tokyo as Second Secretary in the Embassy. I was somewhat puzzled by the move, because I knew little about Japan, could not speak the language, and had no desire to leave my specialty, the Soviet Union. It was not until my arrival in Tokyo that I discovered that Ambassador Joseph C. Grew had asked for a Russian specialist to keep an eye on Soviet-Japanese relations, which were becoming increasingly important as the war dragged on in Europe.

I looked forward to the opportunity to see Asian Russia during the fourteen-day trip aboard the Trans-Siberian Express from Moscow to Vladivostok. The Trans-Siberian was old-fashioned, even for those days. Of pre-World War I vintage, the cars were made of wood and the roadbed was bad. But, as I had learned on my first trip on a Russian train in 1934, the cars could be surprisingly comfortable.

As in all Russian trains, the porter, called the *provodnik*, sat all day long at the end of the car by a samovar. Passengers got hot water from him for their tea. Our *provodnik* was assiduous in his care of his passengers. He made up the berths in the morning, changed the bed linen three or four times during the two-week trip, and answered calls promptly. The train was clean—not up to excessive German standards, but certainly adequate by Russian criteria. That is, there would be dust in the corners, but the towels were clean and an attempt was made to keep the train presentable.

I took a box of books along and did a great deal of reading, particularly about Japan. Having learned from experience of the inadequacies of Soviet dining-car service, I also took with me a large box of canned goods and other food, as well as some wines and liquor. These turned out to be useful, because about half the time the dining car served nothing except tea and black bread.

The liquor also made my compartment somewhat of a social center. Most evenings, I invited some of the passengers in for a drink. We whiled away many an hour singing Russian songs and talking. As on my earlier train trips, I noticed that, while traveling, Russians were much more relaxed and communicative with foreigners than they were in Moscow, but I heard no word of dissatisfaction with the Soviet regime or with living conditions. Even when the radio loud-speaker in the corridor announced a far-reaching Soviet-German economic agreement, the passengers said little about the news.

To my disappointment, I saw very little of Siberia. Under government regulations, the train did not stop at any of the chief Siberian cities except in the night, and no passengers were allowed to leave the platform. During the day, the view from my window—when I scratched a hole in the ice—was almost always of unlimited wastes of snow. From horizon to horizon there was practically no sign of life.

We did get a glimpse of Birobidzhan, an area which the government had set aside for a Jewish settlement. As we neared the city, about seventy-five East European Jewish émigrés aboard the train became greatly excited. Pro-Communists had frequently cited Birobidzhan as an example of the tolerance and humanity of the Soviet Union contrasted with Hitler's barbaric anti-Semitism. But as the train slowed down, sentries with machine guns could be seen standing on raised platforms, and a chill quiet swept over the migrants.

Actually, there was nothing for the Jewish passengers, who had recently escaped from Hitler, to be concerned about—these were not concentration camps. At that time, the Soviet government had a tolerant attitude toward Jews. The Russians even allowed some Jews in Poland and other occupied areas to travel across the country to Japan and China, where they hoped to get visas to enter the United States. The action saved them from the Nazis' gas chambers.

I also got a good look at Vladivostok, a typical Russian provincial town, with many log houses and snow piled in huge hummocks on most of the principal streets. The snow, the cold, the biting wind, the lack of elementary accommodations made Vladivostok a place I would not want to visit for long.

At Vladivostok, most of the other train passengers and I boarded a Japanese ship encrusted with yellow-gray ice. So great was the weight of the ice that the ship had a definite list as we steamed out of the harbor. When we arrived in Tsuruga, Japan, we had our first taste of Japanese hostility toward foreigners. Although I carried a diplomatic passport and was therefore given slightly better treatment than the Jewish émigrés, the delays were interminable and the attitude of the Japanese Kempeitai, the secret police, was far from welcoming. Finally, after long hours of waiting with practically no food, we boarded a train for Tokyo. By that time, I had acquired a first-class case of influenza. After reporting to Ambassador Grew, I went to the Imperial Hotel, where I spent the next two weeks recovering.

I found life in the Tokyo Embassy quite different from that in Moscow. One of the most important differences was that Ambassador Grew, unlike Steinhardt, was a thorough professional, dedicated to the task of improving relations between the United States and Japan, not to publicizing himself. I cannot say that I became really intimate with him. He was faintly aloof, in part because he was much older than his staff, but also because he was by nature an inward-looking man.

Grew's chief assistant was Eugene H. Dooman, the Counselor, who was fluent in Japanese. Dooman worked closely with Grew in the vain efforts to settle differences between Washington and Tokyo. As in other Embassies, there were experts in political, economic, and military affairs, but no one was so specialized that he did not pitch in and help in matters outside his area.

I found the atmosphere in Japan much more pleasant than Russia for a diplomat. Having lived in Russia, I found complaints about the restrictions on foreigners in Japan exaggerated. The foreigner in Japan, even during the Chinese war, was vastly freer than in the Soviet Union, which was, at least technically, at peace. When I would say this to any Westerner, I would be greeted with incredulous stares and smiles of disbelief. Restrictions were not visible in Tokyo or in most parts of Japan, but when we started to enter a particularly sensitive area, the Kempeitai immediately made themselves known. They would politely ask to see our passports, spend several minutes examining the document, and then return it with expressions of apology and request that we proceed in a different direction.

All in all, I liked Japan. The charm of the country, the beauty of the scenery, the politeness of the people made me forget the occasional unpleasantness and overcome even the bitterest feelings against Japanese policies.

While Ambassador Grew and Dooman had little difficulty in conferring with high Japanese officials, I, as a junior officer, was never successful in establishing serious contacts in the Foreign Office. On occasion, I was able to see some lower-level officials, but the calls were never fruitful. There were few social occasions in Tokyo to which members of the foreign embassies were invited. It was a closed-in life in the sense that you saw mostly foreigners, but I did not have the same feeling of isolation as in Moscow. Despite the language barrier (I gave up on Japanese after a month of lessons) and the disparity in cultures, there was more discussion of issues. Some Japanese were not in sympathy with their government and discreetly voiced their opposition, but most kept their own counsel.

Because I was a newcomer, I gathered most of my information from reading translations of the Japanese press, from talks with other officers in the Embassy, from luncheons at the American Club, the gathering place of foreigners, and from conversations with members of other embassies.

I knew one member of the German Embassy—Franz Krapf, who had been in Moscow for economic talks while I was there. I did not know the master Soviet spy, Victor Sorge, head of the Deutsche Nachrichten Bureau in Tokyo and an intimate friend of Major General Eugene Ott, the German Ambassador. Sorge's reports convinced the Soviet government that the Japanese would not attack in Siberia and thereby permitted Stalin to move Siberian divisions to Moscow to beat off the German attack there.

Until Germany launched the attack on Russia, I had no acquaintances in the Soviet Embassy. The German invasion of the Soviet Union, on June 22, 1941, surprised me and the whole Embassy. I had not expected Hitler to do anything so stupid—nor had Stalin. While I had no knowledge of Hitler's psychology, it had always seemed to me that it was infinitely preferable to Germany to maintain tranquil relations with the Soviet Union while endeavoring to deal with England than to embark on another large war. There had been reports of a German troop buildup on the Soviet border, but, like others, I assumed that this was pressure on Stalin to make concessions, probably of an economic nature, to the Third Reich.

As soon as I heard of the attack, I tuned in on Radio Moscow. To my amazement, only regular programs were being broadcast. There were announcements of production records set by workers and a description of the "happy, peaceful" Soviet people enjoying a Sunday holiday. This was about noon Moscow time—about eight hours after the invasion began. As I was listening, the announcer broke in and said Molotov had an important statement to make. Molotov went on the air to inform the unprepared Soviet people of the avalanche that had descended on them. Stuttering, he emphasized that the Nazis had attacked without making "any demands whatsoever"—an indication that if Hitler had asked, he would have been able to get concessions. Molotov ended with—what sounded hollow then—a statement of hope that "victory will be ours."

It was to be expected that Molotov and not Stalin would announce the outbreak of war to the Soviet people. Stalin was not about to assume responsibility for a situation which must have looked like the end of the world to him. Later, early in July, Stalin did address the nation, telling with relative accuracy of the series of reverses suffered by the Soviet Army. It was noticeable that Stalin spoke of citizens of Russia, not "comrades," the Communist form of address.

The attack changed many things in Tokyo, particularly our relations with the Russians. During the post-attack period, I made the acquaintance of Yakov A. Malik, who was subsequently to be a Vice-Commissar for Foreign Affairs, ambassador to Britain, and on two occasions, representative to the United Nations. Malik was a Ukrainian with a rather soft and sly-looking face. Under the impact of the war, we became relatively good friends (all friendships with Soviet officials are relative). We used to eat at the tempura bars, talking over the war while cooks with tall white hats fried shrimp, fish, and lobsters in deep fat. Like all Russians, Malik was apprehensive about the military situation, but with me, at least, he stuck pretty close to the official Soviet communiqués, which insisted that the Soviet army was retreating according to plan and that a powerful counter-stroke would come at the proper time. There was no other subject of conversation except the war.

As summer turned to fall, there was increasing tension between Japan and the United States that led to tighter restrictions on our movements. There were unfriendly incidents between Japanese and foreigners that Grew, as doyen of the diplomatic corps, had to handle and that I was generally asked to help with. The Japanese invariably offered excuses and apologies, but did nothing.

In July, 1941, when the United States, reacting to Japan's invasion of Indochina, froze all Japanese assets in the United States and forbade the export of certain commodities to Japan, war became likely. Shutting off the imports confronted the Japanese government with three alternatives. One course was to abandon all imperialist pursuits on the continent of Asia, to withdraw from Indochina and from China and make a deal with the United States in order to ensure the resumption of oil imports. The second alternative was to accept slow strangulation. The third alternative was to fight.

War did not seem inevitable to me in 1941, because I had some hope that a deal was possible. Premier Fumimaro Konoye proposed a meeting with President Roosevelt in Alaska. The President was intrigued because he always had a predilection for personal diplomacy. But the idea collapsed because of pro-Chinese sentiment in the United States government. In those days, America believed the Japanese were inherently wicked and the Chinese inherently good. The immense sympathy for China, which had fought Japanese aggression for years, limited Roosevelt's ability to talk with Tokyo.

The effort was not dropped completely. Just before Konoye fell from power in October, Grew held some interesting meetings with him. These had to be conducted in the greatest secrecy because there was fear among the Japanese officials of the Black Dragon Society, an ultra-nationalist reactionary organization, with a wide membership among army officers. I was not involved in the talks with Konoye, but Grew kept Embassy officers informed. Eventually, the talks produced a plan under which the Japanese would have pulled out of Indochina and parts of central and southern China, but would have retained Manchuria and stayed to some degree in north China. There was a real opportunity to preserve peace in this plan, but public opinion in both countries made acceptance impossible.

The difference between the views of Ambassador Grew and of the American government pointed up one of the problems of diplomatic reporting. The diplomat, being abroad and out from under the influence of American public opinion, tends always to look at problems of foreign affairs as though they existed in a vacuum. Those responsible for policy in Washington are acutely aware from day to day of the strength and importance of American public opinion. Viewed coldly, it seemed to me there was much to be said for what Ambassador Grew was seeking to do. On the other hand, viewed in the light of American public opinion and in recognition of its importance on government decisions, Grew's quest was fairly hopeless. On balance, a deal might have been a good thing for the United States, but in view of the state of American public opinion, it is idle to speculate on its consequences. Once the talks broke down, war was inevitable.

Before I arrived in Tokyo, a drunken Japanese naval officer had told a Peruvian military attaché that if war broke out in the Pacific, it would begin with a Japanese strike at Pearl Harbor. The Peruvian told the American Embassy, which reported the conversation to Washington, where it must have been filed away without much notice. This report was, I believe, the only intimation that the American Embassy received of a Japanese attack on Pearl Harbor. However, on November 17, Grew himself sent a prophetic telegram to Washington noting that under Japanese tradition military strikes preceded declarations of war. He also pointed out that Embassy personnel could not move around the country freely and thus would not be in a position to report preparations for any military action.

Because we had been conditioned to the possibility of war, the attack on Pearl Harbor did not shock Americans in Japan as much as it did officials in Washington. A Japanese-speaking Embassy official and I were riding from our apartment to work when the chauffeur said that he had heard reports of fighting between the British and Japanese fleets in the Pacific. He added, "Probably not true, only on Tokyo radio." As we approached the gates of the Embassy, I heard the ringing of newsboys' bells. We bought one of the flimsy extras, and my companion translated the reports of fighting between the Japanese and American and British fleets.

In the courtyard of the Embassy, employees were busy burning our codes and important documents in metal barrels. I went to my office and was told to help burn papers. After a few hours, the police came. We thought they were after the codes, but to our surprise they never tried to stop the burning. They looked only for radios, which they suspected might be used to signal aircraft. They missed one radio, in a car, which we used, mostly unsuccessfully, to pick up English-language broadcasts while we were interned.

In the excitement, the Japanese forgot to jam the radiotelephone across the Pacific. We were able to communicate with the Department of State at least twelve hours after Pearl Harbor and were thus able to get an inkling of the extent of the damage from the raid.

While I was burning papers, a relatively minor official of the Foreign Office arrived to read the declaration of war.

I was asked to help make sure that all personnel of the Embassy were safely moved into the Embassy compound. We were permitted to go to our homes with a Japanese escort and pick up some personal belongings.

I was also assigned the job of checking the status of American businessmen and others in Tokyo. I could not leave the compound and therefore had to rely on the telephone. Most of the calls went unanswered. As we later learned from the Swiss, many American businessmen, correspondents, and tourists had been imprisoned by the Japanese.

I was struck by the impeccable behavior of the Embassy servants. Perhaps their attitude could be traced to their feudal heritage. These servants were just as quiet, just as efficient, and just as obedient as before the attack. They stayed on throughout the internment.

We were so busy during the first hours after the news that war had broken out that the full significance of what had happened did not register with most of us. It was not until the Ambassador invited us to his Residence for a drink and we began talking that the full impact of the event struck us. Only then did I perceive, and only dimly, the long, uphill fight that the United States faced—the sacrifices at home, the uprooting of lives, the casualty lists like those Britain and the Soviet Union had already compiled.

Grew was deeply depressed, feeling that his ten-year mission in Japan had failed, although there was certainly no reason for him to blame himself for what had happened. While he had deep feelings, Grew never, to my knowledge, indulged in any recriminations against anybody in the Department of State or in the government. The only time he became angry during the long internment—indeed, the only time I ever saw him angry—was when the Japanese attempted to utilize the entrance to the Embassy to make a propaganda film. One morning, we noticed a crowd outside the gate. An automobile drove up and actors dressed as Japanese admirals and generals got out. They hung on the gate a large sign that said, "We Americans surrender to the imperial eagles of Japan." Then they tried to open the gate as though they were entering the Embassy. Grew was furious. He called the liaison man of the Japanese Foreign Office who was our contact with the outside world and berated him for the outrageous breach of diplomatic immunity. The Japanese quickly ordered the film company to leave.

Along with most of the senior officers, I was lodged in the Ambassador's Residence, a comfortable building, beautifully decorated and furnished by Mrs. Grew, on the top of a hill. The compound covered about two acres. At the bottom of the hill was the Chancellery, with apartment buildings for most of the staff.

We organized our days to keep us busy. There were classes in languages and other subjects and time for recreation. We transformed the bottom garden of the compound into a pitch-and-putt golf course. We devised all sorts of methods for varying the holes, including playing from the roof of the garage over one of the apartment buildings. The superintendent of the building, a retired naval petty officer, complained that ninety-nine windows were broken by the golfers during the six months we were interned. One day, someone sliced a shot over the wall into the street. By chance, the ball hit a member of the German Embassy on the head. There were complaints from the Japanese gendarmerie, who were guarding the compound. We were asked, and tried, to be more careful, but we did get a certain satisfaction out of the fact that we had struck a German.

At noon on April 19, 1942, we heard the burst of bombs, then anti-aircraft fire, then the air-raid sirens. Our first thought was that the sounds were part of an air-raid drill. (The previous day, the Kempeitai had told us that on the following night we could not have any lights showing in the Embassy, because they were going to have an intensive air-raid drill over Tokyo.) Then we saw a plane flying not more than five hundred feet off the ground with anti-aircraft puffs behind it. A military attaché identified it as an American B-25.

Following the raid, the Japanese made claims of having brought down a number of the American bombers, and showed some wreckage at a park in Tokyo. They made a slight slip, however. The "S" in the "U.S.A." markings on the plane was reversed, proving that the wreckage was fake.

We had no way of judging how much damage the raid had caused. A Japanese woman doctor who treated members of the Embassy for minor ailments told us the morning after the raid that she had been in a hospital when a bomb had destroyed a wing of it. This report turned out to be true; in fact, the bomber was commanded by General James Doolittle, the leader of the raid, who had misjudged his target.

In the days following the attack, we noticed a lot more Japanese Zero fighters over Tokyo, but it was difficult, shut off as we were from the rest of the city, to feel the effect of the raid on the Japanese. They certainly had not anticipated that the main Japanese islands would be attacked by American aircraft. An article in the one remaining English-language newspaper, the *Advertiser*, said that the bombers had come from non-occupied China.

Although we were dependent on enemy sources for all our news, we thought we could detect when the Japanese were lying. In those early days, there was little need for the Japanese to invent the news; everything was going their way. But we suspected the Japanese accounts of the first battle of the Coral Sea. The imprecise wording of the claims of victory, compared with the detailed accounts of the fall of Hong Kong, Singapore, and the Philippines, made us suspicious.

Negotiations between the Swiss and Japanese governments for the exchange of nationals took a long time. The Japanese refused to let any foreign ship, whether from a neutral country or not, in her waters. Finally, Lourenço Marques in Portuguese East Africa was selected as the exchange point. On June 20, 1942, we boarded the *Asama Maru* at Yokohama. The ship started to leave, then anchored for the night in the harbor because of a dispute over the American list of passengers. The effect of the delay on those who had been maltreated by the Japanese was agonizing. Keith Meyers, the head of Standard Oil in Tokyo, who had been held incommunicado in a cell for four months, said that he would jump overboard if there was any possibility of his returning to Japanese hands. A number of us kept watch over him, never leaving his side until the *Asama Maru* finally sailed. It took us over two months to go from Yokohama to New York.

A few months after our return to New York, we learned that a young U.S. submarine commander told Grew that in a misty dawn one day in the China Sea he saw through his periscope what he thought was a fat Japanese transport. He was about to fire his torpedoes when the fog cleared and he saw on the side of the ship the Swiss cross, which was a symbol of safe-conduct. The commander said that his submarine had not been cautioned by Washington that Americans were in a Japanese ship in the China Sea at that time. "You were within seconds of receiving two torpedoes right in the middle," he told Grew.

A young naval attaché and I were in charge of allocating berths for the passengers. In some cases, only the last name was given, so we knew neither sex nor age. Occasionally, we had to move a sailor out of a nun's cabin, but generally we had no great problems. When we arrived at Lourenço Marques, we discovered that no effort had been made to assign persons from our ship and from a ship from China to cabins on the *Gripsholm*. The naval officer and I offered to take the job on, but we were rather contemptuously rejected by the shipping agents, who felt that this was their business. The result was unbelievable confusion for at least forty-eight hours after the ship set sail.

Finally, everybody got sorted out, but not until some curious cabin-mates were separated.

When we boarded the *Gripsholm* about noon, we found one of the most sumptuous smorgasbords I have ever seen. It would have been impressive to anyone; for people who had been on short rations, as most of us had been, the sight was almost more than they could bear, and some burst into tears.

There were some sixty or seventy newspaper correspondents on the *Gripsholm*. All searched for a place to write. A lucky few found tables in the library, but like almost every room, this was very noisy because of the large numbers of passengers swarming everywhere. Joseph Alsop came up with the best solution. He leased a toilet from the mens'-room attendant, placed a board across the side, and, sitting on the toilet, wrote in tranquillity. Joe had been employed by Chennault's Flying Tigers, who were aiding Generalissimo Chiang Kai-shek against the Japanese. He had posed as an Associated Press reporter in order to get repatriated. Joe was his usual urbane self and frequently gave cocktail parties on the deck. His presence greatly added to our enjoyment.

Another feature of the voyage was the crap game started by an Armenian lace merchant for the benefit of servicemen—or so he said. It was held on deck from midnight on for about the first week. This crap game was based in large measure on rolls of currency that businessmen from Shanghai had been permitted to bring out by Japanese authorities. Why, no one could be sure. With a lot of loose cash in their pockets and nothing very much to do, the businessmen gave the crap game a big play. When a fight broke out between a sailor from the *President Harrison*, which had been sunk off Shanghai, and a businessman, missionaries petitioned the captain to stop the game, and he did.

About the only political move was the attempt by a Methodist bishop from Japan to organize a sort of Fellowship of Reconciliation. His thesis was that America had acted hastily after Pearl Harbor, and he prayed by name for the leading members of the American Embassy, headed by Grew, for their mistaken support of the war. The bishop's activity gained him a short stay on Ellis Island when we reached New York.

My wife and my mother met me at a hotel in New York, and we went down to Avis's mother's home in Villa Nova. After touching base with Washington, I was granted a month's leave, which we spent on a pleasant tour of New England by train and bus because gasoline rationing limited the use of private cars. Then it was back to Washington, where we bought a house in Georgetown and I received a promotion that ended what in effect had been my apprenticeship and brought me again in direct contact with the Soviet Union.

PART TWO

The President's Man

CHAPTER EIGHT

The First Moscow Meeting

In my new position as assistant chief of the Russian section of the Division of European Affairs, I was more than pleased to find myself working with a number of old Moscow hands. The chief of the section was Loy Henderson, whom I had learned to respect and like when he was the principal political reporter in Bullitt's Embassy in 1934. Others in the section were G. Frederick Reinhardt, who had been in Moscow in 1940 and who later became ambassador to Vietnam, Egypt, and Italy, and Elbridge Durbow, who later became ambassador to Vietnam.

My principal function was to follow Soviet affairs on a day-to-day basis and keep Henderson informed. I quickly learned that the struggle over Soviet policy that I had been caught up in five years before still persisted. Despite the State Department reorganization of 1936 and the bringing in of younger men with fresh ideas, the Soviet section was still wary of the Russians. From Henderson on down, the specialists shared the view that the Soviet Union, even though now an ally, had to be closely watched because its ultimate aims clashed with those of the United States. There was no attempt or desire to hinder the war effort or impede aid to the Soviet Union. We all admired the fight the Russians were making; what we were worried about was the future.

Roosevelt and his chief assistant, Harry Hopkins, were concerned mostly with the present. That meant that they focused on military decisions, because the immediate problem was turning back the Nazis. Eager to prove to the Soviets that the United States was a true ally, the White House thought the State Department's worry about political problems smacked of foot-dragging.

There was also a feeling that the Foreign Service was not in sympathy with New Deal philosophy and that diplomats were fuzzy and tended to concentrate on minutiae rather than the comprehensive nature of a problem.

Actually, this was a classic case of a political leader trying to drag a cautious bureaucracy along. Like Woodrow Wilson before him and Richard Nixon long after him, Roosevelt's solution for the problem was to center foreign-policy decision-making in the White House. Since the decisions were mostly military, Roosevelt and Hopkins saw little need to consult the State Department. Later, they changed their minds.

Hopkins, who had an acid tongue, was contemptuous of the State Department. I met him for the first time in the autumn of 1942, at a dinner at a friend's house. My wife was sitting next to him. Hopkins nodded toward me and asked her if that was her husband across the table. When she said yes, he said he understood I was "one of those Russian experts" and asked if I spoke Russian. She said, "Yes, he does." Undaunted, Hopkins said, "Of course, you have not tried to learn it." Angered, my wife replied that indeed she had, and had become reasonably proficient in the language. Later, at the same dinner, Hopkins challenged me about my views on the Soviet Union. He rudely asked if I were a member of the anti-Soviet clique in the State Department. When I said I did not know of any anti-Soviet clique, he went into a long dissertation about how marvelous the Russians were in the war. I countered by saying this was perfectly true but there were other aspects of the Soviet Union which should not be forgotten, especially their opposition to freedom. I subsequently learned that it was one of Hopkins's techniques to attack an individual to try to ascertain how seriously his views were held.

Hopkins had many enemies, as would any man as close to the President as he was. He had a reputation of being irritable, and he was. He was said to be arrogant, which he was not. He was also called ambitious, and at one time he did aspire to the presidency, apparently with Roosevelt's blessing, but by the time I met him, Hopkins had abandoned his own political ambitions and did not envisage his role as anything independent of the President.

He was devoted to Roosevelt, but clearly recognized the President's weaknesses. As I got to know Hopkins and saw the depth of his devotion to Roosevelt, how he pulled himself from his sick bed day after day to help the President, I became a staunch admirer of this brilliant, moody man who in a real sense gave his life to his country. But I did not like him at first, when, suspicious of my State Department background, he goaded me with question after question in an attempt to plumb my feelings about the Soviet Union.

At that time, the Nazis occupied almost all of European Russia. They were pounding at the gates of Leningrad, and while they had been thrown back from Moscow, they were poised for a final onslaught on Stalingrad. Losses from German submarines were staggering, and the British had to suspend convoys to Murmansk. In the Mediterranean, Rommel's Afrika Corps was closing in on Cairo and Alexandria. Sentiment for the brave Russians swept the United States; even the press, which had been so suspicious of Moscow, tended to go overboard.

It was during this period that the incredible movie *Mission to Moscow* was produced. Based on a book ghost-written for Joseph E. Davies, it dealt with his ambassadorship to Moscow from 1936 to 1938. Two Soviet technicians, who came over from Moscow to aid in the production of the film, helped turn it into one of the most blatantly propagandistic pictures ever screened. At a private showing at the Office of Strategic Services, we recorded sixty-seven factual errors in the picture. So crude was its propaganda that, even with the nationwide sympathy for the Russian people, the film was a flop. Davies showed the film in the Kremlin in 1943, much, I subsequently gathered, to the embarrassment of the Soviet leaders.

The fact that the Russians were carrying so heavy a load led to a guilt complex in our relations. American officials, and the British, too, were always trying to reassure the Soviets about Allied intentions. Often this effort was overdone and had a countereffect. Soviet suspicion contributed to the ambiguity in relations. It should never be forgotten that during the entire war the Soviet Union never permitted any Allied military mission, British or American, to visit the Soviet front.

The most obvious example of the desire to appease the Soviets was in the handling of the communiqué of the June, 1942, meeting of President Roosevelt with Molotov. I had not yet returned from Japan, but I received an account from State Department officials. Molotov insisted on wording that created the impression that the United States had committed itself to open a second military front on the continent of Europe in 1942, to ease the pressure on the Russians on the Eastern front. The draft of the communiqué contained the following passage: "In the course of the conversations, full understanding was reached with regard to the urgent tasks of creating a second front in Europe in 1942." To Henderson, this seemed to promise something that we really could not do and therefore had no intention of doing. It was not only an overcommitment, it was also a false overcommitment. Henderson proposed revising the communiqué to say that the United States was conscious of the necessity of a second front and would open one as soon as conditions permitted, or use some qualifying phrase. But Roosevelt and his advisers in the White House, including, I am sorry to say, Hopkins, were head-down in their desire to make the Soviets happy, and the communiqué was issued as drafted. Molotov was equally successful in London, where he stopped on his way back to Moscow, and the British signed a communiqué containing the phrase "second front in Europe in 1942." In August, Churchill had to go to Moscow to explain to Stalin why it was physically impossible for the Western Allies to open the second front that year. The Allies were planning to invade North Africa, but the great cross-Channel operation to France would not come for almost another two years.

I always thought that the primary reason for the overcommitments to the Kremlin was the fear that the Soviet armies might collapse, that the Bolshevik regime might surrender or make a deal with Hitler. Some people in the administration felt that encouragement, even when based on false premises, would stiffen the Soviet will. If the bleak truth had been told, the discouragement might have been too great for the Russians. Part of the blame for our overoptimistic encouragement can be placed on the Russians, with their pessimistic outlook. Molotov apparently painted so black a picture of the Soviet situation—he almost said that without a second front the Russians would be forced to quit—that Roosevelt must have felt the necessity of appearing to promise a second front in 1942. The effect of making estimates which were not realistic was to deepen Soviet suspicion that the policy of the Western Allies was to bleed Russia white. It is never possible to be sure whether Soviet suspicions are real or contrived, but certainly our optimistic attitude hurt us. I believe that a policy of speaking frankly to the Russians, of indicating only what we could deliver, might have avoided some of the later Soviet suspicions, although I am under no illusion that our basic troubles could have been solved.

We in the State Department were not the only officials in government who had trouble satisfying the Soviets. Those who administered Lend-Lease, the program under which the United States sent supplies to its allies, had some of the greatest difficulties. The Kremlin had sent a purchasing mission to the United States to extract the maximum amount of military equipment as quickly as possible and get it to the front. Most of the dealings were with the Lend-Lease Administration, which had begun as a State Department agency but for military supplies passed under the control of the War Department. It became an independent agency as far as civilian supplies were concerned.

Lend-Lease officials told me that the Soviet mission was constantly pushing, probing, and belaboring them. The Russians acted as if they believed that a denial of a request was due to ill will and not to justifiable reasons. Lend-Lease administrators spent hours explaining that certain items just were not available in the quantities desired. The Soviets, in what I think was a semi-calculated tactic, took the attitude that since they were doing all the fighting in Europe, Americans should contribute whatever was needed to the Red Army.

For another year, Henderson led the quiet struggle in the administration against the soupy and syrupy attitude toward the Soviet Union. A man of the highest character, absolutely incorruptible, he always spoke his mind, a practice that did not make him popular. Overruled time after time, he asked in 1943 to be relieved of his duties as chief of the division, and I was appointed to succeed him. With the departure of Henderson, the Soviet field lost one of its founders, a man who probably did as much for the Foreign Service as any officer, living or dead.

I was the first of the six specialists who started the Russian-language program in the late 1920s to become the head of a division of the State Department.

The change did not lead to any radical switch in the division's views about the Soviet Union. Like Henderson, I, too, thought that we were dealing with the Soviets on an emotional instead of a realistic basis. However, I did not feel as strongly as Henderson about changing policy, if only because I did not see then, and do not see in retrospect, what other course we could have followed given the military facts of the war. Because of my experience, I knew something of the true nature of the Soviet Union, that its leaders were animated by a philosophy not only alien but also definitely hostile to everything democratic governments stood for, and they acted accordingly. Yet in those days I found it almost impossible to convince others that admiration for the extraordinary valor of the Russian troops and the unquestioned heroism of the Russian people was blinding Americans to the dangers of the Bolshevik leaders.

As a matter of fact, I rarely tried to convince anyone, although I objected strongly to some of the nonsense spoken by American Communists. With the fate of the world hanging on the outcome of the Russian-German fighting, I had no inclination to emphasize the odious parts of the Soviet system. On the contrary, I went right along with everyone else, doing everything I could to help our embattled ally. During the war, there was always this ambiguity in my attitude toward the Soviet Union.

The influence of Soviet propaganda on America during the war should not be underestimated. It was not especially aimed at the United States; it was part of the general output, but there were many willing helpers in the United States. Some of them perhaps knew what they were doing and were genuine Party-line boys, eager to capitalize on the situation to promote Communism; others were doing it out of general enthusiasm for the war effort and gratitude for the exploits of the Red Army. With some people, these feelings were so strong that you could hardly say it was cold in Russia without being accused of being anti-Soviet. One night, at a party where the Russians were being lionized, John Russell, a young officer in the British Embassy, whom I had known in Moscow, observed, "There are people in this town who think that the defense of Stalingrad proves there is no GPU."

One day, Isaiah Berlin, another member of the British Embassy, and I were talking about how discussions on the Soviet Union turned not on the subject of what the Soviet Union was or was not but on the attitude of those speaking. We worked out an involved figure of speech to describe Soviet sympathizers. We thought of Soviet Communism as a train where the engineers and firemen knew exactly where they were going and were in charge of getting there. They were the card-carrying Party members. The conductors and brakemen also knew where they were going but had not joined the Party and therefore could not affect the direction or speed of the train. They were cheating the Party out of dues. The passengers were happy to be on a train moving rapidly through the countryside in a direction which they generally approved of; they were fellow travelers. Clustered around the doors of the train were those who were attracted to Communism, but had doubts; some fell off every time the train made a sharp turn to the right or left. The final group were the twilight sleepers, who did not know what was going on. They stood on the edge of the tracks waving handkerchiefs and hats, pleased at seeing the train moving. They didn't know where the train was going but they enjoyed the sight.

Events moved rapidly shortly after my appointment. Allied military fortunes brightened with the successful American-British campaign in North Africa and the Soviet defeat of the Germans at Stalingrad in 1943 and, later, at Kursk, when the Russians smashed the Nazis in one of the major, but little-known, battles of the war. When Italy surrendered in the summer of 1943, we in the State Department thought it was time to discuss with Moscow the shape of the postwar world. There was now no question about the eventual outcome of the war. After some discussion, Washington and London proposed a meeting of the three countries' Foreign ministers, and Moscow accepted. Because of my position, I was included in the American delegation.

When we arrived in Moscow, Hull told me after the first session that in addition to my duties as an adviser on Soviet policy he wanted me to interpret for the delegation. He said the British interpreter would not be able to do the work for both his and our delegation. I told Hull that it had been more than two years since I had spoken Russian regularly and I had not boned up on the language, but of course I would do my best.

Actually, I did pretty well. The work was exhausting. Not only did I have to interpret for Hull and the other Americans at all the sessions, I also had to take notes and prepare the record of each day's meeting for telegraphing to Washington. Most days, I did not finish until long past midnight.

It was at this conference that I got to know the new ambassador to the Soviet Union, Averell Harriman. I had met him only once. A man with his own ideas and occasionally stubborn, he was not the easiest person in the world to work with, but I think everyone who did work with him came away with a high regard for his dedication to public service and his capacity for concentrated work. I cannot say that I ever felt that he really fully understood the nature of the Soviet system. Reading ideological books was not his forte. He had an enormous capacity for assessing the tactical nature of the problem and for understanding what the Soviets were after in a specific situation. But he did not take the indispensable step of relating his keen observations to the over-all Soviet ideological attitude toward the world and the capitalist nations. As a result, he sometimes did not see the wider picture. I was in intimate contact with Harriman from the 1943 Moscow Conference on. We had our disagreements, we had our agreements, but I like to think that none of our disagreements affected our friendship in any way.

As an interpreter, I became much closer to Secretary Hull than I ordinarily would have. I had scarcely known him before. The 1943 Moscow Conference of Foreign Ministers turned out to be a high point in his career. This was the first meeting of any importance between the Russians, the British, and the Americans. While many questions were discussed, the decisions of importance were (1) the setting up of the European Advisory Council to draw up surrender terms for Germany and the other enemy states in Europe, and (2) the Soviet agreement in principle to the establishment of a world organization for the preservation of future peace.

The commitment to join a world organization was contained in a Declaration of the Four Powers (China, although not represented, was asked to subscribe). While there was not much substance to the declaration, it nevertheless was an indication of cooperation at the end of the war which could not be brushed aside. This declaration was greeted with great optimism by the American press and by government officials. It was regarded as a sign that the Soviet Union would really be a loyal friend at the end of the war.

There had been a question among many of us involved in Soviet affairs whether the Soviet Union would seriously contemplate joining a world organization such as the United Nations. It seemed to us that the Soviet view of world politics and of the organization of society was not just radically different from ours but violently opposed to the ideas of other countries. It was difficult to see what common meeting ground there could be. Thus, when the draft of the proposal was first put before the Soviets, we awaited their reaction with some trepidation. To our surprise and pleasure, the Russians seemed favorable to the plan. Viewed in retrospect, it was obvious that the Bolsheviks felt that one way of watching and controlling the Allied powers and, above all, of preventing them from ganging up against the Soviet Union was to be in on all the deliberations from their inception. This rationale of the Soviet Union was to come out very clearly at the time the United Nations Charter was considered.

Hull also claimed that Stalin gave him a commitment of Soviet entry into the war in the Pacific. This unsolicited statement came during a conversation at dinner when I was not present. Hull told several of us and maintained in his memoirs that the commitment was given without any quid pro quo. However, a close study of Hull's account raises serious doubts about what Stalin meant. Stalin was not quoted directly, and Hull did not ask him what the conditions were for Soviet entry into the Asian war. The fact that the dictator did not mention any did not mean that conditions were not in his mind.

Although Hull was Secretary of State through most of the war, his eleven years of service are remembered primarily for his single-minded promotion of a reduction of tariffs. I do not think he can be called a great Secretary of State, because he had only a limited understanding of political currents in the world. He did not understand, and indeed, true to American tradition, rejected the concept of power in world affairs. His view of the enemy as a skunk in the barroom was to become the basis of his approach to all dictators. They were wicked men who had to be stopped if there was to be any decency or peace in the world.

He was not one of Roosevelt's favorites, although Roosevelt had a certain respect for his political influence in the Democratic party. Hull was too rambling, too imprecise. The President preferred to deal with Under Secretary Sumner Welles, who was cut from the same cloth of Groton, Harvard, and the Eastern establishment. As a result, Welles, with Roosevelt's support, usurped many of the Secretary's functions, and Hull did not attend any of the summit meetings. The situation was destructive of morale for many of us in the department, and we were most unhappy about it.

Hull's Tennessee mountaineer background showed through in his vocabulary on the frequent occasions when he became irritated, and especially when the White House was bypassing the Department of State. His great weakness was his sense of over-deference toward the office of the President. He didn't seem to realize that Roosevelt expected his subordinates to take the initiative in bringing ideas to him, in discussing matters by telephone and in person. If you remained silent, you were out of mind. Once when I was in Hull's office, he said, pointing to the telephone, "If the President wishes to speak to me, all he has to do is pick up that telephone, and I'll come running. It is not for me to bother the President of the United States."

In view of such weakness, how can Hull's success at the 1943 conference be explained? Did he have some special way of handling the Soviets, who did like him? There was not much socializing, but I remember the expressions of great satisfaction around the table when Hull said he would like to take the Axis leaders before a drumhead court-martial and shoot them the following morning. It cannot be said that Hull was taken in by the Soviets; he was not blind to their ultimate aims. Just after I had become his interpreter, he made a statement to Molotov that made no sense. I told Hull afterwards, courteously, I trust, that I was afraid I had not been able to get over to Molotov the meaning of the sentence. The Secretary looked at me with a twinkle in his eye and said, "It was meant to be as clear as mud."

The real reason for the success of the 1943 Moscow meeting was that the military situation had improved so much that the pressure was temporarily off on the thorny issues of supplies and to a lesser degree the opening of a second front. By the time we arrived in Moscow in early October, the Russian armies were in full advance across the wide front stretching almost from Leningrad to the Black Sea. On at least three occasions, fireworks were set off over Red Square to celebrate the liberation of Russian cities. As a consequence of the military gains, the Soviets, while still pushing for the opening of a second front, could afford to wait until the Roosevelt-Churchill-Stalin conference scheduled for the next month.

The Moscow Conference was my first opportunity to meet Molotov and Vishinsky, the two chief Soviet negotiators. Stalin had taken over the premiership, but Molotov still held his position of Commissar for Foreign Affairs. Vishinsky was Molotov's chief deputy. I had seen both in action before—Molotov at a session of the Supreme Soviet in 1939 and Vishinsky as the prosecutor at the Bukharin purge trial in 1938. But I had never talked with either.

Both looked somewhat ridiculous at the Moscow Conference. If I remember correctly, it was at this conference that the Soviets wore their diplomatic uniforms for the first time at official functions. The uniform was black, trimmed in gold, with a small dagger at the belt. To me, the uniform looked much like that of Hitler's élite S.S. troops. The Russians were inordinately proud of their new dress, and, needless to say, I kept my thoughts to myself. By the end of the war, Soviet diplomats seldom wore the uniform. I imagine that they began to hear some of the derisive comments made by foreigners and quietly dropped the idea.

Like almost all Soviet leaders a man of mystery, Molotov maintained that air at the conference. Although he was obviously trying to be affable, he had a hard time smiling, and his face remained impassive throughout most of the talks. This first close-up impression of Molotov as a careful, sober negotiator, the epitome of an intelligent Soviet bureaucrat, deepened the more I came in contact with him, and I had many an hour with him over the next dozen years.

Vishinsky was much more outgoing than Molotov, but still not as likable. Whenever I looked into those pale eyes, I saw the horrible spectacle of the prosecutor browbeating the defendants at the Bukharin trial. Vishinsky was sometimes abrasive as a negotiator, but he liked to talk about how the wartime friendship would continue into the peace. In a conversation with Major General John Deane, chief of the

United States Military Mission in Moscow, and me, Vishinsky said he thought the United States, Britain, and the Soviet Union could continue to cooperate after the war. He attributed difficulties in the past to aggressive policies of Czarist Russia and Britain. "All is changed now," he said. "All the three great powers represented here have sufficient territory, population and resources. The Soviet government has no interest in any territory beyond the Soviet frontiers and there is no real obstacle to the closest kind of cooperation." With my background knowledge, and knowing Vishinsky's past, I thought his words did not ring true.

For me, the most memorable point of the Moscow Conference was meeting Stalin for the first time. I had seen Stalin from a distance of about fifty or a hundred yards, at Red Square parades and sessions of the Supreme Soviet, but had never talked with him. Hull took me along as his interpreter when he went to the Kremlin to discuss sites for the meeting of the Big Three leaders. In Stalin's outer office, we were met by a man whom I was to see quite frequently in future years, General Poskrebyshev, a small man with a big head and a rather sinister appearance, which, it turned out, was an accurate reflection of his character. After waiting a few minutes in the plain, bare anteroom, we were ushered into Stalin's office. This was at least thirty feet long, with a desk in one corner and a green baize table on the left as we entered. Pictures of Lenin and Marx, and of such great Russian military leaders as Suvarov and Kutuzov, hung on the walls. Stalin came from behind his desk. He had a round, tubby figure and walked clumsily, like a small bear. He shook hands in a quiet and unassuming way and motioned us toward the green baize table.

Stalin looked very much like his pictures. His face was swarthy, with a black mustache covering most of his mouth. Most pictures had been taken from a lower level and created the illusion of a relatively tall man. Actually, he was very small, coming up only to Hull's shoulders. His hair was quite gray. Before the war, it had been essentially black. His face was pockmarked, his teeth broken and stained. When he lit a cigarette, I noticed that his left arm was slightly deformed. His eyes had a yellow hue, and it seemed to me, as I studied him with quick glances, that his lower eyelids were higher up on his eyeballs than is normally the case in Caucasians. My first impression was that if he had dressed in Chinese robes, he would have been a perfect subject for a Chinese ancestor portrait.

Stalin sat with his back to the wall; his interpreter, V. N. Pavlov, whom I would get to know fairly well, on his left. Hull was opposite

Stalin, and I was on Hull's left. The short conversation was more or less platitudinous. Greetings were exchanged and brief reports of the military situation were given. Then Hull brought up the real purpose of his visit, the meeting place for the conference with Roosevelt and Churchill. Hull put in a strong bid for the town of Basra, the chief port of Iraq, because Roosevelt could get to it by ship, and explained in detail the reason why the President could not be cut off from Washington—the constitutional requirement that the President act on legislation within ten days after it is passed. Stalin only dimly understood the constitutional aspect and seemed to me to be clearly skeptical.

Stalin made one point that was as valid as the President's, although it was by no means the whole story. Since he was personally in charge of Soviet military operations, he did not want to be out of touch with his forces and therefore always had to be in an area where communications were under Soviet control. This requirement strictly limited the sites where the meeting could take place. But he stated courteously that he would consider Basra and let us know later. It was evident, however, that Hull had made little impression on Stalin, and if there was to be a meeting it would have to be at the site selected by Stalin.

In subsequent days, after a few more futile exchanges and suggestions of other places in the eastern Mediterranean, agreement was finally reached for the conference to be held at Teheran, Iran, although the President and his advisers were still worried about constitutional complications.

Just before the Moscow meeting ended, Hull informed me that I was to go to Teheran to be the President's interpreter. The story of why and how I was selected shows the enormous role that luck can play in the career of an individual. In 1942, when Molotov, under the pseudonym of "Mr. Brown," came to the United States, Roosevelt had used Samuel Cross, a Harvard professor of Russian, as an interpreter. Professor Cross apparently did an excellent job, but shortly after his return to Cambridge, word began to reach the White House that he was entertaining dinner parties with stories of what Molotov had said to the President and what the President had said to Molotov. Such leaks in the midst of the war could have provided invaluable military secrets to the enemy. Roosevelt was understandably furious and summoned Hopkins into his office and told him to find some interpreters in government service who would be under discipline and could be relied on not to run around blabbing about what they had heard. Hopkins made an investigation, and came up with two names —George Kennan and Charles Bohlen. Kennan was eliminated because at that time he was chargé d'affaires in Lisbon, where the sensitive issue of bases in the Azores was being negotiated. Thus I was chosen to be tested at the Moscow Conference. It was not until I successfully passed the examination that Hull informed me that I had been undergoing a secret test to determine whether I could be the President's interpreter at Teheran. Satisfied with my work, Hull transferred me to the Moscow Embassy for temporary duty as First Secretary before the conference. In the next few weeks, I interpreted for Harriman at various meetings with Molotov and other Soviet officials in preparation for the Big Three's first meeting. As we got to know each other, Harriman urged the State Department (as I learned much later) to promote me two or three grades and make me his number-two man—Counselor of the Embassy. The department turned him down, quite rightly in my opinion, because I do not believe in the premature promotion, even in emergencies, of regulars in the Foreign Service. Such promotions result in an officer's reaching high levels at such an early age that he is soon overqualified for every available opening. He must then accept demotion or retire early.

Finally, in November, all preparations for the Teheran Conference were complete. Through the accident of fate, my career had been fundamentally altered. I had leaped over the barrier that insulated the State Department from decision-making at the White House. Within a matter of a few weeks, I had been transformed from a mere desk officer, removed from the mainstream of American foreign policy, to a participant in the most critical diplomatic negotiations the United States had ever engaged in.

CHAPTER NINE

The Teheran Conference

On November 21, 1943, Harriman, accompanied by me and a number of other Americans and Britons, took off in the ambassadorial plane, a converted B-25 bomber, which he kept in Moscow. The flight was uneventful until we neared Stalingrad, when our American pilot informed us that trouble had developed in an engine and he would have to land. While the pilot and mechanics worked on the balky engine, we were taken to Communist Party headquarters, the only building in the ruined city that had been repaired. There a sumptuous lunch had been prepared, with large quantities of vodka. In 1943, the Russians did not have any inhibitions about serving vodka freely at parties. Later, when accounts began to appear in the Western press about Russian orgies in the midst of the war, they cut back. The Soviets, while immune in many instances to what was said about them in the press of the world, nevertheless were sensitive to anything that seemed to present them as uncivilized.

After lunch, word came that the engine could not be quickly repaired and we would have to spend the night in Stalingrad. Our hosts then organized a motor trip through the battlefield, which, I confess, I do not remember well. I do recall that Lieutenant General Geffard Martel, chief of the British Military Mission in Moscow, who was also in our party and also feeling his vodka, commented, "This is not as bad as Wipers." Needless to say, he was a veteran of the World War I battle at Ypres, France.

We came back to Party headquarters, where we were spending the night, to discover that the Russians, with characteristic hospitality, had arranged a great banquet. The festivities went on far into the night, and I have a final remembrance of singing a Russian song,

"Stenka Razin," to the amusement of the Russians, and possibly the edification of the Americans. The song concerned a Cossack hero of a seventeenth-century peasant uprising, who threw his Persian girl friend into the Volga. As I was going to bed, an old Russian woman, with a face like a dried apple, started to help me get undressed. I needed help but protested. "Don't worry, young man," she said in Russian, "this is what we always do with gentlemen." She obviously remembered the years before the Revolution.

We finally arrived in Cairo in the middle of the next day. While Roosevelt, Churchill, and Chiang Kai-shek conferred on the war in Asia, I toured the city.

At Cairo, I learned that Hopkins continued to harbor some doubts about my cautious attitude toward Moscow. He was still down on the State Department, calling Foreign Service officers "cookie pushers, pansies—and usually isolationists to boot." We had a long talk in which he again tried to provoke me, but I held my temper and explained the handicaps that State Department officers had to put up with. My argument must have impressed Hopkins, because we got along well after that. Within a year, he took me into the White House.

We left Cairo on Saturday, November 27. I was in the second plane, following the President's. After landing at the Gale Morghe Airport, about five miles south of Teheran, we drove into town along an unprotected road, which, as we arrived at the city limits, was lined with people. The Russians and the British, as well as the Americans, were concerned over the Iranians' loose security measures.

The plan had been for the President to stay at the Residence of the American Minister. However, staying in the American Residence would have required Roosevelt to drive daily through unguarded streets across town to the Soviet and British embassies, which were not far from one another. Soon after Roosevelt moved into the Residence, Molotov told Harriman that Soviet intelligence had discovered the existence of a plot among Nazi-oriented Iranians and Nazi agents to assassinate some or all three of the participants in this conference. Therefore, Stalin proposed that Roosevelt move into a separate building within the heavily guarded Soviet compound, where the meetings could be held in safety. Churchill had no fears; the British Embassy, which was nearby, was guarded by a regiment of Sikhs.

I was skeptical about the plot, but in any event, Roosevelt accepted Stalin's offer, and on November 28 moved to the building allocated to him by the Soviet government. It had three or four large downstairs rooms, as well as quarters for the President's Filipino servants and numerous Secret Service men. I was quartered at an American Army camp, Amirabad, outside of Teheran.

I was somewhat startled to discover that no provision had been made by the American government for taking minutes of the conference proceedings. Finally, four soldiers from the American Army camp with stenographic skills were assigned to us. They were not present at the sessions—I took the notes—but took dictation from me.

No one was in charge of organizing meetings, setting up schedules, or handling any of the numerous technical preparations for the conference. Moreover, Roosevelt had no position papers on questions that would be discussed. It was my first experience with Roosevelt's informal method of operation. He did not like any rules or regulations to bind him. He preferred to act by improvisation rather than by plan.

The delegation was small. Because Teheran was devoted primarily to military affairs, there was no need as far as President Roosevelt was concerned for the Secretary of State or any high official from the department to attend. Ambassador Harriman from Moscow and I were the only State Department representatives present. I was strictly an interpreter and note-taker; I had little time for anything else. We did have a big military staff, headed by Admiral William D. Leahy, the President's Chief of Staff, and General George C. Marshall, the Army Chief of Staff, who was widely expected to command the forces invading France. The Soviet delegation was even smaller than ours. The British were also heavy on the military side, but had brought Foreign Secretary Anthony Eden.

I was understandably nervous at the prospect of interpreting for the President at such important diplomatic negotiations. The Moscow Conference had been good practice, but this meeting was at the highest level. In the few minutes I had with President Roosevelt before his first meeting with Stalin, I outlined certain considerations regarding interpreting. The first and most important was to ask if he would try to remember to break up his comments into short periods of time. I pointed out that if he talked very long, his Russian listeners, not understanding what was said, would inevitably lose interest. On the other hand, short periods of two or three minutes of conversation would hold their attention and make my job infinitely easier. Roosevelt understood, and I must say he was an excellent speaker to interpret for, breaking up his statements into short lengths and in a variety of ways showing consideration for my travails. Churchill was much too carried away by his own eloquence to pay much attention to his pleasant and excellent interpreter, short, baldish Major Arthur H. Birse. There were occasions when Churchill would speak for five, six, or seven minutes, while poor Major Birse dashed his pencil desperately over the paper, trying to capture enough words to convey the eloquence into Russian.

In general, the same system of interpreting was followed on all sides. President Roosevelt would speak in English, I would take notes and then interpret into Russian. Then the President would resume. Stalin and Churchill followed the same practice. The underlying reason for this system was the belief that the speaker's own interpreter would have a better understanding of what his man said than would the translator for the leader who was listening. If the listener's interpreter had done the translating, he might have been accused of distorting statements. Furthermore, no matter how well an interpreter knows a foreign language, slang expressions might be used by the other side that would be difficult to render into proper meanings.

While I had met Roosevelt at large diplomatic receptions in Washington, my contact had been limited to a brief handshake and an exchange of a few words. Teheran was the first opportunity I had of observing him at close hand. Except for one minor incident, he seemed to be in excellent health, never showing any signs of fatigue, and holding his magnificent leonine head high. He clearly was the dominating figure at the conference. I found him pleasant and considerate and his personal touch made our association agreeable.

Obviously, I was not needed when Roosevelt and Churchill met privately, and I was not present for their discussions. Since Roosevelt did not like to keep records, there was almost no American account of these conversations. Churchill painstakingly made a complete record of his recollection of talks and reported them at length in his books on the war.

I was present at every meeting that Roosevelt had with Stalin at Teheran, as well as at their subsequent meetings at Yalta, and kept a record of their exchanges for the White House and State Department. The American-British Combined Chiefs of Staff also kept notes of the proceedings when military subjects were discussed. Their notes are somewhat more extensive regarding certain military questions and omit certain other exchanges. I took notes alone, whereas the military chiefs had several note-takers, but even so they missed a number of relatively important questions. Like ours, the Soviet record was made and kept by the interpreter. The principal interpreter was Pavlov, a personal secretary to Stalin. Occasionally, V. M. Berezhkov took Pavlov's place. The published Russian record of the conference is considerably less complete than the American. Apparently, the Soviets deleted quotations that did not fit the Soviet line.

The absence of records is dangerous. Joint records and joint minutes of meetings would have simplified the problem, since what was decided or said could be put down at once as understood by both sides. In most of the wartime conferences, there were no joint minutes. Each side kept its own. This oversight was quite harmless when Roosevelt and Churchill were dealing with each other. The Soviets, however, were literal-minded and painstaking in drafting the actual text of any agreement. As we subsequently discovered, they went quite far in interpreting a generalized statement or even absence of a statement as implying a tacit agreement. Therefore, a clear record of what was or was not said was important in conducting business with the Soviet Union.

My job at Teheran was the hardest sustained period of work I ever did. After interpreting all afternoon, I dictated as many of my notes to an Army stenographer as I had time for before dinner. I translated and took notes at dinner and any evening session. I would then return to the little room off the big conference room, which had been assigned to us as an office, to dictate and correct notes until three or four o'clock in the morning, when I would take a car and go back to the Army camp, catch a few hours' sleep, and be back after breakfast at 8:30 to continue the work. This went on for four days.*

As busy as I was keeping the record, the four days of the conference provided me with an opportunity to size up the three leaders—to understand their views on important problems, to feel the force of their personalities, to watch the interplay of one on the other. Here I was, a self-described "realist" who had disagreed with the White House on Soviet policy, with the chance to see at first hand how Roosevelt, Stalin, and Churchill dealt with each other.

Despite the importance of its major purpose—to decide on the military action that would deal the final blow to Hitler—the conference was quite informal and somewhat disorganized. There were private meetings between two leaders at which the conversation ranged over the whole world. There were luncheons and dinners which on the surface seemed like victory banquets but whose laughter was undercut by sarcastic references to differences and distrust. There were

---

* Toward the close of the conference, President Roosevelt sent me a note of praise, saying "You have translated my words and my intent with such ease that I have the feeling Marshal Stalin has thoroughly understood my meaning."

plenary sessions, too, but these were formal in name only. There was no formal agenda, apparently at Roosevelt's insistence. My memory of the Teheran Conference nearly three decades after it was held is primarily impressionistic, even when refreshed by a study of the record.

It was three o'clock on November 28, a beautiful Iranian Sunday afternoon, gold and blue, mild and sunny, when Stalin, wearing a simple khaki tunic (he was a Marshal of the Soviet Union) with the star of the Order of Lenin on his chest, walked from the Soviet compound to the American villa to meet with the President. A young American army officer went out to meet Stalin and escorted him into the room to the President. When the door shut, Hopkins, Harriman, and others standing outside became a little excited. They noticed that the escorting officer had remained inside and thought he was trying to stay in the room for the meeting. I do not think the officer had any such idea; he just did not know what was expected of him. When I told him there was no longer any need for him to stay, he departed.

As Roosevelt and Stalin shook hands, the President, who was wearing a blue business suit and was seated in a wheelchair, said, "I am glad to see you. I have tried for a long time to bring this about." Stalin, after an appropriate expression of pleasure at meeting the President, said that the delay had been entirely due to his preoccupation with military matters.

This being primarily a get-to-know-you meeting, the conversation jumped quickly from subject to subject—the military situation on the Russian front (not too good, Stalin said), China (Stalin spoke rather disparagingly of Chiang Kai-shek), and Syria, which at that time was the scene of clashes involving the de Gaulle provisional government (Roosevelt blamed de Gaulle for the crisis).

Stalin also criticized de Gaulle, saying the General was unrealistic because he represented the soul of a symbolic France, whereas the real, physical France was engaged under Pétain in helping the common enemy, Germany. De Gaulle acted, Stalin said, as though he were the head of a great state, whereas in fact he commanded little power.

It was not easy then and is no easier now to assess accurately the reasons for Stalin's anti-de Gaulle attitude. In part, I believe it was simply the reaction of one who felt that any country that collapsed as quickly as France did was not deserving of respect or consideration. Given my experience in Soviet affairs, I could not help feeling suspicious, as I listened to Stalin, that he was also thinking a little bit along other lines. He foresaw in the revival of a strong and healthy France an obstacle to Soviet ambitions in Europe.

In general, the President agreed with Stalin's views about France and said that in his opinion no Frenchman over forty, and particularly none who had taken part in the Pétain government, should be allowed to return to governmental positions. The President said that Prime Minister Churchill believed that France should be quickly restored to the status of a strong nation. He did not share this view, because he felt many years of honest labor would be required before France could be re-established as a significant power in the world.

The President went on to say that he did not propose that the Allies shed blood to restore Indochina to the French, because after one hundred years of colonialism the inhabitants were worse off than they had been before. He said that Chiang Kai-shek had told him that China had no designs on Indochina, that the people of Indochina were not yet ready for independence but that it should be granted without qualification at the end of the war with Japan. Roosevelt said that he had discussed with Chiang at Cairo the possibility of a trusteeship for Indochina to prepare the people for independence in a definite period of time, perhaps twenty to thirty years.

Roosevelt's comments on Indochina reflected two deeply held views which I heard him express many times in the next few years. One was his strong dislike of colonialism. He was on record in many instances, often to the irritation of the British, as opposing colonial rule. The second was his almost passionate insistence on the virtues of trusteeship. This was a solution that he often advanced for colonies not ready for independence.

Stalin was cagey on Indochina. While he agreed in general that France should be punished for collaboration with Germany, he did not go as far as Roosevelt in saying that Indochina should be taken away from France. In fact, Stalin's aim at Teheran seemed to be single-minded—confirmation that the two Western Allies would go through with their decision, made in Quebec the previous summer, to invade France in the spring of 1944.

The President then referred to India, and said he had decided that it would be better not to discuss the question of that country's independence with Churchill, since the latter had no solution and merely proposed to defer it until the end of the war. In passing reference, the President said he would like to discuss India someday with Marshal Stalin, but he felt that the best solution would be reform from the "bottom," somewhat on the Soviet line.

This reference to the Soviet method as coming from the "bottom" was a striking example of Roosevelt's ignorance about the Soviet Union. He undoubtedly viewed the Bolshevik coup d'état as a genuine revolution. He did not realize that the Bolsheviks were a minority who seized power during a period of anarchy. The Revolution came after the seizure of power, not before, and was based on the ideology of the minority Bolsheviks and not on the demands of the majority of the Russian people.

Stalin said he thought the India question was a complicated one, with different levels of culture and the absence of relations between castes. He noted that reform from the bottom would mean revolution.

With the first formal meeting of the three leaders due to begin, the conversation ended.*

The first formal plenary session of the Teheran Conference convened in the conference room at the Soviet Embassy at 4 P.M. The setting was rather heavy for the warm climate. The room, which was fairly big, was furnished with large chairs and a round table with a green baize cover. There were curtains on the windows and tapestries on the walls. Four persons from each country sat at the table. Harriman sat at Roosevelt's right, I at Roosevelt's left, and Hopkins next to me. With Stalin were Voroshilov, Molotov, and Pavlov. Churchill brought Eden, Lord Ismay, Deputy Secretary to the War Cabinet, and Major Birse as interpreter. Soviet secret policemen guarded the room. (For the most part, the United States and British Secret Service men kept out of the conference room.)

Before the proceedings, Churchill and Stalin agreed that Roosevelt, the only head of state, would preside at the first formal session. As the

---

* Two accounts of this first meeting assert that I was not present. In 1968, in a book titled *Teheran*, the secondary Soviet interpreter, Berezhkov, said that he was the only interpreter present, stating that Roosevelt had decided to meet Stalin without me there. There is no question that I was present; the American records show it, so do those of the White House log, and I well remember the first words Roosevelt used. I wrote them down and they appear in the official American record. Curiously, Berezhkov had Roosevelt using the same words. I cannot explain what motivated Berezhkov to write his incorrect account, but it may be that he was drawing on the book *As He Saw It*, by Elliott Roosevelt, in which Elliott quotes his father to the effect that he had decided, in order to show confidence in Stalin, to have the first meeting without his own interpreter. It is conceivable that the President, who sometimes liked to embroider the picture, wished to demonstrate how far he was willing to go to show his confidence in Stalin and actually did tell the story to his son, who did not arrive at Teheran until the day after the first Roosevelt-Stalin meeting. As for Berezhkov, his purpose in writing the erroneous version must have been to increase his stature somewhat. Actually, Berezhkov was not the Russian interpreter at the first meeting; Pavlov was.

proceedings opened, everything was so relaxed it did not seem possible that the three most powerful men in the world were about to make decisions involving the lives and fortunes of millions of people. There was no expression of the strain so frequently attributed to great occasions. Roosevelt's first words were in a light vein. As the youngest of the three, he welcomed his elders. Churchill was the most eloquent, saying, "In our hands we have the future of mankind." As host, Stalin welcomed his guests, then added, "Now let us get down to business." Roosevelt reviewed American efforts in the Pacific, then turned to the central question—the date for the invasion of northern France, known by its code name of Overlord. He said that Overlord should not be delayed by secondary questions.

Stalin, temporarily withholding his comments on Overlord, "welcomed the successes" of the Anglo-American forces in the Pacific and expressed regret that the Soviet Union was too deeply engaged in Europe to join in the war against Japan. He said it would be helpful if Turkey would enter the war.

Churchill not only masked his feelings that Overlord should be delayed, he also said that Britain and France were determined to land one million men on the continent of Europe in May, June, and July of 1944. Stalin suggested an invasion of southern France some two months before Overlord to divert German troops from northern France and guarantee the success of the cross-Channel operation. Picking up the idea, Roosevelt proposed that the military staffs work out, the next day, a plan for invading southern France.

Churchill's real feelings then began to emerge. He said that he personally favored some flexibility in the exact date of Overlord, and proposed that the staffs examine the various possibilities in the morning. Stalin, for the first time a little grumpy, complained that he had not expected to discuss technical military questions and had no military staff, but Marshal Voroshilov would do his best. On that note, the first plenary session ended.

As I rushed off to dictate my notes to a stenographer, I reflected on Stalin's fluency and lack of hesitation in choosing his words. There was a kind of texture to his Russian that might be called an accent. His Georgian accent was not particularly noticeable to my ear, although I was subsequently told that some cultured Russians found it irritating. Stalin also seemed to me to be considerate of his interpreter and to be meticulous in observing the length of time that he spoke. He spoke quietly, never raised his voice, and frequently used expressions designed to indicate a certain humbleness of spirit.

When I returned to Washington, Boris Nicolaevsky, an old revolutionary who had seen Stalin quite often, asked me whether Stalin had ever smiled with the foreigners. When I told him, "Yes indeed," he said this was an innovation, that with Russians he never smiled and was rough and abusive in his language. In Teheran, Stalin used phrases like "in my opinion," "I could be wrong, but I think," and "I believe" with no hint of the arbitrary dictator. I noticed him break from this mold only once, when I approached him from behind with a request from Roosevelt. I had interfered with his study of the Russian text of the final communiqué, and he was tired. Without turning, he snapped over his shoulder, "For God's sake, allow us to finish this work." Then he turned and saw that the interruption came not from a Russian but from an emissary of the President of the United States. This was the only time I ever saw Stalin embarrassed. He need not have been, because I did not convey his remark to the President.

That evening, President Roosevelt was host at a steak and baked-potato dinner prepared by his Filipino mess boys. Roosevelt mixed the pre-dinner cocktails himself, a ceremony he enjoyed. Roosevelt was proud of his drinks, which were unlike anything I have ever tasted. He put a large quantity of vermouth, both sweet and dry, into a pitcher of ice, added a smaller amount of gin, stirred the concoction rapidly, and poured it out. Stalin accepted the glass and drank but made no comment until Roosevelt asked him how he liked it. "Well, all right, but it is cold on the stomach," the dictator said.

At the dinner table, the conversation started out on France but soon switched to Germany. Stalin, it seemed to me, was pursuing a double game. He seemed to favor dismemberment and the harshest possible treatment to prevent the recrudescence of German militarism. I gained the impression, although I made no note of it, that he was deliberately overstating the case to see how far the Allies were prepared to go. As subsequent events proved, this was indeed what he was doing. During the conversation, the President brought up the question of access to the Baltic Sea, but through a mistake in translation Stalin thought the President was referring to the Baltic states.* Stalin said that if he understood the question, he was in favor of assuring free navigation to and from the Baltic Sea.

Roosevelt was about to say something else when suddenly, in the flick of an eye, he turned green and great drops of sweat began to bead off his face; he put a shaky hand to his forehead. We were all

---

* According to my notes, the error was due to the Soviet translator, but it must have been my error, since I was translating for Roosevelt.

caught by surprise. The President had made no complaint, and none of us had detected any sign of discomfort. Hopkins had the President wheeled to his room, where the White House doctor, Rear Admiral Ross T. McIntire, made a quick examination. Hopkins came back and, to the relief of everybody, reported nothing more than a mild attack of indigestion. The President then retired for the evening without returning to the dining room. The next morning, Hopkins told me that he had been quite concerned about Roosevelt—as had I—until the doctor diagnosed the attack as indigestion.

After Roosevelt had retired, Churchill raised the question of Poland, illustrating with three matches what he hoped would happen to that country's borders. He moved all three matches from east to west and said that is what should be done—meaning that much of a new Poland should be carved out of Germany and that the Soviet Union should retain that territory seized on the basis of the Nazi-Soviet pact.

Stalin then questioned the unconditional-surrender principle which the President had so vigorously espoused at Casablanca. The Marshal argued that unconditional surrender merely served to unite the German people, whereas specific terms, no matter how harsh, would tell the Germans exactly what they would have to accept to end the war and would hasten the day of capitulation.*

The next day, November 29, Roosevelt seemed fully recovered from the attack of indigestion. The President was as alert as ever. Roosevelt and Stalin met privately again, primarily to discuss military operations. The conversation soon turned to Roosevelt's plan for a general world organization, rather than a specifically European one. The President outlined a setup of three parts. One body, composed of all nations, would make non-binding recommendations. The second body would be an executive committee, which could suggest ways for settling disputes. The third body, made up of the four big powers, would have power to enforce decisions. Stalin doubted if small nations would like the third body, and suggested the creation of a European and a Far Eastern committee, or a European and a worldwide organization.

Roosevelt said that he saw two methods of dealing with possible threats to the peace. If the threat arose from a revolution or develop-

---

* This conversation was the subject of a misunderstanding between the British and ourselves. The British maintained that the President had been present, whereas my notes, taken at the time and transcribed shortly thereafter, made it plain that the President had retired.

144

ments in a small country, it might be possible to apply the quarantine method, closing the frontiers and imposing embargoes. If the threat was more serious, the four powers, acting as policemen, could send an ultimatum to the nation in question and, if it were refused, would be empowered to take military action. It is interesting to note that the President referred to the possibility of a disturbance or a threat to the integrity of a nation "arising out of a revolution or of developments in a small country." This bit of prescience by Roosevelt forecast many of the problems that the United States has had to deal with in the post-war period as a result of Communist actions. Stalin did not question Roosevelt's idea on this point.

Although Stalin was always cautious about committing himself to any particular type of organization, he never showed any antagonism to the general idea of a world body. It was quite obvious that Stalin felt it would be much more dangerous to be outside any world organization than to be in it, provided the Soviet Union could block actions it did not like and could not be forced to take any action against its will.

As we went into the second plenary meeting, the conference was approaching a crisis; there was a real question whether it was to be a success. At a meeting of military chiefs a few hours earlier, the British, at first hesitant, were raising additional objections to fixing the date for Overlord. Considering the momentous nature of the question, the debate over whether to go ahead with Overlord in the spring of 1944, as the Soviets and Americans favored, or possibly to postpone the invasion for the sake of operations in the Mediterranean, as the British proposed, was rather tame.

Stalin pressed for a decision to launch Overlord in May, saying, "I don't care if it is the 1st, 15th, or 20th, but a definite date is important." While Overlord was of passionate interest to the Soviets, Stalin's words came out in an almost matter-of-fact tone. It was a typical performance for him. Stalin would occasionally read from a prepared document, but most of the time he spoke extemporaneously, doodling wolf heads on a pad with a red pencil, and pausing considerably so that the interpreter could translate. He never showed any agitation and rarely gestured. Seldom consulting his only advisers, Molotov and Voroshilov, Stalin sat quietly, cigarette in hand, concentrating on the discussion.

Churchill, who often paused to relight his cigar, said that he did not feel that the points of view were as far apart as they seemed. He said the British government was anxious to begin Overlord as soon as pos-

sible but did not want to neglect the great possibilities in the Mediterranean merely for the sake of avoiding a delay of a month or two. As
he moved into his argument, I noticed that Churchill had a visual
approach to speaking. He would start a sentence and then repeat it,
sometimes two or three times, before the picture would come to his
mind. Then he would take off on his grand oratory. Some of these
flourishes were as good as anything in his public speeches.

When Churchill completed his argument, Stalin leaned forward and
said he wanted to ask an indiscreet question: "Do the British really
believe in Overlord, or are you only saying so to reassure the Russians?" Churchill glowered, chomped on his cigar, and replied that if
the conditions that had been outlined at the Moscow Foreign Ministers' meeting were met, "it would be the duty of the British government to hurl every scrap of strength across the Channel." He did not
elaborate on this relatively ambiguous remark but suggested that the
British and American staffs meet the next morning to work out a combined point of view to be submitted to the conference. Churchill was
irked, to put it mildly, by Stalin's pointed question.

At dinner that night, although he was the friendly host, Stalin overlooked no opportunity to needle Churchill, implying that he nursed a
secret affection for Germany and desired a soft peace. Instead of getting honestly indignant or passing the teasing off as a joke, Churchill
adopted a plaintive tone that conveyed a sense of guilt. The performance was certainly not one of Churchill's best.

I did not like the attitude of the President, who not only backed
Stalin but seemed to enjoy the Churchill-Stalin exchanges. Roosevelt
should have come to the defense of a close friend and ally, who was
really being put upon by Stalin. Of course it was true that Roosevelt
was arguing on the same side that Stalin was, so in effect this anti-
Churchill attitude was justified. Roosevelt never explained his attitude
in my presence, but his apparent belief that ganging up on the Russians was to be avoided at all cost was, in my mind, a basic error,
stemming from Roosevelt's lack of understanding of the Bolsheviks.
Russian leaders always expected and realized that Britain and the
United States were bound to be much closer in their thinking and in
their opinions than either could conceivably be with the Soviet
Union. In his rather transparent attempt to dissociate himself from
Churchill, the President was not fooling anybody and in all probability aroused the secret amusement of Stalin.

While the exchanges between Stalin and Churchill were acrid in substance, the record comes out rather stilted. For example, Stalin said he was glad that Churchill had never been a "liberal." The record fails to give the inflection of contempt that Stalin employed. There are limitations imposed by translation. With little time to figure out the lilt or elegance of a phrase, the interpreters lose some of the beauty of expression. Also, all three leaders were usually impressed with the danger of misunderstanding and too conscious of their enormous power to play games with language. When they forgot themselves and injected humor, the result was disastrous. To this day, there are those who believe that Stalin was serious when he suggested that some 50,000 or possibly 100,000 German military officers should be liquidated. Actually, Stalin made the remark in quasi-jocular fashion, with a sardonic smile and wave of the hand, and meant this as a gibe at Churchill. I cannot believe he had any intention of putting it into effect. Stalin, who had sent uncounted thousands of Russians to death, would have had no moral repugnance toward the execution of 50,000 Germans. But he realized that his political influence in the world and in Germany, which would still be an important country after the war, would suffer if thousands accused only of being members of the German General Staff were slaughtered.

Churchill, unfortunately, took Stalin's joke seriously and passionately declared that while war criminals should pay for their acts, he could never approve the cold-blooded execution of simple soldiers who had fought for their country. Roosevelt, picking up Stalin's jocular tone, said that in line with his role at the conference he would offer a compromise—49,000 German officers should be executed. There is no doubt that this was a joke, and a bad one, but many writers have taken it seriously.

The Russian dinner was like many meals that I have had in Moscow —an unbelievable quantity of food. There were cold hors d'oeuvres to start with, then hot borsch, fish, meat of various kinds, salads, compotes, fruits, vodka, and wines. Stalin drank very little vodka. He seemed to have a much greater fondness for wines, which is understandable when it is remembered that he was born in Georgia, a wine-producing area. Judging from Stalin's public appearances, he was not a heavy drinker. There have been reports that Stalin got a good deal of macabre pleasure from getting his assistants drunk, but I would seriously doubt if Stalin himself often got intoxicated.

Standing behind Stalin's chair during the dinner was an enormous Russian, about six feet four or five inches tall and built to scale, wearing the white coat of a Russian waiter. When the conference was over and I, on behalf of President Roosevelt, was handing out cigars and small favors to the staff that had helped us, I decided to give this Russian "head waiter" a carton of American cigarettes, certainly a welcome gift in wartime. As I came into the room, a carton of cigarettes in my hands, I discovered that the "head waiter" was wearing the uniform of a Major General of the Commissariat for Internal Affairs. I retired, without indicating that I was about to present a Major General of the security police with a carton of cigarettes.

After the Russian dinner—as I later heard—Hopkins went to see Churchill at the British Embassy and told him that he was fighting a losing battle in trying to delay the invasion of France. The view of the United States about the importance of an assault across the Channel had been firmly fixed for many months, Hopkins said, and the Soviet view was equally adamant. There was really little Churchill could do, Hopkins emphasized, in advising the Prime Minister to yield with grace. It is still not clear whether Hopkins acted under Roosevelt's instructions in going to Churchill. I was not privy to Roosevelt's talks with Hopkins or with Harriman. But at that time Roosevelt was relying more and more on Hopkins, virtually to the exclusion of others. At Teheran, Hopkins's influence was paramount.

Whether Hopkins's visit or something else did the trick is not known, but apparently Churchill made his decision that night, because the next morning, November 30, the British announceed their agreement, and the Combined Chiefs of the two countries recommended that Overlord be launched the following May, in conjunction with a supporting operation against southern France. At a luncheon at Roosevelt's quarters, the President announced that he and Churchill had approved the invasion plan, and Stalin, expressing his satisfaction, promised that the Red Army would open an offensive at the same time.

One of the reasons Stalin doubted Western intentions regarding Overlord was that no Supreme Commander had been appointed. Told at the second plenary session that the choice had not been made, Stalin growled, "Then nothing will come out of these operations." In a revealing commentary on his own one-man rule, Stalin referred to the fact that the Soviet Union had tried the committee system and had found that it did not work. In the last analysis, he said, one man must be responsible and one man make decisions. It was obvious that Stalin was worried that the British might still find a way to postpone the invasion.

As far as I was aware, General Dwight D. Eisenhower was never mentioned as possible commander in chief during the Teheran Conference, although General Marshall was. If my recollection is correct, sometime during the conference Stalin personally congratulated General Marshall, who was becoming a legendary figure even then, on his forthcoming command of Overlord. Marshall, who had his heart set on the appointment, told Stalin that the decision had not been made. Less than a week after the conference, Roosevelt informed Stalin of Eisenhower's selection.

With the Overlord dispute settled, Churchill attempted to draw Stalin out on the Far East, but the Russian was reluctant. The Soviets were understandably anxious to avoid giving the Japanese any pretext whatsoever for entering into military operations against them while they were so hard pressed by the Germans.

In the evening, there was a gala dinner at the British Legation. It was Churchill's sixty-ninth birthday and probably represented the high-water mark of Anglo-American-Soviet collaboration during the war. The toasts were warm and frequent. The table was set with British elegance. The crystal and silver sparkled in the candlelight. The amount of vodka and other alcohol consumed was large, although the three principals drank relatively little. Even in such a warm environment, Stalin could not resist a jab at Churchill; he referred to both the President and the Prime Minister as "my fighting friends," but added, "if it is possible for me to consider Mr. Churchill my friend."

At one point, the President toasted Sir Alan Brooke, the British Chief of Staff. Stalin said he wanted to say a few words before joining the toast. While acknowledging the General's qualities, he said, with a slight smile, he regretted that Sir Alan had adopted a distrustful attitude toward the Russians. He drank to the General's health in the hope that Sir Alan "would come to know us better and find we are not so bad after all."

There was some consternation among the British because Sir Alan was known to be an Irishman with a quick temper, and it was feared that he might destroy the friendly atmosphere with an angry reply to Stalin's gratuitous insult. General Brooke waited for some time, presumably to let his temper cool, then rose to his feet and talked about British cover plans of using dummy tanks and planes to deceive the Germans. Turning to Stalin, Sir Alan said that possibly he had misjudged the Russians because of what he termed the excellent "Soviet cover plan" in the early part of the war in associating herself with Germany. "That is possible," Stalin dryly interjected, and we all laughed, partly in relief that the dictator was taking the gibe in good humor. Sir Alan, in good spirits again, said his real desire was to establish closer collaboration with the Russians. "That is possible," Stalin said, "even probable."*

In offering another toast, Stalin said that ultimate victory was certain only because of American industrial production, particularly of engines. Neither Russia nor Britain could produce so many engines, he said. This was a rare tribute, one that Russian leaders never made publicly and avoided repeating privately when the coalition fell apart after the war.

During the dinner, there was a good deal of discussion of the political complexions of various countries, and Churchill set the tone by stating that he felt that the general complexion of Britain was becoming "a trifle pinker." Stalin warmly welcomed this, and said, "This is a sign of good health." Not to be outdone, Churchill commented that he agreed, provided the process was not carried so far as to induce indigestion.

Roosevelt ended the evening with a toast in which he compared the political coloration to a rainbow: "It has many varying colors, each different, but blending into one glorious whole. Thus with our nations. We have differing customs and philosophies and ways of life. Each of us works out our scheme of things according to the desires and ideas of our peoples. But we have proved here at Teheran that the varying ideals of our nations can come together in a harmonious whole, moving unitedly for the common good of ourselves and of the world. So as we leave this historic gathering, we can see in the sky, for the first time, that traditional symbol of hope, the rainbow." It is tragic to think that these noble, eloquent words were to be proved so wrong in so few years. As naïve as they sound now, the words did express his hope for the future, and even I, with all my doubts, shared them.

The next day, December 1, at a lunch at Roosevelt's quarters, Churchill urged Stalin to be lenient with Finland, which had joined Germany in the war on Russia. Stalin replied that he felt that the Finns had been just as cruel and as merciless toward the Russian population as any of the German units, but he nevertheless felt that any country which fought with such courage for its independence deserved consideration. This was perhaps the real reason why the Soviets did not occupy Finland as they did the countries in Eastern

* The full exchange is omitted from the official record.

Europe. They realized that it would not be an easy task. In any event, Stalin agreed to fairly lenient peace terms, and Britain and the United States can certainly take some credit.

That afternoon, before the final formal meeting of the conference, Roosevelt dismayed me again. At a private meeting with Stalin, he told the Kremlin leader that he wished to discuss briefly and frankly a matter relating to internal American politics. Roosevelt noted that a presidential election was coming up in 1944, and while he personally did not wish to run again, he might have to if the war was still in progress. He went on to say that there were some six to seven million Americans of Polish extraction, and he did not wish to lose their votes. Therefore, while he personally agreed with Stalin's general view that Poland's frontiers should be moved to the west, he hoped that Stalin would understand why the President could not take part at Teheran or in any meeting next winter in any such arrangements. This was the first that I, or any other American, as far as I know, had heard of Roosevelt's intention to run for a fourth term. Harriman was the only other American present; Molotov and Pavlov were with Stalin.

Stalin replied that now that the President had explained the problem, he understood. I doubt whether he did understand the intricacies of American politics, but he must have been relieved to avoid a big argument with Roosevelt over Poland.

I have often wondered why Roosevelt decided to be so frank with Stalin about his problems with Polish voters in the United States. He might have been trying to provide himself with a reason for opposing some part of a Polish settlement. Or he might have been expressing his true feelings at that time. I lean toward the latter explanation.

At this meeting, Roosevelt and Stalin also discussed the Baltic states. The President pointed out that because there were Balts in the United States, their independence was a moral issue for Americans, and he felt that public opinion would demand some expression of the wishes of the Baltic peoples before action was taken. At one point, Roosevelt jokingly remarked that when the Soviet troops reoccupied the Baltic states, he did not intend to go to war with the Soviet Union.

During this meeting, Stalin said that after thinking it over, he had come to agree with the President that the new organization of nations should be worldwide and not regional.

At the final plenary session that evening, Roosevelt, in accordance with his statement to Stalin, did not take part in the discussion regarding Poland. As Churchill and Stalin talked over the problem, I noticed that the British and the Russians were working on a map of Poland torn from *The Times* of London. Since we had brought a collection of books with various maps touching on the Polish issue, I asked the President whether he would have any objection to my lending a copy to Stalin and Churchill to make their discussion easier. The President gave me permission, and I took a book over to Stalin, who looked at one map and asked me on what data these lines had been drawn. The map showed the ethnic divisions of eastern Poland. I informed the Marshal that, as far as I knew, the only data available came from Polish sources. Stalin grunted and took his ever present red pencil and somewhat contemptuously marked the map to show what would be returned to the Poles and what would be kept for the Soviet Union.

During their discussion, Stalin and Churchill virtually agreed on the future borders of Poland. The frontiers included the Curzon Line in the east, with modifications as Stalin had indicated, and the Oder-Neisse Line in the west. In other words, the new Poland would give up Poland's eastern areas to Russia in return for parts of eastern Germany. This understanding, which was entirely oral, led to further confusion later on because there were two rivers Neisse, a western and an eastern, and there was no mention of which one they were talking about. The division that Churchill and Stalin agreed to is the one that still exists.

It was a great mistake for Roosevelt to tell Stalin in the private conference of the last day that for electoral reasons he could not take any position on Polish affairs, to say nothing of the error in implying to Stalin, as he did, that the United States would do little for the Baltic countries. By imposing on himself an unnecessary silence during the discussion of Polish matters the last day, Roosevelt seemed to give his implied, although unstated, acquiescence to the Churchill-Stalin agreement on Polish frontiers. It is, of course, true that the question of the Polish government, which was subsequently to be a bitter source of controversy at Yalta, did not arise at Teheran.

The next day, December 2, I was thinking of Roosevelt's refusal to face up to the Polish issue as Admiral Leahy, Hopkins, and I sat in a jeep, waiting to say good-bye to the President as he left Camp Amirabad. During some desultory discussion of Soviet aims in Europe, I chimed in along pessimistic lines. Admiral Leahy, who was in the front seat, turned his head and said to Hopkins, with a sardonic smile, "Well, Harry, all I can say is, nice friends we have now." Roosevelt, however, was in an optimistic mood and took off in good spirits for the flight to Cairo for more conferences with Churchill and with President Ismet Inonu of Turkey. Harriman and I flew back to Moscow, arriving safely after fighting through a snowstorm, losing our way, and finally following the railroad tracks into the city just before night closed in on us.

There was a tendency of Ambassador Harriman and others in the American Embassy to exaggerate the basic nature of the understandings with the Soviet Union, to attribute them to the "greatness" of the three men gathered around the table. I felt that we had reached a solid military agreement but that all political questions, except for the British-Soviet accord on Poland's eastern border, were completely up in the air. There were a number of disquieting indications of how Stalin's mind was working at that time. There was a definite leaning toward the dismemberment of Germany. There was a generalized discussion about the Soviet desire for warm-water ports. There was a clear indication as to the kind of Poland that the Soviet Union wished to see emerge from the war. There were a few faint hints of Soviet demands in return for their entry into the Asian war. There was also tentative acceptance of a world organization. Viewed in retrospect, there were many forerunners of Yalta at Teheran. These ideas were so inchoate and informal that they did not constitute decisions. The fact that the Yalta agreements were roughly in line with some of the Teheran discussions does not change the fact that Teheran did not decide the issues, despite interpretations that some revisionist historians try to force from the records.

In a memorandum to Ambassador Harriman shortly after our return to Moscow, my basic wariness prevailed, and I pointed out what I thought was Stalin's plan for a postwar Europe dominated by the Soviet Union:

> Germany is to be broken up and kept broken up. The states of eastern, southeastern and central Europe will not be permitted to group themselves into any federations or association. France is to be stripped of her colonies and strategic bases beyond her borders and will not be permitted to maintain any appreciable military establishment. Poland and Italy will remain approximately their present territorial size, but it is doubtful if either will be permitted to maintain any appreciable armed force. The result would be that the Soviet Union would be the only important military and political force on the continent of Europe. The rest of Europe would be reduced to military and political impotence.

There is no doubt, however, that Teheran was the most successful of the wartime Big Three conferences. The atmosphere, on the whole, was good, and I was impressed by the confidence and optimism of the three leaders—a justified confidence in view of the fact that the military decisions made at Teheran led to the defeat and surrender of Germany. A realist on Soviet policy always has his doubts, but there are times when he is hopeful.

CHAPTER TEN

Into the White House

Proof that the Teheran agreements had not opened up an era of good will between the United States and the Soviet Union was shown in a month in two incidents, one involving General William Donovan, head of the Office of Strategic Services, the other involving Tass, the Soviet press agency. Donovan, who had been in Moscow in an attempt to set up a branch office of the OSS, wanted to get to the Mediterranean in time for the Anzio landing. Since I had been ordered back to Washington, Donovan and I decided to leave together. Ambassador Harriman offered his converted bomber, but when Donovan asked for permission for the aircraft to leave, he was informed that it was for the personal use of the Ambassador and could not be used by any other official. Accordingly, the Soviets refused to provide the weather reports essential to any flight.

Donovan, a ruddy-faced, pugnacious Irishman, was undeterred. He told Harriman, "Averell, you leave this to me and I will show you how to deal with the Russians." Referring to the experience he had had in dealing with Slav Americans in Rochester, New York, where he had been a mayor, he said all that was needed was a firm hand and consistency. With me along as interpreter, Donovan and Harriman's pilot went to the military airfield where the plane was stationed. We arrived at about eleven o'clock at night and were met by a Soviet armed guard. Following Donovan's instructions, I explained that he was an American general and wished to see the officer on duty. After some fumbling around with the telephones, a frightened sentry led us to the officer of the watch, a thin-faced young captain. Donovan explained the mission. He said that he thought it was an unfriendly act not to permit an American pilot to see the weather report and that he, as an American general, must insist. The captain was much concerned about a derogation from his orders, but General Donovan's importunities wore him down and he and our pilot went into the weather room and looked at the forecast for the following couple of days.

On the way back to the Embassy, Donovan was quite condescending toward me, saying, "You people in the State Department just aren't tough enough. You have no knowledge of how to deal with the Slavs. You see the results which we achieve by direct action." I said nothing. The next morning, we were informed that the authorities had moved Harriman's airplane from the military field, where the facilities were excellent and the services good, to the civilian field in Moscow, where everything was considerably inferior. Averell and I were too polite to gloat. The issue was finally resolved in the only way it could have been, with Ambassador Harriman making a personal plea in a letter to Molotov.

On my return to Washington, I was asked my opinion why Tass had circulated a dispatch with a Cairo dateline charging that British emissaries were meeting secretly with the Nazis in the Pyrenees Mountains in Spain. We knew that there was no Tass correspondent in Cairo, and that therefore this dispatch had been concocted in Moscow. To this day, I am not sure of the purpose. It is possible that Stalin, who was always suspicious and conspiratorial himself, thought that there was something sinister behind Churchill's effort to delay fixing an exact date for the second front. Whether the Russians had heard a rumor about some meeting in Spain we did not know.

Life in Washington was considerably different for me after the Teheran Conference. No longer was I just a junior Foreign Service officer who happened to be able to speak Russian. I had more or less what you might call an 'in" at the White House, although not in any spectacular way. I was known to the President and to Hopkins, and was therefore gradually cut in on many more confidential bits of business, particularly relations with the Soviet Union. I was told by a friend with connections in the Federal Bureau of Investigation that my telephone was tapped, because, I suppose, I was privy to secrets, including the approximate date of the second front. Obviously, I told no one of the invasion date, and my wife was sufficiently disciplined not to ask any questions regarding the Teheran Conference itself. We were occasionally invited to the White House for social functions, and, more important, I was asked for advice on Soviet affairs.

Shortly after my return to work in Washington, Moscow sent the State Department a note questioning the doctrine of unconditional surrender, which Roosevelt and Churchill had agreed to at their meeting in Casablanca in early 1943. The Kremlin repeated arguments they had raised at Teheran that unconditional surrender afforded the Nazi propagandists an opportunity to play on the fear of the unknown and thereby stiffen the German willingness to fight. Impressed by the argument, Hull asked what I thought. I replied that Moscow indeed had a good point. At Hull's suggestion, I drafted a memorandum, which he signed and sent to Roosevelt. Supporting the Soviet suggestion, the memo said:

> As I understand it, the Soviet government believes that some definition, however general and severe, of the conditions of surrender which will be imposed on the enemy countries would deprive the enemy of this propaganda advantage and consequently weaken the morale of their armed forces and people. In view of the Soviet interest in this matter, do you approve of discussions with the Soviet and British governments to explore the desirability of some public definition for propaganda exploitation of the terms of unconditional surrender to be imposed on the respective enemy countries?

Roosevelt replied with a flat rejection. He pointed out that he had recently emphasized in a speech that "we have no thought of destroying the German people." He cited, as the "best definition" of unconditional surrender, Lee's surrender to Grant at Appomattox at the end of the American Civil War, although Grant had permitted Southern officers to retain their horses and side arms. In actual historical fact, Grant did not demand "unconditional surrender" at Appomattox. He did so at Fort Donelson in 1862, warning General S. B. Buckner that he was moving on his breastworks at dawn: "My terms are unconditional surrender." President Roosevelt had got a little mixed up on his Civil War history. In any event, we were powerless to change what in my opinion was one of the great errors of the war. Hostilities might have ceased sooner and thousands of lives might have been saved if Roosevelt had not insisted on unconditional surrender.

The folly of this policy was soon evident, as Germany reeled from the successful invasion of France. Opposition to Hitler among German army officers grew to desperate proportions. The July 20, 1944, plot failed, but had these officers been able to hold out hope for easier terms—as a pullback from strict adherence to unconditional surrender would have offered—the possibility of their success would have been greatly enhanced and the war perhaps shortened by a considerable period of time. In addition, the fact that there was no government at all when the Allies went into Germany made the division of the country almost inevitable. There probably would have been a government to deal with if Berlin could have negotiated for some sort of terms. Of course, Stalin might have forced a division of Germany anyway, but the existence of one government for the entire country would have made his task more difficult. It is just possible that Germany might not be divided today.

Responsibility for this unconditional-surrender doctrine rests almost exclusively on President Roosevelt. He announced it publicly at the Casablanca Conference in 1943, ostensibly because there was nothing that he and Churchill had to tell the press of any particular interest. According to Churchill, he was surprised by the announcement. True, he made no objection then, but later there was an exchange of notes with London in which the British government questioned the validity of the doctrine. At that time, there was a compelling historical reason for unconditional surrender. A liberal German government had been saddled with the responsibility for the defeat in World War I. The Nazis had convinced the German people that the army had not been defeated but had been betrayed by Socialists and Jews. Roosevelt stressed another reason—that unconditional surrender was needed to hold the Allied coalition together. With vast differences in national interests of the three Allies, and, above all, with the gulf in ideology between the Soviet Union and the West, there was a continuing possibility that one side would be tempted to make a special deal behind the back of the other. If all three members of the coalition were committed to the principle of unconditional surrender, the chance of a separate peace would be reduced, if not eliminated. That, I believe, is what Roosevelt thought, although I never heard him talk on the subject. If that was Roosevelt's purpose, he must have been worried about Stalin's making another deal with Germany, because to my knowledge the idea was never considered by London or Washington.

The American-British invasion of Normandy in June improved relations with the Soviet Union considerably. Stalin issued a statement unsparing in its praise, and sent Roosevelt a warm telegram; the Soviet press, almost always reluctant to give credit to the United States or Britain, devoted considerable space to the progress of the Allied armies.

With the end of the war now only a question of time, Roosevelt was determined to press ahead with the establishment of a world organization. Having learned from his experience as president of the depth of isolationist sentiment in the United States, he had no illusions about the postwar period. He wanted action while public opinion against another war was at fever pitch.

The Dumbarton Oaks conferences, which began on August 22, 1944, were instrumental in laying the groundwork for the charter of the United Nations that was adopted in San Francisco in 1945. I was attached to the delegation as an adviser on Soviet affairs, but I did not participate in all of the determinations, negotiations, and conversations. I was generally familiar with what went on, but I spent no more than a half day several times a week at Dumbarton Oaks. I attended the formal opening and the formal closing and was frequently present at key discussions with the Soviet delegation.

Dumbarton Oaks settled all but two issues regarding the organization of the United Nations—the voting procedure in the Security Council and the Soviet pressure for the admission of all sixteen of the Soviet republics to the General Assembly. It took the conference at Yalta, plus further negotiations with Moscow, before these issues were resolved.

The reason Security Council voting was so important was that the Soviets were absolutely determined to safeguard their sovereignty, to prevent any mechanism of an international or other character from ever placing the Soviet Union in a position of being overridden on its policies and desires by the weight of the opinion of other countries. Thus the Soviets demanded not only a veto over Security Council proposals on enforcement actions regarding threats to peace but also the power to block even discussions of such issues and procedural questions. There was also a good deal of sentiment in the United States against joining an organization which, under certain circumstances, would be able to force its will on us. In this sense, we were as much in favor of the veto as the Russians, although we did not want to let it be used to stifle debate or to balk procedural matters.

On the other major point of disagreement, it was at Dumbarton Oaks that the Soviet Union suddenly proposed, to our surprise, that the sixteen individual republics of the Soviet Union should be admitted as independent nations. Why the Kremlin put this forward was not entirely clear, except that it would obviously increase the number of votes on the Soviet side in the General Assembly. The Soviets knew they would be virtually alone in the United Nations, that their ideological system provided little common ground with other countries. But the proposal to admit Soviet republics which were independent in name only seemed to all the non-Russians at Dumbarton Oaks to be a derisive flaunting of the idea of the United Nations. The

British were just as opposed to the Soviet plan at that time, although they subsequently altered their views. President Roosevelt went so far as to tell members of Congress that if the Russians persisted in this proposal, he would counter with a demand that the forty-eight states of the United States be members.

While these two issues remained unresolved, Dumbarton Oaks did iron away the secondary problems regarding the establishment of the United Nations. Without Dumbarton Oaks, there would have been no conference in San Francisco and no United Nations. Moreover, the success in devising the outline of the United Nations Charter undoubtedly nourished the hope that Soviet Union cooperation in the postwar world was possible. Most of us who had doubts—I was as enthusiastic as some about the United Nations as a peace-keeping mechanism—were silent because we had no hard evidence to support our instinctive feeling that trouble lay ahead.

One expert on the Soviet Union who spoke up was former Ambassador Bullitt, who was then retired. Bullitt wrote in *Life* magazine that no workable agreements could be reached with the evil, atheistic Soviet Union. He went so far as to express the hope, which he said was shared by most of the country, that war with the Soviet Union should take place as soon as possible. The Soviets at Dumbarton Oaks were more concerned than angered by the article, and asked what influence Bullitt had and how far his sentiment represented that of the nation. I did my best to reassure the Russians on this point, but they remained troubled.

Another who expressed his doubts in mid-1944, about both the Americans and the Russians, was my friend and fellow Soviet expert, George Kennan, who was becoming increasingly depressed the deeper he thought about the postwar world. Much more an intellectual than most Foreign Service officers, George returned to the United States from England, where he had been stationed, appalled by the behavior of American soldiers—their reading of comic books, their foul language, and their obsession with sex, among other things. He wondered whether the United States was capable of being a world power. At the same time, Kennan foresaw Soviet seizure of much of Eastern Europe. I told him that while I shared his doubts about the Soviet Union, I did not think he would be so pessimistic if he had a wider perspective on the whole war (obviously, Hopkins and Roosevelt had had an influence on me), and suggested that he accept the post he was being offered as Minister-Counselor in the Moscow Embassy.

Kennan had not been number two to Harriman in Moscow long

when he wanted to put pressure on Stalin because of the dictator's attitude toward the uprising of the Polish underground army in Warsaw. The uprising against the Germans was undertaken by General Bor's army on instructions from a divided Polish government-in-exile in London. With the Red Army approaching the Vistula River, the Moscow radio also urged the Poles to revolt. Stalin, however, not only halted the Red Army (he pleaded lack of supplies) but also blocked, until Bor's army was crushed, American-British efforts to drop supplies to the beleaguered garrison by refusing to let Allied planes land in Russia. It is a good guess that Stalin did not aid the Warsaw uprising because he did not want to help General Bor's non-Communist army. Such a success by the London Pole's army would have complicated Stalin's plans for a Soviet-dominated government.

Kennan felt that this was a moment when Moscow should have been told that unless they went to the assistance of the Poles, or at least permitted the Western Allies to drop supplies, the Allies would cut off aid to the Soviet Union. Such a threat would have been highly unrealistic. I do not think that the Kremlin would have buckled under such pressure. Certainly they would not have moved their armies to break the siege of Warsaw. Perhaps they might have allowed the air-drops, but these alone would hardly have saved Bor's army. The outcome in Poland would have been the same, but the entire course of negotiations would have been changed, probably for the worse.

The strongest voice expressing worry about the Kremlin at this time was Prime Minister Churchill's. As the Soviet armies moved into Eastern Europe, Churchill became concerned about the political structure Moscow would set up with its military power. He prodded Roosevelt to agree to an early meeting with him and Stalin to discuss the political issues that peace would raise. Roosevelt resisted, asserting that he had to wait until after the election in November and his inauguration in January. There have been reports that Stalin deliberately delayed the conference to have as much of Eastern Europe in the hands of his troops as possible. This charge is not true. The record makes it plain that it was American considerations that caused the postponement of the Yalta Conference to February, 1945.

In early October, Churchill decided that he could not wait until February. The Soviets were making military moves with obvious post-war implications. Instead of keeping full pressure on the central target, Germany, Stalin was diverting troops to Bulgaria and Hungary, two secondary targets. Churchill made up his mind to go to Moscow without Roosevelt, and notified the President accordingly.

On October 4, I was sitting in my office in the Department of State when Hopkins called. In his usual no-nonsense manner, he said, "Chip, get the hell over here in an hurry." I found Hopkins sitting in his White House office, one leg draped over the arm of a chair. He handed me the telegram that Churchill had sent to the President stating that he and Foreign Secretary Eden felt it necessary to go to the Soviet Union. Hopkins then showed me the reply Roosevelt had drafted. It merely wished Churchill "good luck," saying he understood perfectly why the trip had to be made.

Hopkins asked me whether I had any thoughts on the matter. I said that I did indeed, that it was dangerous to allow Churchill to speak for us in dealing with Stalin. In effect, that was what Roosevelt was doing. Such a move could foreclose a great deal of the future peace settlements for the continent of Europe, particularly the Balkans.

Hopkins and I did not distrust Churchill, but the Prime Minister's views were different from Roosevelt's on a number of subjects. Hopkins had held up the President's reply when he happened across it in the White House Map Room, which was the center of presidential communications. Hopkins instructed me to draw up cables to Churchill and Stalin that would express our view of the situations and have them ready when he returned from a talk with the President. I found a stenographer and immediately worked out two drafts, one to Churchill and one to Stalin. The message to Stalin said:

> You, naturally, understand that in this global war there is literally no question, political or military, in which the United States is not interested. I am firmly convinced that the three of us, and only the three of us, can find the solution to the still unresolved questions. In this sense, while appreciating the Prime Minister's desire for the meeting, I prefer to regard your forthcoming talks with Churchill as preliminary to a meeting of the three of us. . . .

The wire to Churchill, like the one to Stalin, asked if Harriman could sit in on the talks as an observer. Then Roosevelt told the Prime Minister:

> While naturally Averell will not be in a position to commit the United States—I could not permit anyone to commit me in advance—he will be able to keep me fully informed. . . .

It seemed natural to ask that Harriman be permitted to observe the meeting, which was to be merely a preliminary to the next conference of all three. Throughout the war, the British and Americans had been operating as a team. There were joint plans, mixing of armed forces, a Combined Chiefs of Staff. On the Eastern front, the Soviet Union had run their military affairs completely without consultations with the Western Allies. Therefore, the question subsequently raised by revisionist historians of why the Allies did not invite a Soviet observer to the Quebec Conference and other Roosevelt-Churchill talks does not seem particularly relevant. As far as I know, the Kremlin never asked to send an observer.

While I was drafting the telegrams, Hopkins found the President shaving. Hopkins pointed out the danger we had seen in the "good luck" message. Realizing his mistake, Roosevelt became somewhat agitated and instructed Hopkins to stop the message. He was relieved when Hopkins told him that he had taken the liberty of holding it.

There was no reply from Churchill. On October 8, Stalin wired:

> Your message of October 5th somewhat puzzled me. I supposed that Mr. Churchill was going to Moscow in accordance with the agreement reached with you at Quebec. It happened, however, that this supposition of mine does not seem to correspond to reality.

It was apparent that Churchill had told Stalin that he was in a position to speak for Roosevelt, since he knew, from a recent meeting with the President in Quebec, the President's thoughts. Our wire certainly put Stalin on his guard. By not answering, Churchill indicated that he had had his own views as to how the conversations were to go and he was not pleased to have Harriman at the meeting.

Actually, Harriman did not attend all the meetings, including an important one still clouded in mystery. At that meeting, Churchill scribbled on a piece of plain paper and passed it across the table to Stalin. He had written a list of the degrees of influence that the two sets of powers, Britain and the Soviet Union (it would appear that Churchill associated the United States with Britain in this deal), would have in Eastern Europe. In Rumania, Churchill proposed 90 percent Soviet influence, 10 percent British; in Bulgaria, 75–25 in favor of the Soviet Union; in Yugoslavia and Hungary, 50–50; in Greece, 90 percent Britain, 10 percent Russia. Stalin checked the paper with a blue pencil opposite the formula for Rumania to indicate his agreement and gave it to Churchill. Later, an Englishman who had seen the paper tole me that Stalin had checked only the arrangements for Rumania. But the general belief is that Stalin accepted the whole cynical deal.

Aside from its cynicism, the arrangement was unrealistic. Even in the old days of diplomacy, it would have been difficult to express in percentages the degrees of control of two or more powers in a country. With the Soviet Union such a deal was ludicrous. Even though Communists would be limited in the number of Ministries they controlled in a coalition government, they would continually attempt to extend their influence. A non-Communist Premier with Communist Ministers would be like a woman trying to stay half pregnant.

There is no indication that this agreement had any effect on Eastern Europe. I subsequently heard that the British Foreign Office had translated this agreement into a telegram of instructions to its missions in Eastern Europe, but I was never able to verify this report, and it seems unlikely. The matter never came up at the Yalta Conference between the Americans and the Russians or the Americans and the British. I cannot say whether it ever came up again between the British and the Russians. The President, I was told, knew about the Churchill-Stalin understanding before he left for Yalta. No one at the State Department knew of it; I did not.

Roosevelt took to Yalta a memorandum from the Joint Chiefs of Staff and the Department of State strongly opposing any concept of spheres of influence as a practical means of keeping the peace. It was the American position then, and still is, that spheres of influence are inherently immoral and tend to promote greater friction between nations than they do amity. When the Soviet Union is involved, it is only necessary to remind ourselves of Lenin's dictum in defending the disastrous Treaty of Brest-Litovsk, in 1918, under which the Bolsheviks gave up much of Russia's territory. Lenin pointed out the advantage of the technical distinction between the Communist Party and the government. Lenin noted that the government had signed the treaty and would live up to it, but the Party did not sign and had no such obligation. This dictum would be a formidable obstacle to making a spheres-of-influence agreement with the Soviet Union.

In the United States there is another reason, in addition to immorality, why spheres of influence are opposed. We are a country representing almost all of the people of Europe. To have agreed to consign the small countries of Eastern Europe to the Soviet Union undoubtedly would have aroused fierce antagonisms among the ethnic groups in the United States.

A refusal to negotiate spheres of influence, in either oral or written form, does not mean that the United States does not recognize the fact that the Soviet Union exercises a considerable degree of control and influence over all the countries of Eastern Europe. This is a reality of modern life. To challenge it would require a willingness to consider going to war with the Soviet Union.

Throughout the war, there was some uncertainty about exactly what the British and the Soviets had agreed to in regard to the Balkans. I don't think there was any formal agreement, but there was the nagging fact of the percentage suggestion which Churchill had jotted down. Earlier—in 1943, I believe—Cordell Hull had objected strongly to an arrangement, which Roosevelt seemed to approve of, for military cooperation between the British and the Soviets in the Balkans. Finally, Hull reluctantly agreed that this would be quite permissible if it applied only during the war.

While arrangements for the Yalta Conference were being completed, I was named the official liaison between the Department of State and the White House with the title of Special Assistant to the Secretary of State. This appointment was due to Hopkins, who had come to realize that the President had need of continuous State Department advice. The central questions of foreign policy were becoming more political and less military as the Allied armies scored victory after victory. The State Department could not offer its expertise because it often did not know what was going on. Messages to and from Churchill and Stalin were handled by the White House Map Room. Many were not distributed to the State Department. Despite old suspicions, Hopkins knew that State could make a contribution on dealing with postwar problems. The White House would retain its decision-making powers but, through me as liaison, tap the State Department's expertise.

I do not for a minute mean to imply that Hopkins felt that Roosevelt needed the State Department's advice because he was not physically fit to make the decisions. State could help on the innumerable details of planning and working out of understandings with other countries. Moreover, Hopkins had become alarmed at Roosevelt's tendency to hold meetings of the utmost importance without keeping any official record. One of the functions that he looked to me to perform at Yalta was to keep the record.

As long as Cordell Hull was Secretary of State, there was no possibility of the establishment of the position of White House liaison. Hull was understandably jealous of his prerogatives as Secretary and of his contacts with Roosevelt, however intermittent they were. He would not have welcomed the appointment of a junior officer from the Department of State who would have been in regular contact with the President. My appointment became possible in December, 1944, when Hull, who was ill, resigned and Roosevelt named Under Secretary Edward R. Stettinius, Jr., to replace him. Stettinius was Secretary for only six months. I am not quite sure why he was appointed, but I think one of the reasons was that Roosevelt intended to use Hopkins as his chief instrument in foreign affairs. Stettinius, who knew very little history but who had shown considerable ability in handling Lend-Lease affairs, could devote his time to reorganizing the State Department. His mild personality was an asset, too, since it was unlikely that he would cause much trouble. He would not be disposed to disagree with anything Roosevelt or Hopkins wanted to do. These were qualifications that could not be overlooked, because Hopkins intended to be a power in postwar foreign policy.

Stettinius was a decent man of considerable innocence. All his impulses were correct. He was certainly no intriguer, no infighter, no politician. He had a pleasant, outgoing personality and brought a Boy Scout enthusiasm to his job, which turned out to be useful in getting the United Nations started at the San Francisco Conference. But he made some awkward slips. Just before the founding conference of the United Nations, he told the Polish Ambassador, who represented the London émigré government and was therefore opposed by the Soviet Union and barred from attending the meeting, that he looked forward to seeing him in San Francisco. The Ambassador dryly said he did not think so. Stettinius was embarrassed.

In informing me of my appointment, Stettinius gave me little guidance for the job. He simply told me to keep the department informed of what was going on in the White House and to take to the White House the views of department experts. Hopkins was my chief contact in the White House, but I saw the President often. At the Department of State, my instructions came principally from Stettinius.

In my new job, I had an office in the State Department on the same floor as the Secretary, but spent most of my time in a small office in the east wing of the White House with Hopkins. I went to the White House with some trepidation, thinking that I was going into hostile territory. I found, however, that officials there were looking for informed advice. Admiral Leahy, who was not known for his kindness toward diplomats or State Department officials, was forthcoming and receptive. We had many interesting discussions about the future of the world, particularly Europe and France. I was allowed in the White House Map Room. Telegrams dealing with military strategy were not made available to me, but I saw all the messages on diplomatic relations.

Because I was a White House aide, I was among the relatively small group who witnessed the inauguration ceremonies for Roosevelt's fourth term on January 20, 1945. As the President, his head uncovered, spoke on the south porch of the White House on that cold, sleety day, he was obviously weary. The fatigue seemed natural because he had carried the burden of a long war. I certainly did not see the mark of death on his tired face. After the simple ceremony, we went inside for drinks. I shook hands with the President, wishing him luck in his new term.

I was brought in on the President's speech-writing team when suggestions were needed on passages dealing with foreign affairs. I was successful in getting a thought in the State of the Union message of 1945, which still seems to me to be important for the American people to grasp. This was the idea that power is not always iniquitous. Americans generally feel that power politics and anything touching on power are basically immoral. I wrote a paragraph into the State of the Union message which persisted despite all of the redrafts. It said:

> In the future world the misuses of power, as implied in the term "power politics," must not be a controlling factor in international relations. That is the heart of the principles to which we have subscribed. We cannot deny that power is a factor in world policies any more than we can deny its existence as a factor in national politics. But in a democratic world, as in a democratic nation, power must be linked with responsibility, and obliged to defend and justify itself within the framework of the general good.

Soon after the inauguration, Roosevelt sent Hopkins to Europe to gather information that might be useful at Yalta. In London, he was supposed to soothe Churchill's ruffled feelings. The Prime Minister was angry because Stettinius had criticized British interference in Italian politics. Churchill had fired off a furious telegram to the President, asking what the Secretary of State thought he was doing. Churchill was also irritated by criticism in the United States over his devotion to Britain's retention of her colonies, a passion reflected in his assertion that he had not become Prime Minister "to preside over the liquidation of the British Empire."

Hopkins asked me to go with him. It was on this trip to London, Paris, Rome, Naples, and Malta that I came to admire Hopkins. We talked a great deal on the long plane rides, and I began to see that though Hopkins only faintly understood the importance of the ideological factor in Soviet thinking, he did possess hard common sense about foreign affairs. He was also objective about himself, a characteristic all too uncommon to those close to the throne.

Although he was suffering a great deal of pain from chronic colitis, Hopkins never complained. On the military transport that took us from the Azores to London, the commanding general of our air base on the Azores started a conversation with Hopkins regarding the high rate of venereal disease among his soldiers. The trouble was, the general explained, that the soldiers would wander around in the fields with the girls and not be near preventive treatment facilities. He thought of setting up near the fields a brothel disguised as a reading room. There the men could be inspected before and after their rendezvous with the Portuguese women. The general looked on this as a brilliant idea and asked Hopkins what he thought. Harry, roaring with laughter, commented that he was sure the National Council of Churches would approve.

In London, Hopkins succeeded in soothing Churchill's wounded feelings. In the meantime, I was down in the lower reaches of the Foreign Office talking with various officials, one of them Sir Alexander Cadogan, the Permanent Under Secretary for Foreign Affairs. He told me of a problem regarding the admission of the Soviet republics to the United Nations that I had not known. India had been admitted to the League of Nations on the basis of a fluke, since it had not a vestige of independence at that time. But the British government felt that public opinion in both countries would demand that India be one of the original members of the United Nations. Cadogan suggested that the only place where there might be opposition would be the Soviet Union. In such an event, Cadogan said, Britain was prepared to make a deal to admit, not all of the sixteen Soviet republics, but possibly three or four of them in return for acceptance of India. I told him that this was not our view, that the President had expressed himself strongly against multiplicity of members. "Well, you will have to carry that fight," Cadogan said. "We will not seek to obstruct you, but we will not join you." I passed this information on to Stettinius and to the President at Yalta. It was British inability to go along with us in opposing the admission of the Soviet republics that led to the deal eventually worked out.

The most important business I conducted in London was conferring with Stanislas Mikolajczyk, the former leader of the Polish government-in-exile, who was highly regarded by President Roosevelt. The meeting was arranged by H. F. Arthur Schoenfeld, who was number two in our Embassy to the countries in exile. We went to the Polish Embassy, where we sat in the front drawing room looking out on the somber scene of London, which was at that time under inter-mittent attack by Nazi V-2s, the forerunner of missiles. Mikolajczyk was a short, stocky, round-faced man with blond hair and an open countenance reflecting his peasant origin. He was sensible, calm, and frank. I did not offer any suggestions of my own or hold out any hopes for the success of his plan for an interim coalition government for Poland. I merely promised to transmit Mikolajczyk's views to President Roosevelt.

The problem was that although the Soviets had agreed to the re-es-tablishment of a Polish state, the demise of which they had engineered with the Nazis, they had broken relations with the government-in-ex-ile and had formally recognized the Committee of National Liberation at Lublin, founded by pro-Soviet elements and dominated by Com-munists, as the legitimate government. Intertwined with the issue of who would run the country was the problem of establishing its bor-ders. At Teheran, as already mentioned, Churchill and Stalin had vir-tually settled the issue by agreeing, while Roosevelt stood aside, to move the boundaries west, thus granting Moscow territories she had taken at the time of the Nazi-Soviet pact and giving Poland a big chunk of Germany in compensation.

Mikolajczyk had gone to Moscow with Churchill in October, 1944, to discuss the entire Polish question. The meeting had ended in failure, primarily because Mikolajczyk, despite strong pressure from Church-ill, refused to relinquish as large a piece of territory as the Soviet Union intended to annex. What made the London government's position impossible was the fact that almost all of Poland was occupied by the Red Army, and the Lublin Committee was beginning to administer the country. In his conversation with me, Mikolajczyk said that the Western powers should use every effort to prevent exclusion from decisions regarding postwar Poland. He said almost any compromise would be better than a flat failure to reach an agreement, which could only lead to what he feared most, the domination of Poland by the Soviet Union. He therefore proposed that the Western Allies suggest at Yalta the establishment of a governmental committee consisting of a number of prominent Poles who had stayed in Poland and a number who had fled. This would be the provisional government of Poland pending the holding of free elections. After our conversation, we sent his views in a cable to Paris. I took the document to Yalta and presented it to Roosevelt.

After several days in England, we flew to Paris to see General Eisenhower. He was living on the outskirts in what was known as the Brown House, the home of an Englishman who had a passion for things Napoleonic. One wing was built as though it were Napoleon's tent in the desert, and the whole house was littered with all sorts of mementos of Napoleon—weapons, books, pictures, pottery. Eisenhower was in good spirits, but still somewhat shaken by the December German counteroffensive that had raised for a time the fear of an Allied debacle.

In Paris, Hopkins had a lengthy talk with de Gaulle, who was highly critical of American policy. Hopkins tried to reassure him that our policy toward France was the way it had always been—of utmost friendship and consideration for the interests and future of the French Republic. De Gaulle was not in the mood to listen. He was smarting over the fact that he had not been invited to the Yalta Conference.

I was not present at any of Hopkins's meetings or lunches in Paris, since I was considered primarily a Soviet expert. I did, however, talk to members of our Embassy and a few Frenchmen I had known earlier about the general situation in France and obtained some idea of the outlines of de Gaulle's views. It would have been impossible to let de Gaulle take part in the military aspects of the Yalta Conference. Britain and the United States had some eighty-six divisions in Europe; the most France could have mustered at any given time was about three divisions, with two in reserve. It was obviously impossible to let a country with virtually no military weight have an equal voice with the countries carrying most of the burden of the fighting. It was also understandable that de Gaulle would not share this view.

Hopkins thought that a compromise might be reached whereby de Gaulle would take part in the political conversations at Yalta but not share in the military decisions, and he suggested such a solution to Georges Bidault, who was then the French Foreign Minister. Hopkins said he had no authority from President Roosevelt to make the offer, but he thought that it would be acceptable to the President if de Gaulle was agreeable. Hopkins felt he knew Roosevelt well enough to be free in making this suggestion. Bidault agreed to take up the suggestion with de Gaulle.

The following morning, we flew to Rome, where Hopkins had an audience with Pope Pius XII. In the afternoon, we flew to Naples, where we were joined by Stettinius and others from the State Department who were going to attend the Yalta Conference. In contrast to Teheran, where the State Department had no voice in policy discussions except for a few comments by Harriman, there was a large representation from State at Yalta.

State Department participation meant better preparation for the conference. A series of "black books" covering the subjects to be discussed at Yalta had been prepared for the President. I had been involved in the preparation of the books before I left on the trip to Europe. At Naples, I saw the final "black books" and was impressed with their thorough and competent analysis of every problem likely to come before the conference and the recommendations of the United States positions.

The next day, January 31, we boarded a plane and flew to Malta. The American contingent was put up on the British cruiser H.M.S. *Sirius*, which was moored alongside the quay. The following day was devoted to discussion with the British on conference questions. I was at most of the meetings but not all, as accommodations were very tight. There was almost complete agreement on all major questions. It seemed to me that the British were more realistic about the Soviet Union than the Americans. In large measure, this was due to the fact that the British had been actively dealing with the Soviets on European territorial questions, above all Poland. Foreign Secretary Eden at one point suggested that we should in prudence draw up a list of questions on which we wanted Soviet agreement and another list of the prices we were prepared to pay. This was never done. Why, I cannot recall.

Churchill had arrived in the early morning of January 30; Roosevelt arrived about 9:30 A.M. on February 2. The entry of the President of the United States to Valletta Harbor was a memorable spectacle. The sun was glistening on the waves, and a light breeze was snapping the flags flying from the British warships and walls of the city as the oversized cruiser *Quincy* sailed slowly into the harbor. Roosevelt sat on deck, his black cape around his shoulders, acknowledging salutes from the British men-of-war and the rolling cheers of spectators crowding the quays. He was very much a historical figure.

When I boarded the *Quincy*, however, I was shocked by Roosevelt's physical appearance. His condition had deteriorated markedly in the less than two weeks since I had seen him. He was not only frail and desperately tired, he looked ill. I never saw Roosevelt look as bad as he did then, despite a week's leisurely voyage at sea, where he could rest. Everyone noticed the President's condition, and we in the American delegation began to talk among ourselves about the basic state of his health. I was relieved somewhat, however, to note that his illness did not affect his speech.

The British were concerned by Roosevelt's refusal to discuss either tactical or substantive questions regarding Yalta. This refusal could have been based on Roosevelt's general desire to avoid fixed positions and to improvise on the spot, drawing from his information and the mood of the other side. The refusal may also have been due to Roosevelt's continued insistence on not giving Stalin any evidence that the Western Allies were ganging up on him. Before leaving for Europe, I had told the President that prior consultation with the British would not have any effect on Soviet policy. Roosevelt's response was somewhat vague, but he did say he did not want to arouse Stalin's suspicion.

The refusal to hold extensive discussions with the British might be explained by the state of Roosevelt's health. He may have wanted to save his energy for Yalta. I did not take much part in the talks at Malta, but I saw enough of Roosevelt to conclude that while his physical state was certainly not up to normal, his mental and psychological state was certainly not affected. He was lethargic, but when important moments arose, he was mentally sharp. Our leader was ill at Yalta, the most important of the wartime conferences, but he was effective. I so believed at the time and still so believe.

CHAPTER ELEVEN

The Yalta Conference

We took off from Malta in the middle of the night. Although we had no fighter escort, we flew over Yugoslavia, Bulgaria, and Rumania, all of which were occupied in part by Axis troops. We landed about noon at an airfield at Saki which had been hurriedly repaired. Churchill arrived twenty minutes after the President.

After being welcomed by a greeting party, headed by Molotov, we were offered refreshments, including vodka and champagne, caviar, smoked sturgeon, and black bread. The eighty-mile drive over the mountains to Yalta was made under lowering clouds that spat rain and a little wet snow. The road was lined with troops of at least two Soviet divisions, each soldier standing within sight of the next, for the entire eighty miles. As the presidential car passed (I was in the second car with Stettinius), the soldiers, many of them girls, snapped to the Russian salute—an abrupt move of the arm to put the rifle at a 30-degree angle from the body. Repeated thousands of times, the salute was impressive. The drive took about five hours. Although the country was mostly uninhabited, we saw signs of destruction—gutted buildings and burned-out Nazi tanks. I believe that the wreckage Roosevelt saw on the drive hardened his view on Germany. "I'm more bloodthirsty than a year ago," he told Stalin when they met.

We arrived at Yalta about 6 P.M. It was already dark, and we were immediately shown to our accommodations in the white granite Livadiya Palace, which had been the summer home of the czars. After the Revolution, it had been turned into a rest home for tubercular patients. The Palace served as the site of the Big Three meetings as well as the living quarters of the Americans. The President's suite consisted of a living room, a dining room (formerly the Czar's billiard room), a bedroom, the only private bath in the palace, and two or three other rooms for Secret Service men. The rest of us were upstairs, doubling up in most cases, in whitewashed rooms that had been renovated for the occasion. The Russians had done a remarkable job in making us comfortable. They had taken from Moscow, by train, the personnel and equipment of three hotels and restored the Livadiya Palace buildings, from which the Germans had removed everything down to plumbing fixtures, doorknobs, and locks. The British were installed in the Vorontzov Villa, which was twelve miles down the coast, and the Russians were at the Koreis Villa, about six miles from Livadiya on the former estate of Prince Yusupov, the man who reportedly assassinated Rasputin.

Unlike at Teheran, security was no problem, since the conference was on Russian soil. Guards were discreetly posted around the entrances to the Grand Ballroom, where the plenary sessions were held, and at various other places. The President's Secret Service men were somewhat more noticeable in their movements and activities. Churchill, as usual, had a single security guard, who was not conspicuous at any time. There was one scare. Stalin, on his way to his car after a meeting, ducked into the men's room when his guards were not looking. I walked outside to wait for him. In a few minutes, two Soviet guards rushed out, yelling, "Where's Stalin? Where has he gone?" They calmed down when I told them that he was in the men's room.

I slept well the first night and arose the next day, February 4, refreshed and went to the communal dining room for breakfast. One of the waiters rushed up to me, and I recognized him as a servant we had employed in Moscow before the war. We had nicknamed him Verny Slug, which in Russian means "faithful servant." True to his nickname, he greeted me with affection, and from that moment on made sure I had everything I wanted. He even put cans of caviar and bottles of vodka in my room.

At 11 A.M., there was a meeting of the top members of the American staff. After the President, who looked much better than at Malta, had said a few suitable words, there was a general discussion of the agenda for the conference. Not much of substance was taken up. Realizing that we were in for difficult times at the conference, we were businesslike in our discussion. I felt no great optimism; I do not think other Americans did, either.

Some of my soberness was due to a long letter from George

Kennan that I had received on my arrival at Yalta. Kennan, who six months before had gone to Moscow as counselor of the Embassy, was deeply pessimistic about the future of Europe. He saw almost no hope of cooperation with the Soviet Union in postwar Europe. Disputing optimistic statements being made in the flush of military successes, Kennan foresaw unavoidable conflict arising between the Allied need for stable, independent nations in Europe and a Soviet push to the west. Eloquently, he argued his case:

> I am aware of the realities of this war, and of the fact that we were too weak to win it without Russian cooperation. I recognize that Russia's war effort has been masterful and effective and must, to a certain extent, find its reward at the expense of other peoples in eastern and central Europe.
>
> But with all of this, I fail to see why we must associate ourselves with this political program, so hostile to the interests of the Atlantic community as a whole, so dangerous to everything which we need to see preserved in Europe. Why could we not make a decent and definitive compromise with it—divide Europe frankly into spheres of influence —keep ourselves out of the Russian sphere and keep the Russians out of ours? That would have been the best thing we could do for ourselves and for our friends in Europe, and the most honest approach we could have tried to restore life, in the wake of war, on a dignified and stable foundation.
>
> Instead of this, what have we done? Although it was evident that the realities of the after-war were being shaped while the war was in progress we have consistently refused to make clear what our interests and our wishes were, in eastern and central Europe. We have refused to name any limit for Russian expansion and Russian responsibilities, thereby confusing the Russians and causing them constantly to wonder whether they are asking too little or whether it was some kind of a trap.

As an alternative program, Kennan suggested, in addition to the "partition of Europe," the following:

1. That plans for the United Nations be buried "as quickly and quietly as possible," because the only practical effect of creating an international organization would be to commit the United States to defend a "swollen and unhealthy Russian sphere of power."

2. That the American people be corrected of the "dangerously erroneous impression that the security of the world depends on our assuming some formal blanket engagement to use our armed force in

some given set of circumstances, as set forth in some legal documents." The United States must reserve to itself the right to decide where to use armed force.

3. That the United States should write off Eastern and Southeastern Europe unless it possessed the will "to go whole hog" and oppose with all its physical and diplomatic resources Russian domination of the area.

4. That the United States "accept as an accomplished fact the complete partition of Germany" and begin consultations with the British and French about the formation of a Western European federation, which would include West German states.

Because I was so busy, I could write only a hasty reply:

> I can't say I have given your letter the attention it deserves, but there is simply not time. As you know, there is a very great deal in your expositions that I agree with. You should know that in this connection the U.S. government is following admittedly a policy of no small risk. But have you ever seriously thought through the alternatives? The "constructive" suggestions that you make are frankly naïve to a degree. They may well be the optimum from an abstract point of view. But as practical suggestions they are utterly impossible. Foreign policy of that kind cannot be made in a democracy. Only totalitarian states can make and carry out such policies. Furthermore, I don't for one minute believe that there has been any time in this war when we could seriously have done very differently than we did. It is easy to talk about instruments of pressure that we had in our hands. But the simple fact remains that if we wished to defeat Germany we could never have even tried to keep the Soviet armies out of Eastern Europe and Germany itself. I can never figure out why a piece of paper that you did not get should be regarded as so much more real than those you did get. Isn't it a question of realities and not of bits of paper? Either our pals intend to limit themselves or they don't. I submit, as the British say, that the answer is not yet clear. But what is clear is that the Soyuz [Soviet Union] is here to stay, as one of the major factors in the world. Quarreling with them would be so easy, but we can always come to that.

What I was saying so cryptically to Kennan was that, as usual, I agreed in general with his analysis of the situation, but I thought he was far off target in his conclusions. I recall feeling quite strongly that to abandon the United Nations would be an error of the first magnitude. While I had my doubts about the ability of a world organization to prevent big-power aggression, I felt that it could keep the United States involved in world affairs without, as Kennan thought, committing us to use force when we did not want to.

As for the partition of Germany, the domination of Eastern Europe by the Soviet Union, and the general idea of dividing the Continent into spheres of influence, I could not go along with Kennan. To me, acceptance of a Soviet sphere, instead of relieving us of responsibility, would compound the felony. Any formal, or even an informal, attempt to give the Soviet Union a sphere of influence in Eastern Europe would, as soon as the agreement became known, have brought a loud and effective outcry from our own Poles and Czechs.

I had more hope than Kennan that the Yalta Conference might produce some kind of workable agreement. All the subjects were going to be discussed by the three leaders. I do not think that I had any illusions that the end of the war would usher in an era of good feeling between the Allies and the Soviet Union. Like Kennan, I knew too much about the Soviet Union to believe that. At the same time, my contacts with Roosevelt and Hopkins had tempered my realism about Bolshevism with a political fact of life. As hopeless as the outlook seemed, the United States must try to get along with the Soviets. The American people, who had fought a long, hard war, deserved at least an attempt to work out a better world. If the attempt failed, the United States could not be blamed for not trying.

In short, foreign policy in a democracy must take into account the emotions, beliefs, and goals of the people. The most carefully thought-out plans of the experts, even though 100 percent correct in theory, will fail without broad public support. The good leader in foreign affairs formulates his policy on expert advice and creates a climate of public opinion to support it.

Roosevelt, very much a political animal, went to the Yalta Conference keenly aware of American public opinion. With the war almost over in Europe, Americans wanted Soviet help in the final battle against Japan. Thus one major goal for Roosevelt at the conference was to pin down Stalin on the timing and the extent of entering the war in Asia. Roosevelt also realized that he might have scored only a temporary success in gaining public support during the war for an international organization, which he thought was the only device that could keep the United States from slipping back into isolationism. Thus his other major goal was an accord on the United Nations. The other important problems, principally Eastern Europe and Germany, had to be considered against the overriding importance of Roosevelt's two main goals.

While Roosevelt's goals were naturally American-oriented, Churchill's were traditionally British: to maintain the Empire and to keep Europe from being dominated by one power, which, under the circumstances, meant the Soviet Union. These goals explain why Churchill opposed the dismemberment of Germany and fought to help France resume her major role on the Continent. Churchill's style in negotiation was based in large measure on his debating experience in the House of Commons. His arguments were always well reasoned but were often based on emotional appeal, which left Stalin cold. Churchill obviously felt deeply about Poland, the cause of the British declaration of war, and used all of his parliamentary skill and eloquence to plead his case. From Churchill's principal adviser, Foreign Secretary Eden, on down, the British in general knew their dossiers and were well prepared for the discussions.

To Stalin, the aim was far more than the understandable one of preventing Germany, when she recovered, from mounting a third invasion of Russia. Stalin was a Bolshevik, and his principal aim was to protect the Soviet system. Thus he felt he could not depend on capitalist Britain or the United States to help him, even though their immediate wartime interests coincided. Nor could Stalin count on an international organization, where the Soviet Union was sure to be outnumbered, to give Moscow what it wanted. The Soviet Union would have to protect the Soviet system herself, and that meant the establishment of satellite governments all through Eastern Europe. Stalin was a shrewd and skillful negotiator. He was always calm and unruffled and almost always courteous in his mood and manner. He was particularly adroit and effective in defensive diplomacy. When the subject under discussion dealt with an area under Soviet control, such as Poland or the Eastern Balkans, he showed himself to be a master of evasive and delaying tactics with no great regard for facts. He had done his homework on the principal issues, but he did not hesitate to cite events and actions which Churchill and Roosevelt, to say nothing of the rest of us, profoundly disbelieved but could not refute. On matters not under his control, Stalin was less skillful and did not vigorously push his position. He was ably backed up by Molotov, the faithful follower.

The Roosevelt who sparred and bargained with Churchill and Stalin still believed, as he had at Teheran, in improvising solutions to difficulties. This time, however, he had, in addition to military advisers, a State Department staff of about a dozen officers to back him up. As the conference progressed, it became obvious that Roosevelt had not studied the "black books" as much as he should have, but they undoubtedly helped him.

Roosevelt's chief adviser was still Harry Hopkins, who was quite ill (he lost eighteen pounds at the conference) and too ready to grant

"Chip" Bohlen, tackle on football team at St. Paul's School.

Harvard undergraduate.

Mr. and Mrs. Charles E. Bohlen at tennis courts, Italian Embassy, Moscow, 1938.

The dacha near Moscow in 1939, where German Secretary told Bohlen of Nazi-Soviet talks. Left to right: Armin Dew, Secretary, British Embassy; Norris Chipman, Secretary, American Embassy; Mrs. Chipman; John Russell, Secretary, British Embassy; two visitors. On second-floor porch, Avis Bohlen.

At the dacha. Bohlen; Johnny Herwarth, his German contact; and Fitzroy MacLean, a British Secretary.

At Teheran Conference dinner. Bohlen, Roosevelt, Churchill, and Stalin listen to Major Birse, British interpreter.

Harry Hopkins and Bohlen at Yalta Conference.

Luncheon at Yalta. Clockwise, beginning at left: Secretary of State Stettinius; Sir Alexander Cadogan of Britain; Admiral Leahy (partly hidden); Bohlen; Sir Archibald Clark Kerr, British Ambassador to Moscow; Hopkins; Foreign Secretary Anthony Eden of Britain; Pavlov, Russian interpreter; Stalin; Roosevelt; Churchill; Molotov; and Major Birse, British interpreter.

D I N N E R

Caviare
Pies

White and Red Salmon
Shamaya
Salted Herrings
Sturgeon in Aspic

Swiss Cheese
Game
Sausage
Sucking Pig, Horse-radish Sauce

—

Vol-au-Vent of Game

—

Game Bouillon
Cream of Chicken

—

White Fish, Champagne Sauce
Baked Kefal

—

Shashlik of Mutton
Wild Goat from the Steppes
Pilau of Mutton

—

Roast Turkey
Roast Quails
Roast Partridge

Green Peas

—

Ice Cream
Fruit
Petits Fours
Roasted Almonds

—

Coffee

Vorontsov Villa

February 10, 1945

Menu of British dinner at Yalta, autographed for the author by the Big Three
and their Foreign Ministers.

Averell Harriman, Ambassador to Moscow, and Stalin shaking hands at Yalta;
Bohlen at left.

Signal Corps, U.S. Army

The Big Three and their Foreign Ministers in front of Livadiya Palace at Yalta. Eden is standing behind Churchill, Stettinius behind Roosevelt, and Molotov behind Stalin. Bohlen is at left, behind Churchill.

U.S. Army Photograph

On cruiser *Quincy* in Egypt, after Yalta. Seated: John Winant, U.S. Ambassador to Britain; Roosevelt;

Harry and Louise Hopkins and Bohlen are shown ruins of Berlin by Soviet generals.

At Potsdam Conference. Left to right: Stalin, Bohlen, Pavlov, Truman, Gromyko, presidential press secretary Charles Ross, Secretary of State Byrnes, and Molotov.

Signal Corps, U.S. Army

The Big Three at Potsdam. Bohlen in background.

Signal Corps, U.S. Army

Stettinius, Bohlen, and Byrnes confer during United Nations debate on Iran in 1946.

The Bohlens's son, Charles, with Secretary of State Marshall, 1948.

Bohlen with aide to General Omar Bradley on visit to Seoul in 1951, during Korean war.

Secretary of State Dulles, President Eisenhower, and Bohlen after Senate confirmation of author as ambassador to USSR, 1953.

concessions in return for what he mistakenly thought were Soviet retreats. Secretary of State Stettinius, nominally number two in the American delegation, was the man Roosevelt looked to for the execution of practical tasks, such as working out problems with other Foreign Ministers. Stettinius was typically American in his desire to get on with the business and sometimes was unaware of political nuances, but he carried out Roosevelt's instructions diligently and faithfully. A third key man in the delegation was Ambassador Harriman, who had previously discussed with Stalin in Moscow the terms of Soviet entry into the Japanese war. Other State Department officials, including me, would occasionally see Roosevelt alone.

My role, which became a matter of controversy years later when I was nominated as ambassador to the Soviet Union, included both interpreting for and advising the President. The pressure on me for interpreting was much less than at Teheran. I had made sure before leaving Washington that there would be a full stenographic staff to take dictation from me. I was still Roosevelt's official interpreter at all times and was the official American note-taker for all plenary sessions. At the first session, the Combined Chiefs of Staff also made notes, because it dealt exclusively with military affairs. I also took the American notes for the dinner conversations and for all the private meetings of Roosevelt and Stalin.* Because of the better arrangements and because I knew Roosevelt, Hopkins, and Stettinius, I took part in many discussions of policy, especially on Germany and Eastern Europe.

The conference, which lasted for eight days, was organized in such a way that there was no orderly discussion and resolution of each problem by the leaders. Instead, issues were brought up, discussed, then shunted off to the Foreign Ministers or military chiefs or just dropped for a few hours. There was a plenary session of the three leaders every day at 4 P.M. and meetings of the Foreign Ministers and of the military chiefs every morning. In addition, there were private meetings between any two of the leaders, and discussions by all three at lunch and dinner.

It is a wonder that any agreements could emerge from such confusion. But the constant switch from one subject to another kept tempers cool. It is a matter of fact that, despite the difficulties and disappointments, the atmosphere remained pleasant throughout the conference. The good feeling was evident on February 4, at the first Roosevelt-

---

* H. Freeman Matthews and Alger Hiss kept notes of some conversations at the plenary meetings, and Edward Page of the Moscow Embassy kept the record of the Foreign Minister meetings.

Stalin private meeting before the first plenary session. The two leaders greeted each other as old friends, and in a sense they were, having conferred in Teheran and exchanged many messages during the year. Smiling broadly, the President grasped Stalin by the hand and shook it warmly. Stalin, his face cracked in one of his rare, if slight, smiles, expressed pleasure at seeing the President again. I was the only other American in the room. Molotov and Pavlov, the interpreter, were with Stalin. The conversation began with a discussion of the military situation. The President mentioned that he had made a number of bets crossing the Atlantic that the Red Army would get to Berlin before the Americans got to Manila. Marshal Stalin replied that he was certain that the Americans would get to Manila before he got to Berlin, since there was hard fighting on the Oder Line. Stalin's remark runs counter to the reminiscences of at least one Soviet marshal that Stalin deliberately withheld his armies from driving on to Berlin out of consideration for the slower-moving Western Allies. If this had been his intention, he would certainly have told the Western Allies and claimed credit. He probably did delay the capture of Berlin, but the reasons were political—to permit his armies to capture other areas in Eastern Europe.

Maintaining his mood of good humor, the President recalled Stalin's joke at Teheran about executing 50,000 German officers and expressed the hope that he would offer the toast again. The President's reference to the joke that had angered Churchill, plus remarks about the British wanting to "have their cake and eat it too," were apparently another way of showing Stalin that the United States was not joining Britain in any united negotiating position.

The two leaders ended their talk just before going into the Grand Ballroom of the Palace, which had been simply furnished with a large round table and chairs. The first formal session of the conference was devoted to military reports, all of which were optimistic. The President remarked that he doubted whether the jubilation of the Russian people over the Red Army's advance into Germany exceeded the joy of the American and British peoples. Stalin pointed out that the Red Army had launched its winter offensive ahead of time to help relieve the pressure on the British and Americans set back by the German offensive in the Ardennes. He said the Russians had acted even though there was no pressure from the British or Americans because it was "our duty as Allies." Churchill said no attempt had been made to bargain with Stalin, because he could be depended on to do the right thing.

That night, the dinner was in the Livadiya Palace, with the President as host. There were cocktails, but unlike at Teheran, the President did not mix them. For most of the evening, the conversation was lighthearted, but toward the end it turned to the question of keeping the peace after the war. Stalin had already made known his views that the three big powers, which had borne the brunt of the war, should bear the responsibilities of peace and that he was opposed to giving the smaller powers any rights that could in any way contradict the wishes of any great power. Roosevelt tended to agree that the peace should be written by the big powers. Churchill quoted a verse: "The eagle should permit the small birds to sing and care not wherefore they sang."

When the leaders began discussing the right of dissent within countries, Vishinsky turned to me and said that he thought that the American people should learn to obey their leaders and not question what they were told to do. I replied with some sarcasm that I would like to see him go to the United States and tell that to the American people. With a grin, Vishinsky said that he would be glad to do so.

Later, as I was escorting Churchill and Eden to the door, an argument broke out between them. Churchill had commented that on the whole he rather agreed with Marshal Stalin that small nations' rights should be protected but that they should not have a voice in great matters. Eden said he disagreed and indicated that he was prepared to go before the House of Commons at any time and put the matter to a vote. Instead of answering Eden, Churchill turned to me and, growling in his customary fashion, said that he did not understand the United States formula for voting procedures in the United Nations Security Council. He said he had not had time to read our position paper carefully, and wondered whether I could give him the gist of what we were trying to do. Having absorbed a good dinner with the customary libations, I was emboldened to tell the Prime Minister that our compromise proposal reminded me of the story of a Southern plantation owner who asked a Negro whether he liked the whiskey given him for Christmas. When the Negro replied that it was perfect, the master asked what he meant. The Negro answered that had the whiskey been any better, the master would not have given it to him, and had it been any worse, he couldn't have drunk it.*

* Although British accounts contain a reference to an incident at Roosevelt's dinner in which Stalin became temporarily annoyed over the use of the nickname "Uncle Joe," my notes do not mention it. It is possible that I was out of the room, but I have no memory of the incident. In cables to each other, Roosevelt and Churchill often referred to Stalin as "Uncle Joe," or simply "U.J."

There were moments of irritation and bitterness during the suc-ceeding days, but the over-all mood of good feeling continued right to the last dinner, given by Stalin. In one toast, Stalin proposed the health of Prime Minister Churchill, whom he characterized as "the bravest governmental figure in the world." England had stood alone, he noted, defying the might of Germany, when the rest of Europe was falling flat on its face before Hitler. It is interesting to note that Stalin did not make any excuse or apology for the Nazi-Soviet pact. He ended by stating that he "knew few examples in history where the courage of one man had been so important to the future history of the world." Stalin also proposed the health of the President. He re-marked that he and Churchill had had relatively simply decisions to make because they had been fighting for their countries' very existence. But, he said, there was a third man, Roosevelt, "whose country had not been seriously threatened with invasions, but through perhaps a broader conception of national interest, and even though his country was not directly imperiled, had been the chief forger of the instru-ment which had led to the mobilization of the world against Hitler," a reference to Lend-Lease.

The good will extended down the line to the staff, too. During this dinner, Stalin made one of his characteristic semi-jocular remarks. He proposed a toast to those who "worked while we were enjoying our-selves," and raised his glass to the health of the interpreters. After whispered consultations among the interpreters, I was chosen to respond. Having fortified myself with a number of glasses of vodka, I modified the words of the Communist Manifesto and proposed as a slogan: "Interpreters of the world, unite; you have nothing to lose but your bosses." There was a slight silence, then Stalin burst into a laugh, got up and came around the table, clinked glasses with me, and congratulated me on my "wit."

Underneath this gloss of good will, the three leaders were waging a fierce struggle on the shape of the postwar world. The decisions they reached on these questions, while hailed almost universally at the time as great accomplishments, ultimately came under such heavy attack, first from the right and later from the left, that Yalta is undoubtedly the most controversial conference in United States history. From my position at Roosevelt's side, I witnessed almost all the important exchanges with the Soviet Union.

Here is how I saw the development and resolution of the issues:

President Roosevelt opened the discussion on Germany at the second plenary session. Here was one place where I felt that his ill health might have affected his thinking. The President rambled on about the Germany he had known in 1886, when small, semi-autonomous states such as Darmstadt and Rothenburg thrived. The centralization of Germany in the Berlin government was one of the causes, he said, of the ills from which the world was suffering. Roosevelt's rambling and inconclusive statement, which didn't even hang together, was greeted with polite indifference by the Soviet leaders and by slight signs of boredom by the British. Churchill fiddled with his cigar and Eden looked off into the distance. The British, together with everyone present, as I mentioned earlier, were a bit apprehensive over the President's health at Malta and must have noted in this connection the vagueness of his remarks.

The discussions on the question of breaking Germany up into a number of small states were inconclusive, and I did not get the impression that any of the three really had his heart in it. Stalin was exceptionally cautious. Although at Teheran he had leaned toward dismemberment, at Yalta he was really hoping to get the others fully committed to the idea, so their views would be useful in Soviet propaganda in Germany after the war. I cannot say that I saw this at Yalta, but his purpose became clear at the end of the war, when he assured the German people that he had never intended to divide Germany.

Roosevelt's real views on the dismemberment of Germany remain somewhat of a mystery. There is no doubt that at Teheran he had considered the idea of breaking Germany up into principalities. At Yalta, Roosevelt said he still thought the division of Germany into five or seven states was a good idea, but as the discussion developed, it appeared that he had lost interest in dismemberment; he was just giving lip service to a dying idea.

Even Churchill had spoken favorably of dismemberment at Teheran. At Yalta, he supported the idea in "principle" but saw the need for European counterweights to the Soviet Union and actually favored a united Germany, as well as France, for such a role.

Finally, the conferees decided to refer the question to a committee consisting of Foreign Secretary Eden and the Soviet and American ambassadors to Britain. The committee never met.

The conferees also had to decide whether to give France a zone of occupation in Germany. Churchill, the strongest proponent of giving France both a zone and participation in the Allied council for controlling Germany, assured Stalin that this plan would not affect the Soviet zone, because the French zone would be taken from the British and American areas. The President stated in the very beginning that he favored acceptance of the French request for a zone of occupation, but agreed with Stalin that France should not take part in the control machinery, because other nations would then demand similar roles. Stalin then attempted to foreclose the decision by stating that he felt that there was agreement that France should have a zone taken from the British and American zones but should not be a member of the control council. This was certainly not accurate; it did not represent the views of the Prime Minister. However, I cannot find in the record any objections to Stalin's statement.

In pressing his point on the importance of French participation in the occupation of Germany, Churchill said it was problematical how long the United States would retain troops in Europe and asked Roosevelt his views. The President replied that he did not believe that American troops would stay in Europe much more than two years. He went on to say that he felt he would win support in Congress and throughout the country of any reasonable measures designed to safeguard the peace, but he did not believe that this would extend to the maintenance of an appreciable American force in Europe.

This remark by President Roosevelt has been criticized as playing directly into the hands of Stalin, who subsequently moved aggressively in Eastern Europe, confident that the United States would not intervene. There is no evidence that I know of to support this view. It was clear to all at Yalta, and should be to any who take the time to read the record, that Roosevelt was not talking in the context of a divided Germany with rival occupation armies facing each other—the Soviet Union against the Western Allies—as the situation turned out. Rather, the President was talking in the context of a semi-permanent occupation of certain places in Germany by still united allies following a peace treaty. He was giving his estimate of how long Congress and the American people would support the idea of the permanent stationing of United States forces in Germany to guard against a renewal of militarism. Of course, when Congress was later confronted by a Europe in danger of domination by the Soviet Union, it gave strong support to the retention of American troops there for an indefinite length of time.

After the second formal session, Hopkins, H. Freeman Matthews, head of the European Affairs Division, and I attempted to persuade the President that it was impossible to give France a zone in Germany without a seat on the Control Council.* We also pointed out to the

---

* My memory is that this meeting took place after the plenary session, and not before, as indicated in the official record. There is no formal account of the meeting.

President that it was virtually a political impossibility to endeavor to administer Germany without the participation of France, her hereditary enemy and neighbor and our oldest friend.

Some accounts of Yalta have erroneously attributed to Roosevelt strong opposition to giving France a zone in Germany. This was not so. His only opposition was to the admission of France as a full member of the control commission in Germany. In this, he was probably influenced by his own feelings toward General de Gaulle and a belief that the presence of France would merely contribute to confusion and argument on the council, as it had on so many other occasions. He was probably also influenced by Stalin's view that to put France on the council would mean that other countries would begin to demand the same position.

At the close of our meeting, Roosevelt appeared to be converted, although all he promised was to think the matter over. Later, at a formal session of the conference, he said that after due consideration he had concluded that France would have to be given a seat on the Control Council. At this point, Stalin raised his arms above his head and said, "*Sdaiyous*," which in Russian means "I surrender."*

Stalin's acceptance of France as a full occupying power came as a surprise. I had translated at his private meeting with the President on the first day of the conference when Stalin had expressed an unfavorable view of de Gaulle and the French. We had been opposed to giving France a seat on the Control Council for Germany when the subject first came up at the conference. When Roosevelt switched to Churchill's position, there was little Stalin could do without engendering French hostility.

One of the results of Stalin's acceptance was to reinforce Roosevelt's idea that he had great personal influence on the dictator. None of the Western representatives raised the question whether Stalin's surrender on a French zone merited a quid pro quo response. Stalin may have thought in terms of such a tactical maneuver. When he saw that he could not win on an issue, he sometimes gave in, hoping to affect the Western negotiators, and, indeed, it is possible that Stalin's acquiescence on France may have affected Roosevelt's views on German reparations.

Neither the Americans nor the British went to Yalta with any spe-

* In the light of the subsequent crises over Allied access to Berlin, it is important to note that plans for occupying the city were not discussed at Yalta. The conference merely ratified plans of the European Advisory Council for division of the country into zones and the city into sectors.

cific plan for reparations from Nazi Germany. When the subject came under discussion, both countries agreed that the Soviet Union, which had suffered the most, was entitled to the most reparations. It seemed obvious that until there was some inkling of the extent of damage within Germany, it was ridiculous even to begin to think about the amount of compensation that that country could pay. Besides, Churchill and Roosevelt remembered that after World War I, loans from the Allies, particularly from the United States, paid for a great deal of Germany's reparations. Thus the winners, not the losers, paid. The Soviet Union wanted the leaders to agree to a fixed amount of reparations for the Soviet Union. The argument at Yalta revolved around this point.

The upshot of the discussions was the establishment of a Reparations Commission to look into the matter. At Yalta, the British refused to agree to the fixing of a definite sum. The United States finally agreed to accept as "a basis for discussion" by the commission the Soviet proposition that Germany should pay $20 billion in reparations, half of which should go to the Soviet Union. I expressed opposition to this concession. Roosevelt agreed to it after receiving a note from Hopkins saying that the Russians felt that we were siding with the British against them. The reparations question was not resolved by the commission; despite numerous meetings, the commission could not agree on a fixed sum. The issue was finally settled at the Potsdam meeting.

During a discussion of reparations at a luncheon of Foregin Ministers on the second day of the conference, Molotov expressed the hope that the United States would furnish Moscow with long-term credits. He had raised the question in January, before Yalta, in a note to Harriman. The note suggested that the United States lend the Soviet Union $6 billion at 2 percent interest, with payment to begin in 15 years and to take 30 years to complete. The funds would be used to purchase industrial goods in the United States. The phrasing of the note was such that it seemed less a request for American help to the Soviet Union to rebuild after the war than an offer of Soviet aid to the United States to relieve its unemployment problem. At Yalta, Stettinius told Molotov that the United States was willing to discuss the question any time. Talks were held for almost a year, but got nowhere, partly because the proposed 2 percent interest rate was less than the $2\frac{3}{8}$ percent prevailing rate at the time. These points are worth noting because some historians have made much of the fact that the United States did not extend credits to Moscow after the war.

The most difficult question of all at Yalta was Poland. The Soviets realized that since they had physical control over Poland, they could, in the last analysis, do pretty much what they wanted to with that country. On the other hand, they also realized that the British and American governments had a strong interest in Poland. The Western goal was absurdly simple—the right of the Poles to govern themselves, even if they chose a Communist government. The task of the Soviet diplomacy therefore was to retain a tight grip on Poland without causing an open break with the Western powers. In this regard, Stalin displayed a considerable astuteness, an extensive knowledge of the geographic elements of the problem, such as the location of the frontiers, and a tenacity in beating back one Western attempt after another to create conditions for a genuinely democratic government.

A sure clue to the gravity of the problem was Stalin's getting up and walking up and down behind his chair while expounding his points. His best debating skill stood out on the Polish question. When Roosevelt said he wanted the Polish election to be pure, like Caesar's wife, Stalin commented, "They said that about her but in fact she had her sins."

The frontiers of the new Poland, although not what we wanted, did not present a difficult problem. Churchill and Stalin had pretty much settled the issue at Teheran. The President did attempt to get Lvov and the adjacent oil fields returned to Poland, but Stalin refused. Churchill had second thoughts about his hasty giveaway of German land at Teheran. While still favoring the movement of Polish frontiers west, he said it would be a pity to stuff the Polish goose so full of German food that it got indigestion. Stalin brushed aside the argument by asserting that most of the Germans in the affected areas had run away from the advancing Red Army.

The real issue was the composition of the government which was to rule Poland pending the holding of elections. Stalin insisted that the provisional government which he had set up at Lublin should be recognized by London and Washington and that the Polish government-in-exile in London, which was anti-Communist, should be abandoned. The American and British proposal called for the formation of a new interim government including Mikolajczyk, the peasant Party leader with whom I had talked in London, and other moderate Poles abroad, as well as members of the Lublin regime. We opposed the

Lublin group as the sole representative because it was a purely Soviet creation.

It was not until the third plenary session, on February 6, that Poland was discussed. Drawing on the Mikolajczyk memorandum that I had given him, the President raised the possibility of creating a council composed of Polish leaders in Lublin and London. Churchill then emphasized how much Poland meant to Britain, which had gone to war to help Poland, and pleaded with Stalin to be magnanimous, to accept a solution that would leave Poland independent. The British Prime Minister asked if a new Polish government might not be formed at Yalta.

The appeal to Stalin's generosity was not, on the face of it, a bad tactic. It flattered his sense of power and gave him an opportunity to show magnanimity. But it did not work in this case. In his reply, Stalin said that he understood that Poland was a question of honor for Britain. But he pointed out that, for the Soviets, Poland was a question of life and death, as well as honor, because in thirty years it had twice served as an invasion corridor. He was adamant in refusing to budge from full support of the Lublin government. As for Churchill's suggestion that the Big Three create a new Polish government, Stalin cleverly replied, "I am called a dictator and not a democrat, but I have enough democratic feeling to refuse to create a Polish government without the Poles being consulted."

As we left the conference table that day, the Americans and British faced a formidable task in trying to salvage anything on Poland. We were up against a simple fact: the Red Army held most of the country; Stalin had the power to enforce his will. But the President would not give up so easily. That night, he instructed me to draft a letter to Stalin incorporating Mikolajczyk's idea. I composed a letter which, after slight changes, was sent to Stalin. It said:

MY DEAR MARSHAL STALIN:

I have been giving a great deal of thought to our meeting this afternoon, and I want to tell you in all frankness what is on my mind.

In so far as the Polish government is concerned, I am greatly disturbed that the three great powers do not have a meeting of minds about the political setup in Poland. It seems to me that it puts all of us in a bad light throughout the world to have you recognizing one government while we and the British are recognizing another in London. I am sure this state of affairs should not continue and that if it does it can only lead our people to think there is a breach between us, which is not the case. I am determined that there shall be no breach between ourselves and the Soviet Union. Surely there is a way to reconcile our differences.

I was very much impressed with some of the things you said today, particularly your determination that your rear must be safeguarded as your army moves into Berlin. You cannot, and we must not tolerate any temporary government which will give your armed forces any trouble of this sort. I want you to know that I am fully mindful of this.

You must believe me when I tell you that our people at home look with a critical eye on what they consider a disagreement between us at this vital stage of the war. They, in effect, say that if we cannot get a meeting of the minds now when our armies are converging on the common enemy, how can we get an understanding on even more vital things in the future.

I have had to make it clear to you that we cannot recognize the Lublin Government as now composed, and the world would regard it as a lamentable outcome of our work here if we parted with an open and obvious divergence between us on this issue.

You said today that you would be prepared to support any suggestions for the solution of this problem which offered a fair chance of success, and you also mentioned the possibility of bringing some members of the Lublin government here.

Realizing that we all have the same anxiety in getting the matter settled, I would like to develop your proposal a little and suggest that we invite here to Yalta at once, Mr. Bierut and Mr. Osabka-Morawski from the Lublin Government and also two or three from the following list of Poles, which according to our information would be desirable as people in the development of a new temporary government which all three of us could recognize and support: Archbishop Sapieha of Cracow, Vincente Witos, Mr. Zurlowski, Professor Buyak, and Professor Kutzeba. If, as a result of the presence of these Polish leaders here, we could jointly agree with them on a provisional government in Poland, which should no doubt include some Polish leaders from abroad such as Mr. Mikolajczyk, Mr. Grabski, and Mr. Romer, the United States government, and I feel sure the British government, as well, would then be prepared to examine with you conditions in which they would disassociate themselves from the London government and transfer their recognition to the new provisional government.

I hope I do not have to assure you that the United States will never lend its support in any way to any provisional government in Poland that would be inimical to your interests.

It gose without saying that any interim government, which could be formed as a result of our conference with the Poles here, would be pledged to the holding of free elections in Poland at the earliest possible

date. I know this is completely consistent with your desire to see a new
free and democratic Poland emerge from the welter of this war.

Most sincerely yours,
FRANKLIN D. ROOSEVELT

The purpose of mentioning the reaction of the American public to
the failure of the United States and the Soviet Union to agree on
Poland was to indicate to Stalin the seriousness of the situation. In retrospect, I believe it was perhaps a mistake to include this sentence,
since Stalin considered references to American public opinion in the
same category of nonsense as his reference to the will of the Supreme
Soviet.

At the fourth plenary session the next day, February 7, Stalin
adroitly rejected the Roosevelt proposition, and had Molotov introduce the Soviet plan, which was the basis for the final agreement on
Poland. This plan called for adding to the Lublin Committee some
democratic leaders from Polish émigré circles, with the enlarged temporary regime holding elections as soon as possible. While we could
not accept this plan without writing in safeguards, we did see in it the
seeds of an acceptable compromise. In a counterproposal the following day, the United States called for a committee of three representatives of the big powers to invite Polish leaders from inside and outside
the country to a meeting in Moscow to form an interim government
of national unity that would hold free elections for a permanent government. Molotov, while treating the proposal with respect, skillfully
stripped away its key points and modified others so that little substance was left.

At Roosevelt's suggestion, the Polish issue was referred to the Foreign Ministers to work out the details of a compromise. I had occasionally attended the Foreign Ministers' meetings as an observer when
it was certain there was no chance of any Roosevelt-Stalin meetings,
and sat in on this session on February 9. I did not interpret for Stettinius but did help draft a paper, which I think, in retrospect, went much
too far in meeting Molotov's demands. This document proposed that
the Lublin group be reorganized into a "fully representative government" based on all democratic forces, including democratic leaders in
Poland and abroad. This draft required representatives of the three
powers to verify the holding of a free election.

Molotov, as expected, objected to the American draft's call for a
"fully representative government" as a repudiation of the Lublin government. His wording was for a reorganization "on a wider demo-

cratic basis," implying that the Lublin group was indeed democratic but should be made somewhat more so. He also wished to add to the description of parties allowed to participate in elections the words "non-Fascist and anti-Fascists," and favored elimination of the responsibilities of the three Allied governments in regard to watching the elections. At a meeting of the American delegation, I warned that the term "anti-Fascist" was too broad, since "Fascist" might easily be interpreted to mean anybody who opposed a Communist government in Poland. The statement was modified to read, "all democratic and anti-Nazi parties."

That evening, at a meeting of the Foreign Ministers at Stalin's villa, the formula for Poland was finally agreed to. The key paragraphs in the final agreement on Poland, which became a subject of bitter controversy, read as follows:

> A new situation has been created in Poland as a result of her complete liberation by the Red Army. This calls for the establishment of a Polish Provisional Government which can be more broadly based than was possible before the recent liberation of Western Poland. The Provisional Government which is now functioning in Poland should be reorganized on a broader democratic basis with the inclusion of democratic leaders from Poland itself and from Poles abroad. This new government should then be called the Polish Provisional Government of National Unity.
>
> Mr. Molotov, Mr. Harriman and Sir Archibald Clark Kerr [the American and British ambassadors to Russia] are authorized to consult in the first instance in Moscow with members of the present Provisional Government and with other Polish democratic leaders from within Poland and from abroad with a view to the reorganization of the present government along the above lines. This Polish Provisional Government of National Unity shall be pledged to the holding of free and unfettered elections as soon as possible on the basis of universal suffrage and secret ballot. In these elections all democratic and anti-Nazi Parties shall have the right to take part and put forward candidates.

The meaning of these paragraphs, even reread today in the light of what actually happened, is clear. But they were not specific enough and bore the mark of hasty drafting. The number of non-Lublin Poles from within and without Poland is not even indicated. The phrase "in the first instance" seemed clear enough to us at Yalta and still does. But Harriman, Clark Kerr, and Polish émigré representatives soon discovered that the Soviets were interpreting "in the first instance" to mean that the negotiations in Moscow should only be with the members of the Lublin government, and not to mean, as the English text clearly indicates, that the first meeting should be in Moscow rather than Warsaw. I do not believe the Soviets put the words "in the first instance" in the agreement with the idea of misinterpreting them later. Rather, I believe the Russians, in studying the text afterward, saw in this phrase a loophole allowing them to promote their own cause. The fact that we did not spot the loophole is another example of the lack of care that the Western Allies occasionally showed in their dealings with the Soviets, to whom even the last comma had meaning. Too often, we were more concerned not to appear to be nit-picking than with defending a position by carefully watching small points.

The next day, the last problem was resolved at a meeting of the Foreign Ministers with the American withdrawal of its insistence on Allied supervision of the elections. Stettinius, I believe, obtained this concession from the President. I was not present and therefore do not know the details of the conversation.

Roosevelt has been criticized for not doing more for Poland at Yalta. I cannot agree. The concessions that he and Churchill made in their eagerness to avoid a split were perhaps a mistake, but the agreement, although not what the West had wanted, appeared to us, with some doubts, as acceptable. Had it been fully observed, Poland conceivably would be an independent country today.

I do not presume to know what was going on in Roosevelt's mind, but from what he said at Yalta and from his actions there, I feel that he did everything he could to help the Poles. He was not acting out of any sympathy for the London Poles (although he had met and admired Mikolajczyk), and was not trying to install an anti-Soviet regime in Warsaw. He only wanted to give the Polish people, whose country had been overrun and brutalized by the Nazis, and who then faced domination by the Soviet Union, the right to choose their own government. He was trying to balance domestic political considerations—strong Polish sentiment in the United States—with his diplomatic goal of maintaining Allied unity by recognizing the Soviet determination to protect its western flank. The compromise failed because Stalin insisted on more than security against attack; he wanted to establish the Soviet system of authoritarian control of every aspect of life in Poland. The Red Army gave Stalin the power he needed to carry out his wishes, regardless of his promises at Yalta. Stalin held all the cards and played them well. Eventually, we had to throw in our hand.

There was one other subject that dealt with our relations with Eastern Europe. This was an American proposal for a Declaration on Liberated Europe. The draft, prepared by the Department of State, called for consultation among the three major powers regarding development in liberated countries to guarantee the establishment of democratic governments. When President Roosevelt presented the proposal on February 10, Stalin, surprisingly enough, had only one amendment to offer. This addition referred to the need to support "those people in these countries who took an active part in the struggle against German occupation." We felt that it was a great mistake to include anything of this kind, because it would give the Soviets an opportunity to push their own followers at the expense of others. Stalin's amendment was turned down, and he did not argue the point.

The declaration was adopted. Had it been implemented by the Soviet Union, it would have radically changed the face of Eastern Europe. Almost all of the protests over Soviet policies in Eastern Europe contained a reference to the declaration. But all Soviet actions, from Vishinsky's forcing of a Communist-dominated government on Rumania within a week after the close of the Yalta Conference to moves in Poland, Bulgaria, Hungary, and Czechoslovakia, were made without even a semblance of consultation with Britain or the United States. I have often wondered why Stalin agreed to the declaration.

The agreement on the voting procedure in the Security Council of the United Nations was the one solid and lasting decision of the Yalta Conference. Without the agreement limiting the veto of the permanent members of the council to plans for action, there would hardly have been a United Nations, for the Soviets would have prevented even discussion of major issues which involved the Soviet Union.

The Soviets, who understandably were interested in safeguarding their position in the decision-making body of the world organization, were concerned whether the United States formula, once understood, would fully protect their interests. Also, I think that Stalin had not fully gone into the mechanics of our proposal and wished to hear it explained by the President. Our case was actually presented by Stettinius. Working from prepared documents, he made the best presentation of all our positions at Yalta. In accepting our formula, the Soviets probably concluded that the voting plan presented few dangers to the Soviet Union because the veto remained intact on all substantive questions.

Right after acceptance of the American plan, Molotov announced that the Soviet Union was no longer asking for admission of all sixteen

Soviet republics to the United Nations. Three, or perhaps two, would be satisfactory. He mentioned the Ukraine, White Russia (Byelorussia), and Lithuania. While Soviet acceptance of the voting formula was unconditional, Molotov obviously wanted to capitalize on the good will created thereby to win admission of the Soviet republics. Roosevelt initially objected to the Soviet proposal on the ground that it violated the principal of one vote for each member of the United Nations. In an eloquent plea, Churchill said that his heart went out to the people of mighty Russia, which, though bleeding, was beating down the tyrants. He suggested the admission of at least White Russia and the Ukraine. Churchill's reaction was no surprise, since we knew of his desire to get India into the United Nations.

On the following day, February 8, Alger Hiss circulated a memo in the American delegation titled "Arguments Against the Inclusion of Any of the Soviet Republics Among the Initial Members." Hiss had been working on world-organization plans as deputy director of the Office of Special Political Affairs in the department for some time, but in spite of this, I did not know him personally. At meetings at Yalta, his slightly cavernous face always wore a serious expression. He was not an outgoing person, but one who seemed to regard his associates from a superior distance. I never had a conversation of any consequence with him. In view of accusations much later that Hiss, who was eventually convicted of perjury in denying that he passed secrets to the Soviet Union, had worked for the Communists at Yalta, it is interesting to note that the memo gave a closely reasoned argument against admitting the Soviet republics on the basis that they were not sovereign states under international practice and had not signed the United Nations declaration.

The relationship of President Roosevelt to Alger Hiss has been the subject of much comment, distortion, and downright dishonesty on the part of many Roosevelt critics. I do not believe that Roosevelt had any prior acquaintance with Hiss. He may have seen Hiss among a group of State Department officials brought into the White House for one subject or another. I know that the first time Roosevelt saw him at Yalta was at a general meeting of the leading American advisers on the morning of the first day. The President certainly shook hands with Hiss at that time. But I can testify with certainty that Roosevelt never saw Hiss alone during the entire proceedings of the conference. I am confident of this statement because, as Roosevelt's interpreter, I had to stay close to him in anticipation of a possible suggestion from Stalin for a meeting. Hiss sat in on the big conferences but never at any of the private meetings that the President had with Stalin or with Churchill. I was in general contact with Hiss almost every day in one form or another, and can say that Hiss had no special views to offer on any subjects except those affecting the United Nations, which was his responsibility on the delegation.

Finally, with some reluctance, Roosevelt agreed to the admission of the two Soviet republics, the Ukraine and White Russia, to the world organization as initial members. James F. Byrnes, the director of War Mobilization, remembering the debates in the Senate over the League of Nations, was apprehensive of congressional reaction to three votes for the Soviet Union and six for Britain and her Commonwealth members, and persuaded Roosevelt to write Stalin and Churchill after Yalta asking support for three votes for the United States in the General Assembly. Both consented. When the idea of three American votes leaked in Washington, it was greeted with ridicule by the public. The request was dropped by the American government. I have never heard that there was any other motive on Roosevelt's part except to offset the three Soviet votes. I believe Roosevelt, ill and exhausted with days of arguing, simply made a mistake.

With the war in Europe approaching an end, Roosevelt was eager to take up with Stalin Soviet conditions for joining in the war against Japan. In 1943, in Moscow, Stalin had indicated that he would enter the war at the proper time. His statement to then Secretary of State Hull was general and made no mention of conditions for Soviet entry. At Teheran, Stalin told the conference that "once Germany was finally defeated" the Soviet Union would join the Allies in the war against Japan. Although I cannot find it in the records of Teheran, l distinctly remember Stalin telling Roosevelt that in good time he would make known his "desiderata" for entry into the Japanese war. At a meeting in October, 1944, and again in December, Stalin outlined his "desiderata"; Harriman, who was present, reported them fully to Roosevelt. Since I had not assumed the duties of liaison officer with the White House at that time, I was unaware of Stalin's views, but in essence they were the same as those he presented at Yalta.

With the Allied armies closing in on Germany by the time of Yalta, the moment was right to raise the question with the Soviets. The United States Joint Chiefs of Staff, in a paper dated January 23, 1945, emphasized the importance of Soviet participation in the war against Japan. I was not privy to the details of our military need for Soviet forces in the Japanese war, but I did know of the great importance attached to Soviet help. At Malta and at Yalta, the Combined Chiefs of Staff of the United States and Britain agreed that the war in the Pacific would last eighteen months after the defeat of Germany. This estimate was made before the first successful test of the atomic bomb. It should also be borne in mind that the United States already had plans for two major amphibious assaults on the main Japanese islands. It was estimated that American casualties would be reduced by 200,-000 if the Soviet Union entered the war before these landings. This estimate, it is now believed, was highly exaggerated, but from all I heard at Yalta and from what I have learned since, Roosevelt's one reason for seeking Soviet entry into the Asian war was to save the hundreds of thousands of American lives his military experts estimated would otherwise be lost.

It was at the second private meeting between Stalin and Roosevelt, on February 8, that Asia was discussed. Stalin brought up the question of the conditions under which the Soviet Union would enter the war against Japan. The President said Harriman had filled him in on the conversations with Churchill in October and he did not foresee any difficulty in regard to the one condition relating to the return of the southern half of Sakhalin and the Kurile Islands.

If the President had done his homework, or if any of us had been more familiar with Far Eastern history, the United States might not have given all the Kuriles to Stalin so easily. The President evidently thought that both southern Sakhalin and the Kuriles had been seized by Japan in the 1904 war and that Russia therefore was only getting back territories that had been taken from her. As a report prepared before Yalta by George H. Blakeslee, a State Department consultant, showed, Japan had seized only southern Sakhalin in the 1904 war; it had obtained the Kuriles in an 1875 Treaty of Commerce and Navigation with Russia.

The President reminded Stalin that they had discussed another Soviet condition—a warm-water port in the Far East for the Soviet Union—and he mentioned Dairen at the end of the Manchurian Railroad as a possibility. Roosevelt added that he had not yet had an opportunity to discuss this matter with Chiang Kai-shek, and therefore he could not speak for the Chinese. He mentioned two methods by which it might be accomplished—leasing from the Chinese or the establishment of an international free port.

Stalin made no comment on the President's suggestion, but brought up a third condition—the use by the Soviets of the Chinese-owned Manchurian Railroad. The President, again noting that he had not talked with Chiang Kai-shek about the subject, said that there were again two methods—direct lease or a joint commission.

Stalin said that it was clear that if these conditions were not met, it would be difficult for him and Molotov to explain to the people why the Soviet Union was entering the war against Japan. The people understood the war against Germany, he explained, but it would be hard for them to understand why Russia would go to war against a country which had not attacked them. On the other hand, he said, if political conditions were met, the people would realize the national interests involved and it would be much easier to explain the decision to the Supreme Soviet. The idea of referring issues to the Supreme Soviet, as though it was the pre-eminent arbiter in the country, was a frequent Stalin gambit. Actually, the Supreme Soviet had no power whatsoever. Everybody knew that all power in the Soviet Union resided in Stalin, but as a matter of courtesy, no one at the Yalta Conference disputed him.

Then the President for the third time—it was obvious that he was bothered by what he was doing—said that he had not had an opportunity to talk to Chiang Kai-shek, and observed that one of the difficulties in speaking to the Chinese was a lack of security—anything said to them was known to the whole world in twenty-four hours. Stalin agreed with this and said he did not think it was necessary yet to speak to the Chinese. He suggested that the conditions be set forth in writing, and the President indicated that this could be done.

I did not participate in the negotiations, which were carried on by Harriman and Molotov. I merely saw the final version of the agreement, which was approved by the President at one of his last meetings with Stalin. The agreement provided that "two or three months after Germany has surrendered," the Soviet Union would enter into the war against Japan on the conditions that Outer Mongolia would remain a Soviet republic; the southern part of Sakhalin "be returned" to the Soviet Union; the port of Dairen be internationalized; Port Arthur be leased to Moscow for a naval base; the Chinese-Eastern Railroad and the South Manchurian Railroad be operated by a joint Soviet-Chinese company, "it being understood that the preeminent interest of the Soviet Union shall be safeguarded"; and the Kurile Islands "be handed over to the Soviet Union."

Thus, because Americans were napping, the Soviet Union obtained the Kurile Islands, which Japan had not obtained by force but by peaceful treaty. Moreover, the Harriman-Molotov agreement failed to list the islands that made up the Kuriles. When the Soviet Union entered the Asian war later in 1945, the Red Army took over four islands that Japan insisted were not part of the Kuriles but of a different group, the Northern Territories, which had always been Japanese. It was not until 1972 that Moscow would consent to talk about returning any of these islands.

I doubt if Molotov kept the description of the Kuriles out of the agreement on purpose. But there was another imprecision in the agreement that certainly resulted from Soviet design—the description of Soviet rights in Manchuria as "preeminent." This word was subsequently utilized by the Soviets to get a position in Manchuria that was certainly not in the minds of the American negotiators. The word "preeminent," it seemed to us, was taken strictly from the Soviets. It is not the type of word that would appear in American diplomatic documents. It was an unfortunate choice, since it provided the Soviets with the legal basis to assert all sorts of interests and positions in Manchuria.

While the terms were ambiguous, the principal fault with the agreement on Soviet entry into the war was that it turned out to be completely unnecessary in view of the devastating effect of the atom bomb in Japan. I remain of the opinion, however, that the Chinese would not have received better terms from the Russians had there been no Yalta agreement.

The real criticism of the Yalta agreement was that it was made behind the backs of our Chinese allies. Although Roosevelt mentioned a number of times that he would have to consult with Chiang Kai-shek, the fact remains that the agreement was made without the knowledge or approval of the Chinese. While I doubt if at that stage of the war the Japanese would have thought of any military action against the Soviet Union, nevertheless both the Americans and the Russians seemed to feel that lack of security in Chungking would lead to leaks. I had no knowledge of conditions in China and therefore had no views whatsoever as to whether or not this was true or a reason invented to cover up deals behind the backs of the Chinese. This agreement was held in the closest secrecy. Except for Stettinius, Harriman, and me, no State Department representatives knew of it.

It was three months later, in May, before the Chinese were informed of the terms of the Yalta agreement. President Roosevelt had died and President Truman had succeeded him. Truman read the terms to the Chinese Foreign Minister, T. V. Soong, who was en route to Moscow to begin negotiations with the Russians. Truman asked me to attend the meeting. Soong, an intelligent man, saw the overriding strategy considerations that led to the agreement. I had the impression that he looked on the agreement as a backstop to the Chinese in the face of even more far-reaching demands from the Kremlin. In fact, the agreement did serve that purpose, and he invoked it during his negotiations in Moscow. As for Roosevelt's failure to consult the Chinese before the deal, Soong tactfully accepted Truman's generalized explanation about the importance of military secrecy.

Another agreement at Yalta that was certainly open to question and perhaps caused the United States and Britain more moral anguish than any other was the one made by our military representatives and signed by Roosevelt for the return of the citizens of one country in territories overrun by the armies of another. Our military leaders believed that, without some such arrangement, the Soviet Union might find a pretext to retain the thousands of American prisoners who had been sent to camps in parts of Poland or East Germany subsequently captured by the Soviet armies if we did not force reluctant Russian prisoners of war to return to the Soviet Union. It was regarded as prudent to deprive the Soviets of any pretext for holding off the release of American prisoners. It has always been my feeling that the execution of this agreement went beyond conditions laid down in the text. The controlling paragraph of the agreement said, "All Soviet citizens liberated by the forces operating under United States command and all the United States citizens liberated by forces operating under Soviet command will without delay after their liberation be separated from enemy prisoners of war and will be maintained separately from them in camps or points of concentration until they have been handed over to the United States or Soviet authorities, as the case may be, at places agreed upon between the authorities."

There was nothing in this agreement that required the forcible repatriation of unwilling Soviet citizens to the Soviet Union. Yet this is exactly what happened in Germany; and for six months or so after the surrender, trainloads of Soviet citizens—men, women, and children—were sent back to the Soviet Union against their sometimes physically resisting efforts. The execution of the repatriations was entirely determined by the American and British military. In the spring of 1946, the forcible repatriation was stopped. By that time, all American POWs were out of Soviet-held areas, and there was little Molotov could do about it.

The closing hours of Yalta were similar to other conferences. There was great confusion and a good deal of irritation and squabbling among members of our own delegation over the wording of the final communiqué. I was heavily involved, having to translate from Russian to English and English to Russian. We finished the job in the middle of the night, and then piled into automobiles for the eighty-mile drive back to the airport at Saki. I doubt if anybody was thinking very much about the conference as a whole or assessing its successes and its failures. Although there was a sense of frustration and some bitterness in regard to Poland, the general mood was one of satisfaction.

Each of the three leaders had achieved his major goals. Roosevelt had obtained Stalin's pledge to open a second front against the Japanese and acceptance of a voting formula that would give the United Nations a chance to work. These seemed like immense achievements indeed. Large American casualties in the final assault on Japan might be avoided with Soviet help. As for the United Nations, the agreement meant that Roosevelt had apparently avoided President Wilson's mistake of waiting until after the war, when isolationist feelings returned, to solve the problems. Churchill had also achieved his goal of creating a counterweight to the Soviet Union on the Continent by building up France. Stalin had fought off the Western Allies' attempts to modify his grasp on Poland, thus ensuring his domination of Eastern Europe, and had struck a profitable bargain in Asia.

In each case, the results could hardly be looked on at that time as triumph or defeat for anyone. Rather, the agreements seemed to us to be realistic compromises between the various positions of each country. Stalin had made a genuine concession in finally agreeing to France as one of the powers occupying Germany. Each country altered its position on the United Nations. The United States and Britain had given in a great deal on Poland, but the plan as finally agreed to could have led to a genuinely democratic government if it had been carried out.

In short, there was hope, as we left Yalta, of genuine cooperation with the Soviet Union on political questions after the war. Kennan's gloomy assessment, which I had read on my first day at Yalta, had not yet proved correct. It would take Stalin's refusal to carry out his bargain on Poland, his disregard of the Declaration on Liberated Europe, and other actions to extinguish our hopes for Soviet cooperation.

Even with all the advantages of hindsight, however, I do not believe that the Western Allies could have walked away from the attempt to reach an understanding with the Soviet Union. Nor do I believe that through harder bargaining we could have struck a better deal with

Stalin. Certainly spheres of influence were not the answer. The fault was not the agreements at Yalta, but something far deeper. Regardless of all that was said or not said, written or not written, agreed to or not agreed to at the Yalta Conference, there was nothing that could have prevented the breakup of the victorious coalition and the onset of the cold war once Stalin set his course.

Hope dies hard, however, in the American diplomatic breast, and for the next few years I found myself traveling back and forth across the Atlantic in a vain quest for an understanding with the Kremlin.

CHAPTER TWELVE

A Change at the White House

At Saki, I boarded the *Sacred Cow*
with the President and Hopkins and flew to Egypt. We did not talk
very much; we were all exhausted. We landed in the Suez Canal Zone,
where the cruiser *Quincy* was waiting in Great Bitter Lake. Roosevelt
thought that his stay at the lake would be an excellent opportunity to
meet the rulers of the Middle East. He had invited some of the Arab
sovereigns to luncheons and had even dispatched the U.S.S. *Murphy*,
a destroyer, to bring Ibn Saud of Saudi Arabia from Jiddah. As set
forth in the protocol list before his arrival on board the *Quincy*, in the
King's party were the royal astrologer, a coffee server, and "nine mis-
cellaneous slaves, cooks, porters and scullions." The Arabs refused to
go below deck on the *Murphy*. Most had never been on a ship before,
and some had never even seen the sea. The King sat on deck in a great
gilt armchair for practically the entire voyage. Rather than eat the
ship's food, the Muslims slaughtered one of their sheep on the fantail
before the fascinated eyes of officers and crew. Less spectacular but
even more eye-popping was the Arab attempt to make coffee in bra-
ziers they set up next to the ready-ammunition hoist.

Three admirals and the President of the United States were on the
bridge of the *Quincy* as the U.S.S. *Murphy* approached with Ibn
Saud sitting in his armchair guarded by barefoot Nubian soldiers with
drawn sabers. It was an impressive sight until the commander of the
Murphy misjudged his approach. Instead of coming in smoothly
alongside the *Quincy*, the *Murphy* hit the cruiser a glancing blow
with her bow and had to back off and make a new approach. When
the two ships were finally nestled together, Ibn Saud walked up the
gangway, lordly in his flowing robes, but with a pronounced limp,

202

apparently from a wound received in internecine warfare in Arabia. He greeted the President, who was in his wheelchair, and the two went to a cabin to confer over lunch.

Because Hopkins was too ill to leave his cabin, I had been asked by the President to join the conversations. The discussion, interpreted by Colonel William A. Eddy, our Minister to Saudi Arabia, centered mostly on the Zionist campaign for a Jewish homeland in Palestine.

The President was pro-Zionist. After dinner at Yalta on February 10, Roosevelt had asked Stalin if he was for the Zionists. Stalin had answered warily: yes, in principle, but he recognized the difficulty of solving the Jewish problem. The Soviet attempt to establish a Jewish home at Birobidzhan had failed because the Jews scattered to other cities. Some small groups had been successful at farming, he said. Roosevelt then mentioned that he was going to see Ibn Saud right after the Yalta Conference. Stalin asked what he was going to give the King. The President replied, with a smile, that there was only one concession that he thought he might offer and that was to give Ibn Saud the six million Jews in the United States. Stalin said again that the solution to the Jewish problem was difficult. He called the Jews "middlemen, profiteers and parasites" and joked, "No Jew could live in Yaroslavl"—a city noted for the sharpness of its merchants. Roosevelt smiled, but did not reply.*

At the meeting with Ibn Saud, the President expressed the hope that the Arab countries would permit the immigration to Palestine of some 10,000 Jews from the troubled area of Eastern Europe and Germany. Ibn Saud gave a long dissertation on the basic attitude of Arabs toward the Jews. He denied that there had ever been any conflict between the two branches of the Semitic race in the Middle East. What changed the whole picture was the immigration from Eastern Europe of people who were technically and culturally on a higher level than the Arabs. As a result, King Ibn Saud said, the Arabs had great difficulty in surviving economically. The fact that these energetic Europeans were Jewish was not the cause of the trouble, he said; it was their superior skills and culture.

The President made a long appeal on behalf of the Jewish people, who had suffered so much under Hitler. Ibn Saud gravely replied that he did not see why the Arabs had to expiate the sins of Adolf Hitler when there were other countries in a much better position to help. "Arabs would choose to die rather than yield their land to Jews," he said.

The President assured the King that he would make no move

---

* In the official published version, this conversation was omitted.

hostile to the Arab people. As far as American policy was concerned, Roosevelt said it was impossible to prevent Zionist speeches and resolutions in Congress or articles in the press, but emphasized that he formed his own foreign policy as the chief executive of the United States government.

Ibn Saud's calm and reasoned statement had a profound effect on Roosevelt. When the President returned to the United States and was addressing Congress (for the first time sitting down), he departed from his prepared text to say, "Of the problems of Arabia I learned more about that whole problem, the Moslem problem, the Jewish problem, by talking with Ibn Saud for five minutes than I could have learned in an exchange of two or three dozen letters." American Zionist leaders, fearful that the President was swinging to a pro-Arab policy, rushed to Washington. They were assured that the President still supported the Zionists.

During the *Quincy*'s fueling stop at Alexandria, we were taken aback by a telegram from de Gaulle rejecting an invitation to confer with Roosevelt. At Yalta, Hopkins had received a wire from Paris saying that Georges Bidault, the French Foreign Minister, had decided not to approach the General about attending only the political discussions of the conference. Bidault was certain of an angry rejection. But he had transmitted the invitation to visit with the President at some French port in the Mediterranean. The reply, which Bidault admitted surprised him, was that de Gaulle would be very happy to meet with the President at "any point on French soil." We were pleased, and sent a warm message from the President to de Gaulle welcoming the idea and expressing appreciation that the General would take time out from his duties to travel to the Mediterranean for the meeting. The President proposed that they meet at Algiers, which at that time was an integral part of France, and that de Gaulle join him for lunch, where he would be given a detailed account of exactly what happened at Yalta.

When we arrived at Alexandria, however, we found a message from de Gaulle abruptly rejecting the President's invitation. Roosevelt was furious. He called in Stephen Early, his press secretary, and dictated the outline of a terse and insulting statement on de Gaulle's refusal to meet. When Hopkins saw it, he sent back word by Early to the President that any such public statement would antagonize the French people as well as de Gaulle. The word came back from Early that the Boss had his "Dutch" up and insisted that the statement be released as written. Hopkins then turned to me and said, "Chip, go and see what you can do with the President." I protested, pointing out that I could hardly change the President's mind when neither he nor Early had been able to do so. But Hopkins insisted that I go, and I went. The President was sitting in his cabin, working on his stamp collection. I offered the same argument that Hopkins had about the difficulty of hitting at de Gaulle without, at the same time, hitting at France. "No, no," the President said, "what you don't seem to realize is that the United States has been insulted through its President and this requires an appropriate answer." We kept talking, and eventually I said, "We can all admit that de Gaulle is being one of the biggest sons of bitches who ever straddled a pot." For some reason, that remark tickled the President. His tired eyes suddenly twinkled and his face broke into his famous smile. He threw back his head in his characteristic manner, laughed, and said, "Oh, go ahead, you and Harry try your hand at a draft." I went back to Hopkins, and we worked out a statement expressing the regret of the President at the inability of de Gaulle to join him. It avoided vituperation and did no more than express regret.

At Algiers, Hopkins, who was at that point too ill to contemplate the sea voyage home, and I left the *Quincy*. I heard subsequently from someone who was on the ship that Roosevelt was rather annoyed that both Harry and I had gone. The idea that the President would have wanted me to stay on the ship never crossed my mind. Roosevelt never mentioned the matter to me. Nor did anyone propose that I stay. I had always understood and interpreted my duties as they realistically were, to maintain liaison for the Department of State with the President with the help of Hopkins. I never thought of myself as personally close to Roosevelt. As for Hopkins, there was no question that he needed the rest. He had lost so much strength at Yalta that there was a great deal of doubt whether he could continue in anything like his previous role as the President's closest adviser.

Roosevelt was also exhausted, and the illness of Major General Edwin M. Watson, his intimate friend of many years, depressed the President (Watson died on the *Quincy* on the way home). Although he did not look well, Roosevelt was not regarded by anyone whom I can recall, or have talked to since, as being critically ill then. Thus, the idea that I should stay with the President, rather than with Hopkins, who was obviously ill, never occurred to me. On reflection, the thought came to me that the President might have wanted me to continue working with his special counsel, Judge Samuel I. Rosenman, who had boarded the *Quincy* at Alexandria, on his report to Congress. I had helped Rosenman with the speech for a few days.

Hopkins and I took a plane from Algiers to Mårrakech, where we stayed at a beautiful villa, done in Moorish style, with sunken bathtubs, lovely views on all sides, and an open-air dining room. Hopkins kept close to the villa and rested. I took one day for a shooting expedition with some American soldiers stationed nearby. We saw no game, but the mountain scenery was spectacular. After three or four days, we left Marrakech and flew to the Azores, where the President's plane, the *Sacred Cow*, was waiting for us. The flight to Bermuda was uneventful, and we broke the journey again there to give Hopkins more rest. Despite the rest, Hopkins was so ill when we arrived in Washington that he was flown immediately to the Mayo Clinic, from which he did not emerge until Roosevelt's death in April.

With Hopkins away, I went to the White House every day, usually in the late morning, checked in at the Map Room to look at telegrams, and dropped in to see Admiral Leahy. My conversations with Leahy followed a definite pattern. In his snapping-turtle manner, he usually had some crack to make about General de Gaulle, and I would go to a map on the wall and point out the crucial geographical location of France, which he knew better than I did. A military man who made no pretense to political acumen, Leahy would then grudgingly admit that we had to take care of our relations with France.

I was continually worried by Roosevelt's appearance, and it was now obvious to many that he was a sick man. His hands shook so that he had difficulty in holding a telegram. His weariness and general lassitude were apparent to all, although he could call on reserves of strength whenever he had to meet with congressional leaders or other public figures. But the thought did not occur to me that he was near death. Although I was in the White House daily, I did not become sufficiently intimate with anyone there to talk to him about the President's health. Hopkins was in the Mayo Clinic and my relations with Leahy were not sufficiently close to bring up such a sensitive subject. If those closer to Roosevelt considered the question of how to handle the President's illness, no one mentioned it to me.

Because President Roosevelt's powers of concentration were slipping, and his general energy was lessening, he was forced to rely more than he would have normally on the good faith and judgment of his advisers. Some persons took advantage of his condition, I am sorry to say. For example, an officer of the American government—I was told it was Nelson A. Rockefeller, then Assistant Secretary of State —put before Roosevelt a memorandum authorizing an invitation to Argentina to be a founding member of the United Nations. This is a nearly forgotten matter now, but it was a direct breach of our agreement at Yalta that only those nations that declared war on Germany could be initial members. Argentina did not qualify. Roosevelt signed the memo without fully realizing its content.

During this period, I was responsible for drafting many of the messages that President Roosevelt sent to Stalin and Churchill on the implementation of the Yalta agreements. I often did them myself, or took them back to the Department of State, where the appropriate officer in the department participated in the drafting. There were many messages, because rifts were developing in the alliance. The Soviets were not, to put it mildly, living up to the Yalta agreement on Poland. They were paying little or no attention to Ambassador Harriman or Sir Archibald Clark Kerr, who were supposed to help broaden the base of the Lublin government. Instead, they were consolidating their own government in Warsaw. Nor was there any sign of the early elections that had been promised.

From Moscow, Harriman cabled reports of Soviet refusal to carry out the Yalta agreements. On March 6, 1945, he cabled Stettinius of his appeals to Molotov:

> We have had three more unproductive hours of discussion at the meeting of the Commission on Poland this evening going over much of the same ground as last time. ... Every argument Clark Kerr and I advanced was brushed aside. For example, I told him [Molotov] that I knew the President would be shocked to learn of Molotov's obstruction to the progress of the work of the commission in objecting to our calling representative Polish democratic leaders in Moscow. I pointed out that Marshal Stalin had agreed to inviting Sapieha and Witos to Yalta and I failed to understand why Molotov now went back on his position. In reply he said that the communiqué was the "anchor" for the commission's work and that no other conversation at Yalta had a bearing.

The suspicions that Kennan had mentioned in his letter to me at Yalta were turning out to be soundly based. Despite all of Roosevelt's efforts to get along with Moscow, Stalin was doing exactly as Kennan had predicted and I had feared. I was disheartened, but still did not agree with Kennan that we should write off Eastern Europe and give up efforts to cooperate with the Soviet Union. There should never be a single doubt that we had stood up for the right of the people on the Soviet border to determine their own destinies. Nor should there be doubt that we had made every effort to maintain friendly relations with the Soviet Union.

We sent a stream of protests to Moscow, and so did the British. On April 1, for example, I drafted for the President a message to Stalin expressing our concern at the fate of the agreements on Poland and pointing out the consequences of our failure to agree. This message was transmitted to Churchill for his approval, which he gave immediately. In fact, he informed the President he had called a special session of the War Cabinet in order to put the full weight of that body behind the "grave and weighty" message.

Despite all the messages on Poland sent in the closing days of Roosevelt's administration, there was not the slightest sign that the Soviets paid any attention. Instead, Stalin suddenly informed the President that Molotov would not attend the founding conference of the United Nations in San Francisco—at best a mark of indifference to the United Nations.

Poland was just one of the areas where the Soviet Union was acting like an enemy and not like an ally. In Rumania, Hungary, Bulgaria, and elsewhere, the Soviets were showing that the Declaration on Liberated Europe meant nothing.

Soviet suspicions of the West, which had submerged after the opening of the second front, returned now in a more virulent form. Field Marshal Albert Kesselring, the German commander in Italy, indicated to Allen Dulles, the OSS representative in Berne, his desire to talk about the surrender of the German forces in Italy independently of the main German forces in Germany. The British agreed that Allen Dulles should pursue this matter. Moscow was informed and was assured that once actual surrender terms were considered a Soviet representative would be present. The early contacts were extremely tentative in nature and, of course, highly secret. It was feared on the Allied side that if the Soviets were brought into the proceedings at this juncture, the whole effort would collapse. This decision may be subject to criticism in a postwar atmosphere, but at the time it seemed normal and wise, since the huge prize of German surrender in Italy was at stake. To my mind, it was quite proper and understandable that the Western Allies thought it too risky to enlarge the number of Allied participants and thereby change the whole exploratory nature of the talks. Unsatisfied with our assurances, Stalin sent a message which I think more than almost any other document angered and depressed the President. Stalin insisted that there was reason to believe that the United States and Germany were engaged in some form of secret undertaking. He went so far as to say, "Some of my advisers find it difficult to explain the rapidity of the advance of the Anglo-American armies in Germany unless there is some underlying agreement with the Nazis." This was a direct insult to the United States.

Roosevelt was furious. It was one of the few times that I saw him angry. He was seated at his desk at the White House, his eyes flashing, his face flushed, outraged that he should be accused of dealing with the Germans behind Stalin's back. In his reply to Stalin, which I helped draft, the President denied emphatically, but with dignity, insinuations of collusion with the Nazis, and expressed disbelief that anyone could take the advice of such counselors. He said that if Stalin continued to listen to these advisers, the outlook for American-Russian relations was discouraging. Stalin's answer was characteristic. He said his advisers must have been misinformed, but he was reassured by the President's message. This exchange cast a pall over Roosevelt just before his departure for Warm Springs, where he died. The last message Roosevelt sent to a foreign leader was one to Churchill in which he said that despite the difficulties, the Western Allies must persist.

The news of Roosevelt's death reached Washington in the early afternoon on April 12, 1945. Someone in the State Department handed me a flash dispatch from a news wire. I was given the mission of transmitting the sad news to Harry Hopkins. I called him at the Mayo Clinic. There was a long silence at the other end of the phone. Then Hopkins said, "I guess I better be going to Washington."

The Russians were deeply affected by Roosevelt's death. When Ambassador Harriman went to the Kremlin to convey the news officially, he found Stalin upset. There is no reason to believe this was an act; Stalin did have a regard for Roosevelt, and on a number of occasions at the wartime conferences I saw the Marshal show genuine feeling toward the President. He rarely argued with Roosevelt, and his refusals of Roosevelt's requests were always made with regret. I do think Stalin respected Roosevelt as a man who genuinely believed in democratic liberalism. Stalin obviously did not agree with or even understand democratic liberalism and therefore did things in accordance with his Marxian commitments. But on balance, I think he had a higher regard for Roosevelt than he did for Churchill. It is conceivable that Stalin did not consider Roosevelt to be as difficult or as tough an adversary as Churchill, but he did respect the President.

Stalin expressed his commiseration to Harriman and then asked what the Soviet Union could do to show its appreciation of Roosevelt. With great perspicacity, Harriman promptly replied that the best thing Stalin could do would be to reverse his decision and send Molotov to the United Nations Conference in San Francisco. This, he explained, would show Soviet interest in what might turn out to be Roosevelt's greatest memorial. Stalin readily agreed.

It is hardly necessary for me to point out the importance of Franklin D. Roosevelt. He was a world figure of monumental proportions. Roosevelt's strength in dealing with foreign leaders stemmed from his enormous popularity throughout the world, even in countries he had never been in. Yet I cannot say that he was a likable man. He preferred informal relationships which were informal merely in structure. He could not stand protocol in the accepted sense of the word but was quick to resent the slightest departure from the respect normally accorded the President of the United States, and the aura of the office was always around him. Even Hopkins was always respectful and careful in his manner with the President. Roosevelt influenced people by the fact that he was President. Among those who worked with him in the White House for long periods of time, there was real affection for him, but not the kind of human feeling that springs from personal love.

In foreign affairs, Roosevelt did his job only moderately well. The methods and techniques that he usually used with consummate skill in domestic politics* did not fit well in foreign affairs. He relied on his instinctive grasp of the subject, which was good, and his genius for improvisation to find solutions to problems. In domestic affairs, where all elements were under the same national roof and therefore the reactions had a pattern of similarity, this technique worked. In foreign affairs, particularly when dealing with Soviet leaders, this style meant a lack of precision, which, as I have pointed out, was a serious fault.

A deeper knowledge of history and certainly a better understanding of reactions of foreign peoples would have been useful to the President. Helpful, too, would have been more study of the position papers prepared by American experts, more attention to detail, and less belief in the American conviction that the other fellow is a "good guy" who will respond properly and decently if you treat him right.

---

* I was somewhat shocked at Roosevelt's bitterness, in conversations with me at dinner aboard the *Quincy* on the way from Alexandria to Algiers, in denouncing the Senate as a bunch of incompetent obstructionists. He did not name any senators, but indicated that the only way to do anything in the American government was to bypass the Senate.

As far as the Soviets were concerned, I do not think Roosevelt had any real comprehension of the great gulf that separated the thinking of a Bolshevik from a non-Bolshevik, and particularly from an American. He felt that Stalin viewed the world somewhat in the same light as he did, and that Stalin's hostility and distrust, which were evident in the wartime conferences, were due to the neglect that Soviet Russia had suffered at the hands of other countries for years after the Revolution. What he did not understand was that Stalin's enmity was based on profound ideological convictions. The existence of a gap between the Soviet Union and the United States, a gap that could not be bridged, was never fully perceived by Franklin Roosevelt.

Whether or not our relations with the Soviet Union would have been better under Roosevelt than they were under Truman is an open question. Certainly the Kremlin had considerable respect for Roosevelt, in a large measure because they understood what a powerful figure he was in the entire Western world. Since the Russians always respect power, whatever its source, this might have made Stalin somewhat more careful with Roosevelt than he was with Truman. Given great prestige and his reputation for dealing fairly with Stalin, Roosevelt would have been in a position to have adopted a much firmer line toward the Soviet Union—as I am confident that he would have—with a much greater degree of public acceptance than Truman did. One of Truman's problems was that our wartime disagreements with the Soviet Union had been hidden from the public by secrecy. Any breaches of Russo-American amity consequently have been attributed by some historians to what they erroneously describe as Truman's mishandling of our relations with the Soviet Union, including an alleged failure of the United States to carry out the Yalta agreements.

I tend to believe that even if Roosevelt had lived out his fourth term, the map of Europe would look about the same. If there was one lesson that emerged from the wartime conferences and our postwar dealings with the Soviet Union, it was that the Soviets were going to hold any territory their armies occupied (Austria turned out to be an exception) and install their own system behind their armies, regardless of who was President of the United States.

In dealing with Churchill, Roosevelt also had serious deficiencies. He did not always support the Prime Minister at critical times; he was careless, rarely keeping records of his conversations because there was no interpreter. They did, however, make a good team.

In appraising Roosevelt as a diplomatist, I do not mean to imply that he made many great blunders on foreign policy. He did lead the

United States out of its isolationism; he saw the menace of Hitler long before most other American leaders. Without him, it is unlikely that there would be the United Nations, which, as weak as it is, can be a useful forum in world affairs. His greatest single mistake, I believe, was his insistence on the doctrine of unconditional surrender, which, as I have already said, probably lengthened the war by convincing the Germans they should fight on, and precluded the formation of a government that could have negotiated with the Allies and possibly prevented the division of the country.

Another serious error Roosevelt made was to isolate Vice-President Truman from the wartime conferences and foreign affairs in general. Roosevelt made enormous contributions to American foreign policy, but he failed to give any on-the-job training to the man in line to succeed him. The error was compounded by the fact that the task of making peace descended on the new President with startling speed. Within a month of Roosevelt's death—on May 7—Germany surrendered unconditionally. We in the State Department shared the concern of all Americans whether the "little man from Missouri" could rise to the occasion. I had not met Truman at the time he became president. He was an obscure vice-president, who got to see Roosevelt much less than I did and who knew less than I did about United States foreign relations. The one element of his reputation that stood out was his competence as a senator investigating the American war effort. It took some months for Americans to discover the decisiveness of their new President. Molotov learned Truman's quality much more quickly.

Before Molotov arrived in Washington on his way to the United Nations Conference in San Francisco, Truman summoned his top foreign-policy and military advisers to the White House to discuss problems regarding the Yalta agreements and particularly the line the President should take in his talks with the Soviet Foreign Minister. (The title "Commissar" had been replaced by the more Western term.) General Marshall wanted to make sure nothing interfered with the agreement for Soviet entry into the war against Japan. It must be remembered that this was in the latter part of April, before the atomic bomb had been successfully tested, and there was still worry about casualties in the planned invasions of the main Japanese islands. The majority of the other advisers, led by Averell Harriman and including me (it was the first time I met Truman), thought the President should make it plain to the Soviets that the United States was by no means pleased with the way they were ignoring the Yalta agreements in

Eastern Europe and that he was not disposed to let them get away with it. Following the meeting, James Dunn, Stettinius's European political adviser, and I remained behind at the President's request. The President told us he had decided to follow the advice of the majority in his meeting with Molotov. Indeed he did.

When Molotov arrived in Washington, Truman paid him a courtesy call at Blair House. It was merely an exchange of amenities, with no business discussed. I was the President's interpreter. The next day, Molotov went to the White House to call on the President in the Oval Office. Molotov began the discussion by asking the President whether he, as the successor to President Roosevelt, was prepared to honor the secret agreements that the United States had made concerning Soviet entry into the war in the Far East, and specifically the commitments which had been made to persuade the Chinese to give Moscow certain rights in Manchuria and to force the Japanese to cede territory acquired in the war of 1904. President Truman quickly assured Molotov that he would certainly honor all the Yalta commitments. But Truman sternly added that the United States was getting tired of waiting for the Soviet Union to carry out agreements it had freely entered into that would give Eastern European nations a chance to establish democratic regimes.

Molotov interrupted with a general statement that the Poles had been working against the Red Army. Truman firmly and briskly said he was not interested in propaganda; he merely wished that Molotov would inform Stalin of his concern over the failure of the Soviet government to live up to the agreements at Yalta. Molotov turned a little ashy and attempted to steer the discussion back to the Far East, but Truman cut him off and said, "That will be all, Mr. Molotov. I would appreciate it if you would transmit my views to Marshal Stalin." Having been dismissed, Molotov quickly left. How I enjoyed translating Truman's sentences! They were probably the first sharp words uttered during the war by an American President to a high Soviet official.

Even so, however, I thought that President Truman was merely saying what Roosevelt would have said had he been alive. Roosevelt's technique would have been different, his approach would have possibly been more diplomatic and somewhat smoother, but he was in no mood the last time I saw him, only days before he died, to take further Soviet violations of the Yalta accord lying down. Truman's tough talk with Molotov could not be made public at the time because the war was still on, and it would have been a great shock to the

Americans, as well as to others, if it appeared that the United States and the Soviet Union were having serious differences.

The next day, Molotov flew to San Francisco. I accompanied Secretary Stettinius to the United Nations meeting and was his interpreter during his conversations with Molotov. Most of the discussions dealt with Soviet problems, including the admission of White Russia and the Ukraine as initial members of the world organization. In accordance with the Yalta commitment, their admission was approved by the Coordinating Committee, the body that was doing the substantive work of the conference.

Molotov then tried to bull the designation of its satellite Lublin group through the committee, although there was still no agreement on the Polish government. The attempt to win United Nations backing for the Soviets' Polish regime ran into opposition, the first, I believe, publicly expressed by an Allied government to a Soviet move during the war. Paul Henri Spaak, the Belgian Foreign Minister, said that he was astonished that the Soviet Foreign Minister at that stage of world history should introduce into the middle of the formative conference probably the most delicate—*brûlante* was his term— question on the international scene, particularly after the concession to the Soviet Union on White Russia and the Ukraine.

Shortly after the meeting, I went into the bar of the Fairmont Hotel, where I was staying, and saw Jan Masaryk, the Czech Foreign Minister, drinking a whiskey and soda. "Bohlen," he asked, "what can one do with these Russians?" Without waiting for an answer, he went on, "Out of the clear blue sky I got a note from Molotov saying Czechoslovakia must vote for the Soviet proposition in regard to Poland, or else forfeit the friendship of the Soviet government." He paused, and then asked another rhetorical question. "What kind of a way is that to behave to a country that is trying to be friendly?" Bitterly, he commented on the crude Soviet diplomatic technique: "You can be on your knees and this is not enough for the Russians." Needless to say, Czechoslovakia did vote with Moscow on Poland. But the motion was not passed.

During the San Francisco proceedings, Eden and Stettinius had asked Molotov to ascertain the whereabouts of sixteen Polish underground leaders who had been invited by the Kremlin to Moscow to discuss the formation of a government and then had disappeared. Molotov promised to look into the matter. One night, Molotov invited some of the delegates to dinner at the Soviet Consulate in San Francisco. I walked in with Stettinius, who greeted Molotov with his usual ready smile. As they were shaking hands, Molotov said, "Oh, by the way, Mr. Stettinius, about those sixteen Poles; they have all been arrested by the Red Army." He immediately turned away and said, "Hello, Mr. Eden." Stettinius was left standing there with a fixed smile on his face.

Worried and irritated by the Soviets' general behavior, Harriman met with a number of American newsmen and, with circumspection, advanced the view that the goals of the Soviet Union and the United States were so opposed that any possibility of future cooperation was not realistic. So strong was pro-Russian sympathy in those days that some of the correspondents were outraged. If I remember correctly, Walter Lippmann walked out of the interview. Raymond Gram Swing, in a broadcast, stated that diplomats who lost their belief in the ultimate purpose of our diplomacy in relation to the Soviet Union were expendable.

On the flight back to Washington, Harriman and I got into a long discussion over what could be done to restore amity in Soviet-American relations. The war in Europe had just ended, and something had to be done quickly. With some hesitation, I said if Roosevelt were alive, he would undoubtedly think of sending Harry Hopkins to see Stalin. The reason I hesitated was that I did not want Harriman to think that he, as ambassador, was not capable of handling relations with the Kremlin himself. Harriman liked the idea, and said he would propose it to Truman, whom he was seeing shortly after his return to Washington. First, however, we went to see Hopkins, who was living in a little rented house in Georgetown. He was in bed and emaciated by illness. Nevertheless, as soon as the possibility of a trip to Moscow was mentioned, he became enthusiastic. Harriman then put forward the idea to the President, who promptly sent a message to Stalin. The latter accepted the suggestion, and the visit was thus arranged. One of the reasons Truman agreed to the Hopkins trip was our desire to meet separately with Stalin before the next Big Three conference, which had not been scheduled but was being talked about.

Stephen Early, who was about to resign as White House press secretary, suggested to Truman that as a related move he send Joseph E. Davies to London to see Churchill. Early was about to take a job with the Pullman Company, of which Davies was a director. The ostensible reason for the Davies trip was to fill in Churchill, too, on the views of the new President. Hopkins, who was the subject of much abuse as a sinister influence on Roosevelt, told me that there was another motive in the Davies mission. The purpose was to mitigate expected criticism that Truman was blindly following Roosevelt's policy, including the use of Roosevelt's alter ego. Whether there was any validity to this, I do not know. In any event, Davies went to London, where his pro-Soviet views irritated Churchill, who was preparing for a general election. Churchill was deeply discouraged about the Soviet Union's actions in Europe and possibly no less worried about the American reaction. He did not know Truman and had no way of judging him. Davies's sentimental view of Stalin struck Churchill as dangerous appeasement. Churchill had been bombarding Truman with appeals for American military occupation of as much territory as possible to obtain the strongest negotiating position with the Soviets.

Stalin, with his knowledge that politics follows armies, was not holding back. He was wasting thousands of Red Army lives in his haste to stake out as much territory as possible. In a message to Truman on May 12, Churchill pointed to the extent of the Soviet occupation and expressed serious misgivings as to Soviet policies. He argued that the Moscow plan for reparations would permit the occupation of Germany for an indefinite period. In the same message, he said that "an iron curtain is drawn down" on the Soviet area, the first use, I believe, of the term that to this day accurately describes Soviet actions.

Truman, still feeling his way, was puzzled by conflicting advice. After his tough talk with Molotov, he tended to ease up on the Soviets, and rejected Churchill's power-politics approach to diplomacy. He left the decision on the movement of troops entirely to Eisenhower and the Joint Chiefs of Staff. This decision may have been a mistake, but it did follow the American tradition in the conduct of wars. Although I was not consulted, I certainly would not have disputed the President's decision at the end of the war to pull American troops back to our zones in Germany and Austria. I believe it would have been an egregious error to have followed Churchill's advice to hold on to our positions in the Soviet zones in Saxony and Thuringia. Such a standfast would have given the Kremlin a permanent reason for charging that relationships developed in the war had been torn up and discarded by the United States. Furthermore, we would have lost virtually all of Austria, because Red Army troops occupied most of that country.

Churchill was opposed to a Stalin-Truman meeting before the three leaders' conference, but did want to talk with the President himself. At a White House meeting on May 15, the President asked me if our relations with the Soviet Union would be damaged if he met with Churchill first. Like Roosevelt, Truman did not want to give Stalin the impression that Washington and London were united in their attitude toward Moscow. I told Truman what I had told Roosevelt—that the Soviets considered it logical that Britain and the United States should be close, and that therefore such a meeting, demonstrating Western unity, might make Stalin more reasonable.

Truman thought it important that, since the site of the first two conferences had been selected to please Stalin, the Soviet dictator "come over to meet us" for the next conference. For this reason, Truman opposed their meeting in Germany and proposed Alaska. He asked me what I thought. I am amazed now at what I said in reply. I said that a site within swift communication of Moscow, whether it be Germany or somewhere else, was preferable. I explained that all of us who had been at Yalta "felt that the Soviet failure to carry out the agreement reached there had been due in large part to opposition inside the Soviet government which Stalin encountered on his return." This is a view that was popular in Washington at the time; in the wartime atmosphere, I went along with it.

I certainly knew that the Politburo was not the ruling committee it was supposed to be. It was undoubtedly true that before Stalin made up his mind, there was discussion in the Politburo at which some members expressed a harder line than others. But there is no reason to believe that Stalin was persuaded by one group as against another. And there has never been any evidence that he was overruled by other members of the Politburo. He made the decisions.

The explanation of the Soviet Union's postwar intransigence that seems most plausible to me is that Stalin changed his own mind after Yalta. He realized that any attempt to carry out the Yalta agreements would have resulted in the loss of Communist power in Poland—because the Polish people would have voted against Communist candidates. Stalin seldom received accurate information on public opinion. At Yalta, he very well may have believed that the Poles were welcoming the Red Army as liberators. When he talked with the Polish Communists whom he had sent in with the Red Army, he was probably discreetly told the truth—that the Poles were anti-Russian and especially anti-Soviet. This meant that if the Yalta accord had been carried out, the Polish Communists would not be able to rule in Poland. Learning this, Stalin had no hesitancy in breaking the agreement.

I was not present when Hopkins talked to the President, so I am not certain what instructions he received regarding the trip to Moscow. In subsequent conversations with Hopkins, I gathered that he was to sound out Stalin—to get at what was bothering the dictator. Specifically, Hopkins was to try to get the stalled Polish negotiations moving again, with a view to a settlement consistent with the Yalta agreement. More than that, he was to endeavor to inform Stalin of the consequences that lay down the road he was following in Europe—a breakup of the alliance. Hopkins asked me to accompany him. He also took along his charming wife, Louise.

Beginning in late May, we had almost ten consecutive days of meetings with Stalin in the Kremlin, with some sessions lasting as long as four hours. This was the best opportunity I ever had to observe the Soviet dictator. I had not seen him since the Yalta Conference, in February. His manner was, if anything, even milder and more conciliatory than in the past. He certainly went out of his way to be extremely courteous to Hopkins, not only because of his regard for the adviser to Roosevelt but also because he wanted to make a slight bow in the direction of the new President.

Hopkins, as the President's special emissary, did most of the talking for our side. Ambassador Harriman offered vigorous support. I was so busy interpreting that I took little part in the conversations. Molotov sat in with Stalin, with Pavlov, my Soviet counterpart at the wartime conferences, interpreting. The meetings were relaxed and informal. They were held in Stalin's office in the Kremlin, with the Russians sitting on one side of the usual green baize–covered table and we Americans on the other. Occasionally, a servant would bring in tea and cakes.

Despite the amity, the talks were inconclusive. Hopkins pointed out that public opinion in the United States would become a major factor in Soviet-American relations if the Soviet Union continued to move aggressively in Eastern Europe, especially Poland. He made his points deftly and skillfully, avoiding anything that would seriously annoy Stalin. He dwelt at length on the efforts that President Roosevelt had expended to convince the people of America that good relations with the Soviet Union were not only extremely desirable but also possible. Hopkins pointed out the effect of public opinion on any American government, and warned Stalin courteously but unmistakably that recent Soviet actions, particularly in Poland, were not helpful in contributing to the kind of atmosphere necessary for good Soviet-American relations.

Stalin's tack was similar to that he had employed at Teheran and Yalta. Outwardly agreeable, he would not yield an inch. He was a skillful debater, ignoring facts that undercut his arguments and twisting others to fit his position.

At one point, Stalin dropped his guard and showed the true Bolshevik view of honoring commitments. Hopkins asked whether the Soviet Union was prepared to honor the Yalta agreement on entering the Far Eastern war. Stalin replied testily, "The Soviet Union always honors its word." Then he lowered his voice and added, "except in case of extreme necessity." Pavlov was just about to omit the last phrase in his interpretation when I said to him in English, "I believe there is a little more, Pavlov," and he hurriedly mumbled Stalin's qualification. I do not think that Stalin got the point of the brief exchange. It is only fair to say that I do not believe that there was another man in public office in the world at that time who would have given as frank an admission of the basis on which his government operated. It was characteristic of Stalin that in some things he wished to appear to be scrupulously honest while in others he would utilize deception, or "*la ruse*," as de Gaulle was later to call it, as a diplomatic weapon.

The Hopkins visit did not alter Soviet plans for solving the Polish question. By the time our talks ended, in early June, all the evidence indicated that there was no possibility of a just solution. Hopkins pressed Stalin to carry out the Yalta agreement to widen the Warsaw government, to assure democratic freedoms in Poland, and to release the sixteen jailed underground leaders. Stalin was reasonable in tone but not in substance. He would be glad if four or five of the twenty positions in the Polish cabinet were held by non-Lublin Poles. Naturally, democratic freedoms would be extended—but not to "Fascists." As for the sixteen underground leaders, Stalin knew of their crimes, but they would probably not get stiff sentences. (Many of them died in prison. Of the six or so released, some were rearrested in Poland, some fled to the West.)

Shortly after Hopkins's return to Washington, Truman and Churchill gave up on Poland; they withdrew recognition of the London émigré government and recognized the Lublin regime. Actually, there was no choice. The Lublin government was running Poland, albeit on Soviet instructions. Eventually, Mikolajczyk and a few other London Poles tried to bring a little democracy to the Soviet plan; they joined the Warsaw government. They were given minor posts and subsequently had to flee. Thus Stalin achieved his mastery over Poland.

In discussing Germany, Hopkins asked Stalin when he was going to appoint the official Soviet representatives on the Allied Control Council, pointing out that the United States had already named General Eisenhower and the British had named Field Marshal Sir Bernard Montgomery. Stalin said that he was about to appoint Marshal Georgi K. Zhukov, but he later emphasized that the political arm of the Soviet government completely controlled the military and that therefore Vishinsky, who was in Berlin at that time, would really speak for Moscow.

Regarding Hitler, Stalin doubted that he was dead—"In my opinion Hitler is not dead but is hiding somewhere." He did not even hint of any hard facts to support his contention, and I think the reason he made the statement was that it might be useful in the future to charge some country with harboring Hitler. This guess may seem farfetched, but from what we know now of Stalin, such motivation was not beyond his devious mind.

While we were in Moscow, Hopkins received a telegram from Truman and Stettinius urging him to take up with Stalin the difficulties that the Soviets were causing in San Francisco in regard to the interpretation of the Yalta voting formula. To Americans, to the British, to any honorable person, the Yalta agreement provided that the veto should not be utilized until the United Nations Security Council was voting to take substantive action. We thought the matter had been settled. But the Soviets had reopened the question, insisting that the veto should also apply to placing items on the agenda and to discussing them. Hopkins, who knew little about United Nations matters, was thoroughly briefed, and, accompanied by Harriman and me, went to the Kremlin. After Hopkins, ably aided by Harriman, presented his case, Stalin turned to Molotov and said gruffly, "What is this all about, Molotov?" (Stalin never used the normal Russian mode of address of first name and patronymic, but always just the last name.) Molotov replied that it was the beginning that counted, and therefore a country should have the same rights in the beginning as in the end. Stalin listened, and said, "Molotov, that's nonsense." He then told Hopkins that he believed at first look that our interpretation of the Yalta agreement was correct, but he would like to study the matter. Hopkins persisted, pointing out that the situation in San Francisco was fairly critical and that therefore urgent action was required. Stalin said if his present view was confirmed, a telegram would go out that night. A telegram did go out that night, altering the Soviet position, and the conference came to an agreement in regard to the vital question of voting in the Security Council. As a result, the adoption of a charter for the United Nations was assured.

Without this successful appeal to Stalin, it is doubtful whether the Soviets would have changed their position. I do not believe Stalin responded so much because of the personal influence of Hopkins as because of his conviction that the American position actually did square with the Yalta agreement. He himself had raised numerous questions about United Nations voting procedures at Yalta and was satisfied to let anyone talk about an issue—"That right is not worth much"—as long as the Soviet Union could veto decisions against it. There was a possibility that Stalin did not know that Molotov was trying to stretch the Yalta agreement on voting, because there is evidence that Stalin seldom paid a great deal of attention to the United Nations.

During our stay, the Soviet authorities went out of their way to accord Mr. and Mrs. Hopkins the most lavish and hospitable treatment. Mrs. Hopkins, whose primary purpose on the trip was to nurse her husband, was the subject of much attention. Sitting next to Mikoyan at a Kremlin dinner, she expressed an interest in taking home something Russian, possibly some Ural stones. The next day, some Russians drove up to the Embassy in a truck and carried in an impressive variety of furs. They laid out, on the floor and over the furniture in the drawing room, white fox, blue fox, black fox, red fox, ermine, and mink. In addition, there were Ural stones, brocades from the Caucasus, and fabrics from other parts of the Soviet Union. It was a dazzling display, and the Russians told Mrs. Hopkins that anything was hers for the asking as a gift from Mikoyan. Harry said he was not going to permit her to accept gifts of that value from any foreign statesman. Hopkins remembered all too vividly the uproar in the United States when it became known during the war that his wife had accepted a gift of jewelry from Lord Beaverbrook. Hopkins told her that all she could take from Mikoyan was some inexpensive item as a gesture of appreciation. She took a small semiprecious Ural stone and sadly sent all the rest of the items back.

Louise Hopkins had an extraordinary effect on the Soviet marshals. She was not beautiful, but was chic, with a great deal of wit and charm. At every reception, the marshals, their uniforms covered with medals, clustered around her, practically rendering her invisible. Among her admirers was Marshal Semyon M. Budenny—the old soldier whom I had talked with on the train in 1934. He had so many medals over his chest that Louise Hopkins maintained they carried over onto his back.

On June 7, we flew to Berlin, landing, with Stalin's permission, at

Tempelhof Airport in a ruined city that was still totally occupied by the Red Army. We toured the ruins, smelled the odor of death everywhere, inspected the bunker where Hitler committed suicide (the Russians there did not doubt Hitler's death), then had a light buffet luncheon with Marshal Zhukov (light on food, heavy on vodka) and discussed arrangements for the upcoming meeting of the Big Three. Potsdam, near Berlin, had finally been selected as the site.

In Frankfurt, we spent the night with General Eisenhower. The European war had just ended, and Eisenhower still felt warmly about the Russians. He spoke with respect about Zhukov, in whom he placed great hope for Soviet-American relations. The next day, we held a series of meetings with American military men. General Lucius D. Clay, who had just been appointed second in command to Eisenhower for German affairs, advanced a theory, which was by that time all too familiar to me, that the key to getting along with the Soviets was that you had to give trust to get trust. As we were leaving the I.G. Farben Building, where the meetings were held, I told Clay that within a few months, or certainly within a year, he would become one of the officials in the American government most opposed to the Soviets. My forecast was accurate. Anyone who started with too many illusions about the Soviets came out totally disillusioned.

On the whole, Hopkins gave the military a relatively optimistic view of the possibility of collaboration with the Soviets, but did not, as some observers reported, express unbounded optimism on this subject. I was more skeptical than Hopkins, and told him that the nature of the Soviet system precluded the development of normal relations, even with a country as powerful as the United States. Leaving Moscow, and subsequently, on the way across the Atlantic, Hopkins, in private talks with me, began to voice for the first time serious doubts as to the possibility of genuine collaboration with the Soviet Union, saying he thought our relations were going to be stormy. He based his views primarily on the absence of freedom in the Soviet Union. He felt that the American belief in freedom might lead to serious differences over affairs in third countries.

However, Hopkins still believed that German militarism represented a greater danger than the Soviet Union and that every effort should be made to make sure that there was no possibility of a revival of that particular menace. I disagreed on the danger, pointing out that Germany was crushed flat and that while it was conceivable she could revive, I could hardly believe anyone would be stupid enough to let her tread the same path she had from 1933 to 1939.

The Hopkins mission was hardly a success, although it did show that the United States was prepared to go to considerable lengths to preserve friendship with the Soviet Union. In retrospect, I am inclined to believe that the mission, which I helped initiate, was probably a mistake. Hopkins was a man who had been associated with the previous presidency and did not have the same position with Truman that he had had with Roosevelt. Stalin may have sensed this; he was a shrewd judge of where power lay. There is no question that Hopkins had little effect on him—except on the United Nations voting procedure.

Hopkins withstood the travel to and from Moscow well. But on his return to the United States, after reporting to Truman, he went to the Mayo Clinic. The Moscow mission was his last public service.

On returning from the Soviet Union, I went back to San Francisco to participate in the translation of the United Nations Charter from English into Russian. The work was arduous, interesting, and exacting.

There were differences in the choice and meaning of words. At one point, an argument broke out between one of the White Russians who was working for the conference and a Chinese who had learned his Russian in Manchuria. The conference official maintained that the Chinese had proposed the use of a Russian word that did not exist. They consulted three or four big Russian dictionaries, and the word could not be found. "It just does not legally exist," the conference official said. With a winning smile, the Chinese replied, "Why should they put it in a dictionary? Everybody knows what it means." This same Chinese passed out once after spending an entire afternoon with "a most charming lady" in San Francisco. He had to be carried out of the conference room. The Chiang Kai-shek government, incidentally, gave its officials abroad special allowances for women.

San Francisco was so hospitable that those attending the conference pursued recreation as vigorously as work. I thought nothing, after a seventeen-hour workday, of going to a country estate where I spent a vigorous weekend swimming, playing tennis, and attending an all-night party. In retrospect, I still wonder how I was able to survive the period. I guess our sense of humor brought us through. At that same country place, a British statesman asked if there was an extra bathing suit he could borrow so he could go swimming. The hostess said, "Oh, just go into the bathhouse and you will find plenty there." The English lord soon appeared wearing a jockstrap outside his bathing suit. As he walked toward the startled but laughing guests, he said, "I couldn't figure out what to do with this. Does one put it over one's shoulder?"

I arrived back in Washington just in time to be present at the swearing in of James Byrnes as Secretary of State to succeed Stettinius. While there was no question about Stettinius's ability, Truman felt that he owed Byrnes, his senior in the Democratic party, a political debt. Byrnes had been one of the potential candidates in the convention of 1944 for the vice-presidency but had either stepped aside or been pushed aside by Roosevelt to make way for Truman. Thus began a relationship between the President and Byrnes which turned out to be less than perfect and which, within a matter of days, removed me from the White House.

CHAPTER THIRTEEN

The Potsdam Conference

My job as liaison between the White House and the State Department ceased when Byrnes became Secretary of State. Byrnes told me that henceforth he would be dealing directly with the President. I remained a special assistant to the Secretary, but I was no longer called on to do the liaison work. Although I did not say so, since I was involved, I felt this change was a mistake. Truman, lacking detailed knowledge of the wartime relations between Washington and the Allies, needed State Department expertise more than Roosevelt. The meetings between President Truman and Secretary Byrnes were too infrequent to take up all matters; a liaison officer would have been valuable in handling the day-to-day problems that naturally arose between the State Department and the White House.

At the time of his appointment, I did not know Byrnes very well, although I had met him at the Yalta Conference. He seemed to me to be a good choice as Secretary, because he had been a success in all his previous positions—as a United States senator, an associate justice of the Supreme Court, and the director of War Mobilization. It did not take me long to learn to like Byrnes; friendly and outgoing, he was a good traveling companion during our trips to Europe seeking to mend the rift with the Soviet Union.

The first attempt at an understanding came at the Big Three summit meeting at Potsdam. The American delegation sailed from Norfolk on the heavy cruiser *Augusta* on Saturday morning, July 7, 1945. Every day during the voyage, the President conferred with Byrnes; Admiral Leahy; Benjamin V. Cohen, an architect of the New Deal legislation who had been appointed Counselor of the State Department by Byrnes; H. Freeman Matthews, the chief of the European Affairs Division; and me, as a Soviet specialist. Most of the discussions dealt with the problem of administering conquered Germany. Position papers had been prepared by the State Department on how Germany should be treated in the initial period of the occupation, the goals we should work toward, and the kind of country we wished to see emerge. There were numerous financial, economic, political, and security details discussed with the President on the voyage.

The Potsdam Conference was called largely as a result of the efforts of Churchill, who viewed with growing alarm the Red Army advance. He had urged that the meeting take place as soon as possible —every Soviet success increased his apprehension—and was disappointed when it was postponed until July 16. The purpose of the conference was to discuss urgent European problems resulting from the Allied victory. It was not to discuss the German peace treaty (no one wanted to make the mistake of Versailles of hurriedly drafting a treaty). The main questions on the agenda were the administration of Germany, Soviet actions in the Balkan countries, the occupation of Austria, Poland's eastern frontiers, which, despite the Churchill-Stalin understanding at Teheran, had not been made final, and the war in Asia.

Truman, a newcomer as a world leader, was understandably somewhat nervous about confronting such awesome figures as Churchill and Stalin. But he took advantage of the conferences aboard the *Augusta* to absorb information and ask pertinent questions. He rarely philosophized about the future of the world; he preferred to address himself to the practicalities of questions. During our conferences, Truman spent little time on small talk and jokes. He stuck to business.

The President did find time to relax at poker, but I was not in his intimate circle, so I did not play. He also toured the big ship and one afternoon had lunch with the crew in the cafeteria. One day, he watched the *Augusta* hold target practice. Truman and Secretary Byrnes were standing on a three-gun turret when it fired a salvo. Two of the guns went off properly. The third gave a sort of belch, and a shell eased out of the muzzle and fell into the water a hundred yards or so from the ship. Actually, there was no danger, because the shells carried no warheads.

We landed at Antwerp on Sunday, July 15, then flew to Frankfurt, where we picked up an escort of P-47 fighters, and went on to Berlin. The President was put up at a manor house on the shores of Lake Griebnitz in Babelsberg, a section of Potsdam, in the suburbs of Berlin. The "Little White House," as it was quickly named, was a three-story stucco residence, formerly occupied by the head of the German movie colony. The house had been refurbished by the Soviets but, as the White House log lamented, "The bathroom and bathing facilities were wholly inadequate." The windows were not screened, and mosquitoes were a problem. Matthews and I shared a room on the ground floor. The food, provided by the American Army, was regular military fare with a few embellishments.

The Prime Minister lived about two blocks from the President. Stalin also resided in Babelsberg, about a mile away, along the road from the Little White House to the Cecilienhof Palace, where the plenary meetings were held. The Russians had planted a twenty-four-foot star of red geraniums in the garden of the Cecilienhof.

All participants were living in the Soviet sector of Berlin, although American and British military police were stationed throughout the area. Most of the security guards were green-hatted Soviet frontier troops with oriental faces. I heard later that Stalin had brought in a division of Central Asians to act as his personal guard during the conference.

Potsdam was different from the two previous wartime conferences —different in tone, style, and substance. In the first place, the war in Europe was over with total victory. The war in the Pacific, which the Soviet Union had not yet joined, was nearing a close. Even before the first atomic bomb was exploded, it was obvious that Japan could not hold out for the eighteen-month period estimated by the Combined Chiefs of Staff at Yalta. As a result, there was a sense of relaxation, an absence of compulsion, and, with this absence, a freer exchange of opinions.

Unlike Teheran and Yalta, which were tightly held secrets, the Potsdam meetings were known to the whole world. Stalin was startled on the second day when he thought he heard Churchill say that reporters were in the compound. This misunderstanding was cleared up when Churchill pointed out that the newsmen were outside the compound.

For the participants, there were the same series of meetings at a round table, the same sort of dinners, the same outward friendliness —and the same undercurrent of tension.

However, the delegations were much larger, which meant the work load was distributed among more people, and we had more free time. Mostly, we were engaged in the preparation of papers and discussions of various subjects.

My role had changed considerably compared with Teheran and

Yalta. I had grown increasingly close to President Roosevelt and Harry Hopkins. I was not close at all to President Truman or to Secretary of State Byrnes. While I was Truman's interpreter at the formal meetings, as well as at his informal talks with Stalin, I was not as involved with the affairs of the conference as I had been at the two previous ones. I was not shunned or ignored, but I was not present at most of the intimate conversations between Truman and Byrnes. I was neither surprised nor offended by this change. It seemed inevitable that I should not enjoy the confidence of people whom I had just met to the same degree as I did of those I had worked with longer. Most of my time was taken up with interpreting, with occasional involvement in substantive discussions.

Because of my change in status, I had more time for extracurricular activities. Occasionally, we enjoyed an evening playing poker or rolling dice. I was able one night to go to the only night club open in Berlin. The hall was filled with soldiers of three armies, most of them intoxicated and all of them heavily armed. Some of the Russians carried submachine guns over their shoulders; some of the Americans wore side arms. It seemed to us while we were there that this was risky, and before the conference broke up, the night club was closed as a result of a clash between American and Red Army soldiers. The animosity that lay just below the surface was not peculiar to soldiers. I could sense it among the delegations at Potsdam. While everyone was outwardly friendly, there was a certain reserve on both sides that symbolized basic distrust.

There were also two new leaders among the Big Three—Truman and, after a week, Clement Attlee, who replaced Churchill as Prime Minister as a result of the Labour party victory in the British elections. Truman was the focus of most of the attention. It was inevitable to compare him with Roosevelt and inevitable that the unknown President should suffer in comparison with the fallen giant. Truman's style was totally different. Where Roosevelt improvised, Truman stuck closely to the positions worked out in advance. Where Roosevelt, in his argumentations, would work in extraneous ideas, Truman was crisp and to the point. Where Roosevelt was warmly friendly with Churchill and Stalin, Truman was pleasantly distant. The new President, in his first private meeting with Stalin, did, at one point, try an "Uncle Joe" joke, but it did not draw even a hint of a smile from the dictator.

In addition to the President, the American team had other important changes. Byrnes had never held an important diplomatic position.

Cohen, while brilliant, was new to his job. From the President on down, the American delegation was feeling its way. I do not believe our policy was much affected, however, because the Soviets were so unyielding there was little we could do.

Truman's personal goals at Potsdam were quite simple. He wanted to prove to Stalin that he was his own man, a real leader, in firm command of the United States government. He had already taken a big step in that direction by rejecting Churchill's advice on occupying as much enemy territory as possible. Instead, Truman insisted on sticking to the zonal agreements worked out previously by the Allied Control Commission. But Truman, like Roosevelt, wanted to salvage what he could out of the Yalta pledges of democracy for Eastern Europe. And, above all, he wanted to make sure that the Kremlin would honor the agreement to enter the war against Japan.

Churchill, the old war horse, had turned nearly 180 degrees in his attitude toward the Soviet Union. (At Teheran, he had referred to "Stalin the Great.") Like British leaders before him, he wanted no other power to dominate Europe. He was fearful that the rapid transfer of American troops to Asia would let the Soviets sweep over the Continent. And he foresaw, in the Soviet demand for reparations, an impoverished Germany that would be Britain's charge. So strong were Churchill's fears that he was ready—he said in his memoirs but as far as I know not at the conference—to walk out of the proceedings if the Soviets did not agree to a more eastward boundary between Poland and Germany.

Stalin, having already buttoned up Eastern Europe, went to Potsdam with a long shopping list. One of his principal demands was to break the deadlock over reparations, which Russia needed to restore her devastated industries and cities. There were indications that the Soviets had not yet determined to keep Germany divided. On the other hand, their sealing off of their zone and their refusal to permit the Allied Control Council to operate in their area began to raise some doubts. It was by no means certain, however, that they had decided to strip away the eastern provinces from Germany, give them to Poland, and Sovietize the whole area. It may well be that at the time of Potsdam, Stalin still considered the possibility of a unified Germany under strong military and economic restrictions to avoid the recrudescence of militarism.

Stalin wanted to make sure, too, that the new American President agreed to the price, set at Yalta, for Soviet entry into the war against Japan. In the spirit of the czars who preceded him, he hoped to gain a base on the Bosphorus, as well as assured right through the Turkish straits from the Black Sea to the Mediterranean Sea. Adding to the list a request for Soviet trusteeship of Italian colonies, Stalin apparently took the attitude, "What is the harm in asking?"

Considering Soviet hopes and worries, it was just as important to Stalin to size up Truman as it was for Truman to weigh the Soviet dictator. As he did so often with foreigners, Stalin put on his act of modesty to convince Truman he was not the unmoving rock of his reputation but actually quite a reasonable fellow.

The day after his arrival, Truman met privately with Churchill at the Little White House. I was not present, but I heard afterward that the conference had gone well, with Truman assuring Churchill that he intended to continue Roosevelt's policy and the Prime Minister replying appropriately.

The next day, Stalin, accompanied by Molotov and Pavlov, called on the President. Byrnes was there, and I was the interpreter. Stalin looked tired and older than he had a few months before, during the talks with Hopkins. He seemed to be most cautious. The meeting provided a good beginning of relations between the two leaders, even though Truman's "Uncle Joe" reference and Byrnes's remarks about Stalin's habit of working late fell flat. If Roosevelt could not bring out the humorless dictator, Truman and Byrnes did not have a chance.

But Stalin did appreciate—at least he said so—Truman's pledge of frankness. The President said that he was no diplomat. He proposed to deal directly with Stalin, operating on a yes-and-no basis, and not beat around the bush. Stalin said that he thought the Soviet Union would always try to "meet" the views of the United States. The conversation covered many of the subjects on the agenda for the first formal conference. When Stalin left, Truman said he was satisfied with this first conversation with him.

The successful start, plus the fact that Truman had done his homework, undoubtedly raised the President's confidence. By nature sure of himself anyway, he moved through the conference with the poise of a leader of much greater experience.

Since I was seldom asked for advice at Potsdam, my role was limited to interpreting and observing. From that standpoint, here are my views of how leaders dealt with the principal issues at the conference.

Potsdam was not expected to address itself to the question of peace treaties. It did set up a Council of Foreign Ministers to draw up treaties for eventual consideration by a peace conference. The first task would be to draft treaties for Italy, Rumania, Bulgaria, Hungary, and

Finland. The council would later prepare a treaty for Germany when a government was established. The plan, proposed by the United States, called for the council to be composed of the five members of the United Nations Security Council. Everyone liked the basic idea, agreeing that a peace conference without prepared treaties would be a waste of time. Churchill, however, said that China, although a member of the Security Council, had no business helping decide European questions. In supporting Churchill, Molotov took the position that only countries that had signed the armistice agreement with an enemy country should participate in drawing up the peace treaty. This seemed somewhat arbitrary. It would have ruled out French participation on the basis that the Vichy government had not signed the armistice (because it had not declared war), even though the Free French forces had fought with the Allies during the war. Eventually, a compromise was reached. France could participate in discussions on the treaty with Italy; otherwise, only those countries that signed the armistice could serve. After the conference, the Chinese were permitted to take part in the peace talks on the Balkans.

Austria was not included among the list of enemy nations with whom a peace treaty was to be made because Austria was not considered an enemy country. (Before the conference ended, Stalin had ordered his troops to pull back and let Western forces occupy their zone in Austria.) The treaty-drafting mechanism set up at Potsdam was a success. While the council ran into difficulties and never did consider a German treaty, it did ease the problem of drawing up the peace settlements.

The main formal business of the conference was Germany. It must be remembered that the war had been over only some three months, and the conscience of the world was still horrified by Nazi atrocities, particularly toward the Jews. The spirit of mercy was not throbbing in the breast of any Allied official at Potsdam; there was no disposition to be lenient with the Germans. However, there was, on the Western side, a strong realization that punishment by itself was useless in international affairs.

Neither side had its heart set on dismemberment any longer. It was now the firm intention of the Western Allies to bring about the eventual unification of the German people. Despite Stalin's public statement opposing dismemberment, I am inclined to think that he had not made up his mind whether to support unification at the time of Potsdam.

The final agreement made no mention of any proposal to set up an all-German government and provided that the administration of Germany as a whole should devolve upon the Allied Control Council, composed of representatives of the four occupying powers. The economic principles did provide, however, that while the German economy was to be decentralized to eliminate excessive concentrations, during the occupation period Germany should be treated as a single economic unit. The agreement called for the creation of certain forms of central administrative machinery, particularly in the fields of finance, transportation, and communications.

Reparations, along with the Polish boundary, took up a lot of time at the conference. The discussions on reparations were endless, tortuous, complicated, and confused. The Soviets, while understandably demanding payment for the havoc wrought by the Nazi army, had not proved their claims that $20 billion in reparations could be exacted from Germany. This was the sum that Roosevelt and Stalin —but not Churchill—had agreed at Yalta would be the basis for "discussion." After thirty-seven meetings with the British and Soviet representatives in Moscow, the American government had concluded that there was no basis for the Soviet claim. The Americans and British were determined not to get trapped, as in World War I, in paying for Germany's reparations to other countries. While the conferees were debating general principles, evidence was accumulating that the Soviets had already started stripping German industry of machines and equipment in their zone, in the zone destined for American administration, and in Berlin. British-American teams submitted detailed reports on the extent of the removal conducted by Red Army personnel with technical supervision. The material was not military booty; it was industrial equipment.

Secretary Byrnes scored the breakthrough that produced an agreement of sorts on reparations. At a meeting with Molotov on July 22, Byrnes used strategy learned in the cloakroom of the Senate to force a Soviet retreat. What he did was link reparations to the question of Germany's border with Poland and tell the Soviets they could not have their way on both matters. He said that the transfer to Polish administration of a large part of 1937 Germany would expose the British and French zones to serious difficulties in connection with the delivery of reparations under the Soviet plan. The eastern area contained raw materials needed in the western part of Germany. He pointed out, too, that the Soviets had already removed large amounts of German equipment. Byrnes said he wished to make it plain that the

United States would not pay out money to finance German reparations.

Then, deftly, Byrnes made his point. Under the circumstances, he wondered whether it would not be better to give consideration to the possibility of each country's taking reparations from its own zone. Recognizing that the Soviet zone was primarily agricultural and that the Polish area had coal mines, he said that if the Kremlin wanted to obtain industrial material or equipment from the British or American zones, it could do so in exchange for food or fuel needed in the West. Byrnes was even able to quote Stalin in support of his argument, because the previous day Stalin had said that if the British wanted coal from Silesia, they could exchange other goods for it. In addition, Soviet Russia was to get 10 percent of all the industrial capital equipment in the Western zones unneeded by the German peace economy. Confronted with the politician's maneuver, Molotov reluctantly gave ground on reparations, because the Polish-German border was more important to the USSR. He said the Soviet Union would consider reducing its claim for $20 billion in reparations, and eventually asked for no set figure. The final agreement followed the Byrnes plan.

Actually, Byrnes was dealing only with the realities of the situation stemming from the unilateral actions of the Soviet government. It realized that it could not get more, so it accepted Byrnes's sensible proposal. The plan had no ulterior American motive behind it, no aim to protect American industrial or economic interest. It was designed simply to make certain that Germany would not be totally impoverished by Soviet reparations demands and hence become a charge on the American taxpayer. It also recognized that Germany could not be reduced to an impoverished territory in the center of Europe.

Incidentally, deliveries to the Soviet zone were never made because the Soviets were unable or unwilling to give up the corresponding quantities of food and raw material from their zone.

Whether the resolution of the reparations question contributed to the decades of the division of Germany I do not know. At the time, it did not appear so, and I do not know of any other sound solution that could have been reached.

At one point during the conference, the Soviets tentatively proposed that the Ruhr be internationalized under the control of the four powers. This was refused. The British were in control of the Ruhr and were not ready to give the Soviet Union a veto power in the area.

Moscow would undoubtedly have used the privilege to paralyze the German economy and to push West Germany toward Communism. The Soviets did not press their Ruhr plan, largely, I think, because they were considering administering their zone independently of the Allies. They realized the incompatibility between their scheme for the Ruhr and the Soviet goal for its zone.

The old problem of Poland's western frontiers had a new wrinkle. Representatives of the Polish government were there to plead their case. Among them were Mikolajczyk, who had finally joined the Soviet-dominated regime. Churchill, who had made the egregious error of agreeing to move the Polish western boundary deep into Germany, sought to undo his mistake now that the transfer of these areas would seriously impair the feasibility of treating Germany as an economic whole. Partly because of the Poles, particularly Mikolajczyk (who wanted to prove that he was as nationalist as his Communist opponents), the final agreement at Potsdam left the disputed territory under Polish administration pending a peace treaty. There was little else the Western Allies could do; Poland, with Moscow's blessing, was already ruling the area. Once again, the Western Allies acquiesced in the inevitable.

At Potsdam, the United States attempted to reassert the validity of the Declaration on Liberated Europe signed at Yalta. This was the document by which the three powers guaranteed the establishment of democracy in Eastern Europe. We charged that the Soviets had violated the pledge in Rumania, Bulgaria, and Hungary. The Kremlin denied the charge, and in a diversion, Molotov launched a violent attack on Greece, which was under British influence.

The sharpest words at Potsdam were exchanged over the Balkans. Churchill, again using the phrase that was to become so famous, said of the status of the British and American representatives in the Soviet-controlled countries that "an iron curtain has come down around them." Stalin replied that this was "all fairy tales." Molotov and Eden both became angry during the debates.

At one point, Stalin asked that the words "responsible and democratic government" be deleted from a proposal for the Balkan countries, because the phrase would discredit the regimes in Rumania, Hungary, and Bulgaria. Stalin added that "if the government is not Fascist, the government is democratic." Nothing at Potsdam revealed the deep gulf between the Western Allies and the Soviet Union so much as the discussion on the nature of democracy in the Balkans and the execution of the Declaration on Liberated Europe. Stalin, holding all these territories firmly in his hand, would brook no interference with their Sovietization, using euphemisms to avoid the issue.

The final agreement was unsatisfactory. It took the form of a letter to the control commission in Hungary, which was supposed to be a prototype for the revision of Allied control commissions in the Balkans. Moscow never honored the agreement, balking attempts by the Allies to exert an influence in Hungary.

While consolidating his grip on Eastern Europe, Stalin sought help from his wartime partners in gaining another centuries-old Czarist goal—access to the Mediterranean. A few months before Potsdam, the Soviet Union had demanded that Turkey return parts of Armenia and Georgia obtained from the fledgling Soviet state in 1921. In addition, the Soviet Union wanted a predominant voice in administering the Turkish straits and a military base there or on the Dardanelles. Turkey had refused.

Churchill was a little uncomfortable because he had volunteered a remark at Teheran that the Soviets deserved a base in the area. But he noted that the Soviet proposal went beyond his 1943 remark, and Stalin conceded the point.

The request of the Dardanelles offered Truman the opportunity he had been waiting for to present an idea close to his heart—the internationalization of all waterways bordering on two or more countries. He explained that many disputes between nations sprang from differences over water routes, and therefore they should be put under some form of international control. Churchill was impatient with this digression and Stalin cynically resigned. Neither of them spoke much on the subject. No one could quarrel with Truman's view on the desirability of the internationalization of waterways as a matter of principle, but I had serious doubts if anybody thought it had the slightest chance of success, and therefore listened politely but without much interest. Although Truman made an appeal to Stalin to support his suggestion, the idea was not acted on at Potsdam. The President seemed to be philosophical at the failure of his proposal, although he occasionally referred to it as a good idea. He did not appear vexed by its rejection.

The Soviets got nowhere in their demands on Turkey. Continual pressure on Turkey during the next two years led to the President's proclamation in 1947 of the Truman Doctrine of supporting nations threatened by the Soviet Union. Soviet demands on Turkey were renounced after Stalin's death in 1953.

The Soviet agreement to enter the war against Japan had been reached at Yalta, and by the time of Potsdam the Soviet Union had taken the next step by notifying Tokyo that it was ending the neutrality pact between them. There were many other details to be worked out for the coordinated military assault, and the military chiefs spent most of their time in the early days of the conference discussing the Asian war. The Japanese, who knew that defeat was only a matter of time, had made soundings in Moscow about arranging a peace, some of which we had been told of and some of which we had not.

On July 18, at a private meeting at Stalin's villa, Stalin pushed across the table to Truman a piece of paper that he said he had received from the Japanese. He asked the President's advice as to how it should be answered. The communication expressed a desire to send Prince Konoye on a mission to Moscow to discuss the possibility of peace. Stalin said his disposition was to brush off the proposal, and showed Truman the draft of a reply to this effect. It said that there were problems connected with the visit of Prince Konoye, and perhaps the Japanese had better wait a bit to see how matters developed. Truman approved the message, and it was sent.

This was not the first time the Soviets had told us of Japanese messages, but we also knew through intelligence sources in Stockholm and Ankara that there had been some we had not been informed of. There seemed to be no specific rule in regard to passing on these communications to us. Stalin's disclosure of the Japanese proposal had created a good impression on Truman and Byrnes. They saw it as an indication, albeit a faint one, that the Soviets might be prepared to deal openly with the United States. Actually, Stalin's action was not selfless; it was in his interest, too, for he certainly had no desire to smooth the way for a Japanese peace which might have deprived the Soviet Union of the treasure that it had been promised for entering the war.

Shortly after the conference began, Truman received a message from Washington disclosing that the United States had detonated the first atomic explosion in the history of the world. I had first learned of the atomic-bomb project during a conversation with Hopkins just a few months before. Harriman and I were sitting by Hopkins's sick bed, sounding him out on going to Moscow. In the course of the conversation, Hopkins mentioned the "big bomb," and told of the progress in making it. He did not use the term "atomic bomb," but it was apparent to me that he was referring to just that.

Crossing the Atlantic on the *Augusta* on the way to the Potsdam Conference, Admiral Leahy and I talked quite a bit about the Manhattan Project. He felt that the "longhairs" were gypping the American government out of some $5 billion because the bomb would turn out to be no better than cordite, a simple smokeless powder. Most military men held a more realistic view of the power of the atom.

Three days after the successful test blast, after consulting his advisers and Churchill (the British had cooperated in the project), Truman decided it would be wise to tell Stalin the news. Explaining that he wanted to be as informal and casual as possible, Truman said during a break in the proceedings that he would stroll over to Stalin and nonchalantly inform him. He instructed me not to accompany him, as I ordinarily did, because he did not want to indicate that there was anything particularly momentous about the development. So it was Pavlov, the Russian interpreter, who translated Truman's words to Stalin. I did not hear the conversation, although Truman and Byrnes both reported that I was there.

In his memoirs, Truman wrote that he told Stalin that the United States had "a new weapon of unusual destructive force." Apparently, the President did not tell Stalin the weapon was an atomic bomb, and the Soviet leader did not ask or show any special interest. He merely nodded and said something. "All he said was that he was glad to hear it and hoped we would make good use of it against the Japanese," Truman wrote. Across the room, I watched Stalin's face carefully as the President broke the news. So offhand was Stalin's response that there was some question in my mind whether the President's message had got through. I should have known better than to underrate the dictator. Years later, Marshal Georgi K. Zhukov, in his memoirs, disclosed that that night Stalin ordered a telegram sent to those working on the atomic bomb in Russia to hurry with the job.*

On the plane going home after Potsdam, I had a long conversation with Llewellyn E. Thompson, a close personal friend who was then in the American Embassy in London and who later became ambassador to Moscow and one of our finest diplomats. We discussed the atomic bomb and how we might use the security and power it gave us to establish a sound relationship with the Soviet Union. We were aware and deeply concerned about possible conflicts between the United States and the Soviet Union. It seemed obvious to us that wherever the Soviet armies were, the Soviet system, with its highly structured auth-

* Although a year later, in the fall of 1946, Stalin acknowledged that the Soviet Union still did not possess the "secret" of the atomic bomb, Soviet progress in nuclear research was remarkably rapid. On November 6, 1947, Molotov said that "the USSR knows the secret of the atom bomb." The first Soviet atomic explosion occurred on August 29, 1949.

oritarian control, would be imposed. We recognized the fact that the Soviet Union would not respond to anything except measures endangering the country and the Soviet system. We speculated about methods we might use, considering everything from a flat ultimatum to the Soviets to withdraw to their frontiers down to various degrees of pressure. Every idea ran into insuperable obstacles, such as American public opinion or what we would do if Moscow replied with a flat "no." We thought an outright "no" would probably be the most natural Soviet reaction. Would we then go to war with the Soviet Union, or would we abandon the enterprise? It does not take years of diplomatic experience to realize that bluff on dimensions of this nature would be too risky and unproductive for any country, including the United States.

The news of the atomic bomb and the dropping of the first two devices over Hiroshima and Nagasaki did not trigger Soviet entry into the war against Japan, as some observers have speculated. On July 24, before Truman told Stalin of the bomb, General A. I. Antonov, of the Red Army, told a tripartite military meeting at Potsdam that Soviet troops would be ready to attack in the last half of August. However, the atomic explosions may very well have hurried the Soviet operations. The first A-bomb was exploded at Hiroshima on August 6; the Soviets attacked on August 9, the day the second atomic bomb was dropped, on Nagasaki. Even after the Japanese sued for peace, the Soviet armies pushed on, seizing territory only for political purposes.

As far back as 1944, I had formulated views on Soviet entry into the Pacific war. I wrote a memorandum before the Quebec Conference (which I did not attend) saying that the Soviet Union would come into the war against Japan when it was good and ready, and nothing could keep it out at that time. The memorandum pointed out that in the European war we were dependent on the Soviet Union militarily; it was doing most of the fighting. In the Pacific we were carrying the load; therefore we should never ask the Soviets to join us. At Potsdam, I reminded Byrnes of my memo and expressed the hope that, especially with victory near, we would not put ourselves in the position of the suppliant begging the Russians for help. We should merely take note of the Yalta agreement under which the Soviet Union pledged its entry. I think that Byrnes agreed with me. I was distressed, therefore, when President Truman sent Stalin a letter in effect requesting that the Soviet Union join in the war.

The final agreement at Potsdam confirmed the Yalta accord on the war in Asia, giving the Soviets Japanese territory and rights in China.

Truman acquitted himself well at Potsdam despite his handicaps. The subject matter was new, and he had had no dealings with Stalin and no knowledge of the techniques of Soviet diplomats. But the President studied the position papers and listened to his advisers. He was never defeated or made to look foolish or uninformed in debate. He was fortunate in that Stalin's strategy at the conference was not particularly subtle. Neither Stalin nor Molotov sought to outmaneuver an adversary or entrap him with trick phrases. They stubbornly stuck to one position regarding areas where the Red Army stood. Therefore, President Truman's lack of experience in diplomacy was no real handicap. There was not much room for skill or diplomatic subtlety.

Would Potsdam have been different if Roosevelt had lived? Roosevelt had a personal feeling about the agreements he made with Stalin. He undoubtedly would have acted more angrily to their disregard by the Soviet Union than Truman did. Beyond that—his own reaction —I do not believe Roosevelt's presence would have made any difference. Stalin was not to be dissuaded by personal feelings.

Would the map of Europe be different if Churchill had remained Prime Minister? The answer is again no—even if Churchill had walked out—because in areas of disagreement, such as Poland, the Soviets held all the power.

We were all shocked by Churchill's defeat. The new Prime Minister, Clement Attlee, had taken part in the Potsdam talks before the election, but only as a distinctly subordinate member of the British delegation. Attlee himself had told me one night at dinner that he did not think that the Labour party had a chance of gaining a majority in Parliament. He hoped for gains sufficient to force the Churchill government to listen to Labour's views.

The day of the election, I had lunch with a colonel of the Eleventh British Hussars, who was a cousin of my wife's. We sat in the mess hall after eating and listened to the returns on the radio. As it became apparent that Labour had won, depression descended on the officers. They made gloomy predictions of what would happen with the Socialists in power and no one of the caliber or power of Churchill to direct the affairs of the Empire. I, of course, only listened.

Until then, Attlee had reminded me of a mechanical toy, which, when wound up and placed on the table by Churchill, would perform as predicted. When he returned to Potsdam as head of the British delegation (Churchill stayed home), Attlee was still his modest, unassuming self, but he showed a measure of strength that I had not seen before. By that time, however, most of the agreements had been made, and Attlee did not attempt to upset matters.

I did not hear any direct comment by Stalin on the change in the British government, but he must have been surprised, because he had always spoken contemptuously of the Labour party and had expressed doubt that it could ever form a government. Labour leaders had no illusions about Stalin, either. Ernest Bevin, Attlee's Foreign Secretary, did not hide his anti-Communist feelings, even at Potsdam.

While Potsdam reached a number of decisions, some of which lasted, many of which did not, it cannot be regarded as a vital conference. Most of the policy lines on both sides had been laid down before the meeting. After Potsdam, there was little that could be done to induce the Soviet Union to become a reasonable and cooperative member of the world community. Discrepancies between the systems were too great, the hostility of the Soviet Union toward capitalist countries too deep. For me, the breakdown in the wartime alliance meant another change in roles. For the next few years, I would be an adviser to the Secretary of State, attending numerous meetings in Washington and scores of conferences in London, Paris, and Moscow, trying to help work out solutions to the problems of a ravaged Europe, and, above all, to prevent the cold war from erupting into a shooting war.

PART THREE

The Secretary's Man

———·•∞•·———

CHAPTER FOURTEEN

Byrnes, the Underrated Secretary

Shortly after my return from Potsdam in August, 1945, my wife and I went to Maine on a brief vacation. On the plane to Bangor, a fellow passenger told us that the Japanese had surrendered. Like most Americans, I had never doubted that the West would win the war, even during the collapse of France, the deep Nazi penetration of the Soviet Union, and the black days following Pearl Harbor. But the joy of victory was tempered by a foreboding of the future. Potsdam had not been an encouraging conference, and I could see all sorts of difficulties ahead.

We were going to spend a week or so with friends, the Nicholas Ludingtons, in Southwest Harbor, Maine. Harry Hopkins and his wife, a sister of Mrs. Ludington's, were already there. I had not seen Harry since our return from Moscow in June, and we had much to talk about. He was feeble, but eager to hear about the Potsdam Conference. I told him of my growing apprehensions. Harry, as always, was more optimistic about Soviet policy than I. He clung to one central idea, that good relations between the United States, the Soviet Union, and Great Britain were the most important factor in the world, and everything should be done to promote them. I pointed out some of the problems that we had run into at Potsdam. He did not disagree, but he still held to his main theme and expressed the hope that the Truman administration viewed the world situation somewhat in the same light. Harry was inclined to dismiss ideology, feeling that patient, careful dealings with Moscow were the proper answer to the problem. It was a pleasant time, sitting in the afternoon sun with a drink. I never saw Hopkins again. He went from Maine to New York and shortly thereafter into a hospital, where he died on January 29, 1946.

It is not easy to state the degree of Harry Hopkins's impact on history. His influence with Roosevelt was entirely personal and therefore went up and down, depending on Roosevelt's mood. Sometimes he enjoyed Roosevelt's total confidence and at other times, for no apparent reason, he was cast aside and for weeks never even saw the President. Hopkins became a master at recognizing the President's moods and knew intuitively when to offer a suggestion and when to keep silent. There is no doubt that throughout the war Roosevelt relied more on Hopkins than on any other adviser.

There were few visible signs of affection between the two. I saw Roosevelt show his appreciation only once, at Teheran. After drinking a toast to Hopkins proposed by Churchill, Roosevelt leaned across the table and said to his dedicated assistant, "Dear Harry, what would we do without you?"

Hopkins was essentially a fixer—soothing an angry Churchill or persuading a reluctant Stalin. Highly regarded by the British—Churchill called him "Lord Root of the Matter" because of his extraordinary ability to get to the heart of a question—he was also esteemed by the Bolsheviks because of his forthright honesty and his refusal to indulge in any diplomatic subterfuge or ambiguity. No one tried harder to preserve the wartime alliance.

Stalin once said in my presence that Hopkins was the first American to whom he had spoken *"po dushe"*—from the soul. This relationship did not change Soviet policy much. In speaking of the influence of any individual on Stalin or on the Soviet system, it must always be remembered that no personal feeling which may have been felt by the Soviets ever affected their single-minded pursuit of their objectives.

Hopkins was shrewd, pragmatic, and cynical in his judgments. He made mistakes, especially in his view of Soviet policy. However, more than any other public official I ever met, he was ready to admit his errors. Perhaps affection colors my opinion, but there is no doubt that Harry Hopkins contributed much to the winning of the war, and for that alone he deserves the gratitude of his country.

I had hardly returned to Washington from Maine when I was immersed in preparations for the first meeting of the Council of Foreign Ministers, which had been set up at the Potsdam Conference. As a special assistant to Byrnes, I had no regular bureaucratic duties; I was assigned tasks relating to Soviet affairs according to developments. In those days, almost all developments dealt with the Soviet Union, so I was in constant touch with Byrnes, accompanying him to all conferences. Byrnes often turned to me for specific information about the Soviet Union and about the wartime agreements. As the months went by and we got to know each other better, he sometimes, but not always, would ask my advice on other policy matters.

Secretary Byrnes and the State Department contingent went to London for the Foreign Minsters' meeting on the *Queen Elizabeth*, which was still fitted out as a troop carrier. I shared an immense cabin, designed to hold fifty or sixty officers, with Adlai E. Stevenson, who was head of the American delegation to a preparatory commission for the organization of the United Nations. It was the first time I had met Stevenson, and we had many conversations during the voyage. Naturally, the chief subject was our relations with the Soviet Union. Stevenson impressed me with the freshness and sensitivity of his mind and his civilized approach to world problems. One aspect of his thinking was particularly striking and disturbing. While not denying the seriousness of the task we faced, Stevenson was less concerned with the realities of the problem than with its effect on the American mentality. He feared that the rise of strong anti-Communist sentiment would inhibit genuine liberals. There was much to what he said, as the McCarthy era subsequently showed, but one of the inevitable consequences of his view was to play down the gravity of the problem of our relations with the Soviets.

The first full meeting of the Council of Foreign Ministers took place in Lancaster House. It was our first experience with the extraordinary ability of Molotov to frustrate and delay, a procedure which we came to know only too well in subsequent meetings in Paris, Moscow, and London. The Potsdam agreement had listed the preparations of peace treaties with Italy, Rumania, Bulgaria, Hungary, and Finland as the first task of the council, with German and Austrian agreements to follow. There was no intention at Potsdam, certainly not on the American side, to delay indefinitely the peace treaties with Germany and Austria. The Soviets, however, refused even to discuss a German or an Austrian treaty.

This Kremlin obstruction was the most important development of the conference. It was another revelation, however faint, of Soviet policy toward Germany. It looked as if the Soviets were going to seal off their zone and block any moves toward treating Germany as an economic whole. In short, London gave an intimation of the future division of Germany.

A treaty with Italy was discussed, but agreement foundered over Trieste, a city populated by Italians and surrounded by Yugoslavs. We had thought the Balkan treaties would take no time at all, but at a closed session toward the end of the conference Molotov suddenly announced that the Soviet Union considered that France, an original member of the Council of Foreign Ministers, had no right to participate in the discussions. This announcement came as a surprise. While the Potsdam accord did not specifically provide for a French role in drawing up the Balkan treaties, as it did in drafting the Italian treaty, the Soviets had not objected to the Paris representative's participation at the sessions until the very end. It was not difficult to find the reason for it. The Soviets had believed that the French government, with Communists occupying important positions, would be inclined to favor the Soviet Union in any disagreements with Britain and the United States. It soon became apparent at London that this was not the case. France was still a part of Western civilization and guided her policies accordingly. This stand surprised and infuriated the Soviets, and they decided to pull a technicality. They cited the fact that France, which had been knocked out of the war in 1940, had not been a signatory to the armistice agreements with the Balkan countries and therefore, under the terms of the Potsdam accord, was technically not eligible to participate in the council's deliberations on the peace treaties.

So arbitrary and illogical did Molotov become in presenting his tortured arguments that Ernest Bevin, the British Foreign Minister, could keep quiet no longer. At one of the sessions, which were closed to the press, he said that he " 'adn't 'eard" any argument that resembled the Hitlerite philosophy as much as that which Molotov was using. When this was translated, Molotov became infuriated—or at least professed to be. Asserting that he would not stay to hear his country compared to Hitler's Germany when there were countries that had collaborated with Hitler long before the Soviets, he started out of the room before the interpreter had put what he said into English. When Bevin got the gist of what Molotov had said and saw him moving toward the door, he said, "Oh, I didn't mean any offense, I'll take it back." Whereupon one of the Soviet aides tugged at Molotov's coattails, saying, "He's taken it back, he's taken it back," and Molotov returned.

If Molotov had walked out of the meeting, the Council of Foreign

Ministers would undoubtedly have broken up, and treaties with the former enemy countries might have been delayed. The result might have been widespread public criticism in England and the United States of ill-treatment of the Soviets.

As the wrangling continued, Byrnes decided that further talks were useless. He persuaded the Chinese Minister, who was chairman of the council at that time, to declare the conference ended. As usual, he acted without consulting the President or holding lengthy discussions with his staff.

In the airplane on the way home, Byrnes was concerned about his position. He did not know whether American public opinion would tolerate what he felt was necessary action against the Soviet Union. He wondered whether Americans were so impregnated with pro-Russian sentiment that they would accuse him of spoiling a chance for world peace. Much to his relief, he found that, almost without exception, the press approved of what he had done. Shortly after his return, he made a speech in which he said that the American attitude toward the Soviet Union would have to change from patience and firmness to firmness and patience—a view that was so similar to that of Senator Arthur Vandenberg, the chairman of the Senate Foreign Relations Committee, that it was called the "Second Vandenberg Concerto."

In December, while in Aiken, South Carolina, visiting my sister and mother, I received a call from Byrnes ordering me back to Washington. We were going to Moscow. The trip had apparently been thought up by Byrnes (he had not discussed it in advance with me) as a means of breaking the impasse in the Council of Foreign Ministers and to discuss other differences with the Soviets. I rushed back to Washington, received a set of winter clothes from the Army (I have used them since for duck shooting), and took off across the Atlantic with Secretary Byrnes, Cohen, Matthews, and one or two others.

We had to pass through Paris, a circumstance that raised a delicate question. Byrnes had not suggested that France be represented at the conference and de Gaulle resented this exclusion, especially because the British had been invited. Byrnes thought that since French representation on the peacemaking machinery was a problem, it was better not to get involved with the French before going to Moscow. I am not sure he was right, but that was his decision. To avoid staying in Paris overnight, when we landed there we quickly transferred to a smaller plane, which flew through a driving rain to Frankfurt, where we skimmed in over the hills and put down on a drenched airfield. We spent the night with General Clay, who by that time had succeeded General Eisenhower as Commander in Chief and chief civil-affairs officer in Germany.

The next day, we took off for Berlin in the same plane in which we had crossed the Atlantic. The pilot was inexperienced in regard to European flying, but we had a Russian navigator and radio operator aboard. When we left Berlin, the American weatherman there warned that a front had closed in on Moscow, and while there was a chance that it would move on, it had not done so yet. The pilot, with the optimism of his calling and his inexperience, said, "Well, we will get up there and it will be gone," so off we went. As we neared Moscow, we ran into a snowstorm. I was in the pilot's cabin, translating between the pilot and the navigator. As the minutes ticked by, it appeared that we were boxing Moscow like a compass. First we were about fifty miles to the west of Moscow, then to the north, then to the east, and finally to the south. The navigator was irritated with the radio operator, asking why he could not get Moscow on the prescribed wave lengths. The radio operator shrugged his shoulders and, turning his earphones out so we could hear, said, "Is it my fault if they are playing waltzes on that wave length?" Eventually, we broke through the snow clouds and landed at Vnukovo, near Moscow, just before dark. Vishinsky met us. He seemed quite agitated and kept asking why we had taken such a risky flight. We had no adequate answer.

The British arrived by train about the time we got to Moscow. Bevin was annoyed that this unexpected meeting had been called by Secretary Byrnes without any real consultation with the British, but his irritation rapidly passed away. Bevin had a right to be irritated. The conference had been hastily improvised and was thoroughly disorganized. Items were put on the agenda without adequate preparations. Byrnes himself had irregular work habits; he ran much of the foreign policy from within his head. He did not utilize the facilities of the Department of State to the extent that they might have been and, like Roosevelt, went in perhaps too much for improvisation in dealing with subjects of considerable importance. I could not see how, under the circumstances, the conferences would accomplish much.

We were all surprised when the Kremlin withdrew its objection to the participation of France in the consideration of the Balkan treaties. Exactly why the Soviets reversed their London position we shall probably never know, Something might have developed in their relationship with France—possibly Maurice Thorez, the French Communist leader, had informed them that France could not be left out from the consideration of the Balkan treaties on the mere technicality of a lack of a signature on an armistice. In any event, Moscow decided to allow France to join fully in the discussions on the peace treaties, and a meeting of the entire Council of Foreign Ministers was set for April, 1946.

On the question of carrying out the guarantees for establishing democratic governments in the Balkans, it was the same old, sad story of trying to argue with the Soviets over an area in which they were totally in control. We made no progress even though Byrnes signed, against the advice of almost all the members of the American delegation, an agreement that we would not put up for membership in the Bulgarian government two men who had every right to be there. Byrnes acted in an effort to make it easier to support a joint government. It was a mistake, but it had no serious consequence.

The Moscow meeting also represented the first attempt by the United States to work out some arrangement with the Soviets on the question of the control of nuclear weapons. For this aspect of the discussions, Byrnes had brought along Dr. James B. Conant, who had been intimately involved in the development of the atom bomb. The basis of our proposal had been the Acheson-Lilienthal Plan, which provided for the internationalization of nuclear production for weapons purposes. It was an excellent plan, but the Soviets would not agree to it. Even though the United States would have given up all control over nuclear weapons and their manufacture, we would have been the only country in the world that had the know-how to build the bomb. The Soviets could not permit us to maintain that monopoly. Theirs was an understandable position.

Up until the Moscow conference, the Soviet Union had publicly denigrated the importance of the atomic bomb. Stalin had issued a statement saying that it was only a weapon to frighten the weak-willed. At a Kremlin banquet at the conference, Molotov, following this line, treated the nuclear weapon in jocular fashion. In a toast, he suggested that Dr. Conant might have in his waist-coat pocket a piece of fissionable material. Stalin rose and said quietly that nuclear fission was much too serious a matter to be the subject of jokes. He praised the American and British nuclear scientists for their accomplishment. There in the banquet hall of the Kremlin we saw Stalin abruptly change Soviet policy, without consulting his number-two man. The humiliated Molotov never altered his expression. From that moment on, the Soviets gave the atomic bomb the serious consideration it deserved.

Byrnes brought up the Soviet establishment of a puppet government in Azerbaijan, in northern Iran. The original Anglo-Soviet-Iran agreement of 1941 provided for the withdrawal of British and Soviet troops six months after the war. The Soviets chose to interpret the six months as beginning after the end of the war in the Pacific, thereby gaining some three or four months of additional time during which they helped set up a pro-Communist government. The Soviet position was legally correct and was not contested by the Allies.

Byrnes decided to take the Western view directly to Stalin, and one snowy night we went to the Kremlin to argue the case. Byrnes told Stalin that he could not understand how a country as large and powerful as the Soviet Union, having just emerged victorious from the greatest of all wars, could feel any concern in regard to its tiny, weak, and unarmed neighbor to the south. Stalin, who seemed somewhat listless on that occasion, admitted that the Soviet Union had no reason to fear armed aggression from Iran, but dwelt at some length on the danger of infiltration, especially from saboteurs aiming to damage the Baku oil fields. His arguments were so flimsy and the real reason so transparent that Byrnes finally ended the conversation by saying that the Iranian situation was obviously going to come up before the first meeting of the United Nations Security Council in London the next month, and that the United States might easily find itself in opposition to the Soviet Union. Such a turn, Byrnes added, would be unfortunate. Stalin merely shrugged his shoulders and said, "This will not cause us to blush." In the car on the way back from the Kremlin, Byrnes said he foresaw real trouble over Iran.

Another matter taken up during this brief visit to Moscow was Korea. Although it had been understood at the wartime conferences and reconfirmed at Potsdam that Korea was to be unified and independent, the Soviets persisted in blocking the organization of an all-Korean government. Prodded by Byrnes, Stalin agreed to join in a public declaration that a trusteeship of the three great powers be established for Korea until a viable republic could be set up. We were mildly encouraged by this development and naïvely believed that the difficulties might disappear and we could proceed to the formation of a provisional government which could then hold free elections. We were certainly headed for disappointment.

In the course of the conference, I noticed that we were not sending back regular reports to the President as had been the case in other conferences. I asked Byrnes why. In sharp tones, he said that he knew when it was necessary to report to the President and when it was not. I was put in my place and I stayed there. When we returned to

Washington, we learned that the White House was unhappy—Admiral Leahy was incensed—at Byrnes's failure to report fully on the conference. Byrnes even made arrangements to make a nationwide radio broadcast reporting to the people on his trip without submitting the full text of his speech for adequate White House approval and support. This dispute was straightened out, but such methods of operating led to Byrnes's resignation within a year.

We had hardly returned to Washington when it was necessary to about-face and go off to London, this time for the first meeting of the United Nations Security Council in January, 1946. As Byrnes had predicted, the United States, in opposing Soviet troops and activities in Iran, broke for the first time with the Soviet Union over an important postwar issue. The meeting ended in a deadlock, with the certainty that the matter was going to rise again.*

While it is often difficult to determine motives in diplomatic situations, it is simple when narrowly defined national interests are involved. In the case of Iran, the full motivation of the United States is not easy to put on paper. There was unquestionably a feeling that in this first important case before the Security Council the United States should demonstrate that one of the great powers should join the other nations in a group action against a recalcitrant great power. Soviet moves in Iran were a clear violation of United Nations principles. If the test had not been met, the United Nations would have been a dead letter when it had no more than started.

While Iran could be viewed as a clear-cut issue of principle, power considerations also entered into our decision in that we took a stand in an area remote from normal United States national interests because of the realization that if we did not, we would have to do so someplace much closer to our shores.

There were practical differences that led the United States to act on Iran, whereas it did not on Eastern Europe, which was equally an issue of principle. The Soviets had installed puppet governments in

---

* It was at the London meeting that John Foster Dulles, who was a representative not of the government but of the Republican party, was shown the reports of the Federal Bureau of Investigation in regard to Alger Hiss. Despite the reports, Dulles supported Hiss's nomination as chairman of the Carnegie Endowment for International Peace later in the year. Although at that time I had not seen the FBI reports, Byrnes showed them to me in March, 1946. Hiss had just resigned from the State Department. I examined the file carefully and found nothing in it but the unsupported statement of Whittaker Chambers that Hiss was a member of a Communist cell in Washington. I mentioned the lack of supporting evidence to Byrnes. I added that it was quite possible that if the allegations were true, the case might be more serious than simply a flirtation with Communism.

251

Eastern Europe and East Germany with the power of the Red Army. Iran, which had been a de facto ally during the war, was not only independent of Moscow, it was also the complainant in the case. We could not ignore the complaint.

At the second meeting of the Security Council, in New York, the issue came to a head. There was not a question of the rights and wrongs of the case. The Soviets stood convicted of a direct violation of their agreement to withdraw their troops from Iranian soil and of an attempt to install a puppet regime in Azerbaijan. They faced the united opposition of all the other members of the Security Council, supported by world opinion. They wisely yielded on the issue after walking out for a while (as I had told Byrnes they would). The decision to withdraw the Soviet troops by September, 1946, was a distinct victory for the United Nations.

The question then arose whether the Iranian case should be left on the agenda until the Soviet withdrawal was completed. I maintained that it was ridiculous to drop the case. There were other members of the American delegation who disagreed. In the end, Secretary Byrnes was persuaded to leave the item on the agenda. Trygve Lie, the Secretary-General of the United Nations, told me we should trust in Moscow and drop the case.

There was opposition in the United States to our firm support of Iran. At a dinner party before the Security Council decision, Walter Lippmann was critical of Byrnes's decision to plead the Iranian case, pointing out that any confrontation between the great powers contained the theoretical danger of war. I outlined all the efforts the United States government had made to avoid this issue and said that a war was highly unlikely. In the lively discussion that ensued, Mrs. Lippmann, in support of her husband, interjected to say, "Well, Chip, all I can say is that in your war I will not be a nurse's aide."

Our stay in the United States was not long, and in a few weeks we were back over the Atlantic on the air route with which I was becoming all too familiar. This time, we went to Paris for a half year, from April to October, while the Council of Foreign Ministers drafted peace treaties for the Balkans and discussed a treaty for Italy.

At this conference, I took on for Byrnes the job of press spokesman. He decided he needed to get the American position to the press, because the other delegations were leaking information to reporters. After every session, he would brief me on what I should say and what I should hold back. I almost always gave the press a general outline of what had occurred at the closed meetings, but rarely gave any indication of the difficulties.

252

One of the stories I kept to myself was the conversation at a dinner party that Byrnes gave shortly after arriving in Paris. He invited Molotov and Vishinsky to his apartment at the Hotel Meurice. On our side, there was Ben Cohen, now the Counselor of the Department of State, and myself. While we were eating, Molotov bitterly complained about the unfriendly attitude of the United States in the Iranian case. He maintained that keeping troops in Iran beyond the treaty deadline was too trivial a matter to disturb relations between the United States and the Soviet Union. He did not attempt to deny the illegality of the Soviet action. Byrnes explained that the United States had signed the charter of the United Nations, which was dedicated to the protection of small nations, and he, as Secretary of State, could not think of turning his back on the Iranians in their hour of need.

Molotov also denounced Winston Churchill's speech at Fulton, Missouri, a few weeks earlier, in which the British leader had referred to the Soviet "iron curtain." Molotov said that Churchill's call for action to contain the Soviet Union was resented by the Soviets. He was generally blackguarding Churchill when Cohen, usually mild-mannered and gentle, interrupted him to deliver a lecture on Churchill's courage, pointing out that we would probably not have been sitting there if it had not been for the British wartime leader.

At Paris, a great deal of time was devoted to trying to resolve the case of Trieste. As noted, this city on the Adriatic Sea had a predominantly Italian population but was surrounded by Yugoslav territory. The Yugoslavs felt strongly that Trieste should be theirs, and the Italians, of course, wanted the city. In those days, the Soviets and the Yugoslavs were as one. Molotov argued in Paris that Trieste was economically and historically a part of Yugoslavia and the Italians should be considered a minority enclave. We were supporting Italy because we felt the city should be under the sovereignty of the country from which most of its inhabitants came. Despite newspaper reports, there was little evidence that political pressures from Italian Americans played a part in this matter. Such pressures may have, but the fact that Tito was at that time solidly on the side of the Soviet Union undoubtedly made our support of Italy popular in the United States.

While we argued in Paris, a commission was sent to the Adriatic coast to examine the situation on the spot. Our representative was Dr. Philip Mosely, who was chosen not only because he was a Russian specialist but also because he spoke Serbo-Croat, the language of the area outside of Trieste. The Soviet representative did not speak Serbo-Croat. Thus Mosely could speak with the Yugoslavs but the Soviet representative could not. The commission came back and wrote an honest and objective report presenting evidence that the people of Trieste wanted to be part of Italy. The Soviet representative, because he was overwhelmed by the incontrovertible nature of the evidence or because he had been badly instructed, went along with the majority. Molotov denounced the report, asserting that the commission had no right to make recommendations which appeared to prejudge the Foreign Ministers, who alone could make the decision. He said the commission was sent to Trieste to get the facts, not to draw any conclusions.

In those days, the Soviets were constantly stressing the need for continued friendship between the two countries, insisting that there was no reason why we could not get along together. The problem, as some of us had warned during the war, was that the Bolsheviks wanted more than reasonable protection for their borders; they wanted to extend their control into the Mediterranean and westward into Europe. On such questions we would not budge. One day, Bogomolov, who had been the Soviet ambassador to the French and other governments-in-exile in London, said to me in a friendly fashion, "I don't understand you Americans. You are supposed to be the world's greatest traders, yet here you are, not prepared to trade on Trieste." I replied—perhaps a little pompously—that the United States would never bargain with the fate of human beings.

The Trieste issue dragged on. Finally, two senators who were part of the delegation, Tom Connally and Arthur Vandenberg (particularly the latter), and Byrnes devised a plan for the internationalization of Trieste. The Soviets accepted the idea; then, in discussions on working details, made proposals that sabotaged the principle of internationalization—for example, that most of the city services, including the police, be put directly under Yugoslav control. The Soviet proposals were simply a thinly disguised turnover to the Yugoslavs. We resisted, but made concessions. Even then, we were not able to reach an agreement, because the Yugoslavs apparently objected so strenuously. As a result, we could not conclude in Paris the treaty with Italy.

Treaties with the Balkan countries—Rumania, Bulgaria, and Hungary—presented no great problem.* With these treaties drafted, the Foreign Ministers agreed to call a conference for the signing on July 29, 1946. The date was announced one afternoon, and the press all

---

* The United States, not having been at war with Finland, took no part in drawing up the treaty for that country.

over the world carried the news. The following morning, when the deputies gathered to approve the text of an invitation which France, as the host country, was sending out to other nations, the Soviets refused to accept any version. A meeting of the Foreign Ministers was hastily called, and for four hours Molotov answered every question regarding the rejection of the text of the invitation by saying that the Soviet delegation would not permit the conference to turn itself into a rubber stamp. During this discussion, however, the real reason for the Kremlin turnabout became clear. Molotov had made a bad slip by failing to obtain agreement on the rules of procedure before agreeing to the date of the conference. Knowing that they would be in a minority, the Soviets wanted the veto power inserted into almost all decisions in order to protect the Soviet position, and Molotov received sharp instructions from Moscow to rectify his mistake.

Vishinsky sat by, smiling to himself, enjoying Molotov's discomfort. With no progress made, the Ministers adjourned for dinner. After liberally imbibing at dinner, Bevin, who had become increasingly irritated and frustrated, returned to the conference in a belligerent mood. When Molotov attacked Britain for past sins in international affairs, Bevin rose to his feet, his hands knotted into fists, and started toward Molotov, saying, "I've had enough of this, I 'ave," and for one glorious moment it looked as if the Foreign Minister of Great Britain and the Foreign Minister of the Soviet Union were about to come to blows. However, security people moved in, and Byrnes, who was presiding, spoke in his soothing Carolina voice and the incident was over. Eventually we gave in on the rules question, since it was the only way to get the Russians to the conference.

That fall, when the Foreign Ministers reassembled in New York, Byrnes used his political tactician's skill to settle the Trieste dispute. He called me one day and in typical fashion—he had obviously made up his mind—said, "Come on, Chip, we'll go to see Molotov. I have an idea." We went to Molotov's suite at the Ritz Hotel. Byrnes told Molotov, "In thinking the whole matter over, I really believe the wisest thing for us all to do is admit failure and to disband this meeting." He said he thought it was bad for the reputation of the countries concerned and particularly for the Foreign Ministers to have continual wrangles and deadlocks over what in essence was not so difficult a question. Then, in his smooth way, he added that he really had great sympathy for Molotov. No one could have put himself out more to take care of the Yugoslavs. As far as Byrnes could see, the Yugoslavs were totally ungrateful for all the effort. He thought that Molotov could justify abandonment of the attempt to reach an agreement on Trieste.

Molotov's reaction was characteristic. He began to stutter, as he always did when he was a little excited, and said, "No, no, Mr. Byrnes, don't take hasty actions. Just wait until this afternoon's meeting and you will see developments." As we were going down in the elevator, Byrnes said, "Well, I hope that works." In the meeting that afternoon, Molotov handed out concessions like cards from a deck. Almost all the outstanding points were agreed to in a reasonable manner, and finally the Italian treaty was completed and a signature date set.

The reason the Byrnes tactic worked was that the Soviets knew, on the basis of experience, that Byrnes was not bluffing, and if the Trieste situation was left as it was, with most of the area occupied by the West, the Yugoslavs might lose all chance of winning control over the area. Internationalization always held open the possibility that a more favorable conclusion could be reached within that framework.

In February, 1947, Byrnes resigned. The reason given was his desire to return to private life. I understood, although I was never filled in on the details, that the real reason was a difference between him and Truman on the manner in which he was conducting foreign policy. My hunch was that the division began with Byrnes's failure to report fully on the proceedings of the Moscow Conference in 1945. Byrnes's personal style was to operate as a loner, keeping matters restricted to a small circle of advisers (of which I think I could call myself one). Thus he failed to get the most out of the talent and expertise of the State Department. Moreover, he was not in daily, intimate consultation with the President, as Hopkins had been with Roosevelt and subsequent national-security advisers have been with other presidents. Byrnes was his own man and demanded the freedom to operate that way. This method of operating inevitably ran into conflict with Truman's strong views on the prerogatives of the President. It must also be remembered that Byrnes was considerably senior to Truman in the Democratic party. Although I never heard him mention the subject, Byrnes felt that he and not Truman should have been chosen by Roosevelt as the vice-presidential candidate in 1944. Under such circumstances, Byrnes believed that he held an independent position as Secretary of State.

Byrnes used humor to ease tensions. Once when we were approaching the Azores under hazardous flying conditions, he said, "Boys, I have a story for you," and told about a plane containing a troupe of

USO actresses and some combat soldiers that ran into a severe storm over Africa. The plane shook so much that parachutes were issued to all the passengers, including the women. With each chute was an instruction sheet, which had been written for the soldiers. One of the instructions was that in landing you should keep your left hand on the shroud of the parachute and your right hand on your testicles. A young girl from South Carolina was puzzled at first about what to do, but after a moment she sidled up to a huge sergeant and said, "Big boy, I'm going to stand by you."

I went with Byrnes on all his foreign trips, attended all the conferences he was involved in, and was at his side during the entire period he was Secretary of State, except occasionally at home when he was involved in purely domestic matters.

Byrnes did a better job as Secretary of State than he was given credit for. He had to deal with possibly the most difficult period of any since World War II. He had to shift from a wartime alliance to a policy of facing up to the emerging Soviet menace.

It took considerable courage for Byrnes to end the London Foreign Ministers' meeting and perhaps to incur the onus of breaking up the wartime association with the Soviet Union. It also took courage to decide to throw the whole weight of United States support behind Iran, a weak country on the border of the powerful Soviet Union. It was certainly not Byrnes's intention when he took the job as Secretary of State to engage in a series of confrontations with the Soviets.

Byrnes's successor, George Marshall, found the going even rougher, as Stalin increased his pressure on the West. For me, the change in bosses meant an increasingly important role in the cold war struggle with the Soviet Union.

CHAPTER FIFTEEN

Marshall, an Outstanding Secretary

One of the first moves General George C. Marshall made when he became Secretary of State in January, 1947, was to call in each of the principal officers of the department to get his views of the diplomatic problems facing the United States. When my turn came, I discussed relations with the Soviet Union at considerable length, stressing the ideological element, as well as the great-power factor, of Soviet foreign policy. Marshall listened carefully, made no comment, and thanked me. He was not going to accept the views of anyone, particularly those he did not know intimately, and he did not know the officers of the Department of State.

There was a great deal of nervousness in the Foreign Service over the appointment of a military man as Secretary of State. Marshall's reputation was unparalleled, but morale was low because Byrnes had tended to ignore the Department of State. There was wide apprehension that the General would impose such rigid discipline and procedures that ideas would never make their way to the top.

Everyone knew the story of Marshall's being passed over by Roosevelt for the job as commander of the invasion of Europe, although he had wanted the command and was unanimously considered the best choice. What was not so widely known was that Marshall's qualities of getting along with difficult people—qualities that were to serve him well as Secretary of State—were the factors in Roosevelt's decision to keep the General on as Army Chief of Staff. Besides being able to evoke the loyalties of the other Chiefs of Staff, Marshall could handle the British, who were often a problem, and was a master at dealing with Congress.

I first met Marshall at Teheran, and had been impressed by his lucid presentation of the Allied military situation. Subsequently, I attended a number of meetings at which he was present, and each time my admiration for him grew. The night before the Normandy landing, I, as the head of the Eastern European Section, went to the Soviet Embassy to witness the presentation by Ambassador Gromyko to Marshall of the Order of Suvarov, the highest military decoration Moscow gives foreigners. No one could tell from Marshall's calm demeanor that the greatest military action in the history of the world was at that moment under way. Instead of going back to his office, he went to his home in Leesburg, Virginia. Later, I asked him about his actions that night, and he said, "Well, there was nothing I could do about it any more. It was much better to get a good night's sleep and be ready for whatever the morning might bring." What the morning brought him, while he was still asleep, was a colonel who had rushed out to Leesburg with a message from Eisenhower saying that Allied troops were landing in Normandy. The breathless colonel insisted that Marshall be awakened to read the urgent message. When Mrs. Marshall demurred, the colonel finally showed her the message. Whereupon Mrs. Marshall, knowing her husband, asked, "And what would you have General Marshall do about it?" Her husband slept on.

It did not take Marshall long to win over almost every important member of the State Department. He gave a sense of purpose and direction. His personality infected the whole Foreign Service. Under him, as under Herter in later years, the department functioned with as much efficiency as I was to note in my nearly forty years in the Foreign Service. True, Marshall had excellent Under Secretaries—first Dean Acheson, then Robert A. Lovett. It is also true that Marshall had an easy act to follow, because Byrnes paid little attention to the operation of the department. Under Marshall, all the senior officers were consulted, and when policy was decided, there was no question what it was. There was a greater clarity in the operation of the State Department than I had seen before or have seen since.

A few days after we had talked over Soviet affairs, Marshall asked me to stay on as his special assistant. I quickly discovered that the new Secretary wanted a lot more information and advice than Byrnes had. We consulted a great deal, and by early summer our relationship had grown to the point that he asked Truman to appoint me counselor, a position requiring congressional approval. The appointment did not change my duties very much; I was still Marshall's chief adviser on Soviet policy, traveling with him abroad and interpreting for him in private conversations with the Russians.

One of my jobs was to handle a lot of the inquiries from the press. While I firmly believe that newsmen should be told the truth, I am equally convinced that premature disclosures and partial disclosures of conversations and positions are harmful. Such leaks may make splashy headlines, but they ill serve the reader and the country. I came to the conclusion that attempts to stop leaks by restricting newsmen's access to a few selected individuals would be resented and would not work, while restricting the distribution of secret papers would interfere with the operation of the department. I suggested six "don'ts" that all officers of the department observe to prevent disclosures that would embarrass the United States government. They were:

1. Don't discuss the nature or status of any negotiations or discussions actually in progress with another government. A correspondent should be frankly told that it is impossible to discuss any subject currently in negotiation rather than attempting to give him an evasive answer or to turn away his question.

2. Don't discuss personalities or individuals either of the department or of foreign governments. Newspapers are always anxious to obtain names for stories, and if a correspondent is told that "such and such" an official of the department or a foreign official or diplomat here said "so and so," the correspondent already has the elements of an embarrassing story.

3. Don't show the texts of telegrams or official documents to any newspaper correspondent that have not been made textually public.

4. Don't under any circumstances attempt to forecast what action the U.S. government will take in the future in regard to a certain situation and especially with reference to hypothetical situations which might arise.

5. Don't be misled into confirming or discussing a confidential item of information simply because a correspondent gives the impression he is already in possession of this information.

6. Don't discuss differences of opinion within the department or between the department and other U.S. government agencies.

Such rules would allow plenty of room for informing the press of what was going on, although I doubt whether newsmen are ever satisfied with anything less than full disclosure of everything.

General Marshall took over the department just as the "cold war" began, or, more precisely, just as the term was accepted by the press.

Within a few weeks, the British sent the United States a note saying that His Majesty's government had concluded that it could no longer bear the burden of assisting Greece and Turkey and that it was up to the United States to do the job. A high-level committee, headed by Under Secretary Acheson, with which I was intermittently associated, unanimously recommended that the United States assume Britain's traditional role.

A civil war was raging in Greece. The Communist insurgents in the north of Greece were being actively supplied and presumably directed from countries under Communist rule. Stalin's attitude was somewhat ambivalent, perhaps because of his spheres-of-influence arrangement with Churchill, but more probably because he felt that chances of success were dubious without bringing on a larger war. However, the committee thought that Greece was likely to go Communist, radically upsetting the balance of power in the area and eventually creating a situation inimical to American security. This was sound reasoning. In 1947, every Communist party in the world not only was patterned after that of the Soviet Union but was also the subservient instrument of Moscow policy. Thus the installation of a Communist regime in Athens would have meant extension of Soviet control in the eastern Mediterranean. In a related move, the Soviets were putting intense pressure on Turkey for a base on the Turkish straits.

Fully supported by his advisers, President Truman decided that the United States should help Greece and Turkey protect their independence. The problem was how. General Marshall and I left the United States on our way to a Foreign Ministers' meeting in Moscow before Truman's message to Congress had been written. In Paris, we received the prepared text of the President's message to Congress proposing the Truman Doctrine. The Soviet Union was not mentioned by name, but there was no question that the basic aim of the doctrine was to stop Soviet efforts to undermine the free nations through subversion. It seemed to General Marshall and to me that there was a little too much flamboyant anti-Communism in the speech.

Marshall and I felt that Truman was using too much rhetoric. Marshall cabled our thoughts back to Washington. He received a reply that in the considered opinion of the executive branch, including the President, the Senate would not approve the doctrine without the emphasis on the Communist danger.

In Moscow, we were guests of Lieutenant General Walter Bedell Smith, the American Ambassador, in Spaso House. Smith was not in a good mood. Shortly after our arrival, he had his hair cut by a Russian barber. Smith thought the barber asked if he wanted hair tonic, and said yes. The Russian had really asked if Smith wanted some hair dye, and gave him a henna rinse. When Smith looked in the mirror, he swore so loud we could hear him all over Spaso House. Despite hours of rinsing, Smith's hair had a definite pink tinge while we were there.

Our six weeks in Moscow were spent in frustrating and fruitless discussions on Germany between the Foreign Ministers. There is no need to go into any details of the various proposals put forth by the West and of the blocking tactics of the Soviet Union.

At a banquet in the Kremlin, Molotov said he wished to toast the health of Foreign Secretary Bevin of Great Britain and Secretary of State Marshall of the United States for their work at the conference. He pointedly left out Georges Bidault, the French Foreign Minister. In his second toast, Molotov said that no one should be forgotten, so he would like to toast the Foreign Minister of France. There was no mistaking the deliberate insult to Bidault and France. Bidault turned crimson and was furious. Although he was highly emotional and vain, Bidault, whose government was one-third Communist, had enough sense not to provoke a public brawl with Molotov. I believe that the snub helped condition Bidault's attitude toward the Soviet Union in subsequent years.

Molotov's insult, in characteristic indelicate Soviet fashion, had been used by the Soviets to show their displeasure with France's position at the conference. France's generally accommodating attitude on the Balkan treaties had perhaps led the Soviets to believe that France would support concessions to the Soviets on Germany. The Soviets did not seem to realize that Germany had always occupied a special place in French foreign policy, and that even with a strong Communist influence in the government France would have her own views on how Germany should be treated.

On April 18, General Marshall, accompanied by me, paid a courtesy call on Marshal Stalin. I had not seen Stalin since December, 1945, and was struck by how much he had aged, how much grayer, careworn, and fatigued he appeared. There had been no particular preparation for this interview, since by that time we realized that the Soviets were not willing to move on the German question, and Marshall's only point was to tell Stalin how dangerous it was to leave Germany in a chaotic and divided state.

During our visit, which lasted about an hour and a half, Stalin took a relaxed attitude toward the failure of the conference to achieve any results. Doodling the inevitable wolf's heads with a red pencil, he asked what difference it made if there was no agreement. "We may agree the next time, or if not then, the time after that." To him, there was no urgency about settling the German question. We should be detached and even relaxed about the subject. This was his main thesis, and he answered almost all of Marshall's questions with similar responses. When we got back to the Embassy, I dictated a full account of the conversation, which was sent to President Truman.

Stalin's seeming indifference to what was happening in Germany made a deep impression on Marshall. He came to the conclusion that Stalin, looking over Europe, saw that the best way to advance Soviet interests was to let matters drift. Economic conditions were bad. Europe was recovering slowly from the war. Little had been done to rebuild damaged highways, railroads, and canals. Business alliances severed by years of hostilities were still shattered. Unemployment was widespread. Millions of people were on short rations. There was a danger of epidemics. This was the kind of crisis that Communism thrived on. All the way back to Washington, Marshall talked of the importance of finding some initiative to prevent the complete breakdown of Western Europe.

On our return, Marshall instructed the new Policy Planning Staff, which he had set up under George Kennan, to take on as its first task an examination of European recovery and the role the United States could play in the process. A few weeks later, Marshall sent me the first preliminary memorandum of the Policy Planning Staff, as well as a report from Will Clayton, Assistant Secretary for Economic Affairs, and a number of other documents. The Policy Planning memorandum, which was more of an outline than a memorandum, strongly stressed the necessity of some United States initiative in regard to Western Europe and also underlined the importance of the Europeans' doing as much as they could to help themselves.

In sending me the papers, Marshall asked me to draft a speech that he had agreed to make at the Harvard commencement on June 6. I spent approximately two days on the first draft of this speech, having in hand the Policy Planning Staff memorandum, Clayton's report, and a general idea of what was in Marshall's mind. I wrote the entire draft myself. The final version of the speech, put together after a number of meetings, closely followed the structure of my draft and picked up much of my phrasing. Both drafts refer to the loss of life, destruction of cities, factories, mines, and railroads; and, more important, the invisible destruction, the dislocation of the "entire economic fabric" of the European economy—using Clayton's own words in his report. My draft and the final version ended on the same note. I wrote: "I am confident that with proper foresight and a willingness to face up to the responsibility and duties which history has placed upon the United States, the problem can and will be overcome." Rewriting a bit, Marshall ended the speech with these words: "With foresight, and a willingness on the part of our people to face up to the vast responsibility which history has clearly placed upon our country, the difficulties I have outlined can and will be overcome."

It has been said that Marshall had no idea of the massive proportions of the program he was suggesting. This erroneous idea stems from the fact that Marshall gave no figure in his speech—he merely said that Europe "must have substantial additional help" and added that it was "logical that the United States should do whatever it is able to do." He told some of us in the department that he was concerned that his speech might be considered a Santa Claus offer to Europe and would arouse a storm of protest in the isolationist Middle West. He therefore gave strict orders that there be no advance publicity or background guidance for the speech. As a result, the importance of the speech was not understood by most of the Washington press corps. While the speech was given page-one treatment, the interpretive comment was slight, and no leading columnist I know of gave it the attention it deserved.

The reaction in Europe was, however, quite different. Agence France Presse saw the significance of the speech. In addition, Dean Acheson had on his own initiative taken the matter up with some British journalists and stressed the vital importance of a positive European response. In London, Bevin picked up the hint immediately. He got in touch with Bidault and arranged to meet with him in Paris.

At a regular staff meeting the day after the speech, Marshall turned to Kennan and me and asked whether the Soviet Union would accept an invitation to join the plan. He said that he was sure to get a question on the point at a press conference later in the morning. He also knew that he could only answer in the affirmative, because any American plan that appeared to exclude the Soviet Union would have very little chance of being accepted in the world. He also knew that Soviet acceptance might easily kill the plan in Congress. Kennan and I gave much the same answer. We did not feel that the Soviet Union would accept American verification of the use of the goods and funds. Furthermore, we did not think the Soviet Union would be able to maintain its control over Eastern Europe if those countries were able to participate in the cooperative venture.

We turned out to be right. Molotov and a staff of eighty attended the Paris exploratory meeting with the British and French in July. The size of the Soviet delegation and Molotov's positive comments gave the impression that Moscow was leaning toward joining. But after his proposals were rejected, the Russians went home. They must have been ordered to do so by Stalin.

Molotov's proposals provided the best clue for the Soviet refusal to participate in the Marshall Plan. He suggested that each country draw up a shopping list of its needs, which the United States would accept, deliver, and pay for. There would be no on-site inspection of how the goods were used. The Molotov plan would have meant a free gift of American resources without the slightest check to assure that the supplies would be used as intended. The Soviet leaders realized, too, that the Marshall Plan imperiled Soviet control of Eastern Europe. The Czechs made a move toward joining the plan by accepting an invitation to a second meeting. According to a member of the Czech government who subsequently defected, Stalin called the Czechs to Moscow and forbade them to accept the Marshall Plan under threat of Soviet displeasure. Prague had no choice; it had to withdraw.

One of the distinguishing marks of the Marshall Plan was that it was based on self-help, with the Europeans banding together and, in association with the United States, working out solutions to their needs. The plan also had a considerable political impact. I had written in the original draft that our policy was not directed against any country, ideology, or political party, and specifically not against Communism. It was directed against hunger, poverty, and chaos. Marshall dropped the specific mention of Communism and added "desperation" to the list of targets. This passage automatically placed the Communists, once they opposed the plan, in the position of partisans of hunger, poverty, desperation, and chaos. From a propaganda point of view, these words were worth a great deal in countries with large Communist parties. Even so, in France there were some severe political strikes against the Marshall Plan. The Communists realized that their chances of taking over governments would be reduced, if not eliminated, if the Marshall Plan brought prosperity to Europe.

By November, the executive branch had drawn up a detailed bill embodying the plan, but Congress, despite its enthusiastic support, was not ready to move. Each house had to hold hearings, and months would be required to pass the measure. As a result, the administration had to develop a plan for short-term aid to Europe, which cost the American taxpayer hundreds of millions of dollars more than if the full plan had been adopted early. Even so, the four-year cost of the Marshall Plan was about $4 billion less than the original estimate of $17 billion.

For a time, the Marshall Plan legislation became stuck in Congress. Two factors helped push it through. One was the indefatigable work of Senator Vandenberg, who knew all the parliamentary techniques. The other factor was the Communist coup in Czechoslovakia. The shock of the take-over, which occurred after Marshall's speech, helped crystallize American opinion.

One of the reasons the Marshall Plan worked so well was that the sixteen European countries that joined it contained the necessary qualified personnel, skills, and institutions. All the United States was doing was injecting a little economic blood into a system that had stopped functioning. Later, aid plans for underdeveloped countries ran into difficulties because the needed skills had not been developed.

It could be said that the Marshall Plan was two years late in relation to the needs of Europe. The United States did spend vast sums of money under the United Nations relief plan to care for immediate pressing needs resulting from the destructive effects of the war and to pay for the occupation of Germany and Japan. Congress was not ready to agree to the expenditure of billions of additional dollars for a recovery program before the situation in Europe clarified to the point of making it a necessity. Furthermore, the United States was short of many of the items which were to be included in the Marshall Plan. There was a grave need for agricultural machinery and industrial machinery of some kinds, and it was not an easy task, even in 1947, for the United States to postpone the satisfaction of its own needs to help Europe. Despite the promise of economic recovery held out by the Marshall Plan, everyone in the Western camp, particularly the Europeans, was gloomy in 1948. Marshall told me that Bevin had turned to him at a luncheon and said that with the Soviets' maintaining swollen forces in East Germany and Molotov's intransigent attitude on Germany, there was no country on the Continent that had any confidence in the future. In the face of the threat of Soviet armed might, Bevin asked what, if anything, the United States could do. Marshall replied that the only formula that he could think of would be the same one that had been applied in the economic field—that is, for the Europeans to get together to see what they could do by their own efforts to ensure their defense, and then turn to the United States to make up the difference between their capacity and what the situation required.

Whether or not European fears of an armed Soviet attack were exaggerated, they were genuinely felt. An all-out military attack was feared less than the use of Soviet armed force to encourage and give direct support to the Communist parties of Western Europe in case of an attempted take-over. In the immediate postwar period, the Communist parties on the Continent, with the exception of West Germany, were powerful, and certainly forces to be reckoned with.

In the spring, at the time of the signing of the Brussels Treaty, which established a Western European military alliance without the United States, the Europeans discussed their military needs. Marshall put Robert Lovett, who had become Under Secretary of State, in charge of dealing with Congress on the issue. The original idea was to get Congress to authorize the offering of military supplies to Europe on a Lend-Lease, or grant, basis. In the ensuing discussions with Senator Vandenberg, who became a close friend not only of Lovett but also of Marshall, a much broader concept evolved. The final resolution not only authorized military assistance but also gave the blessing of Congress to the United States' joining some form of regional collective-security organization. The legislation marked the end of American isolationism, since it was the first time in history that any such idea had emanated from Washington, and certainly the first time that Congress had approved any such move. This legislation was the basis on which negotiations were undertaken for the North Atlantic Treaty.

I was not directly involved in the negotiations of the treaty, although I was in and out of the talks when I was in Washington. I did explain to the Scandinavian Foreign Ministers our rationale about NATO and was told that I helped persuade the Norwegians to join.

NATO was simply a necessity. The developing situation with the Soviet Union demanded the participation of the United States in the defense of Western Europe. Any other solution would have opened the area to Soviet domination, contrary to the interests of the United States and contrary to any decent world order. At the time of the signing of the pact, April 4, 1949, I do not believe that anyone envisaged the kind of military setup that NATO evolved into and from which de Gaulle withdrew French forces in 1966. It was, rather, regarded as a traditional military alliance of like-minded countries. It was not regarded as a panacea for the problems besetting Europe, but only as an elementary precaution against Communist aggression.

It is difficult now to recapture the mood of the late 1940s. The Soviet Union was on the move, not only in carrying out the traditional objectives of Russian foreign policy but also in utilizing to the full the existence of Communist parties subservient to it the world over. Had the United States not inaugurated the Marshall Plan or something similar and had the United States not departed from its historical tradition and agreed to join NATO, the Communists might easily have assumed power in most of Western Europe. Certainly none of the original framers of these measures intended to roll back by military force or by other means Soviet power from Eastern Europe. "Rollback" was a goal espoused for Eisenhower by John Foster Dulles during the presidential campaign of 1952.

Early in 1949, Marshall retired and Acheson was named to succeed him. I have never gone in for hero worship, but of all the men I have been associated with, including presidents, George Catlett Marshall is at the top of the list of those I admired. He had the ability to evoke the loyalty, respect, and affection of those who had the privilege of working with him. He was a man of absolute integrity. You felt the firmness, as if it were written in large letters all over him. He told me that one of his most difficult jobs was passing over old Army friends for important command positions in World War II because they did not measure up. He personally selected virtually all of the commanding officers in World War II; it was due to him that Eisenhower, Bradley, Patton, Collins, Ridgway, and others were chosen for their posts.

Marshall had a power of command that I have never seen equaled. He would listen carefully to all sides of a question and then make up his mind. Once the decision was made, there was no turning back, a characteristic that apparently was developed during his military training. His personality infected the entire State Department. It gave it a sense of direction and purpose. He was not a gregarious man—he did not know many people at State—but it did not take long after his acceptance of the post of Secretary for his character to permeate the department. We realized we were working for a great man.

Naturally quiet, he would seldom unbend. He preferred to listen rather than talk. Occasionally, at dinners with only men present, he would get in a reminiscent mood and talk sometimes for an hour at a time. In Moscow, Bedell Smith and I listened to him one evening as he reminisced about World War I. He had an extraordinary memory. He could remember even telephone numbers in France which he had used in World War I.

On rare occasions, he showed a pointed and caustic wit, which he delivered in a flat trajectory, making it doubly effective. During World War II, General Richard K. Sutherland, who was General Douglas MacArthur's Chief of Staff, flew to Washington to plead with the Joint Chiefs for a reversal of a decision in regard to strategy. During the course of his presentation, Sutherland twice said, "I stake my military reputation on the soundness of what I am proposing." The second time, General Marshall leaned back in his chair and asked in a quiet voice, "Would General Sutherland mind telling the Chiefs of Staff exactly what this military reputation is?"

With such a man, no subordinate would have dreamed of being impertinent. Those around him almost felt as though lightning would strike anyone who tried. Marshall knew his position and acted with the dignity it commanded. At a meeting of the Foreign Ministers in Moscow in the spring of 1947, Molotov was the guest of Marshall at a dinner at the American Embassy. The Soviet line at that time was to make fun of soldiers' becoming diplomats, and the faithful Molotov inquired whether, now that the United States had generals as Secretaries of State and Ambassadors (Bedell Smith was then ambassador to Moscow), it was necessary to march in goose step. After this was translated, Marshall turned to me with icy gray eyes and said quietly, "Please tell Mr. Molotov that I'm not sure I understand the purport of his remark, but if it is what I think it is, please tell him I do not like it." I translated this into Russian with great pleasure, and Molotov stopped the kidding immediately.

On the other hand, Marshall never forgot, as Byrnes did, that Truman was President. In the fall of 1948, while we were in Paris at a United Nations meeting, Marshall received a message from Washington that Truman was planning to send Chief Justice Vinson to Moscow in an attempt to work out a solution to problems with the Soviets. Marshall immediately drafted a reply to Truman that began something like this: "Never in the history of diplomatic bungling . . ." When it was read back to him, he said, "I cannot send a message like that. I am talking to my President." He then dictated a message to Truman that said that he had not kept the President completely informed about events and was returning to Washington to consult. He asked for an appointment. In Washington, Marshall threatened to resign if Truman went ahead with the Vinson trip. The President explained somewhat sheepishly that he was merely trying to find a way to get Stalin to listen, but he agreed to drop the idea.

Marshall always treated Truman with great deference and never talked about the President with any of his associates. While he gave the office of the President all the respect that it deserved, he did not hesitate to tell Truman when he thought he was wrong. In the spring of 1948, the President called in some of his advisers on domestic politics, as well as Marshall and other State Department officials, including me. The question was whether or not, because of the Jewish vote in the United States, the embargo on arms to Palestine should be lifted to help the Zionist organizations battling the British. The domestic advisers urged him to end the embargo (Truman's chances for re-election seemed dim; he needed Jewish votes and financial backing). The President turned to Marshall and asked his view. Marshall said he assumed that the President wanted his opinion "with the bark on." As I remember the words, Marshall, who in the military tradition did not exercise his right to vote, went on, "I'm not going to vote anyway, but if I were I would vote against you if you so demeaned the office of the President of the United States." Truman hastily said to the General, "This is what I expected from you," and decided not to lift the embargo.

Marshall had great human qualities. While he was in Washington talking Truman out of the idea of sending Vinson to Moscow, he heard that a nurse had brought my son, Charles, then two years old, with her to the department while she was posting some mail to me and my wife in Paris. Knowing that we had not seen the boy in some weeks, Marshall had the State Department photographer take a picture of Charlie sitting on his knee and in the company of Bedell Smith. Then he carried the picture back to Paris with him and presented it to us. "This is how Charlie looked yesterday," he said.

As for those subordinates who did not have the ability or who were not willing to produce to capacity, Marshall would be courteous but distant. His attitude was perfectly clear to those for whom he had little regard. I am happy to say that in the two years I was his special assistant and counselor, I never fell into this category.

Politicians were a race that Marshall got along with but did not really understand. Their motivation mystified him. For example, when he was urged by Lovett and others to cultivate Vandenberg, Marshall replied that he assumed that the Senator was animated by the national interest and therefore required no cultivation by anyone. He thought such deliberate cultivation would be discourteous to Vandenberg. Subsequently, as the result of natural association, the two became intimate friends, with vast benefit to our foreign policy.

Marshall's formula for dealing with Congress was quite simple. He would never lie or deceive senators or representatives. He would never tell questioners at the hearings that they had no right to information or that it was too sensitive. Instead of saying no, he would suggest that the hearing go into closed session, where he would be completely candid with them. His third rule was to study the backgrounds of the senators and representatives carefully so that he understood not only the questions they asked but why they were asking them. In a few years, when I came under congressional grilling, I found Marshall's formula extremely valuable.

Marshall had a high conception of honor. For example, he turned down an offer from a magazine for $1 million to do three articles because, he told me, he would have to say some unkind things about people against whom he held no animosity.

Working for Marshall was a rewarding experience; it is he whom I remember with the greatest admiration.

It is natural to look for an event to mark the beginning of an era. For the cold war, there is no precise moment. Churchill's "Iron Curtain" speech at Fulton, Missouri, was the beginning for some, although it did not receive widespread recognition in either the United States or Britain. The satellization of Eastern Europe, accepted by the West with the signing of the peace treaties in 1947, is another possible milestone. Still another criterion was the Soviet attempt to move beyond the traditional Czarist goals of influence into the Mediterranean and Middle East. Regardless of what the event was on the Soviet side, there is no doubt from the American view that by the time of the Truman Doctrine and the Marshall Plan our dispute with the Soviet Union had hardened into the cold war.

What caused the cold war? My view is quite simple. The cold war can be traced to the seizure of power by the Bolshevik wing of the Russian Social Democratic Party in 1917. As every high-school history student knows, the Bolsheviks believed in the inherent wickedness of capitalism, which they regarded merely as an instrument for the exploitation of the workers, and in the inevitability of the triumph of Communism over capitalism. Thus any capitalist society was not only an enemy but also an enemy that had overstayed his time on the historical scene. It did not make any difference what the capitalist countries did; the mere fact that they were capitalist made them the object of continuous hostility on the part of the Soviet rulers. They could not do otherwise and pretend to be Marxist-Leninists.

From 1917 until 1933, Great Britain and the British Empire were the number-one target of a cold war. The Soviet press at that time was replete with gross cartoons depicting capitalists in general and particularly the British Empire as the great exploiter of the people. In 1920, at the first Conference of the Toilers of the East at Baku, Zinoviev, then a full member of the Politburo (later purged and executed), made a fiery speech calling on all the assembled Muslims to join in a holy crusade against the British Empire. The tribesmen sprang to their feet and gave Zinoviev a hysterical reception.

From 1933 until the outbreak of World War II, the fantasy of the Soviet Union's being surrounded by capitalist enemies became a reality. To the east was Japan, and to the west Nazi Germany. During the war, because of harsh necessity, Stalin muted the Communist aspect of Soviet foreign policy. Appeals were made to traditional motives—to defend the family and Mother Russia. It was only when victory became clear that the Party began to re-emerge as the driving force and the war became transformed to one for Communist principles. In 1945, Jacques Duclos, a member of the French Politburo, denounced Earl Browder, the leader of the American Communist Party, for asserting that it might possibly be more accurate and certainly more wise to look to social evolution rather than social revolution along the Bolshevik model. This was rank heresy, and there can be no doubt that Duclos was put up to the denunciation by the Kremlin. As a result, Browder was summarily dismissed from leadership and expelled from the American Communist Party. This was the first case of the revival of pristine Bolshevik thought on the revolution. Duclos's attack reasserted all of the standard elements of Bolshevist ideology. The next year, Stalin made his famous electoral speech resuscitating all the harsh and antagonistic elements of Bolshevik philosophy. The word "Bolshevism" may sound outdated to some historians; in fact it is still an accurate term to describe the particular political philosophy that has guided Soviet leaders to this day.

The cold war was turned against America as a part of the basic and unwavering hostility which the Bolsheviks have always displayed against capitalist countries. The United States was selected as target number one simply because it was the chief source of power left in the non-Communist world after the war.

In the forty years that I have been reading the Soviet press, I have never seen any worthy or decent sentiments attributed to the United States government. Any action we have taken, no matter how civilized or progressive, is judged on the basic premise that all capitalism is evil and anything good that comes out of it is only apparently so. This is the basis for the cold war.

It seems fashionable nowadays to conclude that the cold war is over. I do not see how anyone can reach this conclusion if he takes the trouble to read the Soviet press or speeches of Soviet leaders and to examine the daily drumfire of Soviet propaganda that is directed against the United States. If the United States' actions jibe with the Soviet views, our hands have been forced by the "progressive" elements. If we are involved in something easily criticized, such as the Vietnam war, the Soviets exploit the situation to the full. Of course, the cold war has gone through varying degrees of intensity. Our moves to aid South Korea when it was invaded by North Korea produced one of the sharpest manifestations of the cold war. Yet few could honestly argue that either South Korea or the United States started the war. Part of the Communist effort was a carefully orchestrated campaign to prove that the American Air Force was using germ warfare. It is an interesting fact and an indication of the total falsity of the charges that immediately after Stalin's death all charges of germ warfare were dropped and have not reappeared in Soviet propaganda.

I am surprised and somewhat disturbed to see the ready acceptance of the thesis by certain historians that the cold war was really started by the United States. I can think of no historical untruth leading to more damaging consequences.

While the cold war between the United States and the Soviet Union has never become hot, there have been some close calls. The first one came just as the West was beginning to rebuild Europe and forge its military alliance. The Soviets imposed a blockade of Berlin. Through my position at the State Department, I was in a position to contribute to solving this crisis.

CHAPTER SIXTEEN

Standfast in Berlin

The development of Soviet policy toward Germany is still shrouded in mystery. Although I attended most of the meetings of the Council of Foreign Ministers after the war, it was never clear to me what Soviet objectives were. The Soviets were ambivalent about Germany. On one hand, there was a serious desire to punish Germany and make her pay for the incalculable loss in lives and treasure that she had inflicted on the Soviet Union. There was also a contradictory accompanying feeling that Germany, as the key to Europe and the homeland of Marxism, should be won over to the Soviet camp, as Lenin had dreamed. This conflict led to a hesitation and uncertainty in the Soviets' actions. In line with the punitive policy, they stripped their zone of East Germany, sending equipment and entire factories on flatcars to the Soviet Union, where they sometimes rusted in the snow for months and then had to be junked. At the same time, the Soviets permitted many former Nazis to hold high positions in their zone, a fact they ignored when denouncing the West for retaining ex-Nazis.

On the Allied side, we shared, at first, the Soviet fear of a revival of German militarism. That is why Roosevelt flirted with such ideas as dismembering the Reich and remaking, along the lines of the Morgenthau Plan, the country into a pastoral land. By the time of Roosevelt's death, Allied policy was clear. It was the intention of the Western Alliance to unify Germany, to impose on her such restrictions as were necessary to safeguard the peace and prevent a revival of German militarism, and then to write a peace treaty which would terminate the occupation. The efforts to enlist Soviet cooperation never ceased.

It is often forgotten that in 1946, when the fear of the rise of a new

Germany was still strong, Truman offered the Soviet Union, France, and Britain a twenty-five-year pact guaranteeing the demilitarization of Germany and the prevention of any return by Germany to a path of national militarism. This action was supported in the Senate by a resolution of Vandenberg and Connally. Had it ever been accepted by the Soviets, the treaty would have radically changed the whole configuration of Europe. I am still puzzled as to why the Kremlin did not take us up on the offer. The French and the British immediately accepted, but the Kremlin hedged. First, they said it was not long enough, but when we offered to extend the pact over forty years, they brought up other reasons of an obviously contrived character. It is probable that at that time the Soviets considered it a distinct possibility that all of Germany would become Communist.

On a number of occasions, Secretary Byrnes proposed that while peace treaties for Italy and Eastern European countries were being drafted, a commission study the German problem. But the Soviet Union insisted on sticking to a literal interpretation of the Potsdam agreement, under which the German treaty would be the last considered. As a result, there was no discussion of a German treaty. Almost two years were wasted.

It was not until the spring of 1947, at a meeting in Moscow, that the question of Germany was seriously considered by the Council of Foreign Ministers. The diplomacy of this period was marked by incessant wrangling over Soviet charges—for example, that the Western Allies were trying to create a militarized West Germany. A detailed account of these negotiations would take volumes. Initially, there was some reason to believe that the Soviets sought the communization of all Germany. Later, they shifted to a policy of keeping Germany divided. At no time were the Soviets prepared to permit the East Germans to become part of a unified independent Germany. If the Soviet Union could not control all of Germany, it would keep what it had.

By late 1947, positions on both sides had hardened. There seemed to be no basis for compromise, no common ground, and each side set about to make its half of Germany work as a separate entity. Meeting in London, beginning in February, 1948, the Foreign Ministers of the Western Allies decided to combine their three zones, a step toward the formation of a West German government, and, in a move to revive the country's economy, to revalue the mark. The Soviets, expressing the fear that currency reform would lead to the dumping of worthless old marks in their zone and that the formation of a West

German government would lead to a new German army, responded on April 1 with temporary restrictions on military traffic between the Western zones and Berlin.

There had been some warning signs as early as January that a blockade might be the Soviet answer to Allied moves. Trains and truck convoys were frequently held up on the ground that the documentation did not cover certain requirements. Repairs were allegedly instituted on canals, delaying long strings of barges bearing much needed supplies for Berlin. Nevertheless, the partial blockade of April caught the American government to some extent by surprise, and there were no contingency plans for dealing with it. This failure was more understandable then than it is in retrospect. The subject of Germany was still before the Council of Foreign Ministers, and the arrangements in Berlin had not been interrupted since the occupation began, in 1945. The temporary restrictions could have been local harassments. As far as I remember, no one in the State Department thought a full blockade would be imposed. The Pentagon was more sensitive to the possibility of a major Communist move, possibly because of Soviet military maneuvers. Once the situation began to worsen, numerous plans were considered.

There has been a good deal written about the recommendations, first made in April, by the American commander in Germany, General Clay, and by Robert Murphy, his political adviser, to use armed convoys to break through the barriers. The Joint Chiefs opposed the suggestion, because the Soviets could erect tank barriers or remove bridges and force the United States to make the first hostile move. Later in the spring, Clay revived the idea. As the department's congressional liaison man, I attended a meeting in Lovett's office at which Senator Vandenberg, supported by Senator Connally, emphatically rejected the idea on the basis that it would make the United States look like the instigator of war if one should break out. I shared their view. The forcing of the blockade had the attraction of being a clear, firm, and courageous decision. But it carried the risk of placing the onus on us for another world war.

In May, concerned that the Soviets might not understand American determination and aims, George Kennan, head of the Policy Planning Staff, asked Ambassador Bedell Smith in Moscow to endeavor to have a serious discussion with Molotov about the basic problems in Soviet-American relations. We wanted to assure him that despite the presidential campaign, and Henry Wallace's third-party pro-Soviet candidacy, most Americans believed in the same foreign policy, which, while it opposed the extension of totalitarian regimes, was nonaggressive. Although we asked that the talks remain secret, Molotov released a statement on them, apparently with the hope of aiding Wallace and sowing suspicion among the British and French that the United States was dealing behind their backs. Wallace got little help from the Kremlin, but our Allies were suspicious of our intentions. The idea was dropped.

As the weeks went by and the Communist noose around Berlin tightened, the United States had to decide whether to stay in Berlin or get out, to go ahead with the formation of the West German government and currency reform or delay. Supplies in the besieged city were running short. On June 4, the Allies decided to go ahead on both fronts. There was a brisk argument over whether to ask the Soviets to join in the currency reform. General Clay opposed the bid on the basis that the Soviets could, through delaying actions, prevent the swift reforms necessary to revive the economy. I argued for extending the invitation, believing that the West should always let the record show that we favored cooperation with the Soviet Union. If they attempted to block reform through procrastination, we could always go ahead on our own.

The invitation was proffered, but the Kremlin did not reply. In the middle of June, the Allies revalued the West German mark in their three zones, and on June 23 extended the revaluation to the Western sectors of Berlin. On June 24, the Soviets imposed a total blockade on Berlin. Originally, the blockade was met by using transport planes available in Europe, but soon it became clear that additional aircraft were essential.

On July 20, President Truman called a meeting of the National Security Council in the White House. Present were Marshall, Lovett, Clay, Murphy, and me, as well as the Joint Chiefs and officials of the Defense Department. With the use of armed convoys rejected, the question was whether to increase the airlift to circumvent the blockade. The Joint Chiefs had some doubts. They pointed out that the supply of military transport aircraft was not excessive and that if almost all of it was assigned to an airlift, there would be little left for regular military use and virtually none in the event of war. After some discussion, the President made his decision to go ahead with the airlift and ordered the Joint Chiefs to provide the planes necessary to make the operation a success. He expressed his absolute determination to stay in Berlin and not be driven out by any form of pressure. I did not take a very active part in this discussion, since I was not competent in military matters, but I fully agreed with President Truman's decision.

Soviet notes instituting the blockade asserted that the Allied currency reform had "destroyed" the rights of access to Berlin. The phraseology is important, since it contradicts the widely held belief, particularly since the event, that if there had been more detailed agreements as to those rights, the Soviets would not have dared to break them. Actually, the Soviet Union had acquiesced in guaranteeing Western access to Berlin, and notes from the Kremlin said specifically that these agreements were being broken. Therefore it did not make any difference whether there were more agreements; the Soviets would have proceeded in the same way. The reason they did not interrupt air traffic was not because that guarantee was in writing but simply because they correctly figured that such a step might have brought on a war with the United States and the Western powers. Our plans were coordinated with the British and the French, the former contributing a considerable number of planes to the airlift.

In discussions at State, I expressed the opinion that the Kremlin did not, at the time of its inception, plan that the blockade would go as far as it did. The initial motive for the blockade was closely connected with the revaluation of the mark and was designed to prevent an adverse effect on the currency and economy of the Eastern zone. Once the blockade was installed and it became apparent that the Western Allies were not prepared to use military force to break it, Moscow, thinking the airlift would not work, decided to try to force the West out of Berlin. Undoubtedly, one of the Soviet motives was to attempt to defeat Western plans, then well advanced, for the creation of a West German government. Eventually, Stalin himself made this clear.

Early on, the President made a move to show the Soviets that the United States meant business. In July, sixty B-29 bombers, capable of carrying atomic bombs, were sent to Britain. At that time, we still had a monopoly on the atomic bomb. We were not going to withdraw and we were not going to pick a fight. But if we had to fight, we would have the ultimate weapon ready.

In an effort to end the impasse speedily, Truman decided on a direct appeal to Stalin. While I told Marshall that I doubted if Stalin would respond, I saw no harm in the approach. In any event, the appeal to Stalin would help reassure the British and French, who were getting nervous about Truman's vigorous reaction, that the United States was not hell-bent for war. Marshall sent me to Europe to discuss the coordination of a tripartite approach. I flew to Berlin with Clay on his private plane. The General had such a severe case of lumbago that he could hardly twist his head. He was embarrassed when his subordinates in Berlin saw him being carried from the plane in a chair. He did not think it was suitable for a commander to be incapacitated in a crisis.

During my two days in Berlin, I had a glimpse of the airlift, which was just starting up. It was an impressive sight to see those great planes coming over the buildings of Berlin, landing at Tempelhof, and taking off at intervals of three or four minutes. Later came the even more dramatic spectacle of continuing these flights in bad weather. Initially, there was some apprehension on our part that the Soviets might seek to jam the radio-guidance mechanism, which would have made flying at night and in bad weather virtually impossible. However, it soon became apparent that the Soviets did not intend any overt interference with air access to Berlin. Had the Soviets interfered with any of the planes, I believe war might easily have broken out. It was held at the time, and the experts still believe, that the Kremlin did not want a war and would not put themselves in the position of provoking one through an overt act.

Ambassador Bedell Smith flew in from Moscow and Ambassador Lewis Douglas from London. I filled them in on our strategy. The three of us then flew to London, where we talked with Bevin, the British Foreign Secretary, and René Massigli, the French Ambassador there. At one meeting, Bevin turned to me and said, "I know all of you Americans want a war, but I'm not going to let you 'ave it." He spoke in semijocular fashion but still put a good deal of conviction in his statement. The French Ambassador also expressed fear that hasty American action would precipitate a war. I did my best to dissuade them, but am not sure that I was totally successful.

If the British and French had some doubts as to the intentions of the United States, they could not find much evidence to support their feelings. Bevin's remark seemed fantastic to me. It had no basis in fact. He might have heard second- or third-hand reports of bellicosity on the part of some American officials. I was close to the situation at all times, and aside from the initial suggestion by Clay to use armed convoys to call the Soviet bluff, there never was a plan to instigate war. We would fight only if the Soviets insisted. But we would not get out of Berlin.

It is a good principle to examine your own motives carefully when they have been challenged by friends. In international politics, this is not easy to do. Bevin's remark, it seems to me, reflected the overriding fear of the British of being drawn into another war in circumstances in which they were not taking the lead. The British attitude then and since has been excessively timid over what the Soviets might do. Such an attitude is understandable in view of Britain's vulnerability, but it plays into Moscow's hands. The British have not appreciated the fact that in none of the postwar crises was there ever any thought or suggestion of offensive military action on the part of the United States. We always acted only to protect that which was on our side of the line.

With the plan coordinated, I returned to Washington, where Marshall set up an ad hoc committee to deal with the situation. Called the Berlin group, it was composed of various State Department officials concerned with the crisis. Task forces and committees were not as institutionalized in those days as they are now, and we operated rather informally. As head of the group, I was responsible for instructing our ambassadors overseas and officers in the department on the execution of policy. I reported to Under Secretary Lovett and Secretary Marshall. Because of my coordinating responsibilities, I saw all the cables coming in from Germany and all those going out.

I also worked with General Gerhardt, who had been appointed the coordinator in the Pentagon. Frequently, I went to the Pentagon in the evenings for teletype exchanges with Berlin. In those long working days and nights, the irrepressible Lovett provided us with welcome breaks in tension. One night, when the subject of Berlin sewers came up, Lovett said with a grin, "I wish General Clay would realize that our policy is open sewers, openly arrived at."

In accordance with our plan, the three Allied ambassadors to the Soviet Union made a joint request to see Stalin. The Soviets expected some form of ultimatum. The ambassadors were told that Stalin was not in town. They then sought to see Molotov and were informed that he was away. Finally, they got to see a lesser official and informed him of the Western views, which were not in the character of an ultimatum. By some curious stroke of fate, both Molotov and Stalin reappeared in Moscow. The ambassadors met with Stalin and Molotov on August 2, and again on August 23. There were moments when Stalin indicated he would lift the blockade, saying, "We are still allies." On August 2, both Stalin and Molotov pressed for a delay in the Western Allies' plan for establishing a West German government. When the ambassadors would not agree to this, Stalin and Molotov asked that their request be recorded "as the insistent wish" of the

Soviet government. In reading the dispatches from Ambassador Bedell Smith on the meeting, I realized that Stalin was really saying that the blockade would be lifted if we abandoned the idea of forming a West German government. This was a price we would not pay.

With the Moscow talks getting nowhere, I drafted a cable to Ambassador Smith suggesting that Stalin be advised that the Allies would feel it necessary to refer the Berlin problem to the "appropriate organ" of the United Nations if no agreement could be reached. We did not specify whether we meant the Security Council, where the Soviets could veto any action, or the General Assembly, where the veto did not apply but which lacked power to institute action. At the meeting with the three ambassadors on August 23, Stalin was advised of the plan to take the case to the United Nations. He gave further reassurances on Berlin, emphasizing that the future of the city depended on a four-power agreement on German unity. There was some hope a week later, when the Control Council of the four powers occupying Germany issued the directive of August 30. The directive left to the military commanders arrangements for working out the currency problem. Like all ambiguous understandings with the Soviet Union, this one was soon sabotaged by the Soviets.

It was during the session of the United Nations General Assembly in Paris in the fall that the Allies decided to take their case to the Security Council. I thought we should move promptly, because the Soviets might try to capitalize on the war fears of the neutral countries, as well as of Britain and France, by going into the General Assembly with a propaganda campaign for "peace."

Philip Jessup, our deputy representative to the United Nations, was put in charge of the Security Council operation. Much of the success of the effort to end the Berlin blockade can be attributed to Jessup. A man of considerable judicial eminence, who later became a judge in the International Court of Justice, he would never rush into any ill-considered action. He was an excellent diplomat, who could always be counted on to carry out with intelligence and precision the instructions he received from his government.

I was assigned to work with Jessup. After we had planned our strategy for the Security Council debates, we went to Marshall, who told Jessup that he would back up any action he took provided it was not appeasement.

I was concerned that during the debate an American hothead in Germany might do something rash. I telegraphed Murphy, who was known for his tough views, cautioning against any move that might aggravate affairs and urging that only in a grave emergency should anything unusual be done without first receiving Marshall's approval.

As I watched Vishinsky struggle unavailingly to prevent the Berlin dispute from being put on the Security Council agenda, I recalled how Stalin had overruled Molotov's insistence that the veto apply to such procedural questions. I imagine that Vishinsky often thought of the same thing with bitterness and regret.

The debates in the Security Council were not productive. I was irritated by the dissimilarity of treatment accorded the two sides. It was almost as though the members of the United Nations recognized and accepted the fact that the Soviet Union was unmoved by any appeal to morality, to public opinion, or to what would be best for the world; therefore the whole attention of the United Nations came down on the side that was movable, the Western democracies. At a reception, Herbert Evatt, the Australian Foreign Minister (later Prime Minister), grabbed me by the arm and, virtually repeating Bevin's earlier phrase, said to Jessup, who was next to me, "So you want to start another war, do you? Well, we're not going to let you do it." I do not say that the unfair attitude of those United Nations members applied in all cases, but it did exist in situations, like the Berlin blockade, which carried the danger of war. Had we relied on the United Nations instead of the Western Alliance, I fear the consequences would have been the surrender of Berlin.

By October, a group of six neutralist nations proposed a resolution under which the Soviet blockade and the Allied counterblockade would be lifted and the military commanders would meet to set up currency controls. In a telecon call (where messages are flashed on screens) with Washington, Marshall agreed to accept the resolution. Facetiously, I told Washington that in Montmartre cabarets, a notoriously bullish environment, the betting was 8 to 1 against Soviet acceptance. Vishinsky did veto the neutralist resolution, and the blockade continued.

Those of us concerned with the Berlin problem weighed other ideas. The General Assembly of the United Nations would have given the Allied position overwhelming endorsement, but the Soviets would not be bound by the action. We were interested in settling the dispute, not in winning a propaganda war. In a moderate version of his earlier plan, General Clay favored moving road, rail, and barge traffic to the barriers; if the Soviets refused passage, we would call a meeting of the four military commanders to take another step. I pointed out that if the traffic were turned back and we decided not to force the issue, we would be humiliated. For this reason and others, the idea was shelved.

As the fall turned into winter, the airlift kept on, through fog, ice, and snow. So did the Allied embargo on trade with the Soviet zone. In November, Truman scored his astounding upset victory and was elected to a full term as president. Fortunately, foreign policy did not become an issue between Truman and his chief opponent, Republican Thomas E. Dewey.

In January, 1948, Truman began his final four years in office with a new Secretary of State, Dean Acheson. The tall man with the bristling mustache and cold eyes was a good choice to succeed Marshall. Possessing impeccable conservative credentials, Acheson was widely respected in Congress as a man who would not knuckle under to the Soviets. With his debonair appearance, his caustic wit, and his flair for rhetoric, as well as his candidness, Acheson, as an Assistant Secretary of State, had been concerned with economic affairs and congressional relations and had made many friends in Europe and in the House and Senate. In addition, his two years as Under Secretary had given him a knowledge not only of the workings of the department but also of the talents and personalities of various members of the Foreign Service. Most important of all, he was known to be deeply committed to close ties with Western Europe, and such a commitment was central to Truman's foreign policy.

Less than two weeks after Acheson took office, I detected and called to his attention what looked to me like a signal from Stalin of a change in attitude toward Berlin. I was on the lookout for such a signal from the Soviets because the counterblockade was hurting the Communists a great deal. An American correspondent, Kingsbury Smith, European manager of Hearst's International News Service, had written Stalin a letter asking some questions about Berlin. During those years, correspondents wrote Stalin letters from time to time in the hope of receiving an answer. Few of the letters were answered. However, Smith included a question that Stalin wanted to answer. Smith asked whether Stalin attached great importance to the monetary question of Berlin. In his reply on January 31, 1949, Stalin did not speak of monetary matters at all, but of the bad effects of the Berlin blockade and the counterblockade on the development of Germany and the question of trade between the two parts of Europe. When I saw this answer in the press, I was struck by the fact that Stalin had failed to mention the monetary dispute, which the Soviets had heretofore cited as their main reason for imposing the blockade.

In talking the matter over with Acheson and the Berlin group, I cautioned that we could not be sure that Stalin was sending a signal. Soundings had to be made. After Truman had given his approval, Acheson decided on a probing operation. At his regular press conference of February 2, he commented that if Stalin were serious about wanting an agreement, there were channels available that were less public than the press. Then we called Jessup to Washington and asked him to try to open the private channel himself by talking with Yakov A. Malik, the Soviet representative to the United Nations. On February 15, Jessup waited for Malik near the entrance to the delegate's lounge at the temporary United Nations headquarters at Lake Success. (Not, as some accounts have said, in the men's room.) After remarks about the weather, he asked if Stalin's omission of the currency question was an accident. Malik said he did not know. Jessup said he would be interested if Malik found out. Jessup wrote a memorandum on the conversation, which he sent to Senator Warren Austin, the head of our United Nations delegation, and to four other members of his New York staff, as well as to the Berlin group in Washington. It was classified "secret," but when I saw the distribution I became concerned. I criticized Jessup for not being more careful. The memo was reclassified "top secret," and the copies distributed to our staff at the United Nations were destroyed.

The success of the efforts to lift the Berlin blockade is a classic example of the value of secrecy in sensitive diplomatic negotiations. Had news of Jessup's approach to Malik leaked, all sorts of views would have been expressed in the press and elsewhere. The Soviets would have believed that we were trying to influence public opinion, not reach an agreement. It can almost be stated as a principle that when the Soviets are serious about something they do it in secrecy, and when they are not they indulge in propaganda.

The problem of secrecy in government operation, particularly in diplomacy, remains one of the most difficult questions. No one I worked with in the American government ever contested the right of the people to know in general what the policies of their government are, nor did they blame the press for printing what it could discover. The fact remains that for certain types of diplomatic maneuvers involving sensitive issues, secrecy is essential. There is no ready solution to this problem. Only common sense and a sense of common purpose will make it manageable.

A month went by with no word from Malik. I thought my supposition about the omission was wrong. Then Jessup, who had been transferred to Washington and elevated to the rank of Ambassador at Large, received a phone call. Malik wanted to see him. The next day, March 15, at the Soviet United Nations mission on Park Avenue, Malik said that Moscow had told him the omission of the currency question had not been accidental.

The Berlin group in the State Department saw opportunities to explore. On our advice, Truman and Acheson directed Jessup to sound out Malik on the possibility of arranging a settlement which would permit the lifting of the blockade, the ending of the airlift, and the return of Germany, although still divided, to the relative tranquillity it had enjoyed since the end of the war. It took months of careful work on Jessup's part before an accord was reached. I wanted to bring the Security Council in on the final agreement—it would strengthen the United Nations—and hoped to get British and French support for us. Jessup went to elaborate lengths to make sure the Soviets understood we were not promising to delay or cancel the plan to set up a separate West German government. Moscow took pains to make certain that a meeting of the Council of Foreign Ministers to discuss Germany and Austria would be held before the Bonn government came into existence.

Toward the end of the discussions, Robert Schuman, the French Foreign Minister, inadvertently let out the news in an interview in France. By that time, however, the leak did not make any difference, because Malik and Jessup had agreed on a tentative schedule for the lifting of the bloackade, the ending of the counterrestrictions, and a meeting of the Council of Foreign Ministers. On May 5, a communiqué announcing the agreement was issued.

The meeting of the Council of Foreign Ministers was preceded by one of those incidents which always cause a great deal of trouble. Kennan and his Policy Planning Staff had drawn up a paper proposing the reduction of American and Soviet forces in Germany as a means toward eventual reunification. The suggestion had been opposed by the Joint Chiefs of Staff, who pointed out that the United States would have to withdraw forces more than three thousand miles, whereas the Soviets need only withdraw theirs a few hundred miles. Someone—not Kennan—leaked the contents of this paper to James Reston of *The New York Times*, who wrote about it. The article raised a good deal of hell in Europe. The French and British were alarmed that the United States was going to reduce its commitment in Europe only weeks after the signing of the NATO treaty. It took a few hours of soothing conversation to explain to these governments that the Kennan plan had not been floated as a trial balloon by the United States government. There have been occasions when trial balloons have been floated by the government, but given the nature of our society, the nature of the Department of State, and our constitutional structure, they are rare. I know in fact that the Kennan paper was not in any sense a trial balloon.

The meeting of the Council of Foreign Ministers in Paris had its hilarious moments. Vishinsky had made a serious slip in agreeing to a provision in the Austria treaty without having obtained certain safeguards which the Soviet government considered important. We knew about it because the French had monitored a telephone call from Gromyko in Moscow to Vishinsky in Paris, in which Gromyko used as rough and abusive language as it is possible to imagine. The fact that the French monitored Soviet telephone calls was no surprise. Anyone in public life who regards a telephone call, particularly across frontiers, as secure should have his head examined. Every diplomat knows this. The call demonstrated the difference between a Communist Party position and a government position in the Soviet Union. Vishinsky was Foreign Minister, Gromyko only a Deputy Foreign Minister, yet Gromyko's position in the Party was so much better than Vishinsky's that he felt perfectly at ease in abusing his superior.

Although the conference had ended, Vishinsky asked to meet again with the Western Foreign Ministers. There he sought the rectification of a sentence in the communiqué. When Secretary Acheson coldly inquired whether the Soviet government was prepared to violate an agreement when it had hardly been put on paper, Vishinsky dropped the subject and agreed to let the passage stand. His reception on his return to Moscow could not have been warm.

The meeting of the Council of Foreign Ministers in May, 1949, was the last of that body. It was essentially a conference to liquidate the Berlin blockade, which it did. It made some efforts in the direction of an Austrian peace treaty, but these came to nothing.

The outcome of the Berlin blockade was a success for the West in that the Soviets had failed to squeeze the Western Allies out of Berlin and matters were restored to the status before the blockade. We had prevailed without forcing a war. But attempts by the Allies to bring about the creation of a corridor of Allied access were blocked by the Soviets.

The blockade did convince us of the urgent necessity of proceeding with the creation of a West German government. The establishment of the Bonn regime was followed by the creation by the Soviets of a government for East Germany. In this sense, the Berlin blockade may be said to have deepened and perhaps rendered permanent the division of Germany.

As to its effects on Allied policy in general, this is harder to determine. The blockade certainly did not lead to any rearmament by the United States; debate in the spring of 1950 was over whether the American military budget should be $14 billion or $12 billion. Nor did the blockade lead to an increase in anti-Soviet feeling in the United States. The principal lesson of the Berlin blockade was that if the Western Allies were prepared to stand firm on their rights, they had better than a fifty-fifty chance of winning. What would have been the result if more vigorous and more dangerous measures to counteract the blockade had been adopted no one can tell. While we clearly did not wish war and gave every possible indication to that effect, our preparations, particularly the dispatch of a squadron of B-29s to England, must have impressed the Soviets with our determination to stay in Berlin, and that if absolutely necessary, we were prepared to use force.

With the lifting of the Berlin blockade, a tranquillity settled over Europe. There was no crisis in sight, and a very dangerous subject had been liquidated from the international scene. In the Far East, however, the story was somewhat different. The Communists were about to score a victory of gigantic proportions in China. Moreover, the United States was headed for a shooting war in Korea.

CHAPTER SEVENTEEN

Thoughts on Korea

In the summer of 1949, I began to think seriously about my future. I had been in Washington more than seven years, and four years was regarded as the limit for Foreign Service officers. I thought it was about time, if I wished to stay in the Service, to go abroad again, and mentioned my desire to Secretary of State Acheson, who agreed. He offered me any of the minor Embassies in Western Europe. After thinking about the offer, I told him it would be a mistake for me to reach ahead of my class in the Foreign Service and become an ambassador; I preferred a more modest job at that particular point in my career.

As indicated earlier, I continued to feel that it was (and is) a mistake to get too far ahead of yourself in the Foreign Service, that one might end up at the top of the heap at too early an age and then be confronted with the problem of a future assignment. To have been made an ambassador at the age of forty-five would have complicated my future. In addition, I was more interested in the post of Minister to France than an ambassadorship in a less important country. Acheson then offered and I immediately accepted the position of Minister in Paris, the number-two position in the Embassy. Kennan succeeded me as department Counselor and the resident expert on the Soviet Union.

It was a new position that I occupied in Paris. Up to that time, we had never had a regular Minister, that is, a Minister Plenipotentiary and Extraordinary, in any of our Embassies. Earlier in 1949, before I had thought of moving on, James Webb, who was then Under Secretary, asked me to make some suggestions as to how the burdens resting on the shoulders of an ambassador might be lightened. I suggested the creation in the big Embassies of the post of full Minister, who would be able in many cases to appear for the Ambassador. The idea was adopted, and Ministers were set up in London, Paris, Rome, and Moscow. Shortly after I arrived in Paris, I was elevated to the rank of Career Minister by President Truman. This was purely a honorific title, carrying no authority in itself.

Our Ambassador was David Bruce, whom I had known, not intimately, but reasonably well. He had had a distinguished career in the OSS during the war and had been the Marshall Plan representative in France before his appointment as ambassador. He was an admirable boss in every respect, and I regret that we worked together only a year. He was ideal to work for, considerate and courteous at all times, and eventually became a close friend. Later, he became Under Secretary of State and ambassador to Germany and Britain.

Our relations with the French were close. France was a full member of NATO, and Paris was the site of the NATO Council. One of the jobs given to me was to set up the first military-assistance program for France. I had assigned to my staff as head of the military end of the matter General Richards, who had been Budget Officer of the Department of Defense. He was assiduous in protecting the interests of the United States, and occasionally it was necessary for me to soothe ruffled French feelings. He did a good job.

Military assistance was in its infancy, and much new ground had to be broken. I spent a good deal of my time away from Paris, particularly in London, where Colonel Charles H. Bonesteel, an American officer of exceptional ability who later became commander of American forces in Korea, coordinated the whole European program. There were many knotty problems about the military-aid program, particularly in getting the French bureaucracy to submit detailed plans of how the aid would be used. But the question of France's use of our aid in an attempt to suppress Ho Chi Minh's revolution in Indochina was never raised, at least by me. I felt that France was losing the war in Indochina, but I do not recall having any objections, and certainly did not voice any, in regard to the extension of our aid. France was an allied country, and it would have been difficult to substitute our judgment for that of the French with regard to her colony.

I had been in Paris only a short time when the State Department considered calling me back to examine a study prepared by the Policy Planning Staff, then under Paul Nitze, for the National Security Council. The study was ordered as the result of the Soviets' explosion in August of their first nuclear device, thus breaking the American monopoly. The comfortable assumption that the United States had worked on was that it would be several years before the Soviet Union could explode a nuclear device. The Soviets' shortening of the period was anxiously discussed in Washington. The American monopoly of this weapon had been a major factor in all of the dealings with the Soviet Union, and continued to be while we maintained a superiority in the 1950s and early 1960s. This superiority undoubtedly dictated the caution the Soviets followed, particularly in regard to the Berlin blockade and, later, during the Korean war. In the aftermath of the Soviet explosion of their first atomic weapon, there was worry about the Soviet Union's actual and potential military strength compared with the United States. Because events were moving fast, the paper was circulated quickly, and comments were wanted immediately. It was decided not to call me back, and I did not study the paper until I returned in 1951. There was much in the paper, known as NSC/68, that I agreed with, particularly the basic recommendation that American military power be increased so as to be more commensurate with commitments forced on us in the world. There were certain matters in the analysis of Soviet policy that I did not agree with then, and still do not. Soviet policy was presented as nothing more than an absolute determination to spread the Communist system throughout the world. As I have said before, even in those days I was convinced that the Soviet Union, as far as its own actions went, was largely motivated by its interests as a national state, and that the idea of spreading Communism was secondary to such considerations. The main Bolshevik aim is to protect the Soviet system, above all in Russia and secondarily in the satellite countries. The extension of Communism to other areas is a theoretical and secondary goal.

Stalin, as the boss of Russia, would never desire as a matter of basic policy to see Communist systems established in areas which he could not hope to control. Stalin's attitudes toward Communism as a doctrine and as an operating mechanism conflicted. Being a Marxist, he undoubtedly believed in all of the main principles of that doctrine. But being a Soviet nationalist, he had great doubt as to the ability of a Communist Party, left to itself, to achieve power in any circumstance. As he told Churchill at Yalta, there was no need to worry about the establishment of Communist regimes. He therefore had organized the entire Communist apparatus on a worldwide basis as an instrument completely subordinate and, indeed, subservient to orders from the Kremlin—that is, from himself. He trusted a Communist movement only when it was fully under his control. Anything outside of his control, particularly Communist, was subject to serious mistrust and doubt. He therefore ordered the establishment of Soviet-type regimes in areas where they would remain under the control of the Soviet Union. However, he obviously could not turn his back on the success of a Communist party if it won power on its own. This was certainly the case in China. There is ample evidence to support the view that Stalin did not anticipate or wish to see the Communists take power in China, certainly in the immediate postwar period. But once it occurred, Stalin had no course except to help it. NSC/68's misconception of Soviet aims misled, I believe, Dean Acheson and others in interpreting the Korean war.

Also, I felt in reading NSC/68, there was absolutely no chance that its recommendations for huge increases in defense spending would be adopted. It would have involved additional tens of billions in appropriations, increased taxes, and all the disadvantages which accompany a large increase in armaments. In a democracy such as ours, with diverse groups competing for government funds, it was hardly likely that in time of peace any Congress would seriously consider such an increase in the military budget. I did not quarrel with the need of the increase, but I seriously doubted its practicability. NSC/68 was, however, a useful exercise, and I believe that it helped clarify American government thinking on economic problems resulting from our conflict with the Soviet Union.

On June 25, 1950, my wife and I were in our weekend cottage in Thiers, north of Paris. About lunchtime, I received a call from Woodruff Wallner, a Secretary in the Embassy, who told me that fighting had broken out in Korea. He motored out, bringing me the latest dispatches, and we returned together that afternoon. The following day, Ambassador Bruce, Averell Harriman, who was then coordinator of the Marshall Plan, and I discussed the situation. We were relatively gloomy, because we saw no sign that the United States intended to take any vigorous action to stop the Communist invasion of South Korea. We speculated on the consequences of American inaction, how disheartening it would be to our allies, and how much danger it posed for the future. While we were sitting there, a cable from President Truman arrived. It reported his decision to intervene with air and sea forces, and instructed Bruce to inform the French government. I accompanied Bruce when he called on Robert Schuman, the French

Foreign Minister. Schuman's eyes filled with tears. "Thank God," he said, "this will not be a repetition of the past." He was thinking of the French and British failures to stop Hitler before World War II.

After a telephone conversation with Washington, it was decided that I would accompany Harriman back to Washington. We went to London to catch a plane. I remember the ride well. We wondered what was going to happen in Korea. Everything was uncertain, and the bumpy plane ride symbolized our emotions. In the early morning before arriving in New York, we ran into a thunderstorm. Suddenly the airliner dropped perhaps a thousand feet. As the plane lurched, sugar, dishes, and other kitchen supplies poured into the aisles. Unperturbed, Harriman, shaving with his hat on in the men's room, kept right on scraping away.

At Acheson's request, I spent a month in Washington examining evidence to ascertain whether the Korean invasion was the forerunner of similar Communist military moves elsewhere in the world. I was working then with Gustav Hilger, whom I had known when he was German Minister in Moscow during the early years of the war and who happened to be in Washington. He was called in as a consultant after Korea. Born in Russia, he was fluent in the Russian language and an acknowledged expert on Soviet affairs. My conclusion was that there was little chance of the Soviet Union's repeating the invasion in any other place, such as Germany. The Soviet action in Korea was limited strictly to Korea.

Hilger and Kennan shared my view, but we were in the minority. The Korean war was interpreted by Acheson and most others in the State Department, as well as the Joint Chiefs of Staff, as ushering in a new phase of Soviet foreign policy. Their view, which Truman accepted, was that having launched an attack on Korea—the first case of Communist open use of naked military force to expand the system—the Soviet Union was likely to call on satellite armies elsewhere, particularly in East Germany, to spread Communist control. They were understandably influenced by the emotions engendered by the Communist invasion. At various meetings, Kennan and I argued in vain against this thesis.

We were particularly opposed to plans for a counterinvasion of North Korea. We warned that Communist countries would react strongly if hostile forces approached their borders. We had both China and the Soviet Union in mind, of course. Basic to our thinking was our conviction that the main objective of the leaders of Communist countries is preservation of the system. American troops on the Chinese border at the Yalu River, only a short distance from Vladivostok, would certainly be viewed as a threat. It was folly, Kennan and I argued, to take the chance of prodding China and/or the Soviet Union into a war. Sufficient military force should be used to throw back the invaders, we agreed, but large-scale retaliation was not necessary because the attack on Korea was not a prelude to invasions elsewhere.

Why were we so sure in the face of opposing opinions? In the first place, the Soviet Union was far from ready, from a strategic military point of view, to contemplate a global war with the United States. It had been less than a year since the Soviet Union exploded its first atomic bomb. While the test was earlier than many expected, we knew from our experience that the gap between the production of the first device and a usable arsenal of weapons was years. In June, 1950, it was beyond the realm of possibility that the Soviet Union had a stockpile of atomic weapons.

I believe that Stalin's chief motive was the desire to round out his hold over the entire Korean peninsula. By 1950, he realized that there was practically no chance of repeating in Japan his success in carving out a section of Germany. The refusal of the United States through Harriman to accord Stalin an occupational zone on the island of Hokkaido and MacArthur's one-man rule made that clear. In addition, the United States was pushing ahead with plans for a peace treaty with Japan, and the Soviets were powerless to hold it up. But South Korea, practically defenseless since American forces had withdrawn, looked available for the taking.

Stalin also believed he could get away with the invasion because of his continued adherence to a classic error of Marxist thought, that the working class and poor were with the Communists everywhere. Not learning from his disappointment in Finland, he banked on the shock of the invasion to trigger off an internal revolt against the capitalist regime of President Syngman Rhee. While it is true that South Korea had no large working class, the Bolsheviks believed the poor peasants would on the whole favor a Communist regime. This fallacy cannot be avoided by a genuine Marxist-Leninist, for abandonment of this tenet would result in the collapse of the whole attempt to make Bolshevik theory applicable to all countries at all times. There was little doubt that Stalin and the North Korean dictator, Kim Il Sung, believed that the military action would be quick, with the South

Koreans rising to support the Communists, and there would be no chance for any other country to do anything.

I am not one of those who believe that Acheson's speech to the National Press Club on January 12, 1950, in which he left Korea outside the limits of American vital interest in the Far East, had anything to do with the Soviet determination to approve, if not actually order, the attack on South Korea. It is difficult to imagine that a ruler as careful as Stalin would act on the basis of a speech to the press. His experience and instinct were to reject public statements as not necessarily defining a country's real position. It is probably true that Stalin did weigh the speech in the light of the total withdrawal of American military support from South Korea and came to the conclusion that the United States would not act, especially if the invasion quickly took over the whole country. It was certainly not the speech itself that triggered any Soviet action.

There are those who now say that the war was not started by the Soviet Union but by an independent act of the North Koreans. This is childish nonsense. How could an army, trained in every respect by the Soviet Union, with Soviet advisers at every level, and utterly dependent on Moscow for supplies, move without Soviet authorization? Stalin would not have been so careless as to permit the North Koreans to kick off a war that conceivably might involve the Soviet Union in a confrontation with the United States. The Soviet Union has never joked about war.*

Back in Paris, I was happy to read of General Douglas MacArthur's successful landing at Inchon, but I continued to be worried about the entry of Chinese or Russian forces. On November 25, three days after American troops reached the Yalu, Chinese "volunteers" crossed the river in overwhelming numbers. Unfortunately, Kennan and I had been right in warning of intervention.

The disastrous American retreat was bad enough. But there was a new worry. Kennan had left the State Department on a leave of absence to become a resident scholar and writer at the Institute for Advanced Study in Princeton. Thus, at this critical time, there was no major official in the administration experienced in dealing with Soviet affairs. I telephoned Kennan and urged him to go to Washington and impress on General Marshall and Secretary Acheson the underlying

---

* If Khrushchev's memoirs are to be believed, the idea for the invasion of South Korea came from Kim Il Sung, the dictator of North Korea. He presented the idea to Stalin, who had doubts. After consulting with Mao Tse-tung, Stalin decided to support and arm the North Koreans for the venture.

reasons for the turn of events in Korea. Kennan acted on my request, and Acheson enthusiastically accepted his offer of temporary help.

While Kennan and I were correct in our prediction about Chinese intervention, I do not know even now whether Stalin would have stood by and swallowed a total American victory in Korea. I believe Stalin never dreamed the United States would intervene. He thought the attack would be viewed as simply part of a civil war. Once the United States responded and the battle began to go against the Communist forces, I believe Stalin began to fear that the Soviet Union might be pulled into a big war. When the Chinese "volunteers" pushed the Americans back, Stalin must have been worried that the United States would use greater force, perhaps atomic weapons. He looked around for a way to extricate himself from the predicament he had got into. He certainly did not want to tangle with the American giant by launching other invasions.

Whether Stalin was instrumental in getting the Chinese to enter the war is buried in the Moscow and Peking archives. It may well be that the Chinese dictator, Mao Tse-tung, decided on his own to intervene, because the threat to the Chinese Communist regime was too great for it to stand by. The Soviets were certainly perfectly willing to have the Chinese sacrifice their blood to defend North Korea.

Soviet caution did not prevent the launching of a vicious propaganda campaign generally known as the Hate America movement. The press, radio, and television depicted America as an evil country willing to destroy foreign land for profit. Anti-Truman plays were popular in Moscow. The Stockholm appeal to ban the atomic bomb, said to be signed by 500 million people, an obviously false number, was designed to make us look aggressive. There was also an enormous effort to convince the world that the United States was waging germ warfare in Korea. The Soviet propaganda machine mobilized scientists of Communist sympathy and others to support their accusations. Films showed Chinese exterminating bugs, allegedly dropped by the United States Air Force. I attended a number of meetings at which the CIA discussed ways to counter the Hate America campaign, but we did not come up with anything effective. The campaign had its effect. Even some Americans, ever suspicious of the military, wondered if the Air Force had been experimenting in Korea. The United States endeavored on a number of occasions to have the germ warfare charges aired in the United Nations. Lacking evidence, the Communists refused.

Acheson must have realized the weakness in going without a chief

Soviet expert in Washington, because a few weeks later I received a telephone call from Carl Hummelsine, the chief administrative officer, saying that Secretary Acheson thought it would be a good idea for me to return home to resume the position of Counselor. Kennan was returning to Princeton. My wife, who was nearing the end of her last pregnancy, expressed no great pleasure at the thought of giving up the charming house we occupied in Paris and the delights of Parisian life for the grind and problems of Washington. However, like the good Foreign Service wife she was, she accepted the decision without fuss. A few days later, on December 17, I took her to the hospital, awaited the birth of our third child and second daughter, and then rushed off to catch a train to Brussels. The NATO Council was meeting there at that time to consider the armament of West Germany, which had been approved in principle by the Foreign Ministers of the United States, Britain, and France in September.

The French had sounded me out on the plan on a Sunday in November, 1950. Raymond Clappier, private secretary to Foreign Minister Schuman, had come to the Embassy, where we talked for several hours about the defense problem from the French point of view. Eventually, he brought up the idea of a European army. I notified Washington, where large buckets of cold water were poured over the idea. General Eisenhower, who later became one of its chief proponents, took a dim view of it at first. The plan also provoked a strong adverse reaction in France and was never adopted. The Brussels conference did approve the rearmament of Germany in principle, but it was to be a long time before Germans were actually in uniforms.

It had been planned for me to return to Washington early in 1951, and in one of our last holidays my wife and I went off with Cyrus Sulzberger, *The New York Times* columnist, and his wife, Marina, to golf and eat our fill at French inns. We got as far as Barbizon, near Fontainebleau, when the telephone rang. It was the Embassy saying that the Soviets had accepted our suggestion for a meeting to try to work out an agenda for another conference of Foreign Ministers on Germany and Austria. The holiday was canceled; I returned to Paris to discuss the agenda.

We had thought that the meeting would take a short time. Instead, it took almost four months to arrive at the conclusion that we could not reach an agreement on the agenda. The site of the meeting, a monstrosity of a palace built by Boni de Castleane with the money of his wife, Anna Gould, fitted the proceedings. Just as it was impossible to believe that a sophisticated adult could decorate his home in such flamboyant baroque taste in the beginning of the twentieth century (angels on the ceiling!), it seemed incredible that representatives of the great nations of the world could sit around and haggle for so long over the wording of a question on the agenda. Jessup was our representative, and I was his assistant.

The proceedings of the Palais Rose were interminable and desperately boring. It was quite obvious that the Western side was not particularly interested in a conference while a war was on in Korea. I cannot determine the exact extent of Soviet interest, but when we began to discuss the agenda, we could reach no agreement on it at all. We tried a split agenda, where each side set topics down in parallel columns, and occasionally worked on a double-split agenda.

A young Russian woman serving as Gromyko's interpreter did provide some comic relief. Her knowledge of English was not very extensive. At one point, the French suggested a new formula for an agenda item. Gromyko said that although this was served up with new French sauce, it was still the same old dish. The Russian interpreter translated this as, "It is the same old dish, although covered with new French juice." At another point, when Gromyko said that the Soviets would continue to denounce Tito as long as necessary, she translated the verb into "defame"—much to our amusement.

One of the Russians, Vladimir Semenov, told me that as far as he was concerned, he had no objection to the conference's dragging on. He enjoyed Paris. It gave him an opportunity to visit museums and in general to savor the extraordinary qualities of that city.

The French were afraid that if they joined in any initiative to terminate this useless and frustrating effort (some sessions lasted only three minutes), the domestic Communists would exploit the action in the forthcoming French election campaign. Finally, the Western powers screwed up their courage and ended the conference about the middle of June. There is no evidence that the termination of the conference had anything to do with the outcome of the French election. This was not the first time, nor the last, that I had seen excessive sensibilities on the part of the three Western governments to the possible effects on the voters of action or non-action on Soviet issues.

With the meeting over, I boarded a train, carrying our baby girl, Celestine, in a basket, and went to southern France, where my wife and two other children were waiting. We boarded an Italian liner in Genoa and sailed to New York.

On resuming my position as Counselor of the Department of State, I found a considerable difference in duties. Under General Marshall, I had been his intimate adviser. I had accompanied him to conferences, enjoyed his confidence, and worked closely with him. I had no specific functions in the State Department hierarchy. I was, in effect, a floating kidney. Under Acheson, the department functioned in an entirely different way. With his personal advisers already around him, he did not call on me a great deal for counsel on Soviet affairs. Kennan had faced the same problem; this was one of the reasons he left. While Acheson wanted a Soviet expert on his staff, he realized it would not take all my time and that I would have time on my hands. He therefore asked me to take on the job of senior State Department representative on the Planning Staff of the National Security Council. This position was one notch down from that of the Secretaries.

I found the work more frustrating than enlightening, owing in large measure to the fact that there were at least fifteen agencies represented on the Planning Staff. The result was that every paper produced was so compromised and watered down to avoid disagreement that when it was finished it had about as much wallop as cambric tea. We covered a wide variety of topics, ranging from the war with Korea and its consequences to a glimpse into what the peace would bring. In fact, the whole range of foreign-policy questions flowed in a turgid liquid across the table of the National Security Council. The council itself functioned quite well under President Truman, but I do not believe the paper work of the Planning Staff contributed very much to its decisions.

For example, on one occasion we discussed the possibility of the Soviet Union's trying to sneak an atomic bomb into American harbors in a ship. Officials from the Federal Bureau of Investigation and the Customs Bureau raised all sorts of irrelevant considerations. It took several meetings to decide that we should do nothing about the matter.

In September, I was invited by General Omar Bradley, then chairman of the Joint Chiefs of Staff, to accompany him on an inspection tour of the front. Somewhat bored by my regular duties, I jumped at the chance, and we took off for Tokyo, flying via the Aleutian Islands. In Tokyo, we were briefed by General Matthew Ridgway, who had been appointed Supreme Commander in the Far East after General MacArthur was dismissed by Truman. I remember that Ridgway told General Bradley that if we were to contemplate winning a military victory in Korea at that stage, he would need six or seven more American divisions. With the war so unpopular in the United States, that was an impossibility.

We flew to Seoul, where we spent the night. There I found an old friend, Alan Lightner, who was political adviser to the American armies in Korea. He filled me in on the political situation. Bradley and I visited the front, from one side to the other, and I was awed by the ruggedness of the terrain. Then we took a helicopter to the battleship *New Jersey*, which was lobbing sixteen-inch shells into North Korean positions. The contrast between the mud, the dirt, the flies, and the general squalor just to the rear of the front line areas and the cleanliness of the Navy was striking. We landed on an immaculate deck and were taken to the captain's cabin, where coffee, ice cream, and cake were served. I vowed then that if I ever joined an armed service it would be the Navy.

After another night in Seoul and more military briefings, we each took a T-19, a training plane that carried a pilot and one passenger, to the front. As the planes bounced around, I could hear the boom of artillery fire on the American side of the line. The pilot pointed out that the shells were passing over our heads. Once, he dove the plane down suddenly because he thought the shells were coming too close. He pulled out just above the floor of a valley.

After four days in Korea, we flew back to Japan for more briefings. General Ridgway had stabilized the front, driving the enemy back so that the lines were roughly where they had been when the war started. Ridgway gave the impression of being an exceedingly competent military officer who knew his business down to the ground and who had clear, simple, and direct ideas on how things should be done. He did not bother too much about the nuances of international and diplomatic relations.

We spent the night in Japan and had a sukiyaki dinner in one of the buildings in the Embassy compound where I had been interned after Pearl Harbor. Some of the older Japanese employees of the Embassy attended this party, and we reminisced about the internment.

The next morning, we flew to Anchorage, Alaska, through the mist and fog of the Aleutians. When we landed, the weather had cleared and we were treated to the full splendor of an Alaskan autumn day. We lunched at the officers' mess at the air base there, and Bradley conferred with the commander. Then we took off for the nonstop flight to Washington.

Although I personally profited from my first really close observation of warfare and I had certainly learned more about the reality of the Korean situation, nothing of great value emerged from General Bradley's trip. He informed General Ridgway that the United States had no intention of increasing the number of divisions in Korea, because at least partial mobilization would have been required. Bradley's visit did confirm the prevailing opinion in Washington that there was little hope of a military victory.

In the Department of State, I became directly involved in the trickiest and most involved question connected with the Korean armistice negotiations—what to do about the prisoners of war. As the war raged on, the major sticking point to an armistice was the fact that the majority of prisoners captured by the United Nations forces did not wish to return to North Korea or China. They were definitely anti-Communist. The enemy refused to repatriate the prisoners they held unless we turned all in our hands over to them. The argument in Washington split along classic lines. The military, whose primary interest was the safety of our men, was inclined to be rather callous about forcing the enemy prisoners to return. The State Department argued that the humanitarian reputation of the United States would be damaged by forced repatriation. The State Department view reflected the American tradition of freedom of choice. In addition, the State Department warned that dissidents in Communist-controlled countries would be less likely to defect in the future if they thought they were going to be turned back like cattle. I was in the State Department group that tried to come up with a formula to break the impasse, but even though there was a tendency to minimize the anti-Communist feelings of the POWs in order to make it easier for our consciences to turn them back, we could not reach a satisfactory solution.

The Korean war did not end until another President, Eisenhower, had taken office. Even then, the prisoner issue was solved by the wily old South Korean President, Syngman Rhee, who opened the gates of the camps and freed those who did not want to return to the North.

When all is said about Korea, however, the fact remains that the two men responsible for finally blocking the expansion of Communism there were the cocky little President of the United States, Harry S Truman, and his icy-eyed Secretary of State, Dean Acheson.

Harry Truman did a superb job as President. Like everyone else, I felt considerable concern when he unexpectedly became President. He had no background in foreign affairs. He knew almost nothing of the arrangements that Roosevelt had made with Churchill or Stalin or the details of the wartime conferences at Teheran and Yalta. Roosevelt apparently never conceived of the possibility that he might die in office. In contrast with Roosevelt, Truman studied the files and the papers prepared for him and was well prepared on all aspects of a subject when the time came for discussion and decision-making. He had one of the most important qualities necessary to be an effective president, a genuine power of decision. He lived up to the sign on his desk, "The buck stops here." Occasionally, his decisions would be too quick, but he was not hasty in foreign affairs.

As far as I am aware, the plan to send Vinson to Moscow was the only time that Truman, despite his underdog position in the 1948 campaign, let politics influence his judgment in foreign affairs, though he was obviously tempted to woo voters with aid to Israel.

Like all of us, Truman was a creature of his times. To deal with the postwar problems required great decisions. It was impossible in the circumstances of 1945–52 to handle foreign affairs in a haphazard or superficial manner. Many of the problems he faced required "put up or shut up" answers. His firmness with de Gaulle, which led the French to back down in their use of force to gain north Italian areas, and with Tito over Trieste; his leadership of the European economic recovery; his support of Greece and Turkey; his courage and carefulness in the Berlin blockade; and his decision to use American armed force in Korea—none of these decisions could have been made by a second-rate president. Truman measured up to the demands thrust upon him.

It remains an incontestable fact that the major foundations of American foreign policy for decades were adopted during Truman's administration. The Greek-Turkish action set the pattern for our assistance to other governments beset by subversion supported from the outside; the Marshall Plan was the forerunner of all of the aid programs, and NATO remains one of the cornerstones of our foreign policy.

Truman relied heavily on his assistants, and extended to them the same degree of loyalty that he demanded from them. In the early days of his administration, he tended to place confidence only in some old friends, whom he brought into the White House. Some of these men were not up to the job. Since they had little effect on foreign affairs, there is no need for me to name them. His chief adviser, following the departure of General Marshall in the beginning of 1949, was Dean

Acheson. Because I was out of the country for at least 50 percent of Truman's presidency, I could not estimate the influence of his other advisers. One thing is certain; they all relied heavily on Acheson, who had worked out an admirable relationship with the President. The Secretary of State came up with many of the ideas; the President, and the President alone, made the decisions.

Acheson was not a man easy to understand. He had a fine, incisive mind and a considerable knowledge of law and public politics. It was his self-confidence, bordering on arrogance, that got him into trouble.

The son of a clergyman, he retained a strong religious feeling, tempered by skepticism. He did not suffer fools gladly, and when his patience ran out he could be short and even cruel. His sharp and often uncomplimentary comments on individuals were usually made in private correspondence. I cannot think of any time when he was Secretary of State that he indulged in personalities in public.

His love affair with Congress soured after the Communist take-over of China, an event with which Acheson had nothing whatsoever to do. As McCarthyism swept the country, he came increasingly under attack. I do not know many men with the courage to have withstood such vituperation. He took it all without turning a single hair of his magnificent mustache. He never showed that the attacks got under his skin, yet I imagine he must have felt them quite deeply. He conducted the business of the Department of State without any sign that he was even aware of the attacks.

I have always felt that the personal assaults made Acheson more rigid in his anti-Soviet attitude after he left the government. Some of the bitterness welled up later. He became much more caustic in his descriptions of people and downright dogmatic in his view of events. He was frequently summoned by President Kennedy to consult on major issues of foreign policy. One such occasion was at the time of the erection of the Berlin wall. Acheson urged the mobilization of the country to show Moscow that the United States meant business. At the time of the Cuban missile crisis, Acheson felt strongly that the President should order the bombing of the missile sites. He always believed that Kennedy ran a much greater risk of war by imposing a blockade rather than ordering the bombing attack, which would certainly have killed thousands of Russians.

Despite differences, Acheson remained a good friend. He was always kindness itself, and I was frequently at his house and he at mine. Our relationship was one of mutual tolerance and mutual respect, mingled with a certain affection.

While he was a good Secretary of State at a critical point in history, I do think he was wrong in some important historical judgments, particularly about Korea. I have already mentioned that Kennan and I concluded that Stalin's intention in Korea was simply to get control of the whole country, largely because he realized that there was very little chance of his playing the same type of sabotage role in Japan that he had played in Germany. Acheson, influenced, I think, by those in the State Department who did not know Soviet Russia, felt that the Korean war represented a new Soviet foreign policy of military expansion and that all of the areas contiguous to the free nations in Europe were threatened by attack.

As the result of this erroneous judgment, the United States overinterpreted the Korean war and overextended our commitments. The government concluded that godless Communism had conspired to take over the world and that the United States was the knight in shining armor who would fight it everywhere. Before Korea, the United States had only one commitment of a political or military nature outside the Western Hemisphere. This was the North Atlantic Treaty. Our bases in Germany and Japan were regarded as temporary, to be given up when the occupation ended. True, as a hangover from prewar days, we felt it necessary to retain bases in the Philippines, but there was no pledge on their use. The only other places we had military facilities were in England, where we had transit privileges, and Saudi Arabia, where we had an airfield. As a result of our overinterpretation of Communism's goal, we had by 1955 about 450 bases in thirty-six countries, and we were linked by political and military pacts with some twenty countries outside of Latin America. It was the Korean war and not World War II that made us a world military-political power.

We had to pledge the continued defense of South Korea. We could hardly have expended so much blood and treasure in the war and then pulled out. But the war changed the nature of the North Atlantic Treaty. Before Korea, NATO had been the classic form of political and military alliance binding a group of states to joint defense if any one of the members was attacked. Korea led to the creation of the military structure of NATO which has remained virtually intact since 1950. The idea became prevalent that only armies actually in existence along the edge of danger could provide protection. We pledged to keep a minimum of six divisions in West Germany, which was to be rearmed. General Eisenhower was appointed the first Supreme Commander, although up to that time I do not think anyone was seriously thinking of a Supreme Commander except in the event of war or imminent threat of war.

The militarization of NATO was not solely an American idea; European governments were even more strident in voicing their pleas for action. When the United States ratified NATO, our pledge was regarded as adequate for Europe's security. After Korea, where the Communist section of a divided country launched a well-organized military assault on the non-Communist section, a mere pledge on paper was no longer enough. Europe overreacted to Korea as much as, or more than, the United States. In Western Germany, particularly, there was fear that the East German Bereitschaften, a militia-type organization which the Soviets had instituted in violation of the inter-Allied agreements, would launch a surprise attack. Despite opposition, West Germany was rearmed.

The militarization of NATO was not a wise policy. A slight increase in the American military budget would have been sufficient to reassure our friends in Europe. But even when the West rushed to strengthen NATO defenses, there was no increase in Soviet divisions in East Germany. They have remained constant for something like twenty-five years. The militarization of NATO undoubtedly stimulated Soviet marshals to ask for more funds for the Red Army. But again, it is doubtful if there was any qualitative or even quantitative effect on Soviet military planning. One characteristic of the Soviet Union has always been never to neglect the armed establishment.

As a result of Korea, the United States was made the military leader of Western Europe. We are certainly the greatest contributor to its defense and far and away the greatest force in NATO. We thus find ourselves constantly pleading, begging, and pressuring the Europeans to meet their military quotas.

One of the reasons we have had to pressure our allies was their firm faith that they could avoid the danger of conquest by Communism at little cost merely by staying under our nuclear umbrella. Some Europeans have realized the danger of this position—there are situations where nuclear weapons could not be used—and have joined us in seeking increases in their conventional forces. Despite many meetings over the years, the European countries have never even approximately met their goals. It was not until John F. Kennedy became president that the defense of Europe was re-examined and the doctrine of "flexible response" was introduced.

Armament burdens are a political problem for any government, particularly a democracy. The fact that the United States was constantly urging its European allies to spend more money on military forces did not enhance the popularity of America. It is no wonder that we acquired a reputation as a militaristic state bent on smashing Communism with atomic weapons. When the Republicans came into power in 1953, John Foster Dulles, the new Secretary of State, added fuel to the anti-American fire by the narrow-minded way in which he pursued his anti-Communist crusade. Nevertheless, Dulles came under attack from Senator Joseph R. McCarthy and other right-wingers as a result of President Eisenhower's selection of me as ambassador to the Soviet Union.

PART FOUR

The Ambassador

CHAPTER EIGHTEEN

The Defeat of Joseph McCarthy

On January 23, 1953, three days after President Eisenhower took office, the new Secretary of State, John Foster Dulles, called me into his office and told me that the President and he would like to have me go to Moscow as ambassador. I was surprised, because I had no reason to believe that I was in Dulles's good graces. I had known him, but not very well, for a number of years when he was the Republican representative in the State Department. In those days, an attempt was made to keep foreign affairs bipartisan. Although there had never been any incident between us, it was clear that my views on relations with the Soviet Union did not coincide with Dulles's and those of the Republican party.

Just the preceding November, right after the election, I had differed with Dulles at a briefing at the Central Intelligence Agency, which was then headed by his brother, Allen Dulles. As he had said during the campaign, Foster Dulles averred that it was sinful for the United States navy to protect China against Formosa—the Japanese name for Taiwan was still commonly used—and intimated that one of the administration's first acts would be to lift the ban, imposed by President Truman during the Korean war, against any action by Chiang Kai-shek's forces on Formosa against Communist China. I commented that the "unleashing" of Chiang Kai-shek did not make much sense, since mainland China hardly needed to worry about the minute military offensive that Formosa could mount. It was Formosa, I said, that needed the protection we were giving. Dulles conceded that the lifting of the injunction would be mainly symbolic, but he argued that even if Chiang could do nothing, it was morally wrong for the United States to place its fleet in a position of even nominally protecting any Communist country. In any event, he said, the fleet would still guard Taiwan against an attack. The new administration quickly "unleashed" Chiang Kai-shek. The move was without question a cardinal error. It encouraged Nationalist hopes of an eventual return to the mainland and complicated our relations with Chiang Kai-shek for years.

The "unleashing" of the Nationalists was only one of the slogans of the Eisenhower campaign that worried some of us in the State Department. There were also promises to go beyond the Truman policy of containment and "roll back" Communism and "liberate" the satellite nations. Right after the election, I learned that Dulles was serious about these campaign slogans. In testimony to the Senate Foreign Relations Committee in connection with his confirmation as Secretary of State, Dulles spoke of the desire of the United States to bring about a "rollback" of Communist power in Eastern Europe. The next day, my friend George Kennan delivered a speech, previously cleared through me as Counselor, in which he indirectly attacked the "rollback" idea. Shortly thereafter, Dulles told Kennan that there was no place for him in the administration. I told Dulles that I had approved the speech; therefore, if George was not acceptable, I should be put in the same category. Dulles brushed aside my statement, saying I had made no public speeches in regard to the matter.

The 1952 election campaign had been particularly vicious. The Republicans, out of office for twenty years, were avid to return to power and were less than circumspect in dealing with the issues. It was, I believe, the first time Americans had been frightened by international events. The combination of our military setbacks in the Korean war—which raised the specter of the "yellow peril" and was our first armed conflict with a Communist power—and the evil misrepresentations of the unscrupulous Senator Joseph R. McCarthy of Wisconsin produced a genuine state of apprehension. While there had been charges of a sellout at Yalta, up until the Korean war the problem of combating Communism had been solely whether the United States should provide economic assistance to a threatened country. The Truman Doctrine did not even imply the use of armed force. In Korea (the war was still raging), American soldiers were being killed, or, it was thought, worse, captured, by Communist armies with reputations for cruelty. Americans in large numbers began to believe in the worldwide danger of Communist military aggrandizement. Moreover, the United States, which had never lost a war, found itself in one that it could not win—a fact that McCarthyites attributed to a Communist conspiracy in the government.

It is difficult to realize, looking back from the distance of twenty years, how the miasma of fear and suspicion infected American life and pushed diplomacy off its correct path into a moralistic crusade. I believe that without the Korean war and the atmosphere it created, McCarthy would have wound up with a busted flush. Yet even Eisenhower refused to defend his mentor, General Marshall, from McCarthy. At one point during the 1952 campaign, Senator Karl Mundt of South Dakota told me he thought that while McCarthy's actions were crude and perhaps a little unfair in some ways, they were essential to awaken the American public to the danger of Communism. I disagreed, pointing out that eventually McCarthyism would be so discredited that it might not be possible to win public support for valid cases where Communist actions threatened American security. I was too right. Now, in the 1970s, it is difficult to get many Americans to pay any attention whatsoever to the perils of Communism when they do exist.

There had undoubtedly been some infiltration of the American government structure by Communist agents, but the penetration was nowhere near the dimensions McCarthy was to give to it during the course of his anti-government and anti-Communist campaign. It is true that the American government was on the whole relatively innocent in its approach to security. The FBI was active, but there was no tightening up of security regulations until late in Truman's administration. One of the reasons why McCarthy's campaign found a sympathetic response among the American public was the fear engendered by the idea of secret agents' boring from within.

It was in such a suspicious atmosphere that Dulles took over the State Department. Shortly thereafter, I half-jokingly said, and someone repeated the remark to Dulles, that the new people entering the State Department reminded me of a wagon train in hostile Indian territory. Every night the wagons would be put in a circle and a guard posted. So conditioned had many of the new men been to campaign charges of Communist penetration of the department that they expected to find quite a few officials of dubious loyalty. Dulles contributed to the suspicion at his first meeting with department officials. Dulles's words were as cold and raw as the weather that February day. He said that he was going to insist that every member of the department extend not just loyalty but "positive loyalty." He did not define the difference, but his intent was clear. It was a declaration by the Secretary of State that the department was indeed suspect. The remark disgusted some Foreign Service officers, infuriated others, and displeased even those who were looking forward to the new administration.

When Dulles asked me to become ambassador to Moscow, we had been without an envoy there for about four months. In the summer of 1952, at the request of Secretary of State Acheson, I had gone to Princeton and helped persuade Kennan, who by that time had left the Foreign Service, to return as ambassador to the Soviet Union. On his way to Moscow, he stopped briefly in Berlin, where he was asked by news correspondents to give his opinion of the Soviet Union. He said that since he had not been there for some years, he would have to wait until he came out. On September 19, on his way to London for a meeting of ambassadors, he stopped in Berlin, and the correspondents put the question to him again. George frankly replied that the Soviet Union of 1952 reminded him of the atmosphere of 1941–42, when he was interned by the Nazis. "If the Nazis had permitted us to walk along the streets without the right to converse with any kind of German, that would have been precisely the same situation in which we must live today in Moscow," he said. Two weeks later, the Soviet government declared Kennan persona non grata.

I happened to be in Vienna at the time, and was instructed to go to Geneva to talk with George. On the whole, he seemed undismayed and not quite able to figure out what had caused the drastic Soviet action. His personal view was that he knew a little too much about the Soviet Union to be acceptable to Stalin. Much later, when I was ambassador in Moscow, I was standing next to Anastas Mikoyan and Lazar Kaganovich, both members of the Politburo, at an Indonesian reception. We were talking about American ambassadors to the Soviet Union, and they both said that there were two representatives that the Soviets had always thought highly of—one was Kennan and the other myself—because we were "serious" about Soviet affairs. If they had so high a regard for Kennan, I asked, why had he been declared persona non grata? Mikoyan and Kaganovich stressed that Kennan's comparison of the Soviet Union with Nazi Germany had been made in Hitler's capital and implied that this was more than Stalin could be expected to tolerate.

After Kennan's departure, the United States did not appoint any

312

ambassador until I was formally named. In agreeing to accept the post, I mentioned to Dulles the possibility of trouble in confirming my nomination because of my approval of the Kennan speech and my connection with the Roosevelt and Truman administrations. I would have to appear before the Republican-controlled Senate Foreign Relations Committee for confirmation hearings, and there would undoubtedly be a great deal of questioning on the Yalta Conference. At that time, the Yalta papers had not been published, and right-wingers, including some prominent Republicans, were charging a sellout by Roosevelt of Eastern Europe and China to the Communists. I said that I would give the version of the proceedings which I knew to be correct and which would by no means tally with the version offered during the election campaign by the Republican National Committee. Emphasizing that I was not placing any conditions or qualifications on my acceptance, I said that I did believe it wise to check with key senators before I was nominated to avoid embarrassing the administration. Thanking me, Dulles said he had not thought of that possibility, but wondered whether I could not just decline to answer questions on the basis that I had been only an interpreter. I said that since I had been an adviser as well as an interpreter, I did not see how I could avoid answering.

While Dulles did not say so specifically, it was my understanding that he would take soundings in the Senate. A few weeks later, a telegram requesting Soviet agreement to my appointment crossed my desk. I held it up overnight to inquire whether the senators had been checked. Word came back from Dulles's office not to worry. I therefore let the telegram go.

Apparently, Dulles had not checked with any of the leading senators. He had gone off on a European trip, and the matter may have slipped his mind. Perhaps he thought a check unnecessary because my nomination had been endorsed by a committee of three former Foreign Service officers who had been advising him on appointments. The three, all Republicans and all former ambassadors, were Joseph Grew (my boss in Tokyo in 1941), Norman Armour, and Hugh Gibson. Told that I was being considered for Moscow, Grew and Armour concurred in the view that I was "uniquely qualified" for the position. Gibson, who did not know me, did not endorse or oppose me, although he signed the report in which I was recommended. Dulles may also have been influenced by the fact that the President, who personally knew of my work, seemed determined to go ahead with my appointment. Perhaps Dulles also thought that since the Senate had unanimously confirmed my appointment as Counselor two years previously, there would be no opposition.

In any event, the President sent my nomination to the Senate on February 27, and the Foreign Relations Committee scheduled a hearing for March 2. There was little reaction at first. There was no outcry by the right-wing Republicans or by the forces, led by Senator McCarthy, who were spreading the big lie that America had been betrayed by pro-Communists who had infiltrated the State Department and by well-meaning fools who had been duped into following a soft-on-Communism line. While I felt competent to handle any questions that were put to me—after all, I had been at Yalta, and none of the senators had—I thought that prudence required some preparation for the hearing. I reviewed the documents and asked my secretary, Mary Wojnar, to gather material from the State Department Library. Among other things, she found an editorial from *Life* magazine, which was known for its strong support of Chiang Kai-shek, praising the Chinese-Soviet treaty of 1945. The China lobby in 1953 was charging that Roosevelt had sold China out at Yalta, forcing Chiang to sign a pact with Stalin much too favorable to the Soviet Union.

In another talk with Dulles, I repeated that at the time of Yalta I had been an assistant to the Secretary of State and White House liaison officer for the department. Thus I had been more than an interpreter; I had been an adviser aware of the issues at the conference and could not act like a village idiot when questioned.

I went to the hearing, which was closed to the press and public, alone. Alexander Wiley, the short, stocky Wisconsin Republican who was chairman of the committee, set the tone of the session at the beginning. He was friendly, but he wanted to know about the Yalta agreements. So did the other Republican senators, particularly Homer Ferguson of Michigan. They sought to get me to state that the Yalta agreement on China was contrary to the Atlantic Charter, to Roosevelt's promises to Chiang at Cairo in 1943, and to the nine-power agreement pledging the territorial integrity of China. The Democrats tried to take me off the hook by insisting that I had been only an interpreter, without any advisory role, at Yalta. After I made the usual preliminary statement of my experience, the questioning went like this:

> WILEY: Do you feel that the Yalta agreement was, as some people have contended, a direct violation of the Cairo declaration of 1943?

SENATOR THEODORE FRANCIS GREEN (Democrat of Rhode Island): Mr. Chairman, it seems to me that he acted simply as interpreter, and it does not make any difference what his views are or were—certainly not what they were.

BOHLEN: Senator, might I say this, that I was also an assistant to the Secretary of State at Yalta and I had a certain advisory capacity, but almost exclusively in regard to European matters. My whole experience, except for the short tour of duty in Japan, has been in the European area of our foreign relations. To respond to your question, sir, I would like to identify the particular agreement. There were several agreements reached at Yalta, but from the question I would imagine that you are referring to the one about the Far East; is that correct, Mr. Chairman?

WILEY: Yes.

BOHLEN: . . . In fact, that agreement was regarded by President Roosevelt in negotiation as a military matter and I think in Secretary Stettinius's book on the subject you will find a direct statement to that effect. The President told Mr. Stettinius this was not a matter of immediate, direct concern to the Department of State, but was a matter relating primarily to the conduct of the war. . . .

WILEY: Is it not a fact that at Cairo, Roosevelt and Churchill promised Chiang Kai-shek that all of the territories in China would be returned to her, particularly Manchuria, yet fourteen months later, they turned around and proceeded to give the Soviet Union, Mongolia and South Sakhalin?

BOHLEN: I was not present at the Cairo conference, so I have no first-hand knowledge.

I had not answered Wiley's question, and Senator H. Alexander Smith, Republican of New Jersey, came back to it:

SMITH: It was either in Mr. Stettinius' book or elsewhere I read that in spite of the fact that at Cairo in November 1943, President Roosevelt, Generalissimo Chiang Kai-shek, and Churchill were present and made that Cairo settlement—

BOHLEN: Yes, sir.

SMITH: In spite of that fact, in dealing with the disposition of Chinese property and Chinese issues at Yalta, Chiang Kai-shek definitely was not invited. I have heard that Mr. Stalin definitely objected to an invitation to his being there because he wanted to talk with Messrs. Roosevelt and Churchill about this particular setup he was working for as the price of Russia entering the Japanese war. That probably is a true report.

BOHLEN: I had never heard that Stalin had objected to an invitation to

Chiang Kai-shek being present at Yalta. I had never heard that it had ever been considered because the Soviet Union and Japan were not at war, and that was the reason why, for example, the Soviet Union was not represented at Cairo. In other words, there were two wars going on; there was the war in Europe in which the Soviet Union was a belligerent, and there was the war in the Pacific in which the Soviet Union was not involved. In fact, even diplomatic relations were maintained between the two countries, and I had heard—I cannot swear to this because I was not in on all these discussions—that if they were going to deal with the war in the Far East the Russians were not prepared to join in any such conference, that is, openly and officially, discussing a Far Eastern war in which they were not involved.

My only background knowledge in regard to this Far Eastern matter was that once the United States made the decision that we were going to invade the Japanese mainland, a decision which I believe was made at the second Quebec Conference in the fall of 1944, certain things automatically followed in its wake. One of these was the importance of getting the Soviet Union into the Pacific war, not as is popularly supposed at any time, but in time to do some good, so to speak, in time to save American lives.

Now, clearly the agreement on the Far East was unnecessary. The estimates which were given to the President and to Mr. Churchill prior to Yalta proved to be erroneous. Whether the intelligence was faulty, in war you cannot take chances, and the estimate given to them officially and formally by their military staffs was that the war in the Pacific would last 18 months after V-E Day.

In those circumstances the whole question of Russia's entry into it became a matter of considerable military importance, and the tragic thing about it was that it was unnecessary. There was no invasion of Japan; Russia's involvement was not in any sense necessary.

Another feature which, I think, no one would undertake to defend politically, as it were, was the fact that it was done behind the backs of the Chinese. My understanding then was that the reason for that was grounds of military security. If the Soviet Union was coming into the war 2 or 3 months after the end of V-E Day, obviously it would be of great advantage for Japan to know that well in advance of the events. She might have been disposed herself to make some military move involving Russia. Those were the reasons given, sir.

The Republicans were still unsatisfied, and Senator John J. Sparkman, Democrat of Alabama, tried to help me:

SPARKMAN: Now, a minute ago you said that, if I understood you correctly, the Yalta decision was wrong because, first, it was not necessary to get Russia into the war. You are speaking now from hindsight rather than what was actually true at that time, are you not?

BOHLEN: That is right, and I would like to make that very clear, that I do not consider that the men who made the agreement at Yalta considered that they were playing a low trick on Nationalist China. They did not look upon it in that way. As I say, the embodiment of this agreement in a treaty was, so far as I am aware, welcomed in China. There was certainly no belief at Yalta on the part of President Roosevelt and Mr. Hopkins that they were selling out an ally. And, as I say the thing turned out to be unnecessary because the military estimate of the course of the war in the Pacific was not borne out by facts. But I am convinced—

SPARKMAN: Of course, the military estimate was naturally changed with the great success of the atomic bomb—

BOHLEN: Why, certainly.

SPARKMAN (*continuing*):—which had not even had its preliminary explosion.

BOHLEN: That is correct.

SPARKMAN: They did not even know the mechanism would work at the time of Yalta.

BOHLEN: That is right.

SPARKMAN: Mr. Bohlen, I was a member of the Military Affairs Committee of the House, and I remember very clearly General Marshall's discussion before our committee of affairs at the time Germany collapsed, and after Yalta, in which he was preparing us for the terrific losses which we would sustain when we invaded Japan.

Senator Ferguson, however, would not drop the subject, and when it was his turn to ask the questions, he bored in:

FERGUSON: Was not this agreement in relation to the Far East, as far as it gave other peoples' rights and liberties and lands away, in violation of the Atlantic Charter?

BOHLEN: I think I have answered that in saying, Senator, that the Yalta agreement in itself was not a final definitive international instrument. The definitive instrument was the treaty between China and the Soviet Union of August 1945.

FERGUSON: Yes; but we are talking about the agreement, whether it was morally right or wrong, or whether it was just a misinterpretation of the agreement that was wrong; what I want to know is whether or not the giving of this land of another power, another nation, was not in violation of the Atlantic Charter? Did we not say there that there would be no aggrandizement? Was it not a violation of that?

BOHLEN: I do not consider that the Yalta agreement, in effect, did that.

FERGUSON: What did it do? It agreed that we could use our influence.

BOHLEN: That we would support that position.

FERGUSON: We would support that position, which was in violation of the Atlantic Charter, was it not?

BOHLEN: Well, sir, I do not think that the Atlantic Charter was against any territorial adjustments between countries. Perhaps my understanding of it is erroneous.

FERGUSON: Well, was it in violation of the nine-power pact that we made?

BOHLEN: You mean the territorial integrity of China?

FERGUSON: The territorial integrity of China.

BOHLEN: Well, sir, it is a question even in the treaty itself whether the according of a base in another country or certain rights, joint rights on railroads, does constitute a territorial violation of a country. I am not—

FERGUSON: Is that really all that was done so far as Manchuria was concerned?

BOHLEN: Yes, sir. There was the base at Port Arthur, there were certain rights in the port of Dairen, there were joint Chinese-Soviet management conditions in the running of the railroad. Now, Outer Mongolia is, of course, another question.

FERGUSON: Yes, of course. Was it not, as indicated here,

> It is understood that the agreement concerning Outer Mongolia and ports and railroads referred to above will require concurrence of Generalissimo Chiang Kai-shek—

and

> the President will take measures in order to obtain the concurrence on advice from Marshal Stalin.

Now, is it not true that he is going to "take measures," and not just request them?

BOHLEN: I understood that the words "take measures" in that sense means that he will use his influence with Chiang Kai-shek to that effect.

FERGUSON: Was it not more than influence; was it not meant that measures would be taken?

BOHLEN: I have not understood, sir, that the word "measures" meant that you were going to do anything except to urge upon the Chinese acceptance of this.

FERGUSON: Then you come to the conclusion that the only wrong that you can find in these agreements at Yalta, Teheran, or any of the others that we made with Russia, was in the interpretation?

BOHLEN: No, sir; I think that the chief thing that was wrong was the violation of them afterward. I believe, had the Chinese treaties of 1945 been observed, that it would have been regarded as a great act of statesmanship, and I could put into the record an editorial which appeared in *Life* magazine on September 10, 1945, which had taken a very absorbing interest in China. This editorial considered the signature of this treaty as an act of importance for the Far East, second only to the military defeat of Japan. They considered that it put China into the position of a great power. They welcomed it most warmly, sir. I am saying that was the reaction to this Chinese treaty—

FERGUSON: I said "measures," and you said that the President had just agreed to use his good offices. What about this language in the agreement—

> ... the heads of the three great powers have agreed that these claims of the Soviet Union shall be unquestionably fulfilled after Japan has been defeated.

> Is that not a violation of the Atlantic Charter and also of the Kellogg Pact?

BOHLEN: I think, sir—

FERGUSON: I mean, the Nine Power Pact.

BOHLEN: I think that sentence should not have been in there.

FERGUSON: Well, it is in there.

BOHLEN: I know it; but I think that is the kind of sentence that should not be in there.

As expected, there were questions about Alger Hiss, who by that time was in the penitentiary, having been convicted of perjury in relation to the transmission of secrets to Russia. I testified that at Yalta Hiss had primarily confined his activities to problems about the United Nations, which was his area of responsibility in the State Department, and had not advised the President about the Far East.

I was also asked about the policy of "containment" of Soviet expansionist policies through use of "counterforce," which George Kennan had written about in *Foreign Affairs* quarterly in the spring of 1947 under the pseudonym of "Mr. X." The Republicans, led by Dulles, had criticized "containment" as too negative—that in effect it was accepting satellite status for areas of Eastern Europe and elsewhere—and had called for the more positive policy of "rollback" and liberation. In a speech in July, 1952, at the Colgate University Conference on American Foreign Policy, I said that "containment" described only part of America's postwar foreign policy. The word applied only in the military sense of preventing any further Soviet expansion, because the United States would not take the lead in using armed force in an aggressive way against the Soviet Union. "Containment" was essential, I said, because the opposite policy would be non-containment, or indifference to Soviet expansion.

At the hearing, this speech was brought up. Under questioning by Senator Smith, I defended the Truman administration, asserting that the Marshall Plan, NATO, and the Truman Doctrine were far from negative; they had an "extremely positive" effect on the world situation. Pressed by Senator Hickenlooper if I would go further than merely "stopping the advance of the other fellow," I would agree only that "containment is an unfortunate word."

Toward the end of the all-day session, Senator Ferguson, who had become the chief inquisitor, brought up an off-the-record address I had made on United States relations with Iron Curtain countries to a group of State Department officials on July 10, 1947. Ferguson asked if I remembered wanting to speak with emphasis and saying, "And I want to state now unequivocally we are tired of these people who criticize our conduct at Teheran and Yalta; in fact, they are our most glorious diplomatic triumphs." To this day, I do not know who misquoted me to him. I denied the quotation and pointed out that "glorious diplomatic triumphs" was not an expression I would use.

The first session ended on a friendly note. Senator Hubert H. Humphrey, Democrat of Minnesota, after questioning me sympathetically, said:

> I have nothing more to ask you to comment upon, Mr. Bohlen, except again to say thank God we have got people in the government who will take the attitude of forbearance, of honor, particularly in dealing with these great conferences, such as you have, as manifested by your testimony here today. I don't agree with everything that you had to say. There are some things that I might want to join the issue on, but I consider that you represent what I would like to believe and I do believe to be the best of our Foreign Service, and I think we have got a pretty good Foreign Service.

As I left the room, I thought the hearing had gone reasonably well. I did not anticipate any trouble in winning confirmation. All the senators had been pleasant. I did not see any votes against me in the committee, except, perhaps, Senator Ferguson's. Actually, however, my testimony made the nomination an issue, even though the hearings were closed. Articles based on briefings by Senator Wiley (Humphrey had protested the secrecy), appeared in the press over such headlines as "Bohlen Defends Yalta Pact." To the extreme right-wingers, the gauntlet had been flung down. In their opinion, I was opposing views that the public had overwhelmingly endorsed in the election only a few months before.

The day after the hearing, my nomination took on new importance. The Kremlin announced that Stalin was gravely ill. Dulles called me in and asked what would happen in Moscow if Stalin died. He seemed intrigued with the possibility that there might be a bloodletting over the succession to power. I said it would be folly to attempt a serious prediction, but I expressed doubt that the Bolsheviks would let the situation deteriorate to such a point. Dulles showed me a copy of a statement that Eisenhower was planning to issue later in the day. The statement avoided any expression of regret about Stalin but did extend sympathy to the Russian people. I thought it a good statement.

On March 4, Stalin's condition worsened, and the next day he died. Everyone wanted to know what the change would mean to Moscow and the world. The United States was in the unfortunate position of having no ambassador in Moscow. In its quest for understanding, the Senate Foreign Relations Committee called Under Secretary of State Walter Bedell Smith to Capitol Hill for a closed-door briefing. Senator Wiley raised the question of my nomination.

WILEY: Now, General Smith, we are very happy to have you here, and perhaps you can discuss not only the situation upon which you are appearing here today, such information which you can get from the CIA, as the former head of it, but you can also give us some information on this subject that I think is important, and that is, if you have consulted with the Secretary, you probably have, whether or not action should be delayed on Mr. Bohlen's nomination, or whether it should be hurried up, and any consideration to go over until Tuesday. I would like to get your judgment, if it is based upon the judgment of the Secretary and yourself, as to the advisability of hurrying up that confirmation, or delaying it in view of these world events.

SMITH: Mr. Chairman, I have consulted with him and am glad to have a chance to mention this. We feel, in view of the crisis that everything possible should be done to expedite it. The sooner we get in there, the better; because there is going to be a very unusual series of developments, one way or the other, and Mr. Bohlen, of course, is the man probably best qualified that we have at the present time, and available to go there and make reports during this critical period.

There was no doubt in my mind that the Senate would quickly confirm me. We made preparations for leaving. It was during this period that Scott McLeod, the new Assistant Secretary of State for Security Affairs, began to express doubts about me. McLeod, a former agent of the Federal Bureau of Investigation, who was well known for the fervor of his anti-Communism, had, in the few weeks he had been

Dulles's aide, removed a score or more State Department officials on security grounds. In my nearly twenty-five years in the Foreign Service, there had never been a security investigation of me. Under procedures established by Dulles, a security check was ordinarily required before a nomination was sent to the Senate. In my case, the administration was so eager to get an ambassador to Moscow that the FBI check was only begun at the time of the nomination. Rumors soon began to circulate that McLeod was objecting on political grounds that my appointment was risky.

The Foreign Relations Committee had decided to vote on my nomination on March 10. In view of the rumors, another hearing was scheduled for March 16, and the vote set for the following day.

Leaders of the Republican right wing, sensing a good issue, moved in. On March 13, Senator Styles Bridges, for whom McLeod had worked as administrative assistant, announced that "top" people in the administration had asked the President to withdraw my name. Senator McCarthy told newsmen that he was joining the fight against me. Senator William Knowland, the California Republican, widely known as the "Senator from Formosa" because of his strong support of the Chinese Nationalists, expressed skepticism about my nomination.

Senator Robert A. Taft of Ohio, the Senate Republican leader, appeared on a television panel show and wondered what all the excitement was about. He said the "matter was not sufficiently important" to fight about. "Our Russian Ambassador can't do anything," he said. "All he can do is observe and report. He will not influence policy materially."

Senator Pat McCarran of Nevada broke the solid ranks of Democrats supporting me and announced that my connection with Yalta was enough to earn his opposition.

By this time, Dulles was getting nervous. He called me to his office and said, "Chip, I just wanted to know whether there's anything in your past that might be damaging." I told him that I knew of absolutely nothing. He replied, "Well, I'm glad of that because I couldn't stand another Alger Hiss."

I heard later, although no proof was advanced, that Dulles at one point had considered the withdrawal of my name from the Senate, but Eisenhower had put his foot down, saying he knew me personally and he could not capitulate before the McCarthy forces. Eisenhower told me later that an attempt had been made—he did not say by whom—to get him to withdraw the nomination, but he had refused, largely because it was a matter of principle, but also out of consideration for me. I do not know whether Dulles was the one who urged the withdrawal. I believe that if Dulles had followed my advice and checked with some of the Republican senators, he would probably have received enough adverse reaction to have questioned submitting my name to the Senate, although Eisenhower might have insisted on the nomination.

Dulles also discussed the question of my brother-in-law, Charlie Thayer, who was then Consul General in Munich. Unknown to me, McLeod had concluded that Charlie, because of an episode in his past involving a Russian woman, was no longer suitable to be a Foreign Service officer. Charlie telephoned from Munich saying that he had been summoned home for an appearance before the McCarthy investigating committee and did not know why. I did not know the reason either, but I tried to argue him out of returning. He would, I was sure, have a difficult time, not because he had done anything wrong but because of McCarthy's unfair methods. On his return, after he had learned the nature of the episode at a private session with some of the new State Department officials, we had a meeting in my office. There it was agreed that Charlie would be permitted to resign because of his desire to write. There was an element of truth in the letter of resignation that was drafted. Charlie had written an amusing book on the early years of the Soviet Union. The real reason for the decision to resign was the desire to spare his mother the embarrassment of a public controversy over his morals.

Slowly, I was beginning to realize that I was becoming a central figure in a political drama of far more importance than the outcome of the vote on my confirmation. Senator McCarthy and his supporters were attempting to subvert the President's constitutional prerogative to choose his representatives in foreign capitals. Moreover, the career officers in the Foreign Service were watching to see if, like Kennan, I would be shunted aside because I had carried out my duties under another administration. Kennan had been forced to retire because Dulles would give him no assignment. Would Dulles fight for me? If he would not, he would have trouble administering the State Department. Loyalty should extend down from the boss as well as up from the employees. It was difficult for me to recognize the fact that I had become a symbol of the Foreign Service at bay. As the fact dawned on me, I became exhilarated. I welcomed the opportunity to defend the Service. Fortunately, Dulles saw the situation clearly this time, and privately told a number of people—not me—that he realized he could not operate effectively without the respect and support of the career officers who did the pick-and-shovel work for him.

The second hearing had been scheduled for March 16. However, it had to be postponed for two days because while I was in South Carolina saying good-bye to my sister, I broke out with German measles. On my return to Washington, my doctor quarantined me for forty-eight hours.

On March 17, the day before the second hearing, McCarthy jumped all the way into the battle. "I am going to oppose the nomination," he told newsmen, "on the ground that Bohlen was too important a part of the old Acheson machine in the State Department to properly represent the administration, especially in this key spot." Then, locking horns with the Eisenhower administration only two months after it took over the government, he added, "Dulles is making a great mistake in pressing to have his nomination approved."

On the day of the second hearing, Dulles, who was also to be a witness, told me that he thought it would be better if we rode to Capitol Hill in different cars. He said that he thought it would also be better if we were not photographed together. I replied that I had no particular desire to be photographed at all but I did not quite understand him. He said no more, but I imagine that Dulles was thinking of the possibility that I might be turned down by the Senate, and he did not wish to be associated, even in a picture, with so reprehensible a character as I. His remark made me wonder if he would have the courage to stand up to the McCarthyites.

The second hearing, like the first, was closed, and I was not present when Dulles testified. I heard that he had supported my nomination fully, but had expressed doubts about some of my views. Eventually, when the record was published, I read Dulles's testimony. Senator Wiley, who, like everyone else on Capitol Hill, had heard rumors that there was something derogatory about my past, opened the hearing by complaining that, two days before, he had asked the State Department for a summary of its own security file on me, only to be told that there was no such file because there had never been an investigation on me. "It seemed to me very strange, indeed," the committee chairman said, "that a man who had occupied confidential positions in the Department of the highest magnitude for over two decades should not even have had an elementary loyalty and security check by the State Department itself. I would like to have Mr. Dulles explain just how that thing could have come about." Dulles responded that Senator Wiley would have to ask his predecessor, Dean Acheson. He then pointed out that he had asked the FBI to investigate himself and had been cleared as a good loyalty risk by President Eisenhower.

After listing the requirements for an ambassador to Moscow—"a man who was thoroughly versed with the Russian language, in Russian ways, in the techniques and peculiar terminologies, phraseologies, of Soviet Communism"—Dulles said, "The only person that we could think of who was qualified to play that role, which might be extremely important and might affect the welfare and the security of the United States and world peace, was Mr. Bohlen."

With the spate of rumors floating around Washington, the big question, however, was not my qualifications; it was whether I was a security risk. What had the FBI found? Dulles wasted no time in getting to the point:

> DULLES: I received a day ago a summary of the report of the FBI. The approving evidence has not been summarized except by a long list of distinguished people who gave a complete clearance, and expressed high approval of Mr. Bohlen.
> There is no derogatory material whatsoever which questions the loyalty of Mr. Bohlen to the United States, or which suggests that he is not a good security risk, which suggests he is in any manner one who has leaked or been loose in his conversation or anything of that sort.
> WILEY: Do I understand that there is no definite concrete evidence or what a lawyer would consider proof of any dereliction?
> DULLES: Absolutely none whatsoever, not an iota.
> TAFT: Do you think there is anything that creates even a prima facie case of such dereliction?
> DULLES: No, none whatsoever.

Dulles must have known that he would be asked about McLeod's appraisal of me, because he quickly pointed out that "as in any case where there is a warning signal my security officer called this to my attention." He then quoted McLeod as saying, "This is not a case which I can automatically pass because wherever there is derogatory information of this sort I think it is my duty to bring it to your personal attention."

It was this statement about McLeod's view that fueled the fire to the controversy over my appointment. Dulles's testimony on my behalf, while cautious regarding my past associations, was forthright and honest. Although he made it clear, in a bow to the right-wingers, that he did not want me in any policy-making position, he did have confidence in my ability to keep him informed about the Kremlin and in my loyalty in carrying out the new administration's foreign policy. Senator Smith put the question this way:

SMITH: You are satisfied, from your knowledge of Mr. Bohlen's past views on policy, that nothing would prevent his being a 100-percent effective representative of the State Department in Moscow?

DULLES: There is nothing either in the knowledge of those of us who have known him personally in the past—I might mention, incidentally, that I was talking to former Secretary of State, now Governor Byrnes, who called me up on a certain matter, and he said, "This appointment of Bohlen to Moscow is a fine appointment, and it must go through." He said, "I cannot think of anybody who is as uniquely qualified to fill that job as Mr. Bohlen is."

Now, that was the appraisal of Governor Byrnes, whom I think we all regard highly and respect, and who had very intimate association with Mr. Bohlen.

The Governor said that he had made a public statement to that effect—I did not myself see it—but he said he had made a public statement to that effect on the radio two days ago. There is not a whisper of a suggestion that I have been able to turn up throwing any doubt at all upon his loyalty or upon his security as a person.

There is no suggestion that he talks loosely, that he has ever revealed a secret, and I have no evidence at all to lead me to question that he is, as almost all competent people believe, qualified for this particular job.

Senator Hickenlooper probed a little deeper into McLeod's expression of doubt:

HICKENLOOPER: Has your security office cleared this file for loyalty and security?

DULLES: No. I told you that he said that in view of the fact that his file contained some derogatory information, he did not wish to take the responsibility of clearance. He passed the matter up to me, which is the usual practice in such cases. I do not think that security officers, whose primary job is to raise doubts and find out suspicious circumstances, are the persons who should have final responsibility in matters of this kind. In important cases, such as this one, the task of final evaluation should be passed up to the senior officers.

At the close of the questioning, Senator Humphrey asked whether there was any need for quick action on the nomination. Dulles replied that in view of the new situation created by Stalin's death, "It is a matter of real urgency . . . if he [Bohlen] were there today, I would think it would be worth a great deal to the United States."

When Dulles finished, I was called into the room and questioned again. There was little new. Ferguson again was the most persistent questioner.

The committee then met and approved my nomination by a 15 to 0 vote. McCarthy promptly announced he was going to continue to fight, although he did not have the time to make a major case of the nomination. He suggested that the President look at the FBI file on me. On March 19, at his regular press conference, the President spoke up for me, asserting that I deserved the nomination on merit.

The next day, Dulles faced up to the real issue. Senator McCarran insisted that Dulles had "summarily" overridden McLeod in clearing me as a security risk. He said the withdrawal of my nomination was the "acid test" of the administration's pledge to clean out the State Department. McCarthy went even further. He accused the Secretary of falsifying his aide's position and suggested that Dulles be required to testify under oath. In a hastily called press conference, Dulles, with Senator Wiley sitting at his side, dropped his placating tone. He denied McCarran's charge and said that the handling of my nomination was an "acid test of the orderly process of our government" and, specifically, whether charges that lacked even the "substance of rumor" would prevail. He also said there was no difference between him and McLeod over my final clearance.

While vague rumors of charges about me had been circulating, there were no specifics. Dulles had given the Foreign Relations Committee an oral rundown on the derogatory charges in my file, but these were not included in the printed record, which was quickly made public. Dulles pointed out that the Attorney General and the President had both seen the material in the FBI file and were satisfied that I was a good security risk. That was not enough for McCarthy. "I know what's in Bohlen's file," he told reporters. "I have known what's in his file for years."

I cannot prove that McLeod was feeding information to McCarthy, but I have a hunch that is what happened. On March 21, McCarthy said that there were sixteen "closely typed" pages of derogatory information about me in the FBI report. While there was much laudatory material, he concluded that "in our opinion he is a bad security risk." Senator Walter George, the much respected conservative Democrat from Georgia, described the derogatory information as anonymous letters, rumors, and hearsay that I had associated with some "dissolute persons." I was baffled; I had no idea what was in the file.

About this time, a story circulated on Capitol Hill that McLeod felt so strongly that I should not go to Moscow that he went over Dulles's head and took his case to the White House. The rumor was that he had talked for two and a half hours with his friend, General Milton Persons, the President's liaison with Congress, and had urged that Dulles be called in to discuss the matter. I still do not know whether the story is true, but Senator McCarthy referred to the rumor on the Senate floor. In any event, the President never wavered in his support of me.

The Senate debate on the nomination began on March 23. The galleries were packed, but I was not there; it would have been improper for me to have attended. Besides, I wanted to avoid the press, which was constantly hounding me for comments. I followed the debate on the news tickers and refused all comment.

The debate began in rather routine fashion. Senator Wiley, as chairman of the Senate Foreign Relations Committee, opened with a long review of the argument over the nomination. He quickly focused on the two charges against me—that I had been connected with the Yalta Conference and that I was a security risk. Because of the rumors about the FBI check, Wiley first took up the security issue, emphasizing that Dulles and Attorney General Herbert Brownell had cleared me and that the committee of three ex-Foreign Service officers had endorsed me. As for Yalta, Wiley said that I had only been a "technician" and thus could not be faulted for any mistakes made there. "Obviously," he said, "we could never have a career Service if we insisted upon changing it with every administration."

Senator McCarthy then made a major error. Since there were rumors that McLeod had not only refused to clear me but had also been fighting my nomination, McCarthy suggested that Dulles and McLeod be called before the Foreign Relations Committee to testify under oath—in a sort of Alger Hiss–Whittaker Chambers type of confrontation. The implication was that Dulles had not been telling the truth, that he had been holding back some derogatory information about me which, if McLeod were free to disclose it, would prove that I was a security risk. Such a slur did not sit well with Taft and Knowland, two senators whose opposition McCarthy could not afford to take on because they were leaders of the Republican conservatives.

McCarthy then proposed that I volunteer to take a lie-detector test (although offering not the slightest clue as to the questions that I may have answered falsely). Taft, irritated by the demeaning of the Senate, tried to break in. McCarthy at first refused to yield. When McCarthy did yield, Taft, his voice shaking and his face flushed, pointed out that J. Edgar Hoover, the director of the FBI, was opposed to the use of polygraphs. Blind to the enmity he was creating, McCarthy continued to question Dulles's veracity and spoke ominously of something so derogatory in my files that "we cannot discuss it on the floor of the Senate" without violating security.

There was a great deal of discussion on the floor about the security check and whether the Foreign Relations Committee should see the FBI summary of its findings and the raw data gathered by FBI agents. Senator Wiley said that there were "a hundred people of the highest type" who had spoken of my "fine character," and "there were a few others who threw in a little filth." Senator Gillette of Iowa offered the only specifics about the charges against me. He said one report had come from a person who claimed he possessed a sixth sense which could detect the presence of moral turpitude in individuals. This person, whom Gillette did not identify, said he had looked at me and with his sixth sense determined that I had a tendency toward immorality that made me unfit. This, Gillette said, was one of the six or seven reports the Foreign Relations Committee evaluated. There were fifteen others, but none was considered important or dependable enough for an adverse recommendation.

These hints at what might be in my file only whetted appetites as to the nature of the derogatory information, and at the conclusion of the first day of debate the senators agreed to a suggestion by Senator Taft that two members of the Foreign Relations Committee examine the FBI summary of my security file. Taft and Sparkman were chosen and spent two hours the next day, March 24, in Dulles's office reading the summary. They did not see the raw data from the FBI, but were assured by FBI Director Hoover that the summary did not omit any material derogatory fact. I waited in my office in case the senators wanted to talk with me, but was not called.

In view of the controversy over McLeod, Taft and Sparkman did ask him, however, for a written statement whether he had access to any material that they had not seen. McLeod signed a statement that he had turned over to Dulles all the material on me that he had received. In other words, he never saw the raw FBI files; Hoover was the only official who did. McLeod's information was limited, as was Dulles's and Senators Taft's and Sparkman's, to the FBI summary of its investigation.

On March 25, the second day of the debate, Taft and Sparkman reported on their study of the FBI summary. Taft told the Senate that the greater part of the sixteen pages of derogatory information consisted of statements of persons who disagreed with me on foreign policy:

> They think he played perhaps a larger part than others played in the Yalta conversations and that he was closer to Mr. Acheson than they would like. In other words, they were statements of political differences with Mr. Bohlen.
>
> So far as I remember, there was no one who did not end up by saying that although he disagreed politically, he had full confidence in the character, the morality, and the general standing and reputation of Mr. Bohlen.
>
> There was no suggestion anywhere by anyone reflecting on the loyalty of Mr. Bohlen in any way, or any association by him with communism or support of communism or even tolerance of communism.
>
> When it comes to the question of whether there is any reason to think that Mr. Bohlen is in any way a security risk, such testimony as there is on that subject relates solely to the fact that Mr. Bohlen has at times been friendly with and has entertained at his home persons who are considered by the investigators or by the Department as bad security risks.
>
> I could not find in the summary testimony anything which seemed to me to raise even a prima facie case or to support any prima facie evidence that Mr. Bohlen had in any way ever done anything which would make him a bad security risk. The associations he had were those which anyone might have had with persons who were friends of many other people, who may have stayed overnight, or for the weekend, at the home of Mr. and Mrs. Bohlen. But in all the summary I could see nothing which could create the most remote guilt-by-association accusation that could be thought of.
>
> There was not any suggestion that would, in my opinion, create even a prima facie case or a prima facie charge of any ill-doing on the part of Mr. Bohlen.
>
> So I myself came to the conclusion that Mr. Bohlen was a completely good security risk in every respect, and I am glad so to report to the Senate of the United States.

Senator Sparkman agreed with Taft that there was "no suggestion in the summary to raise a prima facie question with respect to anything wrong with the character, integrity or honesty of Mr. Bohlen." He went further: "There was nothing which in my judgment would cause any reasonable person to conclude that a suspicion had been raised.

There was not a single instance of a charge against Mr. Bohlen, or any incident which could be cited against him."*

McCarran fought on, insisting that since McLeod was the State Department security officer, he should be heard from. Bridges followed up with a savagely sarcastic attack on me. After referring to me as "the exponent of appeasement and containment," he said that "since Mr. Bohlen professes to be a great Russian expert, to know the Russian mind, the language and so forth, how did it happen he did not realize at Yalta, that we were being taken for a ride?" A few moments later, he called me an "experienced failure" and added, "I find that in most every diplomatic horse trade at which Mr. Bohlen was present the Russians got the fat mare and the United States ended up with the spavined nag."

Eventually, Bridges did offer a new bit of evidence against me. He said that he had checked Wiley's statement that three distinguished former Foreign Service officers had recommended me for the Moscow post. Former Ambassadors Grew and Armour could not be contacted, but Bridges found Gibson in Room 527 of the Mayflower Hotel in Washington. Because Gibson had suffered a heart attack, Bridges was not able to talk with him, but did submit a question to him through Gibson's attorney, a man named Schwartz. The question was whether the three had approved Bohlen for the Moscow ambassadorship. The answer, Bridges said, was, "No, Mr. Bohlen's name was only casually mentioned, if it was mentioned at all, and they were not called upon to approve Bohlen and neither did they approve Bohlen."

Wiley jumped up and said it was Dulles's word against Schwartz's. With the point sufficiently confused, Senator Everett McKinley Dirksen and Senator Knowland made phone calls. Dirksen called Gibson, who insisted that the three-man committee had not been asked about the vacancy in Moscow and had made no recommendation. Knowland called Dulles, who sent to the Senate a memorandum signed by Grew, Armour, and Gibson. The memorandum made "certain recommendations" with respect to various foreign posts; attached to it was a list of diplomatic vacancies and names of prospective appointees. My name was listed for the Soviet Union. Knowland said that since the letter contained the names of some appointments not yet announced, he was not free to read it into the record. McCarthy was not satisfied, however. He asked Knowland to show the letter to Dirksen "so that there may be no question about it." Knowland's face turned scarlet; he demanded to know whether McCarthy was "sug-

---

* This is as close as I ever came to finding out what was in my file.

gesting that my veracity should be questioned on the floor of the Senate." As he spoke, his anger increased: "Let me say to the Senator from Wisconsin that this is the first time that has happened." Oblivious of the damage he had brought on himself, McCarthy condescendingly told Knowland not to "become so excited." Knowland was not just excited; he was disturbed by McCarthy's methods. Eventually, he brought applause from the galleries when he said:

> Speaking as one United States Senator, let me say that when a nomination comes from the President of the United States and goes to the desk of the President of the Senate, and bears the signature "Dwight D. Eisenhower," I do not want to have to call in a handwriting expert to see whether it is the signature of Dwight Eisenhower. When a letter comes to the Senate from the Department of State, from a responsible officer of that Department, I do not want to have to call in a handwriting expert to determine whether a forgery has been committed. If we have so destroyed confidence in men who have been selected to hold high places in the Government of the United States, God help us; God help us if that is the basis upon which we have to operate.

McCarthy, however, was not through. He evoked applause from his partisans in the galleries when he replied:

> Mr. President, let me say to the Senator from California that apparently I conceive my duty as a Senator of the United States in a somewhat different light than does the Senator from California. When the Senate is charged with the obligation of confirming or rejecting the nomination of a certain person, I think we should run down all the information about that person we can before we vote to confirm the nomination.
>
> The mere fact that Dwight Eisenhower nominates Bohlen does not, to me, mean that we should blindly confirm the nomination. If that were true, there would be no reason for providing for confirmation by the Senate. . . .
>
> If I were in the position of the Senator from California, I would not endorse Bohlen and would not vote for confirmation of his nomination until I found what was rotten in Denmark and ascertained whether a certain signature was bad, and all else about this matter. I do not think that this is an incorrect attitude to take in the case of the nomination of a man who would be sent as our Ambassador to Moscow, a most responsible post—a man who for 26 years has not once raised his voice against communism.
>
> I do not think this is a time for levity. I take my position on this matter very seriously.

McCarthy apparently never realized that he had embittered two senators—Taft and Knowland—with his tactics. The Wisconsin Senator did introduce an additional piece of derogatory evidence against me. He said he had an affidavit of Igor Bogolepov, who had fled Russia during the war after twenty years as an official of the Soviet Foreign Ministry. McCarthy said Bogolepov had access to the Soviet Foreign Ministry's files of "Bohlen's secret reports when the latter was in Moscow between 1939–41." McCarthy quoted the affidavit as saying:

> The secret correspondence of the American Embassy in Moscow was photostated and was available in the Soviet Foreign Office and it is in this way I remember having read some of the reports signed by Mr. Charles Bohlen and sent to the State Department in Washington.
>
> It became known to me that of all the senior personnel in the United States Embassy in Moscow, only one person, Ambassador Laurence Steinhardt, was listed as neutral and one person, Loy Henderson, was listed as hostile by Soviet authorities. The rest of the officers of the Embassy, including Charles Bohlen, were evidently considered friendly.
>
> It must be noted that all foreign diplomats in Moscow in my time were divided into three categories: hostile, neutral, and friendly.
>
> Being friendly did not mean that a person was necessarily a Soviet agent or connected with the Soviet Secret Service and I wish to make that point perfectly clear.
>
> But we must consider that when the name of an alien appeared on the list as a friendly person, it could mean that he might be considered by the Soviet Secret Service as a possible source of information and as a channel for the infiltration of inaccurate information concerning the Soviet Union into the Western World.

This report, from an individual I had never heard of (and have not heard of since), was highly suspect. Henderson never served in the Embassy with Steinhardt. Apparently my name was not even listed in this alleged Soviet appraisal of American Embassy officials. It was outrageous to draw the interpretation that I had been considered friendly to the Bolshevik government.

The day's debate ended with an impassioned speech on my behalf by Senator Herbert Lehman of New York. "What has been attempted in the case of Mr. Bohlen," he said, "is merely a pattern— the same pattern that has been followed against many other loyal, devoted, honest Americans. Unless there is a change in the present climate," he went on, "we shall have in the government service none but persons who are willing to say 'yes' to anything. We shall have no one of courage. They will all be worried about what is going to happen two years, five years, or ten years hence, when opinions expressed by them honestly, sincerely and after careful thought may have been proved to have been unwise."

The next day, March 26, President Eisenhower warmly praised me at a press conference, pointing out that he had known me and my "charming" family for years and had been a guest in the Bohlen home in Paris. He said I knew the Russians, was dedicated to America, and was the best man for the job.

With the administration now in full attack and McCarthy having hurt himself with responsible conservatives, there was no question about the outcome. On March 27, a letter from Grew was put in the Senate record in which he said that he and Armour had consulted and agreed that they had indeed put my name on the list of recommended appointments. Gibson also wrote a letter, in which he said that Dulles had indicated that he had already decided to nominate me. Gibson said that since he hardly knew me, he did not express any opinion, although Grew and Armour had given "strong approval."

Finally, after a few more speeches, I was confirmed by a 74 to 13 vote. I was at my mother-in-law's house in Villa Nova at the time. When the inevitable calls came from newspaper reporters, I still refused to comment. I do not deny the feeling of triumph that possessed me. I like to believe that the emotion sprang from more than the personal satisfaction of having won the battle to occupy the position that I had trained for for nearly twenty-five years. Such a victory was naturally important to me personally. But the events had a wider significance. For the nonpolitical career Foreign Service, the victory drew a line beyond which the witch-hunters like McCarthy and McLeod could not pass. For Dulles, the boost in Foreign Service morale was invaluable to the smooth functioning of the department. For Dulles the victory also meant that he—and not McCarthy or McCarran or McLeod—would control State Department functions. For Taft, Knowland, and other responsible conservatives in Congress, the battle was a clear signal that there was no way to cooperate with or appease McCarthy. Although Taft replied, "No, no, no, no," when asked, immediately after the vote, if he had broken with McCarthy, the fact is that from that point on he kept his distance from the Wisconsin Senator. For President Eisenhower, it was his administration's first serious split with the McCarthyites. Senate approval of my nomination preserved his right to choose his representatives overseas and showed him that he had the power to crush

THE DEFEAT OF JOSEPH McCARTHY

McCarthy any time he wanted to. For McCarthy, the defeat must have brought forebodings of eventual disaster, although he continued on the same dark path he had been following. More than a year would pass before McCarthy would be censured by the Senate, but the action was inevitable. I am proud that the fight over my nomination laid the groundwork for the successful effort to stop McCarthy before he damaged the country any more.

The publicity I received from the battle with McCarthy did more than anything else to make me known to the American people. I acquired, for better or worse, the reputation of being a diplomat who would speak his mind frankly. When I returned from Villa Nova, the leading Washington correspondents gave me a luncheon at the Metropolitan Club. Walter Lippmann, Arthur Krock, James Reston, the Alsop brothers, and others made generous comments about me. I was pleased but somewhat embarrassed.

In the midst of briefings at the State and Defense Departments and the Central Intelligence Agency, I went to see Dulles, who asked me my travel plans. I said I would leave for Moscow in about a week and would stop off for three or four days in Paris, where my wife would join me. With absolutely no tact, Dulles, who was still shaky from the fight with McCarthy, said, "Oh, don't you think it would be wiser for you and your wife to travel together?"

"For God's sake, why?" I asked.

He replied, "Well, you know, there were rumors in some of your files about immoral behavior and it would look better if your wife was with you."

When I told him I would not do any such thing, he said I shouldn't take such an attitude. "Why do you think Mrs. Eisenhower traveled with the President during the election campaign?" he asked rhetorically. I told him that I was sorry, but I was not going to change my plans. He then dropped the idea.

A few days later, Dulles said he would like to accompany me on my farewell call on President Eisenhower. Although the procedure was unusual, I could not offer any objection. In the automobile on the way to the White House, I told Dulles that as president of the Foreign Service Association, I felt I had to bring up with Eisenhower the effect of some recent actions in the Department of State. I said I would not mention any specific case, but would tell him a little bit about the damage being inflicted on the morale of Foreign Service officers in general. Grudgingly, Dulles replied, "If you have to, go ahead."

At the White House, after our general talk about the Soviet Union, I turned to the question of morale in the Foreign Service. As soon as I did, Dulles interrupted to ask if I wanted him to leave the room. I told him no, that I had nothing to say to the President that I would not say in his presence. I then mentioned the low morale and fear of where investigations of subversion would hit next. I had got only a little into the subject, when Eisenhower interrupted. "Oh, you're talking about the appointment of that fellow Scott McLeod," he said. "Well, I think that that was an error on our part, but my feeling is it would be a worse error to dismiss him." I insisted that I was not suggesting the dismissal of anybody, but since he had brought the matter up, I would say that McLeod's activities were not those that would instill confidence in Foreign Service officers. I said that some of the most respected members of the Service, whom the President knew well, were thinking of resigning rather than submitting to what they felt was persecution. The President then delivered a homily, saying that having been in the Army for some forty years, he was used to the whims of public opinion, and the only thing to do was to stand firm and let the storm pass. Since there was very little value in pursuing the matter, I did not continue.

I did not meet McLeod until shortly after my confirmation, when he spotted me in the hall in the State Department and introduced himself. I expressed surprise that he should shake my hand after doing everything he could to prevent my confirmation. He expostulated a little, and we parted.

On April 4, 1953, my wife and I left for Moscow. We changed our plans and went together, not because of Dulles's admonition but because we found a way to get our children ready earlier. As we boarded a Pan American airliner in New York, I put the unhappy thoughts of March behind me. At last, I was on my way to Moscow, where Bolshevism was facing its greatest crisis since the Hitler attack of 1941.

CHAPTER NINETEEN

Changing of the Kremlin Guard

We landed in Moscow on April 11, 1953. After a brief welcome by an official of the Foreign Ministry and Jacob Beam, the American chargé d'affaires, we were taken to Spaso House. I had not been in Moscow since 1945, when I accompanied Hopkins on his mission to Stalin. At that time, the country was painfully emerging from the ruin and horror of the war. In the spring of 1953, the physical appearance of the city had not radically changed. There were a few more cars in the street. The people were better dressed. The stores were better stocked. There were a few more buildings, most of them high-rise structures in a style that came to be known as neo-Stalinist, a rather bad combination of classical and Moorish and some indefinable elements. Construction of apartment houses did not become a major effort until later. By and large, I found very little altered, and certainly the character of the city remained as it had always been—grim, brooding, and drab.

There had been many changes in Spaso House, and all for the better. The rooms had been painted and refurnished, the grounds had been spruced up. The mansion was more pleasant and comfortable than at any time since 1934, when it had been my first home in Moscow.

Like other ambassadors, I made some changes in the life style at Spaso. One of the first was to bring in a French chef, who had been the second or third man in the kitchen of the Paris Embassy. The new chef made our dining room one of the best places to eat in Moscow, but there were times when I wondered whether he was worth the good meals. He had an eye for the ladies, and one day another servant threatened to kill the chef for making a pass at his wife. The chef eventually returned to France.

Beam gave me a detailed briefing of Soviet affairs. He had not been in Moscow very long, but he was an astute observer and had kept Washington fully informed of the period when Stalin was ill and of events following the dictator's death. I had been impressed by Beam's telegrams, which I had read in Washington, and hoped to retain him as counselor, the number-two man in the Embassy. However, Dulles wanted Beam to join the Policy Planning Staff, and within a few months he returned to Washington. Years later, he became ambassador to Moscow.

Naturally, the principal subject that Beam and I discussed was the impact of the death of Stalin on the Soviet Union. Dulles had given me no instructions, except to be alert to any indication of the trend of events. I hardly knew what to expect, because the Soviet Union was so much a product of Stalin. He had dominated the scene to an extent unbelievable in almost any other country. He had collectivized Soviet agriculture and had industrialized the country. His purges had almost torn the nation apart and had brought it to the brink of disaster when the Nazis attacked. Although the shock of the invasion was so great he was unable to function for a week, Stalin pulled himself together, rebuilt the Red Army, and led Russia to an incredible victory. In winning, Stalin expanded the Soviet Union into an empire, dominating all of Eastern Europe, as the czars had long dreamed, and acquiring as the spoils of war all the Asian lands lost to Japan in 1905, and more.

Over the decades, his name had been glorified, indeed deified, in thousands of editorials, articles, books, and moving pictures. He was never referred to except with such adjectives as "great," "victorious," or "exemplary." His word was law, and his whim was the equivalent of his word.

Joseph Stalin will always remain one of the most enigmatic figures in history. The Soviet leaders, as well as the rest of the world, knew that he was relentless, vindictive, and merciless, but his motives will never be known. Even his daughter, Svetlana, seemed to catch only glimpses of his character from time to time. Historians will argue whether Stalin was simply a realist with no moral values or a monster whose paranoia led him into senseless crimes. Judged by his actions, I believe he ranks high on the list of the world's monsters. Count Leo Tolstoy had a moment of real prophecy when he said, "Imagine Genghis Khan with a telephone!" Stalin gave me the impression of a man to whom pity and other human sentiments were completely alien. He was not immoral; he was simply amoral. He did not understand any of the elements of Western thought or behavior which Churchill and Roosevelt expressed to him during the wartime conferences.

The roots of Stalin's inhumanity can be found in his ancestry. Russians are not sadistic. They are not like the Nazis. They are too primitive for that. They are cruel, they are ruthless, but they are not inhuman, and not pathological cases. Stalin was not a Russian. He did not have a drop of Slavic blood in him. He was a Georgian, and Georgian history has been marked by vengeance, conspiracy, deceit, and cruelty, although obviously there are many fine people among them. They are mountain folk, with characteristics more like the people of the Near East than of Russia.

Nevertheless, Stalin was capable of making the magnanimous gesture, even to his opponents. There were times when he departed from his notoriously suspicious nature to trust someone who had broken with him. Thus he allowed no reprisals against Leon Gelphand, the Soviet chargé in Rome, or against Gelphand's family, when Gelphand defected in the 1930s. Gelphand wrote Stalin a letter explaining that he could no longer serve in the government because of the purges, but he promised never to talk publicly about the Soviet Union or to give any information to other countries that would affect the security of the Soviet Union. Stalin accepted Gelphand's assurances at face value. Like the oriental emperors whom he resembled, Stalin liked to think that he knew the people he could trust and thus when to make a show of decency.

In addition to being a naturally suspicious Georgian, Stalin was a vengeful Georgian. In 1928, when Bukharin was in Paris, he told some Russian revolutionaries, including some members of the Second International, of an idle conversation with a group of Bolsheviks. They were giving their opinions of the pleasantest thing to do in the world. The normal ideas were mentioned, such as the satisfaction of a job well done, or an evening of music. Stalin said they were all wrong. He said the pleasantest thing in the world was to select your enemy, prepare the coup, drive the blow home, and then drink a bottle of red wine and go to bed.

There was little in Stalin's demeanor in the presence of foreigners that gave any clue to the real nature or character of the man. Many persons have tried, but have been unsuccessful in discerning the real man behind the swarthy face and black mustache. At Teheran, at Yalta, at Potsdam, and during the ten days I saw him during the spring of 1945 with Hopkins, Stalin was exemplary in his behavior. He was patient, a good listener, always quiet in his manner and in his expression. There were no signs of the harsh and brutal nature behind this mask—nothing of the ruthlessness with which he ordered the slaughter of millions of Russians. He was always polite and given to understatement.

Occasionally, Stalin's mask did slip a bit, not by inadvertence but by design. For example, at Teheran he ridiculed Molotov by summoning him, "Come over here, Molotov, and tell us about thy pact with Hitler," accenting "thy," a word that would be used with intimates in personal conversation but not in official business. These slight touches were designed to demonstrate to the foreigner that Stalin alone was the absolute boss of the Soviet world.

Stalin always seemed in complete control of himself, although we know that he was not in the days after the Nazi attack. He was single-minded in the pursuit of an objective. With foreigners, at least, there was no sitting around discussing trivialities and exchanging reminiscences.

The only time I saw Stalin show anything other than a surface emotion was at a ceremony at Teheran when Churchill presented him a sword made specially for the city of Stalingrad, in commemoration of the Nazi defeat there. The inscription read, "To the steel-hearted citizens of Stalingrad, a gift from King George VI as a token of the homage of the British people." Stalin's hands shook so hard that he dropped the sword. In a low, husky voice, he expressed deep appreciation for the gift and asked Churchill to convey the thanks of the people of Stalingrad to "His Majesty the King."

Although Stalin had the inestimable advantage of controlling everything in the Soviet Union—all forms of public expression, all decisions regarding military, political, economic problems—although he was beholden to no one, not even the dictates of public opinion, which he could shape, Stalin was not the master diplomat he is sometimes said to have been. He made serious mistakes. As previously indicated, one was the Finnish War of 1939, when Stalin believed the working class of Finland would rise up to greet the Red Army as saviors. Another mistake was his refusal to listen to warnings of Hitler's plans to invade the Soviet Union despite the Nazi-Soviet pact, an error which cost the Russians dearly in lives and property. One of Stalin's greatest mistakes was setting off the Korean war. He thoroughly misjudged Truman and came close to involving the Soviet Union in a war with the United States, a development which he sought above all to avoid. Even though the Soviets were not involved in the fighting, the war led to the American commitment to oppose Communist aggression everywhere and was a big factor in the arms race.

Evidently his mistake on Korea was due in large measure to the fact that Stalin had no accurate knowledge of the outside world. Except for a brief journey to Berlin in 1907, another to Stockholm to attend a Revolutionary Congress, and the World War II conferences at Teheran and Potsdam, he never set foot outside the Soviet Union. Furthermore, after he had become master of the Soviet Union, he suffered the fate of all autocrats in receiving reports of what he wanted to hear, not the truth.

In fact, Stalin seemed to surround himself with lackeys. They fitted his purposes more than innovators. He did not need thinkers, he needed executors.

I think history will state that without his ruthlessness and imperviousness to humanitarian considerations Soviet Russia would never have been industrialized as quickly as it was. After the death of Lenin, when it became apparent that world revolution was not around the corner, the Soviets had a major choice. They could go along with Trotsky in attempting to arouse the masses of the West, or they could adopt Stalin's plan of building socialism in one country, making the Soviet Union a modern industrial state. To this day, the Soviet Union is distorted by the extraordinary sacrifices imposed on the Russian people by industrialization and collectivization. If Trotsky's plan had been followed, Soviet Russia would undoubtedly be weaker, but it is by no means certain that the tragic sequence of events in Europe which led to the rise of Hitler would have occurred.

At the time of the news of Stalin's illness, there had been predictions in the West that the Soviet Union would surely undergo a bloodbath over who would succeed him. In briefing me, Beam noted that the Presidium (the name of the small group that runs the Soviet Communist Party was changed from Politburo to Presidium and then changed back to Politburo) had obviously been apprehensive over the gathering of thousands in Red Square following the announcement of the dictator's death. That is why it had issued a statement warning the people not to panic. In another move, the Kremlin indicated that Georgi M. Malenkov was designated, or thought he was designated, to be Stalin's successor. In fact, a fake photograph was published of a meeting of Stalin and Mao Tse-tung in which the face of Malenkov had been inserted. A few days after Stalin's death, the major jobs were distributed among three men. Malenkov was named Premier, the top government post; Lavrenti P. Beria retained the Ministry of the Interior, including the secret police; and Molotov was chosen as Foreign Minister. Nikita S. Khrushchev was given some of the duties, but not the title, of First Secretary of the Party. I made no immediate appraisal of this collective leadership. I had learned enough about the Soviet Union to realize that all important events were shrouded in secrecy and that caution was the proper procedure in Kremlinology.

One of the first questions we were interested in answering was whether Stalin had been murdered. There were rumors that his death had not been natural. It did not take me long to conclude that there was fairly good proof that his death was natural. There were nine doctors who signed the medical report. Those nine doctors were allowed their freedom (later one went to an international conference). If there had been skulduggery, the doctors would have been arrested to prevent disclosure. There was also evidence that Stalin, who was past seventy, had had at least one stroke before. One story was that a blood vessel had burst, but I do not know whether that was true. He may have flown into a rage which brought on a stroke.

After being briefed by Beam, I met with some of the other members of the embassy staff. I already knew three-quarters of them from past assignments. It was a much better prepared staff than those I had been associated with in 1934 and 1938 in Moscow. The Russian specialization program was paying off. Almost every officer of the Embassy could speak Russian. Elim O'Shaughnessy, the First Secretary, was not a Russian specialist, but he was very capable. When Beam left, O'Shaughnessy, on my recommendation, was made counselor.

The Embassy was not large. We had about a hundred Americans and about the same number of Russian employees. This was a small staff for a country as large and as important as the Soviet Union. However, considering our relations with Moscow and the fact that we were blocked in obtaining information, we had enough people.

I made no basic change in the organization of the Embassy. With trade and tourism operating at only a trickle, the principal tasks of the Embassy staff were intelligence-gathering, political reporting, and negotiation of differences. Our military attachés had a difficult time operating. The Soviets considered normal contacts and exchanges of information as espionage. As a result, seven American military attachés, three on a single occasion, were ordered to leave Moscow during my tenure of more than four years. Because of restrictions, the attachés were forced to rely on such poor clues as the display of military equipment at the May Day and November 7 parades in Red Square.

I assumed at once most of the responsibility for the other two major tasks of the Embassy—keeping Washington informed of the effect of Stalin's death on the Bolshevik government and on Kremlin policy, and talks over differences between the two countries, principally the Korean war.

The sources of information on Soviet political events were just as restricted in those days as they had been in Stalin's time. No one in the Kremlin would talk to a foreigner in any informative way. We had to read the newspapers carefully, exchange information with other ambassadors, and pick up gossip from American reporters, whom I saw once a week and played poker with regularly.

My first official action was to go to the Foreign Ministry, a few blocks from my office. After being cleared by a guard at the huge door, I was escorted to an elevator and taken up to Molotov's office. According to custom, I presented to the Foreign Minister a copy of my credentials and a copy of the remarks I planned to make when I made my call on the figurehead Soviet President, Klimenti E. Voroshilov, whom I knew from my previous tours. The stone-faced Molotov stuttered with emotion in response to my formal expression of sympathy over Stalin's death. A few days later, accompanied by my principal officers, I presented my letters of credence to President Voroshilov in the Kremlin and made some innocuous remarks about wanting to further American-Soviet relations. I was now officially the Ambassador.

It was typical of the times that I did not attempt to see Premier Malenkov or any other of the real Soviet rulers. I doubt if they would have seen me. Moreover, Dulles did not approve of such contacts. He seemed to have a built-in fear of any personal association with Soviet officials. I do not know that he felt that the influence would be corrupting, but he believed that if Americans were seen in friendly conversation with Russians, the will to resist Communism would be weakened throughout the world. I did not share the Secretary's view about keeping the Russians at arm's length, but I could not see much value in endeavoring to cultivate them. I have never believed in playing up to the Russians in the hope of gaining their favor, a tactic espoused by many Americans and foreigners. With the shut-in quality of Soviet society, we must conduct ourselves accordingly. That is, we should not demean ourselves by appearing to be too eager to ingratiate ourselves, but we should not miss any opportunity to enter into conversations with Soviet officials.

In almost any other country, there would have been wide opportunities to discuss the meaning of a major event like the death of Stalin, with many individuals both in and out of the government. In Moscow, there was no possibility, at least for many months after Stalin's death, of having any contact with private Russian citizens. Such contacts that we had were almost exclusively with Soviet officials, those of the Ministry of Foreign Affairs and related Ministries, and dealt with specific questions between the two governments, usually of a trivial nature.

There was no question that the Soviet coolness was official policy and that it disturbed some of the Russians. One of those who were frustrated was Mrs. Gromyko. In Washington during the war, my wife, who could speak some Russian, made a special effort, on the few occasions they met, to be friendly to Mrs. Gromyko, who was shy and often lonely because her husband traveled a great deal. At a French reception shortly after our arrival in Moscow, Mrs. Gromyko greeted Avis warmly. Gromyko did not look too pleased, but was politely correct. Friendly, intelligent, and well-educated, Mrs. Gromyko obviously found the restrictions of Soviet life discomforting. She was not allowed to pursue her friendship with Avis, and accepted invitations only to official occasions. Although she often said that she wanted to invite Avis and me to their apartment, she never did. In fact, in all the years we spent in the Soviet Union, we were never invited to a private home.

When I arrived in Soviet Russia, the only city in addition to Moscow that was open to visits by foreigners was Odessa. If I wanted to go more than forty kilometers out of Moscow, I had to receive the permission of the Foreign Office. This prohibition continued, in large measure, I believe, because we had instituted in the United States comparable restrictions on Soviet diplomats. Given the differences between our two systems, I was never fully in favor of an absolute tit-for-tat in regard to travel regulations. Being an authoritarian state, the Soviet Union was not criticized by the Soviets for restricting foreigners. In the United States, unless officials could prove that military secrets were protected, the restrictions were badly received by the American people and frequently criticized in the American press. If a nation is not a totalitarian state, it cannot behave like one. However, as the spring wore into summer, other areas of the Soviet Union began to be opened up, and I had the opportunity to do a good deal of traveling from then until I left in 1957. We went to Central Asia, the Ukraine, the Caucasus, the Crimea, and the Far North.

As the Ambassador, I was under the constant eye of the authorities in one form or another. When I arrived in Moscow, I had four security policemen following me constantly. They parked in a car outside the Residence at all hours, no matter how low the temperature dropped. When my wife and I went to the theater, two of the security men would be within eyesight of where we were sitting. When we went to a restaurant, the same two would sit at a table discreetly distant from ours. We came to know these men quite well, and occasionally would permit ourselves a few joking words of salutation or farewell. Occasionally, I gave them cigarettes, which they accepted quite willingly.

We more or less went on the assumption that the Soviet government had installed listening devices in our offices and heard what we were dictating or saying. When the new Chancellery was under construction in the spring of 1953, security men from the Embassy were on guard all day to prevent the installation of microphones on the two top floors—the seventh floor and the eighth, where I had my office. Unfortunately, because of carelessness and to save money, there was no watch at night. Several years later, long after I had left Moscow, forty-three microphones were discovered on the floors that were supposed to be the most secure in Moscow. This did not mean that the Soviets learned any real secrets. I always assumed that almost everything I dictated aloud to my secretary was recorded by the Soviet government. In cases of really sensitive information, which would have been important to the Soviet government, such as recommendations for American policy actions, I would write the material in longhand. Most ordinary dispatch writing was not of any great importance, because the Soviets were well aware of our general attitude toward the Soviet system, and uncomplimentary remarks would not even cause an eyebrow to be raised by Soviet security police.

It has always been a principle of American diplomacy that the ambassador, as the personal representative of the President, is senior to every other government official within the country to which he is assigned. This rule has been observed more often in the breach than in the performance, and a weak ambassador may not know what representatives of the Defense Department, Atomic Energy Commission, and other agencies are doing. The Central Intelligence Agency is theoretically under the ambassador, and he knows which members of his staff, whatever their titles, are CIA operatives, and in general what they are doing. But it is sometimes wise if the ambassador does not know in detail about the CIA operations. In case a secret agent or clandestine operation is blown, the ambassador can honestly disclaim knowledge of the affair. To my knowledge, no agency official attempted to circumvent my authority or work behind my back in Moscow—or, later, in Manila and Paris.

In the Soviet Union, it was especially important that everyone in the Embassy take orders from the ambassador. There could be no freewheeling, because there was the constant danger of a Soviet attempt to corrupt Americans and recruit them for espionage. One of the first rules of an ambassador was to inform his staff and new arrivals of the hazards. Each was instructed to go to his superior officer immediately if there was trouble with Soviet authorities. In the more than four years I was ambassador, there were about twelve cases, mostly of clerical personnel, but in one instance of a security officer, getting into trouble, usually with women. The secret police took incriminating infrared pictures, then tried to recruit the Americans for espionage. All of these people were out of the country in twenty-four hours. Because of this problem, one of the ambassador's main functions was to keep a close eye on personnel. Moscow was not a good assignment, particularly for clerical workers. They were forbidden to get involved with Soviet women because of the inevitable blackmail attempt. Even the theater was not open if their Russian was skimpy. There were no normal amusements; life was bleak.

In such an atmosphere, the staff had to amuse itself, occasionally in absurd ways. Once, some Marine guards explained to a Russian maid who took care of their quarters why a certain Marine was so depressed. The only way a Marine could win a promotion, they told her, was to kill his nearest relative. Since the depressed Marine had no relatives, he could not be promoted. The maid, as gullible as she was, did not believe the story. So they had the "depressed" Marine lie as if dead in a bathtub filled with water which they had colored red.

They sadly informed the maid that he had committed suicide, and showed her the gory scene.

One of my first tasks was to call on other ambassadors. These visits are time-consuming and frequently nonproductive, but in Moscow they were of considerable interest because each ambassador had a different comment on the Soviet scene. While it required a year and a half to call on all the embassies, it was not long before I established close relations with the British and the French Ambassadors. The British Ambassador was Sir Alvery Gasgoygne, who was succeeded before the year was out by Sir William Hayter, who had been my colleague in Paris. The French Ambassador was Louis Joxe, with whom I became quite intimate. I had known Joxe when he was head of the Cultural Section of the French Foreign Office. He was an excellent colleague. The three embassies worked closely together, exchanging information and showing each other their reports.

The stringencies of the Stalinist regime had not been lifted, but I could see, almost from the beginning, signs of fundamental change. One of the first indications was Beria's denunciations of the "doctors' plot," which Stalin had apparently been planning to use as an excuse for a new purge. Beria asserted that the "plot" by the doctors, most of them Jews, to kill Kremlin leaders was a fabrication, and released the accused. Another, more important, sign was an article in *Pravda* pointing out the sins of the "cult of personality" and the danger of having only one man make decisions. Stalin was not mentioned, but the article was transparently aimed at his dictatorship. This was the first reassertion of the doctrine of collective leadership, which Lenin supposedly had espoused. As the weeks went by, the Soviet press used the term "cult of personality" with increasing vehemence to describe abuses under Stalin. This term was not just a euphemism. Many articles appeared in serious Soviet journals pointing out that the concentration of power in one man and his adulation were a departure from Marxian principles. Eventually, the term "cult of personality" encompassed the entire structure of political power under Stalin. I imagine this relatively mild term was adopted in 1953 to avoid shocking the general population, and especially the intelligentsia, with a full-scale denunciation of Stalin. For twenty-five years, Stalin had been worshiped. It would have been too risky to the Communist Party for the Soviet people to learn suddenly that their idol had not only feet of clay but also bloodstained hands. It was not until 1956 that Stalin was denounced by name and deed.

While these faint indications of change were appearing on the domestic scene, there was a more apparent shift in foreign policy. Malenkov appealed for an effort to solve the outstanding issues. Early in April, Foreign Minister Molotov indicated that a new approach would be made to obtain a Korean armistice. In an unprecedented action, *Pravda* on April 25 devoted its entire first page to a speech by President Eisenhower calling on the new Soviet leaders to settle all international problems. Then the Soviet government withdrew claims Stalin made in 1945 to the Turkish provinces of Kan and Ardahan. On June 8, Molotov told the Yugoslav chargé d'affaires that Moscow wanted to send an ambassador to Belgrade, the first move toward repairing the rupture with Tito. The Soviet press let up on its Hate America campaign.

In June, there were rumors that the new leaders were planning a change in policy regarding Germany. Stringent economic regulations were eased, but I could not ascertain whether rumors of political reform had any substance to them or whether they were merely speculation by foreigners. Then, on June 23, workers rioted in East Berlin. The riots stunned the Soviet leaders, who still could not conceive of the possibility of the working class of any country turning against the Soviet Union. In a remarkable shift, Moscow conceded that workers had opposed a Communist regime. All Soviet newspapers carried full accounts of the riots, and some urged greater consideration and respect for the masses. In a telegram to the State Department, I cautioned against counting too heavily on an easing of the Sovietization of East Germany. If Stalin were alive, I wrote, there almost certainly would have been a tightening of the dictatorship. The riots spread, and the fearful Soviet leaders used elements of more than twenty divisions to crush the rebellion. Nevertheless, the reforms were continued.

In the meantime, I had been working away at some of the problems that beset Soviet-American relations, most of them relatively trivial on the international scale, but nevertheless of vital importance to the people concerned. For example, the Soviets agreed to let Embassy personnel use three bathing beaches in the Moscow area which we had theoretically been permitted to visit but had been barred from by the policy of limiting us to certain geographical areas. Another problem concerned the Russian wives of six American citizens. Some of these women had married American soldiers attached to the military missions in Moscow during the war. Others had married American newspaper correspondents. Toward the end of the war, the Supreme Soviet passed a decree forbidding Russians to marry any foreigners. England had citizens in the same situation, and in December, 1945, Bevin raised the problem with Stalin, who gave his customary evasive answer, that he could not do anything about it because it was the will of the Supreme Soviet. Actually, the ban was designed to prevent soldiers of the Soviet occupation armies in Eastern Europe from marrying foreigners with capitalistic ideas and taking them back home. The Soviet troops had not found in Eastern Europe exactly all the horrors of capitalism that had been depicted by the Soviet press. It was obvious that the Soviet authorities were concerned about the effect on Soviet troops of better living conditions, and particularly of the wiles of capitalist women. Their blunderbuss cure was to forbid all marriages with foreigners. The Russian women who had married were penalized, although all they wanted to do was join their husbands. After Stalin's death, the government soon began to let the wives of foreigners emigrate. Eventually, all six of the wives of Americans were permitted to leave the country.

Of a more important nature were the Korean armistice talks, which were still deadlocked over the question of whether Communist prisoners of war being held in South Korea should be forced, against their will, to return to North Korea and China. On May 18, the State Department asked my views (Dulles apparently realizing that an ambassador was, after all, an adviser) on enlisting Molotov's help in getting the Communists to accept the United Nations' "final position" at the talks at Panmunjom. In reply, I said that in view of the publicity given the Communist rejection of previous offers and disunity among the United Nations, I doubted that a direct approach would work if our position remained substantially unchanged. "If, on the other hand, some modification is to be made in the U.N. proposals," I telegraphed Dulles, "there might be real value in such an approach." After suggesting a delay in the release of the prisoners as a concession to the Communists, I ended the cable with these words: "I do feel, particularly for any approach to the Soviet government, we should concentrate on absolutely essential points on which we are determined not to yield and endeavor to impress on the Soviets that there will be no armistice unless these basic positions are accepted."

On May 25, the United Nations made their final offer at Panmunjom, granting some concessions, but not agreeing to forcible repatriation of prisoners. The next day, I received from Bermuda, where

Eisenhower and Dulles were meeting with the British and the French, a telegram instructing me to go ahead with the approach to Molotov. Two days later, I went to see Molotov. Sitting in a massive brown leather chair in his reception office at the Foreign Ministry, I told him that the United States had put forth a final proposal for an armistice and that it represented as far as we could go. I gave him a memorandum on a plain sheet of paper setting forth the six main points of the offer. The plain paper was a symbol of our desire not to push the Soviet government into any position where it felt it had received a formal request and had to back its allies, North Korea and China. Molotov listened attentively as his interpreter translated the six points. He interrupted several times to ask for clarifications. After the sixth point, calling for a political conference, was translated, he asked which nations would be represented. I said I did not know, but the composition was not in dispute at Panmunjom.

Then I emphasized that the proposal was "the extreme limit of possible concessions," and listed point by point how far we had gone to meet Communist demands. He did not dispute my statement that if at the end of the three months the North Koreans and Chinese had been unable to persuade the prisoners to change their minds, it was clear that only some form of force would bring about their repatriation. I stated, and Molotov did not disagree, that to offer, as the Communists had, merely the choice of either permanent imprisonment in camps or repatriation was in effect the use of force. Speaking slowly and choosing my words carefully, I told him that rejection of the proposals by the North Koreans and Chinese would extinguish hopes for an armistice and lead to the creation of a situation which the United States government was most sincerely and earnestly attempting to avoid.

Molotov asked whether the United States expected a reply to the memorandum from the Soviet government. I said the communication was not an official one, requiring a reply, but I brought up the fact that Molotov, on April 2, had said the Soviet Union was ready to cooperate to achieve an armistice. Molotov said he would inform his government of my remarks, and added that the Soviet Union was indeed interested in establishing peace in Korea. He nodded agreement when I said the United States planned to make no announcement of my visit. Secrecy was essential.

In my cable to Dulles on the meeting, I concluded, "As usual with Molotov I have no grounds for even attempting to forecast what the Soviet government may or may not do in regard to these proposals. I can only report that he listened with great attention and seriousness and refrained from any form of propaganda statement or question or even any attempt to defend or support the Communist position. His reference twice to the composition of the political conference may be some indication of where the present Soviet interest lies."

The purpose of this carefully planned approach was to raise the fear of the Soviets of an expansion of the war, without driving them into a corner. I did not know that in a related action the United States was hinting to China through India that it might use atomic weapons in Korea. In a matter of hours after my talk with Molotov, the North Koreans asked for a two-week delay in responding to our proposal, and on June 3, Molotov called me in and carefully delivered an oral statement in Russian that he had obviously memorized. I listened to it in Russian and then in the English translation by Molotov's interpreter and memorized it myself. He said, "The Soviet government has taken note of the information you gave to me on May 28, concerning the armistice talks at Panmunjom; as you know, the outcome of these talks does not depend on us but it has been noted with satisfaction that the path to the successful conclusion of these armistice talks has been mapped out."

Molotov showed no disposition to elaborate, and I did not consider it wise to question him, since the statement clearly meant that the Soviet Union had persuaded North Korea and China to accept our offer. I thanked him, and told him that if his statement meant an armistice in Korea, it was good news. He made no comment.

There was a scare two days later when French Ambassador Joxe asked me point-blank whether I had talked with Molotov about a Korean armistice. He said the tip had come from the French Embassy in Tokyo. I said he surely understood why I could not discuss the matter with negotiations at a critical point. Joxe said he not only understood that any leaks might have "catastrophic" consequences, but he also planned to tell Paris he would not press me for an answer. Like me, he did not want to embarrass the Soviets by telling the world that they were pressuring their allies to give in to us. Dulles was deeply disturbed, but my approach to Molotov did not leak any further, and the negotiations for the conclusion of the armistice went, as the Russians say, "as though on butter," except for wrangling over the exchange of prisoners. I was concerned, when Syngman Rhee, the South Korean President, set the Communist prisoners of war free, lest the Soviets call off the armistice arrangement. However, Vishinsky, then Molotov's assistant, issued a denunciation of Rhee but not of the United States, and the armistice was concluded in July. For months, Washington had been working on ideas to solve the prisoner dilemma. I was one of those convinced that freeing the prisoners would tie up the negotiations. Rhee's action showed that we could have opened the gates of the POW camps and let all of the prisoners out long before Rhee did.

On July 7, having been in the Soviet Union for three months, I felt I could draw some conclusions about the developments since the death of Stalin. In my first analysis of the new government, I wrote Dulles that the events could not be dismissed as "simply another peace campaign designed solely or even primarily to bemuse and divide the West. The events that have occurred here cumulatively add up, in my opinion, to something considerably more important, offering on the one hand more opportunities and on the other considerably more dangers than the standard propaganda gestures which we have seen since the end of the war."

Emphasizing that the Soviet Union remained a totalitarian state which still regarded any country or organization it did not control as hostile, I listed as a reasonable assumption a return by the Soviet Union to diplomacy as a means of furthering its interests, especially preventing West German rearmament and averting a general war. I predicted the almost definite necessity of a shift in policy toward the Eastern European satellites and Communist China. Domestically, I saw a less rigorous regime which would put its primary emphasis on improving the standard of living of the people, and which would curtail the arbitrary exercise of police power, respect the rights of national minorities, and systematically destroy the myth of Stalin's infallibility and relegate him to the position of "a junior member of the Communist Valhalla."

As for the question of who wielded power, I wrote, "While we simply do not know what forms of combinations or rivalries are transpiring in the upper reaches of the Soviet government, I can only report that the principle of collective leadership as against one man rule has been consistently and steadily developed in this country since Stalin's death. It has been driven home not only in the central press and given ideological underpinnings in the theoretical party journals but also has been disseminated in depth according to our information in factory and party meetings throughout the country.

"It would be folly to attempt to predict that this experiment in impersonal collective leadership will last indefinitely and we can never dismiss the possibility of dissension at the top level or some other event which might radically change the current line. It can only be stated now as a matter of opinion that if there is a radical reversal of the present tendency back to the state of arbitrary terror characteristic of Stalin's rule, this would impose severe strains on the population of this country and would impose severe strains on the system."

Three days after I wrote those words, the first crack appeared in the "united and unshakable" collective leadership. The government announced that Beria, the head of the secret police, had been arrested.

CHAPTER TWENTY

The Collective Dictatorship

In late June of 1953, I requested that an Air Force transport be sent from Frankfurt to take me and my family to France for a month's leave. I had been in the Soviet Union for only three months, and the perquisites of an ambassador made life a lot easier than in my previous tours. Spaso House was a comfortable place to live. We had a dacha in the country. Traveling around Moscow was easier in a limousine with an American flag flying from a fender. Despite the changes, the Soviet Union was still an oppressive society, and we wanted to get away. I had not had a vacation for more than a year, and the time seemed suitable to go. The new regime was firmly in power, and the summer doldrums had set in. The Air Force Constellation was due to arrive on July 6, and we were scheduled to depart for Paris the following day.

A week before we were to leave, a brief item in *Pravda* about the second presentation of the new opera *Dekabristy* set off a wave of gossip that Lavrenti Beria, the Minister of the Interior and head of the secret police, had been purged. In listing the leaders of the government and Party who were at the Bolshoi, the news item omitted Beria. After discussions with the staff, I wired Washington that the omission was "not necessarily significant," because the whereabouts of Soviet leaders were rarely indicated. I pointed out that Beria could be vacationing or traveling, and added that if there was anything politically significant, we would find out soon.

From my personal knowledge of the Soviet leaders, I had little to go on regarding Beria. I had met him at one of the wartime Kremlin dinners but had never had an opportunity to talk with him until the Yalta Conference. There, at a luncheon one day, I was seated between Sir Archibald Clark Kerr, the British Ambassador in Moscow, and

Beria. I interpreted for them. One of the subjects of the conversation was the sex life of fish. I cannot recall how the British Ambassador and the head of the Soviet secret police ever got on this subject. It was also at Yalta that Sir Archibald, an eccentric, rose at Stalin's dinner and said that after all the toasts to spiritual things, such as good will, friendship, and comradeship, he wished to toast the man who "looked after our bodies." He meant Beria, the boss of the blue-uniformed soldiers guarding the conference. Churchill growled and, leaning forward in his chair, said, "No, Archie, none of that." Beria was a plump, pale Georgian with pince-nez eyeglasses. He was quiet and spoke little. He looked like a schoolmaster, a characteristic of chiefs of secret police; Hitler's man, Himmler, from his photographs, had the same look.

On July 3, Rolf Sohlman, the Swedish Ambassador in Moscow, who had some good Soviet contacts, told me that he had heard that Beria had been arrested. For the next few days, I endeavored to check the rumor but could not find any information to confirm it, although a number of tanks were spotted near government buildings. I discussed the rumor with American newspapermen, who got around quite a lot in Moscow, but they could not substantiate the report, either. I was in a quandary. It usually took two weeks to make the necessary arrangements for the Constellation to land in Moscow. The plane was due to leave Frankfurt in a matter of hours. Either I could cancel the plane with an excuse which would have seemed flimsy to the Russians, or I could go on my vacation and take the chance that Beria's arrest would be announced during my absence. I finally decided to go ahead with the vacation. We had no evidence to support the rumor, and even if it were true, there was not much that I would be able to do by remaining in Moscow. However, my main reason for not staying was my firm belief that there would be no great internal upheaval, even if Beria was arrested, because the Kremlin needed peace to consolidate the new leaders' power. I was much aware of the emphasis Stalin's successors were putting on collective leadership. They would most likely close ranks against Beria, who had made many enemies in the fourteen years he was head of the secret police.

I was sitting in the France et Choiseul Hotel in Paris on July 10 when Under Secretary of State Walter Bedell Smith called from Washington and told me that the Soviet government had announced Beria's arrest. He asked whether I should not rush back to Moscow. I said I was perfectly willing to go back, but I was quite convinced that nothing more than the end of Beria was involved and the arrest would not set off a convulsion, as some experts might suppose. It was to be expected that Beria's close associates would be arrested, too, but my assistants in Moscow could report such developments. Smith agreed and suggested that I return to Washington to consult.

While my family went to Majorca, I flew to Washington, arriving early in the evening. A State Department car met me at the airport and took me to Dulles's home. Although he was entertaining some British and French diplomats, Dulles immediately led me to his study to talk. He was excited about the prospects of Beria's arrest's setting off a bloody struggle for power that might lead to the overthrow of the Soviet regime. I repeated what I had been saying for nearly two weeks—that I did not share this view. While I made no claim to certitude, since no outsider knows what goes on behind the Kremlin walls, I explained that the Bolshevik system seemed able to withstand the stress of Beria's arrest because all the leaders understood the dangers of internecine warfare.

My best guess was that Beria had been arrested because he refused to put his secret police under the collective leadership of the Party. The other members of the Presidium, remembering well how Stalin had used the secret police, could not afford to let Beria go his independent way, even if he had not made a bid for supreme power. The secret police had to be brought under control.

Dulles picked up Stalin's book, *Questions of Leninism*, which had been lying open on a desk, and began to read some passages about seizing power, which he had underscored. I told him that Stalin's writings bore little relevance to the Soviet Union after his death. Dulles was reluctant to believe me. Eventually, it was agreed that I should return to France, but keep an eye on events in Moscow from there. If there were any signs of serious trouble, I could get back to Moscow quickly. I spent the rest of the month tranquilly in France with my family while the Beria case faded from the news.

On my return to Moscow, I consulted with my staff and other ambassadors to get their opinions of why there had been no further developments in the case. I wired Dulles that the Kremlin might have decided not to hold a public trial for Beria. A public trial, I pointed out, would require the prosecution to prepare Beria for his appearance, which would be inherently dangerous and could create international problems, because he was accused of being an agent of an imperialist plot to restore capitalism to Russia.

It was not until December 17 that plans to try Beria in secret were announced. The charges, that Beria had been a foreign agent since his youth and was in the pay of foreign capital, were ludicrous. The fact that Beria and all six of his "accomplices" were officials of the KGB confirmed my view that the real issue in the case was the position of the secret police as an institution. In another telegram to Dulles, I said it was likely that the collective leaders had tried to clip the wings of the secret police by subordinating the Interior Ministry to top-level Party control. Whether the plan had been to make Beria the victim from the beginning, or whether he was seized because he resisted, was not of the first importance. The aim was to take away the power of one man to look down the throats of his associates through his control of the secret police. I emphasized the danger to the Kremlin of curbing the secret police, because the Bolsheviks could not afford to destroy the authority of the police in relation to the Soviet population in general.

On Christmas Eve, the Soviet press announced that Beria and his six accomplices had been found guilty by a special judicial panel of the Soviet Supreme Court, and had been executed by shooting on December 23.

A lot of experts were wrong about the post-Stalin period. They thought the Stalin-type rule was a fixed mechanism of Soviet society. They expected a violent upheaval as various leaders sought to take over Stalin's power. When Beria was arrested, these experts expected the struggle to break into open fighting. The events were misinterpreted because the experts failed to realize that certain aspects of the Soviet system were only an expression of Stalin's will. Stalin's rule was a one-man operation, with the secret police as his enforcement machinery. The Communist Party, although the ostensible ruling force, was, in effect, denigrated as an institution. It seemed to me that Stalin's successors came to the conclusion soon after his death that neither the state of the country nor their personalities made the creation of another Stalin possible. We do not know and probably never will know what really happened in the Presidium in the weeks following his death, but my strong impression is that the Kremlin leaders concluded that they would have to work as a group. I became convinced rather early that the controlling factor in the new regime was not a struggle for power to produce another Stalin but, rather, a process of adjusting the ruling mechanism to collective leadership, better described as collective dictatorship. The members of the Presidium were intelligent enough to realize that no one was strong enough, at least in the beginning, to sit in Stalin's seat. Stalin had seen to that.

Each of their fortunes, and their necks, depended on how successfully they could work together. They also realized that the country would not go through another terror that a struggle for power might entail. And they must have felt the great yearning of the people for a freer, more prosperous life.

The first major task of the new leaders was to put the secret police under the control of the group. It was only common sense that committee rule could not work if one member had complete control of the secret police. With his far-flung surveillance apparatus, he would be in a good position to put pressure on other leaders. I do not know the details involving the downfall of Beria, but I think the basic political fact is quite clear. There was no struggle for personal power in the true sense of the phrase. The best evidence for this conclusion was that the nine other members of the Presidium remained in their jobs. If Beria had made a move to seek supreme power, he would have had some allies in the ruling group; otherwise he would have been doomed to failure. He probably started to operate to strengthen his personal position in the police apparatus, getting rid of doubtful assistants left over from Stalin's time, and promoting his own men. The other members of the Presidium considered this dangerous and called on him to cease. He refused openly, according to one fairly good account, and was arrested.

All the evidence since Beria's downfall indicates that the police did indeed become subordinate to the ruling group of the Party, the Presidium. As a consequence, the arbitrary exercise of police power, the use of terror as an instrument of government, has disappeared, to a large extent, from the Soviet Union. The police are still there and can be all-powerful if the rulers in Moscow want to use them, but the miasma of terror, the feeling of never knowing when the police will knock on the door to take you away, has largely disappeared since Stalin. Those who break the laws will be arrested, and the laws prohibit much that Western countries allow. "Socialist legality"—the idea that you cannot be arrested without some violation of law—is flexible, but it is a definite advance from Stalin's day.

With Beria safely out of the way, the new Soviet leaders continued their work of undoing much of Stalin's policies. I was in the diplomatic box at a session of the Supreme Soviet on August 8 when Malenkov announced in his elegant, precise Russian a policy of expanding production of consumer goods, instead of putting so much emphasis on heavy industry. Agriculture, in many ways the most backward element of the Soviet economy, was to be stimulated by encouraging the private sector, without changing the basic policy of collectivization. In my analysis for the State Department, I called the speech the "most important and realistic statement of current Soviet policy since Stalin's death," and said that Malenkov was unquestionably the dominant figure among Soviet leaders.

This analysis was not contradicted a month later when Khrushchev was formally named First Secretary of the Communist Party, in many ways the most important position in the Soviet Union because the Party is the absolute center of power. The fact that he, and not Malenkov, made the most important speech at the Party's Central Committee meeting (as always, closed to diplomats and the press) did not surprise me; the division of functions seemed in accord with collective leadership. Khrushchev pointed out that the state of Soviet agriculture was far from good and that some very serious changes would have to be introduced into the system. Above all, there should be lower taxes on the small private holdings peasants were permitted under the system of collectivization of agriculture. Khrushchev's speech was another indication that the farm system was working badly, but, more important, was a clue to the degree that de-Stalinization was being pursued.

I cabled Washington:

> Khrushchev has been moved up ahead of Voroshilov and now is third in official listings. He furthermore appears to be close to Malenkov and sat next to him at all sessions at which both were present, and also gave every sign of self-satisfaction and confidence. Although officially listed as No. 2, Molotov appeared to keep himself somewhat aloof and rather noticeably did not join in the applause on announcement of the decree removing Beria. These indications are, of course, inconclusive but in view of visible attempts to restore the role of the party as the dominant force in the country, standing over and above government institutions, it would appear logical that Khrushchev as First Secretary of the Central Committee should become Malenkov's close collaborator.

Signs of growing confidence of the new leaders continued to appear. A new history book was issued downgrading Stalin. Malenkov ridiculed the United States' refusal to let Russian chess players visit Glen Cove, Long Island, which was outside the geographical limits set up in retaliation for Soviet curbs on American travel. I had warned Dulles that the Soviets would capitalize on such an exclusion. Of far more importance, on August 20, after hints from Malenkov, the

Kremlin announced the first Soviet explosion of a hydrogen bomb, thus breaking the American monopoly on the most powerful weapon in the world.

On October 6, I was astounded to notice that the black car of the secret police was missing from the entrance of the Embassy. The new British Ambassador, Sir William Hayter, told me that the NKVD had not followed him since his arrival the month before. The abandonment of "protective surveillance," as the Russians termed the practice instituted in 1918, was followed by the institution of a friendlier social style. The leaders of the Kremlin began to hold more receptions for foreigners and to mix freely with the guests and talk more candidly than I had ever heard them. The breakthrough came at a reception Molotov gave in the Speridonovka, the Foreign Ministry's mansion, on November 7, the anniversary of the Bolshevik Revolution.

My wife and I sat with the other ambassadors through the usual concert and lavish buffet. As we were leaving, Molotov sent word that he would like the British, French, and American ambassadors to join him at his table. Nikolai A. Bulganin, Kaganovich, and Mikoyan were there, and also, by some strange process of selection, the Argentine, Burmese, and Chinese ambassadors.

As we sat down, Kaganovich called across the table and asked whether I had forgotten how to drink "*à la Russe.*" I smiled and said that I certainly did remember *pertsovka* vodka—vodka flavored with red peppers. Kaganovich then passed me a bottle. As I filled my glass, a small man with a bald head and pointed beard, seated on my right, commented in perfect Russian, "Ah, the favorite drink of the Ukrainians." I asked if he were Ukrainian. He drew himself up slightly and replied, "No, I'm German." It was only then that I realized that I was sitting next to Walter Ulbricht, the Communist boss of East Germany. Because the United States did not recognize East Germany, and the two governments were at odds, we should not have been talking to each other. I suggested that out of courtesy to our hosts we should at least observe the proprieties. He agreed.

My immediate suspicion was that Molotov wanted to embarrass us by seating us next to Ulbricht. Had that been Molotov's aim, he would have offered innumerable toasts to the Chinese and East Germans, and worded the toasts to jab at the United States. In fact, the Russians paid little attention to Liu Siao, the Chinese Ambassador, or to Ulbricht. Molotov did offer one toast to each, the first to the Chinese Ambassador. However, he noted diplomatically the presence of a number of representatives of countries which did not have relations with China, and expressed the hope that, out of courtesy to himself and the guest, they would rise even though they did not drink. As suggested, the Western ambassadors did rise, but did not drink the toast. Afterward, Molotov told me he thought it was a pity that we had no contact with the Chinese Ambassador, who was a "man of many thoughts on many subjects." In a loud voice, Mikoyan, glancing toward the Chinese Ambassador, commented, "He has no thoughts on anything." Molotov also toasted Ulbricht, while we followed the same procedure—standing without drinking.

Molotov then proposed toasts to the United States, to Britain, and to France, without even an indirect attack on any of our policies. Ulbricht and Liu followed our lead and stood without drinking the toast. Having drunk to all the guests, the Russians then offered a multitude of toasts to peace. Following my usual practice, I had been sipping only a little vodka for each toast, but the alcohol lowered my inhibitions. After another toast to peace had been proposed, I rose and, with news reporters crowding around, said I would willingly drink to peace, but I would like to add two words, "with justice," since without justice in international affairs, there could be no firm peace. This reference to justice animated Soviet officials, particularly Kaganovich, who answered in a long speech to the effect that there were different concepts of justice in the world but that peace was something all people understood. Then Zhukov, who had taken Bulganin's place after the latter became drunk, got up and said, to my surprise, that he would like to support the toast to peace of the American Ambassador. I overheard Mikoyan ask him in a whisper if he did not have a toast of his own. Zhukov replied no, that he merely wanted to support the toast to justice. Later, Molotov toasted the health of military men who had arranged the parade earlier that day, and expressed the hope that they would confine themselves to parades. Although Molotov was contrasting parades to war, the toast did not please Zhukov. I am not sure why Zhukov supported my toast. One American correspondent wrote that Zhukov obviously had the case of Beria, who was in jail at that time, in mind. This was a stretch of the imagination. The most that can be said is that Zhukov was demonstrating his independence of the Kremlin's political leaders.

I was amused to watch Molotov and Mikoyan trying to restrain Kaganovich, who, as the evening wore on, lapsed more and more into Bolshevik jargon without, however, attacking the West. Still smarting from my earlier toast to justice, Kaganovich prodded me again on peace. I finally stood up again and said that it must be evident to everyone that all peoples, all governments, and all sections of the population of the countries of the world were desirous of peace. But, I emphasized, settlement of international disputes was one thing and preservation of peace was another. To preserve peace, only a simple rule of conduct by a nation was required—to avoid acts of aggression. If troops did not cross frontiers, the peace would not be broken. I then proposed a toast to the prevention of aggression. With some uncertainty, the Soviet officials drank the toast.

The reception was discussed for days in the diplomatic community. I linked the friendly atmosphere of the evening to Moscow's rejection of an American proposal for a Foreign Ministers' meeting on Germany and Austria. "In effect," I wired Dulles, "the Soviets were saying, 'We will not negotiate with you and it is all your fault, but we don't intend to fight you.'" This is a characteristic stance the Soviets take when they do not want their actions to be the subject of far-reaching conclusions.

Early in 1954, there were signs of a further thaw in the Soviet position. The United States was able to get an agreement on a meeting of the four Foreign Ministers. The Soviets wanted the conference in East Berlin; we wanted it in West Berlin. It was finally decided that the sessions would alternate between American and Soviet offices in Berlin. The agreement involved an unnecessary complication, but at least it represented a compromise. I was one of Dulles's advisers at the conference. I had no specific function and was not charged with any particular tasks but was there for general purposes of advice and discussion. At this meeting, Dulles had a Russian-speaking lip-reader watching the Soviet delegation. The idea was to find out what the Russians were talking about and possibly to pick up some secrets. I do not believe the lip-reader learned anything of importance.

While the conference made no progress on Germany, it came within an inch of an agreement on Austria. The chief sticking point was Moscow's insistence that it retain the right to reintroduce troops into Austria whenever it felt that the treaty was not being observed. There were also questions involving economic matters, particularly oil concessions. Finally, Dulles, in a sweeping gesture, offered to compromise all of the economic questions if the Soviets would agree to give up the right to reintroduce troops into Austria. Molotov was quick to take advantage of this move, insisting the United States could not have had very deep convictions on the subject if he were willing to abandon our position. Nevertheless, he remained adamant on the subject of troops.

362

The Ministers did reach an agreement to call a conference in Geneva on Indochina, where Ho Chi Minh had been waging guerrilla war against the French since 1946, and on Korea. I was Dulles's interpreter at a confidential meeting that he had with Molotov on calling the conference. I found the task much more difficult than I had imagined. My knowledge of Russian had certainly not deteriorated; if anything, it was better than during the war. But my memory was not as sharp as it should have been for an interpreter. However, the session went off reasonably well. I did not attend the Geneva Conference, but returned to Moscow.

In March of 1954, there were indications of a curious ideological deviation between Malenkov and the other members of the ruling group. All eleven made speeches in their various constituencies in the charade of campaigning for seats in the Supreme Soviet. Malenkov said that any nuclear war would mean the destruction of civilization. This speech was a marked departure from the previous Soviet line that nuclear war would bring about the downfall of capitalism, but not Communist countries. Other top officials stayed with the old line that war was the midwife of revolution and therefore inevitable, and there were signs of a division, vaguely hinted at in the Soviet press. Within a month, Malenkov was forced to modify his statement. But later, when Khrushchev became Premier, it became established doctrine that war was not inevitable. This change in doctrine became one of the chief targets of the Chinese attack on the Soviets as revisionists who had lost their revolutionary fervor.

As the warm spring winds of 1954 melted the Moscow snows, there were signs that Khrushchev's stock was still rising. At the presentation of awards to a Comédie Française troupe on April 15, the pudgy Party Secretary talked incessantly, showing no hesitancy in interrupting Molotov. Two days later, all the Moscow papers carried front-page stories extolling the "glorious son of the working class" on his sixtieth birthday. While still listed behind Premier Malenkov and Foreign Minister Molotov in the controlled press, Khrushchev seemed to have at least equal influence. On April 26, he was given two standing ovations when he spoke to the Council of Union, a reception equal to that accorded Malenkov earlier in the day.

By May, publicity for Khrushchev generated speculation once more of a power struggle among the Soviet leaders. In a wire to the State Department on May 4, I noted the steady rise in Khrushchev's stock, pointing to clues ranging from the fact that on May 2 he stood out in a picture in *Pravda* "as the only leader waving his hat" to the adding of governmental duties to his Party job. But I again cautioned that a split in the Bolshevik leadership was more likely to arise over deep policy differences than purely personal rivalries and that it was therefore premature to attempt to analyze the long-range significance of Khrushchev's increase in public prominence since Beria's downfall.

By the end of May, Khrushchev was, on occasion, listed in the press ahead of Malenkov. I clung to my conviction that the two were not locked in a struggle to take over Stalin's mantle. I believed that a major question was one of a difference over Malenkov's programs for increasing the output of consumer goods and agricultural products. Malenkov made a more realistic estimate of Soviet economic capabilities than did Khrushchev. Another important factor was the increasing emphasis on the Communist Party, represented by its Secretary, Khrushchev, compared with the government bureaucracy, headed by Premier Malenkov. The renunciation of one-man rule and restoration of the Party as the dominant power in the Soviet Union had been steadily pushed since Stalin's death. "Indeed," I wrote the department on June 1, "if one man is not to personify the Soviet structure (and whatever the future may bring, in the fifteen months since his death no successor has yet been developed), some institution must. The party by its tradition and nature is the only Soviet institution which could fill the vacuum left by the death of Stalin."

With these two factors in mind, I kept a close watch on the situation.* At the end of September, the fact that Khrushchev, instead of Malenkov, led a Soviet delegation to Peking for the fifth anniversary of the Communist regime caused some speculation. My guess at an explanation, and it could be no more than that, was that Communist Party matters, which came under Khrushchev, would be the principal subjects to be discussed. Bulganin, the Defense Minister, who shared the spotlight with Khrushchev, went along to take up any military matters. I felt that the Kremlin, which was being forced to raise China's status in the Communist hierarchy, did not want to go too far by including the top man, Malenkov.

On October 1, in Peking, Khrushchev delivered a speech pledging the Soviet people's support to the Chinese campaign to "liberate" Formosa. While I found it difficult to believe that the Soviet government would run the risk of a major war over Formosa, Khrushchev's belli-

---

* I was away from Moscow on July 4, 1954, when the entire Presidium unexpectedly showed up for the American Independence Day celebration at the Embassy. My five-year-old daughter, Celestine, must have felt some aversion to Khrushchev. Although he had been friendly to the children present, when he approached Celestine, as if to pick her up, she stood rigidly and glared at him. The poor man retreated.

cosity worried me. A little too nervously, I proposed to Dulles that the United States move to counteract the Communist campaign before it went too far, and "to remove any shadow of doubt" in Communist minds of United States determination to fight if armed force was used by the Chinese against Formosa. I suggested a propaganda campaign to exploit the glaring contrast between Soviet professions of coexistence and open support of armed aggression against Formosa; a presidential repetition of the warning that an attack on Formosa would involve conflict with the United States Seventh Fleet and war with the United States; and a private message to Moscow indicating the consequences if Chinese Communist threats were translated into action.

A week later, news of Formosa had dropped out of the Soviet press, and I no longer felt the urgency of the situation. Noting that the Soviet government was, at least for the moment, inclined to soft-pedal the issue, I wired Washington that, unless China stepped up its campaign or intelligence sources reported plans for military moves, action on my second and third suggestions should be held in abeyance. The propaganda drive should be pursued with vigor, I said. Dulles never responded to either telegram.

When the Chinese-Soviet agreements negotiated in Peking were published in Moscow on October 12, I realized that my first tentative appraisal of the trip had been wrong. The agreements were government-to-government, not Party-to-Party. They were significant, and at least appeared to elevate Peking to complete equality with Moscow. The Soviets agreed to abandon their base at Port Arthur and to give up Soviet mineral concessions in Sinkiang and other economic rights. The Soviets did keep their hold on Outer Mongolia.

In my appraisal of the accords, I saw two possible sources of continued Soviet influence that would question whether the Soviets had extended more than formal equality to Mao Tse-tung. Soviet economic assistance gave Moscow an important instrument to put pressure on the Chinese government. The other source of influence was the Communist Party. I concluded my dispatch with this explanation:

> These agreements, which deal with strictly governmental matters, do not of course touch the problem of the relationship of the Communist Party of the Soviet Union and the Chinese Communist Party, which in the eyes of Soviet leaders may be a more secure mechanism for the safeguarding of Soviet interests and for influencing Chinese policies for more open governmental channels. As in the case of European satellites it is apparently the present policy of the Kremlin to exert its influence

(and, in the case of East European satellites, control) more through the disguised channels of party relationship rather than the more overt Stalinish methods of domination. Whether this applies or is indeed possible in case of Communist China is an open question but may well figure in long-term plans of the Kremlin.

That comment withstood the test of time. One of the principal aims of the Chinese cultural revolution in the late 1960s was to root out Soviet influence from the Chinese Communist Party, although I doubt that the Soviets ever controlled the Chinese Party or any significant elements in it.

On a number of occasions, I informed the State Department that the stiffest test of collective leadership might come over the Allies' plan to arm West Germany. My theory was that all Russians would agree that every effort should be made to defeat these plans—the memory of the Nazi invasion had not dimmed—but significant differences might develop over what to do if a West German army was created. Moscow pressure helped bring about the defeat in the French National Assembly on August 30 of the European Defense Community, under which West German troops would have been mixed with those of other countries. But in October, after conferences in London and Paris, West Germany became a full partner in NATO, with a 500,000-man army envisaged for the Bonn government. Moscow responded by convening a conference of Communist-bloc countries, which denounced NATO plans for Germany.

On a visit to Washington in December, I told a somewhat skeptical Dulles that the Kremlin was deeply concerned about the arming of West Germany, and its warning should not be dismissed as mere propaganda. The Soviet Union was sure to take countermeasures. Unconvinced, Dulles asked me to study the situation again on my return to Moscow. I discussed the question with the Embassy staff and with the diplomatic corps, and on December 17 sent Dulles a telegram forecasting two minimum countermeasures the Soviet Union would take: "Consolidation of the Eastern European military system with the open creation of some form of centralized staff and command, probably along lines of the NATO organization, and an increase in Soviet bloc military expenditures."

I was not opposed to the rearming of West Germany. I realized that the East German paramilitary forces existed, and that West Germany could not stand as a vacuum in central Europe. I would have proceeded more slowly, however, in the arming of West Germany.

The Warsaw Pact, which formalized the existing military alliance of Eastern European states, including East Germany, was signed the next year. The prospect of spending more for defense intensified divisions in the Kremlin. In late December, *Pravda*, the Communist Party newspaper, and *Izvestia*, the government daily, offered conflicting views, a rare occurrence, on the Soviet economy. In various articles, *Pravda* took the traditional Bolshevik position of giving overriding priority to heavy industry. *Izvestia*, somewhat discreetly, but repeatedly, hinted that more weight should be given light industry, which produces consumer goods.

One of the leading principles of Soviet industrialization had always been the absolute priority of heavy industry, which produces machines and material to build the long-term potential of the country and to make military weapons. The Bolsheviks had always argued that a nation dependent on other countries for the output of heavy industry was in effect in colonial tutelage, if not servitude. Whereas most capitalist countries began their industrial development by concentrating on light industries with an immediate market, particularly textiles, the Soviet Union concentrated its main effort on such heavy industries as steel, iron, electricity, and oil. The dispute on allocation of resources had little implication on Soviet foreign policy in the short run, except to reveal worry about Germany. There was an important theoretical implication for the long haul. In theory, concentration on heavy industry meant development of Soviet military might, thus enabling Moscow to carry greater clout in international affairs. Concentration on consumer goods would mean in theory devoting more effort to the well-being of the Soviet citizen. In actual fact, the differences between the two schools were never great enough to have much impact on foreign policy, but the implications for the people, in symbolizing a goal of improving the standard of living, were great.

The difference in emphasis between the two papers did not last long. By the first week in January, 1955, *Izvestia* had fallen into line on the heavy-industry side. My interest was not in Soviet journalism but in the debate that was obviously going on among the leaders. For example, Khrushchev had spoken the preceding September of "all around expansion of production of consumer goods and of maximum satisfaction of the growing needs of workers." By December, after plans to rearm West Germany were announced, he shifted to emphasis on development of heavy industry. As for Malenkov, one of the original supporters of more consumer goods, he had been strangely silent, not making a major speech in months. On January 7, Malenkov and Khrushchev appeared at a meeting of Komsomol, the Soviet youth organization. Only Khrushchev spoke, and he made some patronizing references to Malenkov, who, apparently in deference to the victors in the dispute, wore his Party uniform instead of the business suit he had worn in most public appearances. Most newspapers printed pictures of Malenkov staring straight ahead, with others on the platform turning their heads toward Khrushchev.

With these clues (how fragile are the straws at which an ambassador in Moscow grasps!), I was not completely surprised on February 8 when, from my seat in the diplomatic box in the Palace of Soviets, I heard the President of the Council of Union, Volkov, read a statement by Malenkov to the Supreme Soviet saying that he had submitted a "request" to step down as Premier, conceding that he lacked experience "in local work" and in administration of economy. While the statement was being read, Malenkov sat on the platform, chatting amiably with Bulganin and Kaganovich. A few hours later, Khrushchev nominated, and the Council of Ministers quickly approved, the aging Bulganin for the premiership.

The fact that Malenkov had not abjectly groveled in resigning and that he had been merely demoted, not executed, was surprising to those who still viewed the Soviet Union in Stalinist terms.*

In assessing the change, I again warned Washington against the theory of a personal power struggle and also against any tendency to interpret the switch as a failure of the Soviet system. While Dulles circulated my assessment, he appended a caution in a cable to Embassies on February 12 that he "would not discount the possibility that personal power rivalries may have played a somewhat greater role" than I thought. Dulles agreed that the Soviet system "still works," but he warned, without elaboration, that it was, if anything, more dangerous to the free world.

On February 18, in summarizing the significance of Malenkov's downfall, I hammered away at the dangers of too great an acceptance of the simple thesis that a struggle for personal power dominated the Kremlin. There was no evidence to support the theory that Khrushchev alone had engineered Malenkov's demotion. I cabled Dulles:

> In the last analysis it is policies pursued or contemplated by this regime which are of primary interest to the free world and whether or not comrade X or Y is up or down is relatively unimportant. Personalities are significant to the extent that they reflect or embody policies;

---

* Khrushchev expressed a different view. A year after Malenkov's ouster, he told me, "Why Georgi Maximilianovich is one of my closest friends."

and only in event of an internecine struggle of such dimensions as to imperil the stability of the Soviet Union would this factor in itself become vital.

As for the specific reason for Malenkov's ouster, everything indicated that it was the dispute over industrial priorities, triggered by the West's decision to arm West Germany. Power factors became decisive once the issue was joined. The reason that Khrushchev had superior power was his ability to enlist support for his views, particularly in the Party. Like Stalin, Khrushchev found the Party secretaryship invaluable. Malenkov just could not swing the Presidium behind him.

We had a report from Ralph Parker, the London *Worker* correspondent, that Molotov had been a principal critic of Malenkov's emphasis on consumer goods, charging malapportionment of raw materials and skilled technicians. According to Parker, Malenkov had lost his temper and refused to accept criticism at a meeting of the Presidium. In his anger, he walked out of the meeting. As a result, the Presidium, which had planned only to rectify Malenkov's mistakes and keep him in the premiership for the sake of unity, decided to oust him. We did not consider Parker a particularly trustworthy source, although we were sure he had some KGB connections and a Russian wife. We doubted that the story was true.

I had first met Malenkov at Kremlin banquets during the war, but never had an opportunity to talk with him. He always seemed to be standing impassively in the background. At that time, he looked like a mechanical man, the most sinister Stalinist prototype, with a gloomy, round, almost sadistic face, a shock of black hair across his forehead, a dumpy, corpulent figure, and a reputation as an evil figure in the purges of the 1930s. He was in charge of the Party records, which provided most of the material against victims who were members. Malenkov's exact role has not been disclosed, but by implication he was charged with collusion in the purges by Khrushchev in his secret speech to the Twentieth Party Congress in 1956. Of course, all of Stalin's associates, including Khrushchev, were involved in the purges. It was inescapable.

As ambassador, I received a favorable impression of Malenkov when I met him at Kremlin receptions. His face became quite expressive when he talked. A ready smile, eyes with a hint of laughter, and freckles across his nose gave him a pleasant appearance. He also stood out from other Soviet leaders of the period in that he did not drink —at least, I never saw him take even one drink of hard liquor at receptions I attended. He spoke the best Russian of any Soviet leader I have heard. It was a delight to hear his delivery. Malenkov's speeches were well constructed and logical in their development. His presentation was made in a clear, fairly high voice, and his accent reflected an educated man. More important, Malenkov impressed me as a man with a more Western-oriented mind than other Soviet leaders. He at least seemed to perceive our position and, while he did not agree with it, I felt he understood it. With other leaders, particularly Khrushchev, there was no meeting point, no common language. Like trains on parallel tracks, we went right by each other.

In a long conversation with me at a Kremlin reception on November 8, 1954, Malenkov pointed out the important role of diplomats in accurately reporting the real sentiments of the governments to which they were accredited, and expressed the hope that the British Ambassador and I understood the sincere desire of the Soviet people and government for peace. Taking advantage of the opening, I made two points. The first was the isolation in which ambassadors in Moscow were forced to operate. We almost never had opportunities for long discussions with important officials. In other capitals, I said, there were innumerable informal contacts at which views could be exchanged. My second point was the lack of accurate reporting in the Soviet press regarding the United States. In regard to contacts with Soviet officials, Malenkov replied that "we are trying to create conditions which will improve the situation." As for Soviet newspapers, he said that "foreigners frequently think that leaders of the Soviet government have nothing better to do than dictate every item in the Soviet press."

I was impressed by Malenkov's avoidance of clichés—such as "Wall Street imperialists"—which to this day are commonly uttered by Soviet officials. As I told Dulles in a telegram, Malenkov "made an impression of a man of great determination and ruthlessness, but with a more subtle and highly developed intelligence than his associates."

At the same reception, Khrushchev and French Ambassador Louis Joxe were arguing about NATO. Khrushchev became quite emotional and finally threw his hands in the air and said, "There is nothing to be done." Malenkov quietly commented, "There is always something to be done." I found it hard to believe that he could not brook criticism and that he had walked out of a meeting of the Presidium for that reason.*

---

* I was interested to learn in 1967 at a dinner with Stalin's daughter, Svetlana, in Princeton, that she regarded Malenkov as one of the ablest and most humane of her father's associates.

Ambassador and Mrs. Bohlen with their three children, Charles, Celestine, and Avis, at Villa Nova, Pennsylvania, in 1953, before leaving for Moscow.

New York Herald Tribune

The new Ambassador presents his credentials at the Kremlin. On Bohlen's left are President Voroshilov and Deputy Foreign Minister Pushkin; on his right is Presidium Secretary Pegov.

A friendly chat with Bulganin at "spirit of Geneva" picnic near Moscow in 1955.

Molotov, Malenkov, Peruvkin, Khrushchev, Shepilov, and Bulganin chat with Ambassador Bohlen at July 4 reception at Spaso House, 1956.

Porgy and Bess troupe receives Ambassador's thanks, Leningrad, 1956.

Sovfoto

The Ambassador in his office in the Embassy, Moscow, 1956.

The author in a contemplative mood.

On way from Moscow to new post in Manila, Bohlen calls
on President Eisenhower, 1957.

White House

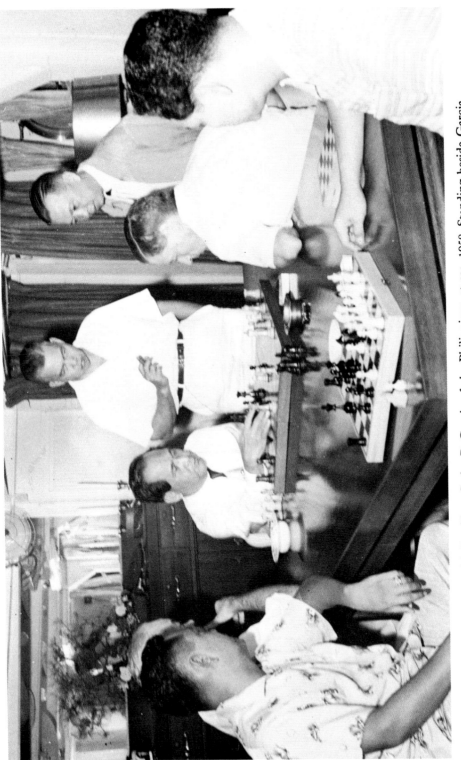

A game of chess with President Carlos P. Garcia of the Philippines, at sea, 1958. Standing beside Garcia, General Vargas, who later became Secretary-General of SEATO.

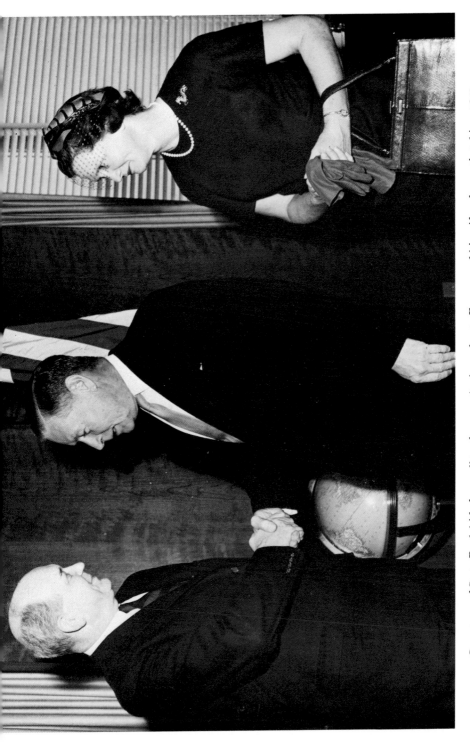

Secretary of State Rusk bids farewell to the new Ambassador to France and his wife, after oath-taking, 1962.

Department of State Photograph

President de Gaulle and Foreign Minister Couve de Murville receive the new
Ambassador.

Hubert Humphrey, accompanied by Ambassador Bohlen, calls on de Gaulle.

A la Chasse Présidentielle, Rambouillet, 1963.

Vice-President Johnson, off for Berlin, at airport with General Clay, George Ball of State Department, West German Ambassador Grewe, and Bohlen.

President Kennedy and Ambassador Bohlen after cruise at Palm Beach, Florida, 1963.

Conferring with President Johnson in White House, 1967.

With President and Mrs. Nixon at White House dinner, 1969. Back row: Mrs. Llewellyn Thompson, Ambassador Thompson, Ambassador Robert Murphy's daughter, Ambassador Murphy. Second row: Mrs. Bohlen, Ambassador Bohlen, Mrs. Bruce, Ambassador Bruce.

White House

Ambassador and Mrs. Bohlen in France.

There was a rumor, never confirmed, that Malenkov was really a Volga German, and that his family name was Klein, which had been changed to Malenkov (both names mean "little"). He certainly had traits of character and disposition that seemed un-Russian, even though he was born in the southern Ural city of Orenburg.

Looking back, I believe I was remiss at the time of Stalin's death in not recommending that Eisenhower take up Churchill's call for a "meeting at the summit"—the first time this phrase was used—with Malenkov. Dulles batted down the idea. I was not asked for an opinion and doubt that I would have been listened to if I had expressed one at that time. Dulles had told the senators he did not want me as an adviser. But I think I made a mistake in not taking the initiative and recommending such a meeting.

After the death of Stalin, there might have been opportunities for an adjustment of some of the outstanding questions, particularly regarding Germany. In addition to the extraordinary act of *Pravda*'s publishing the text of a speech by President Eisenhower calling for peace, the Soviet press let up on its hysterical Hate America campaign. May Day slogans—a clue to the Bolshevik line of thinking—showed a striking contrast to those published for the anniversary of the Bolshevik Revolution the preceding November, when Stalin was still living. Instead of "down with the warmongers" and references to "imperialist aggressors" and "foreign usurpers," there were expressions of confidence in the ability to resolve all differences between nations. Soon after his assumption of power, Malenkov himself said in a statement that there were no issues that could not be negotiated. Khrushchev subsequently charged that Malenkov and Beria had been contemplating a change in Soviet policy on Germany, possibly relinquishing the hold on East Germany and permitting some form of unification in return for a demilitarized, neutralized Germany. Khrushchev, as he often did, was undoubtedly stretching the truth. I doubt if any Soviet leader ever seriously contemplated giving up the Sovietized area of Germany. But there might have been room for some other accommodation.

It has always been a mystery to me why, in the weeks immediately following Stalin's death, Malenkov chose to take the government position of Premier rather than the more powerful position of First Secretary of the Party. In all probability, the other leaders refused to let Malenkov have the most powerful job. He may well have been forced to choose between a Party and a government job, or conceivably he had no choice at all. On the other hand, Malenkov, as Stalin's putative successor, might have had the power to choose the Party position. All indications were that Malenkov, Molotov, and Beria were close at the time. It may well be that Malenkov envisaged the growth of the government apparatus at the expense of the Party. Gossip in Moscow had it that one of the causes of his downfall was his attempt to place the government bureaucracy in key positions at the expense of the Party bureaucracy. It was even alleged that this had been the basis of a violent assault on Malenkov by Molotov in the Presidium. I cannot believe, however, that Malenkov freely chose the government position, since no one in the hierarchy could possibly fail to understand that power remained in the Party.

When Malenkov lost the premiership, he retained his Party position but fell low in the hierarchy. It was not until 1957 that he was removed from the Presidium and eventually from the Party. After that, he was said to have been assigned as manager of a hydroelectric plant in Kazakhstan.

With Malenkov's downfall, Khrushchev emerged as the most powerful single individual in the regime. I was worried. The man whom I once described to Dulles as "not especially bright" had used harsh language in discussing the United States. I feared the Soviet Union would adopt a more belligerent foreign policy. Over the next few months, I was pleasantly surprised.

CHAPTER TWENTY-ONE

Coexistence, East and West

In the spring of 1955, my wife and I decided to take a trip to a part of the Soviet Union we had never visited, Georgia and Central Asia. There was a personal reason. We had long heard of the spectacular mountain scenery of Georgia, of Persian ruins in Baku, of Tamerlane artifacts in Tashkent, of the fortresslike desert city of Bokhara, of bustling, modern Alma-Ata. There was also a professional motivation. We wanted to see the Virgin Lands, as they were called, where crops were being planted for the first time in an attempt to increase Soviet food production. The success of this program was vital to the new leaders, and I was eager to see the area at first hand. While I wanted to meet and talk freely with the Russian people, as an ambassador should, I was not under any illusion that I would have the opportunity. There had been some thaw in American-Soviet relations, and travel permits were granted more readily, but there was no indication that I would have uninhibited exchanges with individual Russians.

By April, all the preparations had been made, the itinerary set, hotel rooms reserved, airline tickets ordered. There was nothing more to do except pick up the plane tickets, which, in Russia, are never delivered until a few hours before the flight. With our departure for Tiflis scheduled for 2 A.M. on April 19, Frank Siscoe, a young Embassy Second Secretary, who, with his wife, was accompanying us, went to the ticket office late in the afternoon of the day before. There he was told that he could not get the tickets. Contradictory reasons were given—because the plane was filled, and because the flight had been canceled. I immediately telephoned the Foreign Office, but I could not raise any responsible official.

Early the next morning, I received a message from Molotov asking me to go to the Kremlin to see him. I was naturally somewhat irritated when I entered his office. But Molotov greeted me with a rare warm smile and said he had some news. The Soviet government had decided, in return for economic concessions, to abandon the right to reintroduce troops into Austria once a peace treaty was signed. Because Soviet insistence on the reintroduction of troops had been the big sticking point to concluding a treaty, the change cleared the way for quick action.

I had no reason to know it at the time, but Molotov's notification to me about Austria was the first concrete step toward the Khrushchev policy of coexistence, which would lead rather soon to the downfall of Stalin's old crony. Molotov, of course, gave no indication that the concession on Austria would be followed by overtures toward West Germany, Yugoslavia, and the United States.

Molotov said that he was afraid that he had delayed my trip to Central Asia. I complained that the abrupt cancellation, without notification, was a curious way to treat an ambassador. Molotov waved off my remark and said a twenty-four-hour delay would make no difference, and stressed that everything would go smoothly on the trip. He indicated that he had wanted to convey the news on Austria directly to an ambassador, and, since the British and French envoys were away from Moscow, he had taken the liberty of holding me over for twenty-four hours. His attachment to strict protocol made it difficult for me to be angry with him, and I forgot my irritation. Actually, the delay produced a dividend. At every place we stopped on the trip, no matter how small or at what hour of the night, a representative of the local Soviet would greet us at the airport. In Baku, a lady presented herself about ten o'clock one night and said that she had been ordered by Moscow to greet us. "I greet you," she said, and left.

We were soaking up the sights of the ancient cities of Central Asia when Dulles sent a wire asking me to cut the trip short and accompany him to Vienna for the signing of the Austrian treaty.

To this day, no outsider knows for certain why the Soviet Union shifted its position on Austria. I came to a conclusion that differed from the one commonly held in Western capitals, that the Soviets were trying to block West German armament. It was my opinion that they realized that the armament of West Germany could not be stopped. But they thought they might stop the inclusion of the three Western zones of occupation of Austria in the NATO setup. If I was right, the Soviets would concentrate on trying to get Austrian Chancellor Raab, and later the three Western powers, to agree to the neutralization of the country. There would be no serious problem in the

West in accepting neutrality as long as the Soviets did not hold the right to put troops back into Austria. The key point, I wrote Dulles, was that Austria herself, and no one else, should determine when her independence was threatened. Otherwise, the Soviets could use the pretext that Austria was being threatened by another country to send in troops.

I believe that the Kremlin leaders, and probably the Soviet military chiefs, decided that a genuinely neutral Austria was of more value to Soviet Russia than the maintenance of a divided country where the Red Army would occupy only the poorer half. The Soviet position in Austria was not strong, in part because the occupation zone had never been Sovietized, in part because the zone was so poor.

The talks with Raab in Moscow proceeded smoothly. In Washington, however, Dulles's suspicions were aroused by Molotov's request for quick action. He fired off a telegram to me saying that the West should not be "stampeded" into a premature peace conference and proposing a preliminary meeting of ambassadors. I replied that a delay by the United States would create the impression throughout the world that we were dragging our feet on a legitimate offer of a treaty, and suggested that we at least set a date as a goal for the signing. Dulles had his way, but there was little or no delay, and the Austrians received their independence.

In my comments to the State Department after the Austrian treaty was signed, I again expressed doubt that the Soviets would try to tempt West Germany into abandoning the NATO plan in return for an Austrian-like pledge of neutrality. I wrote:

> The Austrian and German questions are not comparable not only because of the difference in size and importance of the two countries but also because of the central fact that dismantlement or downfall of the Sovietized system is not involved in the Austrian withdrawal.
>
> I am convinced that the Soviets realize that the only sure method of preventing West German rearmament or any hope of neutralizing Germany along the Austrian model involves the sacrifice of the Soviet system in East Germany....
>
> At the present moment indications are that they still adhere to their determination to hold on to East Germany, in which case I believe we can anticipate Soviet feelers in the direction of the Bonn Governent with view to establishment of relations in return for recognition of the German Democratic Republic.

I also pointed out that if the Soviet Union went ahead with the Warsaw Pact and armed East Germany as part of the organization, this would be a clear indication that the Soviet Union, for the foreseeable future, was accepting the division of Germany as a definite fact and was not contemplating a radical revision in its German policy.

Three weeks after the Austrian peace treaty was signed, the Soviet Union invited Chancellor Konrad Adenauer of West Germany to Moscow to discuss the establishment of diplomatic and trade relations. East Germany was included in the Warsaw Pact military organization which was set up later in the year. All pretense of hope for the unification of Germany was abandoned.

Moving swiftly, Khrushchev and Bulganin next sought to rectify one of Stalin's greatest errors—the excommunication of Marshal Tito of Yugoslavia from the Communist camp because of his insistence on deviation from Bolshevik ideology. The announcement that a Soviet delegation, headed by Khrushchev and including Bulganin and Mikoyan, was going to Belgrade was not surprising. There had been hints for months in the Moscow press. At the time of the visit, in late May and early June of 1955, the Soviet leadership had not decided to reveal Stalin's crimes, so Khrushchev, in a speech at the Belgrade airport, blamed Beria and other "contemptible agents of imperialism" for the break with Tito. The Marshal must have listened to the lie in amazement. He knew full well that Stalin had not only dictated the policy but had also used every form of pressure short of invasion to bring down the regime. The fence-mending Russian also had the temerity to urge Comrade Tito, the ex-heretic, to agree on Marxist-Leninist ideology with the Russians. The result was a chilly reception for the Moscow delegation. Compounding the error at the airport, Khrushchev played the boor—wrestling with Mikoyan and getting drunk at a reception. When the visit was over, it was clear that Khrushchev had failed to bring Tito back to the fold. The joint declaration was a government-to-government document containing no reference to a common ideological viewpoint. Even with this concession, the Yugoslav Communist Party refused to join the circuit of satellites which took orders from Moscow. Khrushchev did, however, put state-to-state relations on a better basis. And the confession of error, although masked, was the sharpest public repudiation of Stalinist policy up to that time.

Looking forward, I was curious about the possible impact on Eastern Europe of the Khrushchev confession of error and indirect endorsement of Tito's independent position. In a commentary on June 3, I wrote Washington:

It will be extremely interesting to see the effect on the satellites of the Soviet admission that "questions of internal structure, difference of social system and difference of concrete forms of development of socialism are exclusively the matter of the peoples of the individual countries." Taken at its face value, this involves an official and public statement by the Soviet Government of the right of the satellite countries of Eastern Europe to follow the path of internal developments dictated by their national interest (always, of course, within the framework of socialism) and not as dictated by Moscow. . . . It is entirely possible that the Soviets are motivated by a desire to lay a foundation for new relations with Eastern European satellites, for which the deal with Tito was an essential step. It is probably clear to the men in the Kremlin that any liberalization of relations with satellites would be extremely dangerous as long as the Yugoslavs were in a defiant or even a distant relationship with the Soviet Union, but less so if the breach had been healed with Tito. Relations with Communist China may have been another factor. With the establishment of Yugoslav-Chinese relations last fall, it is probable that the Kremlin feared a rapprochement between these two Communist countries and the eventual creation of a rival Communist center with resultant effect on Asian neutrals such as India. If these considerations were operative in the Soviet decision to go to Belgrade, results there, while certainly a victory for Yugoslavia, may not be regarded here as a comparable defeat for the Soviets. If the Soviets make a serious attempt to live up to the undertakings contained in this declaration and do not seek merely to utilize its provisions as a trick in order to re-establish some form of control over Yugoslavia, Yugoslavia and the Soviet Union should draw closer and closer together as time progresses. It may be, therefore, that results of the Belgrade talks may mark the beginning of a new phase in Soviet relations with other Communist states and in particular those of the Eastern European satellites.

Undiscouraged by the lack of success in Yugoslavia, the new team of Khrushchev and Bulganin turned their attention to the giant of the non-Soviet world, the United States. Despite Dulles's reluctance, a summit meeting of the leaders of the Big Four powers had been scheduled for June in Geneva. There was no question that the new leaders were interested in better relations with the United States. In a half-hour private conversation with me at a Kremlin reception for the Austrians on April 13, Bulganin had developed the theme that the future of the world in great measure depended on relations between the two great powers and that minor matters had been allowed to create serious differences. I replied that general statements of this nature were unassailable, adding that we should recognize that there were complicated problems in the international situation that inevitably affected relations between our two countries. These matters also concerned the vital interests of other nations. He then asked me what I considered the most serious question in the world today, and I told him that I considered the Chinese threat to Formosa potentially the most dangerous. President Eisenhower and Secretary of State Dulles had made our position quite clear, but we did not know what China was planning to do. Bulganin said he did not consider the Far East the most important question. The absence of any common language between the United States and the Soviet Union was more basic, he said. I repeated to him what I said on November 7 to Malenkov, that the absence of any regular contacts in Moscow between the foreign ambassadors and Soviet leaders made it difficult for anybody to understand clearly the exact motivation and purposes of the Soviet government. Bulganin agreed, and said that he intended to take up this matter with Molotov.

Bulganin did not mention a summit conference, but later the Soviets did make the suggestion. Dulles brought up the question in Paris in May, at a meeting of the members of his staff who were going to attend the signing of the Austrian treaty. At the prodding of Sir Anthony Eden, who had recently become Prime Minister, and Premier Edgar Faure of France, and in the face of Eisenhower's willingness to attend, Dulles became reconciled to a meeting of the four leaders. I was generally in favor of such a conference, even though I doubted whether any important agreements would be reached, but any contacts with the Soviets were better than close to total secrecy. While they would not be candid, nevertheless we could get a valuable insight into their thinking. Furthermore, I did not share Dulles's view that the spectacle of Eisenhower shaking hands with Khrushchev would destroy the moral image of the United States, have a bad effect domestically, and tend to weaken the Allies' will to stand up to Communism. I felt that the shoe was on the other foot. The Communist system, being a closed society, was much less able to withstand the impact of a spirit of détente in regular diplomatic contact between the countries.

Moreover, in the summer of 1955, there seemed to be a good basis for the meeting. The Austrian peace treaty had been signed. German rearmament had been reluctantly accepted in Moscow. The fighting in Korea was over. Free from the pressures of immediate crises, leaders of the two camps could sit down and explore the possibilities of better relations.

Plans for the summit were briefly discussed in San Francisco during the celebration of the tenth anniversary of the establishment of the United Nations. At a dinner given by Dulles, Antoine Pinay, the French Foreign Minister, was infuriated by Molotov's unwillingness to talk about any details of the meeting—the organization or the agenda. To those of us who had had more experience with the Soviets, the reason was plain. Molotov had no instructions from Moscow. The Presidium had not addressed itself to the subject, and he was not going to say anything that might compromise the Soviet Union in the future. This attitude was incomprehensible to Pinay, who burst out, "Do you mean to say that you, the Foreign Minister of one of the greatest countries in the world, aren't able to discuss any details of this conference?" Molotov smiled and maintained his evasive position. Later in the evening, Molotov said to me with one of his icy smiles, "It is apparent that our French friend has not had much experience in dealing with the Soviet Union."

Though Molotov was still Foreign Minister, it was evident that he was on the way out. In March, the Soviet press had published a fairly straightforward account of a Tito attack on Molotov, generating speculation that the old warrior had fallen on bad times. The rumors increased after Khrushchev and his entourage, without Molotov, went to Belgrade. It is fairly well authenticated that Molotov, one of the principal architects of Stalin's campaign to depose Tito, opposed the reconciliation. In a telegram to the State Department, I cautioned that the speculation of Molotov's removal might be premature. It was. He kept the title of Foreign Minister for another year, but he did not have the same influence after the spring of 1955, and was eventually denounced as a murderer by Khrushchev.

In my decades of dealing with Molotov, I came to have a certain grudging admiration for this solid, square character. Emotion, either of pleasure or of anger, seldom altered the impassiveness of his pasty white face with its small black mustache. Under tension, he would stutter, but I rarely heard him do so. At a party in the Waldorf Astoria Hotel in 1946, in celebration of the completion of treaties with the Eastern European countries, Molotov did not know what to do when a merry Ernie Bevin linked arms with him and Byrnes and began to sing "Sweet Molly Malone." Knowing he looked awkward, but not wanting to break away, Molotov wore a silly smile and moved his lips slightly, as if joining in the song. He seldom tried to be funny, and when he did the result was usually elephantine—as when he tried to kid Marshall about saluting a Secretary of State.

There are those who say that passion was not absent in the man Churchill described as carved from a slab of cold Siberian granite. I do not know for certain the details of his visit to Harlem in June, 1942, under the pseudonym of "Mr. Brown." I believe he went there, not for pleasure, as gossips say, but to observe, as a Marxian sociologist, the decadence of capitalism. Little is known now about his private life. He accepted the arrest and exile of his wife, who was Jewish, in 1949. Like most Bolsheviks, he never talked about his family or personal life. He stuck to business. He was not a heavy drinker; I saw him drunk only once, in 1943, at the November 7 reception in Moscow.

Suspicious by nature and by Stalinist training, he took no chances. Wherever he went, abroad or in the Soviet Union, two or three guards accompanied him. At Chequers, the British Prime Minister's home, and at Blair House, the President's mansion for distinguished visitors, he slept with a loaded revolver by his head. In 1940, when he dined at the Italian Embassy, a Russian appeared in the kitchen of the Embassy to taste the food.

Molotov was the perfect assistant to Stalin. He was not more than five feet four inches tall, fitting the pattern of associates who would not physically dominate the dictator. Molotov was also a fine bureaucrat. Methodical in his procedures, he was usually thoroughly prepared to argue his case. He would carry out his orders no matter how ridiculous he might appear to other Foreign Ministers. On that day in Paris when he held up an agreement because he had slipped up on rules of procedure, I heard him repeat on and off for four hours the same sentence, "The Soviet delegation will not permit this conference to become a rubber stamp," and remain impervious to every approach from Byrnes and Bevin.

In the sense that he relentlessly pursued his objective, he was a skillful diplomat. He never initiated policy on his own, as Hitler found out at their famous meeting. Stalin made policy; Molotov executed it. He was an opportunist, but only within the framework of his instructions. He plowed along like a tractor. I never saw him pull off any delicate maneuver; it was his stubbornness that made him effective.

It was never possible to tell Stalin's real attitude toward any of his associates, but most of the time Molotov was visibly subservient to his master. After Stalin's death, Molotov adopted a new style, not hesitating to express differences of opinion with Malenkov or Khrushchev, or to interrupt their conversation to express an opinion. He even loosened up a bit. When I mentioned that I had seen pictures of Khrushchev sitting on an elephant in India, Molotov commented, "Yes, an elephant getting on an elephant."

Despite all the times he irritated me, I felt some admiration for Molotov. He was a genuine Marxist-Leninist—the "iron behind," as Lenin called him. He was an old Bolshevik in the truest sense of the word, believing in the basic verities of Marxian theory. He believed that the working class was essentially a revolutionary body. He believed that class warfare was the guiding principle of history. He believed in the inevitable triumph of Communism over capitalism. These beliefs stuck out in almost all his conversations. His downfall resulted from his conviction that Khrushchev was a dangerous revisionist.

All in all, I respected Molotov as a man who did what he believed in and believed in what he did. I was a little sorry to see the sour little man vanishing from the world stage. But times were changing, and before us was the first summit meeting since Potsdam.

I attended the Geneva Conference of 1955 simply because I was ambassador to the Soviet Union. I was not on intimate terms with any members of the administration, and in view of my association with Yalta, Dulles certainly did not want me in the foreground at Geneva. McCarthyism had finally abated, but its effects lingered on. President Eisenhower even felt it necessary to assure the country publicly that he would make no secret deals.

Despite the fact that I was on the outside looking in, I felt duty bound to send Dulles my views of what the Soviets might do at Geneva. In a 1,200-word dispatch from Moscow on June 12, 1955, I said that the changing direction of Soviet policy was an attempt to administer a dictatorship without a dictator and an empire (at least in Europe) without an emperor. Pointing out once again the two preoccupations of Soviet foreign policy—the retention of the satellites and avoidance of war—I noted a change in the Kremlin leaders' desire for a relaxation of tensions. In the period following Stalin's death, they were conciliatory because they feared that the international situation would automatically evolve in the direction of war. This fear had been replaced by a concern over the strain placed on the Soviet economy by the arms race.

I went on to say that because of the limitations imposed by collective leadership, which reduced the freedom of Khrushchev and Bulganin to negotiate, as well as the typically suspicious nature of the Bolsheviks, the Soviets would not be willing to accept adequate inspection machinery for the policing of an atomic arms reduction agreement. Nevertheless, there might be a more serious basis for discussion of arms limitations than existed before. The other main subject the Soviets would bring up at Geneva, I said, would be an all-European security treaty designed to dismantle NATO. Minor questions such as cultural exchanges would also be on the agenda.

As for a Dulles plan to raise the question of Soviet control of the satellites, I said it was reasonably certain that the Soviets would refuse categorically to discuss any measure affecting the internal security in these countries. The Soviets would, however, attempt to talk about Formosa, and would sidestep the question of the unification of Germany. In conclusion, I said:

> Judging from here, the Western powers go into the conference with a great advantage on their side, faced with an adversary considerably less sure of himself than in the past. It does not, however, follow that we should anticipate that the Soviets will be prepared at Geneva to make a series of concessions or will reflect in the negotiations, elements of weakness or indecision. Indeed, these present advantages of the West can be dissipated if they are stressed publicly or acted on too overtly since the Soviets, like all dictatorships, are mortally afraid of showing weakness or of appearing to yield to foreign pressure.

This memorandum was practically the only contribution I made to the Geneva Conference, except for a few informal interpreting assignments.

Bulganin, as Premier, was the titular head of the Russian delegation to Geneva. In formal sessions, he did all the speaking for the Soviet Union, but Khrushchev was the dominant Soviet figure. He did not hesitate to interrupt Bulganin in private conversations, and took over completely at dinners and receptions. There was never any indication of resentment by Bulganin of Khrushchev's leading role or his boorish peasant humor.

Before the American dinner for the Soviet leaders, Mrs. Eisenhower, Bulganin, Khrushchev, and I were standing on the terrace of the President's villa, admiring the view of the lake. Through me, a Filipino mess boy asked Bulganin what he would have to drink. Bulganin said that although he hardly ever touched vodka, he would, on this festive occasion, have a drink. As I passed the request on to the waiter, Khrushchev interrupted with a mean grin to say, "Please translate for Mrs. Eisenhower," and told the following story, in approximately these words: "There was a member of the Communist Party whom, as General Secretary, I had to discipline a little while ago. This man, who was an excellent engineer, nevertheless unfortunately had a strong propensity for drink, and reports kept reaching us that he was often drunk while on the job. I finally called him in and gave him a formal warning, pointing out that the Party could not tolerate such behavior even though he was an excellent engineer. The man swore repentence and renounced the use of alcohol, or so I thought. About a month or so later, I kept hearing reports that this man had not stopped drinking at all, and I called him in again and was much more stern with him. He protested his innocence. He said, 'I swear to you, Comrade Khrushchev, that I have not drunk any vodka since you spoke to me. I stick exclusively to cognac.'" Khrushchev paused, then added impishly, "That reminds me of Bulganin."

Bulganin, who was known to be a heavy drinker, maintained the benign air of a chaplain, and said nothing. Mrs. Eisenhower laughed politely. I was reminded of Stalin's method of denigrating his associates in public. The incident also demonstrated Khrushchev's personal power. While still not the sole master of the Kremlin, he was able with impunity to humiliate the Premier of his country. Actually, foreigners never thought Bulganin had any outstanding ability. At the time of the Geneva Conference, he was a front man for Khrushchev. Two years later, he was involved in the anti-Khrushchev opposition and gradually faded from view.

On the whole, the Soviets were on their good behavior at the conference. They avoided polemic propaganda and in their personal contacts were courteous and quiet. Khrushchev and Bulganin were impressed by the fact that they were meeting the leaders of the Western countries in solemn conclave. Learning a lesson from his Yugoslav tour, Khrushchev drank very little.

The Geneva Conference was unlike the wartime meetings, where the leaders gathered around a table and worked out agreements. Geneva was much more formal, with each side making speeches and issuing statements. Under such circumstances, it was hardly surprising that no important decisions were made. The conference ran true to my predictions. The Soviets pushed their atomic disarmament plan and European security treaty. The former foundered over inspection procedures, the latter over Western unwillingness to halt West German armament.

There was a brief period of optimism in the American delegation when a committee of Dulles, Molotov, Macmillan, and Pinay hammered out what we thought was an agreement setting the stage for general elections that would lead to the unification of Germany. When the draft was submitted to the general conference, however, Bulganin put a different interpretation on the document, repudiating what Molotov had agreed to less than an hour before. So complete was the turnaround that Eisenhower seriously considered breaking off the conference and issuing a strong statement to the press on the duplicity of the Soviets. On further thought, he realized that the onus would fall on the United States, and, since there was sufficient ambiguity in the document, it was possible that more might come out of it than Bulganin had indicated. Nothing more did come of it.

Eisenhower did score a public-relations victory with his surprise "open skies" proposal. This plan called for the United States and the Soviet Union to exchange blueprints of their military establishments and maps to permit aerial surveillance of each other's defenses. The idea was to provide each side with assurance against preparations for an attack. From my experience, I was sure that the Soviets would never tolerate any eyes prying into their secrets. Above all, they did not want to show how weak they were militarily. Furthermore, they had little to gain, because the location of our bases is printed on commercial maps available to anyone. The United States, on the other hand, had much to learn about the Soviet Union, where secrecy is a fetish.

The initial reaction of the Soviets to the President's proposal was guarded, and no objections were made. At a break in the session, Khrushchev talked to Eisenhower at a small buffet bar. With me interpreting, the Russian said, in his Ukrainian accent, "Mr. President, we do not question the motive with which you put forward this proposal, but in effect whom are you trying to fool? In our eyes, this is a very transparent espionage device, and those advisers of yours who suggested it knew exactly what they were doing. You could hardly expect us to take this seriously." Eisenhower pointed out that since the plan was reciprocal, there was no great disadvantage to the Soviet Union compared with the United States. The President stressed his belief that the problem of disarmament was sufficiently vital to warrant some form of departure from established custom. He hoped that

Khrushchev would not kick the idea out the window. Khrushchev backtracked a little, saying that of course the Soviet government would study it most carefully, but he personally was not a bit sanguine of its being adopted. The Soviets never rejected the proposal formally. It was allowed to die of malnutrition.

The Soviets had brought old soldier Zhukov along, apparently as a gesture of friendship toward Eisenhower. The two lunched privately one day at the President's villa. A Russian interpreter and I were the only other persons present. I had first met Zhukov at the end of the war when Harry Hopkins and I visited Berlin. He looked like a soldier—stocky, sturdy as a Russian oak, a slightly ruddy complexion, and clear blue eyes. Although he had a pleasant smile, he was very reserved, particularly with foreigners. Zhukov was a Bolshevik who undeviatingly followed the Party line, but he was first a Russian patriot. He believed in the independence of the army, and one of the reasons for his eventual downfall was his attempt to throw off the political commissar system. There was a cleanliness of spirit about him that contrasted sharply to the deviousness of other Bolshevik leaders. He conveyed a tolerance, even a respect, for the United States, and there was no doubt in my mind that his affection for General Eisenhower was genuine and not put on for occasions.

The luncheon conversation was mostly personal. The two soldiers reminisced over the war, especially the closing days. Eventually, they did discuss Germany, and Eisenhower told Zhukov the depth of his and the American people's feelings regarding the right of the Germans to be reunited. The President emphasized, however, that reunification did not mean that the Germans had the right to develop policies or armaments that could threaten their neighbors. Had the Soviets agreed to reunification, Eisenhower told Zhukov, there certainly would have been severe restrictions on German military developments. Even without reunification, he said, there were all sorts of controls built into the NATO situation to prevent any outburst of militant German nationalism. Given the new correlation of forces on the Continent, it was almost inconceivable that Germany alone could, as she had in the early 1940s, wage war on two fronts.

Following the Kremlin line, although mildly, Zhukov insisted that there were serious dangers in the Western Allies' plans that would give the Germans liberty of action in many areas. Soviet fears of a revival of German militarism were understandable, in view of the two world wars, but only in a general sense. Russians, especially realists like Zhukov, knew that West Germany could not embark on a military operation without the blessing of the United States. The fear of Germany was an illusion.

At the close of the luncheon, Eisenhower asked Marshal Zhukov what he was going to do for a vacation. Zhukov said he was going to the southwest of European Russia for trout fishing. The two discussed the merits of fishing equipment, and Eisenhower promised to send Zhukov an American rod and reel. About a month after my return to Moscow, the Embassy received through the diplomatic pouch a rod and reel with a letter from General Eisenhower to Marshal Zhukov. The letter was sent unsealed, I presume out of courtesy to the Embassy. It contained nothing more than a friendly greeting and a mention that the rod and reel were being shipped under separate cover, and closed with expressions of warm good will. When Chancellor Adenauer, through the West German intelligence service, got wind of a communication from Eisenhower to Zhukov, he read into it skulduggery and quasi-betrayal. To Adenauer, Eisenhower was engaged in secret talks with the Soviet government, utilizing Marshal Zhukov as the channel. The Chancellor, who faced stiff opposition at home, was apprehensive that Eisenhower would undercut his plans to make West Germany strong and independent, a course he thought would lead to unification of his country. I heard the Adenauer-inspired rumor from several sources and did my best to counteract it. Other American officials who knew the circumstances were equally assiduous. Adenauer never believed the true version and continued to harbor a suspicion of American motives.

In many ways, the Geneva Conference was one of the most disappointing and discouraging of all of the summit meetings. It was evident before we left Geneva that there had been no real progress, even though the ambiguity of the final communiqué made it possible to hold out hope that the Foreign Ministers' meeting in November might pull something out of the bag. The hope was illusory. The Soviets adhered to their interpretation of the Geneva communiqué that there should be no unification of Germany unless "certain fundamental conditions" in regard to the peace of Europe were first met. They never specified what these conditions should be. As a result, the discussion went round and round. The Foreign Ministers' talks were as friendly and unproductive as at Geneva.

The Geneva Conference and the subsequent Foreign Ministers' meeting represented the final effort on the part of the West to reunify

Germany under conditions that would safeguard the rest of Europe from any renewal of German militarism. From that time, the West adhered to a policy of furthering and developing the West German state, and the Soviets built up East Germany. Before the Foreign Ministers' meeting, Adenauer went to Moscow, insisting publicly and privately that the price of establishing diplomatic relations was a Soviet agreement to permit all-German elections and the release of German prisoners of war still held in the Soviet Union. Somewhat arrogantly, he asked me to convey to Washington his belief that "firmness" was essential in dealing with the Kremlin. I was therefore astonished when he buckled and accepted a Soviet offer to release the prisoners in exchange for the establishment of diplomatic relations.

There had never been any doubt in my mind that the principal Soviet aim was the establishment of full diplomatic relations with Bonn so as to formalize the division of Germany. The 9,626 prisoners, while undoubtedly including some diehard Nazi war criminals, were a secondary factor in Soviet eyes. I had told Adenauer and members of his entourage my feelings both before and after the Soviet offer, while emphasizing, on instructions from Washington, that the decision was up to the Chancellor.

I also felt that it was a mistake for a leader of a country to go to Moscow to make a deal on diplomatic recognition, and I said so. Adenauer was trapped into accepting a less than satisfactory agreement. Someone on his staff, which was deeply divided, told him about the reservations I was expressing to Washington, and Adenauer denounced me before American newsmen for "poisoning" the atmosphere. In any event, shortly after the Adenauer agreement Moscow gave East Germany her independence in name, although no one, especially not the East Germans, was fooled.

As predicted, the Soviets at the Geneva Conference refused to talk about the satellite countries, and raised the question of Formosa, which the United States refused to consider. Dulles's idea of discussing international Communism—a patent attempt to appeal to domestic right-wing groups—got nowhere.

There were some gains from Geneva. There was the beginning of an agreement for exchanges of visits by cultural, educational, and scientific experts of the two countries. There is no doubt that increased contacts with foreigners will over many years affect Soviet thinking. Soviet officials feel the need to learn of scientific and technological developments in the West. In the negotiations on exchanges, in which

I participated, the Soviets always concentrated on scientific and technical exchanges. They were willing, however, to have some cultural exchanges because of the considerable amount of money earned by the Bolshoi Ballet and other performing groups.

The conference also gave Eisenhower and Khrushchev an opportunity to size each other up. From every indication, Khrushchev was impressed with the President. From then until the downing of the U-2 spy plane, the Soviet leader spoke highly of the American. Eisenhower, while wary, was sufficiently impressed to agree to exchange visits.

On my return to Moscow, I found the Soviet press and Soviet diplomats talking a great deal of the "spirit of Geneva." As part of the public-relations effort, the Soviet leaders gave a fête champêtre at a dacha about a hundred kilometers south of Moscow. This dacha, one of Stalin's favorites, was used by Soviet officials for rest and for various functions. Never before had it been open to the foreign diplomatic corps. All chiefs of mission, their wives, and their children were invited to a daylong party, which included a lunch, a tea, entertainment, and various types of recreation such as sailing, rowing, and walking. The weather was ideal, hot and dry. After we had been seated at long tables on the lawn on the edge of a birchwood, a long line of waitresses and waiters appeared carrying, head-high, platters of food. It was like a performance at the Bolshoi Theater. There were Caucasian and Crimean wines, vodka, brandy—everything that you could want to drink.

After lunch, we strolled through the parklike grounds. My wife and I were with Mikoyan. He took her for a ride in a rowboat. Although he had a reputation as a lady's man, he was as shy as a schoolboy on his first date. Not knowing what to say, he proudly pointed out a row of mobile toilets. He boasted that the toilets, which had rubber wheels, were a Soviet invention, and explained that they were useful at the May Day celebrations and the November 7 parades in Red Square.

At the end of the afternoon, I found myself with Kaganovich, the old Stalinist party hack, singing "Stenka Razin," the same song of a peasant uprising that I had sung in Stalingrad during the war. Kaganovich, known to have derived sadistic pleasure from purging railroad workers in the 1930s, had drunk enough to feel convivial. He delivered an impassioned speech on peace, saying that women in pain produce children, who, as they grow to manhood, are taken off and slaughtered in senseless wars. His views were warmly applauded, and the party broke up in the full "spirit of Geneva." While there were a few hangovers the following day, the country party was an engaging example of the dictatorship of the proletariat at play, combined with some heavy-handed, but always welcome, humor.

Much has been written about the "spirit of Geneva," most of it derogatory. There is no question that the Kremlin capitalized on the conference, as Dulles feared it might. In the next six months, Soviet diplomats, led by the Khrushchev-Bulganin duo, spread the new Communist gospel in Asia, the Middle East, and Africa. Khrushchev, even under wraps, as he was in India, exuded a crude cockiness that gave the Bolsheviks their first image of naturalness. This assurance, I felt, sprang from Khrushchev's conclusion at Geneva that the Western powers were not going to attack Soviet Russia even though West Germany was going to arm. The Soviets could take satisfaction in the way events were breaking. With their embracing of neutralism (but not, of course, for the East European satellites), they carried a powerful appeal to nations like India. Having reversed Malenkov's consumer-goods program, the Soviet leaders had an export potential of weapons and industrial equipment. Nations in the Western camp, interested in trade, thought they might do business.

The relaxation of tension that followed Geneva resulted in a significant gain for the free world in one area—more contacts with those behind the Iron Curtain. The most publicized have been the cultural, educational, and scientific exchanges, and of these the one that stands out most vividly in my memory is *Porgy and Bess*. Opening night in Leningrad in December, 1955, was a near disaster. The theater was too big and the acoustics bad. There was no translation of the libretto to enable the Russians to understand what was said in this specially American play. They were mystified. Then, the vividly acted scene on the island shocked the Russians, who are quite prudish about sex onstage. As a result, we left the theater plunged in gloom. However, *Porgy and Bess* began to gain in popularity and soon became a success.

The cast created a problem for the Russians. The freewheeling actors rebelled at being guided everywhere they went. They wandered out alone and refused to go on the tours. They always attracted large numbers of curious Russians, who, after decades of propaganda, found it difficult to believe there were well-dressed, well-educated black Americans. Soviet authorities complained to the Embassy that the cast should be told to be more disciplined.

After opening night in Moscow, we held a large reception at Spaso

House. Overjoyed with American food—turkey and ham—and Western drinks—bourbon, Scotch, and Coca-Cola—some members of the cast asked my wife if she would mind if they did a little entertaining. They sang and improvised dances and finally persuaded a young Russan basso named Petrov to sing. The scene of Petrov singing "Old Man River" in Russian with the cast of *Porgy and Bess* sitting on the floor humming the accompaniment as in the original version of *Showboat* was a moving one. Later, at a farewell concert given by the Ministry of Culture, the *Porgy and Bess* cast again surprised the Russians by singing difficult classical arias in five languages, including Russian. The Russians had no idea that the black artists had been so solidly grounded in classical music.

In addition to the cultural exchanges, there were also more contacts with Soviet leaders, who appeared at an increasing number of receptions.* These were usually held in the magnificent white-walled St. George's Hall in the Kremlin. There was a buffet, loaded with food and drink, and, at the far end of the hall, a semi-enclosed section barred to the press, where government officials and diplomats could talk without the risk of being overheard. The exchanges were valuable, and I found that my ability to speak the language gave me an advantage over diplomats who had to rely on interpreters.

But these catch-as-catch-can sessions did not provide the opportunity for the kind of thorough discussions of the views of each side that I had told both Malenkov and Bulganin were needed. On March 6, 1956, Bulganin took me to the private section of St. George's Hall and told me that he could arrange a "heart to heart" talk with him and Khrushchev, or with any other major Soviet leader, at his dacha any time I wanted one. This was exactly the kind of session I had been asking for. Thanking Bulganin, I said I did not want to waste his time in idle talk, but would be glad to avail myself of his offer in the future. Later in the evening, Bulganin returned to the subject, emphasizing that he had been serious in making the offer. I noted that the United States had allies and could not agree to any bilateral deals. Bulganin hastily replied that he was not thinking of deals made behind the backs of either nation's allies, but it was important to have infor-

---

* During this period, a few more members of Congress visited the Soviet Union. I found their conversations valuable and always welcomed them at the Embassy. A few created a minor problem by asking that the Embassy set up appointments with Soviet officials. It was sound policy, dictated by the State Department in Washington, to refuse to open doors in the Kremlin for congressmen, for fear that the Soviets would take any views expressed in the conversations as those of the administration.

mal discussions "without commitments." Enthusiastically, I cabled Dulles of the offer and suggested that President Eisenhower be informed. Unfortunately, Dulles never authorized me to take up the offer, and I certainly could not go ahead on my own. This was a mistake on Dulles's part, although it is only fair to add that there is no evidence that the Kremlin leaders would have said anything in private that would have prevented the crises that soon arose. I still believe that the United States should never refuse any offer for serious talks.

The "spirit of Geneva" also failed to produce any improvement in communication even with individual Russians on an informal basis. More Russians accepted invitations to Embassy affairs, but we could never be sure they would actually come, and they rarely brought their wives. While the Russians could be friendlier, they could not become friends. One week, my wife, my older daughter, Avis, and Kate Roosevelt, daughter of James Roosevelt and the present Mrs. John Hay Whitney, and I went to Lake Onega, north of Leningrad, to see the famous wooden churches built by the "Old Believers," who had fled Moscow at the time of Peter the Great's reform of the Russian church. On the boat to the little settlement of Kizhi, we noticed a group of five or six men, dressed in dark suits and black hats, whom we assumed to be secret policemen sent to watch us. When we stepped off the boat, we were surprised to have them approach us and identify themselves as architects and technicians from Moscow responsible for the restoration of the old churches in the area. They had been sent by the Foreign Office to show us around. Their thorough knowledge of the architecture and history of the churches in the wasteland added a great deal to our visit. We had a gay party on the boat trip back. I drank too much vodka and exchanged tall tales of duck hunting with one of the architects. Despite this pleasant beginning, repeated attempts to develop the friendship on our return to Moscow failed. All the architects and technicians donned their official masks and would not take them off.

The Bolshevik leaders knew what they were doing. They did not favor true friendship between the Soviet Union and the United States, because they realized that anything that breaks through the hermetically sealed character of a Communist regime tends to weaken it. This theory was especially true in the satellite countries in the mid-1950s. There the potent and underestimated force of nationalism was working. The people in these nations were conscious that the system under which they were living was an alien one, modeled on Soviet experience, with little relationship to their traditions or history. Any ideas from the West were bound to excite the desire for independence.

I think the "spirit of Geneva" was one of the forces that stimulated the uprising in Poznan, Poland, in early 1956, which led to the confrontation of Russian and Polish leaders in Warsaw in October and a bloody revolt in Hungary later in the year. Another powerful force was Khrushchev's unmasking of Stalin's crimes in his secret speech to the Twentieth Congress of the Soviet Communist Party.

CHAPTER TWENTY-TWO

Khrushchev's Secret Speech

By the beginning of 1956, Khrushchev's metabolism was running so strong that I began to wonder whether I was right in steadily insisting that collective leadership was exactly that, with no single man supreme. The colorful Ukrainian dominated domestic policy as much as he did foreign affairs. Was he just "first among equals," as I had said for a year, ever since Malenkov had been removed? Or was he in full command? On February 10, I sat down with my chief assistant, O'Shaughnessy, and analyzed the situation. It was five days before the Twentieth Congress of the Communist Party and an ideal time to take stock.

The Soviet Press and speeches at Party meetings were good places to check first. The principle of collective leadership continued to be mentioned in editorials in *Pravda* and *Izvestia*, as well as at regional Party congresses and conferences. It could be argued that propaganda designed to move people away from the doctrine would probably follow, not precede, the establishment of a personal dictatorship. But Khrushchev would need at least a personal buildup, and a study of the proceedings of Party meetings failed to uncover any extraordinary praise for him. He was usually mentioned, with Bulganin, only in connection with their India-Burma-Afghanistan trip. There were two exceptions. In a speech at the Ukrainian Congress, Leonid I. Brezhnev, a rising member of the Bolshevik ruling group, mentioned Khrushchev eight times to once for Bulganin. But such a disparity could be traced to the fact that Khrushchev had once served in the Ukraine. He was also singled out for special praise at the Kazakhstan Party Congress, for what reason O'Shaughnessy and I could not determine.

It was also true that Khrushchev had hogged the limelight from Bulganin with his willingness to spout off on any subject, often tactlessly. Moreover, he showed his strength by conceding publicly that there were shortcomings in the Virgin Lands program.

There was no doubt that, as First Secretary of the Communist Party, Khrushchev was in the best position of any leader to seek supreme power. Through his appointment of key officials, he could play one group or individual off against another. But all the other members of the Party's ruling group, the Presidium, realized that the best way to avoid a return to a Stalin-like rule was to keep one man from holding all the levers of power. For that reason, they still had different men in the two most important jobs–the Party secretary-ship and the premiership.

I remained convinced that collective leadership had operated successfully in the nearly three years since Stalin's death. It was logical to assume that members of the Presidium, having just emerged from the dangers of Stalin's one-man rule, would hardly be likely to submit themselves to this experience again, unless it were the only means whereby the regime could be maintained. It did not appear from external signs that the Soviet Union was faced, from a political, an economic, or a foreign-affairs point of view, with any emergency necessitating such a step. Even if there was an overriding national reason for the re-establishment of the one-man dictatorship, Khrushchev's age–he was nearly sixty-two–militated against his selection. In a telegram to Dulles, I knocked down speculation by British experts in London that Khrushchev would emerge from the Congress as the "top boss," or dictator, of the Soviet Union. While Khrushchev might strengthen his position as first among equals in the Presidium, I felt it was premature to conclude that the Twentieth Party Congress would take the first step on the road to establishing him as the uncontested ruler of the Soviet Union.

There were no indications, when the Congress opened on February 14 in the Kremlin, that anything unusual was about to take place. In my reading of *Pravda* (no diplomats were permitted to attend the Congress), I noted that Khrushchev, as expected, was given the honor of opening the session—a role accorded Molotov at the preceding Congress, held in Stalin's day. After more preliminaries, Khrushchev delivered a long speech, which was tiresome and showed no departures in either foreign or domestic policy. He reaffirmed the principle of collective leadership and insisted that its members were guided by "unselfish motives." In the same defensive tone, he said the relationship of the top leaders was on an "intellectual basis, permitting neither mutual animosity nor personal enmity." Khrushchev was making it clear that there had been differences of opinion, but was contending that the arguments had sprung from considerations of policy, not of personal rivalries. Yet his tone demonstrated a sensitivity that may well have reflected charges by others in the Party that he had been motivated by personal ambitions. All this was interesting, but hardly definitive. I needed more clues.

On February 16, the third day of the Congress, Mikoyan, one of the central core of the Presidium, delivered a sharp attack on Stalin. At the opening session, Khrushchev had belittled Stalin indirectly by asking the delegates to rise in memory of "Stalin, Gottward, and Tokunda," thus coupling the great dictator with two little-known Communists, who had also died since the Nineteenth Congress of the Party. Mikoyan went much further, criticizing Stalin directly as a poor economist and Marxian philosopher. He asked for a new history textbook to replace the Stalin short course, implying that many facts and events required correction.

I saw little in these faint clues, and, on reflection, after the Congress was over, I concluded that the Embassy's pre-Congress forecast had been correct. Khrushchev remained the most powerful member of the ruling group, but it would be difficult for him or any other leader to become a second Stalin. There were two factors militating against a return to one-man rule. One was the formidable political and psychological barrier erected by the strong condemnation by all speakers, including Khrushchev, of the "cult of personality" and arbitrary use of police power. The other was the safeguards developed over three years to prevent one of their number from seizing power and to avoid transforming the collective into an ineffective debating society. The leaders were pulling together to make the system work, and carefully choosing Party officials who supported the committee system. In a telegram to Dulles, I expressed unhappiness that I had been right. I wrote:

> Nothing would give me greater pleasure than to be able to predict a "struggle for power" among the present leadership, leading to the reinstitution of a one-man dictatorship, which would certainly not be accomplished without a real fight with attendant consequences to Soviet stability, policies and prestige. It would indeed be a gift from the gods to the free world. I see no grounds for such optimism at this juncture.

Admittedly, this was a cynical view. I thought that any attempt to reimpose one-man rule would lead to an upheaval and a consequent transformation of the Soviet Union into a more democratic and peaceful nation. Actually, there was little prospect of such an upheaval, because the people would accept the collective leadership which had eased the harsh rule under which they had lived.

At a Kremlin party a week or so later, it was interesting to get Khrushchev's reaction when I noted that there had been comment in the Western press that he was on his way to becoming another "great leader." Unperturbed by my remarks, he called such articles "absolute nonsense," and insisted that "objective circumstances" in the Soviet Union made such a development impossible. Later, Mikoyan gave me the same opinion. That same evening, curious as to how the Presidium functions, I asked Khrushchev and Molotov how it reached decisions. Independently, each gave me the same answer. Presidium decisions were generally made without a vote. In the event of a disagreement, a vote was taken and recorded. Minority votes and even views were put on the record. Khrushchev said that in the event of a disagreement that could not be ironed out, a vote was "obligatory." Candidates for the Presidium had the right to attend all sessions, but did not always do so. They could participate in the discussions but not vote.

To me, the most interesting development of the Party Congress was Mikoyan's direct, and other speakers' indirect, attacks on Stalin. In one way, the attacks pleased me. Any liberalization of Soviet society, no matter how modest, would make it more difficult to control the people. I wrote Dulles; "Nothing could illustrate more clearly the cynicism and moral corruption of the Soviet regime as inflicted on this country than the spectacle of the Twentieth Party Congress of leaders, every one a creature of Stalin and involved up to the hilt in all his actions, now turning on him without a single voice calling them to account for their personal participations in the crimes they now so blandly denounce."

The situation was even worse than I realized. On February 25, at the close of the Congress, Khrushchev had delivered a speech to a session closed to all except Party delegates. This "secret speech," as it was soon called, unmasked Stalin as the instigator of the terror of the 1930s, when millions were shot to death; as a coward who was paralyzed by fear at the time of the Nazi invasion; as a stupid military strategist, who sent thousands of troops to senseless deaths; as a supreme egotist, who rewrote books to glorify himself. Not once did Khrushchev explain his intimate involvement with Stalin.

It was two weeks before I heard anything about the secret speech. On March 10, at a reception at the French Embassy for former President Vincent Auriol of France, a rumor circulated that Khrushchev had made a scathing attack on Stalin. The rumor, like many others, was transmitted by Parker, the Moscow correspondent for the London *Worker*. It seemed evident that the rumor had been planted by Russians who wanted the word out. According to the story, Khrushchev had delivered a two- to three-hour speech giving in considerable detail an account of Stalin's crimes during the purge period. Khrushchev charged Stalin with having decimated the Party and having executed without cause many of its outstanding leaders, some of whom he listed by name. Khrushchev reportedly said that Stalin had murdered 5,000 of the best Soviet military officers, thus undermining the defensive capacity of the country, and had disregarded repeated warnings, including some from Churchill, of the imminence of the Nazi attack. As a result, the Soviet Union had barely escaped a catastrophic defeat in the war.

In a wire to Dulles, I said that there had been indirect confirmation of the report from other sources. While undoubtedly some of the more spectacular versions had grown with the telling (for example, that Khrushchev burst into tears three times during the speech), I thought it highly probable that in substance the report was accurate. It was logical that the Party élite had received a somewhat more convincing justification for the attacks on Stalin than was contained in the formal speeches at the Congress. In this connection, the Yugoslav Ambassador, who attended the formal sessions as an observer, told me that everything he had heard at the Congress had been reported without change in the Soviet press.

Almost immediately the authorities ordered Stalin's statues removed from buildings. Soviet artists, such as Emil Gilels, were no longer introduced as laureates of Stalin prizes. "How far the elimination of Stalin's glorification will proceed is not clear at this moment," my wire to Dulles said, "but if the reports of Khrushchev's speech are reasonably accurate it will probably be far-reaching, and there is even a rumor that Stalin will shortly be removed from the mausoleum."

There were inaccuracies in the rumor, but as the text of the speech eventually showed, the rumor was generally on target.

The next day, I received confirmation of the rumor. Dr. Paul A. Baran, head of the Social Science Department of Stanford University, called on me. A naturalized American of Russian-Polish origin, Baran had been in the Soviet Union for a week, visiting his father, a doctor. The younger Dr. Baran said that one of his father's patients, a member of the Communist Party's Central Committee, had told him that Khrushchev had denounced Stalin in great detail in a secret speech at the Congress. Moreover, an Embassy employee sent to the Tretyakov art gallery found only one small bust of Stalin where scores of pictures and sculptures had been days before.

The Soviet press did not carry any stories on the speech, nor would censors pass any dispatches abroad. But the substance of the speech was outlined to local Communist Party leaders at meetings throughout the country, and the word quickly spread. The shock of the news was great on the Soviet people, even though three years of de-Stalinization had wiped some of the luster off the dictator's image. Under such circumstances, the Embassy was able to break through the secrecy and pick up some items indicating the impact. A scenario writer, no supporter of Stalin's policies, told an Embassy officer that when he heard of the speech, "something great I believed in died." In Georgia, where Stalin was born, students demonstrated in support of the fallen hero. The wife of the head of an industrial enterprise told a Swedish diplomat's wife that the Georgian students were protesting an order to remove the symbols glorifying Stalin. As the Swedish woman passed the story on to us, on March 8 demonstrations in Tiflis got so out of hand that crowds were machine-gunned. The police (or soldiers) there were brutal, firing machine guns breast-high into the crowd. Several people were killed. Most of the demonstrators were under twenty. The Russian woman said her son threw himself on the ground before the machine guns opened fire and thus escaped injury.

While remaining silent on the speech, the Soviet press printed many articles on de-Stalinization. By late spring, the Kremlin called a halt to the anti-Stalin campaign. There were a few indications that it was getting out of hand. I heard that a Party cell in a university adopted a resolution calling for genuine democracy in the Soviet Union, with free elections and power turned over to the people. Those who approved the resolution were expelled from the Party and the university, I was told, and exiled from Moscow. They were not arrested, however.

While lone accounts of Khrushchev's speech were printed abroad, there was always the question of their authenticity. In May, the French obtained a document purported to be a copy of the secret speech, which was published in part in *France Soir*. It was, however, not a text of the address but only notes taken by a member of the French Embassy in Warsaw during a one-hour period in which he was allowed by Polish sources to examine what was said to be a copy of the speech. At the end of the month, I received from Washington the text of a document obtained by the Central Intelligence Agency in Warsaw. After careful study, I concluded that in all probability it was an authentic copy of Khrushchev's speech, or at least of the version sent to the satellites. Verifiable errors of fact in the French document were missing from the CIA copy. In addition, specific details of the speech I had obtained indirectly from a Russian and the Bulgarian Ambassador matched the CIA text.

I was not sure the speech should be published. On June 2, I wired a complicated personal reaction to Dulles:

> In regard to publicity I am of two minds. In general, I believe that documents such as this, concerning Soviet policies which are believed to be genuine, are worthwhile publishing in that they clarify public opinion and explain what is actually going on in this country, and this document would be invaluable to students of Soviet affairs who would normally not have access to it. However, I would seriously doubt if publication would be valuable to our side from the propaganda point of view. The speech is extremely serious and convincing and goes far to providing real evidence that the current Soviet leadership is determined to persist in its present "liberal" course and do away with certain abuses of the Stalin period. The theme throughout the speech, that there must be no repetition of Stalin's crimes, will, I am sure, be regarded as strong evidence in many quarters that the current leadership has indeed in certain respects "reformed." The very fact that the text given in this document is more balanced than previous speculations and leaks will, I feel, not only tend to enhance its credibility but will give more credit than discredit to the present leadership. The fact that the document when published will undoubtedly be denounced as spurious by the Communists will not, in my opinion, offset a reaction more favorable than not to the present regime.
>
> Therefore, I would conclude that if the primary purpose of publication is to place current rulers in an unfavorable light, I would be inclined not to publish. On the other hand, if the main purpose is merely to get out an interesting and important document concerning political developments in the Soviet Union, publication would be useful, particularly as leaks are almost certain.

If the decision was to publish, I suggested that the United States government not be the public agent for doing so, because of the danger—admittedly small—that the document might turn out to be a fake. I remembered that American credibility had suffered in 1918 when the United States government published a forged document designed to show that Lenin was a German agent.

My advice was rejected, and on June 4 the State Department made the text public. Dulles was absolutely right in releasing the speech. What I had failed to take into consideration was that there would be a lingering doubt about the speech—whether Khrushchev actually delivered it, and what he said—until the full text was made public. Khrushchev's quoting of Stalin (e.g., "If you do not obtain confessions from the doctors, we will shorten you by a head") and the anecdotes (e.g., Stalin's rewriting of his official biography to glorify himself as a master military strategist) may have stretched the truth, but they were typical of Khrushchev's style and were convincing evidence that the speech was authentic. Publication of the speech may have improved Khrushchev's image in many countries, but since the Soviet Union continued to suppress freedom, I do not believe it gained the Soviet Union any widespread or lasting support.

The Soviets never did question the authenticity of the State Department's text, in itself an unusual action. Ten days after publication, I asked Malenkov and Molotov about it at a reception. They smilingly responded that versions of the speech circulated in foreign countries were not accurate. The next day, June 15, I had an opportunity to ask Khrushchev himself. It was during a reception at the Kremlin. I was having a drink with him in the semi-enclosed end of St. George's Hall. Khrushchev was not his usual ebullient self; he seemed subdued and said he was tired. Tito was in Moscow, and Khrushchev had been conferring with him. Somewhat mildly for him, Khrushchev complained of Dulles's speeches and press-conference statements, saying they were difficult to reconcile with the spirit of Geneva. I told Khrushchev that he did not understand the American system of free expression of opinions and particularly press conferences, where government officials were subjected to vigorous questioning on any subject.

Khrushchev said the improvement in relations with the United States was going too slowly. Taking advantage of this opening, I told him I thought words were insufficient in matters of this kind. As long as major questions, such as Germany and disarmament, which were the chief causes of tension, remained unsolved, mere words on the desirability of improved relations were not going to change the situation. I said it was my personal opinion that the Soviet leaders seemed to believe that they could have everything their own way. The constant assault in their statements and in Soviet propaganda against measures such as NATO, which the United States and its allies felt to be vital to their security, seemed to me to be incompatible with the constantly reiterated Soviet desire for coexistence and normal relations. I told Khrushchev that persistent Soviet attacks on the American policy of "positions of strength" led me to believe the Soviet leaders desired that we should operate from positions of weakness while they maintained their strength intact. Khrushchev countered by saying that at Geneva the Soviet Union had indicated its willingness to accept NATO as an international fact and had proposed that NATO and the Warsaw Pact countries sign an agreement renouncing the use of force. I replied that additional pieces of paper of this nature were not necessary in view of the pledge taken by United Nations members renouncing aggression. Besides, such questions brought us up squarely against the problem of Germany, since the Eastern zone was a member of the Warsaw Pact. Khrushchev did not argue the point, but insisted that the United States did not understand the depth and significance of the changes taking place in the Soviet Union.

I told him that I did my best to keep my government informed, but despite certain improvements—such as the conversation we were having—secrecy was so great that it was difficult for an ambassador in Moscow to get a clear picture of what was going on. For example, I said with a grin, we knew that he had made a very important speech near the close of the Twentieth Party Congress, yet no authoritative official in Moscow would give us any information on the subject. Khrushchev started to deny he had made the speech, then broke off in midsentence and said, "Versions have been circulated which do not correspond to the truth." Like Malenkov and Molotov the night before, he said he had not read the State Department version, because it required "a big work of translation." He then switched the subject to the upcoming visit of General Nathan Twining, the American Air Force Chief of Staff.*

In 1970, the book *Khrushchev Remembers* provided some fragmentary reasons for the decision to disclose Stalin's crimes. For three years, Khrushchev is quoted as saying, "we were unable to muster the courage and the determination to lift the curtain." Then he said, "We refused to believe Stalin was guilty of the awful crimes," even after disclosures about Beria. But Khrushchev "felt an urge" to look further, and proposed an investigatory commission, which reported just before the Twentieth Party Congress. Kaganovich, Voroshilov, and Molotov were worried about their own skins, but, Khrushchev said, he overcame their opposition and persuaded them that the truth should be reported. The explanation raises more questions than it

---

* Later Khrushchev joked that the CIA had not paid enough for its copy of the speech—only 500 zlotys—or about $100.

answers. I believe that Khrushchev and his colleagues concluded that they could not remake the Soviet mechanism as long as the legend of Stalin persisted. A mere downgrading of the man was insufficient to change the Party and government bureaucrats running the system. For years, Stalin had been emulated at every level of society. There were innumerable little Stalins who ran their particular bailiwicks with the same ruthless autocracy which Stalin himself had exercised over the whole country. Khrushchev was certainly aware of the risk to the infallibility of Bolshevik doctrine, but this style of operation had to be altered if the Soviet system was going to be reformed, even mildly.

By the end of June, the Soviet leaders became concerned over the probing questions Communists abroad were continuing to raise. How had the Stalin cult been able to develop in the Soviet system? Why had Khrushchev and others not acted against Stalin? Had not the dictatorship permanently damaged the Soviet system? In Italy, even the faithful Palmiro Togliatti spoke of the "degeneration" of Soviet society. To counteract the doubts, the Central Committee of the Soviet Communist Party issued a decree on June 30. It attributed the rise of Stalinism to historical conditions—the struggle against class enemies, capitalist encirclement, rapid industrialization—which required "iron discipline, unceasing vigilance, and the strictest centralization of leadership." As to why Khrushchev, Mikoyan, and others had taken no action to depose Stalin, the decree said it was not a lack of personal courage. Such a move would have been interpreted by the people as "subversion," the decree said, because Stalin was so clearly identified with the system. Besides, conditions had changed radically. "Soviet democracy has expanded immeasurably and will continue to expand." The significance of the decree was that there would be no backtracking. De-Stalinization would proceed despite the doubters, who, I was certain, still sat in the upper reaches of the Party.

The Soviets were especially worried about the satellite states, where they had been attempting to hold the lid on national pressures by easing their strict controls. The rapprochement with Tito offered public proof that there were different roads to socialism. When Tito, in June, returned Khrushchev's visit, the Soviets did not make the same mistakes they made in Belgrade. One of the Yugoslavs told me that they were surprised by the openness with which the Soviet leaders conceded their past errors.

Molotov, who had opposed the reconciliation, was replaced just

before the Tito visit by D. T. Shepilov. While there was wide speculation that Molotov had been ousted, I concluded, on the basis of his
good humor at a reception, that he had resigned to escape the humilia-
tion of being treated in front of Tito as a mere technician. For a year,
he had been Foreign Minister in name only.

The Soviets went to elaborate lengths to court Tito. Khrushchev,
who liked to pop off at the slightest opportunity, submitted the text
of his major speech at Dynamo Stadium to Tito before delivery. He
also made sure that Tito received considerably more applause than he
did. A man stood on top of the stadium and signaled physical cultur-
ists massed on the field when to applaud and when to stop.

There was a sour note or two. I heard that Tito had expressed great
resentment at the discovery by Yugoslav experts of eavesdropping
devices at almost every place he stayed. He was also saying privately
that the older Soviet leaders were serious in their liberalization of the
regime, but he was worried lest, when the younger men took over,
they might perhaps unconsciously revert to the Stalinist methods in
which they had been trained.

Tito did give strong support to the Soviet foreign policy, prompt-
ing me to conclude in a wire to Dulles on June 23:

> Yugoslavia has in international affairs indeed rejoined the Communist
> community and we can expect in the future on all important interna-
> tional questions to find Yugoslavia lined up with the Soviet column. In
> general, however, Tito has rejoined the community on his own terms
> and there is not the slightest indication in the communiqué or declara-
> tion that Yugoslavia has lost, at least up to the present, its independence
> or has reverted to satellite status in regard to the Soviet Union, although
> by adopting publicly the Soviet positions he has voluntarily limited his
> freedom of action.

Irritated because Tito had not uttered a single favorable word about
the Western allies or any recognition of the millions of dollars in
assistance the United States had extended to Yugoslavia, I told Dulles
that abrupt cessation of aid would be more than justified on many
grounds, but would lead to charges of forcing Belgrade into greater
dependence on Moscow. On the other hand, I said, continuance of aid
would not halt or even slow the growing intimacy of the two Communist nations.

The central question, however, remained the satellites. I heard that
Tito had privately urged the Kremlin to restore progressively the

independence of the Eastern European countries. Khrushchev, while agreeing in principle, felt that this could be accomplished only over a long period of time, because any sudden moves might produce "dramatic and dangerous" developments. No sudden moves were required. The puff of fresh air that had blown through the Communist world was sufficient in itself to shake the Soviet empire. Within weeks, the Soviets had come within a hair's breadth of using force to crush an incipient revolution in Poland; by fall, Red Army tanks were smashing a full-fledged rebellion in Hungary. My most trying period as ambassador to the Soviet Union was at hand.

CHAPTER TWENTY-THREE

The Hungarian Revolution

After Khrushchev's secret speech, my main concern as ambassador focused on the question of whether the liberalization of the Soviet system would work. What did it mean to the Russian people? Would they enjoy more freedom and a better life? More important, how would Soviet foreign policy be affected? Unfortunately, the liberalization had not given diplomats any additional tools to work with. While the Soviet leaders continued to attend receptions, where they would take part in conversations, there still were no regular, serious, far-ranging discussions that are so necessary in diplomacy. For the most part, the ambassadors continued to rely on the controlled Soviet press for news of Soviet decisions and to cast about in the diplomatic community for additional clues, weighing rumors, exchanging opinions, and occasionally picking up an important fact.

I realized that any liberalization of a dictatorship is fraught with the dangers of going too far too fast or doing too little too late. In June of 1956, the Soviet leaders had every reason to be proud of their performance. In both domestic and foreign affairs, events were going well. Grievances and dissatisfactions remained, but the complaints seemed minor compared with the successes. Even the intelligentsia, that group of artists, writers, teachers, students, and others who work with their brains, embraced the changes without pushing too hard for more. Abroad, there was a new respect for the Soviet Union.

There was a difficult problem with the satellites, but adjustments had been made to recognize the nationalist pressures of the various countries. The new leaders of the Kremlin realized that they did not carry Stalin's weight. Communists in foreign countries who took orders from Stalin were reluctant to listen to a Khrushchev or a

Mikoyan. Khrushchev believed that by giving up direct control and the incredible Stalin policy of trying to dictate every action by every Communist boss in every satellite he could preserve the Eastern European empire.

It was humiliating to go to Belgrade and confess error, but a Tito in ideological battle with the Kremlin was a counterattraction the Soviets had reason to fear. With Tito back on the team, or at least not playing for the opposition, the outlook was much better.

In June came the warning signal that major trouble was fermenting in the satellites. Riots broke out in Poznan, an industrial city of Poland. As the demonstrations spread, they took on an anti-Communist tone, with Party headquarters and security-police offices attacked. Polish troops had to be called out to suppress the rioters, but there was evidence that their sympathies lay with the demonstrators. Sitting in my office in the Tchaikovsky Building in Moscow, I could do little except follow the events on the BBC and study the Soviet reaction in *Pravda* and *Izvestia*. The Soviet line was predictable. The riots were "provocations" by "agents of imperialism and the reactionary Polish underground." But Polish Premier Jozef Cyrankiewicz would not be swayed, the controlled press stated, from his determination to further "democratization." As evidence of support, workers throughout Poland were said to be adopting resolutions condemning the action of the "imperialist provocateurs." I did not realize the seriousness of the situation in Poland then, nor did I know that Bulganin and Zhukov went to Warsaw in July to meet with the Polish Central Committee. I do not think that the Soviet leaders realized the seriousness of the situation, either. In Stalin's day, information sent to Moscow had been conditioned along the lines of what Stalin wanted to hear regarding the "perfect" Soviet system—that the people were supporting Communism and only a small group of "enemies of the people" were against it. It would have taken a courageous man to present news of unhappiness in the Soviet empire. I think that to some extent that dangerous method of reporting still existed (and still exists today) in the Soviet diplomatic service. Whatever the reason, the riot leaders who were tried generally received light sentences. There were no harsh reprisals.

There was also no solution to the problem. In his predicament, Khrushchev turned to his new friend and adviser on the satellites, Marshal Tito. Although Tito had been in Moscow in June, Khrushchev quickly followed up with another trip to Belgrade, and Tito returned the second visit in September. I was in London, attending a conference on the Suez Canal, which had been nationalized by Egyptian President Gamal Abdel Nasser. On my return to Moscow on September 26, Tito was in the Crimea on vacation, according to the Soviet press. So, it turned out, was Erno Gero, who had replaced the despised Stalinist Matyas Rakosi as First Secretary of the Hungarian Communist Party. Checking around in the diplomatic corps, I found a general belief that Khrushchev and Tito were disagreeing over Soviet policy in the satellites. The Soviet press no longer referred to Tito as "Comrade" but as "President."

Speculating on Soviet motives, I concluded that the Kremlin had initiated the talks either because of dissatisfaction and concern with rumored Yugoslav activities that might draw some satellites away from the Soviet Union—in their eyes a hostile policy—or to obtain Tito's acquiescence, and even participation, in some contemplated change in satellite relations. It was more than likely that the dispute centered on divergent interpretations of the thesis of "different roads to socialism" introduced in Khrushchev's first visit to Belgrade. The Soviets always saw more limitations to this thesis than did Tito. They envisaged increasing independence and greater equality for the Eastern European countries, but only within the general framework of, and subordinate to, the general Communist bloc. The Yugoslavs' concept was much closer to national Communism. I told the State Department on October 3 that the Soviet leaders were probably concerned that the satellites, once released from bondage, might establish economic ties with the West and thus bring about the gradual dissolution of the Eastern European bloc. I expressed doubt, however, that Khrushchev was being hard pressed by others in the Kremlin or that the disarray in Poland and Hungary would lead to a return to a Stalinist crackdown. "It is not characteristic of Bolshevik procedure to cry over spilled milk," I wrote.

In mid-October, at a reception at the Afghan Embassy, I got a chance to ask Khrushchev himself about his conversations with Tito. Khrushchev was unusually reticent, but conceded that the two had talked politics during Tito's stay in the Crimea. He professed himself satisfied with the discussions and denounced Western press reports of a division with Tito as "nonsense." Three nights later, on October 19, Khrushchev, Mikoyan, Kaganovich, and Molotov were absent from a reception in the Kremlin in honor of the Japanese, who were setting up an Embassy. Everyone noticed the absences, which in Moscow were enough to start tongues wagging. The rumor was soon circulating that the four, who had been at the Bolshoi the night before, had left for Warsaw to attend a meeting of the Central Committee of the Polish Communist Party. I checked with Ambassador J. Vosahlik of Czechoslovakia, who told me that Khrushchev had gone to Warsaw; the Ambassador had heard of the trip from an authoritive source. He did not know about the three other Soviet leaders. The next day, Radio Moscow confirmed the report that the delegation had gone to Warsaw to attend the Polish Party session, and before the day was out, a Russian source said that the Soviet group had returned with "certain Polish Comrades." There were rumors, which originated in Warsaw, of Soviet troop movements. As the world soon learned, the Polish Communists brought Wladyslaw Gomulka, who had been jailed during Stalin's era, out of disgrace and named him chief of the Party and government. At the same time, Marshal Konstantin Rokossovsky, a Soviet general of Polish origin, whose first loyalty lay with the Soviet Union, was removed as Polish Minister of Defense. In Moscow, all the Soviets got in the way of news was a bare-boned communiqué, which included the usual trash about "further strengthening of fraternal friendship and cooperation" between the Soviet and Polish Communist Parties, but nothing of Gomulka's election and Rokossovsky's removal. In the foreign colony, we heard more rumors of troop movements and even of clashes between Soviet and Polish forces near Stettin. Operating in the dark, I could offer the State Department only tentative opinions and speculation of what was going on. Throughout the crisis—and despite rumblings of discontent in Budapest—I expressed doubt in my wires to the State Department that the Red Army would be used to smash the Polish dissidents.

Subsequent information indicated that the Russians went to Warsaw fully intending to get tough with the Polish upstarts and planning to use the armed forces, but were told by all factions in the Party there that the Polish army could not be counted on. Only the discredited Gomulka, a hero solely because he had stood up to the Soviets before, could prevent an explosion. I believe that it was not until Khrushchev and the other Russians talked to the Poles that they realized that the Soviet Union had only a few friends in Poland. The dissidents were not just a small group in the Party backed by a few army officers. Like Stalin, his successors were misled by ideology and misleading reports from subordinates into believing that people everywhere were with the Soviet Union. Unlike Stalin in this case, they faced up to the truth, that almost all the people of Poland were against them. If the Soviets used force, a bloody outburst was sure to follow. So they backed away from it, settling on Gomulka as the best chance to maintain the Soviet system and keep Poland in the Warsaw Pact. The settlement worked. Gomulka went to Moscow on November 15 and was treated well. He was given considerable leeway, but did not overstep the bounds.

Khrushchev boasted thereafter that the Gomulka arrangement was one of his greatest triumphs. Actually, the Soviet delegation to Warsaw came within an eyelash of ordering Soviet troops to act. On October 25—two days after the revolt began in Hungary—Marshal Zhukov cited Poland as proof of Soviet unwillingness to intervene militarily in the internal affairs of other countries. Talking with me at a party at the Turkish Embassy, he said that there had been more than enough Soviet troops in East Germany, White Russia, and Poland to force a settlement on Kremlin terms. His blue eyes flashing, he insisted, "They could have crushed them like flies." When I asked who "they" were, he made no direct reply, but he was obviously referring to Soviet troops, because he said that the Red Army had shown "great restraint" in Poland. He said that to make sure that troops in East Germany did not march into Poland, he had dispatched Marshal I. S. Konev, commander of Warsaw Pact forces, there. Reading between Zhukov's lines, I believe he had urged military action in Poland, but was overruled. Zhukov's subsequent views on Hungary further confirmed my suspicion.

The Polish compromise prevented the riots from spreading into a national revolution. The Soviets sought a way out of the Hungarian trouble, too, but the nationalistic, anti-Soviet forces would not settle for half a loaf; they wanted full independence. As a result, they were crushed by Soviet tanks.

The Hungarian uprising began on October 23, while our attention was focused on Warsaw. As if the Embassy work load was not heavy enough, the crisis over the Suez Canal (discussed in the next chapter) broke out. For the next few weeks, during the emergency, I held one, two, or even three staff meetings each day. We discussed events, weighed rumors, tried to analyze Soviet moves. There were no particular changes in our assignments, but we all worked long hours. Generally, I talked to the other ambassadors, because of my position. I also made sure that one senior member of the Embassy attended every major reception. If there were any indications that Khrushchev, Zhukov, or any other Kremlin leader would be present, I would go. Newbold Walmsley, who had succeeded O'Shaughnessy as the number-two man, was my backstop, filling in for me at some affairs and going with me to others. The military attachés sounded out their opposite numbers at other embassies, and the younger members of the staff worked the few Soviet sources available—such as the universities, lecture halls, and parks—for rumors and gossip.

We pored over *Pravda* and *Izvestia*. But with the Soviet media typically silent, we had to depend on foreign broadcasts, supplemented by some information from the State Department, for the news. Some 200,000 demonstrators marched in Budapest the first day of the Hungarian revolution. As the protests continued, mobs turned ugly. They attacked the secret-police headquarters and lynched some of the agents. The Soviets reacted with a variation of the successful Polish formula. They replaced Gero with Imre Nagy, who had once been Premier but who had been deposed by the Stalinist Rakosi. Apparently Premier Nagy—we are not sure it was he—asked for Soviet military help to suppress the revolt. In the next two days, the rebellion spread to the whole country. There was a news blackout on Hungary in the Soviet press, but foreign reports said Soviet troops made only halfhearted attempts to fight the rebels.

I scarcely noticed that Mikoyan and another member of the Presidium, Mikhail Suslov, were absent from receptions. The absences did not seem important until Washington relayed an intelligence report that the two had gone to Budapest. Indeed they had, on October 25, and would take two more trips within the week. One of their first moves was to select Janos Kadar, another anti-Rakosi Communist, as Party chief. While Mikoyan and Suslov were off to Budapest, I called at the gloomy little Hungarian Embassy in Moscow to pay my respects to the new Ambassador, Janos Bolboczki. The appointment had been set up before the flare-up in Hungary and was supposed to be merely a social call. However, the Ambassador brought up the subject of the riots himself, seemingly anxious to make the point that there was no internecine struggle in the Party or government. He depicted the uprising in the standard Communist manner—a counter-revolutionary plot involving criminals who sought to exploit grievances of students. Once the disturbances were quelled, he said, Nagy would announce the government's program of "democratization."

Later that day, October 25, the Soviet press broke its silence on Hungary. In a dispatch entitled "Failure of Anti-Popular Adventure in Budapest," Tass attributed the violence to "counter-revolutionary" elements, told of the request for Soviet military help, and said that the "mutiny" had been liquidated. In a pure fabrication, the dispatch said that workers from all over the country had sent telegrams to Budapest in which they "expressed their angry indignation at criminal activities

410

of the counter-revolutionists and assured the Party and government of their readiness to defend the people's democratic society from any encroachments by enemies and to strengthen friendship with the Soviet Union and all socialist countries."

Commenting on the first Soviet report, I told the State Department it was clear that Moscow would insist that the Hungarian troubles had been instigated from abroad. In view of Nagy's request for Soviet troops, I saw no differences, on the surface at least, between the Hungarian and Soviet governments. The Soviets, knowing what was going on, did see differences. At a reception for the Belgians at the Kremlin, there was a noticeable contrast between Khrushchev and Bulganin, supporters of less control of the satellites, and Molotov and Kaganovich, who believed in a more repressive policy. Bulganin, in particular, looked tired and depressed. He made no attempt to put on his usual urbane act and did not circulate among the guests, staying at the table with the Belgians. Khrushchev, although looking less worried than Bulganin, was not his usual exuberant, confident self. On the other hand, the two hard-liners, Molotov and Kaganovich, seemed to be considerably more at ease. Molotov sought me out, and when I asked what the news was from Budapest, he said that the situation was quieting down, although isolated fighting continued. He said the disagreeable developments illustrated what a "small organized group" could do under certain conditions. I told him that from the limited information available to me, it was apparent that the disorders went far beyond small groups, and represented widespread dissatisfaction in Hungary. He replied that masses of people rarely took any initiative on their own, and only operated under the direction of organized groups. When I noted that circumstances were changing all over Eastern Europe, Molotov said new circumstances required new policies and sometimes new people. I could not resist the temptation to tell him that apparently leaders of the Soviet Union had sufficient experience not to require change. He gave one of his rare laughs, and said, "It is true we have had more experience than some of the people in the new popular democracies."

On October 27, after emphasizing the total absence of any real information on events in Hungry and Poland, I told the State Department that it was not possible to make any intelligent forecast of future Soviet action. Without hesitation, I went right ahead and drew some conclusions that turned out to be technically accurate but somewhat misleading. First, I mistakenly said that the "Soviet Union will not use overt force against a Commie regime no matter whether the policies it is pursuing are contrary to Soviet wishes." This, I said, was the "chief lesson" of the Polish settlement. Then, as careful diplomats do, I hedged. There were "possible variations" from this rule if a "minority pro-Soviet Commie group" asked for intervention; but such possibilities seemed "unlikely." My second conclusion was the the Soviets would "undoubtedly in the future be prepared to use regular Soviet troops in support of and on the request of Commie regimes, as in the case of Hungary."

Regarding United States policy, I saw the advantage of creating psychological and political difficulties for the Soviet Union by taking the Hungarian situation to the United Nations Security Council, but said that our judgment of Nagy was vital in making the decision. If the State Department felt that Nagy was heading a movement that would eventually lead to greater independence along the Polish or Yugoslav lines, raising the question in the Security Council might well drive Nagy closer to the Soviet Union. If, however, the judgment was that Nagy had irretrievably compromised himself and was in effect a prisoner of the Soviets, then, I said, there was every advantage in taking the case to the United Nations.

The evening of the next day, October 28, Nagy announced on Radio Budapest that he had succeeded in getting an uneasy cease-fire, a Soviet pledge for an immediate withdrawal of troops from Budapest, and a promise of talks on pulling out of the country. I was puzzled. Had Nagy broken with the Kremlin? That did not seem possible in view of the generally favorable tone of Tass references to him. Although clarification was required, I leaned to the view that the Soviet leaders had decided to cut their losses and pull out, clinging to a forlorn hope that Nagy, by assuming command of the popular revolution, would be able to prevent the complete collapse of the Communist regime. While the possibility of saving Communism was slim, the Kremlin might well have concluded that that course was preferable to total military occupation of Hungary. I could not shake off a suspicion, however, that something else was afoot, and cautioned the State Department that the Soviet pledge of a withdrawal from Budapest might be "nothing more than a cover pending arrival of reinforcements." I should have given greater attention to my instinctive suspicion of the Soviet Union. Already, Khrushchev and the other collective leaders had authorized Zhukov to pour troops into Hungary. Although the Soviets did withdraw from Budapest, within a week they stormed back and quickly smashed the revolution.

The decision to use force must have been made well in advance. I think it may have been made on October 28 or 29. Quite a few big black Zis limousines were seen entering the Kremlin on October 29, indicating that the full Presidium was meeting or had met, and officials were being instructed on carrying out the plans. I had just received a cable from Dulles, who urgently wanted to get a message to the Soviet leaders that the United States did not look on Hungary or any of the Soviet satellites as potential military allies. The cable quoted a paragraph from a Dulles speech at Dallas to that effect, and emphasized that it had been written after intensive consideration at the "highest level"—an obvious reference to President Eisenhower.

I was able to convey the message to Khrushchev, Bulganin, and Zhukov at receptions that afternoon in honor of Turkey's National Day and at the Afghan Embassy. But the American assurance carried no weight with the Kremlin leaders. They had made up their minds to crush the revolution and set into motion what I believe was a cover plan to mask their intentions. Khrushchev and Bulganin sought out British Ambassador Hayter and me, anxious to be seen in conversation with us. Khrushchev's remarks were general in nature. The Soviet government would not deviate from its course, he said, although further "difficulties and unpleasantness" might be anticipated. The implication was that the liberalization policy would continue in Eastern Europe. At one point, I expressed the opinion that Stalin had made a colossal mistake in imposing harsh controls over Eastern Europe. It would have been possible to have had good relations with those countries if Stalin had listened to Roosevelt and Churchill at the wartime conferences and given the people more freedom in choosing their governments, I said, and cited Finland as an example of how friendly such relations could be. Khrushchev replied soberly, "Perhaps you are right," but added that Stalin, despite his mistakes, was an intelligent man, even a "genius."

It was Marshal Zhukov who worked on me, mixing untruths and half-truths with some real facts. I asked Zhukov whether the Soviet Union had agreed beforehand to Nagy's announcement on the radio that Soviet troops would be leaving Budapest immediately and negotiations would begin for their withdrawal from all of Hungary. Zhukov replied that Nagy had not referred to an immediate withdrawal from Budapest, and that Soviet troops, having gone there at the request of the Hungarian government, would remain until that government requested their withdrawal or until "order had been restored." A general withdrawal from the whole country was a matter for consideration by members of the Warsaw Pact, he said.

Zhukov, usually honest, on that occasion, as a good Party member, told me several outright untruths. He said that no Soviet reinforcements had been sent to Hungary "recently," since there were sufficient Soviet troops there. I challenged this statement, pointing out that there was information to the contrary. I noted that the Soviet representative on the United Nations Security Council had not, so far as I was aware, issued any specific denial to a statement by the British representative that Soviet reinforcements had been sent from Rumania. Zhukov said he had not read the Security Council debates, but reaffirmed his no-reinforcement statement.

Zhukov also insisted that Soviet troops had only opened fire in Budapest when some of their officers had been killed by insurgents, and that in the last forty-eight hours there had been no firing by Soviet troops. I again told him I had information to the contrary (the BBC that morning spoke of Soviet artillery firing on Hungarian army barracks). Again Zhukov said the reports were false.

He also said that Soviet troops in Budapest were not under his command, but under the Hungarian Minister of Defense. This was a patent lie. The Soviets would never relinquish control over their military forces. He asserted that Soviet troops had only been in action in Budapest and had not moved against any "new" local authorities in the provinces. Speaking rapidly and with passion, he insisted that, contrary to foreign news reports, there had been no incident of a defection by any Soviet soldier to the rebels. He took a soldier's attitude in defense of Soviet troops, stating that he was not a politician and that the function of the army was to carry out orders. In addition, he attempted along standard Soviet lines to present the Hungarian action as a counterrevolutionary putsch. When help was asked for by a government that was a member of the Warsaw Pact, the Soviet Union could not refuse. He inquired what would happen under any other alliance in similar circumstances. I replied that the NATO pact contained no provision for the use of foreign troops for intervention in internal matters. He said that the Warsaw Pact was for the support of the socialist camp and, therefore, for protection of socialist governments from any threat. I commented that I knew nothing in the text of the Warsaw Pact which would justify internal intervention. Zhukov said such action was "envisaged" in the Pact.

The Marshal attempted, though somewhat mildly, to make a "foreign connection" with the insurgents, mentioning that they had captured large quantities of American rifles, as well as German cannon. He did not, however, assert that these arms had been sent by the

United States, saying they were probably World War II supplies smuggled into Hungary from Austria.

In the course of our conversation, I asked him if it was not a simple fact that when a government was forced to appeal for foreign troops for help to suppress an insurrection, this was the clearest evidence that the government did not enjoy the support of the people. Zhukov feebly spoke of the exploitation of legitimate discontent for past policies by unscrupulous and criminal elements—the standard Soviet line.

In reporting to Washington on the conversation, I said:

> I have no way of judging the truth of Zhukov's remarks that Soviet troops have confined their action to Budapest and have by-passed towns and other areas of Hungary where nationalists are in control. However, from the general tenor of his remarks, as well as statements to the press by Shepilov and him, it looks as though the Soviet decision was to support the Nagy government to the end, although possibly primarily in Budapest, leaving provinces and other towns for subsequent mopping up if resistance can be broken in the capital, thereby hoping to avoid total military occupation of Hungary by Soviet forces. In this light it would appear Nagy's statements on the night of the 28th regarding Soviet troop withdrawal from Budapest was nothing more than a trick, with Soviet connivance, to cause the insurgents to cease fire.

The next day, October 30, the situation became even more confusing. Moscow newspapers carried the text of a resolution passed by the Soviet Central Committee outlining a much more relaxed policy toward the satellites. It accepted the basic concept of "national Communism," under which the internal developments of the socialist countries were solely a matter for each country. It proposed negotiations on the "recall" of Soviet specialists and on the stationing of Soviet troops in Rumania and Poland, as well as Hungary (omitting, significantly, East Germany). Even this resolution, which was more liberal than anything the Soviet government had adopted before on the subject, contained a number of ambiguities. It was clear that it was predicated on the preservation of the "great commonwealth of socialist nations." As the next few days were to show, there were definite limits on Soviet patience in regard to any attempt to substitute a non-Communist for a Communist regime. Thus the so-called Brezhnev Doctrine, as it came to be known in 1968, was in operation in 1956. Brezhnev, who succeeded Khrushchev as Party Secretary, was correct in a sense in saying that he did not proclaim such a doctrine. The Soviets made it clear long before Brezhnev that they had not only the right but the duty to act with armed force to prevent the erosion, undermining, or overthrow of any of their models of socialism. That was Stalin's policy, and it has not changed.

During the evening of October 30, there were slight indications that the Soviets were serious about granting the satellites more freedom. At still another Kremlin reception, an angry Zhukov told me flatly that Soviet troops had been ordered to withdraw from Budapest. "The order has already been given for Soviet forces to leave the city," he said. Then, with an impatient slash of his arm, he said, "Let them deal with it themselves." He meant the Hungarians. Khrushchev, Bulganin, Molotov, and Kaganovich were all looking glum. "It is possible," I wired Dulles, "that Zhukov's statement represented an overnight shift in position based on some events in Hungary unknown to us here."

Indeed there were such events. Pressed by the revolutionary fervor of the people, Nagy in the next few hours proclaimed the end of the one-party system and the withdrawal of Hungary from the Warsaw Pact and appealed to the United Nations. Nagy thus sealed his and Hungary's fates. He was trying to end, not just alter, the Communist system, and he was cutting the umbilical cord with the Soviet Union. Moscow would never accept such a situation.

Before I heard of Nagy's fateful moves, the Soviet government announced it was withdrawing the Red Army from Budapest, indicating to me that the Kremlin had decided either to cut its losses and accept a high degree of independence for the satellites or to get ready for more military action.

Meanwhile, Dulles was anxious to know whether the rapidly changing situation had altered the power balance in the Kremlin. He was especially eager to know because of another crisis that had broken out. In an incredible blunder, the British and the French, in connivance with the Israelis, had ganged up on Egypt in an attempt to seize control of the Suez Canal. On October 29, Israel invaded Egypt, and shortly thereafter Britain and France began bombing in preparation for troop landings.

In response to Dulles's request, I said that while nothing was really known about the lineup of the Presidium, without question the entire leadership was involved in deciding policy on Hungary. "There is no evidence available," I wrote, "to indicate Khrushchev is no longer head of the collective leadership here."

Although the Soviets had already decided on massive use of force and the installation of a new Hungarian government (Kadar, the faithful Party Secretary, had been taken to the safety of the Soviet Union), Bulganin continued to deceive me. At a party for the Syrians on November 2, he denied a stream of authenticated reports of Red Army reinforcements being sent to Hungary. He said there had been much movement of Soviet troops inside the country, and this might have created the false impression that reinforcements were moving in. I told the State Department I did not believe him. Bulganin also said that a Soviet-Hungarian commission would be established to consider Nagy's statement on withdrawal of all Soviet troops from the country and of Hungary from the Warsaw Pact. I was fooled for a few hours, believing that the Soviets might withhold military action. The next morning, noting that the Soviet press carried no references to any commission and remembering the air of triumph of Marshals Zhukov and Vasily Sokolovsky the previous night, I warned Washington that the commission report was little more than a device to gain time for preparations for armed action. If Nagy stands firm, I wrote, "It looks at the moment as though Soviet troops would go into action."

That evening—it was November 3—Khrushchev removed all doubts of Soviet intentions. Toward the end of another reception for the Syrians, he and Malenkov appeared. After conversing with other members of the Presidium, he came over to me. I was talking to Erik Braadland, the Norwegian Ambassador. Without veiling his sarcasm, Khrushchev said he assumed NATO was pleased at the possibility of some "dislocation" in the Warsaw Pact. I asked what Soviet intentions were in regard to Nagy's request for the removal of all Soviet troops from Hungary and that country's desire to get out of the Warsaw Pact. He said that negotiations were taking place and that matters would be "straightened out." I said there seemed to be a contradiction between the talk of negotiations and continual reports of heavy Soviet reinforcements in Hungary. Khrushchev angrily replied that the Soviet Union was going to be just as strong as it needed to be to meet the dangers that confronted it. "We have enough troops there," he said, "but we will add more and more if necessary." I must have had some kind of smile on my face, although I did not think his remark was funny, because he added, "This is no joke." He then switched the conversation to the Suez Canal crisis.

I rushed back to the Embassy and telegraphed the news to Washington. Khrushchev had made it clear that the Soviets were ready to send the Red Army into action. As I told the State Department, "The only discernible virtue in Khrushchev that I can see is his brutal frankness."

Khrushchev was never honest with me regarding the real reason for the brutal suppression of the Hungarian revolution. The closest he came to reflecting his real thinking came in a private discussion with the Swedish and Finnish ambassadors on November 7 at a party in the Kremlin, and relayed to me. The Swedish Ambassador, my friend Sohlman, said he thought Soviet military action would have a bad effect on Stockholm. Khrushchev conceded that this was probably true, but said the Kremlin had little choice. He explained that the Kremlin had agreed to support Nagy, but Nagy lost control to "Fascist" counterrevolutionaries. Sohlman interrupted to say that the Swedish government's information was that the entire Hungarian people, not just "Fascist bands," were involved. Khrushchev gave the standard Soviet denial, saying that if all of the Hungarian people were against them, the Soviets would not have used troops. As proof, he cited Finland. Turning to the Finnish Ambassador, he said, "In your country we knew the entire people were against us, and thus did not occupy Finland after the war." Khrushchev said that the "Fascist bands" in Hungary were murdering "our people" and Communists and sniping at Soviet troops. It was quite impossible, he said, for the Red Army to withdraw in the face of hostile fire.

Still following the propaganda line, Khrushchev said that as the First Secretary of the Communist Party, he could state that the Soviet Union had no special interest in Hungary. The Finnish Ambassador, Eero A. Wuori, said he thought that the Soviet Union had considerable strategic interest in Hungary but wondered whether this interest could not have been protected by Hungarian neutrality along Austrian lines. Khrushchev at last became candid. He admitted the Soviet strategic interest in Hungary, and said the Soviet leaders felt that, from the course of events in Budapest, Hungary would not stop at neutrality but would line up with the West as a "hostile" country. If Hungary would ask for neutrality, the Soviet government would give favorable consideration to the request, he said. This latter statement was window dressing; Khrushchev was really saying that Moscow would not give up its control of the Sovietized buffer state.

On November 4, the Red Army began the attack that crushed the revolution. As Nagy took refuge in the Yugoslav Embassy, the Soviets broadcast a recorded speech by Kadar announcing the establishment of a new government. *Pravda* denounced Nagy as a "tool of reactionary forces," and told how the mobs had destroyed memorials to Soviet troops who had "fallen in battle to free Budapest from the Hitlerite horde." In a matter of days, the revolution was smashed, the puppet Kadar government was installed, and refugees were streaming across the Austrian border by the thousands.

Curiously, the Soviets pulled the same deceptive trick on the Hungarians as they did on the English and French in 1939 at the time of the Nazi-Soviet pact. The Soviet general who was negotiating with Hungarians, as Voroshilov was with the British and French in 1939, thought that he was negotiating in good faith for a pullout of Soviet troops. He was shocked, I was told, when another Soviet officer entered the room and arrested the Hungarians. The only difference in 1939 was that the British and French were not arrested.

There was little the West could do except protest the Soviet action. I received approval from Washington of my request to join the other NATO country ambassadors in boycotting the Soviet celebrations of the Bolshevik Revolution on November 7. Instead of attending, I sent a congratulatory greeting card. On November 8, I received the following letter from F. Molochkov, the Soviet Chief of Protocol:

MR. AMBASSADOR:

I have been instructed to return the congratulatory visiting card which you sent to the Minister of Foreign Affairs of the U.S.S.R., D. T. Shepilov, inasmuch as it is considered that on the basis of your attitude to measures by which the national holiday of the U.S.S.R. is celebrated, sending this card does not in reality conform to that which it expresses.

Respectfully,
F. MOLOCHKOV

I told the State Department that the letter was the only recent Soviet communication that contained the truth. Unfortunately, this effort to demonstrate to the world the West's revulsion over Soviet actions in Hungary was negated in part by Eisenhower's pleasant acceptance of Bulganin's congratulations on his re-election as President. Dulles had not asked my opinion in the matter, and I was taken by surprise when I received the text of the President's reply to a letter from Bulganin. Since the reply had been sent over an open wire and not in code, the Soviets undoubtedly intercepted it, and I had no opportunity to try to stop it. However, I let Dulles know my irritation:

I cannot help but feel that these public messages at this particular juncture will have a most unfortunate effect on the Soviet mentality. As already reported from this embassy, the purpose of the congratulations to the President on his re-election was to demonstrate to the world that despite the reaction of world opinion to the Soviet action on Hungary, relations with the United States could still be regarded as normal. I fear very much that these messages will confirm the success of this maneuver.

Western representatives stayed away from most of the Kremlin receptions for the rest of the year. I did go to a party in the Kremlin for the Poles, but walked out because of a diatribe by Khrushchev against NATO. By early January, I felt that we had made our point. After Foreign Minister Shepilov had approached me and suggested we resume contacts, I talked the matter over with the British, the French, and the other Western ambassadors. We all agreed that a permanent boycott would make us look ludicrous, and we began accepting invitations to receptions again.

The new French Ambassador, Maurice Dejean, was always opposed to boycotting the social functions to demonstrate our opposition. He went to noticeable lengths to ingratiate himself with Soviet officials and placed too much credence in what they said. Even after the Soviet Union double-crossed Paris and, contrary to a promise of Gromyko, voted for the United Nations' taking up the question of Algerian independence in the summer of 1956, and even after Moscow had sent a threatening note to France during the Suez crisis in the fall, Dejean continued to play up to the Soviets. The Soviets were well aware of his attitude and had his measure.

While my efforts were focused on Kremlin policy toward Hungary, my staff was busy trying to pick up clues regarding the impact of events on the Russian people. Traditionally, the Russians have been noncommittal when Westerners ask them questions. So deep were their feelings about Hungary, however, that the Russians loosened their tongues a bit. The Embassy staff soon concluded that a substantial part of the young intelligentsia, which listened to the BBC and Voice of America broadcasts, sympathized with the Hungarian rebels. There were a number of incidents that led to this conclusion. In early November, an officer of the Embassy attended a lecture on international affairs at the Lenin Library. About two hundred persons, most of them students, were in the audience. At the end of the lecture, the speaker asked for questions. He received fifty-one questions, written on cards, all dealing with Hungary or Poland. When the speaker refused to discuss the questions, a young man in the audience demanded to hear the "truth" about Hungary. In reply, the speaker asked, "Does anyone in the audience believe the Soviet press does not print the truth?" The entire audience rose as one. When the lecturer continued to balk at talking about Poland and Hungary, the audience walked out of the hall. At a second lecture a few days later, the audience walked out when the speaker answered questions with clichés.

A Moscow student who was the son of a high Soviet official told an Embassy officer before the Soviet attack on Hungary that Hungarians hated the Russians, and the Hungarian government had stayed in power only because of the presence of the Red Army. He said the Red Army should be withdrawn and the Hungarians should decide their own fate. A Russian intellectual told another Embassy officer, "I am ashamed of what we have done."

There were some young Russians who defended the Soviets' use of force on the ground that an independent Hungary could be a threat to Soviet security. Some also pointed out that the Soviets had a right to act because the Soviet people had suffered much to liberate Hungary from the Nazis.

Undoubtedly, however, the Polish and Hungarian ferment set Russians to thinking of their own lot. One of the subjects that students often brought up was the disparity between wages paid government and Communist Party leaders and those of factory workers. During a question period at a public lecture on December 11, two persons in the audience recalled Lenin's pre-revolutionary program of equality of wages. They pointed out that Party and government leaders and specialists earned 20,000 to 40,000 rubles a month, while qualified factory workers received less than 1,000. "When will Lenin's program be realized?" one of the questioners asked. The lecturer drew hoots from the crowd when he expressed doubts that such disparities existed. Several persons in the audience made disparaging remarks about Soviet agricultural failures, saying that Stalin alone was not responsible. The implication was that Khrushchev was to blame too.

French youths attending Moscow University told the French Embassy, which shared the information with us, that a Communist youth group at the university had adopted a three-point program calling for more equal distribution of income, broader information in the press, and publication of statistics on living standards in other countries. The resolution must have sent chills through some Party hacks. The greatest fear of the Bolsheviks as far as maintenance of their power is concerned is an alliance of disaffected intellectuals and discontented workers. We had few indications of trouble among the latter. One of the most reliable reports was that there had been a three-day strike at the Kaganovich ball-bearing plant in Moscow over a new work-rules and wage system.

Khrushchev realized the potential danger of students' expressing dissatisfaction over working conditions. In a speech on November 8, he referred to the leading role of youths in the Hungarian revolution, then said, "It is necessary to unceasingly increase our vigilance and devote more attention to correct the indoctrination of the youth." *Pravda* and other Soviet journals took the cue, calling for expanded ideology work to wipe out residues of foreign reactionary thoughts.

The troubles continued for some time. In January, 1957, the Russian who had tipped the Swedish Ambassador off regarding Beria's arrest, reported the 35,000 workers at the Stalin auto plant in Stalingrad were on strike, that Sverdlovsk University had been closed because of unruly conduct by students, and that there was an increase in police surveillance in Moscow.

The highest price that Moscow paid for the suppression of the Hungarian revolt was the damage inflicted on Communist parties and sympathizers in the non-Communist world. The heroic image of the Soviet Union, built on the deaths of millions who fell in the fight against Hitler, was shattered. In disgust, many members resigned from the party. Never did the Communist image reacquire the purity it had before. While the Soviets enjoyed the support of the rest of the Communist bloc—it must have been galling to enlist China's endorsement—for the use of force in Hungary, their subsequent actions led to a further estrangement with Tito. The Yugoslavs have never forgiven the Soviets for their treatment of Nagy. In return for Soviet assurances that he would be unharmed, the Yugoslav Embassy turned him over to the Soviet authorities. Eventually, Nagy was executed. In December, the Yugoslav Ambassador, Micunovich, told me he thought the "Stalinists" were mobilizing to isolate Yugoslavia from other Communist countries. While Micunovich was singled out for special favors, he remained pessimistic about the future of relations with Moscow. Despite all the visits and expressions of good will, the Yugoslavs and the Soviets have never resolved their ideological dispute.

How could the United States take advantage of the tremendous setback to its implacable foe? Ambassador Llewellyn Thompson in Vienna suggested in early November that we seek to devise some concrete methods of channeling anti-Soviet feelings into a constructive program. He said the United States had a moral commitment to do something to help Eastern Europe because of the heavily publicized campaign of sending balloons with freedom messages over the satellites and the broadcasts of the Voice of America and Radio Free Europe. There were others, too, who blamed Eisenhower administration, and Dulles in particular, for talking of rolling back Communism and of liberating the "captive nations." Charges were made that the United States had run out on a pledge to aid Hungary.

I do not believe that any broadcasts or any talk from the United States of freeing captive nations had anything whatsoever to do with the Hungarian revolt. The rebellion came from internal developments in Hungary and was a clear manifestation of the hatred of the people for Communism. Shortly after my return to Washington in 1957, a careful examination was made of exactly what the Voice of America and Radio Free Europe had broadcast before and during the revolt. There was nothing in any of the broadcasts which could have been interpreted as an offer to help. There was one broadcast which may have been a little injudicious, but it spoke only in general terms of the sympathy and support of the outside world for the efforts of the Hungarian people to free themselves. The most that could be said was that a few of the Hungarians may have been misled by the administration's use of the word "liberation" in the 1952 campaign. "Liberation" was a word that took on the meaning in World War II of military force freeing a captive land. To the popular mind, "liberation" may have meant that the United States would use force to free satellite areas. There is no proof that the Hungarians placed such an interpretation on the term.

Ambassador Thompson suggested that the United States press the Soviet Union for a firm commitment to withdraw its troops from Hungary in six months or a year. I opposed the idea on the basis that the Soviets and the puppet Kadar government would have plenty of time to consolidate their regime and liquidate the remaining anti-Communist leaders. Under the circumstances, I advised Dulles, "I cannot see, beyond keeping our moral position intact, much that we can possibly do to help the Hungarian people at this juncture short of the use of force," which, of course, was out of the question. I did suggest that consideration be given to offering Moscow a high-level conference on disarmament and related matters in return for a Soviet pledge to comply with United Nations decisions on Hungary. The State

Department expressed interest, but pointed out—and I agreed—that the timing was not right. The President had just declined a Swiss proposal for a five-power meeting on disarmament on the ground that some of the issues were being studied by the United Nations.

The Western powers' freedom of action was also restricted by the fact that the crisis over the Israeli-British-French invasion of Egypt had eroded our moral position as a defender of small nations. I would not undertake to state what the Western powers would have done in regard to Hungary had the revolution been the single event of that period. The dispute between the United States and the British and the French over the Suez Canal deflected a certain amount of attention from Hungary. There might have been much stronger action in the United Nations, although I seriously doubt if anything would have checked the Soviet Union.

CHAPTER TWENTY-FOUR

The Suez Crisis

When President Nasser announced on July 26, 1956, that Egypt was nationalizing the Suez Canal, the Soviet press was ecstatic. *Pravda* spread the story over two columns, quoting Nasser's speech in Alexandria at length and proudly pointing out references to Egyptian purchases of Soviet arms. A few days later, I was instructed by Secretary of State Dulles to call on Premier Bulganin to explain the American protest of Nasser's unilateral abrogation of the 1888 international treaty on the Suez. The conversation became somewhat heated, and at one point I remarked that Nasser's action seemed to me to be a revival of Hitler's tactics in the international world. Bulganin professed great indignation at this remark and, drawing himself up to his full height—he was plump but not tall—said he could not tolerate such comments about the head of a friendly country. I pointed out that my remark was not a comment, but merely a comparison, and one that I thought just. Hitler, too, had unilaterally denounced treaties. I did not say so, but the Russians after the experience of the 1941 Nazi invasion in violation of the 1939 Hitler-Stalin pact, knew full well what I meant. Of course, I did not put Nasser in the same class as Hitler as a threat to other nations. The conversation passed on to other aspects of the subject, and we parted amicably. It was clear that the Soviet Union intended to back Nasser fully. One reason was the traditional Bolshevik support of nationalization; another more ominous reason was the Soviet Union's growing interest in getting a foothold in the Middle East by supporting the Arab countries in their opposition to Israel.

The Soviet Union had been one of the earliest backers of Israel. In 1948, it followed the United States by mere minutes in recognizing the new state in the Middle East. The Soviet Union apparently thought that Israel would be an anti-British enclave in the Middle East because the Zionist terrorist organizations were the only group fighting imperialism there. Besides, there were a large number of left-wing immigrants from Europe in the new nation, and the Soviets mistakenly thought they would be pro-Communist. When Israel developed strong ties with the West, particularly the United States, and Nasser denounced the anti-Communist Baghdad Pact, the Soviet Union swung over to the Egyptian side. In doing so, the Bolsheviks were only reverting to tradition. The Bolshevik movement has a long history of anti-Zionism, not on racial grounds but on organizational and political grounds. Lenin, for example, considered the Bundists, the trade-union organization of Jews in Eastern Europe and Russia, antithetical to Bolshevik aims. Stalin felt that the Jews subordinated the proletariat revolution to the creation of a Jewish national home. In his fight for power in the 1920s, Stalin did not hesitate to use anti-Semitism as a weapon against Trotsky. The Soviet treatment of the Jews has been extremely ambivalent, at times harsh and repressive, at other times tolerant. But never have the Bolshevik leaders considered a Jew with any tendency toward Zionism to be a thoroughgoing Soviet citizen. They have resented the idea that Jews could have allegiances above those to the Soviet state.

From time to time when I was ambassador in Moscow, I heard of secret trials of Jews. On July 23, 1956, for example, I heard indirectly through the Israeli Embassy of a trial in April, in Moscow, of twelve Jews accused of spreading Zionist propaganda, organizing a Zionist underground, and giving confidential information to the Israelis. The defendants were sentenced to terms of three to ten years. A similar case was reported in Leningrad about the same time.

There were historical reasons, too, for Soviet support of the Arabs. Russia's ambitions in the Middle East go back centuries. The czars always wanted warm-water ports and sought unsuccessfully to make Russia a Mediterranean power. In this sense, the Communist leaders were merely behaving like czars. In the mid-twentieth century, the important difference was that, with the decline in British and French power, the Russians saw a real opportunity of moving in. American support for Israel, the bitter enemy of the Arabs, provided the perfect setting for the Soviet move. The weight of the Arab population—perhaps 30 million against 2.5 million Jews—must have influenced the Soviets, who usually look far ahead.

Compounding the difficulty was the fact that Nasser had been rebuffed by the United States. Early in 1954, Nasser asked the United

States to sell arms to Egypt. He said that Israeli raids had forced him to give in to the demands of the Egyptian army for equipment to defend the country. When he was turned down by Washington, he asked Moscow, which arranged in the fall of 1955 for purchases of weapons from Czechoslovakia. Thus began the buildup in Egypt's military capability that eventually made the Soviet Union a major power in the Middle East.

In Moscow in 1954 and 1955, the pro-Arab and anti-Israeli stance of the Soviet government became clearer all the time. On April 27, 1955, no Soviet official attended the National Day reception at the Israeli Embassy, apparently in protest of the release of "terrorists" who had attacked Soviet and Czech legations in Tel Aviv. I wired Washington; "We have seen diplomatic National Day receptions shunned by Soviet officials (e.g., Pakistan), but none so thoroughly as this one. On the other hand, 'independent' Arab states have been by contrast receiving the warmest treatment." On February 1, 1956, the Russian-born Israeli Ambassador, J. Avidar, called on Molotov to ask him for a clarification of the Soviet policy toward Israel in light of the open support of the Arab position, but apparently received no satisfaction. Ten days later, the Soviet Union announced it was going to help Egypt establish a nuclear-physics laboratory in Cairo to work on the peaceful use of atomic energy. In the spring, Khrushchev told a delegation of French socialists that the Arab-Israeli conflict was really an old-fashioned imperialist struggle over oil, with the United States opposing Britain and, to a lesser extent, France. He said that the Soviet Union had vital interests in the Near Eastern countries along its borders, and that it was only natural therefore that Egypt should be given assistance with arms. Later in the spring came the secret trials of the Zionists. In July, Nasser nationalized the Suez Canal, and the Soviets were covering him with glory.

While there was undoubtedly a direct connection between Secretary of State Dulles's brutal notifications of the cancellation of the American offer to help build the Aswan Dam and President Nasser's nationalization of the Suez Canal, I am inclined to doubt that Dulles's tactless action was by any means the sole reason for the take-over. To Nasser, British-French ownership and operation of the waterway infringed on Egypt's sovereignty, and for some time he had wanted to correct the situation. Dulles merely precipitated Nasser's decision. In fairness to Dulles, it should also be noted that the World Bank had taken a negative view concerning the Egyptian government's ability to contribute its share of funds for construction of the dam.

After the first Western protest to Nasser's seizure of the canal, diplomatic efforts were begun to try to resolve the issue. The Soviets gave no hint at first that they were going to take advantage of the situation. On July 31, Khrushchev made a speech in which he proposed that the Suez Canal be the subject of international negotiations. While he supported, as a matter of principle, Egypt's right to nationalization, he did not go all the way with Nasser's assertion that Egypt had the right to determine the operating rules unilaterally. There should be freedom of navigation, Khrushchev said. In all likelihood, the Soviets also did not want to see a precedent confirmed for unilateral control of an international waterway in view of Turkish ownership of the Dardanelles. His speech was apparently designed to calm Egypt by offering support for its nationalization and giving Nasser a friendly voice in any negotiation. "Khrushchev's assertion of Soviet interest in freedom of navigation," I wired Washington, "may be the first step in an attempt to justify Soviet participation in any international discussions on this subject."

On August 1, Premier Bulganin emphasized to me at a Swiss reception that the Soviet Union was interested in freedom of navigation through the canal, but did not reply directly to my statement that an international agreement had been broken. I was convinced that the Soviets were genuinely concerned over the outbreak of war in the Middle East, and wanted to participate in a conference of Suez Canal users which the Allies were organizing. At first, the Soviet Union was not invited as a sponsoring power, apparently because of its pro-Nasser position. That was a mistake that the Soviets exploited for propaganda purposes. On August 3, the decision was made to invite Moscow to the conference.

Informing me of the invitation, Dulles asked me to tell the Kremlin quietly that the United States had had a difficult time restraining Britain and France from taking military action, and that in Washington's view the best interests of both the United States and the Soviet Union would be served by the establishment of an international authority guaranteeing free and open arrangements for the canal. A few days later, Dulles instructed me to make clear to high officials in Moscow that it would be a "grave delusion" if the Soviets thought that the United States would not be solidly with Britain and France if the conference failed. In an attempt to prod Soviet officials to exert influence on those governments with which it had special relations, Dulles asked me to give the Russians a little history lesson: whatever the initial divergences with allies, the United States inevitably became involved in world crises when the chips were down. In his cable, Dulles added his personal belief that the matter was of the utmost seriousness and that unless the conference was held and its result substantially accepted by Egypt, "the result will be forcible action with grave risk of its becoming enlarged."

There were plenty of receptions at this time, and I had no trouble in letting the Soviet leaders know the American view. Even without such conversations, it was easy for me to predict that Moscow would send a representative but express strong reservations concerning the makeup and purpose of the conference. That is precisely what Moscow did on August 10, in a note denouncing British and French "repression" and supporting Egypt in highly propagandistic language. The note led me to conclude that the Soviet purpose was to frustrate Western attempts to solve the problem. There was a great deal of speculation at the time about the possible use of military force by the British and French to reopen the canal on their terms. In a telegram to the State Department, I expressed my belief that the Kremlin had decided that the chances were against actual use of armed force by the Western powers, and that even if limited force was employed, the Soviet Union could successfully stay out of the conflict while exploiting to the full Arab reaction throughout the area. I believed they were counting on evidence avidly reproduced in the Soviet press and undoubtedly exaggerated, that public opinion in both England and France was turning against the use of force. Perhaps too emotionally, I concluded:

> The Soviet government was given every opportunity in this situation to exercise its undoubted influence on Egypt in the direction of conciliation and a decent regard for the rights and interest of others, but has chosen for its own reasons the path best calculated to inflame Arab emotions and make more difficult a solution on lines acceptable to the Western powers.

I flew from Moscow to London for the conference, which began on August 18. My role was primarily that of an observer, since I was not sufficiently in Dulles's confidence to be privy to his thoughts. It has always seemed to me that Dulles was at his worst at this meeting. He shaded the edge of downright trickery and even dishonesty. In simple language, he talked out of both sides of his mouth. To the British and French, he talked as if he favored them; to the Russians, he sounded anti-British and anti-French. I went with him when he called on Shepilov, the new Soviet Minister, at the

Soviet Embassy. The conversation was embarrassing to me. Although Dulles's deception was clumsy, he succeeded in selling Shepilov, who was not very knowledgeable about foreign affairs, on a formula giving the nations using the canal a dominant voice in its operation. Later, apparently after consulting with Moscow, Shepilov realized that the formula violated his instructions and basic Soviet aims, and backed off acceptance.

The British and the French also felt uneasy about Dulles. He certainly sympathized with their position and held no brief for Nasser. But he was also acutely aware of public opinion in the United States and rightly sought to persuade the British and French to forgo military action. The difficulty was in his handling of the matter. He was too slick, seeking to make points in the manner of a Wall Street lawyer.

It is perhaps an overstatement to assert that Dulles pushed the French and the British toward military intervention in the Suez. If the United States had been wholehearted in supporting the British and French positions and had been willing to exert greater pressure on Nasser, Paris and London might have called off their plans for military action. I do not mean to imply that we should have joined the British and French in any threat of military action, and certainly not in the actual attack. While the British and French had a strong case, they could not reverse the course of history. Dulles saw the Suez as a dying gasp of imperialism.

Perhaps Dulles acted the way he did because there was much talk of armed intervention by Britain and France. At a luncheon, Sir Kenneth Strong, the head of the British Joint Intelligence Committee, told me that no decision had been made but the matter was under serious consideration. He was strongly opposed to such action, and said that if I ever picked up the paper and saw that the French and British had attacked the Suez Canal, I could write off the whole venture as a failure. For years, he said, the British had had 80,000 troops in the Canal Zone, and had had little influence on the policy of the Egyptian government. Re-establishing the Western position in the canal would probably have less effect in 1956, he said, unless Britain and France went for the jugular; that is, occupied Cairo and Alexandria. I remembered those words when the invasion came.

Instead of taking military action, the conference dispatched emissaries to Nasser to propose some formula which would have reinstated the 1888 treaty and provided for nationalization through negotiation. This attempt ended in total failure because neither side was ready to make the necessary concessions. Parenthetically, it should be remarked here that in Arab dealings with the British and French the mob in the street in many cases dictated the ultimate policy of the government. Arabs are by nature a volatile people. But before radio, Arab governments could make decisions and impose them on the people with little worry of protests, because there were few means of communication with the mass of the population. Radio, however, changed the internal position of every Arab government. With loudspeakers in every corner of the bazaars, it was possible for any demagogue to arouse the nationalist, racial, and religious passions of the residents. If there was freedom of speech, it was possible for an opposition leader to inflame mobs against the government. Interestingly, radio became a powerful restriction on any government that wanted to compromise. It certainly curbed Nasser in 1956. He had to worry about the reaction of the people and rejected the conference's overture.

The British felt tricked by Dulles's tactics. They believed the United States had no clear policy, but was merely trying to prevent a patently illegal move by Egypt. Despite Dulles's continued pleas for "restraint" in the United Nations discussions, the British gave in to pressure from the French and joined in secret plans for a swift punitive expedition against Nasser. The French government's reasons for desiring the strike were completely unrelated to Suez; Paris wanted to deal a crushing blow to Nasser as the harborer of the Algerian independence leaders in Cairo. The Israelis, worried about Egypt's growing military power, hoped to weaken the foe for some time.

Without notice, official or unofficial, to the United States, the Israelis attacked in the Sinai Peninsula on October 29. The next day, the British and French, their invasion fleets standing offshore, delivered an ultimatum to Nasser. While the world awaited his reply, I attended a reception in the Kremlin. I was talking to Zhukov when Molotov came up and asked, "What is the United States going to do?" I told him my government took a most serious view of the Israeli invasion and had moved to bring the subject before the Security Council. In his most sarcastic style, Molotov implied that the United States could have prevented the invasion if it had wanted to, because it had great influence over Israel. I replied that he was mistaken, that the United States had done everything it could to prevent military action, noting that President Eisenhower had sent personal messages to Israeli Prime Minister David Ben-Gurion.

Shifting his ground slightly, Molotov said that Britain and France were about to join in the attack because they wanted to punish Egypt. I asked how he could believe that, since he must have been aware that Britain had warned Israel that it would go to Jordan's defense if the latter were attacked. Besides, I said, I did not believe that Britain and France, two democratic countries, would be able to wage war without considerably more preparation of public opinion. Molotov smiled cynically and said, "We will see." Then I made a few jabs at Molotov, recalling that Secretary Dulles had warned the Soviet Union the previous year of the dangers of supplying arms to Egypt when the situation was so inflamed. "It is Israel, not Egypt, that is the aggressor," Molotov said. Feeling somewhat bested in the exchange, I confined myself to repeating that the United States had done everything it could do to prevent war in the Middle East and he would be wise to believe me.

Within a few hours, the British and French began bombing Egypt, and I regretted my too quick defense of our allies. The next time I saw Molotov, I confessed error. He was a little smug, but did not rub it in.

Incidentally, my initial view was that, regrettable as the British-French-Israeli attack was, it represented a defeat for Soviet Middle East policy, since it demonstrated that the Soviets could not defend Egypt. It also served, however, to divert attention from the Hungarian revolution, which was then at its peak, and may have convinced the Kremlin that it had a freer hand to destroy the rebels.

Having been burned once in defending the British and French, I kept my thoughts to myself and cautioned members of the Embassy staff to do the same. I did not share the feeling of those Americans who took satisfaction in opposing our allies on an issue of such grave importance. As I wired Dulles, "One of the most disagreeable features of the present situation is finding ourselves on the same side of this question with the Soviets." At a reception for the Belgians, Kaganovich caught me at the buffet table and said he thought the United States and the Soviet Union, together, should be able to do something. Later, Shepilov called me to the Foreign Ministry and presented a note. After denouncing the invasion, the note proposed that the United States and the Soviet Union join in a common action—the implication was military action—if necessary against France and Britain, America's two closest allies. Astonished, I asked whether the Soviet government was joking in asking me to send the note to the American government. When Shepilov assured me that his government was serious, I told him the message would be transmitted, but it would not be well received in Washington, and there was no chance of acceptance of the idea. The note warned that if the invasion was not halted, the Soviet Union would "reserve its liberty of action." At the same time, harsh warnings hinting at the use of nuclear-tipped intercontinental missiles were sent to the British and French.

I immediately sent the note to Washington, and followed it up two hours later with an appraisal that Moscow was motivated largely, if not entirely, by a desire to divert world attention from Hungary. However, it would be imprudent, I cautioned, to dismiss the note as an "empty propaganda gesture." Since the Soviet Union had cast aside, in Hungary, any pretense to moral responsibility, it might be willing "to risk more hazardous action in the Middle East than would normally be the case," I said, mentioning specifically the possibility of a threat to Iran. In that telegram, and in one the following day, November 6, I pointed out the need to induce the British and French to declare an immediate ceasefire. I also urged Washington to warn the Soviet Union that any military action against Britian and France would encounter the armed opposition of the United States. I was gratified to learn that the White House did issue such a warning. This strong American reaction is usually ignored by the French and the British in their bitter comments on the role of the United States in the Suez crisis.

Eisenhower also sent harsh notes to London and Paris demanding that the invasion be called off. It was this pressure, I believe, rather than the Soviet threats, that forced the British and French to call a cease-fire the day after the landings.

Although most of the military action in the Suez was over, the Soviets, their tanks rolling over the weak defenses of the Hungarians, continued to fan the flames of the Middle East. The newspapers were filled with articles about protest meetings. Veterans of the Red Army were reporting to be volunteering to fight in Egypt if the British, French, and Israelis did not withdraw. The idea had apparently been started by Khrushchev two months before. At a reception for the Rumanians, Krushchev told French Ambassador Dejean that if there was war over the Suez, the "Arabs would not be alone." He said there would be many "volunteers," adding, "If my son wished to volunteer I would give him my blessing." After the invasion, I sent a number of telegrams to Washington mentioning the possibility of a volunteer Soviet force. There was no spirit of alarm in the wires, but not until mid-November did I give adequate emphasis to the propaganda aim of the Soviet reports. So tense was the atmosphere (everyone remembered that Chinese threats of sending volunteers to Korea had been brushed off) that Washington seriously believed the Soviets were about to send volunteers. On November 15, I advised the State Department that I was inclined to believe the "volunteer" threat was primarily a propaganda weapon to impress the Arabs and increase the pressure on the British and the French. If fighting resumed, some form of volunteer plan might be put into effect, I thought. In the same telegram, I had one of my better moments of forecasting Soviet intentions. I said that if the Soviets could eliminate all foreign troops in the Suez, they would then proceed through military assistance, including training and instruction of personnel, to equip and train the Arabs. To the Arabs, the military buildup would be aimed at Israel. But the ultimate Soviet aim, I said, was to organize the Arab nation in order to eliminate Western influence and economic positions (which, of course, included the United States) from the Middle East and Africa.

The more I thought about the volunteers, the more I thought the Soviets were bluffing. The Soviets would not take overt action that might put them directly or indirectly into the fighting in the Middle East. The Soviet military posture was not equal to that of the United States and its allies. Besides, there was no easy means by which the Soviets could transport volunteers to the area. They would have to cross countries friendly to the West—Turkey or Iran.

Only once during the Suez crisis did Khrushchev give a clue to his worry about a general war in the Middle East. He expressed regret to the Swedish and Finnish ambassadors, in a private conversation at the Kremlin, of the "necessity" of sending harsh notes on Suez to England and France. According to the account I was given of the conversation, Khrushchev fell back on the excuse that the Soviet Union had to act to enable the United Nations to survive—if hostilities had continued for another week, there would have been nothing left of the United Nations. He insisted that at no time had the Kremlin contemplated unilateral action in the Middle East; it always planned to work within the framework of the United Nations with other powers.

Khrushchev told the Scandinavians the Soviet Union wanted to maintain good relations with the West, but he demonstrated a deep-seated anger at the Israelis. He said the Soviet Union could have handled the Israelis with regular rockets, without airplanes or atomic rockets. This remark pointed up the continued danger in the Middle East. Adding to the tension, Syria and Jordan were rumored to be contemplating an attack on Israel.

The massive Soviet propaganda campaign and the belligerent tone of Bulganin's notes (they must have been written by Khrushchev) worried our allies in the Middle East. Iran, on the Soviet border, was especially sensitive. I do not know where the suggestion originated, but in mid-November I was asked by the State Department about a possible Soviet reaction to a move by the United States to invoke the Baghdad Pact by announcing its willingness to help Iran defend her sovereignty. My judgment was that the Soviets would be violently vocal, predicting the installation of American air bases and denouncing the action as another piece of evidence showing that the capitalist nations were encircling the Soviet Union. I did not believe that the Soviets would turn to direct military action, but would try to reactivate the pro-Soviet Tudeh party and increase agitation among the Iranian people. However, I opposed the aid-to-Iran suggestion on the basis that it would diminish American influence with Egypt and other Arab countries and would line us up squarely with the discredited British. Besides, I did not believe the Soviet Union contemplated any military action against Iran.

Turkey was nervous, too. The Turks were certain that the Soviets were flying over their country, and sent a memorandum to the United States asking for help and expressing a willingness to consider a preventive strike against Syria. In a telegram to Washington, I expressed doubt about any immediate threat to Turkey and questioned whether the Soviets where violating Turkish air space. I saw no danger in helping Turkey strengthen her air defenses. As for sending American military forces, I saw an "acceptable risk" if defensive units—radar groups and interceptor squadrons—were sent. But the dispatch of Strategic Air Command bombers, with all the overtones of nuclear weapons, might, I advised, be regarded by the Soviets as a clear indication of the imminence of an attack, and might, therefore, provoke a convulsive reaction. I counseled against the sending of any planes, at least until there was more credible evidence of danger to the Turks.

As for a possible strike against Syria, I wrote:

> One danger is the clear indication of Turkish willingness, if backed by the United States, to consider preventive action against Syria, which in the present circumstances would be in the highest degree dangerous and I would not venture to predict Soviet reaction in such an event. This would have all the dangers, plus some special ones, of the renewal of hostilities with Egypt. In general I think we should be prepared to take any reasonable measures which would reassure Turkey as to its own security but on the clear understanding that the Turks would not

initiate any action against Syria. The consequences of the Anglo-French-Israeli action would seem to make abundantly clear the folly of a new preventive action and, in addition, I believe there are other methods, political and economic, which could have a good chance of frustrating Soviet long-term designs in the area.

If actual violation of Turkish air space is established I believe a protest to the Soviet government communicated through the United Nations, and if necessary backed by the United States, would be the best method of dealing with this problem apart from practical measures ... to increase Turkish air defense capacity.

The Suez crisis produced the first demonstrations in Moscow against actions by foreign governments. The Israeli, British, and French embassies were the targets. The demonstrations were carefully planned by the Party apparatus. Each demonstrator was told what he could and could not do. Usually, violence was prohibited. I was sitting in my office at the Embassy on November 5—the day of the landings in Egypt—when an officer rushed in to say he had just had a call from a member of the British Embassy that a Russian mob was "storming" the Embassy building. I was startled, and many thoughts raced through my mind. We were having a staff meeting in my office, and we speculated on what this news meant in terms of Soviet policy. We knew that spontaneous demonstrations did not occur in Moscow and that this must have been ordered by the authorities. Before we had reached any conclusions, more accurate and reassuring news came from the British. There was no "storming" of the Embassy building. A group of demonstrators carrying such signs as "Hands Off Egypt" had broken into the courtyard and were milling around. There was no violence. Similar scenes were taking place at the French and Israeli embassies.

There were some amusing sidelights. British Ambassador Hayter, who spoke Russian, asked a militia general, standing among the demonstrators, when the outrage was going to end. The general looked at his watch and replied, "In twenty minutes." Another militiaman picked up a sign that had fallen and tacked it back up on a fence. At the French Embassy, some of the demonstrators had signs in Yiddish. Obviously, these demonstrators should have been at the Israeli Embassy.

I ordered all American Embassy personnel to stay off the street, but a few hours later, when everything remained quiet, withdrew the order.

On December 17, Gromyko called me to the Foreign Office to

complain about a series of demonstrations against the Soviet mission in New York by Hungarians and their supporters. I wired Washington, and promptly received a report of the extensive efforts of the New York police to protect the Soviet mission and its employees. I took the report down to the Foreign Office and read it to Assistant Minister Zakharov, who was inexperienced. I had hardly finished when he took from a folder a typewritten sheet and read it to me. It was a statement contending that the United States was not adequately protecting Soviet officials in New York. It went on to say that the "population" of Moscow was indignant over this situation, and ended with the assertion that the people in Moscow might express their indignation against the American Embassy in Moscow. I immediately told Zakharov that I would be forced to report to my government that the Soviet government was planning a demonstration against our Embassy. He denied such plans, but said he could not predict the reaction of Muscovites. No demonstration took place. I am not certain why it was canceled.

The value to the Soviet Union of controlled demonstrations is dubious. They show the displeasure of the Soviet government, but they also teach the Russian people a method of protesting their real grievances. Spontaneous demonstrations over the treatment and trial of Jews in 1970 were one factor, I believe, in inducing the Kremlin to ease its restrictions on emigration to Israel.

Khrushchev did not confine the Soviet expression of hostility to formal notes and controlled demonstrations. With him, it was a personal matter, and when he was drinking there was no controlling his tongue. On November 17, the other ambassadors from NATO countries and I walked out of a Kremlin reception for Gomulka following a violent attack, in a prepared speech by Khrushchev, on Britain, France, and Israel for their invasion of Egypt. The next day, at the Polish Embassy, he spoke extemporaneously, and obviously the vodka had affected him. He jeered at British and French references to the invasion as a police action and referred to Israel as a "lackey sent ahead by the great Lords to soften up the victim for the attack." At this point, the NATO ambassadors went into an adjoining room and waited until the long, rambling speech was over. As we were leaving the room, we heard Khrushchev say, "We will bury you." This phrase does not imply a lethal attack, as Westerners might think. It is merely a figure of speech expressing confidence in prevailing over the long haul—of being present at an opponent's funeral.

By February, 1957, the tension had eased somewhat, and in April the Kremlin was emphasizing peaceful coexistence again. At an Albanian reception, which I did not attend, Khrushchev stressed the Soviet desire to re-establish diplomatic contacts with the West. He could not resist a reference to the ultimate triumph of communsim because of its "superior principles," but said the realities of living on the same planet necessitated friendly relations between the capitalist and socialist worlds. Calling French Ambassador Dejean a "dear friend," he spoke mildly of the Suez invasion, and stressed the point that Britian, France, and Israel had learned that the venture was a mistake.

Indeed, Suez was a sorry affair. Great Britain and France suffered a resounding defeat. The policy was bad and the execution deplorable. The invasion brought about the downfall of Anthony Eden's government in England and of Guy Mollet's in France. Despite its best efforts, the United States gained no friends. The Arabs were not grateful, even though there is no doubt that it was American opposition that helped lead London and Paris to abort the operation.

There has been much questioning of our policy, and with reason. It was misleading in the summer and indecisive in the weeks before the invasion. Yet even in retrospect I think that, except for cancellation of aid for the Aswan Dam, our general policy was correct. I do not see any other course we could have pursued. Once Israeli-British-French intentions were clear, the United States was firm in its opposition. The nature of the situation and the policies of the participants inevitably put us in the middle. As usual, the one in the middle was blamed by both sides.

The only country that benefited from the Suez affair was the Soviet Union. Without firing a shot or taking any action at all, Moscow was credited in large measure, particularly by the Arab countries, with stopping the war. The noisy support for Egypt greatly increased the Kremlin's reputation throughout the Arab world. Of course, Moscow's relations with Israel suffered, but the Soviets did not particularly care. The Kremlin leaders had decided to get a foothold in the Middle East, and the Suez crisis provided the opportunity. In the months that followed, there was a noticeable increase in Soviet arms deliveries to Egypt and other Arab countries. Khrushchev agreed to help build the Aswan Dam. Taking advantage of the bitter Arab hostility toward Israel, the Soviets have moved steadily to enhance their influence with the Arabs.

It is important to note that Soviet Middle East policy is singularly free from ideology. It is a great-power operation, one that the czars as well as the Bolsheviks could have mounted. The absence of the ideological base has troubled Soviet theoreticians, and there have been many attempts to devise some formula or to wiggle around it. Khrushchev pretended that Nasser was becoming a real Socialist, ignoring the fact that Egypt continued to outlaw the Communists. Eventually, Moscow settled for "progressive" as against "reactionary" Arab regimes. The real distinction was whether the regime was favorable to the Soviet Union and anti-Western. Khrushchev must have had a tough time convincing some members of the Kremlin to go along with his policy, because he later referred to the grumbling of the "narrow-minded skunks who raised such a stink" over his Soviet ties with Egypt. I was not cognizant of such opposition.

Later, the Soviet Union sent Soviet military forces to Egypt. Until then, the Soviet Union had scrupulously refrained from stationing any troops in a country outside the Communist bloc. The move can be explained by increased Soviet confidence in its military power in relation to the West. As the Soviet Union progressively increases its involvement in the Middle East, other opportunities and other temptations arise. The Soviet Union is now a Mediterranean power, an Indian Ocean power, and a Red Sea power.

I could not wait for such developments to give Washington an appraisal of the impact of the events in Eastern Europe and the Middle East on the Soviet Union in the fall of 1956. In December, with the aid of my staff, I prepared a 2,000-word analysis for the President, the Secretary of State, and other members of the National Security Council.

My first conclusion was that there had been no signs of any threat to the stability of the Soviet regime. Restlessness and doubts about Soviet actions had been confined chiefly to students. My second conclusion was that there was no reliable evidence of any significant change in Soviet domestic policies, either political or economic, as a result of the crises.

I also thought it logical that the Kremlin leaders had drawn two main lessons from the uprisings in Poland and Hungary. The first was the danger of relaxing political controls, even to a limited extent, while specific economic grievances of workers remained unrelieved. The second lesson was the failure of Communist education to indoctrinate the youth or intelligentsia. "The fusion of workers' grievances with the discontent of the intelligentsia is, I am sure, in Bolshevik eyes, the chief warning which they would see in developments in Eastern Europe," I wrote.

As to the future policy, it seemed logical that the Kremlin, to prevent such a fusion, would soon grant some economic concessions, especially to the working class, and impose stricter Party controls over the intelligentsia, particularly students, without returning to harsh Stalin devices.

As for the effect on the Soviet leadership, it was only reasonable that there must have been differences of opinion in the Presidium. Collective leadership, by its very definition, almost certainly involves differences, the depth of which would depend upon the seriousness of the issue. Thus I concluded, "Although we have no reliable information whatsoever on the possibility of personnel changes in Soviet leadership, certainly circumstances of the crises in the Middle East and Eastern Europe and the insoluble dilemma they seem to be facing in Hungary make such changes much more likely than at any time since the institution of the Khrushchev-Bulganin primacy in February, 1955."

This forecast turned out to be right. In February, 1957, Khrushchev announced far-reaching economic reforms, decentralizing decision-making to increase industry's efficiency and responsiveness to the public's wishes. At the same time, a group in the Presidium, which some Kremlinologists loosely referred to as the Old Guard—Malenkov, Molotov, and Kaganovich—were laying plans to remove Khrushchev as First Secretary of the Communist Party. Their move would not surface for some months.

Unknown to me, Washington was making plans for a change of its own in Moscow. Secretary of State Dulles had decided that I should no longer be the American Ambassador to the Soviet Union.

CHAPTER TWENTY-FIVE

Exile in Manila

On December 26, 1956, Secretary of State Dulles sent me a letter saying that "knowing your desire to take up writing as a profession, I am thinking of making a change in Moscow." He went on to say that he was planning to appoint Llewellyn E. Thompson, my friend and the Ambassador in Vienna, as my successor. He suggested that the change be made in six months. I was not completely surprised. There had been articles in the press that a change was contemplated. But I did not have the foggiest idea where Dulles got the idea that I wanted to retire or to write. I had no intention of doing either. I was irritated, too, because the letter seemed to be a dishonest way of removing a diplomat from his post. There was no defensible reason for Dulles to take such a tack. It would have been much easier to have said that he thought four years was long enough for one person to serve as ambassador to the Soviet Union and that he had promised the job to Thompson. I would have understood and would have accepted the decision without question. While I preferred to stay another year in Moscow, because I was interested in following developments there, I did not question Dulles's right to make a change any time he felt like it.

The reference in the letter to my alleged desire to write implied that there was no future position for me in the Foreign Service. Although I had often disagreed with him, I could not recall ever having a real run-in with Dulles. I did remember that when Dulles made some scurrilous remarks about the Yalta agreements at the Berlin Conference in 1954, I told him privately that I did not share this view and wanted him to know of my reservations. He said nothing. I certainly did not make it a practice to criticize him publicly. I did criticize him in some private conversations; perhaps some of my comments found their way to him.

Considering the fact that there had been no strong clash, and remembering the oral commendations I had received from Dulles and a letter that President Eisenhower had written saying that "every report I have on you is that no one representing America in Moscow could possibly do better than you are doing," I thought there was a chance that he might really believe the erroneous idea that I did want to retire to write. I wired him that I had never thought of retiring to write and said that if his action was in any sense based on such a false premise, it should be corrected. In the telegram, I noted that over the months, in response to rumors, I had told correspondents in Moscow that I had no intention of resigning or of asking to be relieved. Thus, if asked, I could not say that I had requested a transfer. "Perhaps the best solution," I said, "would be to state that a prior commitment had been made to another officer on the basis that four years is more than normal." Accepting without argument the decision to transfer me, I suggested that the switch be made "at the earliest practical moment." As for my future plans, I proposed that I return to Washington and talk over the possibilities.

I believe that Dulles thought it was time, after four years, to make a change in Moscow, but when he began to consider what to do with me, he faced a dilemma. He did not want me in Washington, because he would have to put me in a policy-making job, which he did not want. If he chose me for another ambassadorship, there might be another fight in the Senate over my confirmation. Although McCarthy had been censured, Dulles was still worried about the right-wing elements in the Republican party. I have a feeling that Dulles just hit on the writing idea as a way to solve the problem.

Thompson got wind of my feelings, and wrote me a moving letter in which he said that he had never entertained the idea of pushing me out of my job and would willingly withdraw his name from consideration. It was a typically admirable gesture on Tommy's part. I immediately replied that I would not want him to withdraw his name, since I was certainly leaving Moscow and could not think of a better successor. Tommy, while not a Russian-language specialist, had served in Moscow for four years during the war.

In subsequent exchanges, Dulles, having decided that the writer ploy was not working, offered me the ambassadorship to Pakistan. I turned this down for a number of reasons. One was that it was a mistake to send a former ambassador to the Soviet Union to a contiguous country. The appointment would give rise to speculation that the United States was involved in policy matters with Pakistan that affected the Soviet Union. A second reason was that I had no interest in or knowledge of Pakistan as a country. I wanted at that point to stay with my specialty—Soviet-American affairs.

Nonetheless, I seriously considered resigning from the Foreign Service or taking a leave of absence. In a personal telegram to Loy Henderson, who was then in charge of the administrative functions of the State Department, I explained the advantages of a leave of a year or two. Max Millikan, director of the Center for International Studies at the Massachusetts Institute of Technology, had written me a letter inviting me to join his group. I was tempted. It seemed like the best solution to the whole unfortunate business. George Kennan had gone to Princeton for almost a year. For me, such a step would avoid the inevitable speculation about differences of opinion that would follow a retirement after leaving Moscow. I could in all honesty say that I had asked for the leave in preference to any foreign post available. It would also make me available for consultation with the State Department or any special assignment I might be qualified for.

Henderson suggested that before I made up my mind I return to the United States and talk to Dulles. I had been prodding Dulles to let me go to Washington to clear up the situation, but he was afraid that the press, remembering the controversy over my appointment, would see another dispute developing. Finally, after I suggested that he refer to my return as a "routine consultation," Dulles agreed. At the end of February, I left Moscow by plane.

The meeting with Dulles was formal and correct. For me, the real issue was whether I resigned from the Foreign Service. I did not contest his decision to remove me or try to rebut his statements about my desire to write, but merely told him that I had had no plans to leave the Foreign Service. Dulles assured me that the desire to make a change in Moscow was in no way connected with my performance there, implying—although he did not say so directly—that it had been satisfactory. I imagine that his commitment to Thompson was as large a factor as any other in his decision.

Dulles then offered me the ambassadorship to the Philippines. I told him that I would give him an answer the following day. As I left the Secretary's office, I was convinced I should resign. A Manila assignment would take me out of the area of my special knowledge. All my experience in Soviet affairs would be wasted. In a sense, I would be exiled from the area of American foreign policy for which I was particularly qualified. In my quandary, I went to see Acheson, Lovett, and Henderson, all of whom recommended that I ride out the storm. I therefore accepted the post in Manila.

My disgust with Dulles's handling of the case was reinforced a few days later when an article appeared in *The New York Times*, obviously planted by someone in the State Department, saying that after four years Bohlen wanted a change, and that my resignation from Moscow had been reluctantly accepted. I seriously considered replying in public—a course which would probably have resulted in my resignation—but decided not to.

A few weeks later, when I stopped off in Washington on my way to Manila, I went to the White House to pay my respects to the President, the normal procedure for an ambassador on his way to a new post. During our conversation, President Eisenhower said he was very sorry to see me leave Moscow. He said he had debated a long time whether to agree to my transfer, but since it was my desire, he had finally reluctantly gone along with it. Stunned, I told the President that I had had no inclination to leave Moscow. "Oh, is that true?" he said, and dropped the subject. Someone had given him erroneous information.

During this unpleasant period, I received a telegram from the French government speaking generously and warmly of the service I had performed in Moscow. I knew that this telegram had been inspired by Louis Joxe, the former French Ambassador to Moscow with whom I had worked closely.

As difficult as it was to live in the isolation of Moscow (in all my years there, I had not been able to make a single Russian friend), I was sorry to leave. I had been blessed with an excellent staff. I owe particular appreciation to the two men who filled the number-two post of counselor. They were Elim O'Shaughnessy, who died in Budapest years later, and Newbold Walmsley. A few months before I left, the post of Minister was created, and Richard Davis was appointed to it. Practically all of the staff were specialists in Russian affairs in varying degrees. They could speak Russian and were dedicated to their work. My two secretaries—Mary Wojnar, who was with me for the first three years, and Helen Abell, who was with me for a year in Moscow and subsequently went with me to Manila and back to Washington—put up with the difficulties of life in the Soviet Union with seldom a complaint.

I cannot say I accomplished much during my four years in Moscow, nor can I think of any serious mistakes we made in the

Embassy. The nature of the Soviet system did not offer much opportunity for individual initiatives. Despite the handicaps, our evaluation of Soviet events and policies stands up under examination fifteen years later. I have mentioned some judgments that turned out to be wrong and some proposals that I am glad were ignored. But, on balance, I believe we kept the United States government fully and accurately informed of Soviet attitudes, trends, and policies. About halfway through my tour, I received a letter from Senator Barry Goldwater stating that while he had opposed my nomination in the Senate in 1953, he had heard good reports of my work in Moscow and would vote to confirm me in any other post I might be nominated for. I like to think I did a professional job.

My leave-taking was attended with the usual parties. Foreign Minister Gromyko gave me the customary lunch on April 17, my last full day in Moscow. In a slight departure from the normal, Mikoyan was present. There were the usual expressions of good will and hope for the future. That evening at a Syrian reception, I had an opportunity to say good-bye to Khrushchev and Bulganin. Khrushchev said there had been some discussion in the Presidium whether my transfer meant a change in policy. "Why are they taking you from us?" Bulganin asked. I explained that the transfer had no policy significance, that it was traditional in the new term of a President to shift ambassadors. Thompson, I said, was an excellent choice, and would undoubtedly take the same attitude I had.

After reviewing various problems, Khrushchev turned to Germany and said, "We did our best to make it plain to President Eisenhower that beyond encouraging contact between East and Western Germany we will not go." Bulganin chimed in, "We will not go." With these words, they said good-bye.

I know that the Soviet leaders were impressed with Thompson as an ambassador. Six months after I left Moscow, Thompson wrote that Khrushchev had expressed, at a reception, his admiration for my work, saying that I had always carried out my instructions correctly and had strived to improve relations. He sent me his *"prvyet"*—best wishes. Two and a half years later, Khrushchev was qualifying his praise. He told my brother-in-law, Charlie Thayer, who was visiting Moscow in the summer of 1959, that I had been an excellent ambassador, well liked by the Russians, and fully representing American interests. But he added that I was not honest. He said that he had definite proof from intelligence sources that Scandinavian and other foreign correspondents had quoted me as saying he was a drunkard.

445

I wrote Thompson, asking him to tell Khrushchev he was "full of red ants." I had tried to spike rumors that Khrushchev was a drunkard, and could not remember ever talking to Scandinavian newsmen. Khrushchev's drinking reputation resulted from his first visit to Belgrade in 1955, when correspondents reported seeing him drunk. Reporters also saw him tight during General Nathan Twining's visit to Moscow in 1956. "Actually," I wrote Thompson, "and you may tell him this if you wish, it was Bulganin who I thought had trouble with alcohol and definitely not Nikita, who merely (and you needn't tell him this), when drinking, drinks like a Russian."

There was a little trouble in my departure from Moscow. On April 6, I had requested permission for a C-124 to land in Moscow to pick up my family and our household goods. The Foreign Ministry informed the Embassy on April 15 that a C-54 would be permitted to land, but not a C-124. I told the State Department I was unable to fathom the reasons behind the Soviet decision, though it might possibly be traced to Russian feelings of inferiority at having the huge plane land in Moscow. I appealed to Bulganin, who authorized the C-124 landing.

Stopping off in Washington on the way to Manila, I went out to Langley, Virginia, and briefed experts of the CIA on the Soviet Union. (I had previously briefed Thompson.) The briefing constituted a sum-up of my four years in Moscow. I had always respected the CIA's specialists on the Soviet Union. Their close observations, their wide reading of materials, and their data from clandestine operators, known as closed American sources, gave them deep insights into the Soviet Union. First I spoke to them at length; then I answered their questions. In my summary, I made the following points about developments in the Soviet Union:

• The subordination of the secret police to the Presidium has been a success, and the use of terror as an instrument of government has largely disappeared.

• The steady process of decentralization is one of the most important trends in the Soviet Union. The judicial system, much of the regular police work, and, most striking of all, industry are being decentralized. By the logic of events, the role of the Communist party in economic affairs will tend to diminish. Local Party people are not very impressive. I don't say the Party is going to disappear, but a great deal of real authority is bit by bit going to seep away from it into the hands of the men who are running industry. At my farewell luncheon in Moscow, I asked Mikoyan whether the decentralization of industry would not lead to the decentralization of political authority. The durable Armenian, his face expressionless, replied, "There are some on the Presidium who understand this." The first step in the decentralization of authority may be the widening of decision-making from the eleven-member Presidium to the three-hundred-member Party Central Committee.

• If I were in the Kremlin, I would be more worried about the staleness and emptiness of current ideology than anything else. The Bolsheviks have failed to produce the new Soviet man, the individual whose conditioned reflexes are in the direction of collective action. The Bolsheviks start out by taking the one body of connected thought of Marxism and use it to outlaw and destroy any other system of philosophy or ethics or conduct. Then the agencies of power in the Soviet Union force them to put their foot continuously through their own doctrine, to twist it and turn it, sometimes in the most absurd way, voiding it of all real content, and they're left with an empty shell. The Russians have a wonderful word for it, "*shablon*," which means a tiresome, ludicrous stereotype. Ideology has been just a question of fiat for many, many years. It's curious that the only place where you've got any ideological stuff with any vitality or bounce comes from China.

• As of 1957, China had been given the status of a partnership with the Soviet Union—a junior partnership, to be sure, but a partnership. On the other hand, I don't see any signs that we can take comfort in the idea of friction between them. I think the common interest is much greater than any possible points of friction for the foreseeable future.*

• The story in Eastern Europe is far from over. The Soviets are extremely nervous, about Poland in particular. The last thing they want to happen is to be confronted with the necessity, in their eyes, of action like Hungary. My hunch is that the Soviets would accept World War III rather than accept the downfall of any of the Soviet areas of Eastern Europe or, for that matter, North Korea.

• There is really only one country that the Soviets took very seriously (as I left the Moscow Embassy), and which they keep their eyes on, and that is the United States. We are the only aggregation of

---

* Sohlman, the Swedish Ambassador, told me in June, 1956, after a trip to China, that the Soviet Ambassador in Peking, P. F. Yudin, told him that the Soviet Union had given China scientific and technical know-how in the atomic field to enable her to produce nuclear weapons, but not the bomb itself or facilities for its manufacture. Yudin also forecast that in five years China would be so strong that no other country would be able to tell her what to do.

power that can possibly oppose them by military force, and we bulk very large in their mind. Almost everything they do, in some form or another, is a function of their impression of the United States.

• The Soviets are very serious about disarmament. I don't think it's a propaganda stunt. Obviously, being what they are, they would like to make a deal that would be advantageous to them and disadvantageous to us, but I think they have not paid out the full string yet of what they would do in the way of concessions. Why? The real reason is that they genuinely believe that an uncontrolled arms race is almost certain to end up in war, sooner or later. Bolshevik thought is determinate—that is, the Bolsheviks believe in the logic of events—and they don't pay very much attention to subjective factors. They don't question the sincerity or honesty of President Eisenhower, but they don't believe that major political events or developments of countries are dependent on the purity of an individual.* They believe that forces are at work. They have this impersonal, determinist attitude toward history. The economic factor, I think, is secondary. We would be deluding ourselves if we believed the Soviet economy could not stand the arms race.

Following my presentation, the CIA experts asked me a great number of questions. Following are some of the questions and my answers:

Q.: Would you say that the diminishing of the rule of the Party presages an increase in the prestige and the power of the formal organs of government?

A.: That could be one of the developments. I want to really make very plain there that when I'm talking about the diminishing of the Party I am really again talking very long term. The Party is IT. And one of the things they did after Stalin's death was to revive the Party as an institution, to institutionalize it rather than personalize it. I'm thinking of the inevitable erosion to the thing—it conceivably could be more power going to the formal government organs heading up, eventually, to the Supreme Soviet. But that is a LONG way off.

Q.: What do you think would be the effect on Soviet society of their abstaining from the active use of terror over a long period?

A.: There undoubtedly are still great areas of tension in the Soviet Union, and there is a good deal of residue of bitterness. I think the four years of Soviet [history] after Stalin leads you to the disagree-

---

* A number of times, Khrushchev told me of his admiration of Harold Stassen, the President's special adviser on disarmament, saying that Stassen had gone deeply into the subject and expressing his hope that he would visit Moscow.

able conclusion that the Soviet Union has a great deal more stability than Stalin's method of rule would indicate. There is a wide degree of acceptance of the Soviet system as a fact of life. There are many aspects the people hope to see corrected and liberalized and improved, but I don't think many of them are thinking, at present, in terms of its forcible overthrow or really substituting something radically different. I would doubt if you would find a literate Russian who would say, "Yes, we want to go back to private property and industrial property." I think you are getting a decreasing number of peasants who would like to see the collective-farm system scrapped. Any attempt to unscramble the collectivization system in the Soviet Union now would produce unbelievable chaos. You could almost predict famine. How would you unscramble it? The omelet has been made, the eggs are all broken.

Q.: How much do you think the Soviet top leadership is becoming convinced that we prefer the arms race to any sincere effort to reach disarmament?

A.: I don't want to get into military policy, but one gets a little bit the impression that we are doing things in the military field that are over and beyond what the situation requires from the point of view of containment.

Q.: Matadors [new surface-to-surface missiles with nuclear warheads, which had been deployed in West Germany]?

A.: Exactly. You see, they take that very seriously indeed. I think they are very worried about the idea of being ringed by these atomic support units, and I think that's only natural. I don't think these fellows are thinking of starting any military action against anybody for the foreseeable future. Now, obviously, if we let the strength of our defenses go down, their attitude may change. But as things are now, they don't see why the hell we keep slamming in all these new weapons. Of course, they have this great-power complex, and when I said—and I said this a couple of times before I left—I said, "My God, look at Hungary. You have very bad agents in the United States if you don't realize to what extent this kind of operation upsets people in our government and people in the United States." Their attitude is, What the hell are a few thousand Hungarian murders between friends?

Q.: You have counted a great deal on their determination to have peace, but isn't there another question, and that is what kind of risks are they prepared to take, for example now in the Middle East?

A.: They are not prepared to take any real risk.

Q.: But the tone of their policy is, let's say, forward.

A.: Now look—[in] all of Bolshevik history risk has been one of the most violent words possible. Go back and read some of the statements

449

that they were making in 1919 and 1920, when it was just a flip of the coin whether they were going to be submerged in a civil war or not, and you will see some of the roughest talk you ever heard about the United States, about the capitalist world. That is the propaganda thing—which they do consciously in order to appeal to the people. But I don't see them taking any form of governmental risk in the Middle East development. In the Suez, they didn't do a damn thing. For one week they did nothing, and then maybe the pressure began to mount on them due to one fact alone, that the country which they had espoused was still fighting.

Q.: Well, this would mean then that if Egypt got into serious difficulties with the West they would drop Nasser?

A.: Why should they drop Nasser? They're not going to drop Nasser. One thing is certain, that as long as the Soviets are not to some extent consulted and feel that their interests in that area are recognized, they are going to turn loose every damn thing they can to oppose Western policy in the area. I had this talk with Mikoyan the last day that I was there. In talking about the Middle East, I said, "What are you really up to there? You convinced a lot of people, and I'm not sure myself about it, that your purpose is to get such influence in that area that you can use the oil as an instrument of pressure against Western Europe." Of course, he denied that. Then he went on to say the Soviets were in the Middle East "just for security." He said, "We are going to do everything we can to oppose the establishment of Western military strength in that area, particularly yours." And he said on the economic thing, "We can't use the oil, and the Arabs can't consume it. We are not such fools as to believe you can work that sort of stuff." Then he said, "Why don't you talk to us? Are you afraid to talk to us?" I said, "We don't see any common interest." And then he said, "If you talk to us, I think you would find there are points of common interest." That is one thing I would think we could perfectly well explore in some sort of a confidential diplomatic way in Moscow. We have not used that arm enough. I don't say that because I was ambassador there—but I think there's just an Indian sign on it, that every time you shake hands with a Russian, you lose your arm to the elbow.

The CIA briefing ended my duty as ambassador to Moscow. From that point on, I prepared myself for my job in Manila.

My two-and-a-half-year stay in the Philippines was an interlude in the main work of my professional life. Soviet-American relations had been my specialty almost from the time I entered the Foreign Service, and there was little about Russia in the Philippines to occupy an

American ambassador. (The Philippines had no diplomatic relations with the Soviet Union, a policy favored by the United States.)

It is difficult to imagine a greater contrast in ambassadorial posts than Manila and Moscow. The cities themselves were so different. About the only thing they had in common was that both names began with "M." In the Philippines, society was disorganized and free. There was practically no governmental control of anything, and there was complete freedom of expression. In Moscow, everything was organized and contrived; the government controlled all; there was no freedom to criticize. Manila was a city of brilliant color, with blue seas, fleecy white clouds, and waving palm trees marred by the shocking contrast between wealth and poverty. Moscow was gray and cold, homogenized and depressing. In Russia, however, you felt a sense of power that was lacking in the Philippines.

There was a sharp difference between the people, too. The Filipinos were charming, friendly, warmhearted, and outgoing, whereas the Russians were reserved and suspicious. In a few months in Manila, I made closer friendships than I had in all my years in Moscow.

The average Filipino looked on the United States with respect and affection. In large measure, this sentiment was due to the hundreds of American teachers who set up schools in virtually every barrio in the country at the beginning of the century and taught the young to read and write English. The memory that these people left behind was still vivid in the minds and hearts of the people. The American military campaign that drove out the Japanese in World War II and the subsequent granting of independence to the islands certainly contributed to the Filipinos' affection for the United States. So great was this affection, which bordered on loyalty to the United States, that it was a matter of concern to some of the younger politicians in Manila. To offset what they regarded as excessive dependency, emotionally anyway, on the United States, they built little fires of anti-American sentiment. Some politicians in personal conversations with me admitted that they indulged in anti-American attacks to enhance their political fortunes.

One of the sharpest contrasts in my new job was the fact that the greatest obstacles to better relations were not in the foreign government but in Washington. My main occupation during my tour in Manila was dealing with problems arising from three important bases, Clark Field for the Air Force and Subic Bay and Sangley Point for the Navy. My negotiations on the bases and other questions were entirely with the Foreign Minister, Felixberto Serrano. I attempted to extract from the United States government, over the opposition of some members of Congress and the Pentagon, a change in the bases agreement of 1946. Under the arrangement, crimes committed by American servicemen off, as well as on, base were tried by the United States military courts, not by the Philippine courts. I strived constantly to persuade the Pentagon of the long-term desirability of giving the Filipinos the same jurisdiction over crimes on their land that other countries where we had bases enjoyed. I did not get very far, however. There seemed to be an almost hysterical fear, particularly in Congress, of letting Americans be tried by systems of justice not in conformity with ours. I have often wondered whether servicemen felt the same way, because a Philippine court would probably hand down much lighter sentences than American military tribunals. I did succeed in bringing about the transfer of some 80,000 Filipinos who lived in a village called Olongapo on the edge of the Subic Bay reservation by rearranging the boundaries of the base. For this small service, I was made an honorary citizen of the village.

In my reporting to Washington, I stressed a number of general conditions in the Philippines. One was the fact that the governmental institutions, modeled unfortunately on our own, were too sophisticated for the Filipino people to manage effectively. Also, the Filipinos had been oversold by us on the virtues of free enterprise (quite a statement to make by a man who had seen the stultifying effect of Soviet-style socialism). In a developing country, the result of a rapid expansion of capitalism is almost invariably that the rich get richer and the poor get poorer. With thousands of Filipinos graduating from college each year (another American legacy), the society was unable to absorb them. These two factors laid the basis for a revolutionary movement. Corruption was rampant; in fact, in the Filipino mind it was immoral not to feather your nest when you were in a position to do so. Virtually no one's ethical standards put duty to country first— another contrast with the Soviet Russians. Thoughtful Filipinos even then saw trouble ahead. The death of Ramón Magsaysay in an air crash just before my arrival in Manila removed a leader who offered great hope for the country. However, even if he had lived it is doubtful if the Philippines could have avoided the breakdown that occurred in 1972. Too much was wrong with the society.

In the depressurized atmosphere of Manila, I found time to relax and turned to golf, which I had played in college. I played every weekend and occasionally on Wednesday at the Manila and Wac-

Wac golf clubs. It was a very popular sport, and many Philippine officials would arise at dawn during the week to get in a round before going to work. I tried this a couple of times with justices of the Supreme Court. We had to turn the headlights of our cars on the first tee to drive off. I quickly discovered that I was tired the rest of the day, and gave up the morning rounds.

All in all, life was extremely agreeable. But my mind was always being drawn back to the Soviet Union. Tommy Thompson wrote me from Moscow, and I read everything I could find on events there, especially the surprising attempt to oust Khrushchev. I lacked the details then, but later learned that on June 19, 1957, when Khrushchev returned from a visit to Finland, he was informed by the other ten members of the Presidium that he was being removed from office as the Party's First Secretary. Instead of meekly accepting the decision, as any other of the "unshakably" united collective leaders would, Khrushchev insisted that the Presidium could not fire him. Taking his case outside the circle of power, he said that he had been elected by the Party's full three-hundred-member Central Committee, and only it could dismiss him. Backed by three other members of the Presidium, Khrushchev summoned the Central Committee members to a special meeting. Coming to Khrushchev's rescue, Marshal Zhukov sent military planes out to fly the members in. The committee, composed of regional Party chiefs who stood to gain from the economic reorganization plan, voted at a stormy eight-day meeting to reverse the Presidium and keep their benefactor in power. Thus, within a few months after I had advised the CIA to watch for a widening of the circle of power to the Central Committee, Khrushchev had accomplished just that.

At the same time, the committee expelled Molotov, Malenkov, and Kaganovich from the Presidium, and Shepilov as a candidate-member. Following the post-Stalin tradition, the ousted four were not shot in the neck but merely given assignments in out-of-the way places.

On October 7, in a letter to Frank Wisner, a high official of the CIA and a personal friend, I pointed out that I lacked information on what had gone on in Moscow. Nevertheless, I expressed my opinion of the meaning of the attempt to oust Khrushchev. I wrote:

> While I certainly did not anticipate any such spectacular developments, or at least not so soon, I have not found anything in the June events in Moscow to change any of my basic thinking on Soviet developments. On the contrary, I believe the manner in which this occurred demonstrated possibly more than anything else that collective leader-

ship was indeed a reality and not a fiction. Had, as many people thought, Khrushchev been building his power position to a point of absolute mastery there would have been no need for a two-week fight including an eight-day Central Committee meeting for him to put down the opposition. From all indications I get here, the argument in the Presidium was real and not *pro forma* and I have yet to receive any information which would indicate that police or other armed force was used or threatened to bring about the final result. It seems to have been a question of who had the majority where and when. It would of course be folly to predict anything for the future, but I am by no means certain that the expulsion of Malenkov, Molotov, Kaganovich and, on a lesser level, Shepilov, marks the end of collective leadership and a return to one-man rule. It might even mark a trend in the opposite direction which, so far as I am aware, is the first time that it has been made the final arbitrator of a dispute of this nature in the Presidium. It could therefore mean that in the future the circle of power will be broadened from the Presidium to include the 133-odd voting members of the CC. Consequently, whoever is top dog will have to, in the last analysis, obtain and retain the support of more people than in the post-Stalin period.

I expressed doubts that events could be explained as a personal power struggle, pure and simple, between Khrushchev and Malenkov. This concept seemed to be based on the assumption that there was one position—i.e., First Secretary of the Party—which had so much power that it was in itself worth struggling for. I pointed out that the very fact that the anti-Khrushchev group could hope to succeed would seem to indicate that the position did not have any such power in itself. My explanation was that, at a certain point, policy disputes in the Kremlin, as in all governments, end in a power struggle among the disputants if the differences are critical. Malenkov was too liberal in his post-Stalin policies to be listed among the Old Guard, and therefore his disagreements with Khrushchev's policies were probably of a somewhat different nature from Molotov's and Kaganovich's. But all three for different reasons saw in Khrushchev's domestic policies a real danger of loss of the collective political power of the top leadership. Being Marxists, they feared that economic decentralization, if pushed forward with the vigor which Khrushchev usually threw into these matters, would inevitably lead to some loss of control at the top.

I did not believe that either side planned its position very carefully before the actual conflict. Given the experience in conspiracy and general dirty work that all three of the opposition leaders had, it seemed unlikely that they would have done such a clumsy job if the coup had been carefully timed to coincide with Khrushchev's and Bulganin's absence. If Khrushchev had planned his counterattack, he would not have spent a week in Finland just before the ouster. While I lacked evidence, it seemed to me that there must have been a confluence of disagreement with Khrushchev's policies for different reasons. Opposition by Molotov, and to a somewhat less publicized degree by Kaganovich, had been known for some time. Malenkov's exact role remained unclear, but because he was younger, it was probable that he was destined to take the top slot. There were obviously many other factors besides economic decentralization involved, and I was inclined to give some weight to a rather frivolous one, that the three men, who were rather serious and on the whole sober individuals, were concerned at Khrushchev's freewheeling and his tendency to make off-the-cuff remarks and commit the group by snap decision, especially in the field of foreign policy.

Again pleading lack of knowledge, I saw nothing to indicate that Khrushchev's victory was due to the military as an independent cohesive force. It stood to reason that if Zhukov had been against him, he would have had great difficulty in eliminating the others. It did not follow that he was in any sense a prisoner of the military. On the contrary, Zhukov, being somewhat of a pragmatist, on the whole probably agreed with most of Khrushchev's policies. I also contended that a military dictatorship would probably be set up only in the event of an emergency, either domestic or foreign, so great that it would threaten the regime. I could not see any reason why the army, as such, even assuming that a distinct army point of view was possible, would wish to take over the direction of all Soviet affairs except in the case of extreme necessity to preserve the system.

I then expressed disagreement with George Kennan's view that the victory had been costly to Khrushchev, on the basis that he had probably committed himself on several issues to the military and perhaps to other factions. I did not believe that Khrushchev had committed himself to any one faction, asserting that his future depended on the success of his domestic policies.*

In conclusion, I saw trouble in the Kremlin for some time to come:

> I am inclined to regard what happened in the Soviet Union in June as a further manifestation of the basic contradiction between the social and economic changes in the Soviet Union brought on by the process of industrialization and the antiquated forms of political rule which

---

* By fall, Zhukov had been dismissed. Within a year, Khrushchev had taken over Bulganin's job as Premier, while keeping the Party secretaryship.

were devised and perfected in quite different circumstances. The story is not over and I think we will see further developments, not necessarily in the near future.

The same month of these events, the Soviet Union scored a spectacular scientific achievement. On October 4, it fired the first artificial satellite into orbit. Sputnik was a great propaganda triumph for the Bolsheviks. It upset the Eisenhower administration and presented the Democrats with an issue. Some time after Sputnik, the Soviet Union announced it had cut back on heavy-bomber production. A directive from the State Department to the United States Information Agency hopped on the announcement as proof that the Soviet economy was unable to bear the burden of orbiting Sputniks and improving defenses. In other words, Sputnik was a sign of a failure of the Soviet economic system. I sent an acid and unsolicited message to Washington, asserting there was no evidence that the Soviet economy could not build bombers and orbit satellites, and ventured the opinion that Moscow was merely trying to leapfrog intermediate defense stages by going straight for a missile program. Months later, on a brief visit to Washington, I discovered that the directive had been written by John Foster Dulles.

The obvious importance of Sputnik was that it demonstrated that the Soviet Union had made impressive technological and scientific gains. I did not accept the implication, common at that time, that the Russians were outdistancing the United States in these areas. The Soviet Union could achieve spectacular results in limited areas by concentrating their resources and best brains. These achievements bore no relevance to the general state of Soviet science and technology. We were far ahead.

I whiled away two years in the Philippines, thinking ever of the Soviet Union and America and slowly losing hope of ever returning to my specialty. At one time, I thought of retiring at the close of the Manila tour, to try to make a little money. Then in January, 1959, John Foster Dulles resigned as Secretary of State and shortly thereafter died of cancer.

As any reader who has stayed with me this far well knows, I had my difficulties with Dulles, but he had many more virtues than defects. He had character and was capable of firmness of purpose and steadiness in execution. He was especially strong as the architect of the West's resolute policy in response to Khrushchev's ultimatum in the winter of 1958–59 to make Berlin an international city and sever

West Berlin's connections with Bonn and the Allies. The firmness of the Western response must have surprised Khrushchev, who eventually backed down.

While in Moscow, I often heard Khrushchev denounce Dulles as the archvillain preventing a détente. Whether the Soviets really felt this way I cannot tell. I believe that they respected Dulles as a diplomat with a steady aim, as a skilled negotiator, and as a student of foreign affairs. Dulles, however, never understood Soviet policy. He was overattentive to the purely ideological aspects, not grasping the subtle relationship with Soviet national interests. He discovered Stalin late in life and read voraciously in Stalin's theoretical writings. He was obsessed with the idea that Soviet Communism was a conspiracy which all righteous people should oppose. This view of the world in black-and-white terms stemmed, I believe, from Dulles's Calvinism, and was a serious impediment to his performance as Secretary of State. He damaged our relations with the developing nations by his opposition to neutralism. He overcommitted the United States with ties to regional anti-Communist pacts. He scared our allies with his talk of brinkmanship.

In England and France, Dulles's reputation was permanently damaged by the Suez episode. He argued the case against London and Paris like a lawyer, instead of clarifying his views to our allies. In West Germany, however, tough old Adenauer always spoke in the highest terms of the Secretary.

I am not sure how history will evaluate John Foster Dulles. He was a strong Secretary of State; whether he was a wise one is doubtful.

Christian Herter, the new Secretary of State, soon wrote asking me to return to Washington as his adviser on Soviet affairs. Dulles had had no Soviet expert close to him. Herter had in mind a position such as Counselor. Douglas Dillon, then the Under Secretary, also brought up the matter when he attended a meeting of chiefs of mission in Manila. Although I felt financial pressures and the need to increase my income, I told Herter I would like to stay in the Foreign Service if I could return to a high-level job. In the summer, Herter discussed the possibility with important senators, and he and I found out that McCarthyism was not dead. While Vice-President Richard M. Nixon was in Moscow, Ambassador Thompson asked him what would happen if the President appointed me to a post in Washington. Nixon told Thompson that he was sure the President had his back up about the opposition and was determined to go ahead with an assignment, but probably one that did not require Senate confirmation.

Herter dropped the idea of making me Counselor, or an Assistant Secretary, and appointed me a special assistant, a position that the senators were not authorized to pass on. While I would have liked a title in keeping with my responsibilities, my experience in Washington in the upper reaches of government had taught me that titles had little to do with duties or influence, provided there were good personal relations with those in power. I was confident of my standing with Herter. I had first met him in early 1947, when he was chairman of a committee investigating the possibilities of the proposed Marshall Plan. From then on, I developed increasingly close ties with him. Herter was mild in his manner, but he had plenty of steel in his decision-making. Dulles first offered him the job of Assistant Secretary for European Affairs, a position that was close to an insult for a man with Herter's experience. Herter said that under no circumstances would he accept a job as low as that. He was then offered the post of Under Secretary. I think the Department of State ran better under Herter than under any other Secretary of State (with the possible exception of Marshall). I admit a bit of parochial interest in view of the fact that Herter elevated Foreign Service officers to Assistant Secretaries of State and brought them in on decision-making. The fact is that this policy brought the full talent of the department to bear on every subject and we had a smooth operation. However, the biggest test of American foreign policy was a crisis that only the President could handle—the U-2 spy-plane affair.

PART FIVE

The Final Years

CHAPTER TWENTY-SIX

The U-2 and the Abortive Summit

In my new job, my first assignment
was to go to Paris with Herter for the annual NATO meeting in
December, 1959. President Eisenhower, who had been on a good-will
trip to India, Pakistan, Iran, and Turkey, stopped in Paris for a brief
meeting with President de Gaulle, Prime Minister Macmillan, and
Chancellor Adenauer. I was standing in the anteroom of the Elysée
Palace as the meeting of the heads of government broke up. I had not
seen President Eisenhower since returning from the Philippines, and
he stopped to say hello. After a few words, he said, "By the way,
Chip, have you ever met General de Gaulle?" When I said I had not,
he introduced me. De Gaulle made a few conventional remarks to the
effect that he had heard of me from some of his associates, then turned
to leave. After taking a few steps, he came back and said, with an
impish smile, "Mr. Bohlen, have you heard what we have just decided? We have decided to speak firmly with Mr. Khrushchev on
vague matters." In French, it sounds much better: "*Nous avons décidé
de parler à M. Khrushchev sur un ton ferme des choses vagues.*" De
Gaulle stretched out the last word, and walked out of the room.

On my return to Washington, Herter asked me to help prepare for
President Eisenhower's visit to the Soviet Union, which was scheduled
for May of 1960. Eisenhower had agreed to make the trip because of
the success of Khrushchev's visit to the United States in September,
the first time any Soviet leader had toured America. Khrushchev
always looked on his visit as a triumph, and, in some ways, it did help
him. I was in Manila at the time, but from what I heard, I think his

eyes were opened by the American standard of living and freedom. He did not, of course, change his basic views ("Your grandchildren will live under Communism," he told Americans); but I think he began to realize some of the advantages of a free society over the Soviet system. This is only guesswork on my part, but the line of the policy that Khrushchev developed shortly after his visit and hints in his speeches led me to believe that the visit had a salutary effect on him.

While much can be said on both sides of the desirability of the visits of leaders of countries, on balance I believe that they are a good thing. I was certainly enthusiastic about Eisenhower's scheduled trip to the Soviet Union. Eisenhower was not only a President, he was also a war hero. The Russians would have loved him. Soviet authorities would have had a difficult time containing the enthusiasm of the people. Khrushchev would not have minded. He would have been given credit for improving relations with America; his policy of coexistence would be shown to be working. But others in the Kremlin would have been shaken to see how popular an American President was. If the Russians pushed and shoved to see a cold personality, as they did for Vice-President Nixon, what would they have done for a warm man like Ike?

During his visit to the United States, and particularly during his talks at Camp David, Khrushchev's regard for Eisenhower rose. Like Americans, the Soviets had always liked Ike. Even Stalin had spoken highly of the American general who allowed Soviet troops to capture Berlin. When I was ambassador in Moscow, the Russians—again like Americans—often separated Eisenhower from policies of his administration that they did not like. In 1956, Khrushchev, in a speech at a reception for General Twining, paid tribute to the President as an "honorable man" who enjoyed the respect of the Soviet government, although the same could not be said "for all others who surround him"— an obvious reference to Dulles. During the Hungarian and Suez crises in October, 1956, Molotov asked me who would win the presidential election. When I said that the odds were on Eisenhower's re-election, he said, "That is good." He also asked about the President's health. When I replied that Eisenhower had fully recovered from his operation, Molotov referred to a strong letter that the President had sent to Bulganin warning against military action in the Middle East. "We had the impression the strain of the election was telling on him, irritating him," Molotov said. Curiously, the Soviet leaders viewed Eisenhower as Truman once did Stalin—as a "prisoner" of those around him.

In April, I did some catching up on Soviet affairs with a quick trip to Paris, where I attended a conference of Eastern European experts, and to Moscow, where I had long talks with Ambassador Thompson, discussions with foreign diplomats, and an unproductive hour with Foreign Minister Gromyko. Many experts at this time considered Khrushchev the absolute boss of the Soviet Union. This was also the period when Khrushchev was talking of making a separate peace treaty with East Germany, establishing West Berlin as an international city and thus imperiling Western rights. I wanted to get the feel of the situation.

I found that foreign diplomatic and press circles in Moscow were virtually unanimous in agreeing that Khrushchev, while unquestionably the leader and number-one individual in both Party and government, did not have the power of unilateral formulation and decision in important matters of policy. He was no Stalin and showed no signs of becoming one.

Most knowledgeable foreigners believed that there was opposition within the Presidium to his policy of peaceful coexistence. I was inclined to believe that there was less opposition to Khrushchev's policy than to the highly personalized way he carried it out. The spectacle of Soviet leaders being wined and dined by leaders of the capitalist world must have outraged diehard Bolsheviks. Their concern was less with the effect on the Russian people than on the puppet heads of satellite countries, such as Hungary and East Germany, where there was strong public hostility.

As for policy, I concluded that Khrushchev was not bluffing in the threat to force the West out of Berlin and to sign a separate peace treaty with East Germany. While he had been careful not to fix any specific time limit to his threat, he would suffer an unacceptable loss of prestige as a leader unless he eventually acted.

The mood of Moscow was much more relaxed than when I had left there three years before. The Thompsons gave a reception for some visiting Americans, and a large number of Soviet officials, artists, writers, and others attended. The mood was part of the coexistence atmosphere. It could change overnight, and did, but it was nevertheless hopeful.

On the way back to Washington, I stopped off at Harvard for a discussion on cultural exchanges with the Soviet Union, then caught a night train to the capital. The following morning, May 3, Hugh Cummings, the head of the State Department's intelligence unit, came to my office and told me that a U-2 photography plane on an espionage flight over the Soviet Union was missing and believed to have been shot down over the weekend. He did not know whether the pilot, Francis Gary Powers, had been saved.

While ambassador in Moscow, I had learned of plans for the flights, but I did not know when they were being made. It was not considered wise to inform even the Ambassador of the actual date of the U-2 flights. Secrecy was absolutely vital. Besides, if anything happened to a U-2, the Ambassador could honestly say that he did not know anything about the matter. Thus, on July 14, 1956, at a reception at the French Embassy, when Bulganin asked me if I was familiar with a note that had been delivered in Washington protesting violations of Soviet Air space by American aircraft in early July, I replied that I knew of the note but beyond that had "no information whatsoever." Bulganin said the Soviet government had indisputable evidence through radar tracking to support the charge of violating air space. "This is a very serious matter," he said. He spoke quietly, endeavoring to impress me with the seriousness with which the Soviet government viewed the matter. My suspicion was that the Russians had spotted U-2s.

Nine days later, at an Egyptian Armed Forces Day reception, news correspondents queried Marshal R. A. Rudenko, Chief of Staff of the Soviet Air Force, about the Soviet charges, and asked how he knew the planes were American. Rudenko admitted that no markings had been seen, explaining that the planes had flown at 20,000 meters. But he contended that Soviet pilots could identify the planes, which remained high out of reach of Soviet Migs, as American from their silhouettes. The reporters pointed out that American-made planes belonged to many countries. Rudenko replied that since the planes were of American origin, the United States was ultimately responsible for their activities. In my report to Washington, I noted that the correspondents had missed a good opportunity to ask Rudenko whether the Soviet Union was responsible for Migs in Korea and the Middle East. The newsmen did ask the Marshal about Soviet policy of shooting at foreign planes flying over Soviet territory without permission. Rudenko replied that the Soviet Union did not want to heighten international tensions, so Soviet planes had orders not to shoot at planes that accidentally strayed over the border. Specific authorization had to be received from the ground to fire at any aircraft. What Rudenko failed to say was that the Soviet Union had no plane that could climb as high as the intruding aircraft, or any anti-aircraft guns that could reach them. The planes were, of course, American U-2s taking pictures of Soviet missile sites and other military installations. Rudenko warned that if the overflights continued, the Soviets would take "necessary measures." It took more than three years for the Soviets to make good on the warning and shoot down a U-2.

When the CIA heard that the U-2 was missing, the President was on one of his periodic visits to a hideout in Virginia that would be used in case Washington was in danger of being bombed. He met with Douglas Dillon, who was Acting Secretary of State because Herter was in Istanbul at a NATO meeting; Allen Dulles, director of Central Intelligence; and Andrew Goodpaster, the President's military aide. At this meeting, plans were changed. Under a cover plan that had been prepared in advance, all queries about any plane missing over the Soviet Union were to be referred to the National Aeronautics and Space Administration, which had a news release ready saying that one of its "weather planes" was missing. At the Virginia meeting, the President decided that the State Department would handle all responses to press inquiries. Goodpaster was given the job of informing James C. Hagerty, the White House press secretary, of the change, but either failed to do so or got to him too late. Hagerty, following previous instructions, contacted Hugh Dryden, the NASA director, who put out the press release. This mix-up was unfortunate, because the press release referred to a limited area of the plane's flight and specifically said that it had been only a few kilometers from the border. At the time the NASA announcement was made, the Department of State knew that the spy plane had been shot down in central Russia. We did not know the fate of the pilot, however, even on May 5, when Khrushchev announced that the plane had been shot down. So Herter, who had returned to Washington, stuck to the NASA cover story, issuing a communiqué saying that the "weather research plane" must have strayed off course, probably because the pilot had lost consciousness. Khrushchev then gleefully announced that Powers, the pilot, had been captured with incriminating photographic equipment.

The issue, hotly debated at a meeting within the department, was whether to admit that an American spy plane was involved, to try to fudge it, to deny it, or, in accordance with traditional international usage, to refuse to comment on an espionage matter. I strongly favored limiting ourselves to a "no comment." Some of those who wanted to admit the truth adopted a highly moral tone, insisting that the United States not only had a right but, indeed, a duty to spy on the Soviet Union, because of the inherent wickedness of the Communist nation, which has indulged in extensive espionage on the West. I felt that this argument was not relevant and, while it might appeal to American prejudices, would damage our case with other nations. The final decision of the meeting was that the United States should admit the truth of the incident.

By the time Herter took the department's views to the White House, the President had already decided to announce that the downed craft was indeed an American intelligence plane and that, while he had not known of each specific flight, he had authorized the program of aerial spying. There may have been a slight deviation from the full truth even in that admission. I learned that Richard Bissell, who was in charge of the operation for the CIA, had called Goodpaster to request authorization to postpone the Powers flight for one day, from April 30, because of weather conditions. The request, I was told, had been checked out with the President by Goodpaster and consent for the delay received. It is unfortunate that no one familiar with the Soviet Union knew that a flight had been scheduled for May 1. May Day is one of the principal Soviet holidays. It was not wise to take a chance on such a day; it was like spitting in a Bolshevik's eye. The United States knew that the Soviet Union had detected the U-2 flights previously, so there was reason to believe the May 1 flight would be spotted. The Soviets did not announce the previous violations, because they pointed up the weakness of Soviet defenses. When the anti-aircraft knocked down the U-2 on May 1, Khrushchev could make the disclosure in triumph.

I believe the reason Eisenhower decided to accept full responsibility for the U-2 was the fear that he would be criticized as a President who was not in charge, who did not know of activities of his administration that could lead to nuclear war. There had been much criticism of Eisenhower as lacking the vigor and leadership of a president. He must have been conscious of these accusations. I still do not know how the situation could have been handled better. The bungling of the NASA release could have been avoided, but I think the results would have been very much the same. The downing of the plane and the capture of the pilot made the problem insoluble.

Of course, the U-2 affair did not raise our optimism regarding the scheduled meeting in Paris of the big-power leaders. We were uncertain what the Kremlin would do, whether Khrushchev would even attend the conference. In one clue to Soviet thinking, the Counselor of the Soviet Embassy, M. N. Smirnovsky, told James Reston of *The New York Times*, on May 9, that he had detected a shift in American attitude from the "spirit of Camp David." He cited as evidence an "awful" speech on April 20 by Under Secretary of State Dillon demanding that the Russians withdraw their troops from East Germany and the other satellites, a "tough" speech by Secretary Herter, an announcement that the United States was resuming nuclear testing, and the U-2 incident. Reston told Smirnovsky the incidents were unrelated, and lectured the Russian on how democracies operate. From Smirnovsky's comments, I concluded that the Soviets had put together the four events and really believed the United States was returning to a cold-war policy. I told Herter that the Soviet leaders often thought other governments operated like their own. Thus to them the four events were part of a carefully calculated plan.

Before we took off for Paris, I suggested that the President point out to Khrushchev at the summit that the Soviet Union could not have a détente and at the same time issue threats on Berlin. "In particular," I said in a memorandum to Herter, Khrushchev "should be told that in the event he carries out his threat to conclude a separate peace treaty with East Germany and attempts thereby to extinguish Western rights in Berlin, a crisis will arise which would make completely illusory any expectation of detente or improved relations." I also proposed that the President state that unless Khrushchev gave definite assurances that he would take no unilateral action on Germany, there might be no Eisenhower trip to Russia. Khrushchev, I was sure, was counting on the trip to raise his prestige at home.

Khrushchev arrived in Paris on May 14, two days before the conference, and called on de Gaulle and Macmillan, who immediately informed the United States delegation of the conversations. Khrushchev sought to prevail on both to bring pressure on Eisenhower to issue a public apology for the U-2 flights, to pledge not to permit any more of them, and to punish those responsible. Both de Gaulle and Macmillan agreed to transmit the message, but held out no hope of its acceptance and made clear they were giving no support whatsoever to Khrushchev. In fact, I believe that de Gaulle said he did not think such a request was feasible.

As a result of the information received from the British and the French, President Eisenhower was fully prepared for Khrushchev's tirade at the opening session. On our side, there was the President, Secretary Herter, Alexander Akalovsky, an American interpreter, and I, as official note-taker. I had been designated for this because of my knowledge of all three languages. After a cold and formal greeting, a brief handshake, without smiles, between the Americans and the Soviets, the conference opened. Khrushchev took the floor and gave a twenty-minute harangue. Acting the role of the injured party, he asked how anyone could fly over the territory of a friendly country, spying on its most intimate secrets, and not recognize the flight as an act of hostility. He implied that he had not expected such an act from President Eisenhower and withdrew the invitation to the President to visit the Soviet Union. How, he asked, could he explain to the Russian people a visit from the leader of so hostile a country? Then he demanded an apology.

As Khrushchev talked, Eisenhower's bald head turned various shades of pink, a sure sign that he was using every bit of will to hold his temper. De Gaulle then said that while he did not condone espionage, it was necessary. As far as flying over the territory of another nation was concerned, he knew that a number of times a month Soviet satellites, which might contain cameras, crossed over territories of the French Republic. De Gaulle noted that he had not found it necessary to make a public scene over these flights. Macmillan spoke in somewhat the same way, although with more regret in his voice and demeanor. Macmillan had placed a great deal of hope on the summit meeting. He felt, following his visit to Moscow the previous winter, that the conference offered a great hope of peace, and he had possibly exaggerated public expectations of it.

When Eisenhower spoke, he gave no sign of the intense anger that he had obviously felt a few minutes before. He then revealed officially what he had decided a week before, announcing that he had ordered that the aerial spying be discontinued. He refused, however, to apologize. It was hoped on the Western side that Eisenhower's remarks might satisfy Khrushchev, but it soon became apparent that the Soviets would not accept anything but a formal abject apology from the President. The conference adjourned, subject to recall in forty-eight hours.

The next day, a group of us had dinner with the President at the American Embassy. After dinner, we had a long, informal discussion about the prospects of the conference. I voiced skepticism over the possibility of Khrushchev's returning to the conference unless the President issued an apology, which was impossible because the U-2 flights were justified and because the President of the United States could not abase himself. I also expressed skepticism that any substantial progress could be made at the conference even if it should resume. The President asked why. I said I could not see how the Soviets would give up East Germany for the sake of unification of the two sections of the country. They had had many opportunities in the past. By 1960, the East German Soviet regime was fully established. There might have been an opportunity for some progress on Berlin, but I doubted it. Eisenhower was a good listener, asking various people what their views were. Someone suggested that Thompson and I talk with Gromyko to try to work out a settlement of the dispute, but it was decided such a move would be useless. The only problem holding up the conference was the impossibility of the President's making a public apology to Khrushchev. This was never seriously considered.

At the appointed time, the three Western leaders gathered in the Elysée and waited for some sign that Khrushchev would return. When he did not, Macmillan exhorted Eisenhower and de Gaulle to let him make a personal appeal to Khrushchev to return to the conference. With tears in his eyes, Macmillan said that all over the British Isles the day before, simple, trusting people had been praying in little churches for peace. The failure of this conference would be a mortal blow to their hopes and aspirations, and he felt that as leaders of their countries they owed it to their people and to their passionate desire for peace to make one more effort. I was sitting behind the President, and I heard him tell Herter, "You know, poor old Hal is very upset about this, and I think we might go as far as to meet him on this one point." I quickly scribbled a note to Herter saying that a personal, emotional appeal was a mistake, that it was not a technique to be used with the Kremlin leaders. While it would not do much harm, I thought it was singularly unnecessary. Before the note could reach Herter, de Gaulle, speaking in his most regal manner in French, said he could not agree with the Prime Minister. The method was too Byzantine, and we must never forget that the Byzantine Empire fell because of addiction to intrigues and similar roundabout methods. His tone was icy and contemptuous. In any event, he effectively killed the idea of another approach to Khrushchev.

At a press conference the following day, Khrushchev gave vent to his violent feelings. He used unprintable language and, curiously, denounced the British and French as much as the Americans. Afterward, two seasoned American correspondents called to ask whether I thought Khrushchev was going back to Moscow and start a war. One of them said Khrushchev's language was reminiscent of some of Hitler's tirades, which had always been the prelude to military action. The correspondents were influenced by the fact that the Soviet Minister of National Defense, tough-looking Marshal Rodion Y. Malinovsky, a World War II hero, accompanied Khrushchev everywhere.

While the glowering Malinovsky's presence added a belligerent tone to the Soviet delegation, I doubted the speculation that the military was taking over. His presence might have meant that the other members of the Politburo—as the Presidium was now called—wished to be absolutely sure that Khrushchev did not go off on any wild tangents. It must be remembered that one of the items on the agenda was disarmament, and that the American Secretary of Defense, Thomas Gates, also attended the conference.

I told the correspondents that I did not believe for a minute that the Kremlin would deliberately start a war. I said the same thing at a meeting of the American delegation that same day. I thought Khrushchev's press-conference remarks showed that his chief irritation was with the French and British failure to put pressure on Eisenhower to make the formal apology. Apparently, Khrushchev had come to Paris determined to get such an apology; without it he was not authorized to participate in the conference. On the way back to Moscow, Khrushchev stopped in East Berlin and delivered a soothing speech, making it clear that he had no intention of heating up the Berlin issue.

Khrushchev's anger and disappointment were real. He had gone out on a long limb in accepting Eisenhower as a man of good will and a man of peace. He genuinely believed the President was different from "capitalist warmongers." In other Bolsheviks' eyes, such trust was close to treason. There is no doubt Khrushchev had difficulties with some of his associates on the main lines of his policy of coexistence. Khrushchev's initial reaction to the downing of the U-2 was that the flights had been taken without the knowledge of the President. When Eisenhower said he had approved all the U-2 flights and accepted full responsibility for them, Khrushchev felt double-crossed. His disillusionment was virtually complete. The only way Khrushchev could have been appeased was by a full apology. It is quite possible that he pledged the rest of the Politburo that he would obtain the apology or leave.

The Russians took a long time to get over the embarrassment of the U-2. In July, Ambassador Mikhail A. Menshikov raised the subject with me. I told him it was history; I saw no need to go into the matter further. Menshikov insisted that the U-2 would continue to be a big factor in American-Soviet relations unless an apology was forthcoming—if not by the Eisenhower administration, then by the next one. "You will have to wait a very, very long time," I said, adding that if that was the Soviet attitude, there was little prospect of any improvement in the future. Menshikov backed away from his position, saying that what he had in mind was that the next administration should not continue "these aggressive and provocative" flights. I pointed out that Eisenhower had announced, at Paris, the suspension of the flights. Menshikov said that if the flights were resumed, the Soviets would retaliate against the base the plane took off from. "It would be extremely irresponsible," I said, "to have the peace of the world hang upon the possibility of an accidental flight by an unidentified plane over Soviet territory."

At one point, Menshikov asked if I, as an adviser on Soviet affairs, had known or approved of the flights. Smilingly, I told him, "in the business we are both engaged in, there are certain questions to which you cannot expect an answer."

The Soviet anti-American campaign that followed the collapse of the summit worried me. The propaganda was designed to increase tensions and provoke disorders. The Soviet Union broke off disarmament talks on June 27, on the eve of new Western proposals. On July 1, Soviet pilots shot down an American reconnaissance plane over international waters of the Barents Sea. For the first time in history the Kremlin, in a policy statement, offered to give military support to any regime which served Soviet purposes.

While these threats were not to be taken at face value, I thought they might indicate a new Soviet doctrine of military intervention in any part of the world where Soviet purposes could be served. In a memorandum to President Eisenhower on July 19, I said:

> It is this aspect of current Soviet behavior which requires something more in response than mere words. Some form of action should be taken to bring calmly and coldly to the attention of the Soviet Union the dangers of its current attitude. While they may have no intention of acting on these threats, it is nevertheless possible that the Soviets, if they feel that this propaganda campaign is succeeding, might progressively commit themselves in future courses of action in the military field which would be extremely difficult for them to disavow if ever put to the test. In addition, we must consider the effect of this Soviet campaign of threat and blackmail on other countries, particularly the uncommitted areas of the world. If this campaign seems to be proceeding without any strong response on the part of the United States, it might well create the impression that the Soviets are in fact in total command of the situation and that the United States is unable or unwilling to devise any appropriate counter.

I proposed that the President ask Congress for a supplemental appropriation of $3 billion to $5 billion for the Defense Department and foreign military aid. Such a request, my memo said, would be "action, not words." The proposal, supported by Herter and Dillon, was approved by Eisenhower and eventually by Congress.

In September, Khrushchev was still carrying on. He proposed that the United Nations be reorganized, and went to New York to offer the plan in person. The plan did not amount to much—substituting a "troika" (a three-man commission) for a single secretary-general and moving the United Nations headquarters to Switzerland, Austria, or the Soviet Union. It was Khrushchev's behavior that drew the most attention. He shouted and laughed during the speeches, and took off a shoe and banged it on his desk—interrupting Macmillan's address.

There were some expectations, fed by Soviet sources, that Eisenhower, who also attended the meeting, and Khrushchev would confer. I strongly advised against a meeting, unless Moscow did something beforehand to show good faith, such as releasing the fliers from the downed reconnaissance plane. In a memorandum on September 23, I said that if Khrushchev were to be received by the President without some demonstrable change in attitude, it would merely convince the Kremlin leaders and a large portion of the world that the Soviet Union was so powerful that it could behave with contempt toward the United States and at any time of its choosing return to the "spirit of Camp David." In short, it would mean in the eyes of many uncommitted nations that the Soviet Union was, in fact, calling the tune in international affairs.

Everyone else in the State Department also opposed any move by Eisenhower to meet Khrushchev. Perhaps the Russian was not yet ready to see the father of the U-2 incident. He did not ask for such a meeting. His ranting at the United Nations showed he had not recovered from his anger. Earlier, in Moscow, Ambassador Thompson had been subjected to a number of embarrassing moments. At a reception, Khrushchev began to shout at Thompson about the U-2. To illustrate his point, he said, "Do you think it is all right to do this?" and stepped heavily on the Ambassador's foot. Afterwards, he told Thompson, "I didn't mean to hurt you." At a speech to the Supreme Soviet, Khrushchev, who had once described Eisenhower as a wise statesman, said he thought the President lacked the character and dignity to head a great nation, although he might have been a good superintendent of schools.

There have been many Americans who have been even more critical of Eisenhower than Khrushchev was. I did not see enough of Eisenhower in the White House to have a basis for judgment. I thought he did well in the U-2 situation, the only crisis in which I observed him closely. True, there was a trace of mental laziness in him. He preferred reading western novels and playing bridge to doing the grinding intellectual work necessary to keep his mind attuned to the decisions he would have to make.

Dulles was given wide authority to conduct foreign affairs, but when there were important decisions to make, Eisenhower made them. Moreover, as President, Eisenhower must bear the ultimate responsibility for all of Dulles's policies, and I do not think that he opposed any of Dulles's major mistakes, such as the overcommitment of the United States through the various treaty networks and the extension of military bases. Eisenhower's approach to the Soviet Union was more pragmatic than Dulles's. The President did not have the ideological commitment against Communism that animated Dulles. He settled the Korean war by compromise. He favored meetings with the Soviets and Khrushchev's visit to the United States.

Eisenhower was not a great President, but he served the spirit of the era. For the eight years he was in office, the country was looking for a period of good feeling, free of crises. The people wanted to get back to simple, ordinary affairs of life. It was not a situation in which a president could do great things; there were no great decisions to make.

In November, another President, John F. Kennedy, was elected. Younger, more vigorous than Eisenhower, Kennedy acted boldly in dealing with the Communist threat, but not always with happy results. I became his friend and advisor, but kicked away an opportunity to counsel him against the disastrous Bay of Pigs invasion of Cuba.

CHAPTER TWENTY-SEVEN

The Cuban Missile Crisis

Shortly after Richard M. Nixon conceded defeat to John F. Kennedy in the 1960 presidential election, I received a telephone call from the President-elect. Calling from the family home in Hyannisport, Massachusetts, Kennedy said that he had received congratulations from Khrushchev and wanted to know how he should reply. I was somewhat at a loss to answer, because I did not have the foggiest notion as to Senator Kennedy's views about the Soviet Union—whether he wanted to start off with a great gesture or whether he wanted to play it cool. Fumbling a bit, I told him that I thought the best reply would be a few courteous words of thanks, but not to go into substantive matters. His message to Khrushchev followed my advice. It was a formal, polite acknowledgment of the congratulations and pledged that the achievement of a just and lasting peace would remain a fundamental goal of the United States.

I had not seen Kennedy during the campaign, nor did I see him right after the election. In the latter part of December, when I was on the Eastern Shore of Maryland for some duck shooting, I received a call to go to Washington to see Dean Rusk, who had been selected as Secretary of State, much to his surprise. He had been in Williamsburg, as chairman of the Rockefeller Foundation, and had received word to stop in Washington to see Kennedy. The President-elect asked him about possibilities for Secretary of State, and told him that if Senator J. William Fulbright had not signed the Southern Manifesto denouncing the Supreme Court's invalidation of school segregation, he would have been chosen. Rusk went back home to Scarsdale, New York, and told his wife there was no need to think about moving. He had hardly spoken when the telephone rang. It was Kennedy, who offered him the position of Secretary of State. Rusk accepted, and

although he was unjustly criticized for his role in the Vietnam war, he
served with distinction for eight years.

Rusk informed me that I was being considered for the ambassadorship of some big European country, possibly Britain or France. I said
that I would go wherever the President and he wanted me to, but
would prefer to stay in Washington for a few years to get acquainted
with the new administration, which I felt was going to be innovative.
Rusk said he had no position suitable to my rank or experience,
because virtually all available posts had been filled. I told him I did not
care about the title, but did want to be involved in major policy discussions. Rusk said I could continue as Special Assistant for Soviet Affairs.
I was agreeable, and after the inauguration was renamed to the post.

The Soviets, disillusioned with Eisenhower, took an avid interest in
the election. At a luncheon at the Soviet Embassy on July 8, before
the 1960 conventions, Ambassador Menshikov asked me a series of
questions about who the candidates might be and who their choices
would be for Secretary of State. Over the usual chicken Kiev, I told
him all my information came from the press and therefore was no
better than his. On November 1, Menshikov asked Supreme Court
Justice William O. Douglas the same questions. He wanted to begin
exploratory talks with the new administration. Douglas said he was
not in a position to answer. After the election, Menshikov resumed his
probing, inviting a number of us—Rusk one day, me another—for
private talks at the Soviet Embassy. "It is obvious," I commented in
a memorandum to Rusk, "that Menshikov must have received rather
strong instructions from Khrushchev." Rusk did not know what
policy Kennedy would follow. Menshikov asked me at a luncheon
whether Kennedy would take the path of increasing armaments,
which might lead to war, or the path of peace. He also wanted to
know if Kennedy would be willing to go to a summit conference. I
said I had no idea what policy the new administration would accept,
except that I was certain it would follow traditional American lines of
trying to settle outstanding differences by negotiation. Menshikov
then stressed the need for general and complete disarmament, and I
responded with the usual answer that controls were necessary. He
replied with considerable seriousness, "Surely the United States realizes that in two or three years other countries will have the weapon
which may render the entire problem insoluble." The Soviet Union's
great fear was not United States nuclear power, it was China's possession of the atomic bomb.

While Foreign Service officers are traditionally separated from politics, I and virtually all of my friends in the Department of State were delighted by Kennedy's election. I had first met John Kennedy in the spring of 1939 in Moscow. He had been on a tour of Europe following an illness. During his short stay in Moscow, my wife and I had lunch with him and one of the other Embassy secretaries and his wife. We were all struck by Kennedy's charm and quick mind, but especially his open-mindedness about the Soviet Union, a rare quality in those pre-war days. He made a favorable impression. There was something about the young President, the astringency of his wit, the freshness of his outlook, his energy, that gave people a feeling that a genuine change was taking place. It was not so much disappointment with General Eisenhower's policies as the feeling that the country wanted a different kind of leadership.

One of my first jobs was serving on a special task force on Laos, where the pro-Western regime was facing considerable opposition from the Soviet-assisted Pathet Lao. Although I had had no direct experience with that part of the world, I was added to the task force so that Soviet policy would receive adequate attention. We concluded that American support of the pro-Western regime was not wise and recommended backing the neutralists.

In April of 1961, we flew down to Key West to meet Prime Minister Macmillan. Kennedy was anxious to find out whether we could count on the British to join with us in sending troops to Laos if we decided to intervene militarily. He also sent a letter to de Gaulle asking the same question. Macmillan gave an uncertain commitment; de Gaulle was specific and negative. It was apparent that Kennedy could not count on the two allies to give much support, and I believe that it was at this time he began to examine other possibilities, which eventually led to the conference of 1962 on Laos, at which a frail and uncertain agreement was reached for a coalition government headed by Prince Souvanna Phouma. It also provided that neither side should station troops in Laos. This agreement was violated by the North Vietnamese almost immediately.

On the way back from Key West, Kennedy turned to me and said, "Chip, I want to talk to you sometime about Cuba." Like an idiot, I said that while I would of course talk with him on any subject he desired, I really knew nothing about Latin America. I had never put a foot in Cuba, and therefore did not think I would have very much to contribute. Kennedy said, "All right, all right," and dropped the subject. I have often thought that if I had had my wits about me, I would have been in a position to have at least tried to convince the President to call off the plans for the disastrous Bay of Pigs invasion by an American-equipped and -trained émigré army.

I knew about plans for the operation, and I had had occasional conversations with some of the people involved. I asked a number of questions regarding the accuracy of our information on the disaffection of the Cubans, particularly among the youth, with Fidel Castro, the leader of the revolutionary government. Throughout history, revolutionary regimes have lost support rather slowly, and disenchantment has reached a serious level only after many disagreeable events or the interplay of negative factors. I did not feel that Castro's regime had had time to become unpopular or that there was much support for the émigré army. Castro had been skillful in maintaining the revolutionary enthusiasm and national fervor. Massive help from the United States would be required to make the invasion a success. I cannot say that I put my views clearly before anyone in top authority, and I had kicked away my opportunity to be consulted on the venture while it was being planned.

Thus I did not know the details of the planned strike when I was brought in on possible Soviet reaction at a meeting in the White House in late February. The President asked what the Soviets would do. Moscow had embraced Castro within weeks of his taking over the government in January, 1959. Mikoyan had journeyed to Havana, where he offered a $100 million loan, technical assistance, and an agreement to purchase vast quantities of sugar. Shortly after the collapse of the Paris summit conference, Khrushchev put a protective arm around Castro. In a speech, he said that the United States was "obviously planning perfidious and criminal steps against the Cuban people" and warned that "Soviet artillerymen can support the Cuban people with their rocket fire, should the aggressive forces in the Pentagon dare to start intervention." Despite the rocket-rattling, I told the President, the Soviet Union would not act militarily, but would only make loud propaganda noises—assuming that the operation would succeed or fail quickly. The Kremlin would not go to war over as stragetically unimportant an area as Cuba. If the invasion led to a long, protracted struggle, the Soviets would deliver arms to Cuba, but not military forces, I said.

In the car on the way from the White House, I raised with Allen Dulles, director of Central Intelligence, and two of his assistants the question of an alternative operation, infiltrating small detachments of guerrillas into the mountains where they could set up a government, as Castro had years before. If the move was successful, the United

States could then recognize the government and have a base for future operations. The CIA men batted down the idea, mentioning a number of technical problems. I had not thought the idea through sufficiently to put up a good argument, and did not press my point. But I continued to worry whether the Cubans, whose hopes had been raised by Castro, would turn to émigrés, who had mainly been middle- and upper-income business and professional people, unpopular with the mass of the poor.

Regardless of the advice Kennedy did or did not receive, the invasion was almost inevitable. In the first place, Kennedy went further than he should have in the 1960 election campaign in denouncing the Eisenhower administration as having done too little to counteract the threat Castro posed for all of Latin America. Kennedy, the candidate, promised that he would take more specific and direct action against Castro. Also, he inherited an ongoing operation, with the CIA training a refugee army in Guatemala and with the American military being involved. If Kennedy had called off the operation, he would have been subject to strong criticism, particularly from right-wing Republicans and certainly from those who had been connected with the preparations. The pressures on him to go ahead were strong, especially when some of his own advisers argued that the venture had an excellent chance of success. I was not present at the meeting in which the decision was made. When I heard that the invasion was to proceed, I was disappointed that the President, the embodiment of new ideas, had decided to go along on so doubtful a scheme.

The invasion army landed at the Bay of Pigs on April 17, and immediately ran into trouble. Soviet reaction followed the line that I forecast. The day after the start of the invasion, Khrushchev sent Kennedy a message saying that the Soviet Union would give Cuba "all the necessary aid" and again citing Soviet rocket prowess. In a separate statement, the Kremlin urged the United Nations to act. Kennedy replied, in effect, that the Soviet Union should mind its own business.

In the first few days, it became clear that the invasion was ending in a disaster. I had the opportunity of observing President Kennedy closely at breakfast and midnight meetings as he strove to wind up the catastrophe. He was calm, wasting no time on recriminations. At a meeting in the cabinet room, Vice-President Lyndon B. Johnson made some critical remarks about the CIA, but Kennedy cut him short, saying it was not the time for backbiting; we should face the future together.

The Bay of Pigs may have had one important effect on Soviet foreign policy. The indecision and faulty execution may have led Khrushchev to believe, in 1962, that the Soviet Union could get away with the installation of missiles in Cuba without decisive American opposition. However, the shipment of massive amounts of other Soviet arms in 1961 cannot be traced to any change in Soviet foreign policy that followed the ill-fated invasion. The Soviet Union would have sent the arms to Castro anyway.

In May, Khrushchev accepted a three-month-old proposal from Kennedy that the two meet. I had strongly recommended that the conference be held, on the basis that it was invaluable for the new President to have the opportunity of assessing his chief opponent in the world. After some correspondence, the meeting was set for June, in Vienna.

About this time, Kennedy also accepted an invitation from General de Gaulle, who had become President, to visit France. Shortly before the trip, the French generals in Algeria indicated they might rebel against de Gaulle's plan to give the North African province its freedom. The situation was tense for a few hours, and it looked as if the rebels might send a parachute detachment to Paris. Foreign Minister Maurice Couve de Murville went so far as to imply, in a statement to the French Assembly, that the CIA was involved in the near revolt of the Algerian generals. Kennedy was disturbed and asked me whether he should call off his visit. I told him that it was difficult to respond to Couve's veiled accusation, and that cancellation of the trip would damage America's standing with the French people. I told him that the best course was to keep the situation under close observance by instructing the Embassy in Paris to watch French public opinion for any increase in anti-American sentiment. If hostile feelings rose, he could then call off his visit. Kennedy accepted the advice and decided to go ahead with the trip when the Embassy detected no great increase in anti-American feeling.

We took off from New York in the evening of May 31 on the Presidential plane, and arrived in Paris, somewhat bedraggled, the following morning. I did not participate in most of the conversations with de Gaulle, because most of the time just the two conferred. I saw the record of their talks, and by and large there was nothing of particular interest except for de Gaulle's stubborn view on the world. He prophetically warned Kennedy about the dangers of getting involved in Indochina. Without stepping over the bounds of international politeness, he practically told Kennedy that he would be a damned fool if he got drawn into the Asian morass. De Gaulle also stuck to his view that it was a mistake to negotiate with the Soviet Union on Berlin, when, as he put it, there was the menace of Soviet action. Kennedy was leaning toward trying to negotiate with the Soviets, even though Khrushchev was becoming increasingly more strident on Berlin.

The entertainment de Gaulle gave in honor of President and Mrs. Kennedy at Versailles was among the most brilliant events I have ever attended. After dinner at the Gallerie de Glace and a ballet in the Louis Seize Theater, which had just been renovated, we went out on a balcony of the Palace of Versailles and watched the fireworks. As we started back to Paris, the cortege meandered through the park, stopping on occasion to look at some particularly striking example of the French art of illumination. One of the features of the evening was the extraordinary good looks and charm of the presidential couple—the President handsome, slim, filled with the vitality of youth and good humor; his wife regal with an elaborate coiffure and a white gown sweeping to the ground. We were proud of them.

Two days later, we took off for Vienna. After an uneventful flight, we landed at the airport near Vienna and motored through the countryside to the city. Everywhere the road was lined with cheering Austrians. The warmth of their greeting contrasted sharply with the coolness of the reception for Khrushchev. The contrast between the two men was just as sharp. Khrushchev was tough, adamant, and exuberant; Kennedy was flexible, reasonable, and sober.

The first meeting took place on June 3, at the Residence of the American Ambassador, shortly after noon. The two leaders went for a short walk in the garden, with only a Soviet interpreter along, then returned to the house, where they were joined by their staffs. I was along as an adviser, not as an interpreter.

The conversations began on an easy note. Kennedy remarked that they had met when Khrushchev, on his 1959 visit to the United States, had discussed international affairs with a group of senators. Khrushchev remembered the meeting, even to the fact that Kennedy had been late in arriving. The President said that Khrushchev had remarked how young he was. "Did I really say that to you then?" the sixty-seven-year-old Premier replied, then added that although his hair began turning gray when he was twenty-two, he was often told he looked younger than his years.

The talks got down to substance, with each of the leaders professing peaceful intentions and seeing no need for conflict because both the United States and Russia had all the resources needed for development. Then Kennedy made a mistake. He let himself be drawn into a semi-ideological discussion involving Marxian theory and the role of colonial powers, subjects which Khrushchev, from his years of training as a Bolshevik agitator, was a master in handling. Kennedy had a bowing knowledge of Marxism, but certainly no profound understanding of the intricacies of Bolshevik thought. In a matter of minutes, Kennedy, who left for Vienna saying, "I go as the leader of the greatest revolutionary country on earth," found himself expressing fear of "insignificant groups" of Communists seizing control of a country and liquidating the capitalist system. "You wish to destroy the influence of my country where it has traditionally been present," the President complained. "You wish to liquidate the free system in other countries." In the exchange, Khrushchev sounded like a libertarian, Kennedy a colonialist:

> KHRUSHCHEV: But if I understand you correctly, Mr. President, you wish to erect something in the way of a dam on the road of the development of the human mind. This is not possible. . . . Ideas have never been destroyed and this is proven in the whole course of human development. . . . If you seek to destroy ideas, then this will inevitably lead to conflict. . . . If you are able to assure, under your system, a higher standard of economic development, then victory will be with you and we will recognize it. If, however, the socialist system assures a higher standard of economic development of industry and culture, then we will win. I am speaking now, of course, not about military victory, but about victory in the plane of ideas.
>
> KENNEDY: The obligation of our Government to the American people and, as I am convinced, the obligation of the Soviet Government to the Soviet people, forces us to be concerned that this fight does not affect the interest of the security of our countries. We recognize that the Soviet Union has vitally important interests in definite regions of the world. The United States also has comparable interests but what is important in all this is that the struggle in other areas of the world goes on in such a way that it does not affect the so vital interests of our two countries. . . .
>
> KHRUSHCHEV: . . . from your words I draw the conclusion that you wish to transfer to us the responsibility for the growth of influence of Communist ideas in the whole world. In order that there should not be any conflict between us, you wish that these ideas not be propagated beyond the already existing socialist countries. But I repeat, Mr. President, that ideas cannot be stopped. . . . Obviously we will be

glad if Communist ideas spread to other countries, just the way you would undoubtedly rejoice at the dissemination of capitalist ideas. However, this depends exclusively on the people themselves.

After the first session, Kennedy was a little depressed. He had not been able to get Khrushchev to understand that the new American government was seeking a détente based on a realistic balance of power in the world. I told the President there had been no hardening of Soviet policy. The Soviets always talk tough.

There were only two days of meetings in Vienna, involving not more than four or five hours of talks. Kennedy did most of the talking for our side, and Khrushchev for the Russians. Occasionally, Rusk or Gromyko would interject a thought. The rest of us listened. During these meetings, I was not well. The doctors diagnosed my trouble as a thyroid deficiency and prescribed cortisone. The medicine made me drowsy, and at one of the conversations between the President and Khrushchev, I began to doze off. Ambassador Thompson woke me up with a kick in the ankle.

The results of the discussions were meager. There was an agreement to hold a conference on Laos, which gratified the President. Khrushchev showed little interest in Laos, and readily agreed to the talks, which were held at Geneva. The result was the 1962 accord on a neutral Laos. The Soviet leaders assured Kennedy that the Soviet Union would resume nuclear testing only if another country did first. He must have lied, because in August the Soviet Union began a two-month series of blasts, ending with the detonation of the most powerful explosion ever set off. Khrushchev had to know in June of these plans, because it would take a long time to prepare for the tests. On Germany and Berlin, there was no progress at Vienna. Khrushchev emphasized his intention to sign, in December, a peace treaty with East Germany—an act he had been threatening since 1958—turning over to the satellite the responsibility of dealing with Allied access rights to Berlin. Kennedy argued, but got nowhere.

In the face of such intransigence, Kennedy felt pessimistic. As the two leaders parted, Kennedy, with a wry smile, said, "Well, Mr. Chairman, I see it's going to be a very cold winter."

The general impression that emerged from the meetings was that Khrushchev was trying to intimidate the new President with his tough talk. I did not receive that impression, probably because I had heard Khrushchev use such language many times. Perhaps I misread Khrushchev. He may have been testing Kennedy. If so, he soon received the answer. Shortly after returning to Washington, Kennedy reported to the nation in a televised speech, in which he announced the partial mobilization of reservists and a reinforcement of our military in Europe because of Khrushchev's threats on Berlin. Some advisers proposed full mobilization, asserting that Khrushchev had meant what he said. While I was not convinced that Khrushchev was serious, I believe Kennedy's reaction was useful. If Khrushchev had any doubts, Kennedy showed that he could not be pushed around. When Soviet intentions are not known, it is better to take any threats at face value.

Whatever the effect on Khrushchev, the Vienna talks had a lasting impact on the President. For weeks thereafter, he commented to his associates on Khrushchev's remarks. At his home in Glen Ora, Virginia, he read the transcript of the conversations to Joseph Alsop, the columnist, and on another occasion to Philip Graham, publisher of *The Washington Post*. He read and reread the sections on Berlin. I believe that the Vienna talks conditioned the President for the crises on Berlin and Cuba that were soon to follow.

The world woke up on August 14, 1961, to learn that a barbed-wire fence dividing the Eastern sector of Berlin from the three Western sectors had been erected overnight. The purpose was to stop East Germans from fleeing to the West. More than three million, many of them young and talented, had fled since the war. The news caught Western leaders by surprise. There had been a meeting of the Foreign Ministers of the three Western powers in Paris in July, 1961, but no one had mentioned the possibility of a Berlin wall. (The barbed wire was soon replaced with brick.) After hasty consultations, the three Western allies decided that there was nothing that could be done. Military action would have been unthinkable, because it would have led to a confrontation in which the West would have had to back down.

Kennedy issued a statement condemning the erection of the wall as a violation of written and unwritten agreements, and decided to send Vice-President Johnson to Berlin for a brief visit to lift the morale of the Germans. I happened to be at the White House on other business when the President sent for me to say that he wanted General Clay and me to accompany the Vice-President. Clay, who had been the commander of the armed forces and the American High Commissioner for Germany at the time of the Berlin blockade, was a hero to the people of Berlin and thus a good choice for the trip. We took off from Andrews Air Force Base in the early evening, and arrived the following morning at Bonn. After a luncheon with Chancellor Adenauer, Vice-President Johnson pulled me into a corner and asked whether it would be wise for Adenauer to accompany us to Berlin. While I didn't think Adenauer's presence made much difference, I said that it would be a mistake. It would give the Soviets a propaganda opportunity by creating the impression that Adenauer was our puppet, and inevitably detract from the Vice-President. Johnson agreed. I explained our reasoning to Foreign Minister Brentano, who went to Chancellor Adenauer and tactfully suggested that it would be better if he did not accompany us. Adenauer accepted the decision in good grace, and sent Brentano to Berlin by separate plane.

During our flight, General Clay said that if he had still been in command of American forces in Berlin, he would have ordered his troops to tear down the barricades and barbed wire that the East Germans had put up. I doubt if it would have been possible to do this without provoking a serious crisis, although a daring move of this kind might have worked. Any such move would have been a serious risk. We had no obligation to East Berlin, and the Soviets on many occasions had demonstrated their willingness to go to extremes to preserve the Soviet system. Johnson did not reply to Clay's statement. The Vice-President was much more of a listener than an asserter of policy on the trip, even though he was the senior American figure present. He asked my advice so often I felt flattered, and he was careful to make no mistakes.

Our Air Force Constellation arrived in Berlin at 5 P.M. The ride from Tempelhof Airport to City Hall was a triumphant procession. A half million people lined the streets to greet Johnson, and 250,000 cheered him at a rally at the City Hall. In his speech, which had been prepared in Washington, Johnson pledged his "sacred honor" and that of the United States to defend Berlin. The next morning, we welcomed the first contingent of 1,500 American troops sent to Berlin as part of our reply to the erection of the wall. Johnson, visibly moved, greeted a tough-looking colonel in command of the detachment. While the Vice-President visited a refugee center, General Clay and Alan Lightner, the American political representative in Berlin and an old friend of mine, and I took an auto tour of East Berlin. Our military car was not stopped once. We saw East German soldiers on almost every corner and a dozen Soviet T-34 tanks, their engines running, at a square.

The Johnson party took off for home at 4 A.M. the next day. Over

East Germany, George Reedy, Johnson's press secretary, asked what I thought of deliberately flying above the altitude limits set by the Soviets for the air corridor. The previous spring, the Soviets had suddenly imposed low limits on civilian, as well as military, aircraft flying into Berlin. There had been a great deal of debate about testing Soviet willingness to enforce the rules. I told Reedy that with the Vice-President aboard it was not the time to test the Soviets. Even if successful, the act would look like cheap bravado. Moreover, it would prove nothing, because the Soviets would probably let Vice-President Johnson go through unmolested but clamp down with redoubled vigor on subsequent flights.

Johnson performed admirably on the trip. He did the right thing at the right time. As I wrote in my report to Secretary Rusk, the Vice-President's visit and the arrival of the reinforcements "dramatized to the people of Berlin, American determination and will" to stay in the beleaguered city. The two events were a "complete and unqualified success." But, I added, "what is not so certain is the lasting effects." I asserted that Washington had underestimated the "profound" reaction of West Germans to the erection of the wall. I listed these factors in reaching that conclusion:

1. The fact that the East German regime, generally held in contempt by the West Berliners, had been permitted to carry out the action. If the sealing off had been done by Soviet troops, there would, of course, have been resentment, but it would have been accepted by the West Berliners as an illegal, but nonetheless more tolerable, action undertaken by one of the occupying powers.

2. There seemed to be a rather widespread feeling among West Berlin officials, shared in large measure by our representatives there, that our failure to react immediately and definitely in some manner, generally undefined, in the face of the East German action had increased Communist confidence to a point where further piecemeal restrictions and harassments were to be expected. There was a tendency to mix up the fact that the measure was taken because of the refugee flow with some idea that it was part of a calculated series of moves by the Communists.

3. Initially, there had been a great questioning of the willingness and determination of the Allies to protect West Berlin and Allied rights in the future. The visit and the reinforcements went far to offset this feeling. We should recognize that the visit itself and the reaffirmation by the Vice-President in such circumstances increased,

in the popular mind, American commitment to Berlin and might possibly be the subject of some overt interpretation.

I made only one specific recommendation:

> ... that is that we be prepared to react swiftly and decisively and, indeed, to overreact, if necessary, to any clear signs of harassment or any attempts by the Communists to erode our rights, and especially in regard to access (which includes the communications between West Berlin and the Federal Republic). Any hesitancy or delay in our reaction to any such attempts would rapidly cast the morale of the West Berliners back to the depths where it was immediately after August 13, and prior to the Vice President's visit.

The rest of 1961 passed in an uneasy peace. There was no actual crisis, but there was not tranquillity, either. A special Berlin Task Force, whose meetings I attended from time to time, drew up countless contingency plans for dealing with Berlin while awaiting, with some foreboding, Khrushchev's moves to carry out his threat to sign a treaty with East Germany. Moscow itself blew hot and cold. At the Twenty-second Congress of the Soviet Communist Party in October, Khrushchev withdrew his threat on Germany, but Marshal Malinovsky boasted about the accuracy and deadliness of Soviet long-range missiles. At the same time, China's Chou En-lai was calling the Kennedy administration the "wiliest and most adventurist yet." Then came Gromyko, with a surprisingly conciliatory speech, praising Kennedy and Rusk and proposing that the Soviet Premier and the American President get together and reach an agreement. I saw two reasons for Gromyko's mild address. It was designed to offset the bellicose nature of Chou En-lai's speech, and it was a sign that the Soviets were rethinking their Berlin posture in the light of Kennedy's firm action. Lest anyone think the Gromyko speech was a Kremlin signal to Washington that a détente was possible, it should not be forgotten that the warm words were uttered against a backdrop of the largest series of atomic tests any country had ever held.

Until Khrushchev's speech, we were not sure whether he was bluffing on Germany. It seemed to me that President Kennedy's firmness was what gave Khrushchev pause. We had an obligation to protect West Berlin. Kennedy made it plain that he would not shrink from that obligation. Khrushchev realized he could not go through with his Berlin plan without war with the United States. The risk was not worth the gamble. Nevertheless, the Berlin wall achieved its objective of keeping East Germans imprisoned in their Sovietized "paradise." The wall remains the clearest symbol of the failure of the Soviet system.

In March of 1962, Secretary of State Rusk led a delegation to Geneva in the hope that the reopening of the disarmament talks would provide an opportunity to discuss Berlin. But like every discussion on either subject I ever took part in, the talks got nowhere. No matter what device we used—big meetings, small meetings, private meetings, closed meetings, limited meetings—the Soviets made clear that they had no intention of permitting Berlin to become a viable entity, particularly that they would not allow any form of unification, even of the city of Berlin, much less of the whole country. The discussions on disarmament became possible because the Soviets concluded their atomic tests, which included the detonation of a 60-megaton device. The purpose of the tests was a mystery. One theory was that it was an attempt to perfect a weapon that, exploded fifty miles or so in the air, would destroy a considerable portion of the country. Another theory was that the tests involved an attempt to produce a neutron bomb, which would destroy radio communications and consequently the guidance system for intercontinental ballistic missiles. Undoubtedly, the Soviet Union had something important in mind. Once the tests were finished, the Soviets were prepared to consider a treaty banning nuclear tests in the air and water. These were the talks that led to the 1963 test ban treaty. I was never involved in any of the disarmament negotiations.

In May, 1962, I was invited to Kennedy's country home at Glen Ora for a visit of André Malraux, who at that time was de Gaulle's Minister of Cultural Affairs. The President sent a plane to pick me up in West Virginia, where I had puzzled a medical-association audience with a dissertation explaining the differences between communism and socialism. (Instead of denouncing both as evil, I said that socialism never represented a threat to the United States but communism did.) I had met Malraux in his pro-Communist period in 1934, when he was inclined to regard the Soviet Union through faintly rose-tinted spectacles.*

At Glen Ora, Malraux explained that de Gaulle had virtually completed (a somewhat inaccurate statement) the main elements of

---

* At lunch in Moscow one day, the conversation turned to drugs, and Malraux, who had spent months on archeological expeditions to the Middle East, said, "I cannot get on with opium. It does not agree with me. On the other hand, I work very well with hashish."

French disengagement from the colonial world and the steps necessary for regaining French independence in foreign affairs. The unfinished part of de Gaulle's effort to rejuvenate the French nation, Malraux said, was domestic reform. The entire French system, political, economic, and social, had to be reconstructed, and he expressed doubt whether this would be as easy a task as de Gaulle seemed to think. Kennedy then spoke philosophically of the function of government in the future, maintaining that in twenty or thirty years political problems would begin to fade away as economic prosperity grew. The result, he said, would be that government would be largely administrative. Malraux agreed, but said that before France could enter on this path, a great deal of reorganization and restructuring were necessary. This conversation, held through interpreters (Kennedy spoke little French), was quite vague. I cite it simply as an indication of Kennedy's inquiring mind.

My inclusion among the guests with Malraux at Glen Ora was a strong hint that I would be named Ambassador to France. I do not remember when Kennedy offered me the post. He explained that the current envoy, General James M. Gavin, wanted to come home. I said I would be more than delighted to accept, because France had always held a special place in my affections. I did not mind leaving my specialty, Soviet affairs, at this point. I had served at length in Moscow and Washington. Tommy Thompson, who was returning to the United States, could serve as Secretary Rusk's specialist on the Kremlin. The French ambassadorship was a big job, with de Gaulle in power. Kennedy wanted someone in the post whom he knew. By this time I knew how the new President felt about foreign affairs and was on such a friendly basis with him that I was confident I could represent him overseas. In addition, I spoke French fluently, had served in Paris as Minister, and loved the country. I met all the qualifications and was eager to go.

Kennedy said that he wanted to see if there was any possibility of doing business with General de Gaulle. On my formal appointment, I received a warm letter from Mrs. Kennedy expressing confidence in my ability. There was no fight in the Senate over my nomination, and, following confirmation, I began to make preparations for my departure for Paris. I decided to go by ship, because there was no particular urgency concerning my arrival.

On October 17, as I walked into the President's office to pay my official farewell call, Kennedy said to me, "Chip, come here and look at these." Spread out on his desk were a large number of photographs.

They were pictures taken by a U-2 reconnaissance plane of missile bases that the Soviet Union was installing in Cuba. While there had been charges in the Senate and by the press of such Soviet activity, the pictures were the first definite proof of what the Soviets were doing. Until then, the CIA said the Soviets were installing only anti-aircraft missiles with a range of twenty-five miles. I spent a half hour with the President, and the word France was not mentioned. He told me that though the data seemed scanty, our experts could determine the nature of the installations with precision. Invaluable in analyzing the photos was material obtained from Oleg Penkovsky, probably the most successful Western espionage agent who worked in the Soviet Union. The pictures, the President told me, showed sites of twenty-four medium- and sixteen intermediate-range ballistic missiles. The danger these forty missiles posed to much of the United States did not have to be discussed. Once installed and ready to fire, they would amount to nuclear blackmail.

The President had not made up his mind what to do. The CIA pictures, taken on October 14, had been given to the President on October 16, the day before my visit. While he did not know how he was going about it, the President said he was determined to get the missiles out of Cuba. "We're going to have a pretty tough time ahead of us," he said, "and we'll have some hard decisions."

The President said he was appointing me to a committee, headed by Rusk, to consider the problem. We met until late in the night weighing the options. One group, with which I sided, favored using diplomatic means to the ultimate before turning to force. The other group held that the quickest and surest method of destroying the bases was by bombing. The fact that bombing would kill thousands of Russians installing the missiles did not bulk as large in the minds of this group as it did in mine. I felt that the Soviets might have felt compelled to strike back against so great a loss. The result would have been nuclear war.

The next day, October 18, the committee met again. That evening, forty-eight hours before I was to sail for France, Joseph Alsop, the columnist, gave a dinner at his Georgetown house for my wife and me. The President and Mrs. Kennedy attended. After we had dined, the President took me out on the porch and we discussed the missile crisis for almost half an hour. Again we went through the options, but he still had not made up his mind on a course of action. He said he might ask me to delay my sailing for Paris so I would be available for consultations. He seemed to be irritated that the State Department had not come up with the answers to questions he had asked about Cuba and the missile crisis. "Chip," he exploded, "what is wrong with that God-damned department of yours? I never can get a quick answer no matter what question I put to them."

"Mr. President," I replied, "one of the reasons, of course, is that foreign affairs is an extremely complex question. I do not have to tell you this, but you cannot give answers off the top of your head and quick ready-made solutions." I hesitated, then added, "In regard to the department as a whole, the fault is yours."

"What?" he said, taken aback. "How do you get that way?" I explained that a department could not be run with authority if the President appointed two or three subordinates before he appointed the Secretary. I named no names, but Kennedy knew of whom I was talking. He had chosen Chester Bowles to be Under Secretary of State and G. Mennen Williams to be an Assistant Secretary before selecting Rusk as Secretary. I did not mean to imply that these were bad appointments; it was the principle that was wrong. The Secretary of State should have the right to choose his subordinates. The President smiled and said maybe there was something to what I had said.

As we were leaving the Alsop house, I told the President I did not expect to see him again before leaving for Paris. "I wouldn't be too sure you are leaving," he said to my wife. "I think I may ask you to stay." This remark seemed to be missed by the other guests. After we got home, I warned my wife that she might have to develop a worsening of her back (she had been suffering from a lumbar condition) "because we are going to have to invent a story for our staying behind here." I did not tell her and she did not ask me—she was a well-disciplined Foreign Service wife—the reason for the sudden change in plans. Before going to bed that night, I wrote in longhand on a yellow legal pad my suggestions of what the President ought to do about the Soviet missiles in Cuba.

The next morning, my wife called Mrs. Alsop, thanked her for the dinner, and said that she was beginning to wonder whether she could leave the United States in view of the condition of her back, which was keeping her in bed. At the State Department, I had a call from Kennedy, who seemed to assume that I was going to attend an important meeting on the missile crisis at 11 A.M. the next day. I then talked with Dean Rusk, and gave him the memorandum I had written the previous night. We both had doubts about the wisdom of canceling my departure plans, including an engagement to speak the next day to the Franco-American Society in New York. Calling off this luncheon of about two hundred people might have alerted the Soviets to the fact that the United States knew about the missiles. Besides, my successor as Rusk's adviser on Russian affairs, Tommy Thompson, had just come back from Moscow and was in a position to give more up-to-date advice on Soviet intentions than I could.

Rusk agreed that my memorandum covered my position fully, and we decided that I should leave as scheduled. Rusk talked with the President, and he apparently agreed. My memorandum, addressed to Rusk for transmittal to the President, said:

TOP SECRET

MR. SECRETARY: October 18, 1962

Since the conversation last night was rather general, and I will not be there tomorrow, I feel I owe it to you and to the President to set forth my views on this matter as succinctly as possible. They are as follows:

1. The existence of Soviet MRBM bases in Cuba cannot be tolerated. The objective therefore is their elimination by whatever means may be necessary.

2. There are two means in essence: (a) by diplomatic action or (b) by military action.

3. No one can guarantee that this can be achieved by diplomatic action—but it seems to me essential that this channel should be tested out before military action is employed. If our decision is firm (and it must be) I can see no danger in communicating with Khrushchev privately, worded in such a way that he realizes that we mean business.

4. This I consider an essential first step, no matter what military course we determine on if the reply is unsatisfactory. The tone and tenor of his reply will tell us something but I don't believe a threat of general nuclear war should deter us. If he means it, he would have so reacted even if the strike had come first.

5. I don't feel so strongly about a message to Castro and this could be dropped.

6. My chief concern about a strike without any diplomatic effort is that it will inevitably lead to war with Cuba and would not be the neat quick disposal of their bases as was suggested. Furthermore I am reasonably certain that the allied reaction would be dead against us, especially if the Soviets retaliated locally (as in Turkey or Italy or in Berlin).

7. A communication to Khrushchev would be very useful for the record in establishing our case for action.

8. In general I feel that a declaration of war [against Cuba] would be valuable since it would open up every avenue of military action—air

strike, invasion, or blockade. But we would have to make a case before our allies to justify such a declaration of war. But if we acted first and sought to justify it later we would be in a spot of great consequence.

9. Finally, I feel very strongly that any belief in a limited quick action is an illusion and would lead us into a full war with Cuba on a step by step basis which would greatly increase the possibility of general war.

The best course in my view would be a carefully worded and serious letter to Khrushchev, and when the reply is received (if it is unsatisfactory) communicate with our principal allies to inform them of our intention and then ask Congress for a declaration of war with a suitable statement of the reason and all adequate preparations.

Please excuse the handwriting but I have no time to have it typed. If the President asks about my opinion this will constitute it. Good luck.

CHARLES E. BOHLEN

There are of course many other angles—but the above seem to me the essentials. I don't quite see the urgency of military action—if it leaks and we have already initiated diplomatic action we should be able to handle it.

At nine o'clock the next morning, I was paged at Washington National Airport. The call was from Kenneth O'Donnell, the President's appointments secretary, who told me that President Kennedy urgently desired that I attend the 11 A.M. meeting at the White House. I said I thought this was impossible, that I really should go to New York and make my speech. While I held the phone, O'Donnell talked to Kennedy; he then came back and said he was sorry but I would just have to get out of the engagement and in a way that would give no publicity. Frustrated, I asked O'Donnell to put Kennedy on the wire. "Mr. President," I said, "I do not see how at this last moment—my plane leaves in fifteen minutes—I can suddenly cancel this flight and engagement in New York dealing with a large audience without running the serious risk of some publicity and a lot of speculation." Kennedy had not realized that the newspapers had been told about the speech and that a last-minute cancellation was sure to tip off the Soviets that something was up. I was too closely identified with Russian policy for anyone to miss the point. The President wanted to maintain the advantage of secrecy. He had not batted an eye when Gromyko told him the previous day that Soviet activity in Cuba was not related to any offensive intention against the United States. Kennedy immediately saw my point, because he said, "I guess you are right, Chip. Go on. I guess we will have to do without you."

I was in mid-Atlantic, aboard the liner *United States*, when Kennedy spoke to the nation on October 22, disclosing the installation of the Soviet missiles and announcing the blockade of Cuba. I listened to the speech on the radio in the smoking room. The static was so heavy at the beginning that it was impossible to understand what the President was saying. Then the airwaves cleared, and I heard the end of the speech, in which the President listed his eight points. There was considerable excitement. Many of the passengers got the idea, from hearing only part of the speech, that Kennedy had ordered an invasion of Cuba, and cheered. I told a group of friends that I did not believe this was the case. I was not sure of the details, but the President's program was a blend of diplomacy and force. The Navy was ordered to "quarantine"—a euphemism to avoid the diplomatic term "blockade"—Cuba, turning back all ships carrying offensive weapons there. In addition, the President warned that any nuclear missile launched from Cuba would lead to full retaliation by the United States on the Soviet Union. And unless the forty missiles were quickly removed from Cuba, the United States, the President made clear, would take military action to do so.

While I was crossing the Atlantic but before the President's speech, Dean Acheson, the former Secretary of State, flew secretly to Paris to inform de Gaulle of the Soviet emplacement of missiles and our contemplated action. Acheson was smuggled into the Elysée Palace through the kitchen door with the American chargé, Cecil Lyon. De Gaulle said that if war broke out, France would be on our side.

There was a car from the Embassy waiting when we landed at Cherbourg on October 24, and we drove right to Paris. I was suffering from a severe toothache, so one of the first things I did was to dash off to a dentist. The following day, I caught up on the news. The Soviets had alerted all military forces but were talking calmly. There was no decision from the Kremlin. Lyon briefed me on the Acheson conversation with de Gaulle. The next few days in Paris were filled with anguished waiting because I could not perform the functions of an ambassador until I had presented my credentials to General de Gaulle. His invariable rule was to receive letters of credence from ambassadors on Saturday morning. I arrived on Wednesday. I had received a few cables from Washington with a little information and an abortive telephone call from McGeorge Bundy, the

President's special adviser on foreign affairs. The call came on a new radio circuit, which was supposed to scramble the words as they were spoken and unscramble them at the other end of the line. The security device scrambled the words so effectively that they could not be unscrambled. We had to give up on the call.

On Saturday morning, with all the key figures of the Embassy, I presented myself at the Elysée. I was received by General de Gaulle and Couve de Murville, the French Foreign Minister, whom I had known for many years. After a few introductory remarks of the type that are usually exchanged on occasions of this kind—about maintaining friendly relations—de Gaulle led me to a sofa and sat down. He gave me the same assurances he had given Acheson that France would be with the United States in the event of war. These assurances, which I transmitted to the President, were never made public by de Gaulle.

The next day, Sunday, October 28, I received an urgent telephone call, again from Mac Bundy, but this time not on the scrambler and I could understand him. There was a message regarding an exchange of letters between Khrushchev and Kennedy that Washington wanted de Gaulle to know about immediately. In one letter, Khrushchev agreed to withdraw the missiles if the United States pledged not to invade Cuba. De Gaulle was at his home at Colombey-les-Deux-Eglises, about a hundred miles from Paris. Our military forces said they could provide a helicopter to take me there. I called the Elysée and got hold of an official who transmitted my request to de Gaulle. The reply came back that de Gaulle did not receive anyone, French or foreign, officially during his weekends at Colombey-les-Deux-Eglises. If the message could be given to the Elysée, it would immediately be transmitted to him. I reported this to Washington, which greeted the information in silence. The incident was a clear example of de Gaulle's calmness in moments of crisis. He refused to join in the frenetic American method of transacting international business.

On Monday, the Soviet missiles were being withdrawn and the Cuban crisis was over. It was a great personal triumph for President Kennedy and one he fully deserved. He had not flinched under two immense pressures—the threat to the security of the United States and the danger of a nuclear war. His mixing of limited, but definite, military action—the blockade—with the strongest possible diplomatic language—the threat to annihilate the Soviet Union—was masterful.

There are those who still believe that the United States should have bombed out the missile sites and with them the Castro government. The simplicity of such a course is attractive, but the results would have been questionable. The missiles would have been removed from Cuba all right. But thousands of Soviet technicians might have been killed. Because it sometimes reacts instinctively, the Kremlin might have responded, without thought of the consequences, with a direct military counterblow. The United States would have won the nuclear war that followed. We still maintained an advantage over the Soviets in missiles and atomic weapons. But millions of lives would have been lost, and the onus for starting the war would have been on us. Kennedy succeeded in getting the missiles removed without a war. The Cuban missile crisis showed that Kennedy would have been a strong President if he had lived.

Why did the Soviets put the missiles in Cuba in the first place? And why, with the entire world watching, did they back down and withdraw the weapons? The operation had all the earmarks of a Khrushchevian gambit. It was arrogant; it was bellicose; it was daring; it was dangerous (harebrained, the Soviet Central Committee said in dismissing him in 1964). The most acceptable theory that I have heard of Khrushchev's motive is that the threat of the missiles would have forced the United States to agree to a Berlin and German settlement on Soviet terms. The bold move also was an answer to the persistent Chinese charge that the Soviet Union had abandoned revolution in favor of comfortable deals with capitalistic powers. In laying his plans, Khrushchev may have underestimated Kennedy and the American people. He probably thought that the President would take the matter to the United Nations, where there would be endless debate and nothing would be done. The Soviet missiles would be accepted by the American people as a fait accompli. Somewhere along the line, Khrushchev would decide whether to keep the missiles in Cuba as permanent blackmail or offer to remove them as part of a German settlement. Khrushchev's misreading of American opinion, both governmental and popular, is characteristic of Kremlin ignorance of other countries. The Soviet leaders have never understood the courage of others to resist them in moments of crisis.

The Soviets, traditionally insecure in the presence of foreigners, were humiliated by the missile crisis. The Chinese supported them during the tense days, but later criticized the operation as adventurism. The galling decision to withdraw accelerated Soviet construction of missiles. Vasily V. Kuznetsov, a long-time Soviet official, said to

John J. McCloy, one of the United States representatives to the United Nations, as the missiles were being withdrawn, "You Americans will never be able to do this to us again."

While Khrushchev put the best possible face on the Cuban events, claiming the American no-invasion pledge as a victory, he never recovered from the setback.

As time passed, Soviet relations with China continued to deteriorate. Of more importance, the Soviet economy failed to fulfill the goals Khrushchev had boasted it would meet. The Soviets were not surpassing the United States in output of meat and milk; they were lagging, and the standard of living remained low. Improvisations and slogans failed to produce the miracles Khrushchev had promised. The reorganization of the economic system disturbed Party chieftains. Finally, on October 14, 1964, nearly ten years after he deposed Malenkov as the top man in the Kremlin, Khrushchev lost all his jobs. In the two chief positions, First Secretary of the Communist Party and Premier, he was replaced by Leonid I. Brezhnev and Alexei Kosygin, both conservative products of the Soviet system. Their ebullient predecessor, who alternately amused, shocked, and scared the world, who gave Soviet Communism a human touch it lacked before and has not had since, dropped out of sight. Khrushchev lived out his last years in obscurity, flashing back into prominence only once, when *Khrushchev Remembers*, a book of memoirs apparently based on tape recordings, was published in the West. He died in 1971.

Nikita Sergeivich Khrushchev was born and bred in the Bolshevik Party. Basically a peasant, he was no philosopher on the ideology, although he was a formidable debater. He added nothing to the body of Communist doctrine except a few pragmatic deviations based upon the recognition that a nuclear weapon rendered warfare totally unthinkable as a means of achieving any objective, whether national or revolutionary. He accepted in toto the general principles of Leninism-Marxism. It just never occurred to him to question them, and he operated on them to some extent. Above all, though, he had a genuine feeling for his own country and its people. When he came into full power in the middle of 1957, he realized in his peasant shrewdness and pragmatism that something had to be done to rejuvenate the structure which had been inherited from Stalin. Otherwise, the system would collapse. In the end, his attempt to save the system was what brought him down. The other men in the Presidium would not stand for the decentralization of political power that necessarily followed the decentralization of the economy.

Khrushchev was also a man of impulses, which, when coupled with an extraordinary amount of animal energy, made him not unattractive, but did lead to some unfortunate incidents. He was coarse and vulgar, given to scatological expressions in his earthy humor, and enjoyed lying to make a story better or to score a point. Despite what he said about me as a gossip, Khrushchev did like to drink. On May 27, 1956, at a reception for Western air force officers in a garden at the Kremlin, vodka was flowing at a prodigious rate. Khrushchev certainly felt his drinks that day. And the peasant in him came out. First, he dismissed small nations as of no great importance. To the French, he said he did not know why they were pretending to be a great power. They were trying to produce an atom bomb but lacked the resources to pay for it. To the British, he complained that A. N. Tupelov, the foremost Soviet aircraft designer, had been barred from some factories on a visit to England. Waving his glass, Khrushchev said it didn't make any difference; the English had nothing new to offer anyway, except diplomatic "cleverness." As the afternoon wore on, Khrushchev became more and more unrestrained. Zhukov and other Soviet dignitaries were disgusted and said openly the remarks were out of place. Eventually, I heard one of the Russians say, "It's about time we closed this and got Nikita Sergeivich out of here." The party was quickly ended, and Khrushchev went along docilely. Later, Zhukov advised me, with a contemptuous wave of his hand, "You should not pay attention to that; it's the way things are done around here."

On foreign affairs, Khrushchev was a complete pragmatist, basing his decisions on the two cardinal rules of Soviet diplomacy—hold on to the Soviet system and avoid war. For these reasons, he was willing to ease up on control of the satellites yet smash the Hungarian revolution. The Chinese confounded him because Peking offered an alternative to Moscow as a center of Communism and, through its aggressive behavior over Quemoy and Matsu, threatened to plunge the world into war.

There was always a basic contradiction in Khrushchev's foreign policies. On the one hand, there was apparently a serious desire to improve relations with the leading non-Soviet countries, even to the point of bringing about a détente with the United States. He seemed to be sincere about seeking agreements on disarmament. This was "peaceful coexistence." On the other hand, he constantly threatened action on Berlin that would drive the West out of the city. The reason for this contradiction lay in the fact that Khrushchev wore two hats, one as the chief figure in the Soviet government and the other as the leader of the Soviet bloc in Eastern Europe. We continually tried to convince him that he could not have it both ways, but he could never make a choice. He was the prisoner of the Soviet contradiction.

Khrushchev was impressionistic. World travels altered his views. He saw that the United States was not the Marxian nightmare of the unbridled misery of the working poor contrasted to the extreme affluence of the capitalists. He realized our power, although he misread our high living standards as showing a lack of backbone. Eisenhower's reputation and warm personality captured Khrushchev, just as they did Americans. He counted on the President—"an honorable man"—and hoped to do business with him. The U-2 incident shocked Khrushchev and undoubtedly convinced some in the Politburo that their leader was soft on the Americans.

If Khrushchev had stayed in power, he might have been willing to explore paths toward détente that his cautious successors hesitated to tread. It is a pity for the Soviet Union, the United States, and the world that the snub-nosed, roly-poly Russian did not remain the leader of his country a few more years. I would have been greatly interested in what he would have done, although my main interest had shifted to one of the monumental figures of the twentieth century—Charles de Gaulle.

CHAPTER TWENTY-EIGHT

Le Grand Charles

In December, 1962, following a meeting of the NATO Council in Paris, Secretary Rusk offered me and my wife a ride to Washington in his plane. Since we had not shut our house in Washington and were only half transferred to France, we decided to accept the offer. I went to see the President, who told me of vague plans regarding a conference with Prime Minister Macmillan at Nassau. He said the problem was to find some way of satisfying the British desire to obtain a nuclear weapon in place of the Skybolt missile, which the United States had promised London but which had been canceled because of high costs and doubts of its effectiveness. London was bitter, because without Skybolt Britain would have no nuclear deterrent and was doomed to drop to the status of a second-class power.

Secretary Rusk decided not to go to Nassau, apparently because he felt he should be the host for the annual diplomatic dinner at the Department of State. The Secretary's motives were the best, but his decision to stay in Washington was a mistake. Anything to do with nuclear matters and Britain raised problems with France, because de Gaulle was always suspicious of the "special relationship" between London and Washington. It cannot be said that Rusk's absence made any changes in the ultimate decision at Nassau, but it certainly did not help his standing with Kennedy as Secretary of State.

Shortly after the conference began, McGeorge Bundy, the President's Special Assistant for International Affairs, telephoned asking if I could return to Paris with a message for General de Gaulle. I checked with Paris on de Gaulle's availability, but before the reply came in, the President summoned me to Nassau, sending a plane to take me there. At Nassau, the President explained the plan he had worked out with Macmillan. The United States would turn over to the British the Polaris missile for installation in a nuclear submarine. I was to tell de Gaulle that he would be offered the same deal. I immediately pointed out to Kennedy that this might be a fine public-relations idea, but to de Gaulle it would not seem generous because the French still lacked the means of building a nuclear submarine and could not manufacture the warhead to go on the Polaris missile. The British were competent in both fields and only needed the guidance system for the Polaris. Kennedy saw the problem, but said the French acceptance might make it possible to amend the American legislative ban on exporting nuclear secrets to give de Gaulle the information he needed to become an atomic power. Before I could depart for Paris, a message arrived saying that de Gaulle was on his Christmas vacation at Colombey-les-Deux-Églises and could not be disturbed. He would see me early in 1963.

I flew with the President to Palm Beach, where I dined with him, Mrs. Kennedy, and Ormsby Gore, the British Ambassador. We had a gay evening, drinking a good deal of rum without inconveniencing anyone. The President, who had had a trying day, went to bed early. The following morning, Pierre Salinger, the White House press secretary, William Lawrence, then the White House correspondent for *The New York Times*, and I played golf (a wicked Salinger drive just missed me) before I flew back to Washington.

I was planning to catch a New Year's Eve flight due to arrive in Paris at 8:30 in the morning of January 1. This schedule would have given me ample time to go to the Embassy, don my cutaway and striped trousers, and appear at the Elysée for the annual New Year's reception. But bitter cold delayed my flight from Washington, and when I arrived in New York, I found the only flight leaving for Europe was a London-bound Alitalia plane. I was the only passenger in the first-class section and celebrated the arrival of 1963 drinking champagne with the crew 30,000 feet above the Atlantic. Despite my efforts, I failed to reach Paris in time for the reception, but did make it early enough on January 2 to keep my appointment with de Gaulle.

Before leaving for the Elysée, I received a phone call from Robert Dixon, the British Ambassador and a friend from World War II days. He had seen de Gaulle the previous day and had filled him in on the American offer. Dixon said his instructions had been so urgent that he had to see de Gaulle before my arrival. It seemed to me that the British were trying to give their version of the offer before we could. Dixon told me it was his impression that de Gaulle had not closed the door to the Nassau plan.

When I saw de Gaulle, I stretched my instructions somewhat, but not seriously. I told de Gaulle that I was sure that his acceptance of the offer would open up a wide field of cooperation between France and the United States. I did not mention nuclear information specifically, but de Gaulle got the point. He assured me that the French government would not be hasty in its reply but would give the proposal careful consideration. It was my first diplomatic business with him, and a certain naïveté was understandable. I interpreted his statement about not taking hasty action to mean that there was a fifty-fifty chance of acceptance, and so reported to Washington.

I was shocked on January 14, only twelve days later, when de Gaulle gave his answer at a press conference—a hard, tough "no" categorically rejecting the Nassau offer without leaving anything open for discussion. He gave no particular reason, and I am inclined to believe that something unexpected led de Gaulle to make his decision sooner than anticipated. That event possibly was the arrival of George Ball on one of his periodic European visits. Ball, the Under Secretary of State, had been attorney for the French government in Washington for a good many years. He had been fairly active in American politics and was a good friend of Adlai Stevenson. We went to see Foreign Minister Couve de Murville. Ball said that the United States was going to give a heavy shove to launch the plan for a multilateral nuclear force, made up of mixed units from the Allied countries, and hoped that the British would, as they had said in Nassau, give it a fair wind. Couve made plain that the French would have no part of any multilateral force, but would not object to its creation. He did not expect we were serious about MLF. But de Gaulle saw that the United States was determined to go ahead with the plan, and he was alarmed at the prospect. He was, of course, opposed to any type of integration with other countries, reasoning that any such move would water down Paris's authority over French elements. He did not like the American veto over the use of nuclear weapons by the MLF. His opposition ran in contradictory directions. First, it was the old fear, common in Europe, that the hotheaded Americans would draw Europe into an atomic war. Second, de Gaulle felt that Americans had become reluctant to use nuclear weapons in the event of a Soviet attack on Europe because the Soviets had developed the missile capacity to destroy American cities. Regardless of the apprehensions, he was not prepared to give up any French sovereignty.

At the press conference, de Gaulle also flatly vetoed Britain's application to join the Common Market. While he spoke vaguely of Britain's non-European orientation and of her special relationship with the

United States, his real reason for barring Britain from Europe was that he did not want a rival for supremacy on the Continent. There was, of course, consternation and bitterness in London and a good deal of disillusionment and some bitterness in America.

Kennedy, like Roosevelt before him and Johnson after him, showed exemplary restraint in handling the General's rejection of MLF and Britain's Common Market bid. Kennedy made no public riposte, only expressing regret. Kennedy learned about de Gaulle quickly. He knew that the General would not be averse to some rows with the American President. They would help him politically in France. Kennedy refused to oblige de Gaulle.

In the month following de Gaulle's press conference, I talked with at least ten cabinet officers about French policy and the General's intentions. I received widely different interpretations and concluded that de Gaulle kept them in ignorance of what he was doing. Even Couve de Murville, who was agreeable personally, had little knowledge of what de Gaulle would or would not do. With these limitations, I gave, in a letter to Bundy on March 2, 1963, the following estimate of de Gaulle:

> In the first place it is important to remember that de Gaulle is distinctly a product of that half of France (or less than one-half) which has been, since 1789, and still is, conservative, hierarchical, religious and military. This was one of the reasons for his bitterness against Pétain. He is also the product of French military training pre-World War I and II in that he tends to approach a given problem from a highly analytical and rather simple point of view. His ignorance of the operation of other countries is, I would say, very great, and this is particularly true of the United States. I am sure he has no understanding or indeed interest in the constitutional structure of the United States and its bearing on foreign affairs.
>
> Insofar as Franco-American relations are concerned, I see very little that can be done to improve them. . . . I can see no particular moves that we can make beyond going on with day to day questions and matters as they come up.

Bundy had asked about the value of a de Gaulle visit to the United States, which the White House had been seeking for some time. In reply, I said I saw no prospect of any real dialogue developing between the President and de Gaulle, and was reasonably certain that de Gaulle did not wish to meet with the President because by nature he did not like general discussions. He apparently often listened to his Ministers, but did not seriously discuss questions with them. I proposed, with some uncertainty, that the President consider writing for de Gaulle a thorough analysis of United States policy toward Europe, American defense and economic interests there, and American policy toward the Soviet Union. The idea would not be to try to change de Gaulle's mind but to avoid a deepening of his suspicion with every minor action taken by Washington. The White House apparently did not think much of the idea, because the President never wrote such a letter.

In view of de Gaulle's independence, there was no expectation that France would sign the nuclear test ban treaty that the United States, Britain, and the Soviet Union agreed to in July of 1963. Kennedy sent a personal message to de Gaulle urging French signature and offering United States help in overcoming any delay that might result in the development of French nuclear effort. De Gaulle would have liked the help, but he refused to accept any curbs on France. No one in Washington had any illusions that he would drop his effort, eventually successful, to develop a French nuclear capability.

The last time I saw President Kennedy was in April, 1963, when I flew to Palm Beach and spent the day sailing with him. He was in a happy mood, but philosophical about de Gaulle. While Mrs. Kennedy water-skied, we discussed French-American relations and what, if anything, the United States could do to change de Gaulle's attitude toward the United States. We decided there was nothing we could do. I think it was I who convinced Kennedy, and Johnson later, to avoid fighting de Gaulle. This policy paid off.

On November 22, 1963, my wife and I were on a train traveling from Paris to Strasbourg, where I was going to spend a weekend hunting with some French friends. At the stop in Nancy, a French *chef de gare* dressed in a white raincoat entered our compartment and courteously inquired whether I was the American Ambassador. When I replied in the affirmative, he said, with true French style, "*Monsieur, j'ai une chose terrible et solenelle à vous annoncer.*" He told me that President Kennedy had been assassinated in Dallas, Texas, and, erroneously, that Vice-President Johnson had been wounded. I got off the train and was driven back to Paris by the chauffeur of the prefect of the region. It was a dismal four-hour journey, with the rain and the blackness of the night matching the darkness of my spirits.

For days thereafter, the French lined up to sign a book in the Embassy as a testimonial to the fallen President. Letters poured into the Embassy. Bouquets of flowers were sent to my wife. The sense of grief and personal loss displayed by the people of France was an extraordinary affirmation of the degree to which President Kennedy had captured the imagination of people. They were mourning a hope of a better world that had been snatched from them.

De Gaulle waited until well into the following day to announce that he was going to the funeral. I believe that he wanted to see what the other leaders did, and when it became clear that many of them, particularly the King of the Belgians and the British Prime Minister, were going, he decided to go, too.

I attended the requiem mass sung for Kennedy at Notre Dame Cathedral. As the Ambassador, I sat in one of the armchairs in the front of the church, along with Georges Pompidou, the Prime Minister, and Madame de Gaulle. Emotions are often difficult to recall, but I well remember feeling, as I sat under the soaring arches of the great cathedral, that the future had collapsed on the present. Here I was, with thirty-five years of experience in the Foreign Service and extremely skeptical about the great men in public life, yet completely crushed by Kennedy's death. I still feel that a great future was extinguished by his death.

Had Kennedy lived, in all probability he would have visited the Soviet Union. Such a visit would not have changed Soviet policy any more than an Eisenhower visit would have, but he would have captured the Russians' hearts.

Except for the Cuban missile crisis and the nuclear test ban treaty, Kennedy's record of achievements in foreign affairs is sparse. By the time of his assassination, however, he was beginning to move with more confidence. I am sure he would have tried some innovations to end the dreary cold war. I do not know what they would have been, but he could have had a fine second term.

Before Kennedy's assassination, de Gaulle had finally acceded to an invitation and agreed to visit the United States. He did not really want to go, and for sound reasons. He told me frankly that while he had not the slightest objection to returning the President's visit, and deeply appreciated the invitation, he felt that a trip to the United States would attract much publicity without the possibility of accomplishing anything, and thus would lead to serious repercussions for both of them. He maintained this view for about a year. Realizing that he could not hold out indefinitely, he said that he would go on a working visit with a minimum of ceremony. The plan was to go to the Kennedy compound at Hyannisport on Cape Cod, where there would be little opportunity for public activities. There would be one or two days of discussion and nothing more.

Right after the Kennedy funeral services, when de Gaulle called on the new President, Johnson said that he looked forward to welcoming him to Washington. Johnson assumed that de Gaulle would fulfill the promise that he had made to Kennedy. De Gaulle replied that the trip had to be worked out through diplomatic channels. Johnson took this reply to mean that only the details—place, date, and agenda—would have to be decided, that the principle of the visit was confirmed. In good faith, he told a meeting of the Governors of the United States the next day that he expected a visit from de Gaulle. When de Gaulle, who was still in Washington, heard of Johnson's remark, he sent Hervé Alphand, the French Ambassador, rushing to the Department of State to insist that there had been no commitment for a visit; the General's reply to Johnson meant that the question whether there should be a visit would have to be worked out through diplomatic channels. De Gaulle never came.

In December, 1964, when I was in Washington, President Johnson asked me to find out whether there was any truth to rumors, which we had been reporting from the Embassy, that Paris was going to extend diplomatic recognition to Communist China. On my return to France, I brought up the subject with Couve de Murville, who would not tell a foreign diplomat a flat lie. I put the question to him; he hesitated and said that he would have to find out and would let me know in a week. It was obvious something was up, and a week later when he called me to say that France was about to recognize China, I had already informed Washington of that distinct possibility. De Gaulle acted simply because he felt that it was ridiculous not to have relations with a large country like China, regardless of its ideology. He also believed that France might develop a profitable trade with China. Like his expectations from his Soviet policy, his China hopes turned out to be more of an illusion than a reality.

There has been a great deal of misunderstanding regarding de Gaulle's decision to pull out of the NATO command. It is important to remember that the North Atlantic treaty, signed in April, 1949, while a landmark in committing the United States, was standard operating procedure for the other countries, which had signed hundreds of similar agreements in their histories. The treaty itself set up no mechanism for carrying out the commitment of assisting any member attacked. Only after the 1950 attack on South Korea was the NATO Supreme Command set up. Even then, the Supreme Commander had no authority in time of peace to move troops or give any of the orders normal to a commander in chief. He did not have command of even a corporal's guard. It was up to the participating governments to decide that the threat of war was so imminent that they should transfer command of their troops to the commander in chief.

Nevertheless, de Gaulle's argument, both publicly and privately, was that military integration in time of peace resulted in the subordination of France's interests to those of the dominant power in the alliance, the United States. Actually, I think de Gaulle was worried about the fact that, if war came, the command would pass into the hands of an American general, since every NATO Supreme Commander had been an American. De Gaulle undoubtedly remembered his dispute with General Eisenhower over the use of French troops during the German offensive in the Ardennes in World War II. Eisenhower was prepared on sound military grounds to abandon Strasbourg to the Germans to shorten his lines. De Gaulle was not. Luckily the German offensive was stopped before Eisenhower gave the order, because it is certain that de Gaulle would have withdrawn the French troops from Eisenhower's command. I also believe that the Cuban missile crisis made it plain to de Gaulle that a Soviet-American war could break out over an issue which had no relation whatsoever to European security or interests. In such an event, Western Europe, under the integrated structure of the North Atlantic Treaty Organization, would be sucked into the vortex, no matter what it felt.

The way de Gaulle announced his decision surprised almost everyone. Shortly before his annual dinner for heads of diplomatic missions in late January 1966, de Gaulle intimated at a press conference that certain things would have to be done to the NATO organization, but gave no indication that France was going to take quick action. After the dinner, I asked de Gaulle what he intended to do about NATO. He replied, "Ah, I will do nothing precipitate. We shall take our time on this and examine everything very closely, but I shall certainly do nothing suddenly." Again I was fooled by de Gaulle. I wired Washington that he was not contemplating any drastic action in the immediate future. Three months later, in March, 1966, Couve summoned me to the Foreign Ministry and handed me a letter from de Gaulle to President Johnson announcing the French withdrawal. Midway through the letter, I said to Couve, "This is a sad day. I will not attempt to argue the case with you now, but I am saddened to have to transmit this message to my President." Couve did not respond. Similar letters were sent to other NATO countries.

Although I cannot cite documentary evidence, I believe that de Gaulle's decision to choose March, 1966, as the date to "regulate" the

NATO affair was due primarily to the fact that he had scheduled a visit to Moscow in June. Had he waited until after the trip, there would have been a strong belief that the NATO withdrawal had been encouraged by the Kremlin. To avoid such conjectures, he acted before his Moscow visit.

According to information received from the Quai d'Orsay, de Gaulle's decision had been relatively sudden, unknown to officials in the Foreign Ministry. In fact, the Quai d'Orsay had been working on a series of proposals to give France more leeway in the NATO structure, particularly regarding French sovereignty over NATO bases. None of these proposals called for withdrawal from the organization or the elimination of United States bases in France. The ideas were taken to de Gaulle, who told Couve de Murville, apparently to the latter's surprise, that they would not do at all. He wanted, within twenty-four hours, an arrangement whereby France could withdraw from the entire NATO organization. I was informed that he even intimated that he was thinking of abrogating the treaty itself, although he had not decided to do so. The latter report may have been true, but I am inclined to question it. The treaty requires every signatory nation to go to war to protect any member attacked by another country. De Gaulle would hardly have risked isolating France in the face of what he agreed was a Soviet menace. However, he might indeed have been thinking along those lines, since geography would require the United States, pledged to defend all NATO countries, to go to the aid of France if she were attacked.

I was called back to Washington to consult with President Johnson and Secretary Rusk on the nature of the reply. One of the problems was de Gaulle's request that the United States forces stationed in France (originally at strong French insistence) be removed and NATO bases in France be closed by April 1, 1967. This was a tall order. President Johnson decided that the United States would do everything possible to meet de Gaulle's deadline. There was some opposition by the Pentagon, but the President, at my urging, ordered the American military to get the job done. I did not think it wise to try to punish or to get tough with France. There was not the slightest possibility that we could persuade or force de Gaulle to alter his course.

The deadline was met. The military moved 800,000 tons of war material and dismantled all the air bases well in advance of the April deadline. It was an impressive achievement. The French had undoubtedly expected us to drag our feet, to raise objections at every move, and in general to behave in a rather bitchy fashion. When we behaved with dignity, acted with efficiency, and got out of France on schedule, the French were astounded. I believe that our action had a salutary effect. We expected to obtain very little in compensation for the properties that were to be turned over to the French. On the contrary, the de Gaulle government was unusually generous in estimating the value of these installations. There was not a single hitch in the negotiations.

Not all the French were happy to see us go. When the American flag was lowered at Camp des Loges, the headquarters of the American commander in chief, near Versailles, even the French generals wept.

After de Gaulle's announcement, the French changed their rationale for withdrawing. Ambassador Alphand told me that the move was made to create a condition for a détente with the Soviet Union. The same argument was used by Couve de Murville in an appearance at Brussels. In an analysis of this argument prepared for Washington on June 30, 1966, I said there was little reason, based on past history and experience, to think that the proper way to create a détente with the Soviet Union was to tear down Western defenses before any analogous move on the part of the Soviet Union. It was this absence of clear motivation that raised fundamental questions concerning de Gaulle's policy. In my view, de Gaulle's policies, if pursued another six years, would result in the complete disruption of the Western alliance. Other NATO members would be tempted to free themselves from any organizational obligation, especially if the Soviet leaders were tactically smart enough to continue their benign behavior. It is true, I told Washington, that a similar evolution might be taking place in the Warsaw Pact, but it should never be forgotten that the Warsaw Pact was chiefly a façade, with the real power of the alliance in the Soviet Union, not only because of its military might and Party control but also because of its strategic geographic position in relation to Europe in contrast to the United States position. I feared not an abrupt break in America's European policy but a gradual reduction in the number of troops and, what is perhaps more important, a gradual reduction in our awareness of the Soviet menace in Europe. The United States might be not only physically out of Europe but psychologically little interested in developments there. My wire concluded:

> The real danger, as I see it, in de Gaulle's policy is that if this keeps on for a sufficient number of years there is a high degree of possibility

that the Germans, becoming discouraged and frustrated with the Western allies, will at some point in the future be tempted to take the previously followed route of a deal with the Soviets. There can be little doubt that Moscow would drop de Gaulle instantly if this prospect developed in Soviet foreign policy. I am sure that all of the people involved in Soviet affairs would agree with my statement that one of the constants in Soviet policy has been a desire—twice implemented—to reach some form of agreement and accommodation with Germany, whose power they have had cause to fear. The only basis on which de Gaulle seems to rest his policy is his belief that the Soviets have really changed and have abandoned any idea of military force, and further expansion of Communism. Although this suits his purposes, it is hardly necessary to emphasize the extreme weakness of this point, and I may add that almost all Frenchmen that I know who are knowledgeable about Soviet affairs disagree with great violence.

There were those in the Johnson administration who were saying, "France is eternal and de Gaulle temporary." I warned that any optimism was false. "There is not much probability of a swing of French policy back to the pro-alliance basis," I wrote. "On the contrary (and this is one of the reasons de Gaulle is hurrying), the job will be so completely done that any French government that succeeds him will find it very difficult and even impossible, particularly in light of the Left opinion, to reverse the field and go back to being again a genuine as against fictitious member of the North Atlantic Treaty."

De Gaulle was as independent of the West in his Middle East policy as he was in his European views, moving France from a pro-Israeli to a neutralist stance. In the spring of 1967, he learned through a newspaper article that El Al, the Israeli airline, had been sending planes steadily to France to pick up spare parts and other military equipment. De Gaulle ordered a stop to that activity, and early in June directed that restrictions be tightened on the shipment of military supplies to the troubled area. This ban was ordered on a Friday, according to Couve de Murville, but apparently Premier Pompidou, possibly because of his connections with the Rothschilds, did not permit the General's order to go into effect until Saturday. Israel attacked the United Arab Republic on Monday. Had it not been for the quick Israeli victory, I believe that this embargo would have raised serious political problems for de Gaulle, because the French people were strongly pro-Israel.

When the war was over, de Gaulle's attitude toward Israel did not change. There were cold-blooded reasons behind de Gaulle's policy. He realized that the United States and Britain had lost their standing in the Arab countries, and he saw an opportunity for France to move in. For the West, this policy was not bad. With Soviet influence rising, it was advantageous to retain some Western friendship among the Arabs, and France was the only country with a chance at success.

I can only guess at de Gaulle's reasons for his Middle East policy. There were all sorts of interpretations of what he was doing. De Gaulle always acted unilaterally. In the five years I was ambassador in Paris, there was not a single important foreign-policy issue in which he sought to consult with his allies, whether it was Vietnam, the recognition of Peking, withdrawal from NATO, or the six-day war in the Middle East. Discussion and attempts to work out a common point of view were alien to him.

On July 11, a month after the six-day war, I went to see de Gaulle. As in all my calls at the Elysée, the visit was almost liturgical in form. I arrived at the entrance of the Elysée, walked up a flight of stairs, was greeted by an aide, and then taken to an outer office guarded by a military aide. I waited in a chair for a few moments until a buzzer sounded. The military aide then escorted me into the office, which was furnished like a salon of the eighteenth century, with big windows looking out on lawns, flower beds, and chestnut trees. De Gaulle came around the table that served as his desk and greeted me in the middle of the room. Then he motioned me to a chair, returned to his desk, sat down, folded his hands over his stomach, and said, *"Monsieur l'ambassadeur, j'écoute."*

De Gaulle almost never initiated a conversation. I brought up the Middle East war. He was in a bitter mood about Israel and Abba Eban, the Israeli Foreign Minister. "Mr. Ambassador," he said in his elegant French, "I told Mr. Eban when he was enroute through Paris that Israel should not ever have recourse to arms. What do you think they did with my advice? They completely ignored it." I pointed out that a country that feared its existence was at stake would sometimes find it impossible to adopt the best advice proffered with the best intentions. He shrugged his shoulders. When he resumed his criticism of Israel, I said, "Mon Général, suppose you were an Israeli?" He stiffened in his chair and haughtily replied, "But I am not an Israeli."

De Gaulle was not anti-Semitic; he objected only to militant Zionism. Once convinced that Israel had started the war to conquer territory, de Gaulle could not be shaken. His views hardened to the point where only a complete settlement would change him.

I do not feel that de Gaulle ever had much understanding of the United States. We lacked most of the attributes which de Gaulle felt were essential for a stable country. We had not established a military tradition; our armies were essentially civilian. We had no unifying religious heritage. We were immigrants from dozens of countries—in his eyes, a somewhat messy collection of tribes that had come together to exploit a continent. He felt we were materialistic without the solid, civilizing tradition of, say, France. We were too powerful for our own good. He frequently remarked to me that American policy was based on an excess of power in relation to the rest of the world. He did not mean military power. The Soviet Union was too strong militarily to ignore, and he realized that there was a military standoff in nuclear weapons. In every other form of power—industrial, commercial, agricultural, scientific, and financial—he saw the United States so far ahead of other nations, including the Soviet Union, that we would fall into error. When I took Vice-President Hubert H. Humphrey to see him in 1968, de Gaulle was quite contemptuous of our sending troops into the Dominican Republic. He cited the action as an example of the false belief that power can solve everything. When we withdrew from Santo Domingo, I mentioned the pullout to de Gaulle. He shrugged his shoulders and said nothing.

Eventually, I concluded that de Gaulle's obsession with detaching France from the United States could be understood if the relations between nations were viewed as similar to the operation of the planetary system. Every planet has its own gravitational pull. A medium-sized planet has to stay out of the gravitational field of the larger planets or become a satellite. For exactly the same reason, France had to stay away from the United States.

Aside from his views of the United States, it was de Gaulle's attitude toward the Soviet Union that interested me most. During the war, de Gaulle had flirted with Moscow. In a speech in Algiers in December, 1943, he had referred to Russia as *"chère et puissante Russie."* In 1944, he went to Moscow, without consultation with the Western Allies, and signed a treaty of alliance with Stalin. There was certainly nothing wrong with such a treaty; the British had signed one in 1942. It is interesting, however, that Stalin's and Churchill's first reaction when de Gaulle made the proposal was that the alliance should include Britain, too. De Gaulle demurred.

While de Gaulle possessed slight elements of naiveté about the Soviet Union, he took the same tough stand with Russia that he did with the West. In discussing the 1944 alliance, the Russians sought to win French recognition of the pro-Soviet Lublin Committee of Poles rather than the government-in-exile in London. Despite enormous pressures, de Gaulle refused and prepared to depart without an agreement, when Stalin capitulated. In later years, de Gaulle overinterpreted Stalin's backing down. He seemed to feel that if the other Western powers had stood firm consistently, they could have prevailed over the strongest Soviet views. De Gaulle was wrong, because Russia occupied Eastern Europe, and no united diplomatic front would have changed the outcome. Also, he did not realize that the French attitude regarding the Polish question was not that important in Stalin's eyes. It was the American and British view that was vital to Stalin—yet even these powerful countries had no leverage on Poland.

De Gaulle's Soviet policy was rooted in his basic attitude on international relations. I am convinced from a dozen or more conversations with him that to de Gaulle the only entity in the international field with a continuing vitality was the *état-nation*, the nation-state. Ideology in his view was a passing and transitory matter and therefore not of great interest to the statesman. Communism was a child's disease, like measles, from which the patient—in this case Russia—was sure to recover. During this illness, other countries should beware of the danger and deal with it. Eventually, the ideology would fade away and Russia would resume its traditional aims and policy.

De Gaulle felt that only countries with coherent, long-term traditions of nationhood really had the fiber to carry them through on the international scene. He once told a Belgian representative to NATO that Belgium was an artificial country created by France for foreign-policy reasons and therefore had no legitimate right to exist as a nation. On another occasion, he said that Italy was not a nation but a conglomeration of cities and provinces. Germany was in the process of becoming a nation. While he often referred to the Germans as a great and terrible people, he rarely termed them a nation. In fact, he came down to France, England, Spain, and Russia as the only genuine nations of Europe. Nation-states, de Gaulle thought, pursued policies in cold-blooded interest. There is a reasonably well-authenticated account of a meeting of the French cabinet in which Couve de Murville referred to "France and her friends." De Gaulle interjected, "*Monsieur le ministre*, a great country has no friends, it only has interests." He did not allow a place for sentiment in his government's analysis of international problems, because he thought those who did were likely to be deluded or tricked. He was mistaken. No one can give an honest and objective analysis of American policy, past, present, and future, without noting the strong strand of sentiment that runs through our policies. Examined cold-bloodedly, de Gaulle's theory was right. Sentiment should not play a role in policy. But given human nature, it is inevitable that it does. Americans have been willing to make sacrifices for countries—like France—with which we have had traditional ties.

While appearing to follow an evenhanded policy toward both the United States and the Soviet Union, de Gaulle did nothing of the kind. He realized that the United States was a benign power, even though he was often sharply critical of us in public. He also realized that Soviet Russia was inherently a malignant power, but since he did not worry about the threat of Communist ideology, he did not see the degree of danger that we did. He was mistaken. Fifty years from now he might be right. By then, I doubt if there will be any remnants of the Bolshevik theory left as guides to an active political belief. But now the ideology plays its part. The Soviet invasion of Czechoslovakia in 1968 might be attributed to the need to protect the Soviet Union's national security. But the mechanism—the total control of the Communist Party—used to further the Soviet national interest was certainly based on ideology. Once adopted, the Soviet ideology imposes obligations and leads to consequences that would not otherwise be present. De Gaulle never saw these truths.

De Gaulle's insistence that nationalism dwarfed ideology in foreign affairs was brought out in his visit to Poland in 1967. He was given a great reception by the Poles, which was understandable. There was a tradition of Franco-Polish friendship. But there was also an ideological reason, because de Gaulle was pulling away from the United States, the bête noire of the Communists. De Gaulle made a speech in which he stressed the Franco-Polish friendship but intimated that the menace to Poland came from the East as well as the West. In other words, he addressed himself to the traditional fears of the Poles. De Gaulle's view, however, did not fit into the ideological pattern into which Poland had been placed by the Soviet Union. Gomulka, the Polish Communist boss, in reply, made a 100-percent ideological speech, emphasizing the eternal fraternal solidarity of the Soviet and Polish people and intimating in pointed terms that no one was going to undermine that friendship.

De Gaulle often used the expression "from the Atlantic to the Urals" in describing Europe. This expression, which first appeared in *Le Petit Larousse* in 1907, referred to lands which had been traditionally in Europe. Siberia was not considered a part of it. The Soviets did not care for this expression, because it implied that Siberia did not really belong to the Soviet Union, but de Gaulle persisted in its use.

It was never entirely clear how de Gaulle envisioned the role of the Soviet Union in this Europe. Russia was a part of Europe, but I imagine de Gaulle left her exact relationship to the countries of the area somewhat vague on purpose. He had a vision not of a United Europe but of a confederation in which the Europeanness of all participants would be recognized. With this common interest, they would stand as a unit against the rest of the world. Even in de Gaulle's eyes, this confederation would take a long time to achieve. Such a statement is extraordinary, because if there was one thing that was characteristic of de Gaulle's thinking, it was a tendency to telescope time. (Malraux described de Gaulle as the man of the day before yesterday and the day after tomorrow.) He would speak of something which could only begin to take effect during the following generation as though it were an actuality of the present. This was the basis of his thoughts about ideology in the Soviet Union.

De Gaulle's tragedy was that he did not have a sufficient power base. If he had been the leader of a great power like the United States, he would have been willing to risk more than we were over Berlin and Germany. He might have been able to make a deal with Moscow, even though he secretly favored the division of Germany. At one time, he said to me, "Why are you Americans so interested in the unification of Germany?" I gave him the standard reply that the division of Germany constituted a permanent sore that sooner or later was going to cause trouble and would be dangerous to the peace of the world. "So would a united Germany," de Gaulle shot back.

Half of de Gaulle's mind realistically appraised the relative weakness of France in the modern world; the other half of his mind refused to accept this lack of power. He talked as if France were a nation of 100 million, but he knew better. Thus he was constantly beset by contradiction. This conception of France as unique—indeed, almost favored by God—was coupled with a paradoxical contempt for her people. He saw the French as frivolous. He was reported to have said, "What can you do with a country that has three hundred and fifteen different kinds of cheese?" but he never made any disparaging remarks about France to me, a foreign diplomat.

His accomplishments for France were real. There is no question that he alone averted a civil war over the loss of Algeria. He also did a masterful job in dismantling the French empire while retaining for France a position of pre-eminence in all the former colonies except Guinea. Above all, he restored France's morale after the shattering blows of World War II. France was humiliated far more by the dreadful defeat of 1940 than those of us on the outside realized. De Gaulle understood and adopted measures designed to enhance French confidence. It did not take long for the French to regain their feeling of superiority.

He was not always so successful. He failed to develop the intimate relations with the Soviet Union that he sought. His greatest error was his rejection, purely on the basis of French pride, of Britain's entry into the Common Market. It was on this subject that de Gaulle ran most squarely against the views of the American government. The United States has favored, since the days of the Marshall Plan, the integration of Western Europe. With the division of Europe into East and West irremediable and permanent, it seemed to us elementary common sense that countries in Western Europe, with similar views regarding the relationship of the individual to society, should unite to protect themselves and make themselves into a viable entity in the modern world. While we urged the Europeans to act, we never tried to force them. Indeed, we emphasized that it was up to them to decide for themselves. De Gaulle's anti-American tone silenced even this cautious support. I would agree that, in principle, we should officially remain quiet, but I do think we should always make known that we strongly favor the unification of Western Europe.

De Gaulle, too, favored the unification of Europe, but under French domination. This was de Gaulle's great design. He had a Frenchman's instinctive fear of Germany. He respected but distrusted the powerful neighbor to the east. He also felt that France had a historic role to play, that France, by her centuries of civilization and her skill in diplomacy, had, in effect, been ordained by God to lead Europe. He was not so unrealistic as to ignore totally the correlation of forces in the world, but he did feel that France's possession of nuclear weapons would enable her single-handedly to prevent Germany from becoming an atomic power and menacing the peace of Europe again. However, it was primarily France's pride and desire to dominate that held up the development of an integrated whole from the continental countries of the Common Market.

Regardless of how much he irritated, even angered, me, I could not but respect the extraordinary personality known as Le Grand Charles. He was not the cosiest of men, but he certainly was one of the most polite men I have ever known. Only when he was at Colombey-les-Deux-Eglises did I have any difficulty in seeing him. At no time was he ever disagreeable with me. He was courteous, calm, and relaxed, giving me as much time as I wanted. Of course, I was careful to avoid overstaying my welcome.

I certainly owe him a debt of gratitude for having awarded me the Grand Cross of the Legion of Honor, the highest decoration given to foreigners by the French Republic. I think de Gaulle appreciated the fact that I did not raise a ruckus over steps he took which the United States opposed but could not stop. The fact that I rolled with the punch, always thinking of our future relations with France rather than the temporary disagreement with de Gaulle, was much appreciated, at least so I have been told.

He also honored me twice at shooting events he held at the Château de Rambouillet, a government-owned château a half-hour drive south of Paris. At these elaborate affairs, held primarily for ambassadors, soldiers dressed in white smocks acted as beaters to drive pheasants into a line of shooters. The procedure was always the same. There would be three drives, and then a pause until three black Citroëns drew up. Dressed in a business suit, de Gaulle would descend from the lead car, shake hands with all the shooters, and then stand behind one of them. I went to four of these shoots, and twice he chose to stand behind me. When I made a good shot, he would say *"Ah! c'est bien,"* or *"Bon coup."* It was a little bit nerve-racking to think that a careless shot as I turned might hit him, for his six-foot four-inch frame was a big target. After one of these shoots, a prominent French official said to me with a malicious grin, "You were extremely well placed, monsieur, in relation to our President."

After the shoot, we would all go to the château for a good French lunch—that is, a lunch with three kinds of wine. On the last two occasions, being the senior ambassador, I sat next to the General. At one of these luncheons, he said it was indeed tragic that history was really made only in time of war. In time of peace, all one has, he said, is politics, inflecting the last word contemptuously. In 1967, at my last shoot there, I asked de Gaulle if he had read Servan-Schreiber's book. *The American Challenge.* "No," he replied, "I have not read it and I will not read it. I do not care for the author."

Vinogradov, the Soviet Ambassador, looked on me as a rival at these shoots. He was not a particularly good shot, although he thought he was. Once when I did better than he, the Soviet Ambassador intimated that the French had given me a better spot in the line. He had become more bourgeois than Communist—one of his proudest memories was of being invited to Alsace by a count, Jean de Beaumont, for a pheasant shoot.

De Gaulle had a mordant wit. At a time when his popularity had fallen, an ardent supporter, d'Astier de la Vigerie, a television commentator, complained that all his friends were worried about the General's policies. "Then, my dear d'Astier," de Gaulle said, "change your friends."

Scarcely a week passed without a story of two, many of them true, about de Gaulle's personal pride. He would not let any French government official of any importance take part in the twentieth anniversary, in 1964, of the landing at Normandy, because neither he nor the French had participated in that particular operation. The greatest amphibious military operation of all time was un-history. The opposite treatment was accorded the anniversary of the landing in southern France, because the Free French forces had participated. The celebration was at a war memorial, at Toulon. The British Ambassador, Sir Patrick Reilly, and I stood right behind de Gaulle, near a large stone flowerpot. A few months later, French newspapers reported that the French Secret Service had found in the flowerpot a powerful bomb, set for detonation by a radio miles away. The device had not worked, apparently because of a malfunction. It was never clear to me whether this report was true or whether it was fabricated to increase de Gaulle's prestige. There was probably some truth in it. In any case, the British Ambassador and I were uncomfortably close to that flowerpot.

De Gaulle was rigidly unforgiving. In 1964, as he was leaving Strasbourg, he was shaking hands with a number of generals lined up at the entrance to his plane. When he came to General Jacques Massu, the commander in chief of the French forces in Germany, he dropped his hand, turned, and marched into the airplane. This animosity, which dated back to Algerian days, did not prevent de Gaulle from getting in his helicopter during the May, 1968, riots and flying off to consult with General Massu in order to measure the loyalty of the army to the government.

De Gaulle was quite inhuman politically—a characteristic that was an asset as well as a liability. He stood aloof from his followers, surrounded by an aura of mystery, and was quite indifferent to whether he helped or hurt them. When those who worked for him were considered no longer useful, they were thrown away. In the latter days of his career, this detachment from the public caused him to misjudge the French people. On New Year's Day, 1968, he said in an address to the country, "France can view with equanimity and calm the events of the coming year since France alone among many of the great nations is unshaken by any great events within her borders." Within four months, the students had rioted and France had become the most shaken of all countries.

Despite our disappointments and difficulties with the French government, my tour in France was as much a delight as a duty. One reason was my staff. I had had a good staff in Moscow and Manila, but the one in Paris was outstanding. It worked together as a cohesive, harmonious unit. There were normal frictions, jealousies, and differences, but these did not prevent our Embassy from becoming a model. There were a few errors of judgment, but these were relatively minor. I was proud that we had an extremely high reputation in both the State Department and the Quai d'Orsay. Washington knew we were on top of all events. Paris trusted us because we did not gossip or distort developments. A great deal of credit for our good work can be ascribed to the three men who served as my chief deputy in the position of Minister of the Embassy. The first was Cecil Lyon, a longtime friend who gave up the post of ambassador to Chile to become number two in Paris. The second was Robert McBride, who went on to be ambassador to the Congo and then ambassador to Mexico. The third was Woodruff Wallner, who had an unrivaled knowledge of the French political scene and the French character. My task was greatly lightened by my secretary, Annabelle Mitchell.

Another reason why I enjoyed France so much was the hospitality we received from the people. There was only one incident during my five years in Paris that really resulted in unpleasantness. D'Astier, the commentator on the government-controlled television system, declared in a broadcast one evening that any American aviator captured in North Vietnam should be chained to a wheel and dragged around Vietnam as punishment for bombing innocent women and children. While d'Astier had a right to his opinion, I felt that it was going a little too far for the government-controlled television system to permit him to air so blatant an attack on the United States Air Force. I wrote a letter of protest to the Foreign Ministry. I had not intended to make the letter public, and I don't believe that my old friend from Moscow days, Louis Joxe, the Acting Foreign Minister, did either, because in discussing the complaint he went so far as to say that he fully understood my views. Nevertheless, the letter did leak to the French press, which accused me of interfering with freedom of speech. I had not questioned d'Astier's right to say anything he wanted to, but noted the government's responsibility for what was said over its own television system. Fortunately, the controversy did not last long.

Our other experiences in France were uniformly pleasant. My wife and I entertained regularly. We had about two receptions a month, to which we would invite cabinet ministers, members of parliament, newspapermen, labor leaders, business executives, artists, intellectuals —representative of all categories of French life. We also had two or three formal dinners a month and innumerable small luncheons. We gave no large, splashy affairs, such as balls; we thought they would be inappropriate because of the Vietnam war.

Moreover, the government, while dominated by de Gaulle, was readily available for talks about our common problems. I saw de Gaulle thirty-five times in my nearly five years in Paris. Couve and I met at least twice a month. We had many a *tour d'horizon* of the kind missing in Moscow.

We traveled all over the country, from Brest to Nice, from Dunkirk to Biarritz, and everywhere were treated with the utmost cordiality by the French people. One of the reasons was a desire by many to show they were still pro-American, despite de Gaulle's break with the United States. They felt that his actions were a slur on French good manners and went a little further than they normally would have to demonstrate their good will to the representative of a country which had twice fought beside them on the battlefields of Europe. The wonderful kindness and hospitality of the people of France will always constitute one of the pleasantest pages of my memory.

At a farewell lunch that de Gaulle gave for me and my wife at the Elysée on January 30, 1968, he spoke of the trials that Franco-American friendship was undergoing:

". . . in the course of its history, which is now some two hundred years long, this is not the first time. For it really seems that as between our two countries there is always one whose instinct carries it toward moderation while the other tends to depart from it. At the different periods when France chose to lead an adventurous life, she did not find the permanent support of the United States. Today, when the latter in turn is particularly susceptible to the impulses of power, it is true that France does not constantly approve of them. Perhaps, after all these divergences in such circumstances have contributed to world equilibrium. But if nevertheless the result has been as at the present time certain differences of attitudes, certain frictions of feeling, the capital of mutual interest, attraction, and admiration which is common to our two nations and which on several occasions has weighed so successfully and so heavily on the fate of the world, must not be impaired because of it."

I was equally circumspect and optimistic in my responses:

"Despite the political problems which exist between our two countries of which we are all conscious or the existence of divergent views on a number of subjects, I feel that the profound friendship between the United States and France remains in being. I leave France with the conviction that in any great event which would test the life of nations you will find France and the United States side by side as in the past."

This is not exactly the way I put the matter in my last report to the State Department. On February 9, 1968, I wrote to Secretary Rusk:

> Given the attitude of de Gaulle, there would seem to be very little chance of any real improvement in Franco-American relations. Even if the war in Vietnam is brought to the negotiating table, which should help in public opinion, nevertheless I feel that de Gaulle's basic interpretation of American power—which [compels] the French to withdraw from support of us in any given circumstance short of all-out war —really does not offer much hope or room for improvement by actions of the American Government or even by those of the French Government. As long as de Gaulle holds this view, and there is no sign that he will ever change it, there would appear to be no hope for any basic improvement in Franco-American relations. In short, I can offer little encouragement to any belief in a change in our relations with France until after the departure of de Gaulle.

Thus I ended my five years in France on the same note of pessimism with which I began them. My spirits were not lifted on my return to Washington. I found a country seething with indignation over the Vietnam war and a President despairing about what to do. And within six months, I was caught in the middle of another crisis with Moscow—the Soviet invasion of Czechoslovakia.

CHAPTER TWENTY-NINE

A Last Look at Moscow

During my regular call at the White House while on home leave at the end of 1967, President Johnson, who was in a brooding mood, asked me a question that he was putting to almost everyone in those troubled days: "What would you do about Vietnam if you were in charge of this country?"

I had seldom been drawn into official discussions about the Vietnam war. Asia was not my field of expertise. Like everyone else, I had views on the war. Like most Americans, my views had changed over the years. When Secretary of State Dulles began to intimate on March 29, 1954, that the United States might send troops to help the French defeat Ho Chi Minh's revolutionary forces, the Soviet government, through the controlled press, expressed alarm. *Pravda* said that Dulles was "infuriated" that he had not succeeded in "provoking" China to intervene in the war, because he wanted an excuse to send American troops to Vietnam. In a dispatch from Moscow to Dulles on April 12, 1954, I pointed out that generally a Soviet press citation of a Soviet nonresponse to an alleged provocation reflected a serious concern by the Kremlin that it might be drawn directly or indirectly into situations it wished to avoid. I added:

> Recent indications of firmness in American policy in regard to Indochina (following your conversations in Berlin with Molotov) appear to have produced characteristic uncertainty on the part of the Soviet government when faced with real determination. Provided Western powers are able to maintain a united front and pressure and have a clear idea of exactly what they wish to achieve in Indochina, a solution on our terms is not totally beyond the realm of possibility. I doubt if the Soviets are willing or even able to force Communist China to complete abandonment of Ho Chi Minh along the lines of the Greek variant, but,

in any event, if the British and French will stand shoulder to shoulder with the United States on the present firm position, any possibility that may exist of an acceptable solution will certainly be enhanced.

Five weeks later, while the Big Four powers, plus China, met at Geneva to seek a settlement of the Vietnam war, I became concerned that the allies were too eager to give concessions to the Communists. The French were so war-weary that they were ready to accept almost any settlement. The British were overwilling to agree to an unreasonable formula, too. While I favored an end to the war, I saw no reason to give up more than necessary to achieve peace. In Moscow, it seemed to me that the Soviets, and presumably the Chinese, were eager to end the war for fear the United States might join the hostilities. There was a danger that the allies were losing their perspective. On May 18, I sent Dulles a long telegram attempting to show that although Molotov was issuing vague warnings, the Soviet desire to avoid war was a major factor that should be carefully considered in an Indochina settlement. It said, in part:

> I believe Soviet foreign relations in the present phase are dominated by two controlling factors . . . (1) determination to hold on to all post-war Communist acquisitions; and (2) a desire to avoid serious crises in its foreign relations which might lead to military involvement. Immediate aims of Soviet diplomacy such as defeat of the European Defense Community, separation of the United States from its Allies, etc., I believe, operate within the limits of these two considerations. In Europe where lines of division are clearly drawn, as the Berlin conference confirmed, application of these factors render Soviet actions or political positions not too difficult to anticipate. The same holds true in regard to Korea where again the line of division is clearly drawn and, whatever rivalries may exist between China and the Soviet Union, they are undoubtedly firmly united in their determination not to relinquish Communist control over North Korea. The case of Indochina . . . is considerably more uncertain in view of the interposition of Communist China and our lack of knowledge as to the degree of Soviet control or influence over China's policies.
>
> I find it difficult to believe that the Soviet Union would be prepared knowingly to face a genuine risk of military involvement over a geographic area so remote from the borders of the Soviet Union as to have little direct interest to the Soviet State. . . . The Soviet desire to avoid military involvement needless to say does not stem from any change in heart since Stalin's death. The domestic programs of new leadership in the agricultural, economic and other fields and propaganda concerning the general improvement of the standard of living and emphasis on the

need for peace do not constitute psychological preparation of a government anticipating serious military involvement at an early date. The
present attempt at collective dictatorship, whatever its durability may
be under any circumstances, is certainly not suited for great emergencies. A major crisis in their foreign affairs would greatly and possibly
dangerously complicate relationships within the top leadership.

The foregoing are considerations which affect the Soviet Union
alone and may be modified or even vitiated by the complexities of Soviet-
Chinese relations. As matter of speculative deduction, it is probable
that Soviet influence on Chinese action is in direct ratio to the risk to
the entire Communist bloc of a given course of action and if, for example, it was plainly evident to the Soviet Government (and to the
Chinese) that the risk of a major conflict over Indochina, especially
with the United States, was real, then I believe Soviet influence on
China could and might be determinant. On the other hand, if the Communists obtain the impression, due to Western disunity, that they can
proceed to acquire all of Indochina without serious risk of major hostilities, the Soviet Government would not be disposed even to attempt a
restraining influence. It seems very difficult here to understand how the
British in particular can have failed to learn the elementary lesson of
dealing with modern totalitarian states—namely that solutions by
negotiation of major questions are only possible when the consequences
of a failure to do so would involve risks to the maintenance of their
regimes....

Certainly nothing is more important at the present time than that the
Soviet Government should be left in no uncertainty as to our position
in regard to Indochina and if we are able to get our Allies to develop
any form of acceptable common position, the sooner it is conveyed privately to the Soviet Government the better.

I was not there, so it is difficult for me to say whether the Geneva
settlement gave the Communists more than required.[*]

During this period, the Soviet Union was becoming concerned
about talk of "Asia for the Asians," which increased following the
conference. Peking showed a new initiative, with Foreign Minister
Chou En-lai visiting India and Burma. Molotov told the Indonesians
that the Soviet Union would like an invitation to a conference at Dja-
karta, because the Soviet Union was an Asian power. The Soviet press

[*] In the book *Khrushchev Remembers*, Khrushchev is quoted as saying that the
Viet Minh were exhausted, and Ho was ready to end the revolution. When Premier
Mendès-France of France proposed the division of Vietnam at the seventeenth parallel,
"we gasped with surprise. We hadn't expected anything like this. The seventeenth
parallel was the absolute maximum we would have claimed ourselves." Khrushchev
was not an accurate reporter, but his views conform with those I held in the spring of
1954.

emphasized that security in Southeast Asia could be assured only by joint efforts by all states. I cited, in a dispatch to Washington on September 16, these "indications that the Soviets are not particularly happy" over developments, which "would appear to turn over to the Chinese Communists exclusive leadership in Asia."

As the war raged on between North and South Vietnam, despite the Geneva agreements, I reported from time to time, from Moscow, comments from Soviet leaders and the Soviet press. During my two years in the Philippines, I was never called on for an opinion about Vietnam, and when I returned to Washington, the major question concerned Laos, which was neutralized, in part, at least, by the Geneva Conference of 1962.

As American intervention in Vietnam increased under Kennedy and Johnson, de Gaulle grew steadily more critical, and I became more dubious of our policy. On January 31, 1966, in a personal letter to Llewellyn Thompson, then an ambassador at large stationed in Washington, I wrote of the Vietnam war:

> What bothers me is the possibility that there are some people in the United States government who believe that bombing of North Vietnam will induce or force Hanoi to the conference table. I feel this is a very fallacious argument since it seems to me that all Communist history shows that they will never yield to external pressure of this kind. Considering as they do that the struggle between the two different systems is to the death, the Communists believe that any concession made under foreign pressure would lead to further pressure and further concessions. Also I think past history demonstrates this point. For example, in Korea there was no question of any armistice after the Inchon landing when things looked very black for the Communists. I know of no peace feelers from them at that time. The possibility of an armistice suggested by the Russians in June 1951 happened at a time when the military situation was virtually at a stalemate.

By the end of 1966, de Gaulle had moved to public hostility. While some of his attitude was based on a belief that the United States would not succeed where France had failed, there was also a genuine fear of the war's being considered racist—white versus yellow—and that it would escalate into a world conflict.

It is easy to say now that the Vietnam war was a mistake, but I doubt if any president would have been able to wash his hands of South Vietnam any more than he would have of South Korea. The error was not in aiding South Vietnam but in the execution of that policy. The American military relied on firepower, which led to heavy casualties among civilians. As a result, most foreigners and a sizable proportion of the American public came to believe that the war was immoral; the United States was brutalizing the Vietnamese to prop up a corrupt, undemocratic regime.

When I returned to the United States in 1968, the lines of decision-making on Vietnam were set, and the participants in the various task forces had long been at work. Occasionally, I would be brought in on White House conferences on approaches to the Soviets, but I played only a minor role.

In my reply to Johnson's question in 1967, I told him that I was not qualified to judge the military value of bombing North Vietnam, but politically it was the worst thing that the United States had done. It forced the Soviets to extend greater assistance to North Vietnam. They attach enormous importance to maintaining their position of leadership in the Communist world, and to have turned their back on a small Communist country under assault from the great "imperialist" power would have exposed them to criticism from the Chinese. To Peking, nonaction by the Soviets would be another proof of the revisionist and nonrevolutionary nature of the Soviet regime. Furthermore, I told Johnson, the bombing turned public opinion in Europe against us. The Europeans could see no military value in bombing small huts in rural areas. To them, the raids were an act of brutality. Walt Rostow, the President's adviser for national-security affairs, who sat in on the meeting, defended the bombing. He pointed out that Allied air raids had killed civilians in World War II but were continued because they helped the military effort. I replied that, without knowing the military effect on Vietnam, there was a difference between traditional movement of vast armies and guerrilla warfare. In traditional warfare, railroads and trucks were required to transport men and supplies. Thus bombing was effective. In guerrilla war, supplies moved on bicycles and the backs of the Vietnamese. Bombing did not stop the enemy. None of the arguments were new. Johnson had heard them from others at various times. He asked no more questions and said nothing in response to my arguments.

The Vietnam war was a tragedy not only for the nation but also for Johnson. It undoubtedly undermined his place in history. It deflected his attention from domestic considerations, where he had been a magnificent leader. On general foreign-policy questions, I would not want to judge Johnson, because I was not close to him. Johnson did not have a deep understanding of the nature of the

Soviet problem, but there was no occasion when this defect damaged the United States. Johnson met with Premier Kosygin at Glassboro, New Jersey, but the conference produced little. As far as de Gaulle was concerned, Johnson displayed a maturity and an understanding for which he deserves the highest marks. So does Dean Rusk.

A few days after my talk with Johnson, Dean Rusk called me back to Washington from the Eastern Shore of Maryland, where I was duck hunting. "Chip, you made too good an impression on the President," he said. "He wants you back here to take Foy Kohler's place." Kohler, Deputy Under Secretary for Political Affairs, was retiring. I would have much preferred to finish my career in Paris, but a public official scarcely ever refuses a presidential request. The previous year, I had declined an offer to send me back to Moscow. Rusk had summoned me home and told me that Johnson was thinking seriously of appointing me for a second time as ambassador to the Soviet Union. I replied that I would, of course, obey orders but I felt that in view of my seniority in the Russian field, I had a right to offer an opinion in regard to my appointment. The Secretary agreed. I pointed out that there was little chance of improvement in Soviet-American relations, at least as long as the Vietnam war continued, and even after, from what I had observed.

I also said it was a mistake to send envoys back to a post like Moscow for a second tour. The excitement of going there as ambassador for the first time generates a zest for the job. There is hope that things will change and relations will improve. Eventually, the excitement wears off, hope dissipates, and boredom and monotony sets in. Unless there was some prospect of real movement, I thought it would be a mistake to send me back. Rusk said he would convey my thoughts to the President. That night at dinner, Thompson and I compiled a list of possibilities for Moscow, which was sent to Rusk. Later in 1966, when I saw the President, I repeated my objections, adding that the French might be offended by my transfer, because the move might look as if Moscow were more important than Paris. My arguments saved me, but not my good friend Thompson, who was sent back to Moscow. From what Thompson told me of his second tour, my forebodings had been sound. He did not consider his time there well spent.

In Washington, I found the duties of a Deputy Under Secretary for Political Affairs not clearly defined. The job involved relations with other departments and supervision over certain sections of the

Department of State. For example, the Political-Military Section, which dealt with the Pentagon, reported to my office. So did the scientific adviser, who coordinated all forms of scientific relationships and agreements. I was also the Secretary's deputy on the Marine Commission, the Space Commission, and similar groups. I found the work interesting, but not arduous. In addition, of course, I retained my special interest in Soviet affairs and was the Secretary's adviser on Soviet matters.

My boss was Secretary Rusk. I had known him since 1949, when General Marshall brought him to the Department of State from the Army, and while the association was warm, we never became intimate friends. Occasionally, we worked together, and I came to respect his cool and careful evaluation of situations. He possessed the qualities of a distinguished public servant—courage, restraint, and a good analytical mind. One of his problems as Secretary of State was the extraordinary reserve with which he treated people, even those whom he knew quite well. I think, although I never heard him say so, that he modeled himself on Marshall. In Navy parlance, he was very much the admiral on the bridge. He would listen to what subordinates had to say and give no indication of his reaction, either in words or in the expression on his round Buddha face (He once told me he looked like a bartender.) He confided in no one. He carried his reserve to a point where it hurt him. Subordinates in the State Department felt alienated and were reluctant to approach him. President Kennedy was also puzzled by this aloofness, and once asked me, "Why is Rusk the only member of the cabinet I do not call by his first name?" With Kennedy's permission, I asked Rusk, who said, "Well, I prefer it that way," and explained that he did not believe cabinet officers should be intimate with the President. Marshall responded the same way toward Roosevelt's easy informality.

Nevertheless, Rusk was an effective Secretary of State. Although he is best known as a hawk on Vietnam, he deserves more credit for certain dovish actions, such as the cessation of heavy bombing. But that is his story to tell.

My work in the Department of State in 1968 soon settled down into routine meeting after meeting. At least once a week, I went to the Joint Chiefs of Staff, primarily for exchanges of views on various situations in the world, except for Vietnam, which was handled separately and almost always at the White House. I did not attend the Vietnamese meetings. I also took a trip around the country in connection with my duties as the Secretary's representative on the Space and Marine commissions. It was all very interesting and impressive, especially the preparations for an *Apollo* flight to land men on the moon.

In July, 1968, I made my last trip to the Soviet Union as a Foreign Service officer. It was mostly a ceremonial affair. I was head of the American delegation on the Pan American Airways flight inaugurating service between New York and Moscow. I stayed in Spaso House and had a number of long talks with Ambassador Thompson.

Moscow was depressing. The intellectual and cultural atmosphere showed no life except for a few younger artists. The population was apathetic, and certainly the faces on the street were gloomy and unsmiling. The youth, I was informed, were alienated, refraining from political life. They apparently did not even discuss politics among themselves. While in some parts of Moscow, notably on the Kalinsky Prospekt and in the Arbat district, there were some new shops and buildings, in general the physical appearance of Moscow had not altered much. The population was a shade better dressed. There was the same run-down air to many Soviet public buildings.

Prospects for the 1968 agricultural year were not good; there had been a drought in the North Caucasus area, and while it was too soon to come to any definite conclusion, the New Lands did not look hopeful. The economic report for the first six months also indicated that industry had slowed down to some extent.

I also found Moscow diplomatically sterile. The members of the Politburo practically never appeared in public. Foreign diplomats had little chance of discussing problems with Kremlin leaders. In short, the gains made in the days of Khrushchev, when Soviet leaders appeared at least at informal social affairs, had been wiped out.

What was lacking in Moscow was hope. There had been times in the short history of the Soviet Union when hope was quite noticeable. There was the period right after the Revolution. And when I went to Moscow in 1934 to help set up the American Embassy, there was strong optimism. People believed that the privations of the civil war and collectivization had been overcome and that they could look forward to increasing prosperity and wider freedom. The purges ended these hopes. Then came the war and its initial setbacks. Toward the end, as the Red Army swept toward Germany, there was a renewed belief in the future. These hopes were certainly dampened by the rigorous controls imposed to repair the industrial and economic damages of the war. Following the death of Stalin, and particularly after his denunciation by Khrushchev in early 1956, optimism was quite evident among the more advanced members of Soviet society in Moscow.

In 1968, however, tightened control over the intellectual and cultural life, the general stagnation of political activity among the masses, and the slow gain in economic benefits contributed to the leaden atmosphere in Moscow. It was also apparent that the Communist Party acted like a dead hand on all of Soviet life and that the people resented the system. Not that they wanted capitalism restored. They wanted less control over the intellectual and cultural life.

There was a measure of hope in my report on my trip, my final official report on the Soviet Union. I concluded:

> I am certainly not predicting that there will be any upset in the Soviet Union. The weight of the established bureaucracy is far too great at this stage for anything of that kind, but I do feel that long run changes will be inevitable—particularly when the present generation of youth grows up—which will be of profound importance for the future of Russia and indeed of the whole world. Whether these changes will come about by evolution or revolution is for the future to decide.

On my mind throughout the trip was the crisis that had developed in Czechoslovakia. Soviet troops had massed on the Czech border. If they moved in before we landed in Moscow, I was under orders to cancel the flight. The trouble in Czechoslovakia began in 1967, when students demonstrated at Prague University. The underlying causes were a breakdown of the economy and continued use of repressive methods by the Stalinist authorities. The protests spread and by the spring of 1968 had reached the danger point. Recognizing the peril, the Czech Communist leaders acted, appointing Alexander Dubcek, a faithful Party regular, as the new head of the regime. Dubcek attempted to take charge of the reform movement, but had no plan of pulling Czechoslovakia out of the Soviet camp or seriously undermining the hegemony of the Communist Party. Dubcek favored only some economic reforms and some liberalization of the repression. As always, the forces of freedom demanded more, and in May most censorship of the press was abolished. Soon there were demands for a genuine multiparty system. No true Communist can stand such freedom, and the Kremlin came to the conclusion that Dubcek was losing control. Warsaw Pact troops were moved to the Czech frontier. In the State Department, our special intelligence committee on Czechoslovakia went on a twenty-four-hour watch.

During this period, I told Secretary Rusk that the odds were 60 to 40 for a Soviet-led invasion. Rusk told President Johnson, who relayed the odds to Joe Alsop, the columnist, who was quite angry with me for not letting him in on the "secret." I explained that the odds were not secret but just a judgment—more in the realm of probability than of possibility. The unanswered question was whether Moscow regarded the events in Czechoslovakia as permissible reform or counterrevolution.

At the end of July, the Soviet and Czech leaders met at the little Czech border town of Cierna. The importance of the meeting was shown by the fact that virtually all of the Soviet Politburo traveled from Moscow to attend. They lived on a train on Russian soil. The communiqué issued after the meeting indicated that an uneasy compromise had been reached. Both sides agreed to restrain polemics in their press, and Dubcek acknowledged the primacy of the Communist Party in Czech political life. Cierna was followed by a conference of the Warsaw Pact powers (Rumania did not attend), at which two uneasy satellite satraps—Gomulka and Ulbricht—were sold on the Czech truce. This conference, at Bratislava, reaffirmed Czech fidelity to the Warsaw Pact and proletarian internationalism.

There were obviously various opinions in the State Department about how long the truce would last. On August 13, I told Rusk in a memorandum that it appeared that the Russians had gone to Cierna on the basis of a faulty idea of the situation in Czechoslovakia. This was due in part to the classic Soviet erroneous belief (which they have to believe) that the masses were with them. I speculated that the Soviet leaders might easily have thought that with the pressure of Soviet troops around the borders, plus a small contingent inside Czechoslovakia, the Czech Presidium at Cierna would be divided, with one important section pro-Soviet (reflecting in their eyes the will of the broad masses of the workers). After a rough first day, in which Dubcek was solidly supported by all the members of the Presidium, the Soviets had to revise their tactics. They apparently never seriously entertained the idea of an all-out national military attack against Czechoslovakia as a country. The failure to discover any group of pro-Soviet Czechs forced them to back down.

While there was no sign of any imminent action, Soviet troops remained along the Czech borders, and new maneuvers were announced by Moscow. There were also a few signs that the agreement to stop polemics might be wearing a little thin. It was probably this point—control of the press—I told Rusk, which would be the biggest problem for Dubcek.

In conclusion, I underestimated Soviet timing on the use of military force:

> It rather appears now that Soviet pressure will be continued through the maintenance of troops on the borders of Czechoslovakia, and I would presume a considerable amount of Soviet activity within Czechoslovakia, in the endeavor to help bring about the formation of some pro-Soviet group. This process will certainly continue up to the party congress on September 9, and conceivably thereafter.
>
> In short, the Czech situation, while not critical, still remains inherently serious and far from satisfactory to the Soviets. I would doubt however any spectacular developments for the rest of the month.

Having disposed of that problem, I went to Rhode Island on vacation. I should not have gone. Only a week later, on August 20, the Russians, supported by the satellites, invaded Czechoslovakia. A special Air Force plane rushed me, Under Secretary of State Nicholas deB. Katzenbach, and Assistant Secretary of State William B. Macomber, who were also in New England, back to Washington.

On arrival, I learned that the Soviet Ambassador, A. F. Dobrynin, had personally handed the President a note asserting that the Soviet armies had moved at the "request" of the Czech government. There was not only no government at the time the note was delivered (Dubcek had been arrested); there was also none for at least ten days afterward. Apparently, the Soviet Ambassador in Prague had presented the President of the Czech Republic, Ludvik Svoboda, who during World War II had fought with the Red Army, with a list of names of those who would constitute the future government. Svoboda indignantly rejected the list and forbade the Czech news agency to publish it, but Moscow assumed that the demand would be accepted and provided Dobrynin with the wording for the note. Dobrynin himself apparently had no foreknowledge of the invasion. Two nights before, he attended a party on the *Honey Fitz*, the yacht that the Secretary of the Navy frequently used for outings, and gave no indication that military intervention was at hand. He could have been hiding his information, of course, but what is more likely is that the Kremlin had not told him at that time.

There is another bit of evidence that indicated that the decision to invade was made only the day before the troops were ordered to move. A note from Premier Kosygin agreeing to a meeting with President Johnson to inaugurate the strategic arms limitation talks and to the President's visiting the Soviet Union was delivered to the White House only two days before the invasion. It is highly unlikely that Kosygin would have agreed to a summit conference and to a visit to Russia knowing that the President would cancel them as a protest to the invasion.

I am sure the Soviets were reluctant to invade Czechoslovakia. They were aware that their reputation would suffer and that Communist parties throughout the world would be placed in an awkward position. There was a combination of at least four elements that led to the Soviet decision. One was ideological. The Soviets were convinced that Dubcek was about to preside over the liquidation of the Soviet system in Czechoslovakia. A second element was the weakening of the zone of satellite buffer states around the western borders of the Soviet Union. The third element was Ulbricht's fear that a successful liberalization movement in Czechoslovakia would gravely disturb the stability of his Communist regime in East Germany. Given the importance which the Soviet Union had always attached to a Sovietized East Germany, this was a matter which the Bolsheviks could not treat lightly. The fourth Soviet motivation was the apprehension that the liberal infection might run up the arm of the Ukraine to the heart of the Soviet Union itself.

There was little the United States could do about the invasion. We had learned from the Eisenhower-Dulles experience in 1956, during the Hungarian revolution, that it would be a mistake for the United States to give any indication that it was going to do something to throw back the invaders. Our bluff would have been called. We were also convinced that any overt move by the United States would have added to Dubcek's problems. Therefore, President Johnson's response was low-key. He issued a statement denouncing the Soviet reasons for the invasion as "patently contrived" and a "flat violation" of the United Nations Charter. He called for a meeting of the Security Council, and appealed to the Russians to withdraw their troops. Then he canceled the meeting he had scheduled with Kosygin to begin talks on limiting strategic weapons, and his visit to the Soviet Union.

The United States followed the same low-key policy during the whole Czech crisis. There were no warning notes. We did not want the United States to be shown up as impotent to deal with the situation. Nor did we want any actions to be seized on as proof that the United States was instigating the Czech reform movement. The Czechs realized that public support by Washington would hurt them, and indicated privately to us that they appreciated our policy of saying nothing.

Our silence did not prevent *Pravda* from making wild charges. On July 19, it reported that the Soviet Union had obtained a copy of a secret American "operation plan" aimed at undermining and overthrowing socialism in Eastern Europe, particularly in Prague. *Pravda* also reported the discovery of "secret caches" of American weapons near the West German border. Following publication of the *Pravda* article, Secretary Rusk called in Dobrynin, and in my presence told him that the Soviet government should be under no illusion regarding American attitudes. Americans still believed in the principle, expressed in the Declaration of Independence, that the people had the right to determine for themselves the institutions under which they were to live. But, Rusk said, the *Pravda* charge that the United States was involved in any Czech counterrevolutionary movement was false and Dobrynin knew that it was false. As always, Dobrynin listened courteously and made no comment.

It is certain, although he never admitted it, that the invasion of Czechoslovakia shocked General de Gaulle. His immediate reaction was to fall back on one of his classic formulas, blaming the Yalta Conference for giving the Soviet Union a sphere of influence in Eastern Europe. In reply, the State Department issued a statement, which I helped draft, pointing out that there was not a single agreement at Yalta remotely connected with an Eastern European sphere of influence. It was the occupation of Eastern European countries by the Red Army that gave the Bolsheviks the power to impose their will. Averell Harriman, then in Paris, issued a firm denial of de Gaulle's charge. Despite de Gaulle's hackneyed response, the invasion caused him to revise some of his estimates and possibly to rethink his foreign policy. Russia was not reverting as rapidly as he had thought it would to the style of a great power; it was following ideology. One indication of a change in de Gaulle was an interview in 1969 with Soames, the British Ambassador, in which he adumbrated the possibility of a looser and more enlarged grouping of Western European powers, conceivably including England. The fact that the British bungled this opportunity did not detract from its inherent significance. Another clue was the warm welcome accorded President Nixon during his visit to France in February, 1969. How far de Gaulle would have shifted will never be known, because in April of 1969, after the defeat of his plan for the reorganization of the French governmental structure, he resigned. He died in 1970 without returning to power.

Many Americans were also distressed by the lack of an effective American response to the invasion of Czechoslovakia. Some leading newspapers editorialized that there must have been at least an implied agreement by Washington and Moscow on a sphere of influence. On September 6, I drafted a memorandum to help Secretary Rusk meet the criticisms. It drew the conclusion that without question the United States, both during and after World War II, was not ever involved in and, in fact, opposed any sphere-of-influence arrangement.

Conceding that the Soviet Union had in effect obtained for itself a specific sphere of influence in Eastern Europe, I emphasized that this resulted from the imposition of Sovietized regimes on Poland, Hungary, Czechoslovakia, Bulgaria, Rumania, and East Germany after World War II. My memo went on:

> It stands to reason that because of common sense and desire on the part of the United States not to become involved in a nuclear war with the Soviet Union that the United States does not ignore the reality of Soviet control, however much we may deplore it and the existence of the Warsaw Pact. We recognize for these reasons that there is little that the United States could do through threat or the use of military force to protect one of these countries (with whom we have no obligation) without automatically engaging in conflict with the Soviet Union. However, since there is no understanding whatsoever, or even implications of one, with the Soviet Union on this area as a Soviet sphere there is no inhibition of the United States from diplomatic and other action which we wish to take.

The Russians treated Dubcek and his associates with typical Bolshevik brutality. They were arrested, manhandled, and taken handcuffed to the Soviet Union. Svoboda insisted that they be released if there were to be any discussions. Reluctantly, the Russians agreed. In Washington, we sadly watched the destruction of an attempt to give the Soviet structure what the Czechs called a human face. No one was happy at our inability to do anything constructive in regard to Czechoslovakia. But despite the constant searchings which went on in the department, no one came up with any ideas that made sense in the circumstances.

I had expected the Western freeze in relations with Moscow to last longer than it did. It was not many months after the invasion that Western European countries were again treading the road of détente. The United States was a little slower, but not terribly much. The calm acceptance of the Soviet use of force in Czechoslovakia contrasted markedly with the violent demonstrations over the crushing of the Hungarian revolution in 1956. One reason was that many people had been killed in the streets of Budapest; there had been an armed uprising. In Czechoslovakia, practically no shots were fired, and the number killed could be counted on the fingers of one hand. Furthermore, the public had grown somewhat callous in regard to Soviet behavior.

Shortly after Czechoslovakia, Brezhnev, the First Secretary of the Communist Party of the Soviet Union, issued what the press called the Brezhnev Doctrine. As mentioned earlier in this book, it was merely the reaffirmation of a principle inherent in Bolshevism from its very beginning. This principle was that the Soviet Union had a duty to use armed force if necessary to preserve and protect the Soviet structure wherever it was installed. There was no doubt that this principle applied to all the Eastern European satellites. In the fall of 1968, I endeavored to ascertain from Gromyko whether the Brezhnev Doctrine applied to Yugoslavia and to Cuba. He evaded the question, and I have never had a satisfactory clarification of the limitations of the doctrine.

I had long decided that my career in the Foreign Service would end when the new administration took office in January, 1969, regardless of who won the election. Forty years in the Foreign Service is long enough. The way should be opened for younger men. Moreover, there is an inescapable human tendency for an ambassador progressively to relate the deference and courtesy he is accorded to himself and not to the office. Besides, at the age of sixty-five, I thought I had enough energy left to make a little money. With all its excitement and rewards, the Foreign Service hardly provided sufficient funds for a comfortable retirement. For these and other reasons, I decided to submit my resignation to the incoming administration. Ambassador Thompson, my lifelong friend and associate in Soviet affairs, had quite independently come to the same conclusion.

My career ended not with a bang and certainly not with a whimper. When Dean Rusk submitted his resignation, I, as highest ranking career officer in the department, was designated Acting Secretary of State to serve until William Rogers, the new Secretary, was confirmed and was sworn into office. The two-day period was a little longer than anticipated, because the Senate held up Walter Hickel's confirmation as Secretary of the Interior and the cabinet was not sworn in until January 22. I then called on Rogers, congratulated him, and walked out of the State Department to C Street and retirement.

Afterword

No diplomat in his right mind who has been through nearly four decades of dealings with the Soviet Union would attempt to predict, with any degree of precision, the future of American-Soviet relations. There have been too many twists and turns, too many changes as the result of totally unexpected events, that have undermined previous forecasts of the most knowledgeable experts in the field. Nevertheless, I think that a broad assessment of the future can—and should—be given. It is my gloomy conclusion that the United States faces decades of uneasy relations with the Soviet Union. The fault, if that is the right word, lies with both countries, but primarily with the Soviet Union.

Nearly twenty years after Stalin's death, the political philosophy of the Soviet Union remains virtually unchanged. There may be some slight theoretical variations, particularly on the non-inevitability of war. The fact of the matter is that ideology is just as important in Moscow today as it was in 1934, when I first stepped on Russian soil. That is why the word "Bolshevik" describes the Soviet rulers as accurately today as it did in the 1930s, and why I have used the term throughout this book.

For the United States, the ideological element of Soviet policy is of vital importance. It means that there can be no harmonious relations with Moscow in the customary sense of the word. The early Bolsheviks held, and present-day Bolsheviks still insist they believe, that the Union of Soviet Socialist Republics is surrounded by capitalist nations ready to destroy it. There was some basis for this belief in the days of Lenin, but it is ludicrous at the present time to think of the powerful Soviet Union with its satellite buffer zone as a beleaguered government surrounded by enemies. Nevertheless, this doctrine is still featured in Soviet political thought. Moreover, the leaders in the Kremlin still regard every government of a non-Communist state as in a transition phase on the way to achieving Soviet status. Thus all settlements with such countries are temporary, to be altered when the correlation of forces in the world is more favorable to Moscow.

Soviet ideology is impersonal, institutional, official, and historical. It does not lead to personal enmity of Russians toward Americans. It does, however, proscribe adherence to any objective standard of morality. Lies are perfectly acceptable if they advance the Soviet cause. (This does not mean that the United States is inherently more moral than the Soviet Union. But we operate in a society in which good and evil are differentiated; the Communists do not.) The use of violence in itself produces no tremors in the Bolshevik mind. Indeed, the use of the Red Army to promote Soviet regimes or to prevent their liberalization is considered a duty—except when the risk of war imperils the Soviet system in Russia. Then the use of force is wrong.

Soviet ideology also means that no matter what the state-to-state relationships of the Soviet Union, the Kremlin will attempt to support and control foreign Communist parties, again as long as there is no risk to the Soviet state. While Moscow's control has been loosened, any attempt at real independence on the part of an installed Communist regime is usually crushed with force, as Hungary and Czechoslovakia attest.

Yugoslavia is an exception to this rule. Tito's heresy demonstrated that a basic tenet of Marxism is false. Marxism teaches that national boundaries are the product of the bourgeoisie, that the working class knows no boundaries. Tito proved that nationalism—developed over centuries of common experience, culture, and history—should not be underestimated.

China's dispute with Russia is a manifestation of the same principle. Stalin was primarily interested in protecting the Soviet system in Russia. He did not want to see Mao Tse-tung successful. The burden of helping China would be too great on the Soviet Union, which was struggling to repair the damages of the war. He also foresaw the possibility of Mao's defection from Soviet views. In any event, he is on record as stating that in 1945 he saw no possibility of success for a Communist revolution in China, and urged "Chinese comrades" to make the best deal they could with Chiang Kai-shek. From the point of view of Soviet interests, Stalin would have much preferred to have had a weak, fragmented China, with Communist parties playing a sufficient role to mitigate or forestall any possible anti-Soviet action of the Chinese government.

When Mao triumphed over Chiang, the Soviet Union had to aid the new Communist regime if it wanted to retain its leadership of the world Communist movement. It was not long before relations cooled, and eventually the two Communist giants fell to quarreling. There are nationalist elements involved, but the dispute is primarily ideological. The Chinese accuse the Soviet leaders of revisionism because Moscow is primarily interested in protecting the Soviet state. While the dispute is real, it would be sheer madness for the United States to count on a permanent split between Moscow and Peking. In case either country became involved in a controversy with the United States, I believe the other would side with its sister Communist state.

Undoubtedly, a great many thinking Russians regard ideology as a sterile, stultifying force. Nevertheless, the rulers have decided that it cannot be changed, and it is presented to the public in the press and on radio and television as unchanging truth. The result is that most Russians seem to accept unquestioningly the accuracy of Bolshevik analyses of world events.

As the Soviet Union grows stronger, the question of ideology will probably become less important in the eyes of its rulers. But ideology will remain, since it is essential for the maintenance of the supremacy of the Communist Party and the Soviet system.

Just as Bolshevik ideology has remained intact, so the political structure of the Soviet Union remains virtually unchanged. The substitution of collective rule for one-man rule has not altered matters very much. There have been a few signs of dissent in the intellectual and artistic community, but there is no threat to the regime. There is not even any indication that the Kremlin, which is more conservative than in Khrushchev's day, will ever modify its policies. There is no sign of evolution of the Soviet state to make it more reasonable in dealing with other nations. Domestically, the weight of the Party bureaucracy is such—running into the tens of millions of people—that it is very difficult to see how the party would accept any evolution toward liberalization. In all probability, the next twenty or thirty years will bring some changes in the Soviet structure, but not through the evolutionary process. There is some, but only a little, likelihood that the Soviet military, which is potentially capable of seizing power, will bring pressure on the Party leaders. It should be remembered that Soviet military leaders are themselves members of the Communist Party, but they do not sit in the top councils of the Bolsheviks.

Zhukov was the only marshal to serve on the Politburo, and he did so only briefly, in 1957. I would not forecast the circumstances under which the military might act. The possibility is dim indeed.

In the United States, the big problem in dealing with the Soviet Union has always been the wide swings in American public opinion. During World War II, the brave Russians were always right; criticism would not be brooked. As the war ended and the imperialist nature of the Soviet system manifested itself anew, public opinion switched to strong opposition to Moscow. After the invasion of Korea, anti-Communism took a tragic and erroneous turn. It became American policy to oppose the extension of Communism everywhere. At home, anti-Communism became a crusade that corrupted American thinking on civil liberties for a decade. Then, with the growing strength of Communist China, Americans began to take a more tolerant view of the Soviet Union. By the 1970s, critical discussion of Soviet policy had fallen to a minor level.

Unhappily, America is not ready for the continuous struggle of wills and never-ending diplomatic crises that we face with the Soviet Union. The United States is divided. Faith in government had reached such a low point in 1968 that some thoughtful people were asking whether President Johnson had lost his ability to govern. Young people in particular believed little the government said. This distrust was the inevitable consequence of the disastrous adventure in foreign policy known as the Vietnam war. Despite efforts by President Richard M. Nixon, faith in our public officials has not returned. It is therefore pertinent to ask whether the United States is capable of leading the free world. The need for leadership is real. We are the only Western country with the military and economic power for leadership. There is doubt that as a people we possess the discipline and patience to prevail. The conflict in priorities between foreign and domestic requirements may be insoluble. One will have to give. I fear America may be forced into a modern form of isolationism with concentration on admittedly urgent domestic problems.

There are those who say that regardless of developments, the long-term outlook is favorable—the American and Soviet societies will "converge"—that is, each nation, facing the same economic and social problems, will eventually work out similar solutions. Presumably, the United States would adopt more of the Soviet planning techniques while the Soviet Union would become more democratic. The convergence theory is advanced by a number of eminent scholars, but I am afraid that it is typical of the wishful thinking that the West has periodically indulged in regarding the Soviet Union. Theoretically, convergence makes some sense, in that human organizations tend to come to similar conclusions when faced with the same problems. But a Soviet-American convergence is many generations, if not centuries, away, if it ever comes. The basic elements of the American and Soviet societies are too different, the cultural and historical traditions too divergent, to expect the two nations to become similar.

Although I see no bridge that can be built between the ideological commitments of the Soviet Union and the United States's insistence on protecting the independence of its allied countries, it does not follow that the two superpowers are on an automatic collision course. Both governments deeply believe that a nuclear war is unthinkable. Neither would set out on a course that would lead to mutual suicide. Bolshevik practice is never to neglect the military, and the Kremlin has made clear that force will be used if necessary to maintain Soviet supremacy in the satellites. But one of the great obstacles to the use of force is the danger of consequences to the Soviet rule in Russia. If Moscow lost a war, the whole house of cards could come tumbling down. For this reason, war is to be avoided. Therefore, I do not see any circumstance under which the Soviets would deliberately embark on World War III. Circumstances might develop along the peripheries of the lines of power, however, which step by step could lead to a confrontation in which neither country could back down. The Middle East is one such area. The fact that both governments recognize this possibility provides assurance that we will not be sucked into the maelstrom.

This fear of war is another reason why the Kremlin has been serious about disarmament. However, I would not be too sanguine about the five-year agreements reached by the Soviet Union and the United States in 1972 limiting missile and anti-missile forces. There are too many sections open to varying interpretations and, as we have seen, the Kremlin always takes advantage of loose drafting to evade the spirit of treaties.

Illusion has no place in any negotiations with the Soviet Union. We should always seek to find the areas where the two countries' interests coincide. Even in areas where interests do not coincide, skillful diplomacy can sometimes produce manageable arrangements of benefit to both. The cultural exchanges fall into this category. The Kremlin is eager for scientific and technical exchanges; we are interested more in visits by artists. Under the agreements, each country sends both scientists and artists.

Aside from such strivings for agreements, I see little that the United

States can do except to continue along the lines of the policy that has been generally followed since World War II. This involves, above all, keeping our defenses sufficiently strong to deter the Soviet Union from any possibility of yielding to the temptation of a first strike against the United States. I do not think we can look forward to a tranquil world so long as the Soviet Union operates in its present form. The only hope, and this is a fairly thin one, is that at some point the Soviet Union will begin to act like a country instead of a cause.

Index

INDEX